INTRODUCTION TO COST AND MANAGEMENT ACCOUNTING

To Milton Keynes
AAT Section.
with best wishes
Roger Storey

Introduction to Cost and Management Accounting

Roger Storey, FCMA

MACMILLAN
Business

First published 1995 by
MACMILLAN PRESS LTD
Houndmills, Basingstoke, Hampshire RG21 6XS
and London
Companies and representatives
throughout the world

ISBN 0–333–62317–7 hardcover
ISBN 0–333–62318–5 paperback

A catalogue record for this book is available
from the British Library

10   9   8   7   6   5   4   3   2
05   04   03   02   01   00   99   98   97

Typeset in Great Britain by
Aarontype Limited
Easton, Bristol

Printed in Great Britain by
The Bath Press, Bath

Contents

List of Tables

List of Figures

Preface

Introduction to Cost and Management Accounting has been written primarily for students studying up to intermediate level for the examinations of the following bodies: CIMA; CACA; AAT; BTEC; LCCI; RSA; A Level; and also for years 1 and 2 university courses. The topics covered will be in the syllabuses of a number of other accountancy and business degree courses and it is hoped the text will be of value to these students also.

The techniques described and illustrated will also be of practical benefit in the business world, to both financial and operational management with responsibilities for controlling costs and revenues, and for planning the future operations of their enterprises.

The aim throughout has been to present theory and practice in a readable, easy-to-follow way, with many diagrams and examples to assist in understanding. The structure of the book is discussed in Chapter 1 with the first two sections laying the foundations for the main cost and management accounting objectives: the control and planning of costs and revenues.

Acknowledgements

I am very grateful for permission to use past examination questions from the following bodies:

Chartered Institute of Management Accountants (CIMA)

Chartered Association of Certified Accountants (CACA)

Association of Accounting Technicians (AAT)

London Chamber of Commerce and Industry (LCCI)

Royal Society of Arts (RSA)

University of London Examinations and Assessment Council (A Level ULEAC)

Associated Examining Board (A Level AEB)

University of Greenwich.

I also wish to acknowledge the kind permission of the Chartered Institute of Management Accountants to use terms and definitions in accordance with the Institute's *Management Accounting Official Terminology*. This is an invaluable aid in the study of cost and management accounting and an order form for this publication is included at the end of the book.

Model answers to computational questions are included in Part V. All the answers are my sole responsibility, with none of the above bodies having provided or approved them.

I am also grateful for the help and encouragement given to me by Croydon College, by Bromley Adult Education College and its Principal, Ian Fraser, and by Bromley College of Further and Higher Education. I am also very grateful for the assistance of Stephen Rutt and Jane Powell of Macmillan Press Ltd, and for the support of my wife Avril and my family during the writing of the book.

ROGER STOREY

Part I
The Elements of Cost

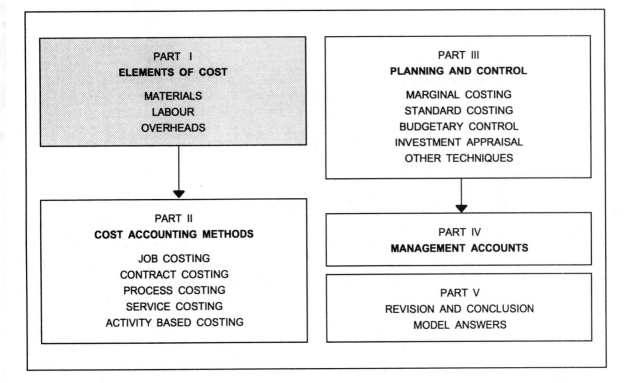

1

Cost and Management Accounting – Definitions

In this opening chapter we shall be defining the different forms accounting takes, namely: cost accounting; management accounting; and financial accounting. We shall then set the scene for what should prove to be an enjoyable and rewarding study of cost and management accounting methods, systems and techniques covered in the five parts of the book.

Here also we shall be taking a first look at the structure and organisation of the Accounts Department within a manufacturing company. (Later, in Chapter 7, we shall examine the roles and duties of the Cost Accountant, the Management Accountant and the Financial Accountant, and the various jobs and tasks carried out by them and the other members of staff in the department.)

Starting first with *definitions*:

COST ACCOUNTING

Cost accounting accounts for the costs of a product, a service or an operation. That is: the past costs, the present costs and the future costs.

MANAGEMENT ACCOUNTING

Management accounting provides the information requirements of management, thereby helping the management team to run the affairs of the business, operation or function effectively and efficiently.

FINANCIAL ACCOUNTING

Financial accounting accounts to the owners of the business and management (and various third parties interested in the affairs of the operation, such as banks and creditors), the actual financial transactions for a past accounting period. This is achieved through the issue of financial statements such as the annual profit and loss account, and balance sheet. Financial accounting is a legal necessity for limited companies, who are required to comply with the Companies Acts of 1985 and 1989.

Cost accounting is thus concerned with actual costs incurred and the estimation of future costs. Management accounting is concerned with providing information on past and present performance, and also estimations of future performance. There is thus a close connection between cost accounting and management accounting. Cost accounting is in fact recognised as being part of the much wider-ranging term, management accounting. The Chartered Institute of Management Accountants (CIMA) has defined precisely the terms 'cost accounting' and 'management accounting' in their publication *Management Accounting Official Terminology*. The definition of cost accounting is:

> *The establishment of budgets, standard costs and actual costs of operations, processes, activities or products; and the analysis of variances, profitability or the social use of funds.*

The first part of the definition shows that cost accounting establishes three things: budgets, standard costs and actual costs. The second part of the definition deals with analysis: analysis of variances, analysis of profitability and analysis of the social use of funds.

The definition of management accounting is:

An integral part of management concerned with identifying, presenting and interpreting information used for: formulating strategy; planning and controlling activities; decision taking; optimising the use of resources; disclosure to shareholders and others external to the entity; disclosure to employees; and safeguarding assets.

The primary purpose of management accounting is therefore to provide information and to interpret that information for management.

Relating these definitions to the sections of this book, dealing first with cost accounting: the establishment of budgets and standard costs, and the differences (variances) arising when comparing estimates of future performance with actual performance, are covered in detail in Part III – the planning and control section. Chapter 18 describes standard costs and variance analysis, and Chapter 19 deals with budgetary control.

With regard to the establishment of actual costs, the whole of Parts I and II are devoted to this area. In Part I, separate chapters describe each of the elements of cost (materials, labour and overheads); and Chapter 8 describes cost bookkeeping methods. In Part II the various cost accounting methods used by differing industries to record costs in their books of account are described fully.

Dealing now with the provision of information to management in accordance with the management accounting definition: in Part IV, two sets of periodic Management Accounts are included, one for a manufacturing company, the other for a service company. These illustrate how financial and trading information is presented to management on a regular periodic basis. Management Accounts are an essential part of the provision of information to management and many firms produce upwards of fifty pages in their monthly (or 4–5 weekly) Management Accounts, with some companies producing considerably more.

Unlike statutory accounts, which are required to be laid out precisely in accordance with the requirements of the Companies Acts, Management Accounts allow free rein for imagination and innovation in presentation and content of information.

Information to assist management in decision-taking is also a key feature of management accounting. In Part III, in addition to the chapters on standard costing and budgetary control there are chapters on marginal costing and cost–volume–profit techniques, investment appraisal methods and other control and forecasting techniques, such as trends analysis and the calculation of key performance indicators.

The structure of the book

The structure of the book has been designed to follow broadly the definitions of cost accounting and management accounting, as the diagrams at the beginning of each part illustrate.

Examination questions are set at the ends of chapters. The quantity of questions in each chapter broadly reflects the importance of the subjects to Examiners as observed from examination papers set over the past few years. Because of this 'weighting' there are a great many questions in Part III – planning and control – far more than in any other section. Examiners will, however, expect students to have a sound knowledge of the basics covered in Parts I and II, and will often structure the Part III-type questions to bring out this knowledge. Answers to the computational questions are given in Part V. These are the author's own solutions and are not endorsed by the various bodies (see Preface).

Management accounting is constantly evolving, with new techniques being developed continually. Some of these developments are introduced in Part V, to prepare students for more advanced studies of cost and management accounting techniques.

The key to successful planning and control is detailed analysis. Advances in computer technology enable the physical task of analysing data to be done rapidly by using powerful programs. This power provides further opportunities for management effectively to plan and control the costs and revenues of the organisation.

Management accounting techniques are designed to assist the management team run their enterprise or operation efficiently and effectively. The techniques can be used to revive, rejuvenate and perhaps revolutionise a business. The methods described in the following chapters work successfully and are used extensively by all progressive companies to plan and control their operations, both current and future.

Accounts Department structure

Returning now to the structure of the Accounts Department, an organisation chart for a typical manufacturing company might appear as in Figure 1.1 (note especially the various tasks each Accountant will be responsible for). Relating the organisation chart to the sections of the book, the responsibilities of the Cost Accountant will largely be covered in Parts I and II (accounting for the elements of cost and cost accounting methods). He or she will also be involved in certain tasks described in Part III, planning and control (in particular standard costing and budgeting).

The work of the Management Accountant will be reflected mainly in Parts III and IV – planning and

control, and the preparation and interpretation of information to management through the periodic management accounts.

Summary

- Cost accounting establishes budgets, standard costs and actual costs; management accounting is concerned with the presentation and interpretation of information for management. Parts I and II of the book are concerned with the establishment of and accounting for the actual costs; Part III with planning and controlling costs and revenues. Part IV provides a set of Management Accounts to illustrate how information is presented to management, and Part V provides solutions to the computational examination questions set.

FIGURE 1.1

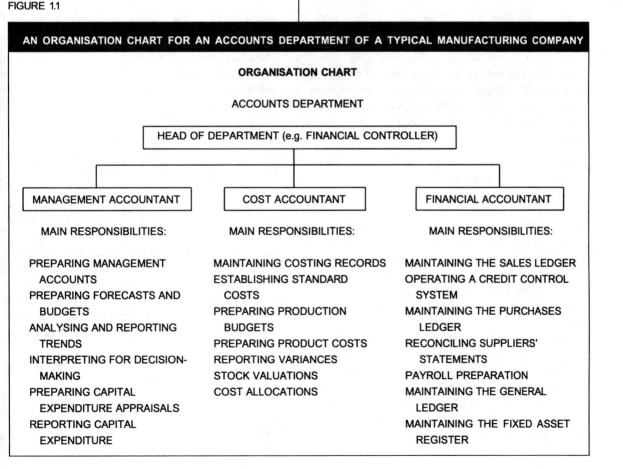

AN ORGANISATION CHART FOR AN ACCOUNTS DEPARTMENT OF A TYPICAL MANUFACTURING COMPANY

ORGANISATION CHART

ACCOUNTS DEPARTMENT

HEAD OF DEPARTMENT (e.g. FINANCIAL CONTROLLER)

MANAGEMENT ACCOUNTANT	COST ACCOUNTANT	FINANCIAL ACCOUNTANT
MAIN RESPONSIBILITIES:	MAIN RESPONSIBILITIES:	MAIN RESPONSIBILITIES:
PREPARING MANAGEMENT ACCOUNTS	MAINTAINING COSTING RECORDS	MAINTAINING THE SALES LEDGER
PREPARING FORECASTS AND BUDGETS	ESTABLISHING STANDARD COSTS	OPERATING A CREDIT CONTROL SYSTEM
ANALYSING AND REPORTING TRENDS	PREPARING PRODUCTION BUDGETS	MAINTAINING THE PURCHASES LEDGER
INTERPRETING FOR DECISION-MAKING	PREPARING PRODUCT COSTS	RECONCILING SUPPLIERS' STATEMENTS
PREPARING CAPITAL EXPENDITURE APPRAISALS	REPORTING VARIANCES	PAYROLL PREPARATION
REPORTING CAPITAL EXPENDITURE	STOCK VALUATIONS	MAINTAINING THE GENERAL LEDGER
	COST ALLOCATIONS	MAINTAINING THE FIXED ASSET REGISTER

2

Cost Classification and the Elements of Cost

Classification of costs by function

All commercial enterprises sell products or supply services, and by doing so incur costs and expenses. From this obvious basis it is possible to prepare an elementary profit and loss account which would look like this:

Sales	£1 000 000
Total costs	£ 600 000
Profit	£ 400 000

But, apart from not complying with the requirements of the Companies Acts and providing virtually no information to the owners, tax authorities and other interested parties, the above statement contributes practically nothing to assist management in running the operations of the business effectively and profitably.

Beneath these 'headline' figures lies a wealth of financial information available and waiting to be used to achieve these management aims and objectives. But to reach these goals it is necessary to analyse the figures; and this is accomplished through the grouping and classification of the numbers that make up the above total costs and sales.

In a manufacturing company the total costs figure is the sum of the following groups of costs:

Manufacturing costs;
Distribution costs;
Selling costs;
Administration costs; and
Interest charges and other costs.

By separating and classifying the total costs into these main categories, we can break down the total costs into logical operations or functions that will reflect the work undertaken in the enterprise. This analysis is called *cost classification by function*: the costs have been classified in line with the main functions carried out within the organisation.

In a retail business the broad classification will be similar, but with the exception that manufacturing costs are, of course, non-existent, all items for resale having been purchased from outside suppliers. These goods purchased for resale will be classified under a main group heading such as 'Purchases of goods for resale'.

In service companies, the broad functional classification might appear as follows:

Servicing costs;
Selling costs;
Administration costs; and
Interest and other costs.

6

This preparatory breakdown of the total costs figure thus provides financial information of considerable use. Using it, management is able to compare, for each accounting period, the total costs of the main functions and operations. For example, management will be able to relate the costs of each function to total sales, expressing each, perhaps, as a percentage of the sales. Managers can thus ascertain whether or not each of the function's costs are in line with expectations, therefore giving them broad control. They can also compare their own business costs with those of other similar enterprises, or, if in a group of companies, with similar divisions in the same organisation.

But more information than the above broad groupings is required to assist management in controlling day-to-day costs; and more information is also needed to provide a basis for financial planning and control for the future. This is provided by a detailed analysis of the costs. For detailed financial information is at the very heart of effective management control and planning.

FIGURE 2.1

THE STRUCTURE OF THE LEDGERS

GENERAL LEDGER ACCOUNTS (ALSO CALLED THE NOMINAL LEDGER) (ALSO CALLED THE TRADE DEBTORS LEDGER)	SALES LEDGER ACCOUNTS (ALSO CALLED THE BOUGHT LEDGER)	PURCHASES LEDGER ACCOUNTS
BALANCE SHEET ACCOUNTS FIXED ASSETS RAW MATERIALS STOCK WORK IN PROGRESS FINISHED GOODS CASH IN HAND CASH AT BANK SALES LEDGER CONTROL OTHER CURRENT DEBTORS PURCHASES LEDGER CONTROL OTHER CURRENT LIABILITIES LONG-TERM LOANS SHARE CAPITAL REVENUE RESERVES CAPITAL RESERVES	CREDIT CUSTOMERS' ACCOUNTS	CREDIT SUPPLIERS' ACCOUNTS

PROFIT AND LOSS ACCOUNTS:
SALES
MANUFACTURING COSTS
DISTRIBUTION COSTS
SELLING COSTS
ADMINISTRATION COSTS
OTHER COSTS AND INCOME

THIS IS AN EXAMPLE OF INTEGRATED ACCOUNTS. CHAPTER 8 DESCRIBES THIS SYSTEM, AND ANOTHER BOOKKEEPING METHOD CALLED INTERLOCKING ACCOUNTS.

Generally speaking, the greater the detail available, the greater the control.

Each of the main functions identified above: manufacturing, distribution, selling, administration, and the other costs (including interest payable, and research and development (R&D) costs when applicable), will be analysed further so that each item of cost within each of the function headings is accounted for separately.

Each individual cost heading will be classified by the issue of its own distinctive account code number. These code numbers are listed in a *Chart of Accounts*.

We shall work through a typical Chart of Accounts of a manufacturing company, but first we shall look at the structure of the ledgers which house the individual accounts to which the Chart of Accounts relates (see Figure 2.1).

The general ledger, or nominal ledger as it is sometimes called, holds the *impersonal* accounts of the business. The *personal* accounts (the customers' and suppliers' accounts) are maintained in the sales and purchases ledgers respectively.

The Chart of Accounts for the general ledger will reflect this structure, each account being assigned its own distinctive account code number. As we are focusing on costs and expenses here, we shall review that part of the Chart of Accounts only. In this example, a six-digit coding system is used: the first three digits indicate the department to which the cost or expense relates, and the last three digits the type or nature of the expense incurred. The Chart might be structured as in Figure 2.2.

The costs are first identified by their main grouping. For example, if a cost relates to manufacturing, then it will fall within the Group 1 code. So all manufacturing function costs will begin with the digit '1'. If it relates to the Maintenance Department, code 1/02 will be used.

The second section of the chart identifies the nature of the cost: for example, stationery costs are designated code 108. So a stationery invoice for the Maintenance Department will be coded 1/02/108 or 102/108 and charged to the Maintenance Department's stationery account bearing that code number.

Similarly, postage charges incurred by the Accounts Department will be coded 4/01/107 (or 401/107) and charged to the Accounts Department's postage account.

Additional analysis of costs and expenses can be provided to individual departments (such as the Transport Department) by extending the code structure. For example, management may need to know the running costs of each delivery van. Costs incurred for van expenses would then be coded 2/01/115, with a suffix to indicate each individual vehicle. Say the company had five vans, then costs for Van 1 would be charged to code 201/115/1; costs for Van 2, 201/115/2 and so on. Computerisation facilitates the analysis of costs and expenditure by providing almost limitless opportunities for cost analysis.

Thus, using a logical code structure, the cost of the broad 'headline' groupings can be further broken down through detailed analysis, thereby providing management with the ability to control costs.

The above illustration is an example of costs by function or department (also referred to as cost centres). These same costs can be classified in a number of other ways, providing management with a wealth of information. Examples are as follows.

Product Costs

These are costs that are incurred in the manufacturing process, designated in our example above as Cost Group 1. The product costs will be used to value the finished goods stocks of products made by the firm. The Chartered Institute of Management Accountants (CIMA) defines a product cost as '*the cost of a finished article built up from its cost elements*'. We now need to define these costs, termed the *elements of cost*.

Elements of cost

The elements of cost are: manufacturing costs plus distribution, selling, administrative and research and development costs.

The elements of cost within the manufacturing function which, when added together, form the product cost, are:

Direct materials (raw materials);
Direct labour;
Direct expenses; and
Factory overheads.

FIGURE 2.2

CHART OF ACCOUNTS

GROUP HEADING		DEPARTMENT HEADINGS	*CODE*

PROFIT AND LOSS ACCOUNTS

SALES	0	**MANUFACTURING**	
		PRODUCTION DEPARTMENT 1	1/00
		PRODUCTION DEPARTMENT 2	1/01
MANUFACTURING COSTS	1	MAINTENANCE DEPARTMENT	1/02
		STORES DEPARTMENT	1/03
DISTRIBUTION COSTS	2	CANTEEN	1/04
		PRODUCTION ADMINISTRATION	1/05
SELLING COSTS	3		
		DISTRIBUTION	
ADMINISTRATION COSTS	4	WAREHOUSE	2/00
		TRANSPORT DEPARTMENT	2/01
OTHER INCOME AND EXPENDITURE	5		
		SELLING	
		FIELD SALES FORCE	3/00
		TELESALES	3/01
		SELLING ADMINISTRATION	3/02
		ADMINISTRATION	
		MANAGING DIRECTOR	4/00
BALANCE SHEET ACCOUNTS	*GROUP CODE*	ACCOUNTS DEPARTMENT	4/01
		PERSONNEL DEPARTMENT	4/02
FIXED ASSETS	6		
CURRENT ASSETS	7	**OTHER INCOME AND EXPENDITURE**	
CURRENT LIABILITIES	8	INTEREST PAYABLE	5/00
LOANS, CAPITAL AND RESERVES	9	INTEREST RECEIVABLE	5/01
		DISCOUNTS RECEIVED	5/02
		DISCOUNTS ALLOWED	5/03

NATURE OF COST/EXPENSE

	CODE
BONUSES	100
COMMISSIONS PAYABLE	101
DEPRECIATION CHARGES	102
HOLIDAY PAY	103
LEGAL AND PROFESSIONAL FEES	104
MISCELLANEOUS EXPENSES	105
PENSION COSTS	106
POSTAGE CHARGES	107
PRINTING AND STATIONERY	108
REPAIRS AND RENEWALS	109
SALARIES AND WAGES	110
SOCIAL SECURITY COSTS	111
SUPPLIES AND INDIRECT MATERIALS	112
TELEPHONE AND FAX CHARGES	113
TRAVEL AND SUBSISTENCE EXPENSES	114
VEHICLE EXPENSES	115

Direct costs are those costs that can be established as being clearly a constituent part of the end product. CIMA defines direct costs as: '*expenditure which can be economically identified with a specific saleable cost unit*'.

Factory overheads, also known as *indirect costs* (or burden as it is sometimes described), are *not* able to be so identified with the saleable product. The CIMA definition of an overhead is '*expenditure on labour, materials or services which cannot be economically identified with a specific saleable cost*'.

Looking at the four elements of manufacturing cost listed above:

Direct materials

This is the cost of the raw materials that can be identified specifically within the finished product. For example, the cost of the paper used to produce this book, together with the board or card for the cover, are direct costs of producing the book. The cost of the paper and board can be specifically and clearly identified within the finished product.

You will have noted the use of the word *economically* in the definitions of direct costs and factory overheads. So, to use the same example of this book for illustration, the glue used, which might account for very little cost in relation to the other direct material costs, may well be treated as an indirect cost and therefore become a factory overhead. This is because the company might decide that it would not be worthwhile to spend time and possibly incur extra costs in measuring the small amount of glue used, because of the relatively low value of the glue; it would not be economical to measure it. The cost of the glue then becomes a factory overhead and will be treated as a manufacturing cost, classified perhaps as consumable materials.

Direct materials costs are, therefore, raw materials costs which can be tracked economically and identified within the finished article.

Direct labour

This is the payroll cost of the production staff (frequently called production operatives) who are directly employed in making the end product. It covers their gross pay and related on-costs. (The term 'on-cost' is used to cover the cost of national insurance and pension costs borne by the company.) To be classified as direct labour the costs must be

identified specifically within the finished product. Thus any time not spent directly by the operatives in the production of the finished item (for example, idle time, when they have not been able to produce the products), will not be classified as a direct labour cost. Instead, this non-productive time will be treated as an overhead cost. Other labour costs which cannot be identified specifically with individual end products (such as foremen's and supervisors' wages, factory cleaning staff, and production administration wages and salaries), are described as *indirect labour costs* and classified as factory overheads.

Direct expenses

A direct expense is any other cost, apart from direct materials and direct labour, which is capable of being identified economically with the finished product. Examples are: royalties per article produced, payable to an inventor for the production rights to produce the article; hire of equipment costs for a specific job; and any other cost which relates specifically to a finished article and can therefore be traced to that completed item.

The *prime cost* of a finished article is the sum of direct materials plus direct labour.

Factory overheads

All other costs incurred within the manufacturing process which cannot be identified economically within the finished product are thus classified as factory overheads.

To illustrate these costs, study the layout of a typical factory illustrated in Figure 2.3 to see how a manufacturing company is organised and planned. This will be of assistance in visualising where and how the factory overheads and the other elements of manufacturing cost are incurred.

Within the area headed *production functions* all the elements of manufacturing costs are incurred: the prime costs and the factory overheads. These combine to produce the product costs. The two Production Departments will produce the finished items and therefore each will be charged with the raw materials and direct labour costs incurred in these departments.

You will see that the raw material passes from one section to the next. As an illustration, assume that the work in Production Department 1 is related to converting the raw materials, through machining or processing, into the basic, identifiable, but as yet unfinished, product; the work in Department 2 might then be to provide the finishing touches to the product: for example, packaging to complete the finished article.

The other departments in the area represent the support services for the production departments. They are therefore classified as production or factory overheads.

But not all of the costs incurred directly by the Production Departments are prime costs. Some will be factory overheads. For example, each department might employ a supervisor and also cleaning staff. Also, there may be rent and rates payable. These costs, not being specifically identifiable with the finished product, are treated as factory overheads.

TABLE 2.1

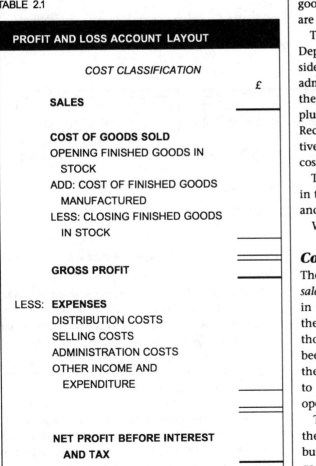

Similarly, some of the materials used in the two Production Departments – for example, oil and cleaning fluid – probably cannot be identified economically with the end product. These too are factory overheads and are classified as indirect materials.

So all the costs incurred in the manufacturing process, if not identified as direct costs, are classified as factory overheads. These will be collected in convenient and logical cost centres – departments – or under other suitable headings: for example, the Production Manager's Department, the Buying Department, Maintenance Department, and so on.

Referring back briefly to the Chart of Accounts shown in Figure 2.2 on page 9, you will see that, broadly, the chart reflects the physical factory layout: the production functions represent Group 1, the manufacturing costs. The distribution costs are incurred in the shaded areas, that is, the finished goods store and the packing and despatch area, and are classified as distribution, Group 2 costs.

The selling costs are represented by the Sales Department plus any Marketing Department and outside sales staff costs (Group 3, selling costs); and the administration costs are represented by the total of all the other departments: the Managing Director's costs plus the costs of the Accounts Department, Personnel, Reception and Postal areas, and any other administrative functionary's costs (Group 4, administration costs).

This classification of costs by function as reflected in the Chart of Accounts will be reported in the profit and loss account, as Table 2.1 illustrates.

Working through this classification of the costs:

Cost of goods sold section

The cost of goods sold section (also known as *cost of sales*) represents the costs of the finished articles sold in the accounting period. So, if 1000 units are sold, the cost of sales figure represents the cost of making those 1000 units. Some of the sold items will have been made in earlier accounting periods. The cost of these items is brought forward from the earlier periods to the current accounting period as finished goods opening stock.

The cost of finished goods manufactured amount is the total of the elements of manufacturing cost attributable to the production of the completed finished goods made during the current period.

FIGURE 2.3

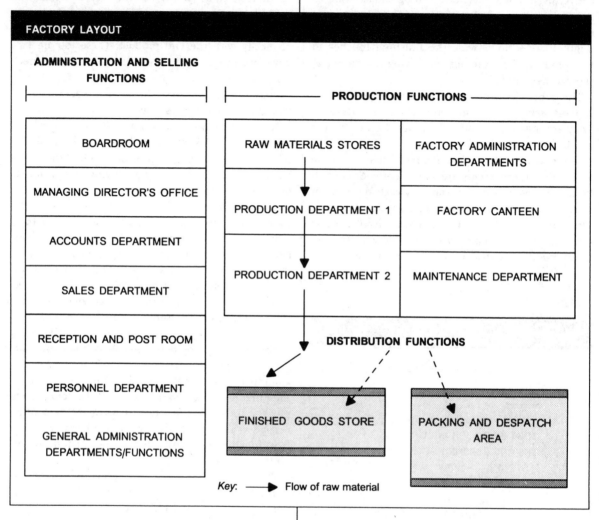

FACTORY LAYOUT

Key: ⟶ Flow of raw material

The closing stock figure represents those finished goods held at the end of the accounting period in the finished goods store area and thus not yet sold. This amount will be carried forward to the next accounting period to become that period's opening finished goods stock.

This section of the profit and loss account thus represents the Product Costs.

Expenses section

The costs of the other functions are reported in the Expenses section as shown in Table 2.1. All of these costs are described as *period costs*. It is important to note the difference between *product costs* and *period costs*:

The elements of cost incurred in the manufacturing process, (the raw materials, direct labour and production overheads), are used to determine the value of finished goods in accordance with standard accounting practice (SSAP 9, stocks and long-term contracts, of which more later) and are therefore classified as *product costs*.

All other costs incurred by the business (distribution, selling, administration and so on), are described as *period costs* and are charged to the accounting period to which they relate.

Period costs are therefore written off to the profit and loss account in accordance with the standard accounting practice that states that costs must match revenue in each accounting period: the 'accruals concept' part of SSAP 2, disclosure of accounting policies, which will also be discussed later.

Cost centres and cost units

The classification of the manufacturing overheads by departments as depicted in the examples above can also be described as *classification by cost centre*, because both the production departments and the service departments are cost centres. A cost centre could also be a machine or group of machines within one of these departments.

A *cost unit* is a unit of product (or unit of service) to which costs are ascertained by means of allocation, apportionment and absorption. (How costs are allocated, apportioned and absorbed is explained in Chapters 5 and 6.) A cost unit is a useful measurement of costs for comparative purposes.

Other classifications of costs

The main classification of costs is by function, as described above, which facilitates the reporting of costs in accordance with areas of management responsibility. These same costs can also be analysed and classified in many other ways to assist in planning and further control. Some of these other classifications are as follows:

Fixed and variable costs

Costs 'behave' according to various levels of activity achieved. Some costs increase or decrease in line with activity, while others remain relatively the same irrespective of the changes.

The total costs of the enterprise can thus broadly be categorised by behaviour as either costs that vary with activity – *variable costs* – or costs that stay relatively the same, unaffected by the changes in activity in the short term – *fixed costs*.

Direct materials, for example, would vary more or less in line with production activity: the more items produced the more direct materials would be consumed. Similarly, the higher the sales, the higher the cost of commission payable to agents, assuming the

company makes sales through this medium. There is thus an implied linear relationship between the variable cost and the level of activity: as sales increase so do the variable costs.

On the other hand, the costs of running the Accounts Department, say, in the short term may be completely unaffected whether sales rise or fall. Therefore the Accounts Department costs would be classified as a fixed cost.

Some costs which initially might be considered as fixed will change as different levels of activity are reached. These costs therefore have both fixed cost and variable cost elements within them and will thus be affected by the activity changes. Such costs are described as either *semi-fixed* or *semi-variable costs*.

We shall be covering fully the usefulness of this method of classifying costs in Chapter 17, on Marginal Costing and CVP Analysis.

Avoidable costs

Some costs can be classified as avoidable. That is, if the firm decides to close down a department or a production line completely, or perhaps ceases to carry out R&D, then the current specific costs incurred and arising solely from those activities would end, and thus be avoided.

To be able to classify costs in this way is useful when considering the *contribution* made by an activity; avoidable costs will be covered more fully in Chapter 17.

It follows that, as some costs are considered to be avoidable, then other costs will (in the short term) be considered to be unavoidable: for example, rent and rates of the premises. If one particular department were closed down, the rent and rates for the whole factory would still need to be paid.

Avoidable costs are defined by CIMA as '*the specific costs of an activity or sector of a business which would be avoided if that activity or sector did not exist*'.

Controllable costs

The organisation and structure of a business signifies various levels of management, each individual manager controlling and being responsible for his or her own sphere of influence within the whole. In the factory example described above, there would probably be a manager in charge of each of the production departments. Also a raw materials warehouse manager, a buyer, a distribution manager, a transport manager, a sales manager and so on. Each person has some control or influence on how much is spent within his or her own section.

If a manager has sway on a particular cost and can influence the outcome of the cost, then that cost is the responsibility of that particular manager: he or she has the ability or power to alter the amount of the expense. Conversely, a non-controllable expense signifies that the individual manager does not have the power to alter or influence the cost.

It should be noted that each layer of management has its own controllable/non-controllable level of responsibility and thus cost control powers. This culminates in the board of directors who are able to control, in the long term, all the costs of the enterprise.

The usefulness of classifying costs this way helps to control costs, because each person becomes accountable for those costs identified as controllable. Controllable costs can be classified readily through the code structure outlined in the chart of accounts, which can be drawn up to accommodate any requirements of management. It follows that if a manager is responsible for the control of costs, some measure of the success or failure in doing so is required. This comparison is provided by way of budgeting for the costs. Each manager will thus be provided with a budget for his or her controllable costs. Budgets are dealt with in Chapter 19 on Budgetary Control. CIMA defines a controllable cost as *'a cost which can be influenced by its budget holder'*.

Differential costs

Whenever management is planning and deciding on future investment opportunities, alternative courses of action are usually open to them and they will have to choose between the competing schemes and risks involved. The alternatives need to be carefully considered financially, as each opportunity will result in differing total costs and revenues, therefore differing profits or cost savings.

The difference in the total costs between each of the alternatives is described as the *differential cost*. Another term used for this is *incremental costs*. Normally the more favourable alternative will be chosen if finance and return on the investment are the sole selection criteria. Note that with differential cost classification it is the total costs of each alternative (the fixed costs and the variable costs) that are taken into consideration when arriving at the differential costs.

Discretionary or managed costs

Costs can be said to reflect management action or behaviour and can therefore be classified as 'engineered', 'committed' or 'discretionary'.

When costs are looked at from this point of view, the costs of manufacturing the product (the variable costs of direct materials and direct labour) are considered to be 'engineered' by the management, that is, the management have decided the content and method of production and have therefore *engineered* its cost.

Most of the fixed costs are necessary to produce the finished article and are therefore designated as *committed* costs; money has to be spent on these costs otherwise the product could not be produced. For example, the costs of the premises (rent and rates, buildings insurance and so on); the depreciation of plant and machinery; supervision; production management; and so on. These costs are therefore committed.

This leaves other costs, fixed or variable, that arise from management decisions unconnected with the engineered or committed costs necessary to complete the products. These are deemed to be *discretionary*: the money spent is completely at the discretion of the management. For example, experimental work, R&D costs, the cost of providing music in the factory, Christmas turkeys for each member of staff, and so on. Synonyms for discretionary costs are: *'managed costs'* costs and *'policy costs'*.

Relevant costs

When management makes a financial decision regarding future opportunities, the costs to be incurred, which relate solely to that decision, are termed *relevant costs*. So, costs that are not affected by the decision (for example, current fixed costs which will not change irrespective of the decision) are irrelevant to the decision and therefore ignored.

This classification of costs for decision-making purposes assists management by concentrating only on costs that will arise or will change when a decision has been made. It therefore facilitates rapid comparisons between profit-earning or cost-saving projects by emphasising only the costs that will be incurred or will change according to the express decision of the management.

Sunk costs

In making decisions about future opportunities, management obviously needs to consider the future costs and prospective revenue of the various ventures or cost savings set before them, in order to come to a reasoned and rational conclusion.

However, costs relating to these opportunities may already have been incurred and charged in an earlier accounting period – market research costs, for example.

Consequently, whether the management goes ahead with the projects or not, that earlier expenditure has been spent, *sunk*, in the earlier decision to carry out the market research, and it becomes just another incurred cost, irrelevant to management's decision.

Opportunity costs

An opportunity cost is a cost that has not actually been paid out in cash to a third party: it is the 'loss' of relinquishing or sacrificing an existing or possible benefit arising out of utilising an asset for another purpose.

So, if a machine is capable of producing a product that is able to contribute £1000 to profits, but the machine time spent on its manufacture may be required for an alternative purpose, the profit of £1000 (actual or potentially realisable) is a benefit given up in favour of the new opportunity: the benefit sacrificed is therefore the *opportunity cost* of using the machine for that alternative purpose. The opportunity cost is added to the total costs incurrable on the chosen project. The selling price of this project should therefore cover the costs associated with it *plus* the opportunity cost (£1000 in this case) plus, of course, a profit element. If the selling price does not cover the total cost plus the opportunity costs then the chosen project will clearly not result in a benefit greater than the present use of the asset.

FIGURE 2.4

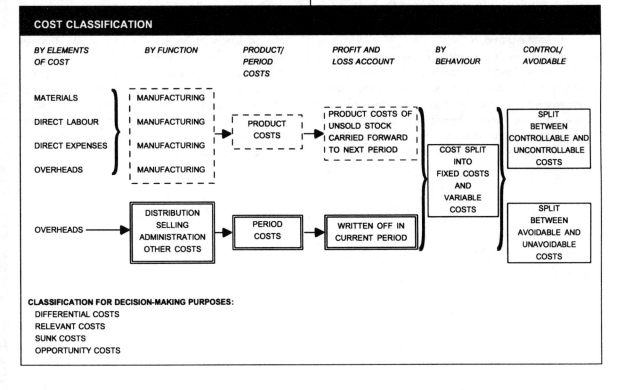

The advantage therefore of including opportunity cost in decision-making is that the present or potential benefits of an asset are taken into consideration and management will therefore be able to see whether or not a financial advantage to the company will be forthcoming from the change. Both sunk costs and opportunity costs are discussed further in Chapter 21, about Other Control Techniques.

Summary

- Costs are classified by function. This assists in identifying management responsibility for the costs incurred in each function.
- The sorting of costs is facilitated by the use of code numbers with a separate account for each cost heading being maintained in the general ledger. A chart of accounts provides a list of these account codes.
- Functional costs are grouped and reported in financial statements as follows: manufacturing costs, distribution and selling costs, administration costs, other costs.
- Cost centres are departments or other appropriately identifiable areas, to which costs can be charged. A cost unit is a convenient measure of the costs of one unit of product or service for control or for comparative purposes.
- A product cost is the total of the manufacturing elements of cost of a finished article. These cost elements are: raw materials, direct labour, direct expenses and factory overheads. Raw materials are also known as direct materials. The prime cost represents the sum of the raw materials and direct labour. Period cost is a cost incurred in an accounting period and written off to the profit and loss account in the accounting period to which it relates. Costs can be classified for other purposes, summarised as follows:
- Costs behave in accordance with levels of activity. Costs can be classified as either variable or fixed and considered to move in line with activity (variable costs) or remain relatively the same (fixed costs). Costs that move in 'steps' as production or sales activity increases or decreases are classified as semi-fixed costs (or semi-variable costs).
- Avoidable costs are costs that will cease if an activity ceases.
- Controllable costs are costs that can be influenced, and therefore controlled, by a manager at his or her level of responsibility within the organisation.
- Differential cost is the difference in total costs between alternative courses of action.
- Discretionary costs are deemed to be not necessarily essential to the manufacture of the products or services supplied by the organisation. In times of cutbacks and economic downturns, discretionary costs are usually the first to be reviewed and reduced.
- Relevant costs are costs that will change according to the decision of the management on future alternatives. Costs that will not change are irrelevant to the decision and therefore ignored.
- Sunk costs are costs that have already been incurred and are ignored by management when costing new ventures or cost-saving opportunities.
- An opportunity cost is an existing benefit or potential benefit 'surrendered' in favour of an alternative. The benefit sacrificed is added to the costs of the alternative to ensure that the new opportunity provides a greater financial benefit than do the existing benefits.

3

The Elements of Cost: Materials

Every tangible finished product is made from a basic raw material or a combination of raw materials. The paper in this book, the wood in the desk, the plastic in the chair, the rubber and steel in the car tyres, and so on.

Raw materials are directly identifiable as part of the finished product and are classified as *direct materials*. CIMA's *Official Terminology* defines raw materials as: '*Goods purchased for incorporation into products for sale*'. Raw materials are one of the elements of manufacturing cost and as such constitute part of the cost of the finished product. Costs that are identifiable as part of the finished article are described as 'product costs'.

There are often numerous other materials purchases which cannot be directly identifiable for incorporation into the finished product but which are nevertheless an essential part of the production process. Such materials and goods are classified as *indirect materials*.

These are frequently referred to as 'consumable materials', meaning the materials used to operate and run the plant and equipment, machine oil, cleaning materials, various loose tools and so on. Consumables may also embrace the cost of small value items which *are* identifiable in the finished product but because of the low value involved management may decide that it is uneconomic to treat them as direct materials. Examples of such materials are tags and adhesives.

Materials control

Stocks of raw materials may represent a significant investment for the business. It is therefore of great importance that proper control is exercised in the management of this stock. There are a number of techniques available to help management to achieve this control but we will first take an overview of how raw materials are ordered and received, and then how the management are able to control the *levels* of stocks carried, thus helping to ensure that stocks are always available for the production process and that funds are not tied up unnecessarily in carrying excess stocks.

We shall assume that the company employs a Buyer and that there is a raw materials stores area. The Buyer will be a member of the Factory Administration section. Referring back to the factory layout in Figure 2.3 on page 12 you will see that these two functions are support services to the two Production Departments.

The major objectives of the Buying Department are to negotiate the best price and delivery terms with suppliers, to issue purchase orders, to reorder, and to take up queries arising with the suppliers. These activities will be assisted by information supplied by the raw materials warehouse section, such as the details of the movement of raw materials or components of each line of stock held. This transfer of information will frequently be through a computer program linking the two departments by way of a networking facility. Or the communication may simply be achieved by passing documents between the two departments.

The raw materials warehouse will be responsible for storing the materials efficiently and effectively, to ensure that the materials are accessible and able to be moved to the production areas quickly and easily. This warehouse will also be responsible for receiving raw materials from the suppliers and also confirming that the goods received are in accordance with the goods ordered by the Buying Department, both in terms of quantity and quality. Figure 3.1 illustrates the

FIGURE 3.1

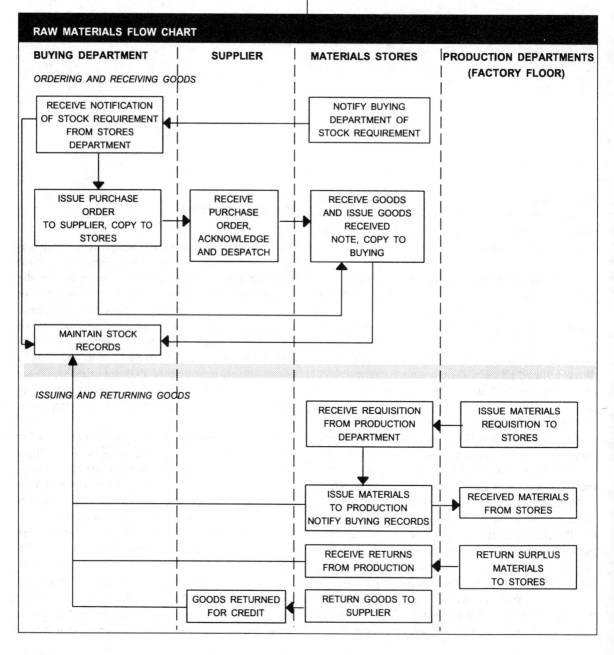

interrelationship between the two departments, and the supplier, and also the production area (the factory floor).

Ordering raw materials

Starting from the premise that management will have already decided on the raw materials requirements for the products, details of quantities and technical specifications will be given to the Buying Department for action. This could be in the form of a *purchase requisition form,* which is prepared by an authorised member of the management team, and simply instructs the Buying Department to go ahead and purchase a required quantity of materials or an article. Occasionally an indication of the price will also be given on the form.

The Buying Department will then negotiate, or confirm, the price and the delivery date requirements directly with the supplier. Cash settlement discounts and trade (quantity) discounts will also be arranged whenever appropriate. When the negotiations have been determined and settled a *purchase order* will then be raised by the department and sent to the supplier, with a copy retained in the department and a further copy being passed on to the warehouse, or 'goods in' section. Additional copies may also be passed to the Accounts Department.

A typical purchase order will comprise the following:

The name and address of the supplier;

The date it was issued;

A purchase order number, or reference, for identification purposes;

A list of the items required, including serial numbers and descriptions when appropriate;

The quantity required of each separate item;

The price agreed of each item and whether VAT applies or not;

The cash discount deductible if the supplier's payment terms are adhered to;

The quantity discount applicable to the purchase;

The date when delivery is required; and

The total value of the order, exclusive or inclusive of VAT.

When completed, the purchase order will then be signed by the Buyer or other individual authorised to commit the company to the spend. This last point is very important because, if correctly authorised, the company has officially entered into a contract with the supplier and is therefore legally committed to pay if the supplier complies with the order and delivers the goods.

The supplier will normally acknowledge receipt of the order by issuing an *order acknowledgement form,* which confirms the contents of the purchase order and thus agrees the contract.

Receiving raw materials

When the goods are delivered, the supplier's deliverer (carrier) will usually provide a document to confirm the details of the load. This is the *delivery note* (or *advice note*). It is usually a form in duplicate and contains the full details of the quantity and items delivered. Upon being unloaded, the goods are carefully examined by the goods in warehouse staff, with the details checked against the copy purchase order to confirm that quantities and items are both in agreement. This is very important because most suppliers stipulate that discrepancies (short deliveries perhaps) be notified to them within three working days. Failure to do so, or a delay in notification, can create additional costs, and these costs could well be substantial because if notification of non-delivery is not made the company will probably have to pay for disputed items.

The supplier's carrier will generally require the signature of the person receiving the goods as proof that the goods have been delivered. If there are discrepancies it is essential these are noted before signing.

An internal document, the *goods received note* (or *goods received report*) will be issued by the goods in staff at the time the goods are received. This will record the quantity and items received and other details, as illustrated in Figure 3.2.

The warehouse employee receiving and checking the delivery will complete the goods received note and copies will be distributed to the various departments who have involvement in the transactions (that is, the Buying Department, the Accounts Department and the warehouse records section). In the example in Figure 3.2 a 'short delivery' occurred: there are four items on the delivery note but only three items were delivered. The shortage will be brought to the attention of the supplier by the Buying Department or the person designated the task of querying deliveries. The Accounts Department will know of the discrepancy through receipt of a copy of the

FIGURE 3.2

GOODS RECEIVED NOTE					

OFFICE USE:			GRN NO:	7291
GOODS ENTERED BY:	KJ		PURCHASE ORDER NO:	AS642
MATCHED WITH PO BY:	SB		SUPPLIER DELIVERY NO:	M2346
CHECKED WITH INVOICE BY:	AS			

GOODS RECEIVED FROM: *A. SUPPLIER*

ITEM	DESCRIPTION OF GOODS	QUANTITY	STOCK RECORD NO:
1	*MATERIALS TYPE A*	10	1234
2	*MATERIALS TYPE B*	25	1235
3	*MATERIALS TYPE C*	37	1236

RECEIVED IN BY *A. WAREHOUSEMAN*

NOTES AND COMMENTS:
DELIVERY NOTE LISTED 4 ITEMS
BUT ONLY THREE WERE RECEIVED
AS ABOVE. SUPPLIER'S DELIVERY
NOTE AMENDED BY ME. AW

goods received note and will therefore ensure that the supplier's invoice will only charge for the three items, or the department will request a *credit note* if four are charged on the supplier's invoice (or perhaps raise a *debit note*, which effectively charges back to the supplier the missing items).

Recording materials stock

The movements of stock and the quantities of each item held must be recorded if management is to control and plan the levels of stocks effectively and efficiently. A *stock control record* for each item will therefore be maintained. The stock record – which may be a computer record or maintained clerically on a card or sheet – is illustrated as follows in Figure 3.3.

As each movement in stock occurs an appropriate entry will be made to record the change in the stock position. The sources of the receipts entries are: the goods received notes or equivalent, and any materials returned to the stores from the production departments.

The sources of the issues entries will be the *materials requisition notes* (which will be discussed later in this chapter), and any returns to suppliers. Note, however, that returns to suppliers are sometimes shown

as negative entries in the receipts column instead of being entered in the issues column. A running balance is maintained to show the up-to-date stock position.

The record can provide further information for management; for example, it can record *stock allocations*. So, though the balance appears to be available and therefore appears free to issue to production, it may be that some or all of the stock is required for a job or process which may not yet have been started. Stock will therefore have been allocated to that particular job and is therefore not available for general issue.

Another name for this record is the *bin card*, which is a physical card and very often located with the actual materials, being updated manually each time a receipt or issue is made.

You will note the other items on the stock control record, namely *reorder level, reorder quantity* and *maximum and minimum levels*. These are indicators used by management to oversee and control the stocks, thus avoiding over-stock and under-stock situations.

Stock control

Too much stock ties up space and cash and is therefore costly and inefficient; too little stock creates the problem of the likelihood of running out of materials and

FIGURE 3.3

STOCK CONTROL RECORD						

ITEM   ITEM NUMBER

STOCK LEVELS: MINIMUM: MAXIMUM: REORDER QUANTITY:

REORDER QUANTITY:

DATE	DETAIL	STOCK RECEIVED Quantity	STOCK ISSUED Quantity	BALANCE Quantity	ALLOCATED STOCK Quantity	FREE STOCK Quantity

therefore halting production or resulting in 'panic' buying at, most probably, much higher purchase prices, which is also costly and inefficient.

To overcome both of these extremes, stock control methods are necessary. Stock control is achieved by setting maximum and minimum levels of stock and by calculating the stockholding point where it is necessary to reorder further supplies.

In order to set these levels it is necessary to research the *usage* of each item over a period of time. This will establish the maximum and minimum quantities used over that particular period of time. Past experience or estimated future requirements can be the basis for these calculations. Additionally, the average usage can also be established.

It is also necessary to ascertain from the supplier the *lead time* required for the goods to be delivered. This is the difference in time, usually expressed in days or weeks, that the supplier takes to deliver the goods from the date of receipt of the purchase order. Most suppliers, to allow for delays sometimes outside of their control, will usually indicate both a minimum and maximum time for delivery, for example 4 to 6 weeks. (The customer may, however, insist on a precise delivery date and the exact date will then form part of the contract.) The delivery details thus provide both maximum and minimum lead times; from these figures an average lead time can then be calculated.

Once the usage figures and the lead times have been determined, the various stock control levels can be set, namely the reorder level, the maximum level and the minimum level. The calculations necessary to do this are as follows:

Reorder level

Maximum usage × Maximum lead time
= Reorder level

This calculation tells management *when* materials have to be ordered. It is the first stock level to be calculated as it forms a constituent of the maximum and minimum level computations.

When the stock reaches this reorder level a purchase order will be raised placing an order for the *reorder quantity*. This is to ensure that sufficient stock is available for future production needs, thus avoiding out-of-stock situations arising.

The assumption behind the reorder level computation is that production is at its highest, therefore demand for the material is at its greatest, but the supplier is taking the longest quoted time to deliver the materials.

Example:

Maximum usage:	5000 units per week
Maximum lead time:	10 weeks
Reorder level	= 50 000 units.

Maximum Level

> Reorder level
> − (Minimum usage × Minimum lead time)
> + Reorder quantity
> = Maximum level

Here the reorder level is effectively 'lowered' by reducing it to the low point in production and the assumption that the supplier delivers the materials in the quickest time. To this lower level is added the reorder quantity. (It should be noted that the justification for setting a maximum level is that a consequence of stock exceeding this level will be cash tied up unnecessarily in stocks. The excess will need financing, perhaps from bank borrowings at high levels of interest. So overstocking, when coupled with the loss of use of the money tied up, which could perhaps be used for other purposes, can be very costly).

Example:

Reorder level:	50 000 units (from the earlier calculation)
Minimum usage:	3 000 units per week
Minimum lead time:	6 weeks
Reorder quantity:	40 000 units
Maximum level	= 50 000 − (3000 × 6) + 40 000
	= 72 000 units

Minimum Level

> Reorder level − (Average usage × Average lead time)
> = Minimum level

The minimum level also uses the reorder level as the base but this time adjusted downwards by the *average* usage and lead time figures. The purpose of setting this minimum level is to alert management to the possibility of running out of stock, which would create serious production problems resulting perhaps in the likelihood that production ceases altogether while awaiting delivery of further supplies.

Example:

Reorder level:	50 000 units
Average usage:	4000 units per week
Average lead time:	8 weeks
Minimum level	= 50 000 − (4000 × 8)
	= 18 000 units

With respect to the minimum level, however, caution teaches 'better to be safe than sorry' and management will normally ensure that a *safety stock level* is maintained, which will provide sufficient cover for all anticipated eventualities. The minimum level will therefore be set higher than the above calculated level. When set to include safety stock the *reorder level* will change. The minimum level will then be:

> Reorder level + Safety stock − Average usage
> × Average lead time

Example:

Reorder level:	50 000 units
Safety Stock level:	20 000 units
Average usage:	4000 units per week
Average lead time:	8 weeks
Reorder level	= 50 000 + 20 000
	= 72 000 units

Note: Safety stocks are also described as 'buffer stocks'.

Reorder quantity

Management may decide the reorder quantity based on past experience or past practice, or on judgement. Or they may decide to calculate an *economic order quantity* (EOQ). This is a theoretical concept that attempts to bring together the cost factors involved in stockholding, namely the cost of holding stock and the costs involved in raising purchase orders. By this method a reorder quantity will be arrived at which results in the lowest costs of both these factors. For example, the Buying Department's costs of placing one order per year with a supplier will clearly be much cheaper than placing one order per week: less clerical work, fewer postage stamps and so on will be required for one order rather than for fifty-two. But the warehouse and storage costs – interest on the higher levels of stock needed to be carried, extra space used and so on, will be much greater than would be the case with individual weekly deliveries. The EOQ method endeavours to find the cost equilibrium between the two factors. Figure 3.4 provides the formula for the economic order quantity.

FIGURE 3.4

ECONOMIC ORDER QUANTITY FORMULA

$$\sqrt{\frac{2 \times \text{ANNUAL CONSUMPTION} \times \text{COST PER ORDER}}{\text{HOLDING COST PER ITEM pa}}}$$

The formula assumes consistency in all the constituent parts of the equation; that is, that annual consumption is evenly spaced throughout the year and that the cost per order and holding costs are certain and constant. Regrettably, all these desirables occur rarely in reality. But the EOQ, if used by management as an indicator, can be both useful and beneficial. With the use of computer spreadsheets and the relative ease of programming, the EOQ can be calculated and constantly updated for each type of material carried.

Dealing with the constituent parts of the equation:

Cost per Order

The costs involved in raising an order are primarily incurred in the Buying Department. Most of these costs are of a fixed nature; for example, the occupancy costs of the department (heat, light, rent and rates, etc.), and the salaries of the staff employed, and the everyday running costs incurred. These costs will remain more or less the same in the short term whether the actual number of purchase orders

processed by the department increases or decreases. But other order processing costs will vary in accordance with the number of orders issued – for example, postage and stationery costs.

To arrive at the cost per order can be a complex calculation on its own right. Precisely what costs should be included? Should only relevant costs be considered? And so on.

Here, however, to illustrate the benefits the EOQ can bring as an indicator of the quantity to be ordered, a straightforward view can be taken to arrive at the order costs.

The calculation for this is as follows :

$$\frac{\text{Total order costs in accounting period}}{\text{Purchase orders issued in accounting period}}$$

The total order costs represent the operating costs of the Buying Department plus any other costs directly related to ordering the materials or components, for example, postal charges. The purchase orders issued figure is the total number of orders raised in the accounting period.

Example:
Running costs per annum of
   buying department: £50 000
Number of orders raised per annum: 1 000
Cost per order   = £50

Holding cost

As with the order cost, the calculation of the holding cost is subject to differing views but, using a relatively straightforward approach, the holding cost can be computed as follows:

$$\frac{\text{Warehousing costs in accounting period}}{\text{average value of total stocks held}}$$

Here, the warehousing costs will be the operating costs of the warehouse, (warehouse wages and salaries, premises costs, insurance costs, interest on the capital tied up in stockholding, and other related carrying costs).

The average value of total stocks held can be found by taking the opening and closing stocks and dividing by two.

Example:
Warehousing costs

per annum:	£88 000
Opening total stocks:	£1 000 000
Closing total stocks:	£1 200 000
Average total stocks:	£1 100 000
Holding cost	= £88 000/£1 100 000
	= £0.08

Thus, the holding cost is 8p per annum to carry £1 of stock.

Calculation of the EOQ

Example:

Annual consumption:	200 000 units
Order cost:	£50
Holding cost:	£0.08

Using the above formula, the calculations are:

$$\text{EOQ} = \sqrt{(2 \times 200\,000 \times £50/£0.08)} = 15\,811 \text{ units}$$

FIGURE 3.5

When plotted on a graph, the three stock control levels will appear as shown in Figure 3.5.

Materials accounting

So far we have looked at the processes of ordering and receiving the raw materials and the way stock levels are controlled. These functions will generally be the responsibility of stores management with accounting backup in researching the usage and lead times data and providing the computations for each level of stockholding. We now need to look at how the stocks are accounted for and how the materials requisition notes are evaluated so that (i) the materials cost content of each job or process carried out on the shop floor can be arrived at; and (ii) to provide stock valuation figures. To record the material costs and movement of stocks a *stock ledger account* will be opened for every stock item carried.

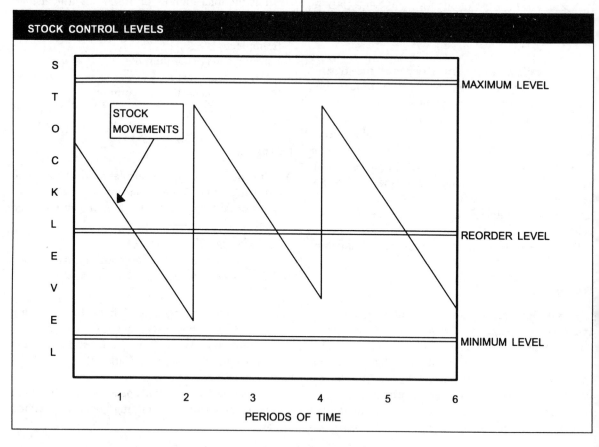

STOCK CONTROL LEVELS

S T O C K L E V E L

STOCK MOVEMENTS

MAXIMUM LEVEL

REORDER LEVEL

MINIMUM LEVEL

1   2   3   4   5   6

PERIODS OF TIME

Think through the double entry for a moment when purchasing materials: the entries are debit raw materials stores account, credit suppliers' accounts (or cash account if cash purchases). The raw materials stores account is in essence a *control account* and summarises in total all the materials transactions each period, both receipts of materials, and issues to the shop floor. This control account will be supported by the stock ledger accounts (of which there may be many hundreds or thousands). Each individual account will record the transactions and movements of one particular item of stock. So, if the transactions in the stock ledger accounts are totalled, the individual transactions will be expected to tally exactly with the total figures in the raw materials stores account. We shall be looking further at control accounts and how they assist in cost bookkeeping in Chapter 8. An individual stock ledger account would appear as shown in Figure 3.6.

Referring back for a moment to the stock control record shown in Figure 3.3 on page 21 you will see that only quantities were recorded there. To have the two records – stock control record and stock ledger account – is not unusual, but many stock control systems, especially computer systems, combine the two.

Working through the entries in the stock ledger account, note the following: in the **receipts** section the entries will be *the actual quantities received* and *the actual costs incurred* (often, an additional column for the cost price per unit is also included). In this section too, but as negative (bracketed) entries, returns to suppliers will also be entered. (This is not always the case, because the returns could also be recorded in the issues columns.)

The documents used for the receipts entries will be: (i) the goods received notes, priced and valued according to the supplier's invoice/purchase order, or

FIGURE 3.6

STOCK LEDGER ACCOUNT

ITEM DESCRIPTION: ITEM NUMBER:

STOCK LEVELS   MINIMUM QUANTITY: MAXIMUM: REORDER LEVEL:

REORDER QUANTITY:

DATE	DETAIL	STOCK RECEIVED		STOCK ISSUED		BALANCE		ALLOCATED STOCK	FREE STOCK
		Quantity	AMOUNT	Quantity	AMOUNT	Quantity	AMOUNT	Quantity	Quantity
			£		£		£		

possibly a predetermined price when standard costs are used (see Chapter 18); and (ii) the supplier's credit note details or the company's own debit note covering the returns made to the supplier.

In the **issues** section the entries will be: *the quantity of materials or components transferred to the production departments* as shown in the materials requisition notes and, as negative (bracketed) items, any *returned materials from production departments* documented on a returns to store note. By reducing (crediting) the receipts section with the value of returns to suppliers the net purchases figure for each accounting period is thus facilitated. By reducing (debiting) the issues section with materials returns from Production the net issues figure is provided.

In the receipts section there is usually no problem in arriving at the costs of material purchases – each delivery will have been purchased at a particular price or a predetermined, standard, price has been used and therefore the value of the purchase is clear. But with the issues section, a method for valuing each issue to the production departments is required. This is because purchase prices are subject to constant change; for example, because of inflation, changes in supplier, difficulties in identifying the cost of an individual stock item and the price paid for it, and so on.

Materials issues evaluation and closing stocks valuations

The following methods of valuing the materials issues are the most frequently used:

> FIFO (First in, First out)
> LIFO (Last in, First out)
> AVCO (Weighted average cost)
> Standard cost

FIGURE 3.7

STOCK LEDGER ACCOUNT USING FIFO

ITEM DESCRIPTION: ITEM NUMBER

STOCK LEVELS: MINIMUM QUANTITY: MAXIMUM: REORDER LEVEL:

REORDER QUANTITY:

DATE	DETAIL	STOCK RECEIVED		STOCK ISSUED		BALANCE		ALLOCATED STOCK	FREE STOCK
		Quantity	AMOUNT	Quantity	AMOUNT	Quantity	AMOUNT	Quantity	Quantity
			£		£		£		
JANUARY 10	RECEIPTS	10	100			10	100		
JANUARY 15	RECEIPTS	20	220			30	320		
JANUARY 18	ISSUE			15	155	15	165		
JANUARY 20	RECEIPTS	30	360			45	525		

FIFO

The *First in* part of this acronym is the **PRICE** and the *First out* part is the **ISSUE**. So, the price of the oldest stock (the 'first in') held in store is used to value the most recent (the last) issue of materials to the production departments on the factory floor.

Example:

Receipts:

January 10	10 units	£100 cost = £10 per unit
January 15	20 units	£220 cost = £11 per unit
January 20	30 units	£360 cost = £12 per unit

Issues:

January 18   15 units

We need to price the 15 units. With the FIFO method the issues will be valued as follows: the oldest stock, the 'first in' stock, is the 10 units, so this cost is used first: £100. The remaining 5 units will be valued at the next oldest price, that is, at £11 each. Those five units will therefore be priced at a total of £55. So, overall, the January 18 issue will be valued at £100 plus £55 = £155.

The stock ledger account, using FIFO, will appear as shown in Figure 3.7:

You may note that you can check the value of the closing balance of stocks by working through each receipt and issue:

15 units at £11 remain in stock at the
    end of the period   = £165
30 units at £12 also remain = £360
Giving a value for the closing stocks of £525.

The next issue, using FIFO, will use the 15 units price of £11 each.

Closing stocks using FIFO will therefore be valued at *latest* purchase prices.

FIGURE 3.8

STOCK LEDGER ACCOUNT USING LIFO

ITEM DESCRIPTION: | ITEM NUMBER

STOCK LEVELS: | MINIMUM QUANTITY: | MAXIMUM: | REORDER LEVEL:

REORDER QUANTITY

DATE	DETAIL	STOCK RECEIVED		STOCK ISSUED		BALANCE		ALLOCATED STOCK	FREE STOCK
		Quantity	AMOUNT £	Quantity	AMOUNT £	Quantity	AMOUNT £	Quantity	Quantity
JANUARY 10	RECEIPTS	10	100			10	100		
JANUARY 15	RECEIPTS	20	220			30	320		
JANUARY 18	ISSUE			15	165	15	155		
JANUARY 20	RECEIPTS	30	360			45	515		

LIFO

The *last in* of this acronym is the latest **PRICE**, and the *first out* being the latest **ISSUE** to the factory shop floor.

Working through the same figures as those given in the example on page 27:

Receipts:

January 10	10 units	£100 cost = £10 per unit
January 15	20 units	£220 cost = £11 per unit
January 20	30 units	£360 cost = £12 per unit

Issues:

January 18	15 units

The nearest purchase price prior to the January 18 issue is the January 15 receipt of 20 units – £11 per unit. This price will be used to charge the 15 units to Production: £165. The closing stock of 45 units will thus constitute the following costs: January 10 units (£100) plus five units remaining from the January 15 receipt (£55), plus the 30 units delivered on January 20 (£360) = £515.

The stock ledger account, using LIFO, will appear as shown in Figure 3.8. The closing stock using LIFO will be valued at the oldest purchase prices.

AVCO – perpetual method

AVCO stands for weighted average cost. Every time a receipt is entered in the stock ledger account a new average cost is calculated. The calculation is simply the latest total stock value, including the newest receipt, divided by the latest quantity in stock.

The average cost is then used to value the next issue made to production and also the closing stock. Using the same figures as before:

Receipts:

January 10	10 units	£100 cost = £10 per unit
January 15	20 units	£220 cost = £11 per unit
January 20	30 units	£360 cost = £12 per unit

Issues:

January 18	15 units

Here the cost of the first two deliveries (30 units) totals £320, an average price of £10.6667 per unit. This average price will be used to value the 15 units issued on January 18 because it was the average price ruling on the day of the issue. The issue price

will therefore be 15 units multiplied by £10.6667: £160. The balance remaining after this issue will also be valued at £10.6667. A new average will be computed with the arrival of the 30 units received on January 20.

The new quantity of 45 units in stock is divided into the balance of £520 (£160 + £360) to provide the new weighted average cost of £11.5556 per unit. The closing stock is therefore valued at £520 (45 × £11.5556).

The stock ledger account, using AVCO, appears as shown in Figure 3.9. You will note that an extra column to calculate the average price per unit is included.

AVCO – periodic method

With this method, instead of recalculating the average every time there is a receipt, an average for the accounting period as a whole is computed. This period average is then used to value the total issues made in the period and thus to arrive at the value of the closing stocks. In the example above, 60 units were received in the accounting period of January at a cost of £680. This gives an average of £11.3333 per unit. The closing stock will therefore be valued at £510 (45 units × £11.3333)

FIFO and LIFO periodic methods

The periodic method of pricing issues can also be used for FIFO and LIFO.

With both methods, the receipts for the whole period will be added and entered in the stock ledger account as one figure. As an illustration, assume the same figures as before, but with an opening stock amount brought forward at the beginning of January of 100 units valued at £9 each. The opening stock will therefore have a value of £900.

Figure 3.10 shows the value of the issues of all three periodic methods. Working through this, the 15 issued in January using the AVCO method have been valued at the average price of £9.875 per unit (£1580/160). With FIFO, the issue was valued at £135. This is because the first price in relates to the opening stock. With LIFO the issue was priced at the latest price in – the January purchases average.

An attraction of the periodic method of valuation is that it reduces substantially the number of calculations to be made, thus saving considerable clerical

FIGURE 3.9

STOCK LEDGER ACCOUNT USING AVCO											

ITEM DESCRIPTION: ITEM NUMBER

STOCK LEVELS: MINIMUM QUANTITY: MAXIMUM: REORDER LEVEL:

REORDER QUANTITY:

DATE	DETAIL	STOCK RECEIVED		STOCK ISSUED		BALANCE		ALLOCATED STOCK	FREE STOCK	Average price per unit
		Quantity	AMOUNT £	Quantity	AMOUNT £	Quantity	AMOUNT £	Quantity	Quantity	
JANUARY 10	RECEIPTS	10	100			10	100			10.0000
JANUARY 15	RECEIPTS	20	220			30	320			10.6667
JANUARY 18	ISSUE			15	160	15	155			10.6667
JANUARY 20	RECEIPTS	30	360			45	520			11.5556

FIGURE 3.10

PERIODIC VALUATION METHODS									
	AVCO			FIFO			LIFO		
	UNITS	£	COST PER UNIT (£)	UNITS	£	COST PER UNIT (£)	UNITS	£	COST PER UNIT (£)
OPENING BALANCE	100	900	9.00	100	900	9.00	100	900	9.00
JANUARY RECEIPTS	60	680	11.3333	60	680	11.3333	60	680	11.3333
	160	1 580	9.875	160	1 580		160	1 580	
JANUARY ISSUES	15	148	9.875	15	135	9.00	15	170	11.3333
CLOSING STOCK	145	1 432	9.375	145	1 445		145	1 410	

effort if the system is maintained manually. However, with computers able to make complex calculations at the touch of a button the benefit of periodic calculations is now less evident.

Other methods used to value issues and closing stocks are listed below.

Standard costs

This method will be discussed in Chapter 18. Note here, however, that a standard cost is a predetermined cost – that is, a cost set by management prior to the actual material costs being known. So, whatever the actual costs of the purchases, the predetermined standard will be used for all issues to Production and also for the valuation of the closing stocks. There will almost certainly be a difference between the actual cost and the standard cost. These differences are termed *variances* and the accounting treatment and terminology for these will also be covered in Chapter 18.

Unit cost

This is the actual cost of each unit issued to Production. The item, and therefore its cost, can be identified precisely. It follows that every unit left in stock at the end of an accounting period will also be precisely identifiable, and therefore the issues will be valued at the actual cost of the unit issued. The closing stocks will be valued at the number of units in stock multiplied by the actual cost per unit.

Base stock

This method assumes there is a base stock (that is, a fixed, predetermined number of units in stock) priced at a fixed unit of value. Stock held in excess of this base is valued using some other method, say FIFO or LIFO. If material stocks remain higher than the base stock, then the issues made will be priced using the other method adopted. It follows that if some or all of the base stock is taken up by issues, then the issue price will be at the fixed unit, base stock, value.

Replacement cost

This method uses the replacement cost of materials so that the issues charged to production reflects the cost which *could* apply if the materials had been purchased at the time of issue. That is, the next proposed or replacement purchase price.

The concept behind replacement cost is to ensure that the resultant product cost reflects the current, latest materials cost; therefore any profit or loss arising will be indicative of the present-day materials costs and provide a truer profit or loss position. This is not so with the other methods, LIFO, FIFO or AVCO, because the materials prices used will have been incurred when the purchase was made, clearly arising in the present or past – perhaps weeks or months earlier. Therefore these methods do not necessarily reflect the present costs.

NIFO

Another valuation method sometimes used, closely related to the replacement cost method is NIFO – Next in, First out. This method uses the materials price of the most recent purchase order or contract placed with the supplier to value the latest issue. With NIFO, the materials will clearly not yet have been received.

So, to recap, the most common methods used for valuing issues of materials to work in progress (the Production Departments) are: FIFO, LIFO, AVCO and standard cost. It is important to note that all these methods can be used by management for their internal control and planning purposes. But, for the annual published financial accounts, some of these cannot be used because they are considered not to be in line with standard accounting practice.

Requirements of SSAP 9

The periodic financial statements prepared by limited companies – the profit and loss account and balance sheet – are required to comply with Statements of Standard Accounting Practice (SSAP). The standard that deals with stocks is SSAP 9 – Stocks and Long-Term Contracts. This standard states that stocks should always be valued at *the lower of cost or net realisable value*. Some of the methods discussed in this chapter do not meet this requirement, so they cannot be used to arrive at the stock values reported in the financial accounts. We shall examine each of the described methods below to see if it complies with this requirement and therefore whether it is permissible or not under SSAP 9.

FIFO

This method can be used in the financial accounts. This is because the valuation of the closing stocks will bear some relationship to the most recent prices paid.

LIFO

This method is *not* allowable. LIFO uses the latest prices paid to evaluate the issues. Therefore older prices are used to value the closing stocks. Thus the old prices may not be a reasonable reflection of the current value of stock. A major concept of accounting is that the accounts should show a true and fair view of the assets and liabilities of the business. By using LIFO, the asset of stock may bear little relationship to recent costs and therefore would misrepresent the current and future trading results of the business.

AVCO

The weighted average price is an acceptable method under SSAP 9.

Standard cost

This too is acceptable, so long as the standard prices provide a reasonable reflection of actual current costs.

Unit cost

Acceptable, as each stock item can be separately identified.

Base stock

This method is *not* acceptable as the resultant valuation will not reflect actual current costs and will therefore not reflect a true and fair view of the value of the stocks.

Replacement value and NIFO

These also are *not* acceptable.

One other method used, found in retailing operations whenever there is an absence of a satisfactory costing system, is selling price less an estimated profit margin. This is an acceptable method but only if it provides a stock valuation which is considered to be a reasonable approximation of the actual cost.

Physical inventory – periodic stock count

The accuracy of the clerical stock records requires verification by an actual, periodic, physical count of the stocks held. This can be an onerous task but is essential to ensure that the profit or loss for an accounting period is correctly calculated.

Many firms carry out only one stock count in each financial year because of the disruptive nature of the check. Some companies even shut down completely while the count is being taken. It follows that with the large time intervals between physical counts it is virtually certain there will be differences recorded between the physical quantity counted and the book stockholding as shown on the stock record card. These differences may be due to clerical errors, theft, short deliveries or over deliveries and so on. An adjustment needs to be made to the clerical stock records to bring the book stock into line with the actual stock. The differences must be valued and the cost of the gain or loss written off to a suitable overhead account such as a stocktaking differences account. The method of valuation of the stock differences will be in accordance with the pricing method adopted by the firm (FIFO, LIFO, etc.).

Physical inventory – Perpetual stock count

Other firms use perpetual inventory methods: stock is counted, rotationally, on a daily basis. So every day a number of items will be physically counted and compared with the book stock. Over a period of time the whole of the stock is thus checked and verified with the records. This system avoids the disruptions to production or trading caused by the periodic check.

'Just-in-time' (JIT) purchasing

This stock control technique enables firms to reduce their investment in stocks to minimum 'near-zero' levels by arranging with suppliers to deliver materials when they are actually required, or 'just in time' for each production run. This system thus does away with safety stocks, economic order quantities, and maximum and minimum levels.

The basis of the system is that the purchaser, that is, the customer, relies wholly and completely on the supplier to hold adequate supplies of raw materials and to ensure that delivery and inspection requirements are met precisely. The material will therefore be planned to arrive just before it is due to be used on the shop floor with the customer able to use it immediately in production: 'just in time'.

Using computer networks, customers and suppliers will be linked directly with each other, with orders placed by the customer and goods picked and despatched by the supplier practically automatically. In many cases, the customer's materials usage information is linked directly with the supplier's computer records. The supplier takes responsibility for maintaining supplies of stocks to ensure that the customer is not let down by late deliveries. The supplier thus effectively becomes part of the firm's stores and production function.

JIT purchasing thus reduces the manufacturer's need for warehousing space to accommodate stock, saving carrying costs and reducing the cost of placing orders.

Summary

- Materials are an Element of Cost.
- Materials used in the production process can be categorised as either direct materials or indirect materials. Direct materials are economically identifiable in the finished product; indirect materials (also known as consumable materials) cannot be so identified economically. They are therefore classified as factory overhead costs.
- Because of the importance of stocks to the business it is desirable to control the physical quantities held. Too much stock ties up cash and creates space problems; too little endangers production or selling requirements because of the likelihood of out-of-stock situations arising. Management therefore needs to set maximum and minimum stock levels. One other level also needs to be set – the reorder level. This signifies the point when an order for further supplies needs to be raised.
- The quantity to be ordered (the reorder quantity) can be calculated using the Economic Order Quantity (EOQ) formula. This takes into account all factors involved in stockholding, the cost of ordering and the cost of carrying the stock, to arrive at the most beneficial quantity to be ordered.
- Stock control records and stock ledger accounts are maintained to track the movement of the stocks and to provide the valuation of stocks and issues to production departments.

- Materials issued to the production process – the factory floor – are recorded on materials requisitions. These need to be valued to account for the materials taken from the Stores and to price the jobs or processes being manufactured. There are a number of methods that can be used to provide this. The most frequently used are FIFO, LIFO, AVCO and Standard cost.
- SSAP 9 – stocks and long-term contracts, provides guidelines with respect to the valuation of stocks for published financial accounts purposes. LIFO and some other methods described in the text are generally not used in financial accounts because the closing stocks valuation may bear little relationship to recent costs and therefore a true and fair view of the asset of stocks at balance sheet date will not be provided. However, management can use any stock valuation method or methods they choose for internal control and planning purposes.
- The control of stock requires regular physical stock counts to be done. The results of the physical count will be compared to book stocks, and if discrepancies arise, investigations into the reasons why will be made by management.
- The costs associated with stockholding can be very high. Just-in-time (JIT) purchasing enables producers to minimise their stockholding by relying on the supplier to deliver the materials just in time to be used on the shop floor.

Examination Questions

1 A LEVEL (ULEAC) 1990

The following stock account relates to stocks of Ergons held by the Brunswick Co. during December. The company records issues on the weighted average cost (AVCO) perpetual system.

December Date	Receipts Quantity	£/unit	Total	Issues Quantity	£/unit	Total	Stock Quantity	£/unit	Total
1	Opening balance						8	15.40	123.20
7	11	15.80	173.80				19	15.63	297.00
12				10	15.63	156.30	9	15.63	140.70
14	15	16.00	240.00				24	15.86	380.70
16				13	15.86	206.18	11	15.87	174.52
19	12	16.10	193.20				23	15.99	367.72
21				17	15.99	271.83	6	15.98	95.89
23	14	15.90	222.60				20	15.92	318.49
29				11	15.93	175.23	9	15.92	143.26

(a) Show the stock account as it would appear using the Last in, First out, (LIFO) perpetual system.
(b) Calculate the value of the closing stock using (i) AVCO periodic, and (ii) LIFO periodic methods.

2   A LEVEL (ULEAC) 1991

Andy Pandy deals in only one product. Opening stocks on 1 May comprised 40 items which had cost a total of £1600. Purchases and sales for May were as follows:

Purchases				Sales		
May 1	150	@ £41	May 6	110	@ £50
May 8	60	@ £42	May 10	80	@ £52
May 15	130	@ £43	May 18	120	@ £53
May 22	140	@ £45	May 23	170	@ £54
May 29	60	@ £47	May 31	50	@ £55

(a)   Calculate the profit for the month when closing stock is valued on a periodic basis using:

   (i)   First in, First out (FIFO);
   (ii)   Last in, First out (LIFO);
   (iii)   weighted average cost (AVCO).

3   A LEVEL (ULEAC) 1993

A company uses the First in, First out (FIFO) method of charging items to production. Details of the receipts and issues for the three months to 31 May were:

Date		Receipts		Issues	Stock
	No.	Value	No.	Value	valuation
	items	(£)	items	(£)	(£)
Mar 1	50	Opening stock			850
16	100	1750			2600
24			90	1550	1050
Apr 14	260	4680			5730
19			150	2670	3060
22	40	736			3796
30			160	2880	916
May 5	190	3648			4564
20			130	2452	2112
25	110	2090			4202
28			120	2302	1900

What would the closing stock valuation have been if the company had used

(i)   the AVCO (weighted average cost) perpetual method;
(ii)   the AVCO periodic method; and
(iii)   the LIFO (Last in, First out) periodic method?

4   A LEVEL (ULEAC) 1990

Village Stocks Limited owns a supermarket, and at 31 May had the following types of stock in hand:

Groceries   The total retail selling value is £17 825 and there is an estimated average mark-up of 15% on cost. Goods valued at £350 selling price (included in the above total) are damaged, and can only be sold for £100. The actual cost of the groceries (other than the damaged goods) is estimated at £12 200.

Frozen foods   These are divided into three main categories, with their cost and net realisable value as shown below:

	Cost (£)	Net realisable value (£)
Fish	13 000	10 000
Vegetables	8 000	14 000
Prepared meals	10 000	13 000

Cigarettes   The company had stock which had cost £18 000 at the year end. This figure includes £3 000 which represents the sales value of cigarettes stolen on 30 May (gross profit percentage on sales is 40%), and also £1 000 which represents the cost of a large sign, required by law, which states that 'smoking cigarettes can be harmful'.

Required:

State the amount which the company should include in its balance sheet at 31 May for each of the three types of stock. Show calculations and give reasons for your considerations.

5   A LEVEL (AEB) 1993

Airwaves Ltd are retailers who sell mobile telephones. During January to March they decided to concentrate their selling activities on the 'Meteor' model, which experienced several cost price fluctuations during the period. The company found that because of this it had to adjust its own selling price.

During the period the following transactions took place:

1. Jan 1   An opening stock of 50 telephones was obtained at a total cost of £8 250.

2. Jan 10   Initial sales were good so extra telephones had to be obtained from abroad; 200 telephones were purchased at a cost of £135 each, but in addition there was a freight charge of £3 each, as well as a customs import charge of £5 each.

3. Jan 31   During the month 180 telephones were sold, at a price of £175 each.

4. Feb 1   A new batch of 120 telephones was purchased at a cost of £170 each.

5. Feb 28   The sales for February were 120 at a selling price of £215 each.

6. Mar 2 A further 220 telephones were purchased at a cost of £240 each and these were subject to a trade discount of 12.5% each.

7. Mar 31 250 telephones were sold during March at a price of £230 each.

All purchases were received on the dates stated.

The accountant of Airwaves Ltd decided he would apply the First in, First out (FIFO) and weighted average (AVCO) methods of stock valuation so that the results could be compared.

Required:

(a) Calculate the stock value at 31 March using each of the methods indicated (if necessary calculated to one decimal place).

(b) Prepare the trading accounts using each of the above methods for the period January to March.

6 AAT COST ACCOUNTING AND BUDGETING 1993

Atlas Limited is having difficulty costing Material X to the various jobs that it is used on. The material is bought in bulk and recent receipts and issues have been:

June 1	Balance b/f	1 000 kg at £4 per kg
June 3	Receipts	2 000 kg at 5 per kg
June 6	Receipts	1 500 kg at 5.50 per kg
June 9	Issues	2 500 kg
June 12	Receipts	3 000 kg at 4.50 per kg
June 14	Issues	3 500 kg

Required:

(a) Cost the issue of Material X for June and calculate the value of the closing stock on the following bases:
(i) FIFO.
(ii) LIFO.
(iii) Weighted average cost.

(b) Atlas is reviewing its stock control policy with regard to Material X. You are told that the cost of making one order is £100, the cost of holding one kilogram for one year is 25p and the annual demand for Material X is 80 000 kg. There is no lead time nor buffer stock.
Determine the following for Material X:
(i) the economic order quantity;
(ii) the average stock; and
(iii) the number of orders to be made per year.

7 LCCI THIRD LEVEL COST ACCOUNTING 1992

Sayftee Ltd makes knitwear to customers' specific orders. Stock control of the yarn requirement is very important and use is made of both the economic order quantity (EOQ) and the free stock balance (FSB) in ordering all main types of yarn. The policy is to reorder when the free stock balance falls to 8 000 kg or below.

Data concerning Yarn Z is as follows:

Annual usage	100 000 kg
Price per kg	£5
Ordering costs	£125 per order
Stockholding costs	20% per annum

The stock record shows the following position at the start of last month:

	kg
Balance on order from suppliers	10 000
Physical stock balance	8 000
	18 000
Less balance on allocations	6 500
Free Stock Balance	11 500

During last month the following events were recorded:

	kg
Received from suppliers	5 500
Issued to production from allocated stock	6 400
Allocated to new orders	9 500

Required:

For Yarn Z;

(a) Calculate the economic order quantity.
(b) Determine the number of orders placed during last month.
(c) Calculate the following (in kg) at the end of last month:
(i) Balance on order from suppliers;
(ii) Physical stock balance;
(iii) Balance on allocations; and
(iv) Free stock balance.

8 ACCA COST AND MANAGEMENT ACCOUNTING 1 1991

The following information is provided concerning a particular raw material:

Average usage	1 000 kg per day
Minimum usage	800 kg per day
Maximum usage	1 350 kg per day
Order quantity	9 000 kg

The stock level is reviewed at the end of each day and an order is placed the following day if the normal reorder level has been reached. Delivery is expected reliably at the beginning of the fourth day following order.

Required:

(a) From the above information, calculate three normal control levels used for stock control purposes.

(b) Draw a graph demonstrating the changing level of stock of the material based on the following actual usage over a 14-day period:

First five days	1 020 kg per day
Next four days	1 200 kg per day
Final five days	900 kg per day

The stock at the beginning of day 1 was 6 000 kg. Show clearly on the graph the three control levels calculated in (a).

NON-COMPUTATIONAL, DESCRIPTIVE TYPE QUESTIONS
(**NB** Minutes in brackets are a guide to indicate the approximate time your essay should take).

QUESTIONS

1. Explain what you understand by the terms 'buffer stock' and 'lead time' and briefly consider any stock policy that would minimise or eliminate such stock costs.
(AAT 1993) (13 minutes).

2. Discuss the relative merits of three methods of pricing the issue of raw materials to production.
(ULEAC 1993) (20 minutes)

4

The Elements of Cost: Labour

Direct and indirect labour

Staff engaged in the production process are collectively classified as 'labour'. The cost of labour is therefore another element of cost, along with materials and overheads. Labour costs are further categorised as being either *direct labour* or *indirect labour*.

Direct labour staff are engaged directly in making the product; their work can be identified clearly in the process of converting the raw materials into the finished product. Indirect labour staff, on the other hand, are not directly associated with the conversion process but supply a variety of necessary backup services required to produce the finished product. Their work therefore benefits all the items being produced and cannot be identified specifically with individual products. Thus individuals working on lathes producing the product, together with the assembly workers, packers and finishers of the item, are classified as direct labour. But the supervisor, the cleaners and the maintenance staff will be classified as indirect labour – their costs clearly cannot be identified specifically as being a constituent part of the finished product. Indirect labour is thus a factory expense and accounted for under the other element of cost – overheads.

So if the labour cost incurred is able to be identified economically, and can be traced directly to the saleable finished unit, it is direct labour; if it cannot, it is indirect labour.

The payroll department

The analysis of payroll costs is important to successful cost accounting, planning and control. So a 'walk through' the Payroll Department at this stage should prove to be of benefit.

This department is responsible for calculating for each individual employee their gross pay entitlement, the deductions from pay for National Insurance contributions (NIC) and Pay As You Earn tax (PAYE), and the voluntary deductions such as pension contributions, savings schemes, staff travel loans and so on.

The gross pay minus the statutory (NIC and PAYE) and voluntary deductions equals the net pay figure. The Payroll Department will arrange to pay this net amount, by cash, cheque or direct to the employee's bank account. When the payroll is completed it will be analysed and a payroll journal prepared.

The journal may appear as follows:

	DR	CR
Gross pay by Departments/operations	××	
Other pay costs	××	
PAYE and NIC control accounts		××
Payroll control account		××

We shall deal first with gross pay by Departments/operations and other payroll costs for the people employed in the production process, examining later the payroll costs for the distribution, selling and administrative functions of the business.

Calculating gross pay

There are three major remuneration methods used for calculating gross pay for production staff; these can be summarised as follows:

Time-based remuneration (day work);
Piecework remuneration; and
Premium bonus schemes plus basic remuneration.

In our walk through the Payroll Department we shall assume, for illustration, that gross pay is calculated using the time basis method, and follow the system through to the completion of the gross pay section of the payroll, ready to prepare the payroll analysis.

Time-based remuneration

This payment method is basically: *number of hours worked × the rate per hour applicable.* So, if an employee works 40 hours and the rate per hour is £8 an hour, the gross pay will be £320 (40 × £8).

Hours worked

Direct and indirect production staff are usually required to 'clock on' when starting work and 'clock off' when finishing. By doing so a record is made of the time spent at the business premises by the employee. *Clock cards* are issued to individuals for this purpose and a special machine, a *time recorder*, will record the time whenever the card is inserted into it. The times recorded will indicate the hours in attendance at the premises, whether the employee is late, whether overtime has been worked and, clearly – if no times at all are recorded – any absences from work.

Clock cards therefore provide the data for the hours and it is practice for management or supervisory staff to authorise these cards at the end of the week or other designated period by signing each one and dealing with any queries that arise. The signed cards therefore act as authority for the payroll department to calculate the pay due.

Time spent at work

The clock card provides the hours in attendance but it does not provide details of the activities of the employee during the period at work. For direct labour staff, this analysis of the activities undertaken during the week may be covered by a *time sheet/job card* or its equivalent. This document will be completed by the employee and will record each job or task the person is engaged upon during each working day. It follows that the hours spent at work in accordance with the clock card should agree with the time sheet total hours. But this is not always the case, for there will be times when, for a variety of reasons, the operative has no work to do. For example, they may be unable to produce because of machine breakdowns, waiting for materials, maintenance requirements and so on. This non-productive time is described as *idle time* and will be accounted for separately as an overhead. It is strictly a controllable cost and management need to know its extent in order to regulate it. Production time lost represents lost profits, and idle time thus has a two-edged effect: lost finished goods and additional overheads incurred. Direct workers are also sometimes diverted from producing products to working on various indirect activities such as cleaning. The cost of these *diverted hours* also needs to be reported separately (why it was necessary to divert, for example) to management for the reasons given above.

Overtime

Hours worked above the normal contractual requirements usually attract an extra payment in addition to the rate per hour: this is termed *overtime*. To encourage staff to work the extra hours, varying *overtime premium rates* may be paid, depending perhaps on the day the overtime is worked. Overtime worked during the normal working week, say Monday to Friday, may not attract any premium, the worker being paid the basic hourly rate for the extra hours put in. But for Saturday work a premium of, say, 50 per cent – 'time and a half' – may be paid. So if a direct labour employee works four hours on a Saturday morning and the normal rate of pay per hour is £8, he or she will have earned £48: 4 hours at £8 (£32) plus a premium of 50 per cent (£16) representing an extra £4 for each hour worked.

The cost of the overtime premium is accounted for separately as an overhead cost, *unless* this extra cost has been incurred as the result of a request by the customer for a specific job to be completed more quickly. In this case the overtime premium becomes a direct labour cost.

Shift work

Firms that operate more than one shift will usually pay an extra premium for the shifts which might be deemed to be during 'unsocial hours'. A company that operates a production line for 24 hours a day, a bakery for example, may break the work down into three shifts. The first – 8 am to 4 pm; the second 4 pm to midnight; and the third midnight to 8 am. The two latter shifts could be deemed to be 'unsocial' and, in order to attract people to work these hours, an extra payment is made; this extra is called a *shift premium*. This premium is accounted for separately as an overhead.

Payroll and payroll analysis

The gross pay calculations and deductions will be made for each person and a payroll record completed. A summary of the complete payroll will also be prepared, called a *payroll analysis*. This may appear as is shown in Table 4.1.

Working through this, note firstly that the *total payroll cost* to the firm comprises the gross pay (including the various premiums), plus the employer's National Insurance Contributions (NIC), plus any pension contributions the company may make to the pension

TABLE 4.1

A PAYROLL ANALYSIS

A PAYROLL ANALYSIS
WEEK ENDED: MAY 14   PRODUCTION DEPARTMENTS

DEPARTMENT	NUMBER OF STAFF	HOURS WORKED	PRODUCTION HOURS	NON-PRODUCTION HOURS	PRODUCTION COST £	NON-PRODUCTION COST £
PRODUCTION DEPT. 1						
PRODUCTION DEPT. 2						
STORES DEPARTMENT						
MAINTENANCE DEPARTMENT						
CANTEEN STAFF						
CLEANING STAFF						
SUPERVISORY STAFF DEPT. 1						
SUPERVISORY STAFF DEPT. 2						
BUYING DEPARTMENT STAFF						
PROGRESS CHASERS						
FACTORY MANAGER AND STAFF						
OTHER PRODUCTION STAFF						
TOTALS						

ANALYSIS OF NON-PRODUCTION HOURS:

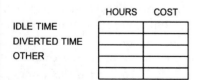

	HOURS	COST
IDLE TIME		
DIVERTED TIME		
OTHER		

fund or pension administrators in respect of the employees.

The *payroll liabilities* section effectively analyses the total payroll cost. These liabilities will be the amounts payable to the Inland Revenue (PAYE and NIC due), to the pension trustees or administrators (pension due), and to the employees (net pay due). Note that the NIC due will include both employee and employer contributions, as also will the pension amount due to be paid.

The total payroll cost for the production departments is often entered in the ledger to a wages control account in its entirety and this aspect of bookkeeping is dealt with in Chapter 8, Cost Bookkeeping.

The entries to this control account are then supported by entries in the various wages accounts. The following example of a payroll journal shows the position where postings are made directly to the individual wages accounts, thus by-passing the wages control account:

	DR	CR
Work-in-progress account (being direct labour cost)	××	
Idle time account (being cost of lost time)	××	
Payroll on-costs account (being company NIC and pension costs)	××	

PAY				TOTAL PAYROLL COST	PAYROLL LIABILITIES		
OVERTIME PREMIUM £	SHIFT PREMIUM £	NIC-COMPANY CONTRIBUTION £	PENSION-COMPANY CONTRIBUTION £	£	PAYE AND NIC DUE £	PENSION DUE £	NET PAY DUE £

Other labour overhead accounts   ×× \
  (being cost of diverted \
  hours, supervisors, etc.) \
PAYE and NIC liability account   ×× \
  (being amounts due to the \
  Inland Revenue) \
Pensions contributions account   ×× \
  (being amounts due to \
  pension trustees) \
Net pay control account   ×× \
  (being net pay amounts \
  due to employees)

You will see that the production cost amount has been charged to the work-in-progress account – this is the 'shop floor' account, relating to where the products are made. This charge represents the direct labour costs identifiable to the products being produced. The indirect labour costs will be charged to individual overhead accounts or cost centres, such as supervisory wages account, cleaning wages account, maintenance department wages account, canteen department wages account and so on. The overtime premium, the idle time costs and other indirect labour costs will also be charged to separate overhead accounts.

With regard to payroll on-costs – the term used to cover the company's NIC contributions and pension contributions – some systems include these as part of the direct labour cost. Therefore these costs will be charged to each of the wages accounts and not accounted for separately, as shown in the above example.

Piecework remuneration

This method of calculating gross pay uses the formula: *number of units made × the rate per piece*.

With piecework methods, the worker will be paid for the actual number of items made, so the Payroll Department will require notification of the quantity made, confirmed and authorised by a member of management. Normally only 'good' pieces are paid for, to ensure that quality requirements are met. The gross pay calculation is, therefore, simple and straightforward – number of pieces made × rate per piece, and there are no overtime or idle time computations.

However, employees could be considered to be at some disadvantage with this method because the flow of work and materials to them is not within

their control. A hold-up say, in materials supplied, or a breakdown of machinery, could have a serious effect on their earning capabilities. To overcome these problems, many firms provide a *guaranteed minimum wage* to piecework operatives.

Here, the time basis method becomes part of the calculation: if the person fails to achieve piecework earnings *equivalent* to (or near equivalent to) the basic earnings that would apply using the time basis (hours × rate per hour), an extra payment will be made to bring the individual's earnings into line with time-basis earnings. For example, an employee on piecework, earning £1 per piece, produces 100 items. The piecework pay would be £100. It took the individual 35 hours to do this work, so if the firm operated a guaranteed minimum wage scheme and the basic rate of pay is £4 per hour, the guaranteed wage will be £140. Therefore an extra payment of £40 will be made to the employee. A further modification to this is when the firm guarantees only a proportion of the basic time-based pay, perhaps 75 per cent. In this case, with only a proportion guaranteed, the individual would receive a top-up of £5 over his or her piecework earnings of £100 (75% × £140 = £105).

Examples:

1 Number of items made   200 \
   Rate per piece   £1 \
   Hours worked   40 \
   Rate per hour   £6 \
   Guaranteed minimum pay 80% of basic pay

Solution: \
Piecework earnings   £200   (200 × £1) \
Basic earnings   £240   (40 × £6) \
Guaranteed minimum \
  wage   £192   (80% × £240) \
Therefore earnings will be £200.

2 Number of items made   180 \
   Rate per piece   £1 \
   Hours worked   40 \
   Rate per hour   £6 \
   Guaranteed minimum pay 80% of basic pay

Solution: \
Piecework earnings   £180   (180 × £1) \
Basic earnings   £240   (40 × £6) \
Guaranteed minimum \
  wage   £192   (80% × £240) \
Therefore earnings will be £192

The extra cost incurred in Example 2 (£12) is treated as an overhead cost and will not be charged to the work-in-progress account.

A refinement to the piecework method is called *differential piecework*. This endeavours to bring the time spent by the individual on making the product into the equation. With straight piecework systems the time factor is *not* taken into consideration – the employee will produce a quantity of products, or pieces, and be paid at the rate per piece made irrespective of the time it has taken. However 'time is money' and in fact management will usually expect certain production levels to be achieved in an allocated period of time.

Differential piecework systems therefore set time targets. A series of production targets will be established and as each target is reached a new piecework rate will apply. So the quicker the individual works, the higher the piecework rate achieved. One of the grounds cited for the introduction of a differential piecework system is that there is a perceived tendency with straight piecework methods for employees to reach certain levels of earnings that they personally find acceptable. When an individual's acceptable level is reached, productivity falls off. To the firm, of course, this is not a desirable situation. Therefore, the extra rates of pay that can be achieved under differential piecework systems can act as an inducement to the employee to aim for higher productivity and resultant proportionately higher earnings.

Example:
Normal quantity expected to be produced in certain number of hours: 100
Piecework rate at this level: £1 per piece
Rate for quantities between 100 and 120: £1.25 per all pieces made
Rate for quantities above 120: £1.50 per all pieces made
Rate for quantities between 80 and 100: £0.75 per piece

Worker A produces 110 pieces. Payment will be £137.50 (110 × £1.25).

Worker B produces 85 pieces. Payment will be £63.75 (85 × £0.75).

The payroll and payroll analysis is completed as described under the time-basis method.

Premium bonus schemes

The major aim of premium bonus schemes is to provide an incentive to the direct labour employee on the time basis method of payment to *save time* in the production process. Time is money, as has already been noted, so any savings in production times will result in reduced unit costs for the company.

If a job or task is expected to take 10 hours to complete and the individual completes it in six hours, a saving of four hours has been achieved. Premium bonus schemes seek to reward individuals for these savings in time. So, in addition to earning the basic time-based pay (hours worked × rate per hour) the employee will also receive an extra payment: the time saved bonus or the premium bonus.

There have been many premium bonus schemes created over the years, some of them originating perhaps 100 years ago. Many firms develop and operate their own systems to recognise and reward the time saved by the direct labour employees in completing jobs and tasks. We shall now look at some of the more well known schemes.

Halsey method (50/50)

This system rewards the employee with a payment based on half the time saved. The formula is:

Time allowed – Time taken
= Time saved × 50% × Basic rate per hour

Example:
Time allowed to complete a job: 10 hours
Time taken to complete the job: 4 hours
Time saved: 6 hours
The Halsey bonus will be 50% of this saving, that is, an extra three hours' pay at basic rate will be paid. Assume the person is paid £8 per hour, the earnings for the 4 hours' work will therefore be: 4 hours at £8 (£32) plus 3 hours' bonus, at £8 per hour (£24), a total of £56 paid for the 4 hours' work.

Halsey-Weir method (30/70)

This is a variation of the Halsey system. Instead of 50 per cent of the time saved as the bonus, 30 per cent of the saving is used. The formula is:

Time allowed – Time taken
= Time saved × 30% × Basic rate per hour

Example:

Time allowed to complete a job: 10 hours
Time taken to complete the job: 4 hours
Time saved: 6 hours

The Halsey-Weir bonus will be 30% of six hours, that is, 1 hour and 48 minutes. Earnings for the 4 hours' work will therefore be:

4 hours at £8 (£32) plus 1.80 hours at £8 (£14.40), a total of £46.40 paid for the 4 hours' work.

Rowan scheme

This scheme rewards the employee with a proportion of the time saved, the proportion being the relationship between the time taken and the time allowed.

The formula is:

> Time taken/Time allowed × Time saved
> × Basic rate per hour

Example:

Time taken is 4 hours, divided by the time allowed of 10 hours = 40%.

The employee took only 40% of the time allowed to produce the item. 40% of the six hours saved = 2.4 hours' bonus.

Earnings will therefore be: 4 hours at £8 (£32) plus 2.4 hours at £8 (£19.20), a total of £51.20 paid for the 4 hours' work.

Incentive bonuses are charged to work in progress as part of the direct labour wages cost; in the last example the £51.20 was earned in producing the item, so it is clearly a direct cost.

Other remuneration methods

Standard minutes

This system is allied to the differential piecework system and seeks to bring the time factor into the reckoning. Management will establish a standard time, set in minutes, for each job or task. For example, a firm may expect 30 units to be produced by an operative every hour: each unit is thus expected to be produced in two standard minutes. The standard minute is defined by CIMA as 'the quantity of work achievable at standard performance in a minute'. A value will be assigned to each standard minute. The computation to arrive at the earnings of the employee will be based on:

> Units produced × Standard minutes per unit
> × Value of the standard minute

Example:

Units produced in the week: 450
Time allowed: 5 standard minutes per unit
Standard minute valuation: 15p (£0.15) per unit
Earnings will be   £337.50   (450 × 5 × £0.15)

High day rate

This also is a time-based system. With this method, the employer will pay a higher than average, perhaps very high, rate per hour. The rationale behind the scheme is that greater levels of productivity will be achieved because staff will be better rewarded. So, instead of, say, a normal hourly wage rate of £8 applying, management will pay perhaps £12 per hour. The rationale behind this is that because the job is highly paid, better-qualified and 'quality' staff will be attracted and therefore greater productivity will result. Because more will be produced, the labour unit cost per item will thus be lower.

A derivation of the high day rate scheme is known as *Measured day work*. This method 'grades' the efficiency of the worker by setting a standard level of output performance (usually expressed as 100%) for either a week or for each day. Performance is then 'banded', having higher and lower bands (called *efficiency bands*) rather than just the standard level. A wage rate for each band is also established. So, for example, a worker with a performance rating of 92 per cent of standard will fall into the efficiency/remuneration band of 90%–110% and earn £8 per hour or its weekly equivalent. Another worker achieving a performance rating of 115 per cent will be in the category 110%–130% and be paid £10 per hour, but a worker who is in the 70%–90% band may be paid only £7 an hour.

Profit-sharing schemes

Many firms have annual profit-sharing schemes in which employees will receive a bonus related to the profits of the firm. The purpose of these bonuses is to provide an incentive for the workforce as a whole to work collectively to improve the overall results of the business.

The clear purpose of any incentive scheme is to encourage operatives to produce more. This encouragement to produce may take many forms. For example, if direct labour staff are late or absent, production could fall. To avoid these negatives a firm might introduce a 'punctuality' or attendance bonus.

Some firms also operate *group bonus schemes*. Here the work is identified as being more of a team effort, with members of the group being dependent upon each other to get the job done, rather than on individual performance. In these schemes a bonus will be paid based on the overall performance of the group.

Advantages and disadvantages of the schemes

As with all payroll schemes, systems and methods, there are benefits and drawbacks of each when compared one with the other. The choice of scheme is also dependent on the type of business and on management's requirements. Some of the advantages and drawbacks of each of the main schemes are outlined below.

With the time-based method, some of the benefits are that it is familiar and simple to understand and the calculations are straightforward; but its drawback is that it does not recognise any extra effort or efficiency by the employee. The high day rates system goes some way towards redressing this disadvantage, however.

With the piecework system the main advantages are that the labour cost of each item is known precisely and it clearly rewards the worker who produces more. But its drawbacks are that employee earnings may be affected by events outside the control of the individual, the quality of products may suffer because of rushed work resulting in high levels of rejects, and the employee may set his or her own 'earnings ceiling', deciding to stop or slow down once this has been reached. Differential piecework rates may help to overcome this latter drawback, and extra supervision may deal with the rushed work disadvantage, but, of course, at extra cost of supervisory wages.

With premium bonus systems, the advantages are that the individual employee is paid for the time he or she is in attendance, using the time-based method, plus a bonus if time is saved on completing tasks or jobs. The bonus element acts as an incentive to increase productivity and therefore reduces the cost per unit produced.

A drawback may be that the predetermined times allowed are not recognised by the employees as being achievable; this therefore becomes a disincentive and could lead to demoralisation among employees.

Distribution, selling and administrative payrolls and incentive schemes

So far we have looked only at the gross pay calculations for production staff and other factory staff. The Payroll Department will also prepare payrolls for the other functions of the business, namely distribution, selling and administration employees.

Staff engaged in the *distribution* process, that is, warehouse staff, fork-lift drivers, delivery van drivers and so on, are usually paid wages based on the time basis – hours worked × rate per hour. Incentive schemes are also often used to encourage the productivity performance of some of the warehouse staff – order pickers and order packers, for example. Orders picked above, say, an expected predetermined quantity per day would attract a bonus.

For delivery drivers, however, productivity incentive schemes may be inappropriate, in particular for long-distance heavy goods vehicle drivers, who have legal restrictions imposed upon them in so far as distance and rest periods are concerned.

Sales staff, marketing staff and administration staff are usually paid on a time basis but, instead of hours worked × rate per hour, their gross pay will normally be calculated on an annual salary basis, divided by 12, to give a monthly gross pay amount; if paid weekly, the annual salary is divided by 52. Other methods found are fortnightly payment intervals or four-weekly intervals.

There are many incentives schemes in operation for *sales staff*, who are at the 'sharp end' of the business in winning orders for the firm. The majority of schemes are volume-related – the more orders received, the more product ordered, the higher the bonus. These schemes are therefore akin to productivity bonuses. Most are tailor-made for the enterprise but not all are related to extra salary payments. Some companies offer luxury holiday rewards for the top salespersons writing the most orders; another incentive could be a quality motor car.

Administration staff, that is, the Managing Director's Department, Accounts, Personnel, Reception and so on, are also usually engaged on an annual salary basis and paid monthly. Generally, because of the difficulty in measuring tasks performed by administration staff in quantitative terms, productivity-style bonuses or incentive schemes are not common. Instead, incentives used to motivate and encourage extra effort will normally be related to the overall profitability of the firm through profit-sharing schemes.

The payroll analysis for the distribution, selling and administration functions might appear as is shown in Table 4.2.

Payroll deductions

The Payroll Department is also responsible for the administration of the various payroll deductions so, to complete the walk through the department, we will take a brief overview of the work this entails.

Amounts payable to the Inland Revenue

These amounts are the tax deducted from employees through the PAYE system, plus National Insurance contributions (NIC) made by both employee and employer. The PAYE system is designed to ensure

TABLE 4.2

PAYROLL ANALYSIS: DISTRIBUTION, SELLING AND ADMINISTRATION

PAYROLL ANALYSIS
MONTH OF MAY

DISTRIBUTION, SELLING AND ADMINISTRATION

DEPARTMENT		NUMBER OF OF STAFF	GROSS PAY		
			BASIC PAY £	BONUS £	OVERTIME £
DISTRIBUTION	GOODS IN STAFF				
	FORK-LIFT DRIVERS				
	PICKERS				
	PACKERS				
	DELIVERY DRIVERS				
	WAREHOUSE CLERICAL				
	WAREHOUSE MANAGEMENT				
SALES AND MARKETING	FIELD SALES STAFF				
	SALES OFFICE STAFF				
	MARKETING DEPARTMENT				
	SALES CLERICAL STAFF				
	MARKETING MANAGEMENT				
	SALES MANAGEMENT				
ADMINISTRATION	MANAGING DIRECTOR AND STAFF				
	ACCOUNTS DEPARTMENT				
	PERSONNEL DEPARTMENT				
	POSTROOM STAFF				
	OTHER ADMINISTRATION STAFF				
	TOTALS				

that at each pay interval (weekly or monthly), a proportion of the individual's annual tax allowance is given as a deduction against the person's taxable pay for that particular pay period. Tax is then calculated on the net figure (gross pay less personal allowances) in accordance with tax tables provided by the Inland Revenue. The tax is then deducted from the individual's pay.

National Insurance contributions are payable by both employee and employer and calculated according to tables issued by the Department of Social Security. The cost to the company of the NIC contributions, often referred to as a payroll on-cost, is either addedto the gross pay amount and charged to the respective wages control accounts, or debited to an overhead account, the payroll on-costs account, as in our examples.

The total NIC deductions are payable in the following month, alongside the PAYE tax deductions, and are normally made together as one payment. Both income tax and National Insurance contributions are described as *statutory deductions*.

Other deductions made from an employee's pay are termed *voluntary deductions*, the employee agreeing (by authorisation in writing), that the company be permitted to deduct certain sums from his/her pay for various reasons. The most common of these are: pension fund deductions, savings schemes deductions,

NIC – COMPANY CONTRIBUTION	PENSION CONTRIBUTION	TOTAL PAYROLL COST	PAYROLL LIABILITIES		
			PAYE NIC DUE	PENSION DUE	NET PAY DUE
£	£	£	£	£	£

repayment of loans, union dues, hospitalisation insurance schemes, travel loans and so on. Most of these voluntary deductions are payable to third parties (described as payroll creditors) – for example, to the pension fund trustees, to the unions and so on.

The net pay amount is cleared by payments made to individuals, whether by cash, cheque or directly into his/her bank account. Another major job within the Payroll Department will be reconciliations of amounts paid to the third parties with the individual records.

Staff turnover

Costs incurred in replacing staff who leave can be very high. Apart from the direct costs of replacement such as advertising, agency fees, search fees and so on, there are also 'hidden' costs, which may not always be obvious or recognised. For example, the induction costs and training costs for new staff, the cost of mistakes as people learn how to do their job, the cost of the manager's or supervisor's time in interviewing; and the Personnel Department's costs in selecting candidates, interviewing and following up references. There is also the loss involved in the investment made in the outgoing member: his or her training, the skills imparted, the speed and efficiency of someone who knows their job and who has full knowledge of the workings of the company.

To avoid these 'disruptive' costs, management will normally endeavour to keep staff. To help gauge the extent of these hidden costs a staff turnover ratio can be calculated. This is simply the relationship between the number of people leaving in an accounting period, say over a period of one year, compared to the average number of people employed in the same period. The formula for the calculation is:

$$\frac{\text{Number of employees leaving in the period}}{\text{Average number of employees in the period}}$$
$$\times \frac{100}{1} = \text{Staff turnover ratio}$$

The average number of employees can be calculated simply by adding the opening number of employees to the closing number and dividing the total by two, or by using moving average techniques. It is normal procedure to include part-time staff as ''halves', with two part-time staff being counted as a full-time equivalent.

The resulting percentage, which should be calculated for each function or department of the business, as well as for the company as a whole, can be compared to earlier-period ratios, and perhaps also to other companies or organisations in the same field of operation (perhaps through trade associations or similar groupings).

Staff leave voluntarily or involuntarily, so the staff turnover ratio needs to be studied further to eliminate those people leaving the company because of rationalisation of operations or staff cutbacks, perhaps caused by economic recession or falling demand for the firm's products or services, or for other reasons.

The resulting staff turnover ratio can then be analysed to identify the reasons why people leave the company. These may be many and varied, but some of the reasons may be within the control of management. For example, there may be areas of employment policy which work against the company, or perhaps poor working conditions may be contributing to the exodus. Staff leave for better pay, perceived better job satisfaction, greater opportunities and so on. The identification of the reasons for leaving voluntarily may also be able to be ascertained by asking the leavers at an 'exit interview' why they are leaving. If the causes can be addressed, staff turnover may fall, thus avoiding expensive replacement costs and improving morale and efficiency. Table 4.3 provides an example of a staff turnover report.

It can be seen from this example that the staff turnover in the Maintenance Department, canteen and telesales section are all much higher than the company's average and it would clearly pay the company to investigate the reasons why.

Holiday pay

The cost of direct labour staff holidays, the annual holiday entitlement plus payment for Bank Holidays, can be accounted for in a number of ways. The entitlement is a condition of employment and is therefore an unavoidable cost.

Note, however, that with other, non-direct staff, holiday pay is not normally accounted for separately, the cost being charged in the wages or salaries accounts as part of the normal wages or salaries cost of

TABLE 4.3

STAFF TURNOVER REPORT			
MONTH: MAY			
AVERAGE STAFF NUMBERS	DEPARTMENT	LEAVERS IN LAST 12 MONTHS (NUMBER)	AS PERCENTAGE OF AVERAGE STAFF NUMBERS IN DEPARTMENT %
PRODUCTION			
40	DEPT 1	14	35
20	DEPT 2	2	10
8	STORES	1	13
3	MAINTENANCE	5	167
6	CANTEEN	8	133
2	BUYING	1	50
4	ADMINISTRATION	2	50
DISTRIBUTION			
6	WAREHOUSE	2	33
4	DELIVERY DRIVERS	2	33
2	ADMINISTRATION	0	0
SALES AND MARKETING			
20	FIELD STAFF	13	65
8	TELESALES	11	138
3	ADMINISTRATION	3	100
2	MARKETING	0	0
ADMINISTRATION:			
6	ACCOUNTS	1	17
3	PERSONNEL	0	0
2	OTHER ADMIN	1	50
COMPANY AS A WHOLE			
139		67	58

the department or function. But for direct labour it is necessary to treat holiday pay separately. Plainly, no production work can be undertaken by the worker while the person is on holiday. It is therefore an extra expense and needs to be accounted for.

Holiday pay can be quite substantial. Consider the employee earning £8 per hour and working a 40-hour week. With three weeks' holiday per annum, plus the usual eight days' Bank Holiday entitlement, the cost of holiday pay would amount to £1472 (ignoring the payroll on-costs of National Insurance contributions and the company's pension contributions if applicable). As a percentage of annual earnings for this individual it represents nearly 9 per cent of the cost.

Dealing now with the accounting treatment, the first method used is to create a *holiday pay provision account*. In each accounting period an extra charge will be made to the work in progress account to cover the holiday pay expenses. A corresponding credit entry will then be made to the holiday pay provision account. When the holiday is taken the gross pay for the holiday period will be debited to the holiday pay provision account.

Example:

Number of operatives: 10

Number of holiday days p.a.: $23 \times 10 = 230$

Estimated amount of holiday pay p.a.: £14 720
   (1840 hours at £8 per hour)

Number of accounting periods p.a.: 12

Holiday pay provision per period: £1227*

Actual direct labour cost in Period 9: £13 867
(1733 hours × £8)

Charge to work in progress for period 9: £15 094
(£13 867 plus £1227).

*The provision can be a straight 1/12th of the annual holiday pay figure or, more accurately, based on the actual direct labour hours worked in the period. With this latter method the calculations will be:

> Cost of estimated holiday pay for the financial year ÷ Number of productive hours for the year (estimated annual hours − holiday pay hours).

In the above example, therefore, the holiday pay charge for Period 9 will be

$£14\,720/(20\,800 - 1840\,\text{hours}) = £0.7764$ per hour multiplied by the 1733 actual hours. This will give a charge of £1345 to the work-in-progress account for Period 9, and a corresponding credit entry will be made to the provision account.

The provision account will appear as shown in Table 4.4.

In this example the actual holiday pay proved to be the same as the estimated figure but, at the end of the financial year, there will usually be a balance remaining on the account. This will represent an overcharge or an undercharge of holiday pay made to the work-in-progress account. This balance, which, if the calculations have been made with any degree of accuracy, will usually be relatively small, will be written off as a factory overhead expense.

Another method often used is based on the view that direct labour holiday pay is an unavoidable expense, therefore it should be treated as a factory overhead indirect labour cost in the same way, say, that idle time and diverted hours are. Here also, a holiday pay provision account would be utilised to spread its cost over the whole of the financial year instead of having large sums coming through in certain periods, with no charge in others, thus distorting the costs.

Worked examples

1. ACCA COST AND MANAGEMENT ACCOUNTING DECEMBER 1990
X Ltd has an average of 42 workers employed in one of its factories in a period during which seven workers left and were replaced. The company pays a basic rate of £4.60 per hour to all its direct personnel. This is used as the standard rate. In addition, a factory-wide bonus scheme is in operation. A bonus of half of the efficiency

TABLE 4.4

HOLIDAY PAY PROVISION ACCOUNT

		DR			CR
JAN	PAYROLL JOURNAL	640	JAN	CHARGE TO WIP	1 227
FEBRUARY	PAYROLL JOURNAL	0	FEBRUARY	CHARGE TO WIP	1 227
MARCH	PAYROLL JOURNAL	0	MARCH	CHARGE TO WIP	1 227
APRIL	PAYROLL JOURNAL	1 280	APRIL	CHARGE TO WIP	1 227
MAY	PAYROLL JOURNAL	1 280	MAY	CHARGE TO WIP	1 227
JUNE	PAYROLL JOURNAL	1 920	JUNE	CHARGE TO WIP	1 227
JULY	PAYROLL JOURNAL	3 200	JULY	CHARGE TO WIP	1 227
AUGUST	PAYROLL JOURNAL	3 840	AUGUST	CHARGE TO WIP	1 227
SEPTEMBER	PAYROLL JOURNAL	0	SEPTEMBER	CHARGE TO WIP	1 227
OCTOBER	PAYROLL JOURNAL	0	OCTOBER	CHARGE TO WIP	1 227
NOVEMBER	PAYROLL JOURNAL	0	NOVEMBER	CHARGE TO WIP	1 227
DECEMBER	PAYROLL JOURNAL	2 560	DECEMBER	CHARGE TO WIP	1 223
		14 720			14 720

NOTE: WIP = WORK-IN-PROGRESS ACCOUNT.

ratio in excess of 100% is added as a percentage to the basic hourly rate (e.g. if the efficiency rate is 110%, then the hourly rate is £4.83 (£4.60 + (£4.60 × 5%).

During the period 114 268 units of the company's single product were manufactured in 4900 hours. The standard hour is 22 units.

Required:
(a) Calculate the labour turnover percentage for the period;
(b) Identify the reasons for, and costs of, labour turnover, and discuss how it may be reduced; and
(c) Calculate the hourly wage rate paid for the period, and the total labour variance.

Solution:
(a) Calculation of labour turnover
Number leaving in the period	7	
Average number of workers	42	
Staff turnover	**16.7%**	(7/42)

(b) Some of the reasons and costs are discussed in the chapter.
(c) Calculation of hourly wage rate:
Basic pay: £4.60
Bonus pay:
114 268 units were made. Each hour it was planned that 22 units would be made. Therefore the 114 268 units should have been made in 5194 hours (114 268/22 per hour). They took 4900 hours to do the work; therefore they were more efficient.
The ratio of 5194 to 4900 is 106% (5194/4900 × 100): they were thus 6% more efficient than expected.
The workforce will therefore receive an extra bonus of 3% per hour (half the 6%).
The hourly wage rate that will apply to the 4900 hours worked will therefore be:
£4.60 plus 3% of £4.60 = £4.738 per hour

Actual gross pay will thus be 4900 × 4.738:
                              £23 216.20
But the company expected to pay:
                              £23 892.40
The difference is a saving of   **£676.20**

(This is termed a favourable variance, which is a standard costing term, the subject 'of Chapter 18)

2. LONDON CHAMBER OF COMMERCE AND INDUSTRY 1994 SECOND LEVEL
Shaver and Turner are machine operators in a company which manufactures components for motor cars. The basic working week is 40 hours and overtime is paid at time and a half. The company operates a bonus scheme. 50% of the hours saved against a standard time allowed are paid at the basic rate of £4 per hour. The following details relate to two jobs completed during Week 36:

Shaver
Job X23 component D224:	110 units
Hours worked on job X23:	38 hours
Hours booked to idle time:	2 hours
Hours attended to be paid:	40 hours
Allowed time per unit of D224:	24 minutes

Turner
Job X27 component D239:	160 units
Hours worked on job X27:	43 hours
Hours attended to be paid:	43 hours
Allowed time per unit of D239:	18 minutes

All units produced are paid for, although, on inspection, Shaver had 8 units rejected and Turner 6 units rejected.

Required:
Calculate separately for both Shaver and Turner:
(a) The amount of bonus payable;
(b) The total gross wage; and
(c) The direct wages cost per good unit produced.

Solution:
(a) Bonus payable

	Shaver	Turner
Units produced	110	160
Time allowed each	24 Min	18 Min
Time allowed in hours	44	48
Time taken	38	43
Time saved	6	5
Bonus – hours	3	2.5
Bonus payment at £4 per hour	**£12.00**	**£10.00**

(b) Total gross wage

	Shaver	Turner
Hours worked	40	43
Basic pay	£160.00	£172.00
Bonus pay	£12.00	£10.00
Total gross wages	**£172.00**	**£182.00**

(c)   Direct wages cost per good unit produced

	Shaver	**Turner**
Total gross wages	£172.00	£182.00
Less idle time	£8.00	£0.00
	£164.00	£182.00
Good units produced	102	154
Cost per good unit produced	**£1.61**	**£1.18**

Summary

- Labour is an element of cost and is ranked along-side the other elements of cost: materials and over-heads.
- Production staff are classified as being either direct labour or indirect labour. The work of direct labour staff can be identifiable directly as forming a con-stituent part of the finished product or task. They are the people who are actively involved in making the product. The direct labour cost is charged to the work-in-progress account and is one of the prime costs of the product, the other being direct materials.
- Indirect labour employees assist in, or serve, the pro-duction process, but their work cannot be identified economically with the finished product. For exam-ple, factory administration staff, stores workers, clea-ners, maintenance staff and canteen workers.
- The Payroll Department is responsible for calculat-ing gross pay, calculating statutory and voluntary deductions and arranging payment of the net sums due to the staff. A payroll journal will be prepared from the payroll analysis details and posted to the ledger.

- Gross pay calculations for direct labour staff may be based on the following methods:

  Time basis schemes: Hours worked × rate per hour.
  Piecework schemes: Number of items made × rate per piece
  Premium bonus schemes: A proportion of the time saved in completing a job or task × basic rate per hour + basic pay for hours worked.

- There are a number of variations within each of these schemes, for example high day rates in the time basis method; differential piecework and guar-anteed minimum wages modifications in piece-work schemes; and various premium bonus schemes designed to encourage and reward the saving of time in performing tasks and jobs. There are also various profit-sharing schemes and group bonus schemes.
- The information to calculate gross pay is dependent on information received by the Payroll Depart-ment. This information may be collected via clock cards and time sheets.
- A key cost accounting task is to analyse direct labour gross pay amounts to ascertain idle time costs, diverted hours costs, overtime premium and shift premium costs, etc. It is usual for holiday pay costs for the direct labour staff to be spread over the whole financial year, with a provision to cover its cost being made to production each accounting period.
- By comparing staff leavers with average staff num-bers periodically a staff turnover ratio can be ascer-tained. The staff turnover ratio, expressed in per-centage form, can indicate staff relations problem areas which, when addressed, may help reduce the hidden costs associated with staff turnover.

Examination Questions

1   A-LEVEL (ULEAC) 1990

Under Sturton Manufacturing Co's premium bonus scheme, em-ployees receive a bonus equivalent to half of the time saved on a job. Three workers are given a similar job to do, the set time for which is six hours. Daniels completes the task in 3 hours, Ericson in 4 hours, and Frith in 6 hours. The hourly rate of pay is £5.

(i)   Calculate the earnings for each of the workers, for that job.

(ii) Assuming that Daniels and Frith work at the above speed throughout a 35 hour week, calculate who would earn most and why.

2   AAT COST ACCOUNTING AND BUDGETING 1993

A company is reviewing its labour remuneration methods and you are given the following data:

Normal working week	37.5 hours
Guaranteed rate of pay on a time basis	£6.00 per hour
Standard time for one unit of production	10 minutes
Piecework price	£1 per unit
Bonus scheme	£6 per hour
for two-thirds of hours saved in addition to guaranteed rate.	

Required:

(i) Calculate the remuneration levels under time rate, piecework and the bonus scheme for 80%, 100% and 120% of budgeted activity achieved within the working week.

(ii) Determine which method would be most suitable if the company wished to minimise wage costs yet at the same time give its employees a guaranteed wage and an incentive to earn more. Give reasons for your decision.

NON-COMPUTATIONAL, DESCRIPTIVE TYPE QUESTION
(**NB** Minutes in brackets are a guide to indicate the approximate time your essay should take to complete.)

QUESTION

A Explain briefly the role of the following in the costing of labour:
   (i) Time sheets
   (ii) Piecework tickets
   (ACCA 1991) (11 minutes)

B A company previously paid its direct labour workers upon a time basis but is now contemplating moving over to an incentive scheme.
   Required: Draft a memo to the Chief Accountant outlining the general characteristics and advantages of employing a successful incentive scheme.
   (AAT 1991) (15 minutes)

C Describe how to ensure accurate labour cost records, if employees are paid on (i) time rates and (ii) piece rates.
   (ULEAC 1993) (30 minutes)

D Wage rates based upon flat day rates (or time rates) do little to encourage employees to improve output.
   Bring out the main characteristics of the following approaches showing how they seek to overcome this defect
   (a) high day rate (premium day rates)
   (b) measured day work
   (c) premium bonus schemes
   (d) collective bonus schemes
   (e) profit sharing schemes.
   (ULEAC 1990) (35 minutes)

5

Factory Overheads – Allocation and Apportionment

Overheads

The third element of cost is Overheads. Overheads comprise *all* of the costs of the business except direct material costs, direct labour costs and any direct expenses that can be specifically identified as forming part of the finished product. The combined costs of materials, labour and *factory overheads* provides the cost of the finished article, that is, the *product cost*.

Picture an ordinary product: a desk, for example, or the till receipt you are handed when buying goods in a shop. You can see the material or materials from which these are made; clearly the direct materials. You can also imagine a carpenter making the desk, or a group of factory workers loading one huge paper roll on to a paper cutting machine and then boxing the myriads of till rolls produced from it – unmistakably direct labour staff who have contributed directly to making the finished product.

These products are obviously made inside a building – the factory. And various tasks and operations connected with the manufacturing process need to be carried out and undertaken before, during and after the product is made to bring it to the finished state. The product could not be made without these other manufacturing activities. The costs of these other activities are described as *factory overheads* (or *manufacturing overheads, production overheads or indirect costs*).

It can be seen, however, that the identification of the factory overheads with each and every individual finished article is not so straightforward. For example, how can the rent and rates payable on the factory or the maintenance costs of the machinery that produced it be identified with the finished product?

The solution is to apportion or spread those factory overhead costs to the finished articles on some predetermined, equitable basis so that each item will have absorbed its 'fair share' of the overheads.

But first, overheads need to be split between the various functions of the business to identify and then correctly account for the factory overheads. The overheads incurred in the other functions of the business: in distribution, in sales and marketing and in general administration, are termed *period costs*. In this chapter we shall be dealing with the collection of factory overheads *prior to* their absorption into the products produced.

Factory overheads are incurred on the factory floor and in the back-up factory services such as factory administration; also in the stores, in the works canteen, the Maintenance Department, and in the general running and operations of the production function. Thus all the costs and expenses incurred in the manufacturing process, from the ordering and receiving of the raw materials through to the placing of the finished article into the finished goods storage or despatch areas, are production or factory overheads.

Factory overheads comprise:

Indirect materials used on the factory floor;

Indirect labour costs, for example cleaners working in production; departmental expenses of each supporting production function;

Premises costs applicable to the production area such as rates;

Depreciation of the plant and equipment used;

Electricity, gas and water used in the factory area; and

Other factory-incurred costs such as idle time and shift premiums.

In Chapter 2, Figure 2.3, a diagram of the business premises as a whole was depicted. Looking again at this, but from a factory overheads point of view, we have examples of costs as shown in Figure 5.1.

We shall briefly 'walk through' these production areas to visualise how the overheads are incurred, starting first with the Raw Materials Stores Area.

This department is responsible for receiving the raw materials and issuing them to the Production Departments (factory floor). The staff will be operating fork-lift trucks, moving materials, and counting and checking stores.

The costs and expenses of running the department will be broadly in line with the examples given in Figure 5.1. Occasionally, interest payable on the stocks carried will also be charged as an overhead of this department.

You will note there is a charge for premises costs. This also appears in all the other departments. It represents the cost of the space occupied by each of the departments.

These costs are:

Uniform business rate;
Rent if applicable;
Heating and lighting of the building; and
Insurance and repairs of the whole building.

FIGURE 5.1

EXAMPLES OF OVERHEAD COSTS

PRODUCTION AREA

RAW MATERIALS STORES AREA
STAFF WAGES; CONSUMABLES; PREMISES COSTS; COMPUTER COSTS; FORK-LIFT TRUCK COSTS; DEPRECIATION OF EQUIPMENT; REPAIRS AND MAINTENANCE OF EQUIPMENT; TELEPHONE COSTS

PRODUCTION DEPARTMENT ONE
SUPERVISORY WAGES; CLEANERS' WAGES; PREMISES COSTS; CONSUMABLES; DEPRECIATION OF EQUIPMENT; POWER AND WATER; WORKWEAR FOR STAFF

PRODUCTION DEPARTMENT TWO
SUPERVISORY WAGES; CLEANERS' WAGES; PREMISES COSTS; CONSUMABLES; DEPRECIATION OF EQUIPMENT; POWER AND WATER; WORKWEAR FOR STAFF

FACTORY ADMINISTRATION DEPARTMENTS
STAFF SALARIES; PRINTING AND STATIONERY; PREMISES COSTS; DEPRECIATION OF FURNITURE AND EQUIPMENT; TELEPHONE COSTS; COMPUTER COSTS; ADMIN VEHICLE COSTS

FACTORY CANTEEN
FOOD SUPPLIES; POWER AND WATER; STAFF WAGES; WORKWEAR; CLEANING MATERIALS; PREMISES COSTS; DEPRECIATION OF EQUIPMENT

MAINTENANCE DEPARTMENT
MACHINERY PARTS; LOOSE TOOLS AND SPARES; STAFF WAGES; PREMISES COSTS; DEPRECIATION OF EQUIPMENT; VEHICLE COSTS

We shall be examining later how the premises costs are apportioned to the various departments.

It is in the two Production Departments that the products are actually made. Here the raw materials are converted into the finished products. Examples of the overheads incurred in running these two departments are as indicated Figure 5.1.

The Factory Administration Departments will be headed by the Production Director or Works Manager; clerical staff will be employed in controlling the movements of raw materials and direct labour, also in planning and ensuring that jobs and tasks are carried out and completed in accordance with the production programme. In the Buying Department (part of Factory Administration), the Buyer and his or her staff will be negotiating prices with suppliers, ordering products, chasing supplies, investigating alternative sources of raw materials and handling other purchase requirements for the company as a whole, such as indirect materials purchasing, stationery and fixed assets.

FIGURE 5.2

PRODUCTION AREA CHART OF ACCOUNTS

DEPARTMENT CODE		100 PRODUCTION DEPT. NO. 1	101 PRODUCTION DEPT. NO. 2	102 MAINTE- NANCE	103 STORES	104 CANTEEN	105 ADMINIS- TRATION
EXPENSE CODE:							
COMPUTER COSTS	116						
CONSUMABLES	117						
DEPRECIATION	102						
FOOD SUPPLIES	118						
FORK-LIFT TRUCK COSTS	119						
LOOSE TOOLS	120						
MACHINERY PARTS	121						
POWER AND WATER	122						
PRINTING AND STATIONERY	123						
REPAIRS AND MAINTENANCE	109						
SPARES	124						
STAFF WORKWEAR	125						
TELEPHONE	113						
VEHICLE COSTS	115						
WAGES AND SALARIES	150						

> EXAMPLES OF CODING:
> TELEPHONE BILL FOR STORES WILL BE CODED 103/113
> WORKWEAR FOR CANTEEN WILL BE CODED 104/125
> WORKWEAR FOR NO. 1 DEPT WILL BE CODED 100/125

PREMISES COSTS CHART OF ACCOUNTS

DEPARTMENT CODE	900
EXPENSE CODE:	
RATES	200
RENT	201
HEAT AND LIGHTS	202
WATER	203
INSURANCE – BUILDING	204
BUILDING MAINTENANCE	205

> EXAMPLE OF CODING:
> MAINTENANCE CHARGES WILL BE CODED 900/205

The canteen will cater for the requirements of the production area staff and may serve hot meals at specified break times. Many canteens charge for the meals and when this is the case the income arising will be credited to the Canteen Department. Thus a profit or loss will arise from the operations of the canteen. Any loss incurred will effectively represent the financial subsidy the company makes to the canteen operations.

The Maintenance Department staff will be responsible for maintaining the machinery and plant, carrying spare parts stocks and generally ensuring that equipment is kept in good order, thus minimising breakdowns.

Allocation of overheads

The first accounting task is to charge the overhead costs incurred by each department to the specific accounts of the department. Each department will be designated its own set of account numbers and these will be given in the Chart of Accounts (see page 9). If a cost can be specifically identified with a department that cost is *allocated* to that department. For illustration we have set up the truncated Chart of Accounts shown in Figure 5.2 to allocate the production area overhead costs. The examples given are costs that can be attributed specifically to the work undertaken by the different functions and therefore the costs have been *allocated* to those functions.

Apportionment of overheads

Some costs, however, cannot be identified as arising from the activities of one specific department or function. Consider the rates. Here the charge will be levied on the premises as a whole. How the company organises its internal workings is of no concern to the local authority and therefore only one bill will be received, covering the whole premises. Rates and other similar costs, such as are listed in the lower part of Figure 5.2, are described as *premises costs*. They will all relate to the building as a whole.

You will remember that our eventual aim is to establish how much each finished product will bear of the factory overheads. To do this we need to know the overheads applicable to each of the Production Departments. We therefore need to *apportion* the unallocated costs to the various Production Departments.

Other costs which might also be apportioned where it is not possible or feasible to allocate directly to departments are:

Machinery insurance charges;
Power costs; and
Depreciation (if this charge cannot readily be identified with user departments).

Apportionment of all these types of expenditure must be made to the departments or cost centres on a fair and equitable basis. Some of the more common bases used for apportioning costs are as follows:

Premises costs, on the area occupied by each department;
Power costs, on the usage of kilowatt hours;
General supervision, on the number of staff in each department;
Depreciation, on the value of plant and equipment used in each department; and
Machinery insurance, on the value of plant and equipment used in each department.

Example:
Breslin Engineering incurred the following costs which could not be allocated directly to the various departments:

	£
Premises costs	100 000
Power costs	45 000
General supervision	20 000
Depreciation	18 000
Machinery insurance	12 000
	195 000

The total area of the factory is 200 000 m^2

These figures are broken down as follows:

		As a percentage of total
Department 1	35 000 m^2	17.5
Department 2	20 000	10.0
Maintenance Department	16 000	8.0
Stores	10 000	5.0
Canteen	14 000	7.0
Factory Administration	5 000	2.5

Other non-manufacturing

| departments | 100 000 | 50.0 |
| Total occupancy | 200 000 m² | 100.0 |

The power used by each producing department was as follows:

Department 1	20 000 Kwh	66.67%
Department 2	10 000 Kwh	33.33%
Total power	30 000 Kwh	100.00%

General supervision charges were apportioned on the number of staff in each department:

Department 1	40	50.0%
Department 2	20	25.0%
Maintenance	5	6.25%
Stores	7	8.75%
Canteen	8	10.0%
Total staff	80	100.00%

Depreciation and machinery insurance charges were apportioned on the basis of the following plant and equipment valuations:

Department 1	£50 000	50.0%
Department 2	£30 000	30.0%
Maintenance	£5 000	5.0%
Canteen	£6 000	6.0%
Administration	£9 000	9.0%
Total plant values	£100 000	100.0%

Using these bases, the costs will be apportioned as in Figure 5.3.

At the end of each accounting period, when the overheads have been allocated and apportioned to the various production departments, the total costs for each department will be known.

The activities in the production area of the factory comprise the producing departments (in our example,

FIGURE 5.3

APPORTIONMENT OF COSTS TO MANUFACTURING AREAS

COST		DEPT. 1	DEPT. 2	MAINTENANCE	STORES
		£	£	£	£
PREMISES		17 500	10 000	8 000	5 000
POWER		30 000	15 000		
GENERAL SUPERVISION		10 000	5 000	1 250	1 750
DEPRECIATION		9 000	5 400	900	1 080
MACHINERY INSURANCE		6 000	3 600	600	720
TOTAL APPORTIONED COSTS		**72 500**	**39 000**	**10 750**	**8 550**
BASIS OF APPORTIONMENT					
PREMISES	AREA (m²)	35 000	20 000	16 000	10 000
	% CHARGE	17.5	10.0	8.0	5.0
POWER	Kwh	20 000	10 000		
	% CHARGE	66.7	33.3	0.0	0.0
SUPERVISION	NUMBER OF STAFF	40	20	5	7
	% CHARGE	50.0	25.0	6.25	8.75
DEPRECIATION &					
INSURANCE	PLANT VALUES	£50 000	£30 000	£5 000	£6 000
	% CHARGE	50.0	30.0	5.00	6.00

(Apportionment example: the total area is 200 000 m². Dept. 1 occupies 35 000 m². As a proportion of the total it represents

Departments 1 and 2) and the non-producing departments (sections covering raw materials stores, canteen, maintenance and so on).

It follows that as the non-producing departments – the service departments – exist solely to serve the producing departments, the costs of these non-producing departments should *also* be charged – apportioned – to the two producing departments. The end result is that the total overhead costs of running the whole production section are consolidated into the two producing departments. The methods to achieve this are detailed below.

Apportionment of reciprocal services

The service departments' primary purpose is to manage, assist and serve the production process. But they very often carry out work and perform services for other service departments too. For example, the maintenance staff may be required to repair and service items in, say, the canteen from time to time; the canteen, in turn, will serve the maintenance staff as well as production and other non-production staff; the factory Administration Department may deal with some of the stores clerical procedures, and stores, in turn, may hold records for the Administration Department. These intra-servicing arrangements are termed reciprocal services.

The task now is to apportion the costs of the service departments, on equitable bases, so that all the factory overheads are eventually consolidated into the costs of the producing departments. The term used for this is *apportionment of reciprocal services*.

Basis of apportionment of reciprocal services

Management will endeavour to assess the work done by each service department for the producing departments and for their fellow non-producing departments. They

CANTEEN	ADMINISTRATION	MANUFACTURING DEPTS. TOTAL	NON-MANUFACTURING DEPARTMENTS	COMPANY TOTAL
£	£	£	£	£
7 000	2 500	50 000	50 000	100 000
		45 000		45 000
2 000	20 000	20 000		20 000
1 620		18 000		18 000
1 080		12 000		12 000
11 700	22 500	145 000	50 000	195 000
14 000	5 000	100 000	100 000	200 000
7.0	2.5	50.0	50.0	100.0%
				30 000
0.0	0.0	0.0		100.0%
8				80
10.0	0.0	0.0		100.0%
£9 000				£100 000
9.0	0.0	0.0		100.0%

17.5% (35 000/200 000): 17.5% × £100 000 = £17 500)

may decide, for example, that the best way to apportion the canteen costs will be to base them on the number of staff in each of the departments. Maintenance Department costs may be considered to be representative of the number of machines in each department, so the number of machines in each department will be used to spread this cost. Or they may decide it would be a better reflection of the situation to use the number of repair jobs the Maintenance Department carried out over a period as the basis.

When the assessment is complete, the proportion of each service department to be apportioned to the other departments is expressed in percentage terms. These may appear as shown below. (**Note**: To simplify the illustration the number of service departments/sections has been reduced to two, Maintenance and Canteen. Also, that the sum of the percentages should always by 100%.)

	Maintenance	*Canteen*
Department 1	40%	50%
Department 2	40%	30%
Maintenance	–	20%
Canteen	20%	–
	100%	100%

There are a number of methods used to apportion reciprocal services but the most frequently used are:

Elimination method (simplified method)
Repeated distribution (continuous allotment) method
Algebraic method (simultaneous equations)

Example:
Overhead costs have been allocated and apportioned as follows:

	Costs (£s)
Production Dept 1	60 000
Production Dept 2	40 000
Maintenance	30 000
Canteen	20 000

The total production costs amount to £150 000. The £50 000 costs incurred in maintenance and the canteen now need to be apportioned into Production Departments 1 and 2.

Elimination method

This method is based on the assumption that when one service department's costs are apportioned, that particular department is then eliminated from any apportionments of the other service departments, as shown in Table 5.1.

You will see from Table 5.1 that maintenance was first apportioned in accordance with the percentages and then 'closed' so that it could not accept any

TABLE 5.1

APPORTIONING COSTS: ELIMINATION METHOD					
	PRODUCTION DEPARTMENTS		**SERVICE DEPARTMENTS**		
	DEPT. 1	**DEPT. 2**	**MAINTENANCE**	**CANTEEN**	**TOTAL**
COSTS	£60 000	£40 000	£30 000	£20 000	£150 000
APPORTIONMENT BASIS					
MAINTENANCE (%)	40.0	40.0	–	20.0	100.0
CANTEEN (%)	50.0	30.0	20.0	–	100.0
APPORTIONMENT OF RECIPROCAL SERVICES					
MAINTENANCE	£12 000	£12 000	(£30 000)	£ 6 000	
SUBTOTAL	£72 000	£52 000	£0	£26 000	
CANTEEN	£16 000	£ 9 750		(£26 000)	
COSTS	£88 250	£61 750	£0	£0	£150 000

charges from the canteen. Hence the term 'elimination': the Maintenance Department is now eliminated from any further charges. However, looking at the canteen percentages it will be seen that 20 per cent of the cost should have been absorbed by the Maintenance Department. As it is closed, this cannot be done. Therefore the two Production Departments will have to bear the canteen costs in proportion to the charges allocated to them: 50 per cent and 30 per cent respectively. So Department 1 will take 50/80ths of the canteen costs, and Department 2 will take 30/80ths. At the end of the exercise it can be seen that the two producing departments now carry the full overhead costs of the whole production function. Note that the total costs at the start of the exercise should always agree with the closing total costs as shown in the table, in this case £150 000.

Strictly, the elimination method does not accord with the concept of reciprocal services, because none of the services provided by the canteen will be charged to the Maintenance Department. This method is also known as the *simplified method*.

Repeated distribution method

This method (known also as the *continuous allotment method*) *does* reflect the reciprocity of the service departments to each other. Here the costs are charged to the various departments in the percentage proportions assessed by management, as shown in Table 5.2.

We shall work through this table, starting with the initial maintenance distribution. You will note that this department's costs were transferred into the other departments and a credit entry in the maintenance column closed it. The canteen distribution then effectively reopened the Maintenance Department – in this case £5200 was charged. This figure now has to be distributed over the departments. This process continues so that each time one of the service departments is 'closed' it is reopened by a charge from the other department. Hence the term 'repeated distribution'. The process continues until all the service costs have been fully transferred into the Production Department. (It is reasonable to ignore pence and keep the figures to round numbers. It is also

TABLE 5.2

APPORTIONING COSTS: REPEATED DISTRIBUTION METHOD					
	DEPT. 1	DEPT. 2	MAINTENANCE	CANTEEN	TOTAL
COSTS	£60 000	£40 000	£30 000	£20 000	£150 000
MAINTENANCE (%)	40.0	40.0	0.0	20.0	100.0
CANTEEN (%)	50.0	30.0	20.0	0.0	100.0
APPORTIONMENT OF RECIPROCAL SERVICES:					
MAINTENANCE	£12 000	£12 000	(£30 000)	£ 6 000	
SUBTOTAL	£72 000	£52 000	£ 0	£26 000	
CANTEEN	£13 000	£ 7 800	£ 5 200	(£26 000)	
SUBTOTAL	£85 000	£59 800	£ 5 200	£ 0	
MAINTENANCE	£ 2 080	£2 080	(£ 5 200)	£ 1 040	
SUBTOTAL	£87 080	£61 880	£ 0	£ 1 040	
CANTEEN	£ 520	£ 312	£ 208	(£ 1 040)	
SUBTOTAL	£87 600	£62 192	£ 208	£ 0	
MAINTENANCE	£ 83	£ 83	(£ 208)	£ 42	
SUBTOTAL	£87 683	£62 275	£ 0	£ 42	
CANTEEN	£ 21	£ 12	£ 9	(£ 42)	
SUBTOTAL	£87 704	£62 287	£ 9	£ 0	
MAINTENANCE	£ 4	£ 5	(£ 9)	£ 0	
COSTS	£87 708	£62 292	£ 0	£ 0	£150 000

sensible to deal with the very small balances at the end in a commonsense way.) The repeated distribution method can be quite laborious if done manually, but with a computer spreadsheet program the calculations are, of course, instantaneous. An example of a spreadsheet to do the calculations is shown in Figure 5.4

Algebraic method (simultaneous equations)

This method produces the same end result as the repeated distribution method, but it can be far quicker and for those who enjoy solving equations perhaps a more rewarding exercise than the repeated distribution method. A step-by-step approach might be found to be the most straightforward way to calculate the sums.

Step 1

Set out the equations to be solved:
Let Maintenance be M and the Canteen C.
The amount to be absorbed into the Production Departments will be based on the following:

$$M = £30\,000 + 20\%C$$
$$C = £20\,000 + 20\%M$$

Step 2

For the calculations it is easier to dispose of the fractions and work in whole numbers. Multiply each of the above lines to bring the percentage figures to $100\% = 1$.

As both are 20%, this means each line will be multiplied by 5 (100%/20%):

$$5M = £150\,000 + 1C$$
$$5C = £100\,000 + 1M$$

FIGURE 5.4

SPREADSHEET: REPEATED DISTRIBUTION METHOD

	A	B	C	D	E	F	G	H	I
3									
4									
5									
6				DEPT.1	DEPT.2	MAINTENANCE	CANTEEN	TOTAL	
7									
8									
9		COSTS		£60 000	£40 000	£30 000	£20 000	@SUM(D9..G9)	
10									
11		MAINTENANCE (%)		40.0	40.0	0.0	20.0		
12		CANTEEN (%)		50.0	30.0	20.0	0.0		
13									
14		APPORTIONMENT OF RECIPROCAL SERVICES							
15									
16		MAINTENANCE		+$F9*D11	+$F9*G11	-G16-D16-E16	+$F9*G11		
17				+D16+D9	+E16+E9	+F16+F9	+G16+G9		
18		CANTEEN		+$G17*D$12	+$G17*E$12	+$G17*F$12	-D18-E18-F18		
19				+D17+D18	+E17+E18	+F17+F18	+G17+G18		
20		MAINTENANCE		+$F19*$D$11	+$F19*E11	-E20-D20-G20	+$F19*G11		
21				+D19+D20	+E19+E20	+F19+F20	+G19+G20		
22		CANTEEN		+$G21*D$12	+$G21*E$12	+$G21*F$12	-D22-E22-F22		
23				+D21+D22	+E21+E22	+F21+F22	+G21+G22		
24		MAINTENANCE		+$F23*$D$11	+$F23*$D$11	-G24-E24-D24	+$F23*$G$11		
25				+D23+D24	+E23+E24	+F23+F24	+G23+G24		
26		CANTEEN		+$G25*D$12	+$G25*E$12	+$G25*F$12	-D26-E26-F26		
27				+D25+D26	+E25+E26	+F25+F26	+G25+G26		
28		MAINTENANCE		+$F27*$D$11	+$F27*$D$11	-D28-E28-F28	+$F27*$G$11		
29									
30		COSTS		+D27+D28+D29	+E27+E28+E29	+F27+F28+F29	+G27+G28+G29	@SUM(D30..G30)	
31									
32									
33									

(This is the equivalent of saying that '5 maintenance departments' are equal to £150 000 plus '1 canteen'.)

You will remember with equations that when $2 + 1 = 3$, this is the same as saying $2 = 3 - 1$. When a number switches from one side of the equality sign to the other it changes from a plus to a minus, and vice versa.

Step 3

So the next step is to rearrange the equation so that the symbols are on one side and the value is on the other:

$$5M - 1C = £150\,000$$
$$5C - 1M = £100\,000$$

Step 4

We need now to eliminate either M or C to find the value of one of them and, by substitution, we will then be able to find the value of the other. To do this we need to cancel out one of the symbols on both lines: for example, the $-1C$ or the $-1M$.

Take the first option: $-1C$. If this line were multiplied by 5 the result would be

$$25M - 5C = £750\,000.$$

We can then match the $-5C$ with the $+5C$ on the bottom line, thus cancelling both:

$$25M - 5C = £750\,000$$
$$5C - 1M = £100\,000$$
$$= 24M = £850\,000$$

Therefore $M = £35\,417$ (£850 000/24)

Step 5

Having found the value of M, the value of C will become known through substitution:

$$5C - £35\,417 = £100\,000$$

Switching the value so that both appear on the same side:

$$5C = £100\,000 + £35\,417$$

Therefore $C = £27\,083$ (£135 417/5)

Finally, with the values of M and C established, to find the amount chargeable to Production

Departments 1 and 2, the following calculations need to be made:

	Department 1	Department 2
Maintenance	40% × £35 417	40% × £35 417
Canteen	50% × £27 083	30% × £27 083

The overall position then becomes:

	Department 1 £	Department 2 £
Allocated costs	60 000	40 000
Maintenance charge	14 167	14 167
Canteen charge	13 541	8 125
	87 708	62 292

It looks more complicated than it really is and, with some practice, the figures can be computed relatively quickly.

Worked example

A LEVEL (UNIVERSITY OF LONDON) 1991
The following information relates to Flyby Knight PLC for the six months ended 31 December:

	Production Departments			Service Departments	
	A	B	C	X	Y
Overheads	14 000	12 000	8 000	4 000	3 000

Overheads to be apportioned:

	A	B	C	X	Y
X	35%	30%	20%	–	15%
Y	30%	40%	25%	5%	–

(i) Use the continuous apportionment (repeated distribution) method to apportion the service departments' overheads between each other.

(ii) Apportion the service departments' overheads to the production departments.

(iii) Show how the overheads apportioned to the Production Departments would have differed if the elimination methods had been used for the Service Departments.

Solution:

<table>
<tr><td>(i) and (ii)</td><td></td><td></td><td>DEPT. A</td><td>DEPT. B</td><td>DEPT. C</td><td>SERVICE DEPT</td><td>SERVICE DEPT</td><td>TOTAL</td></tr>
<tr><td></td><td>COSTS</td><td></td><td>£14 000</td><td>£12 000</td><td>£8 000</td><td>£4 000</td><td>£3 000</td><td>£41 000</td></tr>
<tr><td></td><td>X%</td><td></td><td>35.0</td><td>30.0</td><td>20.0</td><td>–</td><td>15.0</td><td></td></tr>
<tr><td></td><td>Y%</td><td></td><td>30.0</td><td>40.0</td><td>25.0</td><td>5.0</td><td>–</td><td></td></tr>
<tr><td></td><td colspan="8">APPORTIONMENT OF RECIPROCAL SERVICES</td></tr>
<tr><td></td><td></td><td></td><td>£</td><td>£</td><td>£</td><td>£</td><td>£</td><td>£</td></tr>
<tr><td></td><td>X</td><td></td><td>1 400</td><td>1 200</td><td>800</td><td>(4 000)</td><td>600</td><td></td></tr>
<tr><td></td><td></td><td></td><td>15 400</td><td>13 200</td><td>8 800</td><td>0</td><td>3 600</td><td></td></tr>
<tr><td></td><td>Y</td><td></td><td>1 080</td><td>1 440</td><td>900</td><td>180</td><td>(3 600)</td><td></td></tr>
<tr><td></td><td></td><td></td><td>16 480</td><td>14 640</td><td>9 700</td><td>180</td><td>0</td><td></td></tr>
<tr><td></td><td>X</td><td></td><td>63</td><td>54</td><td>36</td><td>(180)</td><td>27</td><td></td></tr>
<tr><td></td><td></td><td></td><td>16 543</td><td>14 694</td><td>9 736</td><td>0</td><td>27</td><td></td></tr>
<tr><td></td><td>Y</td><td></td><td>9</td><td>11</td><td>7</td><td>0</td><td>(27)</td><td></td></tr>
<tr><td></td><td></td><td></td><td>16 552</td><td>14 705</td><td>9 743</td><td>0</td><td>0</td><td></td></tr>
<tr><td></td><td>COSTS</td><td></td><td>16 552</td><td>14 705</td><td>9 743</td><td>0</td><td>0</td><td>41 000</td></tr>
<tr><td></td><td></td><td></td><td></td><td>X apportioned to Y =</td><td></td><td></td><td>£627</td><td></td></tr>
<tr><td></td><td></td><td></td><td></td><td>Y apportioned to X =</td><td></td><td>£180</td><td></td><td></td></tr>
<tr><td>(iii)</td><td colspan="2">ELIMINATION METHOD</td><td>DEPT. A</td><td>DEPT. B</td><td>DEPT. C</td><td>SERVICE DEPT</td><td>SERVICE DEPT</td><td>TOTAL</td></tr>
<tr><td></td><td>COSTS</td><td></td><td>£14 000</td><td>£12 000</td><td>£8 000</td><td>£4 000</td><td>£3 000</td><td>£41 000</td></tr>
<tr><td></td><td>X%</td><td></td><td>35.0</td><td>30.0</td><td>20.0</td><td>–</td><td>15.0</td><td></td></tr>
<tr><td></td><td>Y%</td><td></td><td>30.0</td><td>40.0</td><td>25.0</td><td>5.0</td><td>–</td><td></td></tr>
<tr><td></td><td colspan="8">APPORTIONMENT OF RECIPROCAL SERVICES</td></tr>
<tr><td></td><td>X</td><td></td><td>1 400</td><td>1 200</td><td>800</td><td>(4 000)</td><td>600</td><td></td></tr>
<tr><td></td><td></td><td></td><td>15 400</td><td>13 200</td><td>8 800</td><td>0</td><td>3 600</td><td></td></tr>
<tr><td></td><td>Y</td><td></td><td>1 137</td><td>1 516</td><td>947</td><td></td><td>(3 600)</td><td></td></tr>
<tr><td></td><td></td><td></td><td>16 537</td><td>14 716</td><td>9 747</td><td></td><td>0</td><td></td></tr>
</table>

Summary

- Factory overheads are the third element of cost used to arrive at the product cost.
- Factory overheads, also called indirect costs or production overheads, are allocated to specific Production Departments' overhead accounts in the ledger. Production Departments are classified as either producing departments – where the actual saleable product is made – or non-producing departments, supporting services which enable production to take place.
- The process of charging directly attributable factory overheads to the appropriate account is called allocation of overheads: if the indirect cost can be identified with the activities of a department it is allocated to it.
- If a cost cannot be so attributed it needs to be apportioned to the 'user' departments on an equitable and consistent basis. Examples of apportioned costs are rates and buildings insurance.
- The objectives of allocating and apportioning factory overheads are twofold. They enable control to be exercised by identifying the departmental costs and therefore the management responsible for incurring the costs; the other main function is to arrive at a total production cost for each of the producing departments ready to be absorbed into the costs of the products.
- To enable all the factory costs to be identified with the manufacturing departments responsible for making the products, it is necessary to apportion the Service Departments' costs, such as those of stores and maintenance, into these departments. This process is called apportionment of reciprocal services. There are a number of methods used to do this but the most frequently found are: the elimination method, the repeated distribution method, and the algebraic method.
- At the end of the exercise, when all the factory costs have been allocated and apportioned, and the reciprocal services apportioned into the producing departments' costs, the total overhead costs for each of the producing departments will have been arrived at. This will then enable the factory overhead costs to be absorbed into individual products (the subject of the next chapter).

Examination Questions

1 A LEVEL (ULEAC) 1989

The Meldreth Manufacturing Company uses the algebraic (simultaneous equations) method to apportion the overheads of its service departments one to another.

| | Service Departments | |
	A	B
Overheads (£)	4 200	2 400
Apportionment (%) A	–	10
B	5	–

(a) Calculate the overheads to be apportioned to each of the two service departments.

2 A LEVEL (ULEAC) 1991

(a) Retro Ltd uses the continuous apportionment method to apportion overheads between its two service sections.

Service sections	Technical services	Administration
Overheads	£30 000	£20 000
Apportionment (%)		
Administration	10	–
Technical Services	–	5

For each service section, calculate the amount of overheads to be apportioned to production.

(b) Explain two other methods that Retro Ltd could have used to apportion the Service Departments' overheads between Technical Services and Administration.

3 A LEVEL (ULEAC) 1992

Use the repeated distribution method (continuous apportionment method) to apportion the overheads between the two Service Departments shown below:

| | Service departments | |
	Maintenance	Administration
Indirect costs (£s)	120 000	86 000
Apportionment		
Maintenance (%)	–	5
Administration (%)	10	–

6

Factory Overheads – Absorption into Products

In Chapter 5 we *allocated* the factory overheads incurred by the various producing and non-producing (service) departments on the basis that if the cost could be directly identified with a particular department or cost centre it was charged directly (allocated) to that department's appropriate analysis account.

We then *apportioned* to the Production Departments those other overhead costs which could not be directly identified with and therefore allocated to specific factory departments (for example, premises costs), and used various apportionment bases, such as space occupied, to spread these costs.

Finally, the Service Departments' costs were charged to the producing departments using apportionment of reciprocal services techniques.

The result of allocating and apportioning the manufacturing overhead costs is that the producing departments (in the examples, Departments 1 and 2), in the end bear *all* the overhead costs.

These, then, are the factory overheads that, in an *absorption costing system*, must be absorbed into the product so that the product cost (materials plus labour plus factory overheads) can be arrived at for each saleable unit made. CIMA defines absorption costing as: '*the procedure which charges fixed as well as variable overheads to cost units*'. The next step, the subject of this chapter, is how those factory overheads are absorbed into the products.

Absorption of overheads using absorption rates

As has already been discussed, factory overheads cannot be identified specifically with the finished article, so it is necessary to have some equitable system that allows for these overheads to be absorbed into the products. To do this an *absorption rate* needs to be computed. The CIMA definition of an absorption rate is: '*a rate charged to a cost unit intended to account for the overhead at a predetermined level of activity*'.

Note that the rate is based on predetermined activity, which indicates that management need to estimate both overhead costs and the quantity of an activity for a future period. This normally entails preparing budgets for both costs and quantity and we will be looking at this aspect shortly. Dealing first with the computation of the absorption rates, the following are the most commonly found in conventional costing systems:

Direct labour hour rate
Direct labour cost percentage rate
Machine hour rate

There are other methods used and later in the chapter we shall examine some of these. Also in Chapter

15 we shall examine the overhead absorption technique called Activity Based Costing (ABC), an alternative to the conventional methods described in this chapter.

Direct labour hour rate method

The basis of this method, using predetermined figures, is the number of direct labour hours activity needed to make an article. The formula is:

> Overhead costs of the producing department for an accounting period/Number of direct labour hours worked in the department in the same period

Example:
Predetermined overhead costs of Department 1: £500 000
Predetermined direct labour hours to be worked in the Assembly Department: 100 000
Predetermined direct labour hour overhead recovery rate therefore: £5 per direct labour hour (£500 000/100 000).

So, if a product or job takes 10 direct labour hours to complete, the overhead charged to that job or product will be: 10 × £5 = £50. £50 of overheads will have been absorbed by that job or product. For illustration, assume that the prime costs amount to £100 (£40 material; £60 direct labour) and the company has a policy of fixing the selling price on the basis of cost plus 100%. The calculation of the sales price will be:

Prime costs	£100
Overhead absorbed	£ 50
Product cost	£150
Mark up	£150
Selling price	£300

Direct labour cost percentage rate

Here the formula is:

> Overhead costs of the producing department for an accounting period/Cost of direct labour for the department in the same accounting period

Example:
Predetermined overhead cost of Department 1: £500 000
Predetermined cost of direct labour in Department 1: £800 000
Direct labour cost percentage rate: £500 000/ £800 000 = 66.67% of the direct labour cost.
So, with the *labour cost* being £60 the overheads charged will be: £60 × 66.67% = £40.00.

In this case, the product cost and selling price will be:

Prime costs

Materials	£ 40
Labour	£ 60
Overheads	£ 40
Product cost	£140
Mark up	£140
Selling price	£280

Machine hour rate

The formula is:

> Overhead costs of the producing department for an accounting period/Number of machine hours worked in the same accounting period

Example:
Predetermined overhead cost of Department 1: £500 000
Predetermined number of machine hours to be worked in the Department : 87 260
Machine hour rate is therefore: £5.73 per machine hour

So if the machine hours needed to produce the same item were, say, 200, the charge to the item would be £114.60 (200 × £5.73). The product cost and selling price will be:

Prime costs	£100.00
Overheads absorbed	£114.60
Product cost	£214.60
Mark up	£214.60
Selling price	£429.20

The choice of method is one of management judgement. If production in a department is highly labour-intensive it would seem to make good sense to use either the direct labour hour method or the direct labour cost percentage method (if there is a reasonably close correlation in labour payment rates).

On the other hand, if production is highly automated and the number of direct labour staff thereby correspondingly few, the machine hour rate would seem to be more logical. Management need to decide which method is the most appropriate in light of the operations carried out.

The other recovery methods sometimes used are summarised as follows.

Unit produced rate

The formula for this method is:

> Overhead costs of the producing department for an accounting period *divided by* Number of units produced in the period

This method may be considered to be the most appropriate if production consists of products that are more or less identical and which take approximately the same time to produce.

Prime cost rate

> Overhead costs of the producing department for an accounting period/Prime cost incurred for the period (direct materials + direct labour)

The prime cost recovery rate is generally considered to be inequitable and inaccurate because it does not reflect fairly the overhead burden of each product; the overhead charged will be heavily weighted towards those products with a high prime cost, which may not be a fair reflection of the overhead burden the product should carry. (And, if the resultant product cost is used as the basis for the selling price calculation, it might make the product uncompetitive.)

Direct materials cost rate

> Overhead costs of the producing department for an accounting period/Direct materials costs incurred for the period

This method is also considered inequitable, for the same reasons as is the prime cost basis. A product with a direct material cost twice as much as another product, but with both taking the same amount of time to complete, will clearly be charged twice as much in overheads.

In addition to the methods detailed above, a further system should also be noted; some manufacturers with more than one producing department may decide to use a *single,* or *factory-wide* or *overall* recovery rate to be used by all the producing departments. Another name for this method is the *blanket recovery rate*. The formula is:

> Total factory overheads of all production departments for a period *divided by* [Total labour hours/machine hours (or other suitable divisor) for the whole factory for the same period]

Reverting back to the earlier examples, you will have noticed that each produced different product costs, and therefore different selling prices. It is very common for firms to base their selling prices on the product cost and therefore the choice of an appropriate overhead absorption method becomes of great importance. An inappropriate choice may mean sales opportunities are lost or unprofitable work taken on.

Predetermined absorption rates

The above examples could use the actual costs and actual activity for a particular period's production rather than predetermined figures. However, actual overhead costs are not always readily available for the calculations to be made at the time products are completed. For example, expenditure bills may be slow in arriving; utilities charges may be levied quarterly; and it takes time to analyse payroll overhead costs, to collect, allocate, apportion, accrue and prepay, and post everything to the ledgers. But the product cost will usually need to be known immediately the item is finished, for cost control purposes and perhaps for fixing the selling price or for the evaluation of closing stocks.

This is why it is of advantage to management to have a *predetermined* rate ready and available immediately production is completed. Thus, once the actual divisor is known (for example, actual labour hours, machine hours and so on), the overheads to be absorbed by the product can be calculated without delay. Another major benefit of using predetermined overhead recovery rates is that the ups and downs of factory overhead costs are 'smoothed out', resulting in a more equitable charge for each accounting period. For example, if each month's actual factory overheads were absorbed into the respective month's production and in April an annual, very expensive but thorough spring-clean were carried out, the overhead charged to the products made in that particular period would bear this cost. This would result in the product costs for April probably being much higher and therefore out of line with the rest of the year. (The management could, of course, provide for one-off costs by providing a proportion each month through the accruals system.)

Calculation of predetermined overhead recovery rates

As we have seen, the objective is to be able to calculate the overhead to be recovered as soon as the product has been completed, to arrive at the product cost.

To do this it is necessary to estimate the factory overheads for a future accounting period, and also to estimate the divisor – for example, direct labour hours – for the same accounting period. With a budgetary control system in operation (the subject of Chapter 19), budgeted factory overheads and budgeted direct labour hours will be used.

The predetermined overhead recovery formula is:

> Budgeted (or estimated) factory overheads for an accounting period/Budgeted (or estimated) direct labour hours* for the same period
>
> *or one of the other denominators described: machine hours, direct labour percentage cost methods, etc.

The accounting period will normally be the budget year ahead and cover the production expenses expected in that year, at the level of activity that management anticipate will be achieved. It follows that the direct labour hours or machine hours (or other chosen method as the denominator), will also be at the same budgeted activity level of production for the budgeted accounting period.

Once established, the predetermined overhead recovery rate will then be used for all actual jobs and products made. As an illustration, we shall use the direct labour hour rate method for the following example.

The prime costs of Product A are:
Materials £100; Direct labour £48 (6 hours at £8 per hour).

Budgeted overheads for the forthcoming period are expected to be £20 000 and direct labour hours 2000. The predetermined overhead recovery rate is therefore £10 per direct labour hour.

Overhead charged to Product A will be: 6 hours at £10 per hour.

The cost of Product A is therefore £208.

Overabsorbed overhead and underabsorbed overhead

When production overheads are absorbed into products using predetermined recovery rates, as in this example, there will almost inevitably be a difference at the end of an accounting period between the overheads absorbed and the actual overheads incurred.

This arises either as a result of the actual overheads for the accounting period being higher or lower than the budgeted overheads, or because the activity denominator, for example, direct labour hours, was higher or lower than expected. Or because of a combination of both these factors.

Example:

Budgeted production overhead	£500 000
Budgeted direct labour hours	100 000
Direct labour hour recovery rate	**£5.00**
Actual production overhead	£530 000
Actual direct labour hours	120 000
Overabsorption of production overhead	**£ 70 000**

Here you will see that 120 000 hours were actually worked. As the overhead recovery rate had been set at £5 per hour £600 000 of production overheads have been absorbed (120 000 × £5). But the actual overheads were £530 000. Therefore an *overabsorption* or *overrecovery of overhead* has occurred.

Example:

Budgeted production overhead	£800 000
Budgeted machine hours	400 000
Machine hour recovery rate	**£2.00**
Actual production overhead	£850 000
Actual machine hours	360 000
Underabsorption of production overhead	**£130 000**

FIGURE 6.1

FACTORS CAUSING OVERHEADS TO BE OVER- OR UNDERABSORBED

EXPENDITURE ———▶ Actual will be more or less than budgeted
HOURS WORKED* ———▶ Actual will be more or less than budgeted

* or other denominator

In this case, 360 000 machine hours were worked, so £720 000 was absorbed. But the actual costs were £850 000. Therefore an *underabsorption of overheads* has arisen.

Management will be interested to learn the reasons why overheads are either over- or underabsorbed. There are two factors at work that cause the differences (see Figure 6.1).

Taking the first example, you will see that the actual expenditure was £530 000, but the budgeted expenditure was £500 000. Clearly an overspend compared to budget, of £30 000. This difference, or *variance* as it is called, is an *expenditure variance*. In this case, £30 000 more was spent than was budgeted. When more cost has been incurred than expected the difference is termed an *adverse* variance. Conversely, when costs are less they are termed *favourable* variances. So the £30 000 overspend on expenditure is an adverse overheads expenditure variance.

You will see that the hours were also different: 20 000 more hours were worked than the budget expected. So more overhead was absorbed: 20 000 more hours at £5 per hour, or £100 000. This is a *favourable volume variance*.

Management now know why there has been a total overabsorption of overheads of £70 000: £30 000 was 'lost' due to higher *expenditure* than budgeted, but £100 000 was 'gained' by production *volume* being at a greater activity level than planned in the budget.

An investigation into the reasons for the increase in expenditure may indicate where this arose; it may be attributable in part to the extra productivity achieved, for very often the two are interlinked in a cause-and-effect way. For example, it may be due to special overtime premiums being paid to get the work done, so extra hours will be worked, but at a higher cost in overheads.

In the second example there was an underabsorption of overhead amounting to £130 000. Here there was an adverse expenditure variance of £50 000 (the difference between the budgeted spend of £800 000 and the actual spend of £850 000). There was also an adverse volume variance of £80 000 (40 000 fewer hours worked at £2 per hour). Clearly something for management to investigate to discover the causes. Overabsorbed overheads are a gain in the profit and loss account because more overhead has been absorbed into the products and therefore charged to cost of sales or carried forward in the closing stocks evaluation. Conversely, underabsorbed overheads is a loss. Both figures will affect the 'bottom line' of profit directly so they are of considerable importance to management.

The subject of overhead variances is fully dealt with in Chapter 18, Standard Costing and Variance Analysis.

Over- and underabsorbed overheads are recorded in separate accounts within the ledger. The bookkeeping entries are dealt with in Chapter 8.

SSAP 9 Requirements for stock evaluation

Mention has been made of product costs being used to value closing finished goods stocks. SSAP 9 – the statement of standard accounting practice covering stocks and long-term contracts – requires that the value of stocks, reported in the published accounts of limited companies, includes the cost of conversion of the raw materials into the finished goods condition.

Costs of conversion are defined as being:

(a) *Costs specifically attributable to units of production*. These are the direct labour and direct expenses costs.

(b) *Production overheads.* These are overheads in respect of (indirect) materials and labour, and services for the production process relating to the company's normal level of activity.

(c) *Other overheads.* These are other overheads (if any) attributable to bringing the product to the finished goods condition.

All 'normal' production overhead costs are included in the Product Cost. But some production overhead costs should be excluded because of their 'abnormality'. These are costs such as losses (or gains) because of exceptional wastage or spoilage of materials, or idle time losses. These overheads become period costs and are thus written off directly to the profit and loss account in the period in which they have been incurred.

SSAP 9 says that other overheads, apart from production overheads, may also be included in the value of stocks if management considers it prudent to do so, and that such costs can be allocated to the production function. Take, for example, the Accounts Department costs, which are essentially period costs and come under the function of general administration. This department will carry out support functions for the production process by paying direct and indirect production wages and salaries, and by producing production financial statements and statistics. If management consider that it is prudent to include a proportion of the Accounts Department costs that can be related to the production function then such costs may be included in the conversion cost.

With regard to the internal management accounts, SSAP requirements do not apply; management may decide on any method for valuing stocks and products that they choose, perhaps deciding to ignore completely the production overheads cost element altogether, instead valuing finished products based on the prime costs only. This particular method uses marginal costing techniques, the subject of Chapter 17. But for published financial accounts the normal production overheads always have to be included.

Worked example

ACCA COST AND MANAGEMENT ACCOUNTING (1990)

A company produces several products which pass through the two Production Departments in its factory. These two departments are concerned with filling and sealing operations. There are two service departments, Maintenance and Canteen, in the factory.

Predetermined overhead absorption rates, based on direct labour hours, are established for the two Production Departments. The budgeted expenditure for these departments for the period just ended, including an apportionment of service department overheads, was £110 040 for filling and £53 300 for sealing. Budgeted direct labour hours were 13 100 for filling and 10 250 for sealing.

Service department overheads are apportioned as follows:

Maintenance	Filling	70%
	Sealing	27%
	Canteen	3%
Canteen	Filling	60%
	Sealing	32%
	Maintenance	8%

During the period just ended, actual overhead costs and activity were as follows:

Filling	£74 260	12 820 direct labour hours
Sealing	£38 115	10 075 direct labour hours
Maintenance	£25 050	
Canteen	£24 375	

Required:
Calculate the overheads absorbed in the period and the extent of the under/over absorption in each of the two production departments.

Solution:

Overheads absorbed in the period	*Filling*	*Sealing*
Budgeted expenditure	£110 040	£53 300
Budgeted direct labour hours	13 100	10 250
Predetermined direct labour hour absorption rate	£8.40 per hour	£5.20 per hour

	Filling	*Sealing*
Actual hours worked	12 820	10 075
Overheads absorbed in the period	**£107 688**	**£52 390**

Under/over absorbed overheads extent

Apportionment of reciprocal services	Filling	Sealing	Mainentance	Canteen	Total
Actual costs	£74 260	£38 115	£25 050	£24 375	£161 800
Canteen apportionment	60.0%	32.0%	8.0%	–	
Maintenance apportionment	70.0%	27.0%	–	3.0%	
	£	£	£	£	
Canteen	14 625	7 800	1 950	(24 375)	
	88 885	45 915	27 000	0	
Maintenance	18 900	7 290	(27 000)	810	
	107 705	53 205	0	810	
Canteen	486	259	65	(810)	
	108 271	53 464	65	0	
Maintenance	45	17	(65)	2	
Roundings	2	0		(2)	
Total actual costs	108 318	53 482	(0)	(0)	£161 800
Overheads absorbed	**£107 688**	**£52 390**			
Underabsorbed overhead	**£ 630**	**£ 1 092**			

Note: If Maintenance Department had been distributed first, slightly different underabsorption figures would have resulted.

Summary

- Production overheads, having been allocated and apportioned to the producing departments, need to be absorbed into products to arrive at the total product cost for each individual finished article.
- The objective of absorption costing is to arrive at the total production cost of the finished product. This will comprise the three elements of cost: materials, labour and production overheads. The product cost is used for pricing finished goods stock and is often used in selling-price decisions.
- Absorption is usually achieved by choosing an overhead recovery rate most suited to the activity of the producing department. The most frequently used rates are : direct labour hour rate, machine hour rate, direct labour cost percentage rate, and factory wide blanket rates. But there are others, such as the unit produced rate and Activity Based Costing, the subject of Chapter 15.
- The overhead absorption rate is calculated by dividing the Production Department overheads for an accounting period by the selected activity denominator; in the case of the direct labour hour method, the activity denominator will be the direct labour hours for the same accounting period. Because details of actual overheads are not generally available until after an accounting period has ended it is common practice to calculate a predetermined absorption rate. Budgeted production overheads and budgeted activity levels are used to do this.
- With predetermined overhead absorption rates, it is inevitable that a difference will arise between the budgeted figures used to calculate the recovery rate and the actual figures; differences will arise in both numerator and denominator.
- If more overhead is absorbed, an overabsorption will arise; if less, an underabsorption will be the case. The differences may be analysed into their constituent parts: expenditure variances and volume variances. If more or less overheads expenditure has been incurred than budget, an expenditure variance results. If more or less activity has occurred, (i.e. more or fewer labour hours used, for example), a volume variance has arisen.
- SSAP 9 – stocks and long-term contracts – requires that production overheads are included in the evaluation of stocks for published financial accounts. Production costs can be 'normal' or 'abnormal'. Normal costs are absorbed into the products made and used to value the closing finished stocks;

abnormal production costs, idle time, etc., are written off as a period cost.

- If it is considered prudent, then other, non-production, costs may be included as a production overhead and absorbed into products.

- For internal accounts, management are free to choose any method to arrive at product costs, including ignoring production overheads altogether (the marginal costing basis).

Examination Questions

1 A LEVEL (ULEAC) 1990

Saxilby Mouldings absorbs overheads by means of the following budgeted departmental overhead'rates:

Machine shop	110% of direct wages incurred
Finishing shop	70% of direct wages incurred
Assembly bay	£0.125 per unit of output
Stores	120% of value of direct materials used

During the week ending 13 January, when 60 096 units were produced, the following costs were incurred:

	Materials charged £	Wages incurred £	Overheads charged £
Machine shop	2 036	5 200	5 615
Finishing shop	12 216	6 840	4 814
Assembly bay	6 108	1 950	7 627
Stores	–	–	23 180

(a) Calculate for each department, and in total (i) the amount of overhead absorbed into costs; and (ii) the amount of under- or overabsorbed overhead.

(b) Apportion the stores overheads to the production departments, stating clearly the basis you use.

2 A LEVEL (ULEAC) 1993

The Ashwell Fabrication Company is divided into four departments. The Pressing, Fabrication and Painting departments are production departments; Manufacturing Support department is a service department.

Total estimated costs for the six months ending 31 December are as follows:

	£		£
Supervision	15 000	Fire insurance	5 000
Rent	10 000	Plant depreciation	4 500
Power	9 000	Lighting	1 000
Plant Repairs	6 000		

The following information is also available for the four departments.

	Pressing	Fabrication	Painting	Manufacturing support
Area (sq. m.)	1500	1100	1900	500
Employees	20	15	10	5
Value of plant (£000s)	240	180	120	60
Value of stock (£000s)	150	90	60	–

Required:

(a) Apportion the costs to the four departments by the most suitable method, and state clearly the basis you have used.

(b) Apportion the total of Manufacturing Support's expenses to the production departments on the basis of the number of people employed by each.

(c) Calculate the overhead absorption rate (to two places of decimals) for each of the production departments on the basis that Pressing will work 13 511 machine hours, Painting 8 290 machine hours, and Fabrication 15 646 direct labour hours.

3 A LEVEL (ULEAC) 1994

For the six months ending 31 December, overheads for Magog Ltd's 5 departments have been calculated as follows:

Department	A	B	C	F	G
Overheads (£s)	24 000	20 000	14 000	7 000	5 000
Apportionment of overheads (%)					
Department F	25	40	30	–	5
Department G	40	35	15	10	–
Hours worked:					
Direct labour	3 150		2 400		
Machines		1 890			

What would the overhead recovery rates be if

(i) the elimination method; and

(ii) the continuous apportionment method are used for apportioning the service departments' overheads

4 A LEVEL (AEB) 1992

R. E. Lee Ltd is a company that manufactures building equipment. It has three production departments and a service department and has produced the following budgeted cost of production for the year ended 31 March:

		£	£
Production cost	Direct materials	240 000	
	Carriage inwards	10 000	
	Direct wages	200 000	450 000
Indirect wages	Dept X	8 000	
	Dept Y	12 000	
	Dept Z	18 300	
	General Service Dept	6 700	45 000
Other costs	Consumable stores	32 000	
	Rent	21 000	
	Light and heat	14 000	
	Power	36 000	
	Depreciation	80 000	
	Insurance – machinery	2 000	185 000
			680 000

The following is a set of data relating to the physical and performance aspects of the company:

Department	X	Y	Z	Service
Area m^2	15 000	22 500	20 000	12 500
Book value of plant	140 000	180 000	10 000	70 000
Stores requisitions	180	120	100	–
Effective horse power	80	100	5	15
Direct labour hours	100 000	80 000	220 000	–
Direct labour cost	50 000	60 000	90 000	–
Machine hours	70 000	90 000	10 000	–

Note: The general service department is apportioned to the production departments on the basis of direct labour cost.

Required:
(a) An overhead analysis sheet for the departments, showing clearly the basis of apportionment.
(b) A computation (correct to three decimal places) of hourly cost rates of overhead absorption for each production department using the performance data given.

5 A LEVEL (AEB) 1994

Togfell Ltd has decided to abandon its present costing system and change to one using absorption costing techniques. The company manufactures three products: Tog A, Tog B and Tog C. Each product has to pass through two production departments before it is completed. These departments are identified as the Cutting Department and the Machining and

Finishing Department. Both departments are labour intensive so it has been decided to use direct labour hour rate of overhead absorption. Only overheads primarily involved with production will be used. The budgeted overhead costs for the coming year are:

	£
Factory power	59 600
Sales commission	30 000
Light and heat (factory)	46 200
Depreciation of equipment	62 500
Repairs to factory equipment	17 500
Delivery charges to customers	21 700
Advertising	15 000
Supervisory staff costs (factory)	54 600
Canteen expenses (used by all staff)	39 360

The following is data upon which an appropriate basis of apportionment can be determined:

	Cutting Dept.	Machin-ing and Finishing Dept.	Administra-tion and Sales Dept.
Labour force (excluding supervisory)	20	50	20
Floor space (sq metres)	4 000	5 000	2 000
Book value of equipment (£000)	80	420	–
Equipment (kilo-watt hours (000))	25	75	–
Supervisory staff	1	5	–

Production time per product (hours)

Tog A	0.6	3.5
Tog B	0.5	2.9
Tog C	0.4	2.4

The total hours worked by the factory labour force per person is expected to be 1800.

Required:

(a) Calculate, to two decimal places, the selected overhead absorption rate for each department (Cutting; and Machining and Finishing) stating the apportionment basis used.
(b) Calculate, to two decimal places, the total unit overhead cost per product.

6 AAT COST ACCOUNTING AND BUDGETING 1993

An organisation has budgeted for the following production overheads for its production and service cost centres for the coming year:

Cost centre	£
Machining	180 000
Assembly	160 000
Paint shop	130 000
Engineering shop	84 000
Stores	52 000
Canteen	75 000

The product passes through the machining, assembly and paint shop cost centres and the following data relates to the cost centres:

	Machining	Assembly	Paint shop	Engineering	Stores
No. of employees	81	51	39	30	24
Engineering shop – service hours	18 000	12 000	10 000		
Stores (orders)	180	135	90	45	

The following budgeted data relates to the production cost centres:

	Machining	Assembly	Paint shop
Machine hours	9 200	8 100	6 600
Labour hours	8 300	11 250	9 000
Labour cost	£40 000	£88 000	£45 000

Required:

(a) Apportion the production overhead costs of the service cost centres to the production cost centres and determine predetermined overhead absorption rates for the three production cost centres, on the following bases:

Machining – machine hours
Assembly – labour hours
Paint shop – labour costs

(b) Actual results for the production cost centres were:

	Machining	Assembly	Paint shop
Machine hours	10 000	8 200	6 600
Labour hours	4 500	7 800	6 900
Labour cost	£25 000	£42 000	£35 000
Actual overhead	£290 000	£167 000	£155 000

Prepare a statement showing the under/overabsorption per cost centre for the period under review.

7 ACCA COST AND MANAGEMENT ACCOUNTING 1 1992
One of the factories in the XYZ Group of companies absorbs fixed production overheads into product cost using a predetermined machine hour rate.

In Year 1, machine hours budgeted were 132 500 and the absorption rate for fixed production overheads was £18.20 per machine hour. Overheads absorbed and incurred were £2 442 440 and £2 317 461 respectively.

In Year 2, machine hours were budgeted to be 5% higher than those actually worked in Year 1. Budgeted and actual fixed production overhead expenditure were £2 620 926 and £2 695 721 respectively, and actual machine hours were 139 260.

Required:
Analyse, in as much detail as possible, the under/over-absorption of fixed production overhead occurring in Years 1 and 2, and the change in absorption rate between the two years.

NON-COMPUTATIONAL, DESCRIPTIVE TYPE QUESTIONS
(**NB** Minutes in brackets are a guide to indicate the approximate time your essay should take to complete.)

QUESTIONS
A State, and critically assess, the objectives of overhead apportionment and absorption.
(ACCA 1990) (20 minutes)
B Write a report to the Managing Director briefly describing three methods of overhead absorption and in each case stating why each may or may not be adopted.
(10 minutes)
C Distinguish between overhead allocation, overhead apportionment, and overhead absorption. Give examples to illustrate your answer.
(ULEAC 1993) (12 minutes)

7

Distribution, Selling and Administrative Overheads

In Chapters 5 and 6 we dealt with production overheads which, because they are incurred in the manufacturing process, constitute the product cost (materials, labour and production overheads).

Other overheads are incurred in the non-production areas of the business. These overheads are described as *period costs*, meaning that they are written off to the profit and loss account in the period to which the costs relate. The diagram of the factory shown in Figure 7.1 indicates where the period costs are incurred. We shall examine these various departments and see how and why the period costs are incurred, starting with the distribution function.

Distribution function

Distribution costs comprise: the costs of the warehouse or storage areas which hold the finished goods; the despatch area costs and the costs of the vehicles or other delivery methods used in distributing the finished product to the customers, or for further storage to outside depots/warehouses.

Finished goods storage area costs

Following the completion of the manufacturing process in the production area, the resultant finished goods, ready for sale, will be physically transferred to the finished goods storage area (sometimes called the finished goods warehouse). The transfer of the goods will be recorded on a 'goods manufactured' document and an accounting entry will be made in the ledger accounts: debit finished goods account, credit work-in-progress account.

In the warehouse itself, some logical method of storage of the finished products will be organised, with products kept in distinct bays or sections to assist in the picking of customers' orders. The costs involved in this operation will comprise:

Warehouse premises costs;
Warehouse staff costs; and
Warehouse operating costs.

Finished goods warehouse premises costs
The space utilised by the finished goods warehouse function will attract premises costs related to the area occupied, the premises costs being a proportion of rates, rent (if payable), heating and lighting, and other building costs as described in Chapter 5.

Warehouse staff costs
The organisation chart of the typical finished goods store and packing and despatch area might appear as shown in Figure 7.2. The staff costs will be the gross

FIGURE 7.1

SOURCES OF PERIOD COSTS	
DISTRIBUTION FUNCTION	FINISHED GOODS STORE AREA PACKING AND DESPATCH AREA SHIPMENTS TO CUSTOMERS
SELLING AND MARKETING FUNCTIONS	SALES DEPARTMENT FIELD SALES FORCE SELLING AGENTS, REPRESENTATIVES ADVERTISING AND PROMOTION MARKET RESEARCH SALES PLANNING
ADMINISTRATION FUNCTIONS	MANAGING DIRECTOR ACCOUNTS DEPARTMENT PERSONNEL DEPARTMENT RECEPTION AND POST ROOM GENERAL ADMINISTRATION
FINANCING COSTS OTHER INCOME AND EXPENSES	INTEREST PAYABLE INTEREST RECEIVABLE CASH SETTLEMENT DISCOUNTS ALLOWED CASH SETTLEMENT DISCOUNTS RECEIVED

FIGURE 7.2

FINISHED GOODS AREA STAFF ORGANISATION

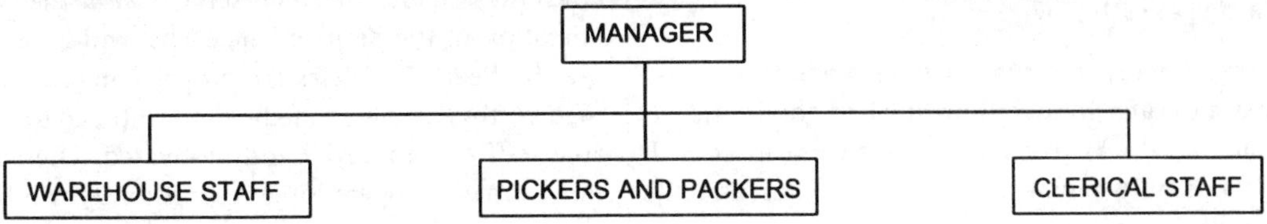

```
                    MANAGER
                       |
        ┌──────────────┼──────────────┐
  WAREHOUSE STAFF   PICKERS AND      CLERICAL STAFF
                     PACKERS
```

pay of the staff, plus any bonus schemes payments, overtime premiums, payroll and pension on-costs and any other employee welfare expenses incurred.

The Warehouse Manager's job will be to ensure that the Department is run efficiently and competently, and that the products are stored safely and securely. The warehouse staff will include fork-lift truck drivers and staff engaged in storage work and moving products within the warehouse.

Order pickers, as the job title indicates, are given customers' orders (in the form of order-picking documents). They move around the warehouse picking (collecting) the order, placing the picked items into despatch boxes or cartons, securing these and putting the completed orders in the despatch area ready for shipment. The completed picking document will be passed to the clerical staff for further action.

Warehouse clerks will be involved in all the documentation of the department, the control of the picking documents, updating stock records, payroll data collection and other clerical duties.

Warehouse operating costs

All costs and expenses incurred directly by the warehouse will be included as warehouse operating costs: the costs of operating the fork-lift trucks which are used exclusively in the finished goods warehouse; rental costs of any outside storage area; the cost of any materials that might be consumed; depreciation of warehouse fixtures and fittings and so on.

Combined raw materials and finished goods warehouse

It is common to find that, for various operational reasons, the raw materials storage area (a manufacturing function) will be combined with the finished goods warehouse; for example, space limitations may force a combination, or perhaps management may find by merging the two warehousing functions that staff utilisation and the use of equipment is improved.

When this is done it will be necessary to apportion the costs of the combined operation between the two, thus ensuring that the raw materials storage costs are absorbed into the product cost and the finished goods warehouse function costs are written off as period costs.

Outside storage costs

Firms occasionally find that they need additional storage space to cater for overflow finished goods and/or raw materials stocks. The costs of this extra space will include not only rental charges (plus other directly

incurred costs related to the extra space) but also the transport costs involved in collection and retrieval of the stock.

The reasons why additional space is needed should always be monitored and controlled, as it may indicate poor stock control procedures with maximum stock levels being exceeded. Or it may indicate a longer-term need for bigger premises. However, with seasonal businesses, in which the product sales are related to a particular period, Christmas, say, the use of outside storage may be unavoidable in the lead-up period as stocks rise in anticipation of satisfying the seasonal demand. As with combined warehouse arrangements, it will be necessary to apportion the storage costs between raw materials and finished goods for product and period cost purposes.

Delivery costs

The costs of delivery of finished goods to customers consist of the following:

Distribution staff costs;
Vehicle running costs; and
Freight charges by third parties.

Distribution staff costs

A typical organisation chart for the distribution function of a larger firm with its own vehicles might appear as shown in Figure 7.3.

The Distribution Manager will be responsible for an efficient, reliable delivery service and the smooth operation of the despatch area. This will entail ensuring the fleet of vehicles are properly maintained and roadworthy, delivery schedules are adhered to and capable staff are employed and motivated. The Distribution Manager's operational responsibility will be from

FIGURE 7.3

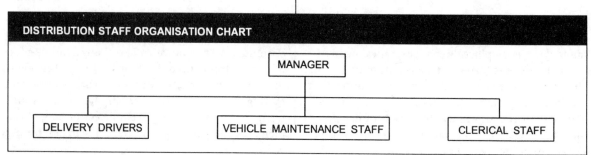

the point where the picked goods are transferred to the despatch area through to the delivery of the goods to the customer. (The Transport Manager may be required to hold a Vehicle Operator's Licence, which permits the individual to run a 'large goods vehicle' (but commonly known as an HGV (heavy goods vehicle)), or a fleet of such vehicles. There are some rigorous legal conditions involved in running HGVs in the interests of road safety. For example, each HGV, is required to keep a 'tachograph' recording each day's work. This is a paper disk, affixed into a machine within the lorry, which keeps a record of every break and rest period the driver takes, as well as logging the actual driving periods. (Drivers of large goods vehicles also need special driving licences.) Drivers will have a daily schedule of deliveries to make.

Vehicle maintenance staff will be responsible for service and repair work of the vehicles including Ministry of Transport (MoT) test preparation work and so on. The clerical staff in the Distribution Department will be involved in planning delivery routes, maintaining journey records and dealing with the paperwork associated with deliveries, returns from customers and the operation of the fleet of vehicles.

Vehicle running costs

The running costs of the vehicles will include: fuel and oil used, vehicle insurance, road fund taxes, parts, spares and repair costs, and tyres. In addition, when drivers are required to make long journeys and therefore are unable to return to the depot at the end of the day, 'overnight' stoppage costs will be incurred. These may consist of lorry parking fees, hotel or bed and breakfast lodgings for the driver, extra subsistence payments and so on.

Some of the running costs of vehicles are fixed, for example, insurance and road fund taxes, while other costs are variable, changing in line with journeys made. The splitting of transport costs between fixed and variable elements assists in the control and decision-making functions of management. This *behavioural* nature of costs is the subject of Chapter 17, Marginal Costing. Service costing techniques are also used to control and plan distribution operations. Service Costing is the subject of Chapter 14.

Freight charges by third parties

Running a fleet of vehicles is an expensive operation in its own right and many firms, large and small,

decide that it is more economic for an outside carrier to do the delivery work for them. The company therefore transfers the responsibility for delivering products to the customer to a third party, the carrier. Many carriers are substantial commercial undertakings in their own right, with expert management and staff and huge fleets of vehicles, but others may be sole traders or small limited companies, or partnerships with perhaps one or two vehicles.

Each day, or at agreed intervals, the carrier will collect the finished goods from the warehouse despatch area and deliver them to the firm's customers in accordance with delivery documents completed by the company. The customer will be asked by the carrier to sign for the delivery and the goods, and relevant documentation will be handed over to the customer. Problems arise occasionally when the delivery is disputed, in which case the company needs to go to the carrier to obtain a 'proof of delivery' signature from the customer. This can be a time-consuming affair and therefore costs are involved in its administration. Very often suppliers of goods will indicate on the documentation given to the customer – delivery note, invoice – that claims for non-delivery or short delivery are to be notified within a matter of days from the delivery date. Failure to do so may mean rejection of any claim by the customer.

Own delivery vehicles versus third party carriers

A comparison between the two methods of distribution can be made by the use of *service costing* techniques. A *cost unit* will be established, perhaps a 'tonne-mile'. This is the product of the tonnes, or weight carried, multiplied by the miles covered in an accounting period. The cost per tonne-mile of running a fleet of vehicles to deliver goods to the customers will be calculated and then compared with the carrier's costs for the same service. The option with the lower unit cost should be selected as the most cost efficient method.

Warehouse and distribution cost reports

Management need to plan and control the costs of both these operations, and regular periodic financial and costing information on the performance of the distribution function will be made. This information will be supplied by the Accounts Department in the

FIGURE 7.4

WAREHOUSE AND DISTRIBUTION COST REPORT

MONTH OF

WAREHOUSE	ACTUAL	BUDGET	VARIANCE	THIS MONTH LAST YEAR	ACTUAL AS % OF DELIVERIES*	BUDGET AS % OF DELIVERIES* (*OR SALES)
	£	£	£	£		
WAGES AND SALARIES:						
MANAGEMENT						
WAREHOUSEMEN						
FORK-LIFT DRIVERS						
ORDER PICKERS						
CLERICAL STAFF						
PREMISES COSTS						
FORK-LIFT TRUCK COSTS						
OUTSIDE STORAGE COSTS						
CONSUMABLES						
DEPRECIATION OF EQUIPMENT						
TELEPHONE COSTS						
STATIONERY						
SUNDRY WAREHOUSE COSTS						

DISTRIBUTION COSTS	ACTUAL	BUDGET	VARIANCE	THIS MONTH LAST YEAR	ACTUAL AS % OF DELIVERIES*	BUDGET AS % OF DELIVERIES* (*OR SALES)
	£	£	£	£		
WAGES AND SALARIES:						
MANAGEMENT						
DRIVERS						
MAINTENANCE						
CLERICAL						
PREMISES COSTS						
VEHICLE RUNNING COSTS						
CARRIER CHARGES						
DEPRECIATION OF EQUIPMENT						
TELEPHONE COSTS						
STATIONERY						
SUNDRY DISTRIBUTION COSTS						

form of reports and statistical data, and may consist of the following:

Warehouse costs incurred: staff costs, occupancy costs, operational costs.

Distribution costs incurred: staff costs, occupancy costs, vehicle running costs, shipment costs.

Usually the data will be reported in tabular form and compared with the plan (budget). The relationship of these costs to sales, or some other benchmark, may also be reported so that management is able, through management by exception techniques, to identify those costs that are out of line with expectations. An example of such a report is shown in Figure 7.4.

Statistical information may also be provided, with plan or budget comparisons, for tonnage delivered, number of orders picked, journeys made, tonne-mile unit cost and so on. Occasionally, graphical presentation of the information will highlight movements in the trends of the costs and statistics which may not always be clear from the table. Further consideration of presentation of information to management is provided in the chapters in Part IV.

Sales overheads

Sales overheads usually also embrace marketing costs although the two are quite distinct and separate. The Chartered Institute of Marketing (CIM) define marketing as '*the management process responsible for identifying, anticipating and satisfying customer requirements profitably*'.

Selling is a part of marketing and is concerned with persuading customers to acquire the product or service which '*best matches an organisation's resources (human, financial and physical) with its customers' wants*'.

Marketing costs will usually comprise salaries of the marketing staff, bonuses, payroll on-costs, plus other staff costs, car expenses, travel and so on, also materials used and research costs incurred in the process of identifying, anticipating and satisfying customers' requirements.

Selling costs will comprise the field sales staff costs, the sales office costs, agency commission, and the sales promotional costs of advertising, promotional activities, point of sale material and other similar costs.

A leading US industrialist (Bennett S. Chapple Jr) has said that marketing planning is '*The starting point for* all *corporate planning... it is the basis for the extent and direction of all other corporate decisions*'. This is often reflected in the budgeting process, the subject of Chapter 19, where the sales budget is the first budget to be completed in short-term planning.

We shall tour the Departments of Marketing and Sales to see what can be discovered of their operations and how the analysis of costs might assist the management of these functions.

Marketing Department

The head of the department, the Marketing Manager, will be responsible for ensuring that the company is fully aware of market trends affecting and influencing the sales and future sales of the existing products or services. He or she will also be responsible, through market research, for investigating potential markets for the firm's products or services. In addition, the design and market testing of new products (and also improved designs for existing products) will be undertaken by the Department.

Hand-in-hand with these activities will go the creation of marketing strategies and planning, with the objective of satisfying the identified customer requirements *profitably*. This work may involve product launches, public relations exercises, major advertising campaigns and so on.

With the key word *profitability* in the definition it follows that reliable and accurate product or service costs, together with the identification of relevant costs, will be of great importance in the work of the Marketing Department. There have been many instances of business ideas and products that have failed because relevant costs have been ignored, or had not been fully considered and provided for, with the end result that the products or services did not contribute to profits or, worse, plunged the company into losses. The resources of the Accounts Department in supplying financial data and costing statistics will therefore play a key role in assisting the marketing function to fulfil its role.

Sales Department

The structure of a typical Sales Department responsible for selling the products or services may appear as shown in Figure 7.5.

FIGURE 7.5

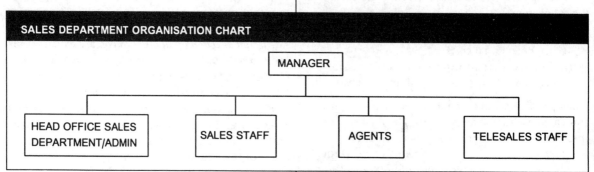

SALES DEPARTMENT ORGANISATION CHART

MANAGER

HEAD OFFICE SALES DEPARTMENT/ADMIN | SALES STAFF | AGENTS | TELESALES STAFF

The selling function's task is to sell the products or services. There are three clear aspects to this: informing the customer of the existence of the product (also a marketing activity); taking or collecting the customer's order; and handling the paperwork generated from the latter activity.

Informing the customer

The most obvious example of this activity is advertising. Companies budget large sums to advertise their products or services and, to quote, 'it pays to advertise'.

But advertising is very expensive and needs to be planned with care to ensure that the message of the advertisement reaches the right audience. The success of advertising, if done with flair and imagination, is unquestionable, as can be witnessed every day. TV advertising slogans leap instantly to mind; interna-

tional advertising agencies, employing thousands, with billings running into millions of pounds and dollars, dream up the catch phrases that spell profitability to the advertisers: 'You've been tango'd'; 'It's the real thing'; 'A Mars a day...'; 'Guinness is good for you' and so on.

Informing customers can be done through the distribution of leaflets and mailshots. It can be done through radio and by telephone. Other forms of advertising are by 'point-of-sale' material, window stickers and billboards.

A British industrialist once said: 'Half the money I spend on advertising is wasted...the trouble is, I don't know which half.' However, by monitoring the response to an advertisement, the 'redemption rate' of sales of a mail order product, say, it is possible to measure the effectiveness or otherwise of advertising and allied promotional activities.

FIGURE 7.6

MAILSHOT REDEMPTION RATE CALCULATION

NUMBER OF LEAFLETS TO BE DISTRIBUTED	1 000 000
TOTAL COSTS OF MAILSHOT	£30 000

PROFIT CONTRIBUTION OF PRODUCT:

SELLING PRICE	£2.50
PRODUCT COST	£1.00
PROFIT CONTRIBUTION	£1.50

NUMBER OF SALES UNITS TO PAY FOR MAILSHOT COSTS (£30 000/£1.50)	20 000 UNITS
REDEMPTION RATE (20,000/ 1,000,000)	**2.00%**

As an example, imagine a company wishes to sell its product through mail order and intends to issue a million leaflets to potential customers. The costs of the exercise – designing the leaflets; printing and distribution; the charge for the mailing lists of potential customers' addresses; return postage expenses; freephone charges and so on, will be calculated in advance.

The purpose of any business exercise is to make a profit, so the contribution the product makes – selling price less the product cost – will need to be included in the calculations, because it must be sufficient to pay for all these costs and still result in an overall profit. Therefore the calculation of a realistic, achievable redemption rate is of great importance in deciding whether the venture is likely to succeed or not. See Figure 7.6 for an example of a mailshot redemption rate calculation.

A redemption rate of 2 per cent to *break even* on the exercise may appear to be not too difficult to achieve, with 1 in 50 of potential customers taking the product, so management may decide to go ahead with the venture. But redemption rates for this particular market and type of product may well be below 1 per cent – perhaps only a half of 1 per cent (think of the vast amount of 'junk mail' that comes through one's letter box and which almost always is immediately thrown away).

In this example, if the redemption was a half of 1 per cent, only 5000 products would be sold, resulting in a loss on the one-off venture of £22 500 excluding management time and other associated costs not already taken into the costings. On the other hand, if the response was 4 per cent, 40 000 would be sold, resulting in a profit of £30 000, and thus making the exercise worthwhile. See Table 7.1, which shows the profit or loss position from various redemption rates.

This example of break-even, *cost–volume–profit*, (CVP) analysis assists management in clarifying the likely results of potential decisions. Here, they may try to reduce the costs of the mailshot, or endeavour to increase the profit contribution of the product by perhaps increasing the selling price, to come near to the norm of a 1 per cent redemption rate before embarking on the venture. The techniques of break-even and CVP analysis in decision-making are the subject of Chapter 17.

Taking/collecting customers' orders

This is the function of the sales team. *Taking* orders from customers implies that the customer takes the initiative and places the order with the firm. This is what happens in retail operations, with customers going directly to shops or supermarkets and purchasing the required products. It also happens in catalogue mail order selling. Product knowledge by the person taking the order assists the customer to choose the right product for them.

Collecting customers' orders means selling through making contact with customers – by visiting through appointment or by 'cold calling' in person or by telephone.

Although considered to be a difficult method of selling, many firms use cold call techniques, most notably telesales, where the salesperson works from a script. The success of this method of selling is measured by the quantity of calls a person can make in a given period of time and the conversion rate of those calls into customer orders. It is therefore similar to redemption rate calculations.

The more calls the greater the probability of getting orders. If 100 calls are made, the company might expect, say, five orders to result. This form of selling

TABLE 7.1

PROFIT OR LOSS FROM VARIOUS REDEMPTION RATES					
REDEMPTION RATE (%)	0.5	1.0	2.0	3.0	4.0
SALES (IN UNITS)	5 000	10 000	20 000	30 000	40 000
PROFIT CONTRIBUTION	£7 500	£15 000	£30 000	£45 000	£60 000
MAILSHOT COSTS	£30 000	£30 000	£30 000	£30 000	£30 000
PROFIT OR (LOSS)	**(£22 500)**	**(£15 000)**	**£ 0**	**£15 000**	**£30 000**

may be more cost effective than a salesperson physically calling on customers, and an examination of the relevant costs and returns of both will enable management to decide which is best, or which combination of the two is most effective.

Sales costs reporting

The activity of selling the product or service is thus a key cost to the business and will be controlled through preparation of periodic cost statements, such as that shown in Figure 7.7.

In addition, other financial information can be prepared, because each salesperson might also be identified as a *profit centre*. For example, a company with a field sales force will be able to prepare an operating statement for each member of the sales team. This will show the contribution made by each salesperson to overall profits, as shown in Table 7.2.

Management thus have a tool with which to measure performance and can investigate the reasons why one representative should be top and another bottom.

FIGURE 7.7

MARKETING AND SELLING COST REPORT						
MONTH OF						
				THIS MONTH		
	ACTUAL	*BUDGET*	*VARIANCE*	*LAST YEAR*	*ACTUAL*	*BUDGET*
	£	£	£	£	*AS % OF SALES*	*AS % OF SALES*
MARKETING COSTS						
MANAGEMENT SALARIES						
STAFF SALARIES						
STAFF EXPENSES						
VEHICLE EXPENSES						
RESEARCH COSTS						
TELEPHONE						
STATIONERY						
SUNDRY MARKETING COSTS						
DEPRECIATION						
SELLING COSTS						
MANAGEMENT SALARIES						
SALES OFFICE SALARIES						
SALES STAFF SALARIES						
STAFF EXPENSES						
VEHICLE EXPENSES						
TELEPHONE						
STATIONERY						
SUNDRY SALES EXPENSE						
DEPRECIATION						
MAILSHOTS						
ADVERTISING						
PREMISES COSTS						

TABLE 7.2

SALES REPRESENTATIVES' CONTRIBUTION REPORT

MONTH OF

NAME	SALES	GROSS PROFIT ON SALES £	REPRESENTATIVE COSTS £	CONTRIBUTION £	CONTRIBUTION AS % OF SALES	CONTRIBUTION RANKING
AA	12 355	3 707	2 112	1 595	12.9	6
BB	25 001	5 000	3 022	1 978	7.9	8
CC	15 500	4 650	2 277	2 373	15.3	5
DD	18 765	5 630	2 451	3 179	16.9	4
EE	24 332	6 083	2 973	3 110	12.8	7
FF	16 900	5 577	2 344	3 233	19.1	3
GG	12 021	4 808	1 899	2 909	24.2	2
HH	13 689	5 476	2 034	3 442	25.1	1
	£138 563	£40 930	£19 112	£21 818	15.7	

Sales office

Selling activities generate paperwork. The sales office, often referred to as the 'back office', deals with the resultant documentation and will also co-ordinate the selling activities of the field force – the outside sales staff.

As orders are received, internal documentation will be prepared, instructing the factory or finished goods stores to manufacture or issue the product. The sales office will also liaise with representatives, passing on instructions and messages received from customers. They will also deal with the general sales administration functions. Computers enable many of these tasks to be done automatically – the orders received will be recorded and immediately 'deducted' as 'allocated stock' from the stockholding.

The cost of running the sales office will be reported in similar format to the cost report shown in Figure 7.7. A unit of performance measurement can be set for the sales office based on the formula:

$$\frac{\text{Sales office costs}}{\text{Number of orders processed}}$$

The resultant cost per order can be compared with previous accounting periods or against a predetermined estimate or budgeted statistic.

Administration

Administration covers the following departments:

    Managing Director's Department
    Accounts Department
    Personnel Department
    Reception and Post Department
    Research and Development (R&D) Department

An organisation chart for the Accounts Department is shown in Chapter 1, page 5.

Managing Director

The Managing Director (MD), as Chief Executive of the company, has overall responsibility for the day-to-day running of the enterprise. As such, he or she will have authority to delegate responsibilities to the management team and generally 'call the shots' in regard to the methods, products and operations used by the business. Other Executive Directors – the

Finance Director, Sales and Production Directors and so on – will report to him or her. In turn, the Managing Director will report to the Chairman or Board of Directors as a whole, and they in turn will report annually to the shareholders.

The success or failure of an enterprise is very often a reflection of the skills and abilities of the Managing Director and the team around him or her. As the MD has overall responsibility for every aspect of the business, he or she will review all the sales and costing data. Often, because of the time pressures and work load, an MD will require the detailed financial and management accounting information to be summarised to major key statistics and money values which highlight variations from plan or budget.

This enables him or her to identify those functions of the business which may need closer attention to bring them into line with predetermined expectations. This 'management by exception' technique works on the basis that if actual sales and costs are in line with expectations, then management need not spend valuable time in monitoring those costs which are in line. This releases time to spend on those areas of the business that are not in line with the expectations of the plan – the *exceptions* – or are different from the plan.

Staff working in the MD's Department might be a personal secretary, and an assistant or other staff attached to his or her office. The costs incurred will be reported periodically in the Management Accounts, examples of which can be found in Chapter 22.

Accounts Department

The head of the department has various titles – Finance Director, Financial Controller, Company Accountant, Financial Director, Chief Accountant and so on.

The person will normally be a qualified member of one of the recognised accountancy bodies, namely a Chartered Accountant (CA, ACA or FCA), a Certified Accountant (ACCA or FCCA) or a Cost and Management Accountant (ACMA or FCMA); in public finance posts the recognised accountancy body is the Chartered Institute of Public Finance and Accountancy (CIPFA).

He or she will be responsible for all of the accounting functions and will usually work closely with the MD on financial matters. As everything a commercial company does is measured ultimately in money terms through the profit and loss account and balance sheet it necessarily follows that effective and efficient financial control is central to success.

Financial accounts section

Working through the Department, we will first look at the financial accounting section, headed by the *Financial Accountant*. He or she will be responsible for recording the financial transactions arising from trading. These records comprise the Sales Ledger, Purchases Ledger, Cashiers function and Payroll, and the General or Nominal Ledger. In computerised accounting packages, such as Sage and Pegasus, the Sales, Purchases and Payroll records are generally linked, or interfaced, with the Nominal Ledger to provide a self-balancing system by way of control accounts.

Sales ledger section

This section is responsible for all the paperwork relating to credit sales: the raising of invoices to be sent to customers, recording the sales in the sales day book or register, receiving payments from customers, entering the transactions into the Sales Ledger – invoices and cash received, reconciling the customers' ledger accounts, and so on. Much of this routine work is now done by computer, thus reducing the clerical effort required in raising invoices, entering the details in the sales day book and so on.

Sales ledger staff will also usually be involved in credit control and debt collection. Sales invoices generally show 'payment terms' which inform the customer when payment for the goods or services is due. The most commonly found payment term is 'nett monthly account'. This informs the credit customer that the amount due is payable by the end of the month following delivery. So, goods delivered on, say, 10 January, should be paid for by the end of February. Other firms offer a cash discount, or settlement discount, to induce the customer to pay by a specified date. The customer will deduct the settlement discount if paying by the due date, thereby making a saving on the purchase. If they do not pay by the due date, then the full amount becomes payable.

To help ensure that the stipulated payment terms are adhered to, many firms send *statements of account* to customers on a regular basis, usually monthly. The statements show the details of the transactions on the account still outstanding at a specific moment, usually the last day of the calendar month. Computer systems are able to age the debts so that a summary of the amounts outstanding is shown on the statement, in age order: for example, current month, one month, two months, three months and older. The older the debt, the greater the chance that it will become a bad debt.

Management needs therefore to control the payment time taken by trade debtors, to safeguard against bad debts and slow payers. To help them do this, a periodic "aged debtors analysis" is prepared, similar to that shown in Table 7.3.

As debts age, more costs are incurred: the cost of interest, the lost opportunity of using the cash for other purposes, the cost of sending statements and making chasing telephone calls, the cost of court proceedings and so on. These costs can be substantial and many firms, in order to avoid such costs if they can, will carry out credit vetting procedures, investigations into whether the risk of giving a customer credit terms will be worthwhile. This is usually done by asking customers for trading references including references from the customers' bankers.

The costs of operating the sales ledger therefore comprise: staff salaries; premises costs; printing and stationery; telephone and postage; and depreciation of equipment used. Costs associated with the function will be settlement discount allowed; bad debts written off; court costs; debt collection agency costs; charges levied by banks for cheques presented which are dishonoured, etc. Interest payable costs might also be included, and this can be identified with those customers who do not pay their accounts by the due date. Because some customers take longer to pay than the credit terms stipulate, it follows that interest charges and the administration costs incurred in maintaining these accounts will be higher. By analysing the extra costs by customer, management will be able to decide whether to continue to offer credit terms to these slow payers, or perhaps to levy an extra charge to cover the additional costs suffered.

Purchases ledger section

This section deals with suppliers' invoices, matching them with internal documentation such as goods received notes and purchase orders. They enter the details of the purchase into the Purchases Ledger (also called the Bought Ledger), reconcile suppliers' statements of account, and arrange payment of the amounts due.

Authorisation from management that each invoice can be entered will normally be obtained before the suppliers' invoices are recorded in the accounting

TABLE 7.3

AGED DEBTORS' ANALYSIS							
AGED DEBTORS' ANALYSIS: MONTH OF MAY							
CUSTOMER	TOTAL DUE	CURRENT	30 DAYS	60 DAYS	90 DAYS	OLDER	COMMENTS
	£	£	£	£	£	£	
A1	180.00	50.00	100.00			30.00	
A2	150.00	100.00	50.00				
B1	100.00		100.00				
B2	600.00			600.00			
B3	250.00	250.00					
C1	300.00	300.00					
C4	400.00		400.00				
C6	100.00				100.00		
ETC							
TOTAL	2 080.00	700.00	650.00	600.00	100.00	30.00	

records. Any discrepancies between goods or services charged for and received may be taken up with the supplier directly or passed to the Buying Department. Very often an Invoice Register is maintained, its purpose being to record the date each suppliers' invoice was received, its whereabouts within the system, and to whom it has been passed for authorisation, or query. The authorised invoices are then coded, using a Chart of Accounts as depicted in Chapter 2, and entered in the Purchases Ledger and the Nominal Ledger. This is done simultaneously if a computer system with an interface facility is used, but if a manual system is in operation, the entries will be made first into a purchases day book and then posted to the ledgers.

Corrections to suppliers' invoices, perhaps because of goods not being received, or incorrect charges being levied, are normally covered by *credit notes* issued by the supplier. However, waiting for credit notes may cause undue delays in keeping the accounting records up to date, as many firms do not enter the original invoice until the credit note is received. The reason for this is because credit notes may take weeks to be received and if the invoice had been entered there is a possibility it might have been paid inadvertently. These problems are overcome, however, by the firm issuing *debit notes*. The supplier will be sent the debit note, which will show the reasons for its issue, together with the amount being debited to the supplier's account.

The payment of suppliers' accounts will be done periodically, according to the suppliers' payment terms. Often, the cheque-writing function is separated from the Purchases Ledger to ensure internal security. Many have a *weekly payment run* to take advantage of cash settlement discounts offered by suppliers and also to pay those bills that are due to be paid immediately. The *monthly payment run* deals with all the other normal term accounts. Computer systems usually provide an aged creditors listing facility. This will identify which invoices are due for payment each period, thereby assisting in the payments process.

Reconciling suppliers' accounts may form a large part of the section's workload. Timing differences between the supplier receiving the cheque and crediting it in their books, and also supplier's invoices not yet entered in the firm's books, ensures a lot of work for the section.

The costs of the section might be reported separately from other sections of the department. A 'unit of service', such as the number of invoices processed, might be used to monitor both costs and efficiency over a period of time.

Large companies often split the Purchases Ledger – for example into A–K suppliers and L–Z suppliers, for ease of administration.

Cashier's section

The Cashier will be responsible for the daily banking of receipts and raising cheque payments. He or she will also organise standing orders, direct debits and credit transfers. Bank receipts and payments are entered in a Cash Book, which may be a manual record or a computer nominal ledger bank account.

The Cashier may also be responsible for maintaining the petty cash float for paying small cash expenses such as window cleaning. The petty cash in hand is often controlled by the use of the *imprest system*. This system works on the basis that a given petty cash float is established, say £100. As cash expenses are paid out, the float reduces. At given intervals, perhaps each week, the petty cash expenditure spent for the week will be reimbursed to the float, bringing it back to £100. This system ensures that, at any given time, the cash held plus the vouchers covering the expenditures should always add up to £100.

Another important task of the Cashier is to reconcile the bank account with the bank statements. A reconciliation should be completed in every accounting period, thus usually monthly, but with large organisations it may be completed on a daily basis. Computer programs are available that are able to complete the bank reconciliation by inputting data from the bank's own computer records. These match the items, thus reducing the laborious task of ticking each transaction manually.

As part of internal checks and management control the bank reconciliation should be reviewed by the Administration Department's senior management in each period to ensure that everything is in order. For example, if cheques issued over six months previously have not been presented, they are out of date and should therefore be cancelled. Similarly, if receipts have been entered in the Cash Book but remain unrecorded in the bank statements, then immediate enquiries should be made to ascertain the reasons.

Payroll section

The financial accounts section will also normally be responsible for payroll maintenance and calculations, the procedures being covered in Chapter 4. Other tasks in the department will be the upkeep of the General Ledger and the Fixed Asset Register.

General Ledger

The General Ledger holds all the impersonal accounts of the business. The personal accounts are held in the Sales Ledger and Purchases Ledger. The structure of the ledger will be reflected in the chart of accounts, with the accounts grouped broadly as shown in Figure 7.8.

Fixed Asset Register

The financial accounts section will usually be responsible for keeping a record of all the fixed assets owned by the firm. Each asset will be designated its own record and (generally) physically identified by numbering or tagging, the asset number being part of the record. The register will enable calculations of depreciation for each item and will also show the useful economic life remaining in the asset. In total, the value at cost or valuation of all the assets in the register, categorised by type of asset (for example, plant and equipment, motor vehicles, etc.), will equal the

fixed asset original cost or valuation accounts in the General Ledger. Similarly, the total of the accumulated depreciation should also agree with the accumulated depreciation account in the General Ledger. The register is therefore an analysis of the fixed assets accounts, effectively a memorandum ledger.

Cost accounts section

The Cost Accountant will be responsible for maintaining the cost accounting records of the enterprise which cover the 'Cost of Goods Sold' section of the profit and loss account. The bookkeeping methods used for cost accounting are covered in Chapter 8. The Cost Accountant will also be involved in product costing, standard costing, budgeting and other techniques, which are discussed in other chapters.

Management accounting section

The preparation of periodic Management Accounts will be a major function of this section. This work includes detailed involvement in the budgeting process as well as analytical work to assist management in decision-taking. The methods and techniques of analysis and presentation of information used by the section are covered in other chapters.

FIGURE 7.8

GENERAL LEDGER	
DR	CR
FIXED ASSET ACCOUNTS	**CAPITAL AND RESERVE ACCOUNTS**
NET TANGIBLE ASSETS	SHARE CAPITAL
NET INVESTMENTS	PROFIT AND LOSS ACCOUNT
	RESERVES
CURRENT ASSETS ACCOUNTS	**CURRENT LIABILITIES ACCOUNTS**
STOCKS	TRADE CREDITORS
TRADE DEBTORS	BANK OVERDRAFT
CASH AT BANK	OTHER CREDITORS
CASH IN HAND	
OTHER DEBTORS	**LONG-TERM CREDITORS' ACCOUNTS**
PREPAYMENTS	LOANS
COST AND EXPENSES ACCOUNTS	**SALES AND OTHER INCOME ACCOUNTS**

FIGURE 7.9

TYPES OF RESEARCH AND DEVELOPMENT	
TYPE	**WORK DIRECTED TOWARDS**
PURE RESEARCH	PRIMARILY THE ADVANCEMENT OF KNOWLEDGE
APPLIED RESEARCH	EXPLOITING PURE RESEARCH FOR COMMERCIAL GAIN
DEVELOPMENT	INTRODUCING OR IMPROVING SPECIFIC PRODUCTS OR PROCESSES

Personnel Department

The Personnel Department (Human Resources) will normally be managed by a member of the Institute of Personnel Management (IPM) He or she will usually report directly to the MD and will be responsible for implementing the firm's employment policies and practices. This will entail ensuring that staffing levels are in line with operating plans, that training and management development programmes are effective and appropriate, and that employee legislation requirements are correctly observed and handled. Recruitment of staff, covering staff advertising, dealing with staff agencies and interviewing prospective employees will also play a major role in the day-to-day activities of the Department.

One potentially large area of cost responsibility for the Department is in the area of staff training. This is usually controlled by budgeting a specific sum for the purpose. The Personnel Manager will allocate this training fund to ensure that it is spent appropriately. This entails close co-operation with other line managers. Periodic reports will be issued to show the expenditure made compared to the planned allocations.

The costs of staff recruitment can also be high and will be reported to management in detail on a periodic basis. As an alternative to recruiting through advertisements and agencies, many firms will pay existing members of staff who introduce new members. And

a 'free' method of recruiting is through the selection of likely employees who have written to the company on a speculative basis looking for employment.

Investigations into the causes of staff turnover, discussed in Chapter 4, will be an area in which the Personnel Manager will be involved. The costs of the department will be reported periodically in similar manner to the distribution and sales functions, as previously illustrated.

Reception and Postal Departments

The Receptionist and postal staff will generally report to the Personnel (or Human Resources) Manager. The costs of this section will also be reported periodically. Postal charges may be reallocated to user departments responsible for this spend.

Research and Development (R&D) Department

Many firms spend money on research and development and the costs incurred in this activity can be treated in different ways according to the type of work being undertaken. SSAP 13 – Research and Development, recognises that there are three broad categories of activity; as shown in Figure 7.9.

The costs of pure and applied research can be regarded as ongoing and therefore no particular future accounting period will benefit specifically from the work done. Therefore these costs are treated as *period* costs and are written off to the profit and loss account in the accounting period in which they arise.

Development expenditure will also be written off as a period cost unless the work is undertaken with reasonable expectations that specific future commercial benefits will arise. When this is the case it is permissible to carry forward the development costs, but only if certain circumstances apply. These are:

(i)   that the expenditure has been incurred on clearly defined projects; and

(ii) the related expenditure is separately identifiable and the project has been assessed with reasonable certainty that it is technically feasible and ultimately will be commercially viable.

When the product or process begins its commercial life the related accumulated development costs will be amortised – written off – over the period it is expected to be sold or used: that is, the product's useful economic life.

Summary

- Unlike production department overheads, which are product costs, distribution, selling and administration overheads are treated as period costs and written off to the profit and loss account in the period in which they arise.
- Distribution costs cover the warehousing and storage of the finished products and also the delivery costs to customers and outlying storage depots.
- Marketing costs cover the process of identifying, anticipating and satisfying customer needs profitably. Selling costs are incurred in persuading and encouraging customers to buy the product or service. Administration costs are incurred in conducting, directing and managing the affairs of the business and are incurred by the work of the Managing Director's Department, the Accounts Department, Personnel Department and other associated administration functions.
- Research and development costs are normally written off as a period cost unless development work on specific products or processes can be identified with future commercial viability, in which case the costs may be carried forward and amortised over the useful life of the project or process.

8

Cost Bookkeeping

In this chapter we shall be examining how costs and income are recorded in the books of account.

Look again at Figure 7.8 in Chapter 7 (page 88). You will see that these accounts are included with the assets, capital and liability accounts in the one ledger, the General Ledger. This bookkeeping system is described as an *integrated accounts system*.

Another system of double entry bookkeeping, used in cost accounting, is called an *interlocking accounts system*. With this system the cost and income accounts (and also stock accounts), are repeated in a separate memorandum ledger called the Cost Ledger. Figure 8.1 illustrates the two bookkeeping methods.

Integrated accounts system

CIMA defines integrated accounts as '*a set of accounting records which provides financial and cost accounts using a common input of data for all accounting purposes*'.

The double entry bookkeeping entries for all transactions are thus made directly into one General Ledger, the postings being from the various day books (sales, purchases, cash book, petty cash book) and the journal. One trial balance will be prepared, from which the Financial Accounts and Management Accounts are prepared. As can be imagined, a large company may have thousands of accounts: customer accounts, supplier accounts, asset accounts, liability accounts and many cost and income accounts.

The resulting trial balance, listing every balance on every account, would be both unwieldy and cumbersome. But in order to prove the General Ledger balances, every account with a balance on it has to be listed. So, to help resolve the practical difficulties of administration, and also to assist in the allocation of accounting and bookkeeping tasks, separate memorandum ledgers are maintained for identifiable groups of accounts and linked into the General Ledger through *control accounts*. A memorandum Sales Ledger is operated to house the customer accounts, a memorandum Purchases Ledger to control the suppliers' accounts, and there are separate memorandum ledgers for the various stock accounts and other groupings of accounts, including the cost accounts.

The General Ledger in an integrated system, being self-balancing, must therefore include the balances in these memorandum accounts. This is achieved through the mechanism of control accounts. A control account records all the movements in a memorandum ledger, but in total form only.

As an illustration, we shall follow through the bookkeeping entries for raw materials purchases. Here the purchases of raw materials – the debit entries – will be entered into individual stock accounts in a memorandum raw materials ledger. There will be an account

FIGURE 8.1

BOOKKEEPING METHODS		
INTEGRATED ACCOUNTS ONE GENERAL LEDGER:	**INTERLOCKING ACCOUNTS** TWO LEDGERS: FINANCIAL LEDGER AND COST LEDGER	
COMPRISING ACCOUNTS FOR:	*FINANCIAL LEDGER COMPRISING ACCOUNTS FOR:*	*COST LEDGER COMPRISING: ACCOUNTS FOR:*
FIXED ASSETS INVESTMENTS STOCKS DEBTORS CREDITORS LOANS SHARE CAPITAL RESERVES	FIXED ASSETS INVESTMENTS STOCKS DEBTORS CREDITORS LOANS SHARE CAPITAL RESERVES	STOCKS
SALES AND INCOME COSTS FINANCING COSTS AND INCOME	SALES AND INCOME COSTS FINANCING COSTS AND INCOME COST LEDGER CONTROL ACCOUNT	SALES AND INCOME COSTS

for each item of stock carried. The total of all the raw materials purchases will be recorded (posted) in an account within the General Ledger called the raw materials control account.

Similarly with issues of materials to the production departments: the individual details will be posted to the accounts in the memorandum ledger and the total of all the issues will be posted to the General Ledger's raw materials control account. When all the entries have been made to the memorandum stores ledger in an accounting period it follows that the sum of the balances in that ledger will equal the raw materials control account balance in the General Ledger. If they do not, then a posting error, or casting error, has occurred and this will need to be found and corrected. Figure 8.2 (using raw materials as the example) illustrates the concept of control accounts.

The following lists the type of control accounts likely to be found in the General Ledger:

Production overheads control account;
Wages control account;
Distribution overheads control account;
Selling overheads control account; and
Administration overheads control account.

For asset and liability control accounts, those commonly used are:

Raw materials control account;
Work-in-progress control account;
Finished goods control account;
Sales Ledger control account; and
Purchases Ledger control account.

Bookkeeping entries using integrated accounts

We shall briefly work through the various day books with some sample entries and post these to the memorandum ledgers and the General Ledger to illustrate how the control account system works (see Figure 8.3).

The flow diagram shown in Figure 8.4 indicates the interlinking of the memorandum ledgers with the control accounts in an integrated accounting system.

Interlocking accounts system

CIMA defines interlocking accounts as: '*a system in which the cost accounts are distinct from the financial*

FIGURE 8.2

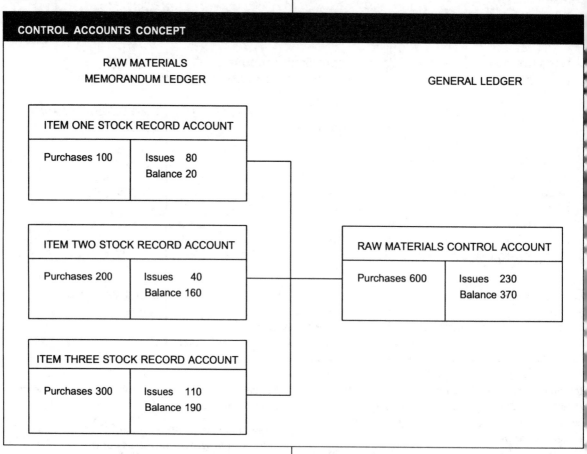

CONTROL ACCOUNTS CONCEPT

RAW MATERIALS
MEMORANDUM LEDGER

GENERAL LEDGER

ITEM ONE STOCK RECORD ACCOUNT	
Purchases 100	Issues 80
	Balance 20

ITEM TWO STOCK RECORD ACCOUNT	
Purchases 200	Issues 40
	Balance 160

RAW MATERIALS CONTROL ACCOUNT	
Purchases 600	Issues 230
	Balance 370

ITEM THREE STOCK RECORD ACCOUNT	
Purchases 300	Issues 110
	Balance 190

accounts, the two sets of accounts being kept continuously in agreement by the use of control accounts or reconciled by other means.'

A separate Cost Ledger will be set up. The General Ledger (which becomes known as the Financial Ledger in this system), will continue to record the double entry aspect of the transactions as before, but in addition a memorandum account will be kept which will record items that should be reflected in the cost ledger. This memorandum account is called the cost ledger control account. Within the Cost Ledger itself, a control account will also be maintained, to make that ledger self-balancing. This account (called either the cost ledger control account or the financial ledger control account) will enable the double entry to be completed for those transactions whenever the other side of the entry appears in the Financial Ledger. The operation of this account will also facilitate reconciliation with the Financial Ledger entries.

Broadly speaking, the Cost Ledger will record the trading activities of the firm and will hold the sales and costs accounts, and also the stock accounts. But some profit and loss accounts will be excluded from it. Generally speaking, financing costs and income such as interest payable and rents receivable, and the various profit appropriation accounts are excluded from the Cost Ledger.

It can be seen that in an interlocking accounting systems there are a number of extra postings to be made to record transactions that need to be entered in the cost ledger: the original two in the Financial Ledger (the debit and credit aspects of the transaction); a further entry in the Financial Ledger, to the memo-randum cost ledger control account; and entries in the appropriate accounts in the cost ledger, including an entry to the Cost Ledger control account.

Figure 8.5 provides an overview of the operation of an interlocking system, followed by examples of the

FIGURE 8.3

LEDGER ENTRY EXAMPLES

		MEMORANDUM LEDGERS		GENERAL LEDGER	
		DR	CR	DR	CR
SALES DAY BOOK					
INDIVIDUAL CUSTOMER ACCOUNTS	(SALES LEDGER)	X			
SALES LEDGER CONTROL ACCOUNT				X	
VAT OUTPUTS ACCOUNT					X
SALES ACCOUNT					X
PURCHASES DAY BOOK					
Two examples:					
1. Purchases of raw materials					
2. Stationery invoice for Accounts Department					
1. INDIVIDUAL STOCK RECORD ACCOUNTS	(RAW MATERIALS LEDGER)	X			
RAW MATERIALS CONTROL ACCOUNT				X	
VAT INPUTS ACCOUNT				X	
PURCHASES LEDGER CONTROL ACCOUNT					X
INDIVIDUAL SUPPLIER ACCOUNTS	(PURCHASES LEDGER)		X		
2. ACCOUNTS DEPT STATIONERY ACCOUNT	(ADMIN OVERHEADS LEDGER)	X			
ADMIN OVERHEADS CONTROL ACCOUNT				X	
VAT INPUTS ACCOUNT				X	
PURCHASES LEDGER CONTROL ACCOUNT					X
INDIVIDUAL SUPPLIER ACCOUNTS	(PURCHASES LEDGER)		X		
CASH BOOK					
Payments of various production overhead costs by cheque					
INDIVIDUAL PRODUCTION COST ACCOUNTS	(PRODUCTION OVERHEADS LEDGER)	X			
PRODUCTION OVERHEADS CONTROL ACCOUNT				X	
VAT INPUTS ACCOUNT				X	
BANK ACCOUNT					X
JOURNAL ENTRY					
Issue of raw materials to the factory floor					
INDIVIDUAL STOCK RECORD ACCOUNTS	(RAW MATERIALS LEDGER)		X		
WORK IN PROGRESS CONTROL ACCOUNT				X	
RAW MATERIALS CONTROL ACCOUNT					X
INDIVIDUAL WORK IN PROGRESS JOBS	(WORK-IN-PROGRESS LEDGER)	X			

FIGURE 8.4

AN INTEGRATED ACCOUNTING SYSTEM (INTEGRATED LEDGER)

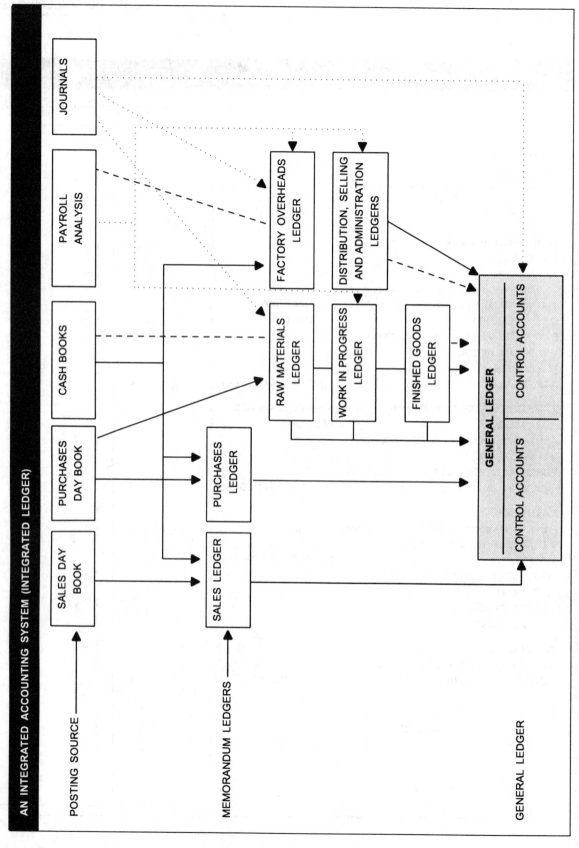

system in use, illustrated in Figure 8.6.

Examples:
1. Purchase of raw materials.
2. Wages paid.
3. Rent of outside warehouse.
4. Issue of raw materials to factory floor.

The entries in both ledgers will be as shown in Figure 8.6.

Reconciliation of the costing profit and loss account

With interlocking accounts systems it is possible to produce two profit and loss accounts: a financial profit and loss account and a costing profit and loss account. The former is produced from the information held in the Financial Ledger, the latter from the Cost Ledger. Because entries in the two ledgers will often differ, the resulting profit and loss accounts will not show the same profit or loss.

So periodically, a *reconciliation* will be required. The main differences between the two will usually be caused by:

opening and closing stock valuations;
profits or losses arising on the sale of fixed assets;
depreciation rates;
notional rent, other notional charges;
interest charges, tax and dividends and other appropriations; or
bad debts and provisions.

The reasons for the differences are generally as listed below.

Differences in stock valuations

Separate ledgers enable management to operate different stock valuation methods. SSAP 9 requires that financial statements evaluate stocks at the lower of cost or market value. Closing stocks in the financial

FIGURE 8.5

INTERLOCKING ACCOUNTS OVERVIEW

FINANCIAL LEDGER ACCOUNTS	**COST LEDGER ACCOUNTS**
FIXED ASSETS AND INVESTMENTS ACCOUNTS SHARE CAPITAL AND RESERVES ACCOUNTS SALES LEDGER CONTROL ACCOUNT PURCHASE LEDGER CONTROL ACCOUNT OTHER DEBTORS' AND CREDITORS' ACCOUNTS	RAW MATERIAL CONTROL ACCOUNT WORK-IN-PROGRESS CONTROL ACCOUNT FINISHED GOODS CONTROL ACCOUNT
OPENING STOCK ACCOUNTS **PURCHASES ACCOUNTS** **WAGES ACCOUNTS** **EXPENSES AND SALES ACCOUNTS**	SALES ACCOUNTS FACTORY OVERHEADS CONTROL ACCOUNT WAGES CONTROL ACCOUNT SELLING, DISTRIBUTION AND ADMINISTRATION CONTROL ACCOUNTS
DIVIDENDS, TAX, OTHER APPROPRIATIONS ACCOUNTS	
	NOTIONAL RENT ACCOUNTS
INTEREST PAYABLE AND RECEIVABLE ACCOUNTS RENTS RECEIVABLE, DISCOUNTS ALLOWED ACCOUNTS DISCOUNTS RECEIVED ACCOUNTS GAINS OR LOSSES ON SALE OF ASSETS ACCOUNTS	
MEMORANDUM COST LEDGER CONTROL ACCOUNT	COST LEDGER CONTROL ACCOUNT

FIGURE 8.6

EXAMPLES OF AN INTERLOCKING ACCOUNTS SYSTEM IN USE

	FINANCIAL LEDGER		COST LEDGER	
	DR	CR	DR	CR
1. PURCHASE OF RAW MATERIALS				
PURCHASES ACCOUNT	X			
PURCHASES LEDGER CONTROL ACCOUNT		X		
MEMORANDUM COST LEDGER CONTROL ACCOUNT	X			
RAW MATERIALS CONTROL ACCOUNT			X	
COST LEDGER CONTROL ACCOUNT				X
2. WAGES PAID				
WAGES ACCOUNT – GROSS	X			
PAYROLL CREDITORS ACCOUNTS		X		
BANK ACCOUNT		X		
MEMORANDUM COST LEDGER CONTROL ACCOUNT	X			
WAGES CONTROL ACCOUNT – GROSS PAY			X	
COST LEDGER CONTROL ACCOUNT				X
3. RENT OF OUTSIDE WAREHOUSE				
APPROPRIATE EXPENSE ACCOUNT	X			
CREDITOR OR BANK ACCOUNT		X		
MEMORANDUM COST LEDGER CONTROL ACCOUNT	X			
DISTRIBUTION OVERHEADS CONTROL ACCOUNT$			X	
COST LEDGER CONTROL ACCOUNT				X
4. ISSUE OF RAW MATERIALS TO FACTORY FLOOR				
WORK IN PROGRESS CONTROL ACCOUNT			X	
RAW MATERIALS CONTROL ACCOUNT				X

accounts therefore might be valued using FIFO or AVCO methods (see Chapter 3). However, in the cost accounts, management may require stocks to be valued on a different basis, such as LIFO or even NIFO (Chapter 3). Therefore a difference in the profits will arise because of this different treatment.

Profits or losses arising on the sale of fixed assets

Gains or losses arising on the disposal of an asset are generally not included in the cost accounts. It is rea-

soned that these are one-off events and thus outside the scope of the Cost Ledger, the main purpose of which is to record and report on the everyday trading activities of the enterprise for cost control and planning purposes: therefore these items generally appear only in the Financial Ledger.

Depreciation differences

Management may decide to operate two different methods in each ledger – perhaps the *straight-line method* in the financial accounts and a *units-of-production method* or *reducing balance method* in the cost accounts. This will give rise to a difference in reported profits.

Notional rent, notional interest charges

Notional interest and notional rent charges are sometimes made in the cost accounts. These are entries designed to ensure that management take into account expenditure which might normally be expected to be included when arriving at a product or service cost. Take factory rent, for example. If the property is owned by the company there will clearly be no rental charge, so it follows that the factory overheads will be lower than if rent was payable. The product cost consequently will be lower and this may be passed on to customers in a lower selling price. But the cost of rent is a factor in production generally and some argue it should be included in the cost of a product. Similarly, with a company operating two factories, one rented and the other owned. Here the product costs will differ because of the absence of a rental charge in the owned premises. By making a notional charge, the two factories' total overhead costs, and therefore product costs, can be compared on a like-for-like basis.

The double entry postings for notional rent entries in the Cost Ledger are shown in Figure 8.7. The notional rent provision account will be carried forward as a reserve account in the Cost Ledger. As no entry for notional rent or charges is required in the financial accounts, the charge made in the Cost Ledger will form part of the reconciliation *if* the credit entry is made to the reserve account. But if the credit is made to the costing profit and loss account it will clearly contra the debit entry in the factory overheads section, therefore cancelling out and thus not a reconciliation item. (With regard to notional interest charges, these are often created to recognise the cost of capital employed in the production process.)

Interest payable, tax and dividend charges and other appropriations

These costs and appropriations are of a financial accounting nature and therefore omitted from the cost accounts, appearing only in the Financial Ledger.

Worked Example:

AAT June 1992

Your organisation operates separate financial and cost accounts. The Cost Accountant tells you that the financial profit has been determined as £75 000. You are also told the following:

(i) Debenture interest of £13 000 was paid during the year.

(ii) Rent of £25 000 was received during the year.

(iii) There was a write-off of goodwill amounting to £20 000.

(iv) Machinery with a net book value of £15 000 was sold for £21 000.

(v) A notional rent charge of £14 000 was charged in respect of the company's premises.

(vi) Discounts allowed amounted to £7000 and discounts received amounted to £5000.

(vii) The cost accounts included overheads recovered on the basis of £25 per machine hour; £8000 machine hours were worked and the actual overhead incurred was £220 000.

(viii) The financial accounts use FIFO to value material, while the cost accounts charge materials out on a LIFO basis. This has given the following stock values:

	Financial accounts	Cost accounts
Opening stock of raw materials	£16 000	£21 000
Opening stock of finished goods	£47 000	£42 000
Closing stock of raw materials	£27 000	£34 000
Closing stock of finished goods	£39 000	£40 000

FIGURE 8.7

NOTIONAL RENT ENTRIES IN THE COST LEDGER		
	DR	CR
FACTORY OVERHEADS CONTROL ACCOUNT (NOTIONAL RENT ACCOUNT)	X	
COSTING PROFIT AND LOSS ACCOUNT		X
OR		
NOTIONAL RENT PROVISION ACCOUNT		X

FIGURE 8.8

ACCOUNTS MAINTAINED IN THE COST LEDGER

DR	RAW MATERIALS CONTROL ACCOUNT		CR
	£		£
BALANCE BROUGHT FORWARD		TRANSFER TO W-I-P ACCOUNT	A
PURCHASES – COST LEDGER CONTROL ACCOUNT		TRANSFER TO FACTORY OVERHEADS	B
STOCK DIFFERENCES		STOCK DIFFERENCES	
		BALANCE CARRIED DOWN	
BALANCE BROUGHT DOWN			

DR	WAGES CONTROL ACCOUNT		CR
	£		£
WAGES PAID – COST LEDGER CONTROL ACCOUNT		TRANSFER TO W-I-P ACCOUNT (DIRECT LABOUR)	C
PAYROLL ON-COSTS		TRANSFER TO FACTORY OVERHEADS (INDIRECT LABOUR)	D

DR	FACTORY OVERHEADS CONTROL ACCOUNT		CR
	£		£
TRANSFER FROM RAW MATERIALS CONTROL	B	TRANSFER TO W-I-P OVERHEADS RECOVERED	E
TRANSFER FROM WAGES CONTROL	D		
OTHER FACTORY INDIRECT EXPENSES – COST LEDGER CONTROL ACCOUNT		TRANSFER: UNDERABSORBED OVERHEADS	
DEPRECIATION CHARGES – COST LEDGER CONTROL			
TRANSFER: OVERABSORBED OVERHEADS			

DR	WORK-IN-PROGRESS CONTROL ACCOUNT		CR
	£		£
BALANCE B/FORWARD			
TRANSFER: RAW MATERIALS	A	TRANSFER TO FINISHED GOODS ACCOUNT	F
TRANSFER: DIRECT LABOUR	C		
TRANSFER: FACTORY OVERHEADS	E		

DR	FINISHED GOODS CONTROL ACCOUNT			CR
		£		£
BALANCE BROUGHT FORWARD			TRANSFER TO COST OF GOODS SOLD ACCOUNT	G
TRANSFER FROM W-I-P ACCOUNT		F	BALANCE CARRIED FOWARD	
BALANCE BROUGHT DOWN				

DR	COST OF SALES ACCOUNT			CR
		£		£
			TRANSFER TO PROFIT AND LOSS ACCOUNT	
TRANSFER FROM FINISHED GOODS ACCOUNT		G		
BALANCE BROUGHT DOWN				

DR	COST LEDGER CONTROL ACCOUNT			CR
		£		£
BALANCE BROUGHT FORWARD			BALANCE BROUGHT FORWARD	
			RAW MATERIALS CONTROL ACCOUNT	
SALES ACCOUNT			WAGES CONTROL ACCOUNT	
			FACTORY OVERHEADS CONTROL ACCOUNT	
			DEPRECIATION – FACTORY OVERHEADS CONTROL	
			COSTING PROFIT FOR THE ACCOUNTING PERIOD	
BALANCE BROUGHT DOWN			BALANCE BROUGHT DOWN	

NOTE: W-I-P = WORK-IN-PROGRESS.

Required:
Determine the costing profit for the Cost Accountant.

Solution:
Working

Item	Financial Ledger	Cost Ledger	
Sales			
Cost of sales			
Opening stocks	63 000	63 000	
Closing stocks	(66 000)	(74 000)	
	(3 000)	(11 000)	
Gross profit effect	3 000	11 000	'Extra' profit to be adjusted for

TABLE 8.1

Answer

Item		£	Reasons
	Profit per Financial Ledger	75 000	
(i)	Add back debenture interest	13 000	Financing charge
(ii)	Deduct rent received	(25 000)	Non-trading income
(iii)	Add back goodwill written off	20 000	Financing charge
(iv)	Deduct profit on disposal of asset	(6 000)	Disposal gain
(v)	Deduct notional rent	(14 000)	Excluded in Financial Ledger

COMPARISON OF PRESENTATION OF THE PROFIT AND LOSS ACCOUNT

COSTING PROFIT AND LOSS ACCOUNT

ACCOUNTING PERIOD
£

SALES

LESS — COST OF GOODS SOLD
ADD (DEDUCT) — (OVER) UNDERABSORBED OVERHEAD
ADD (DEDUCT) — STOCK LOSSES (GAINS)

GROSS PROFIT
LESS — EXPENSES

DISTRIBUTION
MARKETING AND SELLING
ADMINISTRATION
NOTIONAL RENT AND CHARGES

COSTING PROFIT FOR THE PERIOD

FINANCIAL PROFIT AND LOSS ACCOUNT

ACCOUNTING PERIOD
£

SALES

LESS — COST OF GOODS SOLD
OPENING F/GOODS STOCK
ADD — GOODS MANUFACTURED
LESS — CLOSING F/GOODS STOCK
TOTAL COST OF GOODS SOLD

GROSS PROFIT

LESS — EXPENSES

DISTRIBUTION
MARKETING AND SELLING
ADMINISTRATION
FINANCING COSTS AND INCOME
GAINS OR LOSSES ON DISPOSALS

PROFIT BEFORE TAX
TAXATION
PROFIT AFTER TAX
DIVIDENDS AND APPROPRIATIONS
RETAINED PROFIT

	Add back discounts allowed	7 000	Other expense
(vi)	Deduct discounts received	(5 000)	Other income
(vii)	Add back 'under-absorbed' overheads	20 000	Absorbed £200 000: Actual costs £220 000
(viii)	Deduct financial accounts stock gross profit effect	(3 000)	As above workings
(ix)	Add cost ledger stock gross profit effect	11 000	As above workings
	Profit per Cost Ledger	93 000	

Figure 8.8 provides examples of the entries to be found in the stock accounts and other accounts maintained in the Cost Ledger.

Comparison of presentation format for the Profit and Loss Account

An example of the costing Profit and Loss Account format (compared with the conventional Profit and Loss Account produced from the financial accounting records) is as shown in Table 8.1.

Manufacturing Account

Many firms do not operate cost accounting methods for control and planning but still need to prepare the cost of goods sold section for their trading account for an accounting period. The manufacturing account provides this information, recording the elements of cost, namely raw materials, direct labour and factory overheads. The manufacturing account is a total account and, as such, is limited to the information it can supply to management. There will be no details for example with regard to the cost of individual jobs or processes, therefore individual product profitability exercises will not be able to be completed. It also does not distinguish between costs that change according to the levels of activity, namely fixed and variable costs. An example of the manufacturing account appears in Figure 8.9.

FIGURE 8.9

MANUFACTURING ACCOUNT

MANUFACTURING ACCOUNT FOR THE PERIOD ENDING_____		£
MATERIALS OPENING STOCK OF MATERIALS PURCHASES LESS RETURNS *less* CLOSING STOCK OF MATERIALS		
= MATERIALS USED		A
DIRECT LABOUR		B
PRIME COST	A + B =	C
DIRECT EXPENSES		D
FACTORY EXPENSES INDIRECT LABOUR INDIRECT MATERIALS OTHER FACTORY OVERHEADS (listed)		
		E
TOTAL PRODUCTION COSTS	C + D + E =	F
ADD: OPENING WORK IN PROGRESS		G
LESS: CLOSING WORK IN PROGRESS		H
COST OF GOODS COMPLETED IN PERIOD		F + G − H

Summary

- There are two distinct types of bookkeeping systems used in cost accounting: integrated accounts and interlocking accounts.
- With integrated accounts, one General Ledger is maintained, the costs and expenses accounts, revenue accounts, assets, liabilities and capital accounts being housed therein. It is self-balancing, the debits equalling the credits. Memorandum ledgers are kept to house groups of accounts of a similar type, such as individual sales customers' accounts and individual suppliers' accounts. The memorandum accounts are integrated into the General Ledger through the use of control accounts. Control accounts are total accounts.

- With interlocking accounts, two ledgers are maintained to record costs and income: the Financial Ledger and the Cost Ledger. The Cost Ledger is a memorandum ledger and is used to house the trading accounts and the stock accounts.
- Both ledgers are self balancing. This is achieved through the creation of a cost ledger control account in the Cost Ledger. A memorandum account is maintained in the Financial Ledger to reflect the entries to be found in the Cost Ledger. As this is a memorandum account it is an 'extra' account and is therefore not part of the Financial Ledger's double entry system. Entries in the Financial Ledger needing to be entered in the Cost Ledger will thus go through both cost ledger control accounts.

- With interlocking accounts, separate profit and loss accounts can be prepared, a costing profit and loss account and a financial profit and loss account. Differences often arise because of the differing treatment of items in both ledgers, such as stock valuation and depreciation charges. A reconciliation of the two profits is therefore required to be completed at periodic intervals.

Examination Questions

1 A LEVEL (ULEAC) 1990
The following manufacturing account of Barrington Products Ltd for the year ended 31 December has been produced by an inexperienced bookkeeper.

BARRINGTON PRODUCTS LTD
Manufacturing Account for the year ended 31 December

	£	£
Opening stocks:		
work-in-progress	12 842	
raw materials	8 724	
		21 566
Raw materials purchases		146 249
		167 815
Less closing stocks:		
work-in-progress	11 287	
raw materials	9 562	20 849
		146 966
Factory expenses:		
labour	81 450	
general expenses	33 889	
heat and light	5 620	
insurances	6 574	
rates	3 422	
		130 955
Prime manufacturing cost		277 921

Upon closer examination, you find that:
(i) During the year ended 31 December:
£1863 for materials returned had been omitted;
of the factory labour, £31 590 was indirect labour;

of the general expenses, £16 679 were direct expenses; depreciation of factory machines, £4624 had been omitted; goods completed had a market value of £389 162.
(ii) At 31 December:
£643 of direct wages and £719 of indirect wages were owing;
£323 of general factory expenses were owing;
the figure of £5620 included a closing prepayment of £214 for heat and light, which has been ADDED;
insurances £512 and £317 rates had been prepaid.
Note: No correcting adjustments had been taken on any of these matters.

Required:
Redraft the manufacturing account as it should appear, to show clearly prime cost, total factory overheads. total factory cost of goods completed, and the manufacturing profit.

2 LCCI THIRD LEVEL COST ACCOUNTING 1991
Konnectus Ltd operates an interlocking system of accounting. The following data has been used in the Financial Ledger for quarter 1:

	£
Sales	450 000
Direct labour costs	25 250
Factory overhead expenses	23 500
Administration overhead expenses	11 800
Selling overhead expenses	26 250

	Opening stock	Closing stock
	£	£
Raw material (RM)	107 250	98 800
Work in progress (WIP)	79 600	80 300
Finished goods (FG)	83 250	88 400

A reconciliation statement for quarter 1 is as follows:

	£
Costing Profit	40 750
Sundry income in financial period	730
Administration overhead over absorbed	1 700
WIP – opening stock difference	14 750
WIP – closing stock difference	5 650
FG – closing stock difference	9 670
	73 250

	£
Financial Profit	23 030
Factory overhead under absorbed	3 300
Selling overhead under absorbed	3 750
RM – opening stock difference	11 770
RM – closing stock difference	21 650
FG – opening stock difference	9 750
	73 250

In the Cost Ledger, the following bases for overhead absorption have been used:

Factory: as a % on direct labour cost.
Administration: as a % on sales value.
Selling: as a % on sales value.

In anticipation of usual seasonal variations, any under or over absorption in quarter 1 has been carried forward to quarter 2.

Required:
(a) Calculate the following stock values as shown in the Cost Ledger for quarter 1:
   (i) Opening stock: Raw material
                    Work in progress
                    Finished goods .
   (ii) Closing stock: Raw material
                    Work in progress
                    Finished goods.
(b) The balance on the Control Account in the Cost Ledger at the start of quarter 1.
(c) Each of the three overhead absorption rates used in the Cost Ledger.

3 ACCA COST AND MANAGEMENT ACCOUNTING 1 1990
V Ltd operates interlocking financial and cost accounts. The following balances were in the cost ledger at the beginning of a month, the last month (Month 12) of the financial year:

	DR	CR
Raw materials stock control account	28 944	
Finished goods stock control account	77 168	
Financial ledger control account		106 112

there is no work in progress at the end of each month.

21 600 kilos of the single raw material were in stock at the beginning of Month 12. Purchases and issues during the month were as follows:

Purchases:
7th   17 400 kilos at 1.35 per kilo
20th   19 800 kilos at 1.35 per kilo

Issues:
1st   7 270 kilos
8th   8 120 kilos
15th   8 080 kilos
22nd 9 115 kilos

A weighted average price per kilo (to four decimal places of £) is used to value issues of raw material to production. A new average price is determined after each material purchase, and issues are charged out in total to the nearest £.

Costs of labour and overhead incurred during Month 12 were £35 407. Production of the company's single product was 17 150 units.

Stocks of finished goods were:
Beginning of Month 12   16 960 units.
End of Month 12   17 080 units.

Transfers from finished goods stock on sale of the product are made on a FIFO basis.

Required:
Prepare the raw material stock control account, and the finished goods stock control account for Month 12.

4 CIMA COST ACCOUNTING 1992
A manufacturing company has approximately 600 weekly paid direct and indirect production workers. It incurred the following costs and deductions relating to the payroll for the week ended 2 May:

	£	£
Gross wages		180 460
Deductions:		
Employees' national insurance	14 120	
Employees' pension fund contributions	7 200	
Income tax (PAYE)	27 800	
Court order retentions	1 840	
Trade union subscriptions	1 200	
Private health care contributions	6 000	
Total deductions		58 160
Net wages paid		122 300

The employer's national insurance contribution for the week was £18 770.

From the wages analysis the following information was extracted:

	Direct workers £	Indirect workers £
Paid for ordinary time	77 460	38 400
Overtime wages at normal hourly rates	16 800	10 200
Overtime premium (treat as overhead)	5 600	3 400
Shift premiums/allowances	8 500	4 500
Capital work in progress expenditure*	–	2 300*
Statutory sick pay	5 700	3 300
Paid for idle time	4 300	–
	118 360	62 100

*Work done by building maintenance workers concreting floor area for a warehouse extension.

You are required to show journal entries to indicate clearly how each item should be posted into the accounts
(i)   from the payroll, and
(ii) from the Wages Control Account to other accounts, based on the wages analysis.
Note: Narrations for the journal entries are not required.
5   CIMA COST ACCOUNTING 1993
NB Limited operates an integrated accounting system. At the beginning of October, the following balances appeared in the trial balance:

	£000	£000	£000
Freehold buildings		800	
Plant and equipment at cost		480	
Provision for depreciation on plant and equipment			100
Stocks:			
Raw materials		400	
Work in process 1:			
direct materials	71		
direct wages	50		
production overhead	125	246	
Work in process 2:			
direct materials	127		
direct wages	70		
production overhead	105	302	
Finished goods		60	
Debtors		1 120	
Capital			2 200
Profit retained			220
Creditors			300
Bank			464

Sales		1 200
Cost of sales	888	
Abnormal loss	9	
Production overhead under/over absorbed		21
Administration overhead	120	
Selling and distribution overhead	80	
	4 505	4 505

The transactions during the month of October were:

	£000
Raw materials purchased on credit	210
Raw materials returned to suppliers	10
Raw materials issued to:	
Process 1	136
Process 2	44
Direct wages incurred:	
Process 1	84
Process 2	130
Direct wages paid	200
Production salaries paid	170
Production expenses paid	250
Received from debtors	1 140
Paid to creditors	330
Administration overhead paid	108
Selling and distribution overhead paid	84
Sales, on credit	1 100
Cost of goods sold	844

	Direct materials £000	Direct wages £000
Abnormal loss in:		
Process 1	6	4
Process 2	18	6
Transfer from Process 1 to Process 2	154	94
Transfer from Process 2 to finished goods	558	140

Plant and equipment is depreciated at the rate of 20% per annum, using the straight-line basis. Production overhead is absorbed on the basis of direct wages cost.

Required:

(a) to ascertain and state the production overhead absorption rates used for Process 1 and for Process 2;
(b) to write up the ledger accounts.

NON-COMPUTATIONAL, DESCRIPTIVE TYPE QUESTIONS
(**NB** Minutes in brackets are a guide to indicate the approximate time your essay should take to complete.)

QUESTIONS

A Integrated accounting systems are far superior to non-integrated accounting systems.

Required:
(a) to discuss the above statement;
(b) to state the principles to be followed in establishing a chart of accounts for an integrated accounting system.
(CIMA 1994) (25 minutes)

B One of the weaknesses, it is often argued, of operating an integrated accounting system is that 'notional costs' cannot be entered into the accounting records. You are required to discuss the above statement, to explain the meaning of notional costs and to illustrate with two examples why their inclusion in cost accounts may be desirable.
(CIMA 1992) (15 minutes)

C Describe briefly the purpose of the 'wages control account'.
(CIMA 1992) (5 minutes)

D Explain the purpose of the financial ledger control account*.
(ACCA 1990) (7 minutes)
* Described in the text as the Cost Ledger Control Account

E What are the benefits of operating control accounts?
(AEB A-Level 1993) (10 minutes)

Part II
Cost Accounting Methods

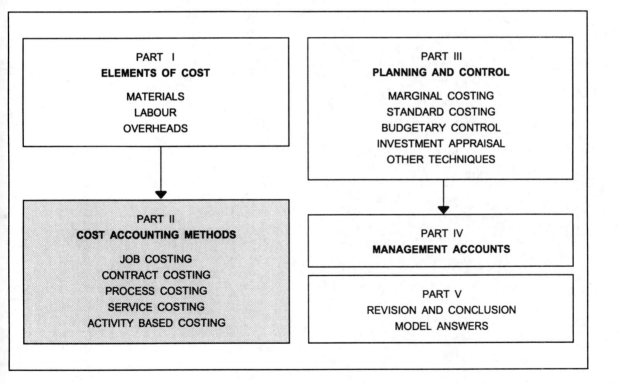

| PART I
ELEMENTS OF COST

MATERIALS
LABOUR
OVERHEADS | PART III
PLANNING AND CONTROL

MARGINAL COSTING
STANDARD COSTING
BUDGETARY CONTROL
INVESTMENT APPRAISAL
OTHER TECHNIQUES |
| PART II
COST ACCOUNTING METHODS

JOB COSTING
CONTRACT COSTING
PROCESS COSTING
SERVICE COSTING
ACTIVITY BASED COSTING | PART IV
MANAGEMENT ACCOUNTS

PART V
REVISION AND CONCLUSION
MODEL ANSWERS |

9

Cost Accounting
Methods Overview

In Part II we shall be examining and investigating ways in which the manufacturing elements of cost are accounted for in different industries and undertakings.

Dependent upon the item being produced, and the methods used for its manufacture, management needs to establish a *cost per unit* of output to control costs and plan for the future. So, whether they complete one-off jobs or make batches of products, or operate a process or perform a service, there is a common denominator which can be calculated for each item of output – the *unit of cost*.

Over many years various cost accounting methods have evolved to record the manufacturing elements of cost to suit particular industries. The Manufacturing Account, on page 102, could be used for all industries, combining as it does *all* the manufacturing elements of cost. But it has many limitations. It does not, for instance, provide management with control and planning information, being simply a total account; it provides no details of efficiencies and inefficiencies; and it gives no facts on individual products, processes or work performed.

Hence the need for management to establish a suitable cost accounting system for their particular business so that the cost elements can be allocated, apportioned and absorbed into products and services, thus giving them control over the costs incurred.

As an example, the cost accounting system for a factory producing, say, chocolate-coated peanuts, in which the raw material undergoes a variety of changes as it moves through various processes to become the finished packaged product, cannot be the same as that used by a company carrying out, say, large civil engineering projects, such as the construction of new motorways, which might take years to complete.

Most manufacturing firms can therefore be classified as either:

(a) In business to make/assemble/construct jobs or products to individual customers' specific orders; or

(b) To 'mass-produce' products, through continuous operations, which will then be sold from stock (therefore not being produced to the order of a specific customer).

The result of this broad classification of manufacturing techniques is that two major cost accounting systems are used, as shown in Figure 9.1: Specific Order Costing and Operational Costing.

FIGURE 9.1

TWO MAJOR COST ACCOUNTING SYSTEMS

SPECIFIC ORDER COSTING

JOB COSTING
BATCH COSTING
CONTRACT COSTING

CONTINUOUS
OPERATIONAL COSTING

PROCESS COSTING
SERVICE COSTING

Specific order costing

Job costing

Job costing is a system in which the elements of cost incurred are specifically identifiable with the item being made to a customer's specific orders or instructions.

The costs of each job are recorded in a Job Account. The resulting profit or loss arising on each separate job is thus able to be calculated in a straightforward manner – sales value less the cost of making the job. The *unit of cost* in job costing is the cost of the job itself.

Examples of industries and enterprises using job costing methods are: the construction industry for short duration jobs (that is, jobs which can be completed within one year); the printing trade; fabricators and engineering machine shops; and vehicle servicing.

The cost of the completed job will be: the materials used for the job, the direct labour employed and the production overheads charged to it.

Batch costing

Batch costing is allied to job costing inasmuch as a customer may ask for a number of identical products to be made to a specific design. The items will be produced as one job. On completion, the cost of each unit made within the batch will be:

Total manufacturing costs of the batch
Number of items made in the batch

Batch costing methods are also used when firms manufacture for stock certain components that form part of the main product. An internal order for the components will be 'placed' by the Stores Department (who are effectively the customer) with the Production Department. The cost of the individual components will be arrived at by using the formula as above: total manufacturing costs divided by the number of components made in the batch.

Another example of the use of batch costing is when customers require modifications to be made to a basic product. Rather than wait for the customers' orders to arrive before starting production (and also perhaps to be in a more favourable selling position by being able to offer early delivery), the manufacturer may decide to produce the basic product in batches. These basic units will be held in stock to await customers' specific orders.

When an order is received, the resulting Job Account will be debited with the calculated unit cost of the basic product, plus the additional specific costs incurred in meeting the customers' specifications. Job and Batch Costing methods are the subject of Chapter 10.

Contract costing

Contract costing is also a specific order costing system but the job undertaken will take longer than one statutory accounting period (usually a year) to complete. The system is used extensively in the construction industry and in civil engineering.

As with job costing, a separate Contract Account will be opened for each job – here called the contract – and charged with the elements of cost arising during its construction. As the contract may take years to complete, it follows that a system of financing is needed to pay for the work as it progresses. In addition, an equitable method of attributing profit arising on uncompleted contracts in the interim statutory accounting periods is required. How this is done and how the Contract Accounts are operated is the subject of Chapter 11. The unit of cost using contract costing is the total cost of the contract itself.

Continuous operational costing

Process costing

Here, bulk raw materials will be converted into individual finished products by a sequence of continuous operations or processes. Imagine a moving conveyer belt – the production line – with raw materials being loaded on at the beginning of the conveyer and individual finished products coming off at the end, with a number of operations in between which change the bulk material into finished products. The finished products are effectively made for stock and not to specific customers' requirements, being held in the finished goods store awaiting orders.

It is clearly not possible to calculate the cost of one of the individual finished products while it is being formed; so instead, the cost of the particular unit is arrived at by *averaging the costs*, using the formula:

$$\frac{\text{Manufacturing costs in the period}}{\substack{\text{Usable completed products} \\ \text{(i.e. the saleable finished units)}}}$$

Manufacturing costs are allocated, apportioned and absorbed into Process Accounts for each of the Processing Departments (of which there may be many), with each process converting the raw material to a particular stage of completion.

Often, more than one saleable product will arise from a common process. This results in either joint products or by-products being created.

The distinction between joint and by-products is one of value. If, say, two products emanating from the one common process both have relatively significant values the products can be considered to be joint products, with each being recognised as a main

product in its own right. But if one product is relatively insignificant in value compared to the other, then this lower value product is described as a by-product, it being considered incidental to the main product being produced. Frequently, joint products (and sometimes by-products) will go on for further separate processing or modification.

Chapter 12 explains the cost accounting methods used in Process Accounting, and Chapter 13 deals with cost accounting for joint and by-products.

Service costing

Service cost accounting is also an operational cost accounting method and is used by enterprises that provide services to customers, such as parcel delivery services, hotels, restaurants and long-distance freight companies. It is also used by utilities organisations, hospitals and local services providers. Additionally, it can also be used in a manufacturing business to account for internal services provided: for example, factory canteen costs, delivery costs to customers and so on.

The purpose of service costing is to establish a relevant unit cost of the service provided which can then be used for cost control purposes and for forward planning objectives, and perhaps for arriving at selling prices for the unit of service.

Chapter 14 covers the areas in which this method of cost accounting is used.

Activity-based costing

In Part II we shall also be looking at the factory overhead absorption technique called activity-based costing (ABC). This method of absorbing factory overheads endeavours to identify costs more precisely with the products being made. This is achieved through a detailed analysis of the activities creating the costs; that is, what 'drives' the costs. The cost of an activity will then be related to the number of times it is performed in an accounting period, to arrive at an absorption rate for the activity. As there are usually a number of activities required to make a product it follows that with ABC there will be a number of absorption rates calculated.

The traditional absorption costing methods, such as the direct labour hour rate, machine hour rate, blanket rate, etc., assume that all factory overheads are linked to that one chosen method of absorption. But when the overheads are subjected to further study, by investigating the activities that cause the costs (such as the activity of ordering materials, for example) and then measuring the number of times a product requires the use of the activity, the overheads can be more precisely absorbed. Thus the absorption of factory overheads into product costs using the ABC method will be activity-based. Chapter 15 provides an introduction to *activity-based* costing.

10
Job and Batch Costing

Job costing

A job is a specific order from a customer instructing the supplier to carry out a task or manufacture a product to the customer's specific requirements. Job costing is the cost accounting method used to collect the elements of cost related to carrying out the task or making the product.

Job costing is used in a wide variety of trades: for example, by printers, by engineering shops and by metalworkers; and by the building trade for short-duration works (which generally are completed within a year).

CIMA defines job costing as '*a form of specific order costing; the attribution of cost to jobs*'.

The first thing needed for a job to be made is obviously an order from the customer. And usually, before the order is secured, an enquiry from the customer will have been received (accompanied by details of the job needing to be done), asking for a quotation.

It may be possible for the manufacturer to quote a price immediately but, generally, cost calculations will need to be done to ensure that nothing is overlooked and that the selling price 'quote' will have a good chance of winning the order. Also, and just as important, a profit element will need to be built into the price. This quotation work will be completed on a *cost estimate* form.

The cost estimate lists all the manufacturing elements of cost which will be attributable to the job. It will also cover other costs, to arrive at the *total cost* applicable to the job quoted and will normally provide a formula to arrive at the estimated profit for the job and thereby a selling price, thus

total estimated cost + estimated profit = selling price.

The cost estimate appears as follows shown in Figure 10.1.

Working through the form:

Materials
The total estimate for materials needed to complete the job, including any normal allowance for wastage or scrap, will be computed:

quantity of materials × price for each type of material.

Usually, current market prices of materials will be used in the estimate, to be in line with the prices of possible competitors. But alternatively, if stocks of the material are held in store, management may decide to use actual prices paid, (using either LIFO, FIFO, AVCO or standard costs methods – see Chapter 3).

FilGURE 10.1

A   COST ESTIMATE

DATE: _____   No:

CUSTOMER: _____

JOB DESCRIPTION: _____

Materials	QUANTITY	x	PRICE £	*TOTAL VALUE* £
				£

Labour	HOURS	x	RATE PER HOUR £	
				£

Direct Expenses			COST £	
				£

Factory Overheads	HOURS	x	RATE PER HOUR £	
				£

TOTAL MANUFACTURING COST ⟶ £

add   SELLING AND ADMINISTRATION COST   £

ESTIMATED TOTAL COSTS   [TC] ↓   £

£

add   PROFIT MARGIN ⎯ on cost (Total Cost × Profit on cost %)

or ⎿ on s/price (Total cost/(100% − Profit on sales %) − Total Cost)   £

SELLING PRICE | TOTAL COST PLUS PROFIT MARGIN | £

Labour

The estimated number of direct labour hours required to produce the order will be calculated, as well as the hours to be spent on any related work such as set-up time of the machinery and other direct labour hours expected in the production process. Thus the various grades of staff involved in manufacturing the product will be listed along with their corresponding expected hours and the respective rates of pay. The computation then is

> number of hours × rate per hour.

Direct expenses

It may be decided by management that some of the work will need to be completed by third parties such as subcontractors. Their costs will also be included in the estimate.

Factory overheads

The overheads recovery rate, perhaps based on the direct labour hour absorption rate basis, will be computed and included in the estimate:

> number of direct labour hours estimated for the job
> × overhead absorption rate per hour.

The overall total *manufacturing (or production) cost* of the job will thus be arrived at:

> materials + labour + direct expenses
> + absorbed factory overhead.

Job cost estimates often include the costs of other functions of the business, such as distribution, selling and administration costs. The objective of this is to provide management with an estimated overall *total cost* of the job.

Distribution, selling and administration costs

The estimated charge to cover these costs is often calculated by the use of a percentage figure on the total production costs as computed above. The percentage rate will have been predetermined by calculating the relationship of the selling and administration

costs to the production costs (in this example using budgeted information) as follows:

$$\frac{\text{Budgeted distribution,}}{\text{Budgeted production costs}} \times \frac{100}{1}$$

$$= \text{Budgeted recovery \%}$$

Alternatively, the ratio can be based on prior periods' actual relationships between the costs:

$$\frac{\begin{array}{c}\text{Actual distribution,}\\ \text{selling and administration costs}\end{array}}{\begin{array}{c}\text{Actual production cost for the same}\\ \text{accounting period}\end{array}} \times \frac{100}{1}$$

$$= \text{Historic recovery \%}$$

There are, however, a number of other methods which could be used, for example as a percentage of the prime cost or as a percentage of direct labour costs.

The rationale for including these charges in the estimate is that distribution, selling and administration costs are being incurred (a) before a customer places an order; (b) when the order is received; and (c) at the time of the delivery and following the delivery.

The sum of the estimated total manufacturing costs plus the estimated distribution, selling and administration costs thus provides the *estimated total cost*.

Estimated profit margin

The estimated profit is the difference between the total estimated cost and the quoted selling price. It may be computed in a number of ways, but the two most common methods used are: (i) as a percentage on estimated total cost, or (ii) as a percentage on selling price.

Percentage on estimated total cost

This is also known as the 'mark-up' method: the costs are marked up; that is, added to, by applying a percentage rate to the total estimated cost, to arrive at the selling price. The difference between the two figures is the estimated profit margin – the mark-up.

Example:
Estimated total costs: £10 000
Mark-up percentage: 30%
Profit margin
  is therefore: £3000 (£10 000 × 30%)
Selling price will be: £13 000 – (£10 000 + £3 000)

Percentage on selling price

This method is also known as the 'margin' method, the profit being calculated on the selling price. But with a cost estimate, the selling price is not known until the estimated profit has been computed:

cost + profit = selling price

(that is unless the selling price has already been fixed). To resolve this apparent 'Catch 22' situation it is necessary to remember that the *selling price* in the margin method is *always* 100 per cent. So, when given the expected profit percentage, it follows that the *total cost* in percentage terms will always be:

100% – the profit percentage rate.

Example:
Selling price, always = 100%
Profit margin, say = 30%
Total cost, therefore = 70%

To arrive at the profit margin divide the total cost figure by the total cost percentage and then deduct the total cost amount from the result.
  Alternatively, to arrive directly at the selling price, divide the estimated total cost by the total cost per cent. The profit margin is the difference between the two figures:

total cost – selling price

Example:
Expected profit margin = 30%
Estimated total cost = £6300
Selling price = £6300 divided by 70%
  = £9000
Profit margin = £9000 – £6300
  = £2700
Checking this:
  30% of £9000 = £2700

On completion of the cost estimate the selling price will then be quoted to the customer. Assuming that the price is accepted and the order secured, the job can then be started and a job number allocated to it.

Worked example

AAT COST ACCOUNTING AND BUDGETING (1991)

A company has been asked to price Job AX This job requires the following:

Direct material	£3788
Direct labour	£1100
Direct expenses	£422

Factory overheads are absorbed on a machine-hour basis, based on the budgeted information: budgeted production overhead £600 000; budgeted machine hours 50 000.
  Administrative overhead is absorbed at the rate of 20% on factory cost.
  The number of machine hours spent on this job was 120.

Required:
Compute the price for this job, given that the company profit margin is equal to 10% of the price.

Solution:
Cost Estimate
Job AX

	£	
Materials	3 788	
Labour	1 100	
Direct expenses	422	
Factory overheads	1 440	See Note 1
Factory cost	6 750	
Administrative overheads	1 350	See Note 2
Estimated total cost	8 100	
Profit margin	900	See Note 3
Selling price	9 000	

Note 1:
Budgeted absorption rate:
£600 000/50 000 hours = £12 per machine hour
120 machine hours × 12 per hour
Note 2:
Factory cost = £6750; 20% thereof = £1 350

Note 3:

Selling price = 100%
Profit margin = 10%
Total cost   = 90%
Total cost divided by 90% = £9 000; profit margin therefore £900.

Job accounts

Job accounts will be prepared for each job to record the production elements of cost. Job accounts are held within the work-in-progress ledger. The account appears as shown in Figure 10.2.

The entries will emanate from the following documents and data.

Materials

Raw materials directly identifiable with the job will be debited to the account, the source documents being suppliers' invoices (or priced goods received notes); or from materials issues notes if the goods are taken from stores.

The job account is also known as the job card (or job sheet) and will record the quantities of materials used as well as values. This provides management with the 'tool of comparison': it will be possible to compare the original estimates of materials consumption and costs per the cost estimate with the actual costs and consumption.

Labour

As the job works its way through the Production Departments the direct labour hours utilised will be booked against the job, originally on time sheets, and then into the job account itself, with the payroll costs applicable to those hours worked being debited accordingly to the job account.

Management will generally require an analysis of the labour hours and costs, including overtime hours worked, rectification hours and so on, as the job progresses. This information will also be compared against the original cost estimate.

Direct expenses

These costs will also be charged to the job account, with detailed information entered in the account.

Factory overheads

As the job progresses, factory overheads will be debited to the job account, using one of the overhead absorption recovery rates discussed.

FIGURE 10.2

A JOB ACCOUNT					
DR		JOB NUMBER			CR
			£		£
RAW MATERIALS	Quantity	Price			
DIRECT LABOUR	Hours	Rate			
DIRECT EXPENSES				TRANSFER TO FINISHED GOODS	
FACTORY OVERHEADS	Hours	Rate		TRANSFER TO COST OF GOODS SOLD	

The job account (along with all the job accounts for all the other jobs being produced) will be a constituent of the work-in-progress control account, therefore job accounts are memorandum accounts and kept in the memorandum Work-in-Progress Ledger. At the end of the accounting period, when each job account has been balanced, the sum of the closing balances of all the jobs will equal the closing balance on the work-in-progress control account.

On completion of a particular job, the job account will be closed by a credit entry transferring the costs to either the finished goods account (when the job is physically transferred to the finished goods stores), or to the cost of goods sold account, if the item was shipped immediately to the customer.

Job profit and loss account

With the customers having been billed and the sales entries recorded in the ledgers, management will require details of whether each individual job has resulted in a profit or loss. This information is supplied through a supporting schedule to the costing profit and loss account which will be produced for each accounting period.

The following illustrates such a costing profit and loss account:

Worked example

LCCI COST ACCOUNTING (1994)

Oxy Ltd manufactures special components for customers. A system of job costing is in use. The following details relate to two jobs, numbered 2596 and 2597, which were completed in Week 20:

Direct materials: the stores ledger for Material X, which is used in both jobs, showed the following entries:

Opening balance, Week 18: 10 units at £1.80 each
Receipts: Day 1, Week 18: 100 units at £2.35 each
           Day 1, Week 20: 100 units at £2.47 each
Issues: Day 2, Week 19: Job 2596, 40 units
           Day 2, Week 20: Job 2597, 20 units
Closing balance, Week 20: 150 units.

The company uses the weighted average method of pricing.

Direct labour:

	Job 2596 hours	Job 2597 hours
Welding at £4 per hour	3	5
Finishing at £4.50 per hour	16	14

Direct expenses: the company paid £380 for the hire of a special machine for testing the welds on each job. This charge is to be apportioned on the basis of welding hours.

Overheads: All overheads are charged to jobs at 20% on prime cost.

The finished jobs were collected by the customer, who paid £480 for Job 2596 and £550 for Job 2597.

Required:
Prepare a detailed cost and profit statement for each job.

Solution:

Profit Statement – Week 20

	Job 2596 £	Job 2597 £	Total £
Selling price	480.00	550.00	1 030.00
Cost of manufacture			
Material	92.00	48.00	140.00
			See Note 1
Labour	84.00	83.00	176.00
			See Note 2
Direct Expenses	142.50	237.00	380.00
			See Note 3
Overheads	35.20	26.20	61.40
			See Note 4
Gross profit for week	126.30	155.30	281.60
As % or sales	26.3	28.2	27.3

Note 1: Materials

Date/ Details	Receipts Units	£	Issues Units	£	Balance Units	£	Average price per unit
Opening balance					10	18.00	£1.80
Day 1, Week 1							
Receipts	100	235.00			110	253.00	£2.30
Issues –							
Job 2596			4	92.00	70	161.00	£2.30
Day 1, Week 2							
Receipts	100	247.00			170	408.00	£2.40
Issues –							
Job 2597			20	48.00	150	36.00	£2.40

Note 2: Labour

	Job 2596	Job 2597
Welding	£12	£20
Finishing	£72	£63
Total	£84	£83

Note 3: Direct Expenses

	Job 2956	*Job 2957*	*Total*
Hours	3	5	8
Cost	£142.50	£237.50	£380.00

Note 4: Overheads Absorbed

	Job 2596	*Job 2597*
Prime cost	176	131
205 thereof	£35.20	£26.20

Batch costing

This costing method is used when a specific quantity of identical articles or products is manufactured together as one 'job'. For example, a customer may order 1000 identical metal brackets from an engineering plant, but only one job account need be opened, not a thousand. The production costs of materials, labour and overheads will be debited to the one job account. On completion of the batch, the cost unit is the cost of the whole batch as shown in the job account. But if the cost of each article is required, the following formula can be used:

> Manufacturing cost of the batch
> ──────────────────────────────
> Number of units produced in the batch

So, if the total cost of the 1000 metal brackets amounts to £10 000 the unit cost of the batch is £10 000, and the unit cost of each article is £10 each.

The CIMA definition of batch costing is '*a form of specific order costing; the attribution of costs to batches*'.

A batch need not always relate to specific customers' orders, it can also relate to 'in-house' orders. For example, many jobbing manufacturers produce components which form part of one-off products made specifically for customers. Rather than make these components on the same one-off basis along with the main product when the order comes along, management may decide that it is more economical to produce these components in quantity because of

their universality. These components will then be held by the Stores Department until required, to be used on receipt of specific customers' orders for the manufacture of the main product. An internal order – issued by the Stores Department – will thus be raised for the production of the components.

Similarly, batch costing may be used by companies that assemble mass-produced articles. Here, some or all of the parts that comprise the finished article may be made, in batches, by the company. The finished parts will then be held by the Stores Department and issued to Production when required.

The production costs of each batch will be recorded in job accounts (which could also be designated 'batch accounts'), with the unit cost of each component being calculated using the cost/number of units produced basis.

In many ways, costing for batches is similar to costing for continuous operations (i.e. process costing – see Chapter 12), because for the production costs are not attachable to a single individual product as it is being processed but rather the cost of the group of products is *averaged* over the number of items that have been produced. For example, the production of bread is done in batches and either batch costing or process costing could be used to record the production costs of the bakery.

Summary

- Job costing is a specific order costing system used for jobs made to customers' orders which, generally, are completed within one statutory accounting period (normally one year).
- On receipt of an enquiry from the customer, the manufacturer (or service provider) will prepare a cost estimate. This shows the elements of cost, thus providing the total manufacturing costs, and also the charge to the prospective job to cover the costs of the distribution, selling and administration functions. The total of manufacturing costs plus the other costs is called total cost.
- To this is added the profit to arrive at the selling price. The profit margin may be calculated in a number of ways but the two most frequently used methods are: percentage on-cost, and profit on selling price.

- The percentage on-cost method adds a percentage profit to the total cost figure: the mark-up. The selling price will be the sum of the profit figure plus the total cost amount.
- The profit on selling price method is called the margin method. Management will fix a profit margin, say 25% on selling price. Selling price is always 100%. Therefore the total cost, in percentage terms, will be 100% minus the fixed profit margin percentage. (For example, 100% − 25% = 75%: 75% therefore represents the total cost percentage.) This percentage is then used to arrive at the selling price, by dividing the total cost value by the total cost per cent.
- When the order is received a job account will be opened to record the elements of cost chargeable to the job.
- On completion of the job, a transfer of the total production cost will be made, closing the job account and debiting either finished goods or the cost of goods sold account.

- Management will require details of the profit or loss on each job. This is provided by analysing the costing profit and loss in a supporting report. The original estimated cost figures will also be reported on the analysis, and variations from the estimate will be investigated, to assist future performance.
- Batch costing is a form of job costing whereby a quantity of identical items are manufactured together as one job. Therefore only one job account is opened for the batch. The elements of cost covering all the items in the batch are charged to the account. Batches may be made to customers' order or for stock, the articles being held in store until an order is received.
- The unit cost of a batch is the cost of manufacturing the batch itself. Thus management can compare the manufacturing costs of similar batches.
- Frequently, however, a unit cost is required for each individual item made in the batch. This is arrived at by averaging: total batch cost divided by the number of items made in the batch.

Examination Questions

1 A LEVEL (ULEAC) 1991

The Acme Shelving Co. Ltd manufactures shelving brackets in batches of 300. During May, Batch No. 23 was machined at a rate of 15 per hour. Sixty of the brackets failed to pass inspection, but of these, 40 were thought to be rectifiable. The remaining 20 were scrapped, and the scrap value was credited to the batch cost account. Rectification work took nine hours.

	Batch No. 23 £
Raw materials per bracket	1.60
Scrap value per bracket	0.86
Machinists' hourly rate	4.20
Machine hour overhead rate (running time only)	3.60
Setting up of machine: Normal machining	21.00
Rectification	18.00

Calculate:
(a) The cost of Batch No. 23 in total and per unit, if all units pass inspection.
(b) The actual cost of Batch No. 23, in total and per unit, after crediting the recovery value of the scrapped components, and including the rectification costs.
(c) The loss incurred because of defective work.

2 A LEVEL (AEB) 1993

Downpike Ltd is a manufacturing company that utilises a large number of different machines in its production process and uses machine hour rates to absorb the production overheads in job costs.

The following details are available for machine XR8.

1. The cost of the machine is £24 000; estimated life is 8 years. The straight line method of depreciation is applied.
2. Machine department overheads per annum are:

	£
Heat and light	7 000
Supervision	6 000

The area of this department is 8750 square metres, of which machine XR8 occupies 250 square metres. The number of machines in the department is 20.

3. The annual cost of repair equipment for XR8 is £110.
4. Machine running time is 2500 hours per annum (2300 hours production and 200 hours setting up).
5. The power cost is 5p per hour for both setting up and production.
6. The labour rate for machinists is £4.80 per hour. When machines are being set up, full-time attention is needed

from the machinists, but once machines are in production then one machinist can control three machines.

7. The company has arranged insurance coverage for the machines for an annual premium of £8000 (total cost of all machines is £768000).

A typical job carried out by this machine is coded Z22. This job involves using 15 kilos of material costing £2.50 per kilo, 12 machine hours and 3 hours' assembly work using labour paid £3.60 per hour.

Required:

(a) Prepare a statement showing the machine hour rate for XR8 (correct to two decimal places).

(b) Calculate the job cost of Z22.

3 A AAT COST ACCOUNTING AND BUDGETING 1991
A manufacturing company has prepared the following budgeted information for Year 2:

	£
Direct material	800000
Direct labour	200000
Direct expenses	40000
Production overhead	600000
Administrative overhead	328000

Budgeted activity levels include:

	Units
Budgeted production	600000
Machine hours	50000
Labour hours	40000

It has recently spent heavily upon advanced technological machinery and reduced its workforce. As a consequence it is thinking about changing its basis for overhead absorption from a percentage of direct labour cost to either a machine hour or labour hour basis. The administrative overhead is to be absorbed as a percentage of factory cost.

Required:

(a) Prepare predetermined overheads absorption rates for production overheads based upon the three different bases for absorption mentioned above.

(b) Select the overhead absorption rate that you think the organisation should use, giving reasons for your decision.

(c) The company has been asked to price Job AX. This job requires the following:

Direct material	£3788
Direct labour	£1100
Direct expenses	£422
Machine hours	120
Labour hours	220

Compute the price for this job using the absorption rate selected in (b) above, given that the company profit margin is equal to 10% of the price.

4 AAT COST ACCOUNTING AND BUDGETING 1993
Swithern Ltd is considering putting in a bid for a job coded 'Zeron' that would have the following costs:

Materials
11000 kilos Rayex at £4 per kilo
8000 kilos Nayon at £2.50 per kilo

Labour
Dept A 2500 hours at £4 per hour
Dept B 1600 hours at £5 per hour

Production overheads
The policy is to use predetermined overhead rates for each department based upon:
Dept A: Per labour hour
Dept B: Per % of labour cost

Budgeted information for the year under review was:
Direct material £763000
Labour Dept A 38000 hours at £4 per hour.
Labour Dept B 25000 hours at £5 per hour
Production Overhead Dept A £760000
Production Overhead Dept B £750000
Administrative overhead £510000 and to be recovered on the basis of production cost.

You are told that usual company policy is to take a profit of 40% of price.

Required:
Cost job Zeron for Swithern plc and calculate the bid price that they should tender.

5 ACCA COST AND MANAGEMENT ACCOUNTING 1 1991
A company provides a building repairs and maintenance service. A job costing system is in operation in order to identify the cost, and profit, of each job carried out. Several jobs are in progress at any one time. One such job is Job 126, which was started and completed in the month just ended.

Quantities of Material P were issued from stores to the job, as well as other materials as required. Raw material issues are priced at the end of each month on a weighted average basis.

Overtime is worked as necessary to meet the general requirements of the business, and is paid at a premium of 30% over the basic rate for direct personnel. The basic rate is £6.00 per hour. Overheads are absorbed into job costs at the end of each month at an actual rate per direct labour hour. Idle time, material wastage, and rectification work after jobs are completed, are a normal feature of the business. Idle time is not expected to exceed 2% of direct hours charged to jobs. Wastage is not expected to exceed 1% of the cost of materials issued to jobs. Rectification costs are not expected to exceed 1.5% of direct costs. All such costs are not charged as direct costs of individual jobs.

Information concerning Job 126 is as follows:
Issues of Material P were 960 kilos. Issues of other materials were costed at £2030. Of the total materials issued to the job, wastage cost £42 and materials used for rectification cost £33. The hours of direct personnel working on the job were 496. These included 37 overtime hours, 10 hours of idle time, and 12 hours spent on rectification work.

Information for all work carried out on jobs during the month is as follows:

Opening stock of Material P was 3100 kilos, valued at £5594.

Purchases during the month were 3500 kilos at £1.81 per kilo, and 3800 kilos at £1.82 per kilo. 7060 kilos of Material P were issued from stores to jobs, including 60 kilos which were subsequently wasted and 340 kilos which were used for rectification work.

Other materials issued to jobs were costed at £19 427 (including £236 wastage and £197 rectification). Hours of direct personnel paid at basic rate were 3640 with a further 290 hours paid at overtime rate. These total hours include 82 hours of idle time and 37 hours spent on rectification work.

Other costs incurred in the month were:

Supervisory labour	£3 760
Depreciation	£585
Cleaning materials	£63
Stationery and telephone	£275
Rent and rates	£940
Vehicle running costs	£327
Other administration	£688

Required:
(a) Prepare a statement of the costs associated with Job 126.
(b) Provide, and comment upon, any additional information that may be useful in controlling the business.

11
Contract Costing

In this chapter we shall be examining the specific order cost accounting methods used for long-term contracts. A customer requiring something to be built or made specifically for them will usually issue a written order or contract. The time taken to complete the project may be short, meaning that the job will be completed in less than one year, or it will take longer than a year to finish. Specific order jobs can therefore be categorised as either short-term contracts or long-term contracts.

By taking less than one calendar year to complete short-term contracts, the profit or loss result will be reported in the accounting period in which the customer receives the finished goods or the completed project. So a short-term job can be ordered and finished in an accounting period, and billed to the customer in the same period; or, if uncompleted at the end of the year when it was ordered, the costs will be carried forward as work in progress to the next accounting year. It will then be finished in this following period and invoiced to the customer. The costing system used to account for short-term contracts is Job Costing, the subject of Chapter 10.

Long-term contracts, on the other hand, are those contracts with an extended life, taking longer than one calendar year to complete. Thus, more than one accounting period is involved between the commencement of a contract and its completion and handing over to the customer. For these long-term contracts the costing system used is *contract costing*.

Contract costing methods are widely used in the building and construction industries: for example, construction of new offices and factories, roads and motorways, ships, shopping precincts, theme parks, civil engineering projects and so on. It is also used in long term building refurbishment works and other works that generally take more than one calendar year to complete.

The CIMA definition of contract costing is: *'a form of specific order costing: attribution of cost to individual contracts'*.

Firms engaged in long-term contract work have two major accounting problems to deal with: how much profit or loss arising from the contract should be taken into each accounting period's profit and loss account, and how the project will be funded over the extended period of construction.

To deal with the matter of funding first: with short-term jobs, funding problems do not usually arise if working capital is sufficient: the firm will complete the job, bill the customer and expect payment to be received within the settlement terms. Short-term contractors can, of course, assist their cash flow further by requiring customers to make payments on account, perhaps by paying a deposit. Or they may have a fixed payment structure, for example, one-third payment when placing the order, one-third on delivery and the final third some time after delivery.

But with long-term contracts it is doubtful whether the contractor could finance the project in this way. Therefore the arrangements for payment from customers during the course of construction are generally rigidly structured and constitute an essential part of the contract. The customer (who is also known as the *contractee*), will be contracted to make *payments on account* in the interim periods.

Dealing now with the problem of profit and loss: long-term contracts by definition may go on for a number of years so it is neither practicable nor prudent to wait until the contract has been completed fully and handed over to the customer before the profit or loss is reported.

Imagine a five-year contract to build a new motorway. To wait until the fifth year to include a profit or loss on the whole project would clearly distort the fifth year's figures. And in years one to four, without showing a profit or loss here, the picture of the firm's considerable activities in these interim years is not revealed. For shareholders too there could be a problem: perhaps just one dividend in five years – and that at the very end of the contract. Clearly, therefore, a fair view of the contractor's activities is not reflected in each year's Profit and Loss Account; and from an investment viewpoint, to have to wait for a return for such a long time would probably be unacceptable.

Contract costing methods, when in accordance with SSAP 9 (Stocks and long-term contracts), enables management to overcome these profit and loss difficulties by providing acceptable methods of accounting for long term contracts.

The contract account

First we shall look at the structure of a long-term contract account.

Each contract will have its own contract account, clearly identifiable and separate from all other current contracts. Contract accounts are held within the memorandum work-in-progress ledger and are memorandum accounts to the Work-in-Progress Control Account.

The contract account will be used to collect all the costs and expenses incurred by the job, that is, the familiar elements of cost: materials, labour and overheads. It will also record the monies receivable from work done as the job progresses, and also the profit and loss details. It has two sections: a costs section and a 'trading account' section.

Costs section

This section of the typical contract account will appear in Figure 11.1.

Working through Figure 11.1:

FIGURE 11.1

COSTS SECTION OF A TYPICAL CONTRACT ACCOUNT		
DR	CONTRACT ACCOUNT	*CR*
	£	£
MATERIALS	MATERIALS RETURNS	
LABOUR	MATERIALS CLOSING STOCKS	
	CARRIED DOWN	
SUBCONTRACTORS' CHARGES		
OTHER SITE COSTS		
HEAD OFFICE COSTS		
PLANT AND EQUIPMENT	PLANT AND EQUIPMENT AT	
	VALUATION CARRIED DOWN	
	BALANCE CARRIED DOWN	
BALANCE BROUGHT DOWN		

Materials

The materials charged to the contract will consist of materials delivered directly to the site by the suppliers, plus perhaps materials taken from the firm's central stores or depot. At the end of each accounting period the unused materials remaining on site will be valued at cost, generally using recognised stock evaluations methods such as actual cost, FIFO, average cost or standard costs (see Chapter 3), and carried down to the next accounting period.

Labour

Staff employed by the firm who spend all their time on the contract will be charged directly to the contract. Examples of staff involved on site who can be allocated directly are: builders and labourers, supervisory staff, skilled craftsmen and clerical staff. The project may be large enough to warrant employment of its own Site Director, in which case his or her costs and staff support costs will also be charged directly to the job.

Expenses

All the expenses incurred by the project will be charged to the contract, as they are direct expenses and can thus be directly allocated to it. For example electricity charges, water supplies, hire of plant, and security costs. There may also be an office located at the site. The costs of running this office, the electricity costs, the telephone costs, printing and stationery expenses and so on will also be treated as directly incurred costs of the contract and therefore debited to the account.

In addition to these expenses, other clearly identifiable costs of the contract, such as professional fees and fuel supplies, will be charged to it. Thus all the directly allocatable expenses of the project will be charged to the contract account.

Head office charges

Some contractors also decide that in order to arrive at a realistic cost of each contract it is correct and necessary to apportion the whole of (or a proportion of) the costs of running the head office/central administration functions to each contract. For example, the central drawing office and certain other central departments exist essentially as a service for all the firm's contracts. When such an allocation is made each individual contract will be charged with a proportion of the head office costs.

One method of apportioning these costs is based on the contract value of each contract, using the following formula:

$$\frac{\text{Total budgeted head office costs}}{\text{Total budgeted value of contracts}}$$

So if, say, the total head office costs were £100 000 and the total value of all the expected contracts in a budgeted period is £1 000 000, then an absorption rate of 10 per cent of each contract value will be used to absorb the head office/central costs. Thus each contract will be debited with a head office charge equivalent to 10 per cent of the sales value of the respective contract. The setting of budgets is explained in Chapter 19.

Plant and equipment

A special feature of contract costing is that the cost of capital equipment used on a project, such as cranes, tools, site vehicles and other fixed assets, is a charge to the contract account, either at the original cost price or at valuation. Then, at the end of each accounting period, the equipment will be revalued. This is done either by physical check and valuation (usually, by professional valuers), or by providing for the wear and tear and use of the assets through a depreciation charge. The resulting valuation of the (written down) equipment at the end of each accounting period will then be carried forward to the next accounting period. Thus the difference between the cost amounts charged to the contract and the amount carried forward to the next period represents the depreciation charge for the accounting period.

To illustrate the first section of the account we shall work through an example.

Worked example

A LEVEL (UNIVERSITY OF LONDON) 1994

The Beeching Contracting Co. has two contracts in hand at 31 May:

	Contract No.	
	93/5	93/9
	£	£
Contract price	600 000	800 000
Direct materials issued	110 000	80 000
Materials returned to stores	1 000	2 000
Direct wages	96 000	64 000
Wages accrued at 31 May	4 000	5 000
Plant installed at cost	60 000	90 000
Establishment expenses	50 000	30 000
Direct expenses	30 000	20 000
Direct expenses accrued at 31/5	2 000	1 000
Work certified by architect	320 000	160 000
Cost of work not yet certified	20 000	30 000
Value of plant at 31 May	40 000	80 000
Materials on site at 31 May	11 000	8 000
Cash received from contractee	300 000	120 000

In calculating profit on uncompleted contracts the company applied the formula 2/3 × notional profit to the ratio of cash received to the value of work certified. Retention monies on Contract 93/5 have been agreed at 10 per cent of the contract price: there are no retention monies applicable to Contract 93/9.

Required:
Show the contract accounts for both contracts as they would appear in Beeching's books at 31 May.

Solution, cost section (see page 127):

The cost entries in each account are straightforward extracts from the question. Wages accrued and direct expenses accrued have been shown as separate entries, but these amounts could be added to their respective headings. You will note also that the difference between the plant installed and the valuation represents the depreciation charge. Materials on site carried down, and the plant carried down, will be brought forward as opening entries in the next accounting period. However, the balance of the cost section is carried down to the second section, the 'trading account' section, *within the same accounting period*. This balancing figure represents the actual total costs incurred to date on the contracts.

In the second section, entries will be made for the following:

Work certified;
Work not yet certified; and
Attributable profit (notional profit and profit provision).

Before completing this second section, explanations of the entries need to be made.

Work certified

As discussed earlier, a long-term contract may take years to complete and requires continuous financing throughout its construction. It would be unreasonable (and in the majority of cases, impossible) to expect the contractor to wait until the end of the contract before being paid by the customer. Equally, it would be unreasonable to expect the customer to pay for the whole contract before construction commences. Therefore payments on account – progress payments – are a major feature of the contract so that the customer pays for work done as the contract progresses. These progress payments are based on *interim valuations* and these may be calculated monthly or at longer intervals. The interim valuation will usually involve the appointment of a professional valuer, a Quantity Surveyor, who will make regular visits to the site and assess and agree with the contractor's representatives how much work has been completed to the date of the visit.

When each interim valuation is completed an *Architect's Certificate* will be issued, with copies being sent to the customer and the contractor. This 'measured valuation' will include an element of profit. The Architect's Certificate becomes the basis, the authority, for the contractor's interim invoices; the customer will therefore owe the contractor the amount so certified, subject to a *retention*, which is discussed later in this chapter.

The accounting entries in the contractor's books to record the interim valuations are: debit the customer's account, and credit the contract account, as *work certified*.

Work not yet certified

It follows that as contracts are progressing continuously there will be work completed at the end of accounting periods which the Quantity Surveyor will not yet have seen and evaluated. This is *work not yet certified*. The contractor will value this work, *at cost value*, and credit the second section of the contract account, carrying down the amount to the next accounting period. ('Work not yet certified' is thus the equivalent to work in progress in a manufacturing firm.)

DR   Contract 93/5 ACCOUNT   CR

Date		£	Date		£
	Materials issued	111 000		Materials returned to store	1 000
			31 May	Materials on site carried down	11 000
	Direct wages	96 000			
	Direct wages accured	4 000		This is the cost section	
	Plant installed at cost	60 000	31 May	Value of plant carried down	40 000
	Establishment expenses	50 000			
	Direct expenses	30 000			
	Direct expenses accrued	2 000			
			31 May	Balance carried down	300 000
		352 000			352 000
31 May	Balance brought down	300 000		'Trading account' section – see page 131	

DR   Contract 93/9 ACCOUNT   CR

Date		£	Date		£
	Materials issued	80 000		Materials returned to store	2 000
			31 May	Materials on site carried down	8 000
	Direct wages	64 000			
	Direct wages accrued	5 000			
	Plant installed at cost	90 000	31 May	Value of plant carried down	80 000
	Establishment expenses	30 000			
	Direct expenses	20 000			
	Direct expenses accrued	1 000			
			31 May	Balance carried down	200 000
		352 000			290 000
31 May	Balance brought down	200 000			

Notional profit

The notional profit on the contract to date is simply the difference between total costs brought down from the first section of the contract account, and the total of work certified plus work not yet certified entered on the credit side. It is thus the balancing figure between the two sides of the account, as shown in Figure 11.2. (If the balancing figure is entered on the credit side the costs incurred to date will not have been recovered from the interim charges to the customer, or carried forward as 'work not yet certified' to the next accounting period; thus a loss to date on the contract will have occurred.)

Profit to be taken to profit and loss account

The notional profit is the balancing figure but it is not the profit that will be taken to the profit and loss account for the accounting period.

This is because, until the project is fully completed and handed over to the customer it is not absolutely certain that a profit will result. The accounting concept of prudency dictates that:

Profits	Losses
Revenue and profits are not anticipated but are included in the profit and loss account only when reasonably certain to be realised.	Losses are to be provided for in the profit and loss account for all known or estimated losses as soon as the information about the losses comes to light.

SSAP 2 (Disclosure of accounting policies) defines the four basic fundamental accounting concepts which underlie the preparation of periodic financial accounts. The prudence concept paraphrased above is one of the four.

But SSAP 9 (Stocks and long-term contracts) does allow interim profits to be taken on long-term contracts because, 'To defer recording turnover and taking profit until completion of a project' may result in the profit and loss account for a particular year reflecting only the completed projects in a year, and therefore not reflecting a fair view of the results of the year's activity on all the other, as yet unfinished, contracts. SSAP 9 goes on to say:

> Where the outcome of a long term contract can be assessed with reasonable certainty, *Attributable Profit* should be calculated on a prudent basis and included in the accounts (p&l and balance sheet) for the period under review.

Prudence therefore dictates that where the outcome, that is, an overall profit, cannot be assessed with reasonable certainty, no profit should be taken to the profit and loss account. But conversely, if a loss on the whole of the contract is expected, then *all* of the expected loss is to be provided for as soon as it is foreseen.

Attributable profit

The notional profit is therefore rarely, if ever, taken directly to the profit and loss account. Instead an

FIGURE 11.2

CONTRACT ACCOUNT EXTRACT SHOWING NOTIONAL PROFIT

DR	CONTRACT ACCOUNT EXTRACT	CR
	BALANCE C/DOWN	COST SECTION
BALANCE B/DOWN	WORK CERTIFIED'	
NOTIONAL PROFIT*	WORK NOT YET CERTIFIED	'TRADING A/C' SECTION

*BALANCING FIGURE

attributable profit, if any, prudently calculated, will be credited to each interim accounting period's profit and loss account, thereby reflecting the activity on the long-term contract in each period. The contractor consequently needs to consider whether, in his/her view, a profit is 'reasonably certain' to be the outcome on the eventually completed project.

As a backdrop to these deliberations, the contractor will normally have prepared an estimate of the contract as good commercial practice: total costs (plus, perhaps, provisions for unforeseen costs) plus an element of profit, to arrive at the contract price. Therefore, at the outset, management will have been reasonably certain that a profit would be the result. As the project progresses, however, additional costs can, and often do, occur.

Many of these additional costs may be recoverable from the customer and will thus be included in the contract. For example, inflation and groundwork problems. But in some cases these extra costs cannot be passed on and must be borne by the contractor, thus eating into the expected overall profit and possibly affecting the 'reasonable certainty' of a favourable outcome.

Management therefore needs to review the end position at each interim accounting period. To help them to do this, the *degree of completion* of a project has to be taken into consideration.

It follows that as time passes the overall outcome for the project – profit or loss – becomes more certain. If, for example, a five-year project is 20 per cent complete, management cannot expect to know with reasonable certainty the extent of further costs being incurred. Therefore the overall profit outcome of the project is not reasonably certain: unforeseen calamities may result in costs not recoverable from the customer arising during the remaining 80 per cent construction period. As the project gets nearer to completion, however, management can expect to become more certain that an overall profit will result. So, after three years of work, say, it may be possible for management to estimate with a reasonable degree of certainty the overall total costs to complete the whole project and then to compare this figure with the contract price to see if a profit is or is not reasonably certain to be achieved.

The degree of completion plays a key role in management's assessment when judging the final profit or loss outcome of a project. The requirements of SSAP 9,

prudence, and past accounting tradition and practice, can be summarised in the following table of degrees of completion. This provides a formula to enable contractors to provide for an interim profit or loss on the projects while construction continues.

Degrees of completion	Action	Formula (if profit reasonably certain on whole project)
0 to 30%	No profit taken unless certain that an overall profit will be earned on the whole project. If it is possible to estimate the total costs to complete use formula A. Otherwise no profit taken.	A
30% to 80%	Estimate the remaining costs to complete and use formula A. If remaining costs cannot be estimated but it is reasonably certain that an overall profit will be earned, use formula B.	A or B
80% to 90%	Estimate the remaining costs and use formula A.	A

Formula A is given in Figure 11.3.
Formula B is shown in Figure 11.4.

Reverting now to the A Level question in the worked example on pages 125–6, you will note that Formula B applies to both contracts. The completed section two of the accounts will thus appear as is shown in Figure 11.5.

You will note that the notional profit in Contract 93/5 amounted to £40 000. Using the two-thirds Formula B the attributable profit taken to profit and loss account amounted to £25 000. This left £15 000 as a profit provision.

Profit provision

The profit provision represents the element of prudence to cover future costs that may or may not arise. In this question 37.5 per cent of the notional profit has been carried forward and 62.5 per cent has been taken to profit and loss. The degree of prudence

FIGURE 11.3

FORMULA A

FORMULA A

£

CONTRACT PRICE A (VALUE OF WHOLE CONTRACT)

ACTUAL COSTS TO DATE (PER CONTRACT ACCOUNT)
PLUS ESTIMATED COSTS TO COMPLETE
TOTAL COSTS TO COMPLETE B

ANTICIPATED PROFIT A – B

FORMULA TO CALCULATE ATTRIBUTABLE PROFIT:

$$\text{ANTICIPATED PROFIT} \times \frac{\text{CASH RECEIVED}}{\text{CONTRACT PRICE}}$$

---

exercised is dependent on management's view. For example, some may consider that the two-thirds proportion is too great and should perhaps be 50:50: 50 per cent carried forward and 50 per cent taken to profits; others may feel that a provision of a quarter more fairly reflects the risk of unforeseen costs and therefore a proportion of three-quarters will be taken to profit.

To illustrate both calculation methods the following details refer to a four-year contract:

Year 1:

Overall contract value:	£1 000 000
Costs incurred to date:	£100 000
Work certified to date:	£150 000
Work not yet certified at year end:	£50 000
Notional Profit to date:	£100 000
Cash received to date:	£135 000

The project is 15 per cent complete with regards to value (£150 000/£1 000 000). Management have decided that overall profitability cannot with reasonable certainty be foreseen at this early stage; therefore no interim profit will be taken in the first year and the £100 000 notional profit will be carried forward to Year 2 as a profit provision.

Year 2:

Costs incurred to date:	£300 000
Work certified to date:	£400 000
Work not yet certified at year end:	£50 000
Notional Profit to date:	£150 000
Cash received to date:	£360 000

The project has now reached 40 per cent completion (£400 000/£1 000 000). This is within the 30%–80% degree of completion band. Assuming that management take the view that they are reasonably certain

FIGURE 11.4

FORMULA B

FORMULA B

£

FORMULA B TO CALCULATE ATTRIBUTABLE PROFIT:-

$$66.6\% \left(\tfrac{2}{3}\right) \times \frac{\text{CASH RECEIVED}}{\text{WORK CERTIFIED}} \times \text{NOTIONAL PROFIT}$$

FIGURE 11.5

COMPLETED SECTION TWO OF THE ACCOUNTS

DR		CONTRACT 93/5 ACCOUNT	CR
	£		£
BALANCE B/DOWN (COSTS TO DATE)	300 000	WORK CERTIFIED	320 000
ATTRIBUTABLE PROFIT*	25 000	WORK NOT YET CERTIFIED	20 000
PROFIT PROVISION	15 000		
	340 000		340 000

$$* \frac{2}{3} \times \frac{£300\,000}{£320\,000} \times £40\,000$$

DR		CONTRACT 93/9 ACCOUNT	CR
	£		£
BALANCE B/DOWN (COSTS TO DATE)	200 000	WORK CERTIFIED	160 000
		WORK NOT YET CERTIFIED	30 000
		LOSS TRANSFERRED TO	
		PROFIT AND LOSS ACCOUNT	10 000
	200 000		200 000

an overall profit will be the outcome, but are unable to quantify the additional estimated costs to the end of the contract, Formula B would be used to calculate the attributable profit, as follows:

$$\frac{2}{3} \times \frac{£360\,000}{£400\,000} \times £150\,000$$

$$= £90\,000 \text{ attributable profit.}$$

Year 3:

Costs incurred to date:	£500 000
Work certified to date:	£850 000
Work not yet certified to date:	£40 000
Notional Profit to date:	£390 000
Receipts from customer to date:	£765 000
Estimated costs to completion:	£300 000

Here the degree of completion is 85 per cent (£850 000/ £1 000 000) and management have estimated the costs to completion. Thus Formula A will be used:

Contract price:	£1 000 000
Actual costs to date:	£500 000
Estimated costs to complete:	£300 000
Total costs to complete:	£800 000
Anticipated profit:	£200 000

Attributable profit calculation:

$$£200\,000 \times \frac{£765\,000}{£1\,000\,000}$$

$$= £153\,000 \text{ attributable profit.}$$

But of this amount you will note that £90 000 has already been taken to the profit and loss account in earlier accounting periods. This has to be deducted, leaving an attributable profit for Year 3 of £63 000.

Year 4:

Costs incurred to date:	£800 000
Work certified:	£1 000 000
Cash received from customer:	£900 000

The accounts for the whole life of the project will appear as shown in Figure 11.6.

Reporting the attributable profit in the profit and loss account

The attributable profit is reported in the profit and loss account in the following fashion:

As *Sales*: the work certified amount for the year
As *Cost of Sales*: total costs for the year plus closing profit provision, less opening profit position, plus

FIGURE 11.6

ACCOUNTS FOR THE WHOLE LIFE OF THE PROJECT

	SUMMARY		
	COSTS	INCOME	PROFIT

DR   CONTRACT ACCOUNT – YEAR 1   CR

	£		£	COSTS	INCOME	PROFIT
COSTS INCURRED	100 000	WORK CERTIFIED	150 000	100 000	150 000	
PROFIT PROVISION C/DOWN	100 000	WORK NOT YET				
		CERTIFIED C/DOWN	50 000			
	200 000		200 000			

DR   CONTRACT ACCOUNT – YEAR 2   CR

	£		£			
WORK NOT YET		PROFIT PROVISION B/DOWN	100 000			
CERTIFIED B/DOWN	50 000					
COSTS INCURRED	200 000	WORK CERTIFIED	250 000	200 000	250 000	
ATTRIBUTABLE		WORK NOT YET				90 000
PROFIT TO P&L	90 000	CERTIFIED C/DOWN	50 000			
PROFIT PROVISION C/DOWN	60 000					
	400 000		400 000			

DR   CONTRACT ACCOUNT – YEAR 3   CR

	£		£			
WORK NOT YET		PROFIT PROVISION B/DOWN	60 000			
CERTIFIED B/DOWN	50 000					
COSTS INCURRED	200 000	WORK CERTIFIED	450 000	200 000	450 000	
ATTRIBUTABLE		WORK NOT YET				63 000
PROFIT TO P&L	63 000	CERTIFIED C/DOWN	40 000			
PROFIT PROVISION C/DOWN	237 000					
	550 000		550 000			

DR   CONTRACT ACCOUNT – YEAR 4   CR

	£		£			
WORK NOT YET		PROFIT PROVISION B/DOWN	237 000			
CERTIFIED B/DOWN	40 000					
COSTS INCURRED	300 000	WORK CERTIFIED	150 000	300 000	150 000	
ATTRIBUTABLE						47 000
PROFIT TO P&L	47 000					
	387 000		387 000			

TOTAL CONTRACT:	800 000	1 000 000	200 000

opening work not yet certified, less closing work not yet certified.

In the first year the entries in the profit and loss account will be:

Sales	£150 000
Cost of sales	£150 000
Profit	Nil

In the second year:

Sales	£250 000
Cost of sales	£160 000
Profit	£90 000

In the third year:

Sales	£450 000
Cost of sales	£387 000
Profit	£63,000

And in the fourth year:

Sales	£150 000
Cost of sales	£103 000
Profit	£47 000

Retention monies

The contract will usually specify that a proportion of monies due to the contractor is withheld by the customer to allow for any rectification work that needs to be carried out after the contract has been completed and handed over. This may be 5 per cent or 10 per cent and upwards of the value of each interim valuation. The customer will receive interim invoices from the contractor, based on the Architect's Certificates, and deduct the agreed contracted percentage, paying the net amount due to the contractor. This deduction is called a *Retention*.

It is a deferred debt owed by the customer to the contractor and may be held for 12 months or longer after the hand over date, to ensure the contractor makes good any defects or carries out rectification work arising. Any costs the customer incurs in that period related directly to correcting defective work will thus be deductible from the retention, but normally the contractor would carry out any remedial work necessary. At the end of the retention period the customer is required to pay over the retention monies withheld.

You will note when calculating the attributable profit that the relationship of cash received to work certified is taken into consideration. The difference between the two figures is normally retention monies. Consequently the attributable profit is further reduced by this relationship, clearly allowing for the worst scenario: that the customer may require rectification work to be undertaken and the contractor will therefore not be paid the retention monies. Prudence clearly in action.

Balance sheet entries

A requirement of SSAP 9 is that stocks at the end of an accounting period are valued at cost or net realisable value and classified under main headings, such as raw materials, work in progress and finished goods. On the balance sheet itself these are grouped under the general heading Stocks.

With long-term contracts, SSAP 9 requires the cost of the work in progress incurred on the contracts to be classified separately from these other types of Stock, and designated 'long-term contract balances'.

The following items comprise '*long-term contract balances*':

Total costs to date
Less amount transferred to cost of sales
Less provision for foreseeable losses
Less payments on account not matched with turnover.

SSAP 9 also requires that the 'recorded turnover in excess of payments on account' is classified as *amounts recoverable on contracts* and shown, again separately disclosed, within the debtors' figure on the balance sheet. This figure will normally be the debit balance on the customer's account, generally representing retention monies.

In some instances customers may have paid more than the sum transferred to profit and loss account as sales (the work certified amount). For instance, the customer may have paid an initial deposit as well as the contractor's periodical interim invoices, resulting in a credit balance on the customers account. This will be shown in the balance sheet as a separate item under the main heading Creditors as *payments on account*.

To illustrate the balance sheet entries, SSAP 9 provides a number of examples and these are depicted as shown in Figure 11.7.

FIGURE 11.7

EXAMPLES OF BALANCE SHEET ENTRIES

BALANCE SHEET ENTRIES (£s)

DR	PROJECT No. 1 CONTRACT ACCOUNT		CR	
COSTS	110	WORK CERTIFIED	145	
ATTRIBUTABLE PROFIT	35			
	145		145	

DR	PROJECT No. 1 CUSTOMER ACCOUNT		CR	
WORK CERTIFIED	145	PAYMENTS ON ACCOUNT	100	DEBTORS:
		BALANCE CARRIED DOWN	45	AMOUNTS RECOVERABLE ON CONTRACTS 45
	145		145	
BALANCE B/DOWN	45			

DR	PROJECT No. 2 CONTRACT ACCOUNT		CR	
COSTS	510	WORK CERTIFIED	520	
ATTRIBUTABLE PROFIT	70	WORK NOT YET CERTIFIED		
		C/DOWN	60	CREDITORS
	580		580	PAYMENTS ON ACCOUNT 20
WORK NOT YET CERTIFIED B/DOWN	60			

DR	PROJECT No. 2 CUSTOMER ACCOUNT		CR	
WORK CERTIFIED	520	PAYMENTS ON ACCOUNT	600	
BALANCE CARRIED DOWN	80			
	600		600	
		BALANCE B/DOWN	80	

DR	PROJECT No. 3 CONTRACT ACCOUNT		CR	
COSTS	450	WORK CERTIFIED	380	
ATTRIBUTABLE PROFIT	30	WORK NOT YET CERTIFIED C/DOWN	100	
	480		480	CLASSIFIED UNDER STOCKS: LONG-TERM CONTRACT BALANCES 80
WORK NOT YET CERTIFIED B/DOWN	100			

DR	PROJECT No. 3 CUSTOMER ACCOUNT		CR	
WORK CERTIFIED	380	PAYMENTS ON ACCOUNT	400	
BALANCE CARRIED DOWN	20			
	400		400	
		BALANCE B/DOWN	20	

DR	PROJECT No. 4 CONTRACT ACCOUNT		CR	
COSTS	250	WORK CERTIFIED	200	
PROVISION FOR FORESEEABLE LOSS C/DOWN	40	LOSS	90	PROVISION FOR LIABILITIES AND CHARGES/CREDITORS
	290		290	PROVISION/ACCRUAL ON CONTRACTS 40
		PROVISION B/DOWN	40	

DR	PROJECT No. 4 CUSTOMER ACCOUNT		CR	
WORK CERTIFIED	200	PAYMENTS ON ACCOUNT	150	
BALANCE CARRIED DOWN	80	BALANCE CARRIED DOWN	50	DEBTORS
	200		200	AMOUNTS RECOVERABLE ON CONTRCTS 50
BALANCE B/DOWN	50			

DR	PROJECT No. 5 CONTRACT ACCOUNT		CR	
COSTS	100	WORK CERTIFIED	55	
ATTRIBUTABLE PROFIT	70	LOSS	30	CREDITORS
PROVISION FOR FORESEEABLE LOSS C/DOWN	30	WORK NOT YET CERTIFIED C/DOWN	45	PAYMENTS ON ACCOUNT 10
	130		130	
WORK NOT YET CERTIFIED B/Dn	45	PROVISION B/DOWN	30	

DR	PROJECT No. 5 CUSTOMER ACCOUNT		CR	
WORK CERTIFIED	55	PAYMENTS ON ACCOUNT	80	
BALANCE CARRIED DOWN	25			
	80		80	
		BALANCE B/DOWN	25	

Summary

- Contract costing is a form of specific order costing for long-term contracts. These are contracts where the completion process takes longer than one calendar year and therefore embraces more than one accounting period.
- The costs of each contract are recorded in separate contract accounts.
- The elements of cost, materials, labour and expenses are debited to the contract account. Any unused materials in one accounting period are valued and carried forward to the next accounting period.
- Plant and equipment used on site are charged to the contract account, either at original cost if new, or at valuation. At the end of each accounting period a new valuation of plant will be carried out and the resulting value credited to the account. The difference between the two figures represents depreciation of the plant and equipment.
- Accruals and prepayments are calculated and entered in the contract account as appropriate in the usual way.
- The balance on the contract account when all the above entries have been completed represents the cost of the contract to date. These cost entries are made in the top section of the contract account.
- In the second section – the 'trading account' section – the work certified by an Architect as having been completed for a period is credited to the account. This figure represents sales and will be debited to the customer's account.
- Work completed, but not yet seen and therefore not yet certified by the Architect, is credited to the account (in the second section usually) and carried forward to the next accounting period. This entry is described as work not yet certified and is akin to work in progress in a manufacturing concern.
- Because of the length of time involved in completing a long-term contract it is appropriate to take a profit in the interim accounting periods.
- SSAP 9 requires that an overall profit on the whole contract can be assessed with 'reasonable certainty'.
- The profit taken to the profit and loss account is called an attributable profit and must be calculated prudently.

- Where a profit on the whole contract cannot be foreseen with reasonable certainty, no attributable profit can be taken in the interim periods.
- If a loss on the whole project can be foreseen, then the whole of this loss must be recognised and provided for in the accounting period in which it first comes to light.
- There are two methods used for calculating the attributable profit when an overall profit is reasonably certain to be achieved:

1. By calculating an overall estimated profit on the whole contract – described here as Formula A – the anticipated profit method.
2. By using Formula B – the 'two-thirds' method.

- Both methods are based on the degrees of completion of contracts.
- The difference between contract costs in an accounting period, and the work certified and not yet certified is termed the notional profit. To ensure prudence in the interim periods a profit provision is retained in the account, leaving an attributable profit to be transferred to the period's profit and loss account.
- The customer may deduct sums from remittances to the contractor. These are termed retentions and will be withheld by the customer for perhaps a year or longer after the completed project has been handed over to the customer. This is to ensure that any remedial work required is carried out at the cost of the contractor, not the customer.
- SSAP 9 requires balance sheet entries for long-term contracts to be identified separately.
- Under Stocks on the balance sheet, a separate heading called 'long-term contract balances' is required to be disclosed. This generally comprises the work not yet certified less any profit provision and less any payments on account by the customer.
- Under Debtors the amounts recoverable from customers are reported separately as 'amounts recoverable on contracts'.
- Any provisions for foreseeable losses are required to be charged to the contract account and disclosed on the balance sheet under either provisions for liabilities and charges, or creditors.

Examination Questions

1   A LEVEL (ULEAC) 1991

From the following information prepare a contract account for the year ending 31 December. Show clearly the amount of profit that may prudently be taken.

PADDY QUICK CONSTRUCTION CO.
Contract No. 1234 (Start date 1 January)

	£
Contract price	850 000
Materials issued to site during 1990	120 480
Materials returned to stores	1 460
Materials on site, 31 December	15 340
Direct wages	134 200
Wages owing at 31 December	5 220
Plant issued to contract (at cost)	82 600
Plant value at 31 December	63 200
Sub-contractors' charges	27 560
Head Office expenses charged to contract	71 430
Direct expenses (site expenses)	42 570
Direct expenses owing at 31 December	2 840
Work certified by architect	500 000
Cost of work not yet certified	27 350

The money received from the client (£425 000) was equivalent to the value of the work certified less the agreed 15% retention. Paddy Quick uses the fraction two-thirds in calculating the profits on uncompleted contracts.

2   A LEVEL (ULEAC) 1994

The Beeching Contracting Co. has two contracts in hand at 31 May:

	Contract 93/5	Contract 93/9
	£	£
Contract price	600 000	800 000
Direct materials issued	110 000	80 000
Materials returned to stores	1 000	2 000
Direct wages	96 000	64 000
Wages accrued at 31 May	4 000	5 000
Plant installed at cost	60 000	90 000
Establishment expenses	50 000	30 000
Direct expenses	30 000	20 000
Direct expenses accrued at 31 May	2 000	1 000
Work certified by architect	320 000	160 000
Cost of work not yet certified	20 000	30 000
Value of plant at 31 May	40 000	80 000
Materials on site 31 May	11 000	8 000
Cash received from contractee	300 000	120 000

In calculating profit on uncompleted contracts the company applies the formula two-thirds × notional profit to the ratio of cash received to the value of work certified. Retention monies on contract 93/5 have been agreed at 10% of the contract price: there are no retention monies applicable to contract 93/9.

Show the contract accounts for both contracts as they would appear in Beeching's books at 31 May.

12
Process Costing

A vast array of everyday products are mass-produced in processing plants and factories throughout the world. All have one thing in common: the basic raw materials enter a production line at one end of the factory and, after a number of processes and conversions, emerge at the other end as the familiar, everyday finished article. A feature of mass production is that the finished products are indistinguishable from each other. Think of chocolate bars, cans of soup, tins of paint, shampoo: all looking exactly the same from the producing manufacturer: picture yourself standing at the end of a production line, picking up one of these finished items, wrapped and packaged, date-stamped, and consumer-ready.

The manufacturing cost of that one product cannot be identified individually from the thousands surrounding it. All have come from the same basic materials introduced at the beginning of the conversion system, and all have been subjected to various repetitive operations and processes. So how is that one product to be costed? Process cost accounting methods enable this question to be answered.

In broad terms, the following formula provides the cost of that one article:

$$\frac{\text{Costs of production for the period}}{\text{Number of saleable units made in the period}}$$

Process costing therefore uses the techniques of averaging to arrive at the cost of one unit. CIMA defines process costing as *'The costing method applicable where goods or services result from a sequence of continuous or repetitive operations or processes. Costs are averaged over the units produced during the period'*.

The costs of production in the equation are the now familiar direct materials, direct labour and overheads. The number of units will be the exact, usable quantity made in the same accounting period in which the costs were incurred. Process costing is therefore an *operational* costing system.

The flow diagram of a processing factory shown in Figure 12.1 gives an indication of the movements of the materials, the operations and work involved in converting the materials into finished products, and how the manufacturing costs build up.

As can be deduced from looking at the diagram, the costs of each Processing Department will be recorded in separate process accounts. Each account will record the materials introduced (either from the previous process or directly brought in from the raw materials stores), and the *conversion costs*. Conversion costs are the direct labour costs plus factory overheads allocated or charged to the Process Department.

Using the flow diagram factory as the example, the process accounts will appear as shown in Figure 12.2. The first thing to note is that the process accounts have an extra column to record the units introduced. The principles of double entry apply to this column as well as the value column, so the units introduced must be fully accounted for within the account. As you will see in this case, 1000 units were brought in to Department 1 and 1000 units were transferred out to Department 2, and so on.

This transfer procedure follows through also with the costs. The costs incurred in Process Department 1 are transferred to Process 2; and, in turn, the costs of Process 2 are transferred to Department 3. As can be seen, the total cost of converting the 1000 units into finished, saleable products amounted to £42 000. The cost per unit is therefore £42.00 each: £42 000 divided by the 1000 units.

It should be noted that the 1000 units may end up as any number of individual products. Say the 1000 units were kilograms – in this case 1000 kilograms – and the finished, saleable product weighed 0.025 kg (25 g), the number of articles produced would be 40 000, giving a cost per unit of £1.05 each (£42 000/40 000). The above example, where units introduced exactly matched the output units, is, however, rarely seen in reality. Losses occur during processing and these need to be accounted for.

Losses of materials during production

It is usual for a certain amount of material to be lost, scrapped or wasted during the production process. This may be caused by evaporation, trimming, machine set-ups, off-cuts and various other reasons.

FIGURE 12.1

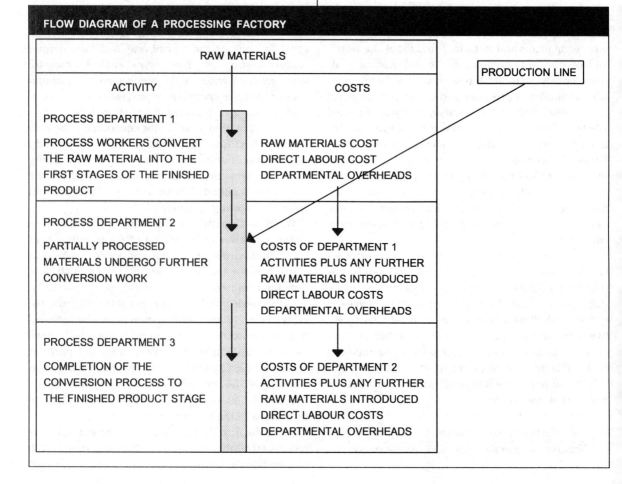

FLOW DIAGRAM OF A PROCESSING FACTORY

RAW MATERIALS

PRODUCTION LINE

ACTIVITY

COSTS

PROCESS DEPARTMENT 1

PROCESS WORKERS CONVERT THE RAW MATERIAL INTO THE FIRST STAGES OF THE FINISHED PRODUCT

RAW MATERIALS COST
DIRECT LABOUR COST
DEPARTMENTAL OVERHEADS

PROCESS DEPARTMENT 2

PARTIALLY PROCESSED MATERIALS UNDERGO FURTHER CONVERSION WORK

COSTS OF DEPARTMENT 1 ACTIVITIES PLUS ANY FURTHER RAW MATERIALS INTRODUCED DIRECT LABOUR COSTS DEPARTMENTAL OVERHEADS

PROCESS DEPARTMENT 3

COMPLETION OF THE CONVERSION PROCESS TO THE FINISHED PRODUCT STAGE

COSTS OF DEPARTMENT 2 ACTIVITIES PLUS ANY FURTHER RAW MATERIALS INTRODUCED DIRECT LABOUR COSTS DEPARTMENTAL OVERHEADS

FIGURE 12.2

PROCESS ACCOUNTS FOR FACTORY

DR	PROCESS ACCOUNT – DEPT 1				CR
	UNITS	£		UNITS	£
RAW MATERIALS	1 000	10 000			
DIRECT LABOUR		8 000			
DEPARTMENTAL OVERHEADS		6 000	TRANSFER TO DEPT 2	1 000	24 000
	1 000	24 000		1 000	24 000

DR	PROCESS ACCOUNT – DEPT 2				CR
	UNITS	£		UNITS	£
TRANSFER FROM DEPT 1	1 000	24 000			
ADDITIONAL RAW MATERIALS		5 000			
DIRECT LABOUR		4 000			
DEPARTMENTAL OVERHEADS		3 000	TRANSFER TO DEPT	1 000	36 000
	1 000	36 000		1 000	36 000

DR	PROCESS ACCOUNT – DEPT 3				CR
	UNITS	£		UNITS	£
TRANSFER FROM DEPT 2	1 000	36 000			
ADDITIONAL RAW MATERIALS		3 000			
DIRECT LABOUR		2 000	TRANSFER TO FINISHED		
DEPARTMENTAL OVERHEADS		1 000	GOODS STORE	1 000	42 000
	1 000	42 000		1 000	42 000

Some of these losses are 'normal', that is, only to be expected. They will always occur no matter how efficient and careful the management and staff are in handling the materials. Therefore it is prudent and sensible to allow for this type of loss.

Management, over time, are usually able to identify an average percentage of *normal losses* expected to arise from the production process. For example, 100 per cent of material is introduced into the production process but on average only, say, 90 per cent ends the processing operation as a saleable product. Therefore a 'normal loss' of 10 per cent would be expected.

Obviously, as with all averages, sometimes the loss will be greater, sometimes less. If the loss is greater than expected, the difference between the two (the actual loss minus the normal loss) is called an *abnormal loss*. If the loss is lower than the normal loss the difference is called an *abnormal gain*. It follows that with abnormal losses the saleable product will be less; and with abnormal gains the saleable product will be more than expected. The diagram in Figure 12.3 illustrates this point.

Using the earlier example as demonstration, we shall assume that management, after careful study, have decided that a normal loss of 5 per cent is to

FIGURE 12.3

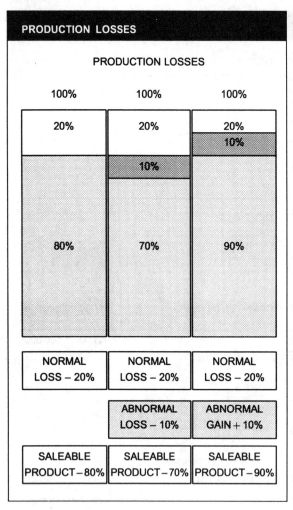

noted that actual quantities rather than percentages are sometimes given as normal losses, for example 50 tonnes in every 1000 tonnes).

Wastage forms the bulk of materials losses and has no saleable value in its own right. However, if it does have a value and will therefore produce revenue it is called *Scrap*: wastage = no value, scrap = value.

In the example discussed above normal losses had no value and were shown as zero in the value column.

However, assume now that the normal losses in Department 3 do have a saleable value, say of £20 per unit. This revenue will be credited to the Finishing Department, thus reducing the overall costs, as shown in Figure 12.5. The effect of the income arising reduces the cost per unit to £50.00: £41 500/830, or £1.25 per article (£41 500/33 200).

Accounting for abnormal gains and losses

Having set the 'benchmarks' for normal losses, management need to measure in cost terms any abnormal gains or losses arising from production. An abnormal gain is obviously good news and represents a saving in costs; conversely, an abnormal loss represents an extra cost to the company.

Using the example in Figure 12.4 again, assume that the following production figures were achieved:

Department 1: 940 units loss = 60 units
Department 2: 850 units loss = 90 units
Department 3: 825 units loss = 30 units

The process accounts will appear as shown in Figure 12.6. Working through Figure 12.6, in Department 1, 950 units were expected but only 940 were produced. Thus production was down by 10 units – an abnormal loss. The valuation of this abnormal loss is based on the unit cost of what was expected to have been produced, that is, 950 units at a total cost of £24 000. Therefore 10 units multiplied by the cost per unit (£25.26) represents the cost of the abnormal loss. There was also a loss in Department 3, but in Department 2 there was an abnormal gain. Both amounts were calculated in the same way as for Department 1.

The bookkeeping entries for the abnormal gains and losses are completed by the amounts being transferred to an *abnormal gains account* or an *abnormal losses account* or, as in Figure 12.7, a combined *abnormal gains and losses account.*

be expected in Department 1. In Department 2 they expect a 10 per cent loss, and in Department 3, 3 per cent. Following this through, the position in each account will appear as shown in Figure 12.4.

You will note that the cumulative effect of these normal, expected, losses reduced the saleable products to 830 compared to the 1000 originally introduced. The cost per unit is thus increased to £50.60: £42 000/830. The cost of the individual articles becomes £1.265 each, up from £1.05 – a major difference.

It can be seen then that accounting for these normal expected losses is of great importance to a business, for many companies use the unit cost price as the basis for setting their selling prices. (It should be

FIGURE 12.4

POSITION IN EACH ACCOUNT SHOWING NORMAL LOSSES

DR		PROCESS ACCOUNT – DEPT 1		CR

	UNITS	£		UNITS	£
RAW MATERIALS	1 000	10 000	NORMAL LOSS – 5%	50	0
DIRECT LABOUR		8 000			
DEPARTMENTAL OVERHEADS		6 000	TRANSFER TO DEPT 2	950	24 000
	1 000	24 000		1 000	24 000

DR		PROCESS ACCOUNT – DEPT 2		CR

	UNITS	£		UNITS	£
TRANSFER FROM DEPT 1	950	24 000	NORMAL LOSS – 10%	95	0
ADDITIONAL RAW MATERIALS		5 000			
DIRECT LABOUR		4 000			
DEPARTMENTAL OVERHEADS		3 000	TRANSFER TO DEPT	855	36 000
	950	36 000		950	36 000

DR		PROCESS ACCOUNT – DEPT 3		CR

	UNITS	£		UNITS	£
TRANSFER FROM DEPT 2	855	36 000	NORMAL LOSS – 3%	25	0
ADDITIONAL RAW MATERIALS		3 000			
DIRECT LABOUR		2 000	TRANSFER TO FINISHED		
DEPARTMENTAL OVERHEADS		1 000	GOODS STORE	830	42 000
	855	42 000		855	42 000

FIGURE 12.5

REVENUE CREDITED TO THE FINISHING DEPARTMENT

DR		PROCESS ACCOUNT – DEPT 3		CR

	UNITS	£		UNITS	£
RAW MATERIALS	855	36 000	NORMAL LOSS – 5%	25	500
ADDITIONAL RAW MATERIALS		3 000			
DIRECT LABOUR		2 000			
DEPARTMENTAL OVERHEADS		1 000	TRANSFER TO DEPT 2	830	41 500
	855	42 000		855	42 000

FIGURE 12.6

PROCESS ACCOUNTS EXAMPLE

DR			PROCESS ACCOUNT – DEPT. 1			CR	HOW THE ABNORMAL
						UNIT	LOSS/GAIN AMOUNT
	UNITS	£		UNITS	£	COST	IS CALCULATED
RAW MATERIALS	1 000	10 000	NORMAL LOSS – 5%	50	0		EXPECTED OUTPUT IS
DIRECT LABOUR		8 000					950 UNITS (1000 – 50).
			ABNORMAL LOSS	10	253	£25.26	COST OF THE 950
DEPARTMENTAL OVERHEADS		6 000	TRANSFER TO DEPT. 2	940	23 747	£25.26	IS £24 000.
							THEREFORE COST
	1 000	24 000		1 00	24 000		PER UNIT IS:
							£24 000/950 = £25.26

DR			PROCESS ACCOUNT – DEPT. 2			CR	
	UNITS	£		UNITS	£		
TRANSFER FROM DEPT 1	940	23 747	NORMAL LOSS – 10%	94	0		AS ABOVE:
ADDITIONAL RAW MATERIALS		5 000					846 EXPECTED
DIRECT LABOUR		4 000					(940 – 94) AT A
DEPARTMENTAL OVERHEADS		3 000					COST OF £35 747
ABNORMAL GAIN	4	169	TRANSFER TO DEPT. 3	850	35 916	£42.25	COST PER UNIT
							= £42.25
	944	35 916		944	35 916		

DR			PROCESS ACCOUNT – DEPT. 3			CR	
	UNITS	£		UNITS	£		
TRANSFER FROM DEPT 2	850	35 916	NORMAL LOSS – 3%	25	500		AS ABOVE:
ADDITIONAL RAW MATERIALS		3 000					825 EXPECTED
		2 000	TRANSFER TO				(850 – 25) AT A
DIRECT LABOUR		1 000	GOODS STORE	820	41 165	£50.20	COST OF £41 416
DEPARTMENTAL OVERHEADS			ABNORMAL LOSS	5	251	£50.20	COST PER UNIT
							= £50.20
	850	41 916		850	41 916		

So far we have set up and entered the elements of cost in the process accounts; management will have set normal loss percentages to account for the expected wastage/scrap arising during production, and any abnormal gains or losses will have been adjusted in the accounts by way of transfer to the respective abnormal gains and losses account. You will note that the total costs incurred in the processes amounted to £41 500. This is accounted for as follows:

	DR	CR
Transfer to finished goods account	41 165	
Transfer to abnormal losses account	504	
Transfer to abnormal gains account		169

To illustrate the importance of accounting for losses, consider the following trading results statement shown in Figure 12.8. The assumption is that the company planned to sell the product at 100 per

FIGURE 12.7

ABNORMAL GAINS AND LOSSES ACCOUNT			
DR	ABNORMAL GAINS AND LOSES ACCOUNT		CR
	£		£
TRANSFER ABNORMAL LOSS FROM DEPARTMENT 1	253	TRANSFER ABNORMAL GAINS FROM DEPARTMENT 2	169
TRANSFER ABNORMAL LOSS FROM DEPARTMENT 2	251	TRANSFER TO PROFIT AND LOSS ACCOUNT	335
	504		504

cent mark-up on cost but did not provide for normal losses in the selling price calculation. The forecast column in Figure 12.8 shows this position.

Some difference! So, not taking into consideration expected normal losses when setting selling prices can prove to be an expensive oversight. The reporting of abnormal losses, as here, brings to the attention of management these additional costs that are controllable: there must be reasons why the norm was exceeded. With regard to the abnormal gains, these too should be investigated to discover the reasons so that future operations may benefit.

FIGURE 12.8

TRADING RESULTS STATEMENT		
TRADING RESULTS		
	ACTUAL	FORECAST
SALES (UNITS)	820	1000
	£	£
SALES	68 880	84 000
COST OF SALES	41 165	42 000
GROSS PROFIT	27 715	42 000
ABNORMAL LOSSES	(504)	0
ABNORMAL GAINS	169	0
PROFIT	27 884	42 000

Accounting for the sale of scrap

In Department 3 the normal expected scrap was sold for £20 per unit and the process account was duly credited. But the actual losses in this Department were 30 units. The extra scrap of 5 units – the abnormal loss – at £20 per unit, is credited to the abnormal loss account. The bookkeeping entries are:

Debit cash or debtor account with the actual total value of scrap (i.e. normal loss quantity + abnormal loss quantity × price per unit).

Credit process account (normal loss quantity × price per unit).

Credit abnormal loss account (abnormal loss quantity × price per unit).

When an abnormal gain occurs the process account is still credited with the normal loss quantity × the price per unit. But the abnormal gain account will be debited with the shortfall:

Debit cash or debtor account with the actual value of scrap disposed of (i.e. normal loss quantity – abnormal gain quantity × price per unit).

Credit process account (normal loss quantity × price per unit).

Debit abnormal gain account (abnormal gain quantity × price per unit).

In the example shown in Figure 12.9 the abnormal gains and losses account reflects the sale of the extra scrap.

FIGURE 12.9

SALE OF EXTRA SCRAP REFLECTED IN ABNORMAL GAINS AND LOSSES ACCOUNT

DR		ABNORMAL GAINS AND LOSSES ACCOUNT		CR
	£			£
TRANSFER ABNORMAL LOSS FROM		TRANSFER ABNORMAL GAINS		
DEPARTMENT 1	253	FROM DEPARTMENT 2		169
		SALE OF DEPARTMENT 3 SCRAP:		
		5 UNITS AT £20 PER UNIT		100
TRANSFER ABNORMAL LOSS FROM		TRANSFER TO PROFIT AND		
DEPARTMENT 3	251	LOSS ACCOUNT		335
	504			504

FIGURE 12.10

EQUIVALENT UNITS (EU) TABLE 1

EQUIVALENT UNITS

UNITS	MATERIALS UNITS	LABOUR UNITS	OVERHEADS UNITS
COMPLETED UNITS MADE	X	X	X
ADD: ABNORMAL LOSSES	X	X	X
LESS: ABNORMAL GAINS	(X)	(X)	(X)
ADD: EQUIVALENT UNITS IN WORK IN PROGRESS	X	X	X
TOTAL EQUIVALENT UNITS	A	A	A

COSTS	MATERIALS £	LABOUR £	OVERHEADS £
COSTS CHARGED TO THE PROCESS ACCOUNT	X	X	X
LESS: PROCEEDS FROM SCRAP SALES	(X)	(X)	(X)
TOTAL COSTS IN PERIOD	B	B	B

COST PER ELEMENT	B DIVIDED BY A	B DIVIDED BY A	B DIVIDED BY A
	M	L	O

TOTAL COST PER EQUIVALENT UNIT $M+L+O$

VALUATION OF WORK IN PROGRESS:
WIP EQUIVALENT UNITS × COST PER ELEMENT

VALUATION OF COMPLETED UNITS:
COMPLETED UNITS × TOTAL COST PER EQUIVALENT UNIT

Work in progress

The above examples assumed that all the units in each process were fully completed and transferred in their entirety to the next process. And completed finished products were then transferred in full to the finished goods storage area.

FIGURE 12.11

This does happen in practice, but it is more likely that some of the units in each of the Departments will not have been completed by the end of the accounting period. Work not yet completed at the end of an accounting period is called *work in progress*. These uncompleted units need to be costed for stock valuation purposes and also to arrive at the proper cost of the completed units made in the accounting period.

EQUIVALENT UNITS (EU) TABLE 2

EQUIVALENT UNITS TABLE

UNITS	MATERIALS UNITS	LABOUR UNITS	OVERHEADS UNITS
COMPLETED UNITS MADE	900	900	900
ADD: ABNORMAL LOSSES	10	10	10
LESS: ABNORMAL GAINS	0	0	0
ADD: EQUIVALENT UNITS IN WORK IN PROGRESS	40	24	16
TOTAL EQUIVALENT UNITS	950	934	926

COSTS	MATERIALS £	LABOUR £	OVERHEADS £
COSTS CHARGED TO THE PROCESS ACCOUNT	10 000	8 000	6 000
LESS: PROCEEDS FROM SCRAP SALES	0	0	0
TOTAL COSTS IN PERIOD	10 000	8 000	6 000
COST PER ELEMENT	£10.5263	£8.5653	£6.4795
	M	L	O

TOTAL COST PER EQUIVALENT UNIT   £25.5711 M+L+O

VALUATION OF WORK IN PROGRESS:
WIP EQUIVALENT UNITS × COST PER ELEMENT

MATERIALS	£421	40 × 10.5263
LABOUR	£206	24 × 8.5653
OVERHEADS	£104	16 × 6.4795
	£730	

VALUATION OF COMPLETED UNITS:
COMPLETED UNITS × TOTAL COST PER EQUIVALENT UNIT

COMPLETED UNITS	900 UNITS × £25.5711	£23 014
ABNORMAL GAIN	10 UNITS × £25.5711	£ 256

FIGURE 12.12

PROCESS ACCOUNT, DEPARTMENT 1

DR			PROCESS ACCOUNT – DEPT. 1		CR
	UNITS	£		UNITS	£
RAW MATERIALS	1 000	10 000	NORMAL LOSS – 5%	50	0
DIRECT LABOUR		8 000			
			ABNORMAL LOSS	10	256
			TRANSFER TO DEPT. 2	900	23 014
DEPARTMENTAL OVERHEADS		6 000	WORK IN PROGRESS	40	730
	1 000	24 000		1 000	24 000

Valuing work in progress

The method adopted to achieve this is called the *concept of equivalent units* (EU).

In Department 1, the transfer of completed units to Department 2 was 940 units. To illustrate the EU concept, assume that 900 units only were fully completed. Therefore 40 units would remain in the Department, not yet completed. We need to value the 900 units and also the 40 units not yet completed: and these 40 will be at various stages of completion in so far as the elements of cost are concerned.

The assumption behind the concept is that if, say, materials are 80 per cent completed in a process and 100 units are being worked on, then 80 units are deemed to be fully completed while work on the other 20 units is considered to have not yet been started. Similarly, if the conversion costs are 50 per cent completed – half the conversion work having been done – then 50 units are deemed to be fully completed in so far as labour and overheads are concerned, with 50 units not yet started. So 'equivalent units' means the equivalent of fully completed, finished, units. In the above example, therefore, 80 units for materials have been assumed to be fully completed, and 50 units fully completed in so far as conversion costs are concerned.

Normally, management will supply the degree of completion at the end of the accounting period, or will have devised a method of assessing the ratio.

FIGURE 12.13

INCOMPLETE PROCESS ACCOUNT, DEPARTMENT 1 – NEXT ACCOUNTING PERIOD

DR			PROCESS ACCOUNT – DEPT. 1, NEXT PERIOD		CR
	UNITS	£		UNITS	£
WORK IN PROGRESS B/FWD	40	730	NORMAL LOSS – 5%	102	0
MATERIALS	2 000	20 000			
LABOUR		15 000			
DEPARTMENTAL OVERHEADS		11 000	TRANSFER TO DEPT. 2	1 900	
ABNORMAL GAIN	62		WORK IN PROGRESS	100	
	2 102			2 102	

A *cost per element* needs to be calculated to ascertain the cost to be used in valuing both finished production and work in progress. One way of doing this is to use a table as illustrated in Figure 12.10 which shows the equivalent units for an accounting period and the costs related to those units.

Using the table in Figure 12.11 to evaluate the fully completed units and the units not yet completed in Department 1 it will be assumed that management have set the following degrees of completion for the work in progress for each element of cost:

Materials: 100% completed;
Labour: 60% completed; and
Overheads: 40% completed.

FIGURE 12.14

EQUIVALENT UNITS TABLE – AVCO METHOD

EQUIVALENT UNITS

UNITS	MATERIALS UNITS	LABOUR UNITS	OVERHEADS UNITS
COMPLETED UNITS MADE	1 900	1 900	1 900
ADD: ABNORMAL LOSSES	0	0	0
LESS: ABNORMAL GAINS	(62)	(62)	(62)
ADD: EQUIVALENT UNITS IN WORK IN PROGRESS	100	50	45
TOTAL EQUIVALENT UNITS	1 938	1 888	1 883

COSTS	MATERIALS £	LABOUR £	OVERHEADS £
W-I-P BROUGHT FORWARD	421	206	104
COSTS CHARGED TO THE PROCESS ACCOUNT	20 000	15 000	11 000
LESS: PROCEEDS FROM SCRAP SALES	0	0	0
TOTAL COSTS IN PERIOD	20 421	15 206	11 104
COST PER ELEMENT	£10.5372	£8.0540	£5.8970
	M	L	O

TOTAL COST PER EQUIVALENT UNIT   £24.4882   M+L+O

VALUATION OF WORK IN PROGRESS: WIP EQUIVALENT UNITS × COST PER ELEMENT

MATERIALS	£1 054	100 × £10.5372
LABOUR	£ 403	50 × £ 8.054
OVERHEADS	£ 265	45 × £ 5.897
	£1 722	

VALUATION OF COMPLETED UNITS: COMPLETED UNITS × TOTAL COST PER EQUIVALENT UNIT

COMPLETED UNITS	1900 UNITS × £24.4882	£46 528
ABNORMAL GAIN	62 UNITS × £24.4882	£ 1 518

Note that the completed units and abnormal losses are valued at total cost per equivalent unit, as it is assumed that these losses occurred at the end of the process. Also note that closing work in progress is calculated by multiplying the equivalent units by the cost per element and then adding all three together.

The process account of Department 1 will appear as shown in Figure 12.12.

Valuing units when there is opening work in progress

The calculation of the cost per unit figures for evaluating the closing stocks and completed units is modified whenever there is *opening work in progress*.

Here the company has a choice of two methods:

(i)   AVCO: Weighted average cost method; or
(ii) FIFO: First in, first out method

The first, AVCO, uses *all* the costs in the process account to evaluate the closing work in process and the completed units.

The other method, FIFO, uses only the *current period's costs* to value the closing work in process. Therefore, with this method, the whole of the opening work

in process cost becomes part of the completed units cost.

To illustrate both methods, we shall assume that the figures for Department 1 in the next accounting period are as shown in Figure 12.13.

Note that an abnormal gain of 62 units has arisen. This has to be valued as well as the Transfer to Department 2 (1900 units) and the work-in-progress quantity of 100 units.

Management have assessed the closing work in progress by element of cost, as follows: materials: 100% completed; labour 50% completed; and overheads 45% completed.

AVCO method

For this method, the calculations are as shown in Figure 12.14.

Working through the table, note first that the units section has a similar layout to that seen in Figure 12.11, on page 145. Within the costs section you will note there is one change, however, the £730 WIP amount brought forward is shown under its constituent parts: £421 materials, £206 labour, £104 overheads, and this is analysed in the respective columns. The remainder of the calculations are as described previously.

The completed Process Account for Department 1, using the AVCO method, appears in Figure 12.15.

FIGURE 12.15

COMPLETED PROCESS ACCOUNT, DEPARTMENT 1–NEXT ACCOUNTING PERIOD					
DR			PROCESS ACCOUNT – DEPT. 1, NEXT PERIOD		*CR*
	UNITS	£		UNITS	£
WORK IN PROGRESS B/FWD	40	730	NORMAL LOSS – 5%	102	0
MATERIALS	2 000	20 000			
LABOUR		15 000			
DEPARTMENTAL OVERHEADS		11 000	TRANSFER TO DEPT. 2	1 900	46 528
ROUNDINGS*		2			
ABNORMAL GAIN	62	1 518	WORK IN PROGRESS	100	1 722
	2 102	48 250		2 102	48 250

*The calculations were made to 4 decimal places; to be precise the calculations need to be taken to perhaps 8 or more.

FIGURE 12.16

EQUIVALENT UNITS TABLE – FIFO METHOD

EQUIVALENT UNITS

UNITS	MATERIALS UNITS	LABOUR UNITS	OVERHEADS UNITS
COMPLETED UNITS MADE	1 900	1 900	1 900
ADD: ABNORMAL LOSSES	0	0	0
LESS: ABNORMAL GAINS	(62)	(62)	(62)
ADD: EQUIVALENT UNITS IN WORK IN PROGRESS	100	50	45
LESS: EQUIVALENT UNITS IN WORK IN PROGRESS B/FWD	(40)	(24)	(16)
TOTAL EQUIVALENT UNITS	1 898	1 864	1 867

COSTS	MATERIALS £	LABOUR £	OVERHEADS £
COSTS CHARGED TO THE PROCESS ACCOUNT	20 000	15 000	11 000
LESS: PROCEEDS FROM SCRAP SALES	0	0	0
TOTAL COSTS IN PERIOD	20 000	15 000	11 000
COST PER ELEMENT	£10.5374	£8.0472	£5.8918
	M	L	O

TOTAL COST PER EQUIVALENT UNIT   £24.4764 M+L+O

VALUATION OF WORK IN PROGRESS: WIP EQUIVALENT UNITS × COST PER ELEMENT	MATERIALS	£1 054	100 × £10.5374
	LABOUR	£ 402	50 × £ 8.0472
	OVERHEADS	£ 265	45 × £ 5.8918
		£1 721	

VALUATION OF COMPLETED UNITS:
COMPLETED UNITS × TOTAL COST PER EQUIVALENT UNIT

UNITS COMPLETED	B/FWD UNITS	THIS PERIOD UNITS			
1900	40	1860	MATERIAL	£19 600	1860 × £10.5374
1900	24	1876	LABOUR	£15 097	1876 × £ 8.0472
1900	16	1884	OVERHEADS	£11 100	1884 × £ 5.8918
				£46 526	
ADD COSTS BROUGHT FORWARD				£730	
TOTAL VALUE OF COMPLETED UNITS				£46 526	
ABNORMAL GAIN = 62 UNITS × £24.4764 =				£ 1 518	

FIGURE 12.17

PROCESS ACCOUNT, DEPARTMENT 1 – FIFO METHOD

DR			PROCESS ACCOUNT – DEPT. 1, NEXT PERIOD		CR
	UNITS	£		UNITS	£
WORK IN PROGRESS B/FWD	40	730	NORMAL LOSS – 5%	102	0
MATERIALS	2 000	20 000			
LABOUR		15 000			
DEPARTMENTAL OVERHEADS		11 000	TRANSFER TO DEPT. 2	1 900	46 526
			ROUNDINGS		1
ABNORMAL GAIN	62	1 518	WORK IN PROGRESS	100	1 721
	2 102	48 248		2 102	48 248

FIFO method

This method charges the *whole* of the opening work in progress costs to the completed units in the period. The closing work in process is thus valued at *current costs*. Therefore the equivalent units applicable to the period need to be calculated and related to the current period costs. An adjustment is thus made to the units section of the table to deduct the brought forward equivalent units. In the calculation table, note the opening work in progress amount of £730 is added to the current period computations for completed units. Note also that the abnormal gain is valued at the total current cost per unit.

The table for FIFO is as shown in Figure 12.16. The process account of Department 1, using the FIFO method will appear as shown in Figure 12.17.

Summary

- Many products undergo processing to convert basic raw materials into the final consumer-ready articles. Process costing methods are used to account for the manufacturing costs incurred in this form of production, which is termed operational costing.
- Separate process accounts will be set up for each separately identifiable process. The materials travel along a production line from one process to the next, with the completed units of one process becoming the basic materials for the next process.

Costs are identified at each process stage and charged to the account for that process.
- As the materials move through the factory, invariably losses occur. Most of these are to be expected, such as evaporation and waste and are therefore termed normal losses. By the study of yields from materials usage, management will be able to set down guidelines for normal losses that are likely to arise. This is usually in the form of a percentage of the materials introduced into the processing departments. Normal losses are therefore taken into account; the 'usable' production thus bears the cost of these normal losses.
- 'Losses' sometimes have a saleable value. When this is the case they are called scrap; if they have no value they are called waste.
- Proceeds from the sale of scrap are credited to the specific process account in which it arises.
- When normal losses are exceeded, the difference between the actual loss and the normal loss is called an abnormal loss. Conversely, if the actual loss is lower than the normal loss, an abnormal gain results. Separate accounts are maintained to record these abnormals. They are reported separately in the costing profit and loss account. It is important that management investigate the reasons for these.
- When there is work in progress at the end of an accounting period it is necessary to calculate the equivalent units (EU) of the constituent elements of cost. This will enable the closing work in progress

and the completed units for the period to be valued. The concept of equivalent units is that if, say, 100 units are 70 per cent completed, then 70 units are fully completed. The purpose of this is to provide a method of arriving at a cost per completed unit for each element. These unit costs are then used to value the completed units for the period and the work in progress is carried forward.

- When a process account has opening work in progress, the valuation of both the period's completed units and the closing work in progress can be calculated by one of two methods: the AVCO method or the FIFO method.

- The AVCO method, Weighted average cost, uses *all* the costs in the process account (that is, the opening work in progress costs, plus current period costs, less any revenue from the sale of normal losses), to arrive at a cost per completed unit for each element.

The FIFO method, First in, First out, charges the opening work in progress amount to the completed units. The balance of the completed units in the period is then valued at current period costs (that is, all the costs in the account except the opening work in progress amount). The closing work in progress is also valued at current period costs.

Examination Questions

1 A LEVEL (ULEAC) 1989
Anglian Products processes its products through three separate stages. Details of production for the month ending 31 May were as follows:

Process	Raw materials		Labour costs	Over- heads	Normal loss	Actual output
	(kg)	(£/kg)	(£)	(£)	(£)	(kg)
Primary	65 000	0.60	5 730	3 240	10	55 000
Secondary			7 200	4 100	5	53 000
Finishing			8 280	5 160	5	48 000

During the month £6300 worth of materials were used in the secondary process. The nature of the processes requires equipment to be cleaned at the end of each month. Thus there are no opening or closing stocks of product in process.

Losses from the finishing process are sold at £1.25kg.

Required:
(i) The process account for each process; and
(ii) the abnormal gain and abnormal loss accounts as appropriate.

2 A-LEVEL (ULEAC) 1990
The following estimates relate to the Coton Processing Company for the year ending 31 December:

	Departments				
	Processing			Servicing	
	A	B	C	X	Y
Indirect costs (£)	15 000	12 000	10 000	8 000	4 000
Dept. Y's costs (%)	40	30	20	10	–
Dept. X's costs (%)	45	25	30	–	–
Hours worked	2 000	2 200	2 500		

Overheads are absorbed by production on the basis of the number of hours worked in each process.

During April, an order was received which involved the following:

	Process	
	A	B
Material input: 5000 kg	50 000	
Material added (£)	–	4 000
Labour cost (£)	2 331	1 651
Normal losses (%)	5	2.5
Output (kg)	4 500	4 500
Process hours worked	120	80

(a) Apportion the service departments' overheads to the process departments, and calculate an overhead absorption rate for each process.
(b) Use process accounts to calculate the cost of the order processed during April – to the nearest £.

3 A LEVEL (ULEAC) 1990
At Earith Industries at the beginning of April there were no partially finished goods on hand. During the month, 6000 completed units were produced, together with 800 units partially completed. Details of the partially finished items were:

	Total cost (£)	Percentage completed
Materials	12 540	75
Labour	8 476	65
Overheads	7 084	55

Calculate:
(a) The total equivalent production.
(b) The cost per complete unit.
(c) The total value of work-in-progress.

4   A LEVEL (ULEAC) 1992

During the three months ended 31 May 1992, the Toft Processing Co. Ltd completed 8000 tonnes of product, with a further 300 tonnes partially completed. The partially completed product was 90% completed as far as materials were concerned, 70% completed for labour and 60% completed by way of overheads.

The following balances refer to the activities of the company for the three months ended 31 May 1992.

	£
Raw materials:	
Stocks at 1 March	5 576
Stocks at 31 May	6 400
Direct factory wages	58 042
Indirect factory wages	40 573
Heating and lighting	11 803
General factory expenses	10 839
Insurance of plant	6 664
Rates on factory premises	15 151
Purchases of raw materials	76 110
Raw materials returned to suppliers	2 510
Output at market price	271 000

Notes:
(i)   £3450 direct factory wages paid during the period referred to the previous three months. At 31 May, £4520 was owing for the current period.
(ii)   £1860 of the lighting and heating was for the period ended 28 February. £1320 was still owing for the period ended 31 May.
(iii) £810 general factory expenses were prepaid and £760 were owing at 31 May.
(iv) £1490 insurance was prepaid and rates were prepaid £4012 at 31 May.
(v)   Indirect wages were accrued at £5490 at 31 May.
(vi) Factory plant is depreciated at 10% per annum based on the 1990 valuation of £254 800.
(vii) There had been no product in course of manufacture at 1 March because of a major production breakdown during February.

Required:
(a) Calculate the value of semi-finished product using the method of equivalent production.
(b) Prepare the manufacturing account of Toft Processing for the three months ended 31 May, showing clearly the prime cost, the total cost of product manufactured, and the manufacturing profit.

5   A LEVEL (ULEAC) 1994

Muggleton Limited commenced the manufacture of garden spades on 1 July. By 31 December, when the half yearly financial reports were prepared, 4000 complete and 400 half-finished (as regards materials, labour and factory overheads) were produced. No orders from customers had yet been taken. Costs in the six-month period were as follows:

	£
Materials consumed	3 300
Labour	4 320
Production overheads	780
Administrative overheads	540
	8 940

At 31 December the net realisable value of each completed spade was estimated at £5.50. At this date, the company held stocks of raw materials as follows:

	Cost	Net realisable value
	(£)	(£)
Material X	2 400	2 700
Material Y	600	480
Material Z	1 060	1 060

Required:
Produce valuations of:
(i)   Raw materials;
(ii)   Work in progress; and
(iii) Finished goods,
suitable for inclusion within the company's balance sheet at 31 December.

6   AAT COST ACCOUNTING AND BUDGETING

ATM Chemicals produces product XY by putting it through a single process. You are given the following details for November:

Input costs

Material costs	25 000 kilos at £2.48 per kilo
Labour costs	8 000 hours at £5.50 per hour
Overhead costs	£63 000

You are also told the following:
(i)   Normal loss is 4% of input.
(ii)   Scrap value of normal loss is £2 per kilo.
(iii) Finished output amounted to 15 000 units.
(iv) Closing work in progress amounted to 6000 units and was fully complete for material, 2/3 complete for labour and 1/2 for overheads.
(v)   There was no opening work in progress.

Required:

(a) Prepare the process account for the month of November, detailing the value of the finished units and the work in progress.

(b) Prepare an abnormal loss account.

7 AAT COST ACCOUNTING AND BUDGETING

A company manufactures a product that goes through two processes. You are given the following cost information about the processes for the month of November:

	Process 1	Process 2
Unit input	15 000	0
Finished unit input from Process 1	0	10 000
Finished unit output to Process 2	10 000	0
Finished unit output from Process 2	0	9 500
Opening WIP – units	0	2 000
Opening WIP – value	0	£26 200
Input – materials	£26 740	–
labour	£36 150	£40 000
overheads	£40 635	£59 700
Closing WIP – units	4 400	1 800

You are told:

(i) The closing WIP in Process 1 was 80% complete for material, 50% complete for labour and 40% complete for overheads.

(ii) The opening WIP in Process 2 was 40% complete for labour and 50% complete for overheads. It had a value of labour £3200, overheads £6000 for work done in Process 2.

(iii) The closing WIP in Process 2 was two-thirds complete for labour and 75% complete for overheads.

(iv) No further material needed to be added to the units transferred from Process 1.

(v) Normal loss is budgeted at 5% of total input in Process 1 and Process 2. Total input is to be inclusive of any opening WIP.

(vi) Normal Loss has no scrap value in Process 1 and can be sold for the input value from Process 1, in Process 2.

(vii) Abnormal losses have no sales value.

(viii) It is company policy to value opening WIP in a process by the weighted average method.

Required:

Prepare accounts for

(a) Process 1.

(b) Process 2.

(c) Normal loss.

(d) Any abnormal loss/gain.

8 LCCI THIRD LEVEL COST ACCOUNTING 1992

Product Wye is produced at the end of two consecutive processes. In Process 2, further direct material is added to the input from the previous process, but this does not increase the number of units produced.

Inspection takes place at the end of Process 2, when rejects are identified and then sold for scrap at £2.50 each. The normal reject rate is 5% of the total units inspected.

The following data is available for Process 2 for last month:

	£
Opening work in progress:	
5000 units from Process 1	60 200
Materials added – 70% complete	5 200
Conversion costs – 60% complete	11 900
Closing work in progress:	
3000 units, Materials added – 80% complete	
Conversion costs – 75% complete	
Transfers from Process 1:	
30000 units	361 800
Costs incurred: Materials added	44 000
Conversion costs	118 700
At inspection:	
2200 units rejected as scrap	
29 800 units to finished stock	

A system of average pricing is in operation.

Required:

Showing details of your workings, calculate the following:

(a) The cost per unit and the total value of the transfer to finished stock.

(b) The value of the closing work in progress, both in total and by each element of cost.

(c) The charge to profit and loss account in respect of any abnormal loss in Process 2.

9 LCCI THIRD LEVEL COST ACCOUNTING 1992

Prostan Ltd makes a single product in Process A. No losses occur during manufacture. At the start of last month, 2000 units were in progress, only 40% complete for conversion costs, valued as follows:

	£
Direct materials	45 000
Conversion costs	22 000
	67 000

Actual costs incurred last month were:

	£
Direct materials	143 000
Conversion costs	166 700
	309 700

6500 units were completed during last month, at the end of which 1500 units were still in progress, only 60% complete for conversion costs.

At present the accounting system is based on historic costs, using the average pricing system. A system of standard process costing has been proposed using the following standard cost per unit:

	£
Direct materials	22
Conversion costs	26
	—
	48

Required:
(a Prepare the Process A account for last month as it appears under the present system.
(b) Assuming that the proposed standard costing system had been continuously in operation, calculate variances to the extent that the above data permits and prepare the Process A account as it would now appear in this system.

(*Author's note*: (b) should be tackled after reading Chapter 18, Standard Costing.)

10 ACCA COST AND MANAGEMENT ACCOUNTING 1 1990
A company manufactures a single product from one basic raw material. The standard purchase price of the raw material is £3.50 per kilo, and standard usage is five kilos per unit of finished product. Material price variance is identified on purchase of raw material. Actual direct labour costs and production overheads absorbed are charged to units of finished product based upon weighted average costs. The production overhead absorption rate is 200% of direct labour cost.

Balances in the company's integrated accounts at the beginning of a period included:

Raw materials:
Direct materials, 5240 kilos
Indirect materials, £1484
Production overheads:
Accrued at the end of the previous period, £3840
Work in progress:
Direct materials, £4550
Direct labour and production overheads, £1950
260 units, complete as to direct materials, 50% complete as to direct labour and production overheads.
Finished goods:
1470 units, £47 775

Costs incurred during the period were:
Raw materials purchased:
Direct materials, 7600 kilos, £26 904
Indirect materials, £2107

Raw materials issued:
Direct materials, 7460 kilos
Indirect materials, £1963
Production wages paid:

	Direct workers (£)	Indirect workers (£)
Gross	8670	2235
Employees' deductions	2688	693
	—	—
Net	5982	1542

The cost of the productive time of direct workers was £7950. The balance of the wages paid to direct workers is charged to production overheads.

Other production overheads incurred: £9252.

Period sales: 1520 units.

Production output of the single product during the period was:

Completed and transferred to finished goods stock, 1450 units.

Closing work in progress 310 units, complete as to direct material, 60% complete as to direct labour and production overheads.

A physical stock check of the basic raw material at the end of the period revealed that 5310 kilos remained in stock. Production overhead to be accrued totalled £4170.

Required:
Prepare accounting entries for the period in the following accounts:
(a) Raw material stock.
(b) Production wages.
(c) Production overheads.
(d) Work in progress.
(e) Finished goods stock.

11 ACCA COST AND MANAGEMENT ACCOUNTING 1 1991
The manufacture of one of the products of A Ltd requires three separate processes. In the last of the three processes, production and stock for the month just ended were:

1. Transfers from Process 2: 180 000 units at a cost of £394 200.
2. Process 3 costs: materials £110 520, conversion costs £76 506.
3. Work in process at the beginning of the month: 20 000 units at a cost of £55 160 (based on FIFO pricing method). Units were 70% complete for materials, and 40% complete for conversion costs.

4. Work in process at the end of the month: 18 000 units which were 90% complete for materials, and 70% complete for conversion costs.
5. Product is inspected when it is complete. Normally no losses are expected but during the month 60 units were rejected and sold for £1.50 per unit.

Required:
(a) Prepare the Process 3 account for the month just ended.
(b) Explain how, and why, your calculations would be affected if the 60 units lost were treated as normal losses.

12 ACCA COST AND MANAGEMENT ACCOUNTING 1 1992
A company produces a single product from one of its manufacturing processes. The following information of process inputs, outputs and work in process relates to the most recently completed period:

	kg
Opening work in process	21 700
Materials input	105 600
Output completed	92 400
Closing work in process	28 200

The opening and closing work in process are respectively 60% and 50% complete as to conversion costs. Losses occur at the beginning of the process and have a scrap value of £0.45 per kg. The opening work in process included raw material costs of £56 420 and conversion costs of £30 597. Costs incurred during the period were:

Materials input   £276 672
Conversion costs   £226 195

Required:
(a) Calculate the unit costs of production (£ per kg to four decimal places) using:
    (i) The weighted average method of valuation and assuming that all losses are treated as normal; and
    (ii) The FIFO method of valuation and assuming that normal losses are 5% of materials input.
(b) Prepare the process account for situation (a)(ii) above.

13 ACCA COST AND MANAGEMENT ACCOUNTING 1 1993
A company operates several production processes involving the mixing of ingredients to produce bulk animal feedstuffs. One such product is mixed in two separate process operations. The information below is of the costs incurred in, and output from, Process 2 during the period just completed.

Costs incurred:	£
Transfers from process 1	187 704
Raw materials costs	47 972
Conversion costs	63 176
Opening work in process	3 009

Production:	Units
Opening work in process	1 200
(100% complete, apart from Process 2 conversion costs which were 50% complete)	
Transfers from Process 1	112 000
Completed output	105 400
Closing work in process	1 600
(100% complete, apart from Process 2 conversion costs which were 75% complete)	

Normal wastage of materials (including product transferred from Process 1), which occurs in the early stages of Process 2 (after all materials have been added), is expected to be 5% of input. Process 2 conversion costs are all apportioned to units of good output. Wastage materials have no saleable value.

Required:
(a) Prepare the Process 2 account for the period, using FIFO principles.
(b) Explain how, and why, your calculations would have been different if wastage occurred at the end of the process.

14 CIMA COST ACCOUNTING 1990
C Limited manufactures a range of products and the data below refer to one product which goes through one process only. The company operates a thirteen four-weekly reporting system for process and product costs and the data given below relate to Period 10. There was no opening work in progress stock.
    5000 units of materials input at £2.94 per unit entered the process.

	£
Further direct materials added	13 830
Direct wages incurred	6 555
Production overhead	7 470

Normal loss is 3% of input.
    Closing work in progress was 800 units but these were incomplete, having reached the following percentages of completion for each of the elements of cost listed:

	%
Direct materials added	75
Direct wages	50
Production overhead	25

270 units were scrapped after a quality control check when the units were at the following degrees of completion:

	%
Direct materials added	66.66
Direct wages	33.33
Production overhead	16.66

Units scrapped, regardless of the degree of completion, are sold for 1 each and it is company policy to credit the process account with the scrap value of normal loss units.

Required:

(a) To prepare the Period 10 accounts for
    (i)   the process account; and
    (ii) abnormal gain or loss.

15   CIMA COST ACCOUNTING 1992

A chemical compound is made by raw material being processed through two processes. The output of Process A is passed to Process B, where further material is added to the mix. The details of the process costs for the financial period number 10 were as shown below:

Process A

Direct material:	2000 kilograms at £5 per kg
Direct labour:	£7200
Process plant time:	140 hours at £60 per hour

Process B

Direct material:	1400 kilograms at £12 per kg
Direct labour:	£4200
Process plant time:	80 hours at £72.50 per hour

The departmental overhead for Period 10 was £6840 and is absorbed into the costs of each process on direct labour cost.

	Process A	**Process B**
Expected output was	80% of input	90% of input
Actual output was	1400 kg	2620 kg

Assume no finished stock at the beginning of the period and no work in progress at either the beginning or the end of the period.

Normal loss is contaminated material which is sold as scrap for £0.50 per kg from Process A and £1.825 per kg from Process B, for both of which immediate payment is received.

Required:

Prepare the accounts for Period 10, for
(i)   Process A.
(ii)   Process B.
(iii) Normal loss/gain.

(iv) Abnormal loss/gain.
(v)   Finished goods.
(vi) Profit and loss (extract).

16   CIMA COST ACCOUNTING 1994

Process costing is used by a company which has just commenced business. It makes a component in the following way. A piece of metal is stamped and formed and to this is attached one unit of Material A, which is purchased. At this stage, machining and cleaning takes place. Two units of purchased Material B are then attached before the whole component is spray-painted.

The consulting engineer has suggested that of the total direct labour time involved in the production process, 25% would be spent on the first operation of stamping and forming, 25% would be for the first assembly of attaching one unit of Material A, 12.5% for the machining and cleaning, 25% for the second assembly of attaching two units of Material B and 12.5% for the spray-painting.

Production overhead is assumed to follow the same pattern as the labour percentage cost. All production workers are paid at the same wage rate.

The following data relate to financial Period 1:

		£
Metal purchased	50 000 kg	50 000
Purchases of Material A	40 000 units	32 000
Purchases of Material B	75 000 units	30 000
Paint used		2 144
Direct wages incurred		22 268
Production overhead incurred		16 701

Stocks at the end of Period 1:

Metal		2 900 kg
Material A		2 500 units
Material B		3 000 units
Components in process:		
Ready for the second assembly		1 500
Assembled but not painted		2 500
Completed components in finished goods		3 750

During the period 33 500 completed components were transferred to finished goods stock.

Required:

(a) To prepare a schedule which shows clearly the percentage of labour cost attributable to the component at each of the five stages of the production process.

(b) To produce a cost of production statement for Period 1, showing:

(i)   total production cost;

(ii) equivalent production units;

(iii) cost of one component (to three decimal places);

(iv) cost of completed units; and

(v)   value of work in process at the end of Period 1.

Note: for each of (i), (ii) and (iii), show the appropriate figures for

> Metal;
>
> Material A;
>
> Material B;
>
> Paint;
>
> Direct labour; and
>
> Production overheads.

NON-COMPUTATIONAL, DESCRIPTIVE TYPE QUESTIONS

(**NB**   Minutes in brackets are a guide to indicate the approximate time your essay should take to complete.)

QUESTIONS

A   Explain the nature of abnormal losses and two possible reasons for their occurrence.
(CIMA 1993) (11 minutes)

B   Distinguish between normal and abnormal losses, their costing treatment and how each loss may be controlled.
(AAT 1991) (11 minutes)

C   How far is it true to state that while a process account might show a normal loss and an abnormal gain, it can never show an abnormal loss and an abnormal gain? Give reasons.
(ULEAC 1994) (13 minutes)

D   How are sales of (i) normal losses; and (ii) abnormal losses usually shown in accounts, and why?
(ULEAC 1994) (10 minutes)

13

Joint Products and By-products

In process industries it is very often the case that more than one saleable product will result from the conversion of raw materials. As an illustration, imagine standing at the beginning of the production line in the factory and watching the basic raw materials being introduced into the first process. Follow its progress along the line. By the time the material has reached say, Process 3, perhaps two or more separately identifiable products may have become recognisable in their own right, or the conversion process has resulted in the potential for more than one product to be made. We shall assume that two separately identifiable products have emerged. Both products will be saleable separately from each other and, *dependent upon the saleable value of each product*, they will be classified either as joint products (main products), or one will become a by-product of the other (which becomes the main product).

A *joint product* is thus a product acknowledged in its own right as a main product by virtue of its saleable value. In this instance, assuming both have a high selling value, the processing of the raw materials will have yielded two main products.

CIMA defines joint products as *'two or more products separated in processing, each having a sufficiently high saleable value to merit recognition as a main product'*.

A *by-product* is a product that arises incidentally to the main product and therefore will not have the same 'sufficiently high saleable value' in order for it to be treated as a main product. CIMA defines a by-product as *'output of some value produced incidentally in manufacturing something else (main product)'*.

So joint products are main products and by-products are incidental to the main product: and the accounting treatment of both will be different.

Joint products

The common process account

Until the point where the separately identifiable products emerge from the processing operations it follows that all the conversion work leading up to this point will be common to both joint products and by-products. The account shown in Figure 13.1 indicates this common position.

You will see that the elements of cost have been recorded as usual in the account. At this time these costs are described as *joint costs*. At the stage when the separated products become individually recognisable, the *'split-off point'* has been reached. This is also known as the *'point of separation'*.

The joint costs need to be apportioned between the joint products at this split-off point to obtain the cost

FIGURE 13.1

			COMMON PROCESS ACCOUNT			
DR			COMMON PROCESS ACCOUNT			**CR**
	UNITS	£			UNITS	£
MATERIALS	1 000	10 000				
LABOUR		5 000				
DEPARTMENTAL EXPENSES		3 000	COST OF JOINT PRODUCTS			
			AND BY-PRODUCTS		1 000	18 000
	1 000	18 000			1 000	18 000

of each of the products, principally for stock valuation purposes. (It should, however, be noted that one or both of the products may need further processing work before being in a saleable condition.)

The basis for the apportionment of the joint costs is decided by management and there are three recognised methods commonly used to achieve this:
(i)   Sales value at split-off point method;
(ii) Sales value after further processing method; and
(iii) Physical units/weight produced method.
(Note: Sales value is sometimes described as market value).

Sales value at split-off point

This method is based on the premise that each product has a saleable value immediately it emerges from the common process. Assume the two products have a saleable value of £10 000 and £20 000 respectively at the split-off point. The joint costs will thus be apportioned as follows:

Product 1:

$$\frac{10\,000}{30\,000} \times £18\,000 = £6\,000$$

Product 2:

$$\frac{£20\,000}{£30\,000} \times £18\,000 = £12\,000$$

Assuming that the items produced are then transferred to the finished goods stores, the accounting entries required will be:

Debit Product 1 finished goods account – £6000.
Debit Product 2 finished goods account – £12 000.
Credit common process account – £18 000.

When the products are sold, the profit and loss position will be as follows:

	Product 1	Product 2
Sales	10 000	20 000
Cost of sales	6 000	12 000
Profit	4 000	8 000
Profit margin	40%	40%

This method will always produce the same profit margin percentage for each product (assuming that there are no further processing costs attributable to the individual products). For this reason many consider it to be the most equitable method of dealing with the joint costs, because it appears to be fair and is also easy to understand and to calculate.

But a problem is that the sales value may not always be known at the point of separation, because, as indicated, further processing may need to be completed before the product is in a saleable state. The second method listed – Sales value after further processing – provides a way of apportioning the common costs when this is the case.

Sales value after further processing method

After the split-off point further work may be carried out in order to get both products into a saleable position. Additional costs are therefore likely to be incurred after the point of separation. These costs will be charged to new process accounts set up for each product. The transfer of the joint costs from the common process account to these further process accounts will then be made on the basis of the sales value *after* the further processing costs have been taken into consideration.

Example:

	Product 1	Product 2
Sales value after further processing	20 000	30 000
Additional processing costs	2 000	8 000
'Contribution value'	18 000	22 000

You will see there is a total 'contribution value' of £40 000 (£18 000 plus £22 000) to the common process account joint costs. These contribution values are used as the basis to apportion the joint costs of £18 000:

	Product 1	Product 2
Ratio	45%	55%
	(£18 000/£40 000)	(£22 000/£40 000)
Apportionment of £18 000	£8 100	£9 900
	(£18 000×45%)	(£18 000×55%)

The bookkeeping entries are:

Debit Product 1 process account: £ 8 100
Debit Product 2 process account: £ 9 900
Credit common process account: £18 000

The profit and loss position of each product will appear as follows:

	Product 1	Product 2
Sales	£20 000	£30 000
Cost of sales:		
Common costs	£8 100	£9 900
Additional costs	£2 000	£8 000
Profit	£9 900	£12 100

Physical units/weight produced method

This method measures the physical units or weight produced of each joint product at the point of separation. The ratio of each to the total physical units or weight produced is then used to apportion the common costs.

Example:

	Product 1	Product 2
Physical units	2 000	8 000

Apportionment of £18 000 common costs:

Product 1 $\dfrac{2\,000}{10\,000} \times £18\,000 = £3\,600$

Product 2 $\dfrac{8\,000}{10\,000} \times £18\,000 = £14\,000$

TABLE 13.1

SUMMARY OF PROFIT AND LOSS RESULTS						
	METHOD 1 SALES VALUE AT SPLIT-OFF POINT		METHOD 2 SALES VALUE AFTER FURTHER PROCESSING		METHOD 3 PHYSICAL UNITS OR WEIGHT PRODUCED	
	PRODUCT 1	PRODUCT 2	PRODUCT 1	PRODUCT 2	PRODUCT 1	PRODUCT 2
	£	£	£	£	£	£
SALES	10 000	20 000	10 000	20 000	10 000	20 000
COST OF SALES:						
COMMON COSTS	6 000	12 000	8 100	9 900	3 600	14 400
PROFIT	4 000	8 000	1 900	10 100	6 400	5 600

ADDITIONAL SALES VALUE:	10 000	10 000
ADDITIONAL COSTS:	2 000	8 000
PROFIT:	9 900	12 100

The entries will therefore be:

Debit Product 1 process account   £ 3 600
Debit Product 2 process account   £14 400
Credit common process account   £18 ,000

The profit and loss position will be:

	Product 1	Product 2
Sales	£10 000	£20 000
Cost of sales	£ 3 600	£14 400
Profit	£ 6 400	£ 5 600

All apportionment methods are subjective, with no 'best' method as such. But the method once chosen should be applied consistently. Later, we shall look at the advantages and disadvantages of each of the methods described. But as you will see from the summary of the profit and loss results shown in Table 13.1, the effect of apportioning the common costs (or joint costs as they are also called) on perceived profitability can be markedly different.

Common costs and decision-making

The overall profit is the same in all three cases – £12 000. But if, as manager, you were reviewing the results in percentage terms, without being aware of the method of common costs apportionment, you would note that in Method 2, Product 1 produced a 19% profit, against Product 2's 50.5%. Conversely, with Method 3, Product 1 produced a margin of 64%, but Product 2 managed just 28%. Dependent therefore on the method of apportionment chosen, you might come to differing conclusions as to which product was the most profitable and therefore the 'winner'.

The splitting of joint costs for decision-making can therefore lead to wrong choices being made. For example, management may need to know whether it will be more profitable to incur further processing costs to enhance the selling value of a specific product, or to sell it at the point of separation. The way the common costs have been apportioned could result in a wrong (meaning less profitable), choice being made. The joint costs, being common to all the products, will not change or be influenced by the decision of the management, as these costs have been incurred irrespective of the pending decision. They are not relevant to that decision. Management therefore need consider only the additional costs of further processing to be incurred, ignoring the joint costs.

Example:
Joint costs of two products: £450 000
Total sales value of Product 1:   £200 000
Total sales value of Product 2:   £300 000

Present overall profit is therefore £50 000.

By further processing of Product 2, management calculate that this product's sales value will increase to £350 000. The additional processing costs are estimated at £44 000.

You will see that income from sales will rise by £50 000 and the additional costs – *the relevant costs to the decision* – will increase by £44 000. Thus by undertaking further processing on this product the overall profit will increase by £4000, to £54 000. Thus any decisions that relate to further processing are considered in the light of the relevant additional costs and additional revenues only.

Considered advantages and disadvantages of the apportionment methods

Some examples of the advantages and disadvantages of the three methods of appropriating the joint costs are as follows:

Method 1 - Sales value at point of separation (split-off point)
Considered advantage: most appropriate as it relates the joint costs to the earnings capabilities of the joint products *at the moment they have been jointly formed*.
Considered disadvantage: the products may not have a saleable value at this stage, as further processing may be necessary. Therefore, in the absence of a sales value for each product, the method can only be used if management estimate the sales values.

Method 2 – Sales value after further processing method
Considered advantage: the products will always have a sales value and therefore there is a basis for the apportionment of the joint costs.
Considered disadvantage: the sales values could be driven by the market (with one product perhaps having a much higher value than the other product); the higher value may not be reflective of the additional processing costs incurred for that product. Thus the apportionment of the common costs will be distorted.

Method 3 – Physical units/weight produced method

Considered advantage: the quantities/weight of each product will usually be known and therefore the calculations are straightforward.

Considered disadvantage: joint products may not have the same units of measurement – for example, some of the products may be solids whilst others may be liquids or gases.

By-products

Dealing now with by-products. As previously discussed, a by-product is any saleable output from processing which has a relatively insignificant value compared to the main product or products produced. To reiterate, the difference between a by-product and a joint product is therefore the relative selling value of each product to the other products produced. The decision by management as to whether a product is one or the other is often subjective.

The accounting treatment of a by-product will differ from that of a joint product, where, as we have seen, the joint costs are allocated to each product using one of the three methods of apportionment. Here, with the exception of one procedure, no attempt is made to allocate joint costs to the by-product. Instead, one of the following methods will be utilised:

Procedure 1 Joint costs account credited with net sales value of by-product;

Procedure 2 Joint costs account credited with profits arising on production of by-product;

Procedure 3 Separate by-product gains or losses (profit and loss) account maintained; or

Procedure 4 Common costs allocated to the by-product.

Procedure 1

With this method, the entries are akin to accounting for scrap: the revenue arising from the sales of the by-product will be credited to the joint costs account. This therefore reduces the joint costs and the resulting lower costs will then be apportioned to the joint products using one of the three methods described earlier. If any costs are incurred that are directly attributable to the by-product, for example, further processing work on the by-product, these additional costs will be charged to the joint costs account.

Example:

By-product sales value: £1 per item

Units of by-product manufactured: 3000

Revenue receivable on sales of by-product in the period: £1000

Costs incurred in further processing of the by-product: £1500

See Figure 13.2. Note that the stocks of the by-product are carried forward to be matched to the future sales revenue of the product. An alternative is to

FIGURE 13.2

COMMON PROCESS ACCOUNT 2

DR		COMMON PROCESS ACCOUNT		CR
	£			£
MATERIALS	10 000			
LABOUR	5 000			
DEPARTMENTAL EXPENSES	3 000			
BY-PRODUCT COSTS	1 500	SALE OF BY-PRODUCTS		1 000
		STOCK OF BY-PRODUCTS C/DOWN*		1 000
		COST OF JOINT PRODUCTS		17 500
	_____			_____
	19 500			19 500

*2 000 UNITS VALUED AT 50p (NET SALES VALUE: £3 000 – £1 500/3 000 UNITS)

FIGURE 13.3

COMMON PROCESS ACCOUNTS

DR	COMMON PROCESS ACCOUNT		CR
	£		£
MATERIALS	10 000		
LABOUR	5 000		
DEPARTMENTAL EXPENSES	3 000		
		TRANSFER TO BY-PRODUCT	
		CONTROL ACCOUNT	1 500
		COST OF JOINT PRODUCTS	16 500
	18 000		18 000

DR		BY-PRODUCT CONTROL ACCOUNT			CR
	UNITS	£		UNITS	£
TRANSFER FROM COMMON			SALES	1 000	1 000
COSTS ACCOUNT	3 000	1 500			
BY-PRODUCT FURTHER COSTS		1 500	STOCK OF BY-PRODUCTS C/DOWN	2 000	2 000
	3 000	3 000		3 000	3 000

ignore the stocks of the by-product and not carry these forward. This will result in one accounting period bearing all the costs of further processing, but not all the income receivable, as sales of some by-product units would not be made until a later accounting period.

Procedure 2

With this method, the actual by-product units produced in the accounting period will be transferred to a separate by-product control or stock account at sales value less attributable by-product costs. This effectively credits the expected profit on the by-products to the common account. The by-product control account will be debited with any further by-product processing costs. At the time of the actual sales the control or stock account will be credited. Thus any balance on the control account represents stocks of by-products.

Example:

By-product sales value: £1 per item
Units of by-product manufactured: 3000
Costs incurred in further processing the 3000 units: £1500
Sales income: £1000

Both accounts appear as shown in Figure 13.3.

Procedure 3

This method treats by-products as other income, with the proceeds of the sales being credited to a by-products income account. All additional processing costs and any other directly attributable costs associated with the by-product will be debited to the account. In common with the other two procedures, no apportionment of the joint costs will be made to the by-product.

Example:

Sales income: £1000 in the period (1000 units sold)
Costs incurred in further processing the 3000 units: £1500

FIGURE 13.4

BY-PRODUCT TRADING ACCOUNT 1

DR		BY-PRODUCT TRADING ACCOUNT		CR
	£			£
		SALES		1 000
BY-PRODUCT FURTHER COSTS	1 500			
		STOCK OF BY-PRODUCTS C/DOWN		1 000
TRANSFER TO PROFIT AND LOSS ACCOUNT	500			
	2 000			2 000

NOTE: UNITS IN STOCKS WILL BE VALUED AT SELLING PRICE LESS ATTRIBUTABLE COSTS PER UNIT: £1 MINUS 50p (£1 500/3 000 UNITS)

FIGURE 13.5

BY-PRODUCT TRADING ACCOUNT 2

DR			BY-PRODUCT TRADING ACCOUNT			CR
	UNITS	£		UNITS	£	
TRANSFER FROM COMMON ACCOUNT	3 000	1 200	SALES	1 000	1 000	
BY-PRODUCT FURTHER COSTS		1 500				
			STOCK OF BY-PRODUCTS C/DOWN	2 000	1 800	
TRANSFER TO PROFIT AND LOSS ACCOUNT		100				
	3 000	2 800		3 000	2 800	

NOTE: UNITS IN STOCK WILL BE VALUED AT COST: £2 700/3 000 = 90p EACH

The account will appear as shown in Figure 13.4.

Procedure 4

This method charges a proportion of the joint costs to the by-product (using one of the apportionment methods described previously). A separate process account will be set up to which will be posted the apportioned joint cost, additional further processing costs and income arising from the sale of the by-product.

Example:

Joint costs applicable to the by-product: £1200 for 3000 units

Sales of by-product: 1000 at £1 each

Further processing costs: £1500

The by-product trading account will appear as shown in Figure 13.5.

Summary

- Joint products are produced from a common process and are classified as such by virtue of their sales value significance to the firm.
- The separated joint products become the main products of the business.
- By-products also emanate from the common process but, in contrast to joint products, they are incidental to the main product or products produced and therefore their saleable value will not be considered significant by the firm.

- The difference between the two is therefore a question of saleable value.
- Joint or by-products become recognisable at the point of separation (or split-off point) in a common process.
- Common process costs need to be apportioned to the joint products principally for stock valuation purposes. This is done by deciding on an appropriate apportionment method. The three most used methods are:
  - Sales value at split off point
  - Sales value after further processing
  - Physical units/weight produced

- But management may decide on any other appropriate apportionment basis.
- Receipts from the sale of by-products may be credited to the common process account. If so, any costs incurred on the by-product will be debited to the account. Alternatively, they may be accounted for separately in trading accounts.
- For decisions relating to the joint products or by-products (for example, whether to process further or not), the common costs are ignored as being irrelevant to the decision. Only the costs and revenue arising from the new decision will be taken into consideration when selecting the best option.

Examination Questions

1   A LEVEL (ULEAC) 1993

A company makes two types of adhesive – Adamite and Bondite – by passing the raw materials through two consecutive processes. The results for April were as follows:

	Process	
	Primary	**Secondary**
Costs incurred		
Materials – 60 000 litres	£24 000	
Direct labour and overheads	£29 340	£83 568
Production		
Value of production transferred to the		
Secondary Process	£55 200	
Defective production ((ltrs)	4 800	
Output		
Adamite (ltrs)	18 000	
Bondite (ltrs)	36 000	
By-product (ltrs)	1 200	
Sales		
Adamite (ltrs)	9 900	
Bondite (ltrs)	28 800	
By-product (ltrs)	1 200	

Normal losses in the Primary Process are expected to be 10%: no losses are expected in the Secondary Process. All defective output is sold as scrap at 25p per litre.

Notes:

There was no work in progress at the beginning or end of the month, and no opening stocks of adhesive.

Unsold adhesive from the Secondary Process was in stock at 30 April. The selling prices per litre of the two products are Adamite £6.30 and Bondite £3.10. No additional costs are

incurred on either of the main products after the Secondary Process.

The by-product is sold for £1.50 per litre after being refined at a cost of 20p per litre. The operating costs of the Secondary Process are reduced by the income received from the sales of the by-product.

Required:
(i)   Calculate for April:
  - the cost of the output from the Primary to the Secondary Process;
  - the net cost or saving arising from any abnormal losses or gains in the Primary Process; and
  - the cost of output from the Secondary Process.
(ii) Calculate the value of the closing stock of each adhesive using the following methods of apportioning joint costs to the joint products:
  - volume of output; and
  - market value.

2   ACCA COST AND MANAGEMENT ACCOUNTING 1 1990

C Ltd operates a process which produces three joint products. In the period just ended, costs of production totalled £509 640. Output from the process during the period was:

Product W	276 000 kilos
Product X	334 000 kilos
Product Y	134 000 kilos

There were no opening stocks of the three products. Products W and X are sold in this state. Product Y is subjected to further processing. Sales of Products W and X during the period were:

Product W   255 000 kilos at £0.945 per kilo
Product X   312 000 kilos at £0.890 per kilo

128 000 kilos of Product Y were further processed during the period. The balance of the period production of three products W, X and Y remained in stock at the end of the period. The value of closing stock of individual products is calculated by apportioning costs according to weight of output.

The additional costs in the period of further processing Product Y, which is converted into Product Z were:

Direct labour	£10 850
Production overhead	£ 7 070

96 000 kilos of Product Z were produced from the 128 000 kilos of Product Y. A by-product, BP, is also produced which can be sold for £0.12 per kilo: 8000 kilos of BP were produced and sold in the period.

Sales of product Z during the period were 94 000 kilos, with a total revenue of £100 110. Opening stock of Product Z was 8000 kilos, valued at £8640. The FIFO method is used for pricing transfers of Product Z to cost of sales.

Selling and administration costs are charged to all main products when sold at 10% of revenue.

Required:
(a) Prepare a profit and loss account for the period, identifying separately the profitability of each of the three main products.
(b) C Ltd has now received an offer from another company to purchase the total output of Product Y (i.e. before further processing) for £0.62 per kilo. Calculate the viability of this alternative.

3 CIMA COSTING 1990

QR Limited operates a chemical process which produces four different products, Q, R, S and T, from the input of one raw material plus water. Budget information for the forthcoming financial year is as follows:

	£000s
Raw materials cost	268
Initial processing cost	464

Product	Output in litres	Sales (£000s)	Additional processing cost (£000s)
Q	400 000	768	160
R	90 000	232	128
S	5 000	32	–
T	9 000	240	8

The company policy is to apportion the costs prior to the split-off point on a method based on net sales value.

Currently, the intention is to sell product S without further processing, but to process the other three products after the split-off point. However, it has been proposed that an alternative strategy would be to sell all four products at the split-off point without further processing. If this were done the selling prices obtainable would be as follows:

	Per litre
Q	£ 1.28
R	£ 1.60
S	£ 6.40
T	£20.00

Required:
(a) To prepare a budgeted profit statement showing the profit or loss for each product, and in total, if the current intention is proceeded with.
(b) To show the profit or loss by product, and in total, if the alternative strategy were to be adopted.
(c) To recommend what should be done and why, assuming that there is no more profitable alternative use for the plant.

4 CIMA COST ACCOUNTING 1992

BK Chemicals produces three joint products in one common process but each product is capable of being further processed separately after the split-off point. The estimated data given below relate to June:

	Product B (£)	Product K (£)	Product C (£)
Selling price at split-off point (per litre)	6	8	9
Selling price after further processing (per litre)	10	20	30
Post-separation point costs	20 000	10 000	22 500
Output (litres)	3 500	2 500	2 000

Pre-separation point joint costs are estimated to be £40 000 and it is current practice to apportion these to the three products according to litres produced.

Required:
(a) To prepare a statement of estimated profit or loss for each product and in total for June if all three products are processed further.
(b) To advise how profits could be maximised if one or more products are sold at the split-off point. Your advice should be supported by a profit statement.

NON-COMPUTATIONAL, DESCRIPTIVE TYPE QUESTION
(**NB**   Minutes in brackets are a guide to the approximate time your essay should take to complete.)

QUESTIONS

A   Distinguish between:
   (i)   joint products; and
   (ii) by-products,
   and contrast their treatment in process accounts.
   (ACCA 1992) (11 minutes)

B   Discuss briefly the methods of, and rationale for, joint cost apportionment.
   (ACCA 1990) (11 minutes)

C   'Milk is separated into cream and skim. Skim, once treated as a waste product is now commonly classified as a by-product, because of the demand for powdered products. The growing demand for skimmed milk created by the "slimming industry" may raise skim to the status of a joint product in the near future.' K. Slater and C. Wootton '*A Study of Joint and By-Product Costing in the UK*'. (CIMA, 1984)
   (a)   In process costing how do the stages of waste product, by-product, and joint product represent changes in a product's importance to a manufacturer?
   (b)   Examine three methods of apportioning joint costs (common costs) to joint products, bringing out the advantages and disadvantages of each.
   (ULEAC 1991) (36 minutes)

14

Service Costing

In this chapter we shall be examining service costing techniques, which can be used in both manufacturing operations and service industries, such as transport companies and hotels.

Looking first at services found in manufacturing concerns, it will be remembered from Chapter 5 that the third element of manufacturing cost, *factory overheads*, includes not only the overhead costs of the various production departments but also the indirect costs of the service departments. Service departments within the manufacturing function exist primarily to provide a service to the shop floor. For example, the Stores Department is needed to supply the shop floor with materials, the Maintenance Department's role is to repair and look after the machines so that production can continue, and the canteen exists to serve the factory workstaff during breaks.

These factory services are accounted for separately and are then apportioned into the Production Departments' own overheads through apportionment of reciprocal services techniques.

The costs of these various factory services need to be controlled and this is usually achieved by comparing actual expenditure with budgeted expenditure. The preparation of budgets is the subject of Chapter 19. In addition, management can also establish and budget for *service unit costs*.

The formula for a service unit cost is:

> Service costs for an accounting period
> Quantity of service units supplied in the period

The service costs for an accounting period will be the total costs of the particular function, for example the canteen. This sum will then be divided by the quantity of service units supplied. In the case of the canteen, management may decide that the key cost unit is the number of meals served. Thus a cost per unit – the total cost of one average canteen meal – is arrived at. This can then be used by management to compare current performance with budgeted expectations and past achievements. So, if the number of meals falls but the costs remain the same, the average cost per unit will obviously rise. Management will need to find the causes and take appropriate action. To add to the usefulness of the technique, periodic unit costs also can be indexed to a base period to provide a measure of the trends in both the costs of the service and the units provided. Trends analysis techniques are examined in Chapter 21.

The most appropriate service unit for each service function needs to be established; we shall be looking at some examples of these shortly. Service costing techniques are also utilised in non-manufacturing organisations, such as transportation companies, hotels, colleges, power stations, hospitals and so on. Service units can be established for each type of service and thus be used by management to control and plan the costs of the service.

Service costing is also known as function costing and has been defined by CIMA as 'cost accounting for services or functions (e.g. canteens, maintenance, personnel). These may be referred to as service centres, departments or functions'.

Dealing now with both types of service, we look first at services in manufacturing companies.

Service costing in manufacturing companies

The service departments in a factory can be considered to be all of the non-producing departments, such as those shown in Figure 14.1.

As the unit costs formula shows, the service unit cost is the result of dividing a department's costs by the appropriate quantity of service supplied. Dealing first with the costs side of the equation, in order to control these, management need to have the costs reported periodically. This is accomplished by a *cost report or operating statement* which will be included in the periodic Management Accounts (example sets of which can be seen in Chapters 22 and 23). An example of the canteen operating statement might appear as shown in Figure 14.2.

FIGURE 14.1

THE SERVICE DEPARTMENTS IN A FACTORY	
PRODUCTION	STORES DEPARTMENT
	MAINTENANCE DEPARTMENT
	BUYING DEPARTMENT
	PRODUCTION ADMINISTRATION
	CANTEEN
DISTRIBUTION	WAREHOUSE FUNCTION
AND SELLING	DELIVERIES SERVICE
	SALES FUNCTIONS
ADMINISTRATION	ACCOUNTS DEPARTMENT
	PERSONNEL DEPARTMENT

The most appropriate service unit for canteen operations might be considered to be the number of meals served, as shown in this report, (or perhaps the number of staff eligible to use the canteen could be used). You will see that the cost per unit calculation is straightforward: costs divided by number of meals (the units).

Management can thus compare quickly the actual cost per unit with both the budgeted and the 'this period last year' figures. It becomes a 'key performance indicator'. Comparison can also be made against cumulative figures. The ratio is obviously sensitive to changes in numerator and denominator, and will therefore act as an effective warning signal for management, indicating if any action is required: perhaps to bring the canteen's costs into line with expectations or to step up the activity, that is more meals to be served, by improvement of the service, or a combination of the two factors.

The costs of the other services within a company can also be controlled using the same technique. Examples of appropriate service unit costs are shown in Figure 14.3.

Service costing in non-manufacturing organisations

Every organisation that provides a service can use service costing techniques to control and plan their costs and financial operations. Each should be able to identify an appropriate 'quantity of service' which can then be related to costs incurred in an accounting period in fulfilment of the service. Some examples of service cost units used in service industries are shown in Figure 14.4.

Using transport undertakings as an illustration, their business is to move passengers or products from A to B. The costs of the operation will be reported on a periodic basis in an operating statement similar to the one depicted for the canteen. Also reported will be the mileage covered in the period and the number of passengers or tonnes carried.

The service unit of a passenger-carrying business could be a composite of the number of passengers and the miles covered: described as the 'passenger mile'. For the freight firm, their unit of measurement

FIGURE 14.2

A CANTEEN OPERATING STATEMENT

OPERATING STATEMENT

CANTEEN DEPARTMENT

MONTH OF:

	ACTUAL £	BUDGET £	VARIANCE £	THIS MONTH LAST YEAR £
FOOD				
MEAT				
BAKERY ITEMS				
FRESH FRUIT AND VEGETABLES				
BEVERAGES				
SUNDRY FOOD SUPPLIES				
FOOD PREPARATION				
STAFF WAGES				
PAYROLL ON-COSTS				
GAS AND ELECTRICITY CHARGES				
CONSUMABLES				
CROCKERY/CUTLERY				
CLEANING MATERIALS				
ADMINISTRATION COSTS				
MANAGEMENT SALARIES				
PAYROLL ON-COSTS				
PREMISES COSTS				
REPAIRS AND MAINTENANCE				
PRINTING AND STATIONERY				
TELEPHONE COSTS				
SUNDRY EXPENSES				
TOTAL CANTEEN COSTS				
NO. OF MEALS SERVED:				
COST PER UNIT (COST PER MEAL SERVED):				

could be the composite of miles covered and the weight carried: the 'tonne-mile' or 'tonne-kilometre'.

Take a freight company's operations, for example. They will carry goods, with varying weights, to various destinations. The tonne-mile provides a conve- nient measure because it links the weight carried to the miles covered: the greater the weight carried and the more miles covered, the higher will be the running costs. There is a correlation between weight and distance which is recognised in the tonne-mile.

FIGURE 14.3

EXAMPLES OF APPROPRIATE SERVICE UNIT COSTS

DEPARTMENTAL UNIT COSTS

		COST UNIT EXAMPLES
PRODUCTION	STORES DEPARTMENT	NUMBER OF STORES REQUISITIONS PROCESSED
	MAINTENANCE DEPARTMENT	NUMBER OF PRODUCTION MACHINES
	BUYING DEPARTMENT	NUMBER OF PURCHASE ORDERS ISSUED
	PRODUCTION ADMINISTRATION	NUMBER OF PRODUCTION ORDERS
	CANTEEN	NUMBER OF MEALS SERVED/STAFF NUMBERS
DISTRIBUTION,		
SELLING	WAREHOUSE	NUMBER OF ORDERS PICKED
	DELIVERIES SERVICE	NUMBER OF TONNE-MILES (TONNE-KM)
	SALES FUNCTIONS	NUMBER OF CALLS MADE/ORDERS TAKEN
ADMINISTRATION	ACCOUNTS DEPARTMENT	NUMBER OF PERSONAL ACCOUNTS
	PERSONNEL DEPARTMENT	TOTAL STAFF EMPLOYED
	GENERAL ADMINISTRATION	PER £ OF TURNOVER

The formula for calculating the tonne-mile is simply:

Number of miles covered × Weight carried

This, then, is the 'quantity of service units' – the service unit cost – and this will be used to compare the costs incurred in an accounting period with the budget, and with past periods. The service unit cost for a freight business (the cost per tonne mile) will therefore be:

FIGURE 14.4

EXAMPLES OF SERVICE COST UNITS USED IN SERVICE INDUSTRIES

SERVICE	COST UNIT EXAMPLES
TRANSPORT AND DELIVERY	NUMBER OF TONNE-MILES (TONNE-KM)
HOTELS	NUMBER OF ROOMS OCCUPIED
COLLEGES	NUMBER OF STUDENTS
HOSPITALS	NUMBER OF BEDS OCCUPIED/ OUT-PATIENTS
POWER STATIONS	KWH PRODUCED

$$\frac{\text{Costs incurred in the period}}{\text{Tonne-miles}}$$

Example:

Miles covered	Tonnes carried	Tonne-miles
10	20	200
20	30	600
30	40	1 200
40	50	2 000
Total tonne/miles		4 000

So if the operating costs were £16 000 in the same period, the cost per tonne-mile would be £4.00 (£16 000/4 000).

The tonne-mile statistic has other uses apart from being a useful control and planning tool: it can also be used to fix selling prices for jobs. This is done by adding a mark-up to the cost (or applying a percentage margin) to arrive at a selling price per tonne-mile. For example, assume a customer requires 4 tonnes of materials to be delivered to a site 20 miles away. The tonne-miles will therefore be 80 (4 tonnes × 20 miles). Assume that the carrier requires a mark-up of 20 per cent on cost for their profit. As the cost of a tonne mile is £4, the selling price for the job will be £4.80 per tonne-mile and the charge to deliver the materials will thus be £4.80 × 80 tonne-miles = £384.

For passenger-carrying operations the passenger-mile measurement can be used as the control tool. The formula for the passenger mile is:

> Number of miles covered × Passengers carried

And the cost per passenger-mile will be:

$$\frac{\text{Operating costs}}{\text{Passenger-miles}}$$

Similarly, other service operators can use service costing techniques to control their costs. For example, hospital management will need to measure the costs of both out-patient and in-patient services. A possible method of doing so will be perhaps to establish the *cost per out-patient attendance* and a *cost per in-patient day*.

In each accounting period, the costs for these will be reported in a cost report similar to the earlier canteen example. The service unit cost calculation formula will be the same:

$$\frac{\text{Costs}}{\text{Quantity of service supplied}}$$

The out-patients quantity of service might be the number of attendances; the in-patients statistic might be a composite number similar, say, to the passenger-mile:

> Number of patients × Average length of stay in the hospital.

Example:
See Figure 14.5.

This key statistic enables management to budget more accurately the costs required for the level of service anticipated. And when the actual costs are incurred, it provides the yardstick with which to control the costs. The statistic can also be used for comparison purposes, one hospital with another, one district with another, and so on. The example given in Table 14.1 illustrates this point.

Although the total costs per unit of service for both hospitals are broadly similar, by comparing each cost heading it becomes clear that Hospital A is out of line with Hospital B where the other service costs are concerned. But with regard to the catering, the opposite is the case: here there is a large difference of 28 per cent. Management would need to investigate all the large variances to ascertain the reasons and endeavour to improve the areas that are out of line. Similarly, if an 'industry average' cost per service unit is available this will also further enhance management's ability to control the costs.

Key performance indicators too play an important role in control and planning. In hotels, for example, a 'bed or room occupancy' ratio is used. This is simply the number of beds (or rooms) occupied for a particular period divided by the total number of

FIGURE 14.5

EXAMPLE OF SERVICE UNIT COSTS FOR A HOSPITAL	OUT-PATIENTS	IN-PATIENTS	
COSTS	£100 000	£900 000	
NUMBER OF OUT-PATIENT ATTENDANCES	5 000		
NUMBER OF IN-PATIENTS		1 000	
AVERAGE LENGTH OF STAY – DAYS		15	
IN-PATIENT DAYS		15 000	
COST PER SERVICE UNIT – OUT-PATIENTS	£20.00		(£100 000/5 000)
COST PER SERVICE UNIT – IN-PATIENT DAYS		£60.00	(£900 000/15 000)

TABLE 14.1

OUT-PATIENT COSTS COMPARISON STATEMENT					
PERIOD					
	HOSPITAL A £	COST PER PATIENT £	HOSPITAL B £	COST PER PATIENT £	PERCENTAGE DIFFERENCE B TO A
COSTS					
NURSING STAFF COSTS	500 000	50.00	1 300 000	52.00	4.0
SUPPLIES	100 000	10.00	240 000	9.60	−4.0
MEDICAL SUPPLIES	400 000	40.00	1 125 000	45.00	12.5
OTHER SERVICES	200 000	20.00	400 000	16.00	−20.0
CATERING	50 000	5.00	160 000	6.40	28.0
ADMINISTRATION STAFF COSTS	150 000	15.00	375 000	15.00	0.0
CLEANING	35 000	3.50	100 000	4.00	14.3
TOTAL COSTS	1 435 000	143.50	3 700 000	148.00	3.1
NUMBER OF OUT-PATIENTS ATTENDING	10 000		25 000		

beds or rooms available. This provides management with further key data to indicate the usage of the assets.

Summary

- The costs of services performed need to be controlled and one way of doing this is through service unit costs.
- A service unit cost is calculated by using the formula:

$$\frac{\text{Service costs}}{\text{Quantity of service units supplied}}$$

- Both figures will relate to the same accounting period. Service units are the common denominator relating to a particular function. For example, in a canteen the number of meals served is the service performed, so the total costs of the canteen divided by the quantity of meals served will give the service unit cost.
- Service costing techniques are used in manufacturing operations and non-manufacturing concerns.

In manufacturing, services are carried out by the Stores Department, Maintenance Department and so on, in ensuring that the shop floor workers are able to produce the goods. Services are also carried out by the selling, distribution and administration functions of the business.

- In non-manufacturing organisations (i.e. service industries), service costing techniques can be used to ascertain the cost per service unit supplied.
- Service costing is also known as function costing and is a continuous operations costing method.
- The costs of a particular service are collected and reported periodically in operating statements which form part of the Management Accounts. Example sets of these are shown in Chapters 22 and 23.
- The service units statistics are also collected for the same period and reported on the statements. When the actual service cost per unit has been calculated, management are then able to relate the resulting figure with budgeted expectations, previous periods, other operations, locations and so on. It thus provides key data for control and planning.
- CIMA provide the following examples of cost units for various businesses:

TABLE 14.2

EXAMPLES OF UNIT COSTS FOR VARIOUS BUSINESSES

BUSINESS	COST UNIT	BUSINESS	COST UNIT
BREWING	BARREL/HECTOLITRE	TIMBER	100 FT/STANDARD/STERE
BRICK-MAKING	1000 BRICKS	AIRLINE	AVAILABLE TONNE KM
COAL MINING	TON/TONNE	HOTEL AND CATERING	ROOM/COVER
ELECTRICITY	KWH	PROFESSIONAL SERVICE:	
ENGINEERING	CONTRACT, JOB	(ACCOUNTANT, ARCHITECTS,	
GAS	THERM	LAWYERS, SURVEYORS)	CHARGEABLE HOUR
PAPER	REAM	EDUCATION	(A) ENROLLED STUDENT
PETROLEUM	BARREL, TONNE, LITRE		(B) SUCCESSFUL STUDENT
SAND AND GRAVEL	CUBIC YARD/METRE		(C) SCHOOL MEAL
STEEL	TONNE/TON/SHEET (A) ROLLED TONNE/TON/SHEET (B) CAST TONNE/TON/SHEET (C) EXTRUDED	HEALTH CARE (HOSPITALS)	(A) BED OCCUPIED (B) OUT-PATIENT

ACTIVITY	COST UNIT	ACTIVITY	COST UNIT
BUILDING SERVICE	SQUARE METRE	PERSONNEL ADMINISTRATION	EMPLOYEE
CREDIT CONTROL	ACCOUNT MAINTAINED	SELLING	(A) £ OF TURNOVER
MATERIALS STORAGE/ HANDLING	(A) REQUISITION (B) UNIT ISSUE/ RECEIVED (C) VALUE ISSUE/ RECEIVED		(B) CALL MADE (C) ORDER TAKEN (A) NUMBER (B) VALUE
		TELEPHONE SERVICE	(A) CALL MADE (B) EXTENSION

Examination Questions

1 AAT COST ACCOUNTING AND BUDGETING 1992
A large hotel has recently reorganised its costing system and split its activities into four cost centres:

1. Accommodation
2. Catering
3. Leisure
4. Outings

The hotel is moving towards standardising its services and selling a hotel package to its customers which will include accommodation, meals, use of leisure facilities and a number of outings. There is to be a predetermined price per day for the use of each cost centre by the customer. Labour and material can be identified and allocated to the cost centres in the budget, but other overheads listed below cannot be so readily identifiable.

	Accom-modation	Catering	Leisure	Outings	Total
	£	£	£	£	£
Labour	110 000	100 500	35 000	38 500	284 000
Materials	19 000	38 000	16 000	13 000	84 000
Power					84 000
Rent and rates					72 000
Depreciation					60 000
Advertising					76 000
Office expenses					240 000

You are given the following information about the cost centres from the budget for the coming year:

	Accom-modation	Catering	Leisure	Outings
Floor area (in sq metres)	1 200	400	600	200
No. of employees	32	16	24	8
Machinery value	£10 000	£20 000	£60 000	£30 000
Kilowatt hours	5 000	2 500	12 500	1 000
Expected customer usage in days	15 000	12 000	8 000	3 000

You are told that advertising is to be apportioned to the cost centres on the basis of customer usage and office expenses apportioned on the basis of total cost per cost centre before the apportionment of the office expenses.

The budget for the coming year has been based upon the strategy that customers will have the standard accommodation and catering package with the leisure facilities and outings package as optional. Hotel policy for the coming year is to operate a profit margin of 30% on price.

Required:
(a) Prepare a cost statement for the four cost centres showing the budgeted total cost and the budgeted cost per customer day per cost centre.
(b) Calculate the price to be charged to a married couple who want to stay at the hotel for one week. They require accommodation and catering for seven days, use of the leisure facilities for three days and want to go on outings on three days.
(c) The actual results for the hotel for the year under review were as follows:

	Accom-modation	Catering	Leisure	Outings
Total cost	£320 000	£275 000	£200 000	£125 000
Customer days' usage	15 250	13 000	6 800	3 200

Calculate the under/over absorption of costs per cost centre.

2 AAT COST ACCOUNTING AND BUDGETING 1993
Ablico Limited have been asked to provide the services of two consultants, Black and White, to a government department for the coming calendar year. The consultants will still be in the employ of the company, who will invoice the government department on a quarterly basis for their services.
You are given the following cost data:

	Black	White
Gross annual salary	£42 500	£35 000
Holiday entitlement per year	6 weeks	5 weeks
Public holidays per year	10 days	10 days
Working day	8 hours	8 hours
Employer's pension contribution – % of salary	8%	6%
Cost of company car bought at start of contract	£13 464	£13 660

You are told that:
(i) 10% of each consultant's working time is non-chargeable.
(ii) Overheads associated with the project amount to £44 400 and are to be charged to each consultant's cost upon the basis of £15 per hour worked by Black and £10 per hour worked by White.
(iii) It is envisaged that Black's company car will last for 2 years and have a residual value of £6 000 while White's company car will last for 3 years and have a residual value of £4 000. Company policy is to use the straight line method of depreciation.

Required:
(a) On the basis of a 5-day week and a 52-week year cost the services of Black and White to the government department on an hourly basis.
(b) Given that it is company policy to take a profit of 20% of contract price charged, calculate the value of the invoice issued each quarter to the government department for the services of both Black and White.

3 ACCA COST AND MANAGEMENT ACCOUNTING 1 1992
CD Ltd is a distribution company. 'We Sell Everything' has invited CD Ltd to tender for a contract for the distribution of products from the 'We Sell Everything' central warehousing unit to its chain of shops. Daily deliveries (Monday to Friday) may be required, on any of the 40 routes involved, for 52 weeks each year.

A fleet of 40 vehicles would be required to fulfil the contract. CD Ltd currently has no spare capacity. New vehicles could be purchased at a cost of £35 000 each, and additional drivers could be recruited. Alternatively, contract vehicles and drivers could be hired by CD Ltd on a daily basis. It is estimated that the 40 vehicles, if purchased, would be idle for 20% of the working days available. 35 additional drivers would be required to fulfil the contract with 'We Sell Everything'. Gross wages would be £13 000 per driver per annum, with employer costs of 15% in addition. Other incremental annual fixed costs per vehicle (excluding the cost of drivers and vehicle depreciation) would be £1240. Average variable running costs per journey are estimated at £37.80.

Contract vehicles (including drivers) could be hired at a cost of £100 per day, plus £0.20 per kilometre. Total kilometres to fulfil the contract over 52 weeks is estimated to be 1 747 200.

The contract with 'We Sell Everything' may be for either three or five years. Vehicles if purchased, would be disposed of at the end of the contract period. Disposal values are estimated at £11 000 per vehicle after three years, and £5 000 after five years.

Required:
(a) Calculate the minimum annual price that could be quoted for the contract tender if:
  (i) the contract is for three years; and
  (ii) the contract is for five years.
  (The minimum price is that which would just cover incremental costs incurred. Ignore interest costs if vehicles were purchased.)
(b) Calculate the percentage utilisation of new vehicles that would be required, for the estimated costs of own-vehicle purchase and contract vehicle hire to be the same on a three-year contract.

NON-COMPUTATIONAL, DESCRIPTIVE TYPE QUESTIONS

(**NB**   Minutes in brackets are a guide to indicate the approximate time your essay should take to complete.)

QUESTIONS

A   You have been promoted to the position of Assistant Cost Accountant within your organisation. On the first day of your new appointment you receive two tasks: one from the Purchasing Director and one from the Cost Accountant. The Purchasing Director has recently been on a course that discussed costing methods. Among the methods mentioned were job costing, batch costing, contract costing, process costing and service costing, which left the Purchasing Director enthusiastic but confused. He has asked why there cannot be one costing method universal to all organisations.

Required:
Write a memorandum to the Purchasing Director, explaining the need for the different costing methods mentioned, briefly outlining the main characteristics of each method and giving two examples of their use.
(AAT 1992) (30 minutes)

B   Dick Barton is planning to start a car repair business. He hopes to employ three mechanics, repairing a variety of different makes of car. His mechanics will be paid on the basis of time rates, plus premiums for overtime working. Dick seeks your advice on the accounting system necessary to ensure that:

(a) each mechanic is paid the correct wages due to him/her;
(b) overheads are recovered on the basis of labour hours; and
(c) each customer is correctly charged.

Prepare a report outlining the accounting system that you recommend and explain carefully the nature and purpose of any documents used in the system.
(ULEAC 1989) (36 minutes)

15

Activity-based Costing

In this chapter the factory overheads absorption method called *activity-based costing* is introduced, a system considered by many to be replacing the traditional methods of absorbing overheads into products, as described in Chapter 6.

Recapping for a moment on the traditional absorption methods, these systems evolved when factory overheads were relatively small compared to materials and labour costs. For convenience and ease of administration, the spread of overheads to products was based on straightforward assumptions that there was a causal connection between the recovery base chosen and the total factory overheads incurred. For example, if the work in the factory was largely labour-intensive, then the overheads would be considered to relate in some way to that fact, management thus choosing the direct labour hour or direct labour cost methods to charge the overheads to products. Similarly, if machine work was the dominant production feature, then the overheads would be associated with these and the machine hour rate chosen.

But in recent years the picture has changed. Production overheads have grown significantly as a proportion of production costs, while direct labour costs have declined. The rapid growth in technology and computerisation of production lines has reduced the need for direct labour, but the costs of operating the computer systems, depreciation of the equipment and software, maintenance costs and so on, have grown. The simplified 'percentage mix' of the cost of a product shown in Table 15.1 illustrates this change.

The effects on the cost of products from the change can be gauged from the following simplified example, Product 1 being produced on an expensive computer-based system, and Product 2 produced manually:

	Product 1 (£)	Product 2 (£)
Materials	2 000	2 000
Labour	300	1 000
Overheads	600	2 000
Total	2 900	5 000

The overheads here have been absorbed on the traditional direct labour cost method: £2 being absorbed for every £1 of direct labour spent. The overheads detail however may have been as follows:

	£
Depreciation of computer system	1 200
Maintenance of computer system	350
Supervision costs	350
Other factory overheads	700

TABLE 15.1

TRADITIONAL AND PRESENT-DAY COST MIX PERCENTAGES		
	TRADITIONAL COST MIX %	PRESENT-DAY COST MIX %
MATERIAL	60	60
LABOUR	30	15
FACTORY OVERHEADS	10	25
TOTAL PRODUCT COST	100	100

The absorption basis used was volume-related, that is, the more labour cost incurred by a product, the more overhead absorbed. But it can be seen that these particular overhead costs are largely unaffected by volume, being of a fixed-cost nature. Note also that some of the overheads relate more to Product 1 than to Product 2. Therefore Product 1 has not carried its full weight of overheads, while Product 2 has been overcharged. Traditional methods of absorption can thus be considered inappropriate for current production methods, resulting in distorted product costs, thereby leading to incorrect calculations of selling prices and erroneous decisions.

So, in the 1980s, a fresh look was taken at the methods of overhead absorption into products with the purpose of producing more accurate product costs. As a result of this research activity-based costing (ABC) evolved. CIMA defines activity-based costing as *'cost attribution to cost units on the basis of benefit received from indirect activities, e.g. ordering, setting-up, assuring quality'*.

Activity-based costing therefore endeavours first to establish the cost of the activities going on in the various factory departments which are creating the overheads, and then relating these activities to the products.

To absorb overheads using ABC techniques, the first stage is to analyse the activities of each of the factory overhead departments, under broad, main headings to establish what is happening in each department. This detailed analysis will often provide management with information on some activities which do not contribute (do not add value) to the product and therefore could perhaps be discontinued or changed so that they do. Activities cause costs and they are termed *cost drivers*: the work being done creates, generates – drives – the costs. CIMA defines a cost driver as: *'an activity that generates cost'*.

When the cost drivers have been identified they are costed and the total costs collected into *cost pools*. In addition to collecting the costs of each activity, data will also be collected on the number of times an activity is performed during the same period of time as

FIGURE 15.1

ACTIVITY-BASED COSTING OVERVIEW

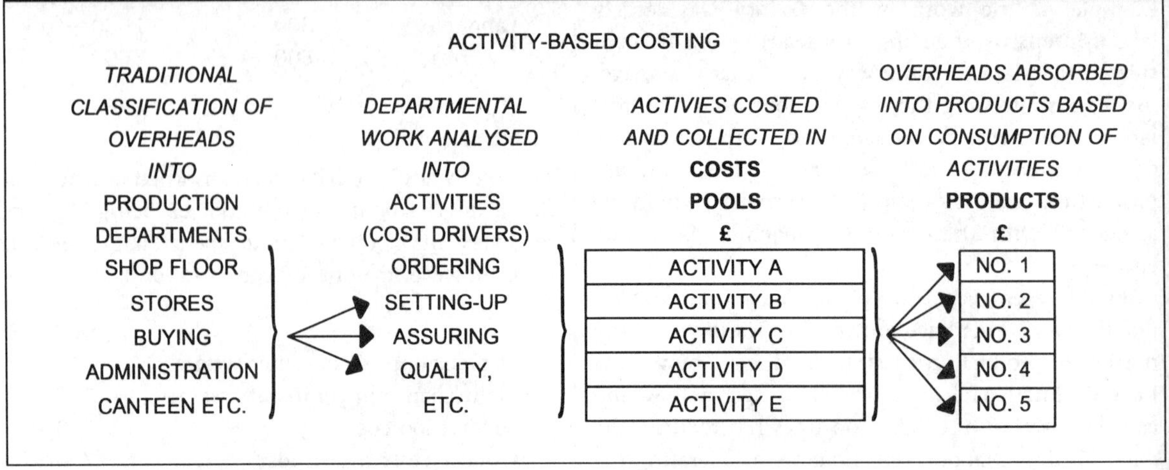

the costs are incurred. A cost per activity can thus be established:

$$\frac{\text{Costs of the activity}}{\text{Number of times the activity is performed}}$$

The number of times a product requires the performance of the activity is also established. The end result is that each product is charged with each activity in proportion to its consumption of that activity. The simplified flow diagram in Figure 15.1 provides an overview of the procedure for the items highlighted in the CIMA definition.

Working through this figure, you will note that the departmental costs are reclassified to calculate the costs of the activities, such as ordering materials, set up costs and so on. The total cost of each activity is thus arrived at. (It follows that the overall total cost of the activities should equal the overall departmental totals.)

Activities cross departmental boundaries. You can visualise that the output documentation of one department will be the input documentation of another department, with work in both departments relating to the overall activity. For illustration, the Stores Department requires additional materials, so will instruct the Buying Department to purchase them. The activity in the Stores Department of issuing the instruction – the paperwork, the staff involved, consultations, etc. – incurs cost. Then, in the Buying Department, further costs are incurred, also directly attributable to the receipt of the instruction from the Stores Department, for example, negotiating with suppliers, raising the purchase order, telephone calls and so on. The costs of the activity are then charged to a *cost pool*, headed perhaps 'ordering activity costs'. Figure 15.2 depicts this cross-departmental activity and the build-up of the cost pool.

FIGURE 15.2

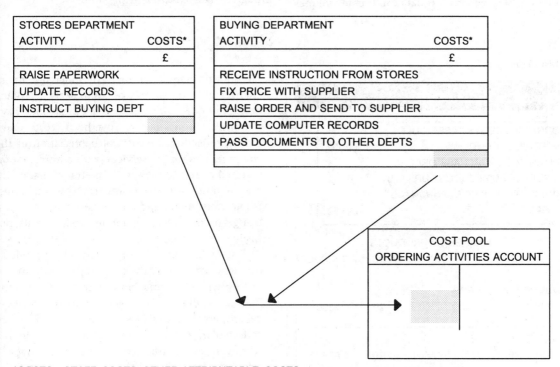

CROSS-DEPARTMENTAL ACTIVITY AND THE COST POOL

ACTIVITY: ORDERING MATERIALS

STORES DEPARTMENT ACTIVITY	COSTS*
	£
RAISE PAPERWORK	
UPDATE RECORDS	
INSTRUCT BUYING DEPT	

BUYING DEPARTMENT ACTIVITY	COSTS*
	£
RECEIVE INSTRUCTION FROM STORES	
FIX PRICE WITH SUPPLIER	
RAISE ORDER AND SEND TO SUPPLIER	
UPDATE COMPUTER RECORDS	
PASS DOCUMENTS TO OTHER DEPTS	

COST POOL
ORDERING ACTIVITIES ACCOUNT

*COSTS = STAFF COSTS, OTHER ATTRIBUTABLE COSTS

In this example, management might select as the cost driver the purchase orders issued. The cost of this activity will therefore be:

$$\frac{\text{The total cost pool of the activity}}{\text{Purchase orders issued}}$$

The final stage of the process is to identify how many times a product needs to use an activity. The charge to the product will be:

Number of times the activity is required
    multiplied by the unit cost of the activity

Example (Figure 15.3):

Initially, there may be a lot of work involved in analysis and research to ensure that activity-based costing will be effective. There could be many activities going on to support the manufacturing process. Information on the major activities will be collected, perhaps through questionnaires and observations of work patterns.

To help run an ABC system, specialised computer programs have been written to collect the details. Some of these programs use 'data capture' techniques which link the information held in a number of computer files with each other to provide the cost per activity and the other information needed.

For example, the Buying Department will probably use a program to prepare purchase orders; the number of purchase orders raised will be recorded in that file. This quantitative data will then be linked to the general ledger cost accounts program to collect the costs of ordering materials – the *cost pools* – to arrive at the relevant activity cost per order. This, in turn, will then be linked to the number of times the products have utilised the activity, thus the overheads will be absorbed into the products.

One of the benefits ascribed to activity-based costing is that the data provides management with a much better understanding of how overhead costs arise. Management, by identifying the cost drivers and then establishing the costs created, will be able to set benchmarks which can then be used for planning and control purposes. ABC techniques can also be used in a wider context to assist management to improve performance of other areas in the business through *Activity-based management* (ABM), and to assist in estimations of future work and resources through *Activity-based budgeting* (ABB).

Summary

- Methods of manufacturing have undergone major changes with the advent of computerised production methods. Direct labour requirements have diminished, but factory overhead costs have grown, reflecting the costs of depreciation of the equipment, support services and administration required to run the systems. The traditional methods of absorbing overheads, such as the direct labour hour method, do not reflect these changes, being volume-based. Therefore product costs can easily be distorted.
- ABC seeks to charge factory overheads to products by identifying the activities going on within the factory which are causing the costs. These activities are called cost drivers. Activities traverse departmental boundaries, so costs need to be collected in a different way from the traditional cost centre – departmental – basis. Cost pools – 'activity accounts' – will be set up to collect the costs created by each activity.

FIGURE 15.3

CHARGE TO THE PRODUCT			
ORDERING COSTS IN PERIOD (PER COST POOL)			£500 000
NUMBER OF PURCHASE ORDERS ISSUED IN PERIOD (COST DRIVER)			20 000
ORDERING COST PER PURCHASE ORDER			**£25.00**

CHARGE TO PRODUCTS	PRODUCT 1	PRODUCT 2	PRODUCT 3
NUMBER OF ORDERS ISSUED IN PERIOD	100	200	300
ORDERING COSTS CHARGE	£2 500	£5 000	£7 500

- The number of times an activity is performed will also be measured. Dividing the cost pool by the number of times an activity is performed provides an absorption rate for each activity.
- The number of times an individual product uses the activity, multiplied by this rate, will be the amount of overhead charged to the particular product.
- Much analysis work is required if ABC is to be effective. Each activity needs to be identified and then costed. This research often enables management to eliminate duplicated activities or change systems to reduce costs. Because of the volume of data required to run ABC, specialised computer programs are available, which provide data capture facilities linking cost pools with the cost drivers.
- ABC techniques can also be used to improve overall performance throughout the enterprise (activity-based management). In addition, the techniques can assist management in planning and control through activity-based budgeting.

Examination Questions

1 CIMA COST ACCOUNTING 1991

Having attended a CIMA course on activity based costing (ABC) you decide to experiment by applying the principles of ABC to the four products currently made and sold by your company. Details of the four products and relevant information are given below for one period:

Product	A	B	C	D
Output in units	120	100	80	120
Costs per unit	**£**	**£**	**£**	**£**
Direct materials	40	50	30	60
Direct labour	28	21	14	21
Machine hours (per unit)	4	3	2	3

The four products are similar and are usually produced in production runs of 20 units and sold in batches of 10 units.

The production overhead is currently absorbed by using a machine hour rate, and the total of the production overhead for the period has been analysed as follows:

	£
Machine department costs (rent, business rates, depreciation and supervision)	10 430
Set-up costs	5 250
Stores receiving	3 600
Inspection/quality control	2 100
Materials handling and dispatch	4 620

You have ascertained that the 'cost drivers' to be used are as listed below for the overhead costs shown:

Cost	Cost driver
Set up costs	Number of production runs
Stores receiving	Requisitions raised
Inspection/quality control	Number of production runs
Materials handling and dispatch	Orders executed

The number of requisitions raised on the stores was 20 for each product and the number of orders executed was 42, each order being for a batch of 10 of a product.

Required:
(a) To calculate the total costs for each product if all overhead costs are absorbed on a machine hour basis.
(b) To calculate the total costs for each product, using activity based costing.
(c) To calculate and list the unit product costs from your figures in (a) and (b) above, to show the differences and to comment briefly on any conclusions which may be drawn which could have pricing and profit implications.

NON-COMPUTATIONAL, DESCRIPTIVE TYPE
   QUESTIONS
(**NB**   Minutes in brackets are an indication of the length of time to be spent in answering the question.)

QUESTIONS
A   'It is now fairly widely accepted that conventional cost accounting distorts management's view of business through unrepresentable overhead allocation and inappropriate product costing.

   This is because the traditional approach usually absorbs overhead costs across products and orders solely on the basis of the direct labour involved in their manufacture. And as direct labour as a proportion of total manufacturing cost continues to fall, this leads to more and more distortion and misrepresentation of the impact of particular products on total overhead costs'.
(From an article in *Financial Times*, 2 March 1990)

Required:

To discuss the above and to suggest what approaches are being adopted by management accountants to overcome such criticism.

(CIMA 1992) (30 minutes)

B   Explain why overheads need to be absorbed upon pre-determined bases. Consider whether these bases for absorption are appropriate in the light of changing technology, suggesting any alternative basis that you consider appropriate.

(AAT 1993) (13 minutes)

Part III
Planning and Control

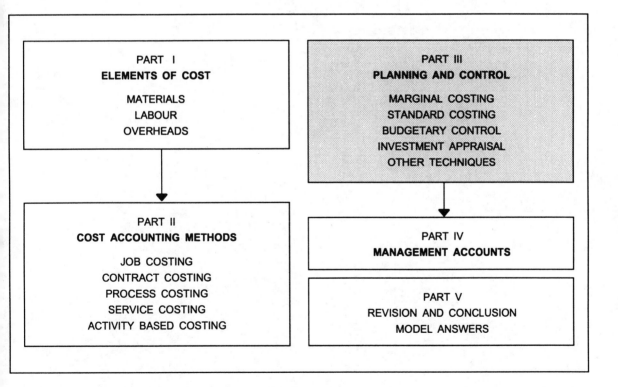

PART I **ELEMENTS OF COST**	PART III **PLANNING AND CONTROL**
MATERIALS LABOUR OVERHEADS	MARGINAL COSTING STANDARD COSTING BUDGETARY CONTROL INVESTMENT APPRAISAL OTHER TECHNIQUES
PART II **COST ACCOUNTING METHODS**	PART IV **MANAGEMENT ACCOUNTS**
JOB COSTING CONTRACT COSTING PROCESS COSTING SERVICE COSTING ACTIVITY BASED COSTING	PART V REVISION AND CONCLUSION MODEL ANSWERS

16

Planning and Control – Definitions and Overview

In Part III we shall be looking at a number of important cost and management accounting techniques for planning and controlling the activities of an enterprise. These terms go together: the *plan* sets out the financial path the enterprise intends to follow for a future period; and the *control* endeavours to see that activities are in line with this plan. A key to successful planning and control is investigation work into departures from plan. When there is a deviation, a variance from plan, management need to know why so that action can be taken to bring results back into line.

In this section we shall be looking at these two key activities in detail. We shall be working through the most frequently used management accounting techniques and applying the methods to various business situations. We shall also be analysing how and why costs change at different levels of activity – termed *cost behaviour* – and how management can use this form of analysis for making decisions and for other useful purposes.

Planning and control skills are key management attributes: a manager should be able to appraise situations as they arise; he or she should be able to anticipate and formulate strategies and tactics for the future. Another ability is to be able to work towards the achievement of set aims and objectives. Essentially, management should stick to a plan once it has

been formulated, and take steps to bring performance into line with the plan. Management accounting and costing techniques provide management with the financial tools to assist them in achieving these tasks.

The first part of the equation is *planning*. There are basically two types of plan: long-term plans and short-term (or operational) plans. In this overview we shall take an introductory look at long-term planning, and in Chapter 19 short-term plans or budgets will be examined.

Long-term planning

Long-term planning is the establishment of objectives. A company with a product which has, say, a 5 per cent share of a market might state 'We want to have a 10 per cent share by Year 5.' This becomes their objective – their long-term plan. Having established the long-term objective, the next step for management is to ascertain where the company is *now*, that is, at the start of the exercise.

This is done by undertaking a *'position audit'*. This has been defined by CIMA as: *'part of the planning process which examines the current state of the entity in respect of*:

resources of tangible and intangible assets and finance; products brands and markets;
operating systems such as production and distribution; internal organisation;
current results;
returns to stockholders'.

The 'current state' of each of these headings may take some time to establish and substantiate. You can see by going through the list that a business needs to ask of itself many questions and to be able to answer them.

The next step is for management to analyse the circumstances and conditions likely to prevail during the plan period. For example, what the likely demand for products will be over the period; what the position is with competitors, with technology, with staffing, and so on. Many firms adopt an appraisal system at this stage called '*SWOT analysis*'. This seeks to identify or assess the position of the business in relation to the firm's strengths (*S*), weaknesses (*W*), opportunities (*O*) and threats (*T*). Each of these headings will be addressed, with the purpose of maximising the strengths and opportunities, and minimising the weaknesses and threats.

For example, a strength might be the superiority of the firm's product compared to those of competitors; an opportunity could be the opening up of a new overseas market for the product; a weakness might be that the manufacturing plant is old, or that selling techniques are outdated; a threat could be that a competitor is known to be investing heavily in modern plant, clearly to improve their own product and thus their market share.

So, having seen where the company is now (the audit position) and having established the SWOT position, the next stage in the planning process is for management to decide how they are going to get from A (now) to the ultimate objective, B. *Gap analysis* will assist them to do this. Figures 16.1 and 16.2 illustrate this concept.

Figure 16.1 shows the gap that needs to be bridged if the objective is to be achieved; Figure 16.2 shows the possible options open to management to enable them to do this. In our example, the aim is to increase market share from 5 per cent to 10 per cent. To close that gap, management will need to make decisions and plan activities if the aim is to be achieved. Thus a strategy will be required.

In the above example, management may decide that they need to introduce new products and open up new markets as well as become more efficient in their operations if they are to fill the gap. Other terms to describe long-term planning are *corporate planning* and *strategic planning*.

Once the long-term plan has been decided upon, the next stage is to set it in motion. Getting from now, position A, to the desired objective, position B, requires operational planning of the intervening short-term periods.

FIGURE 16.1

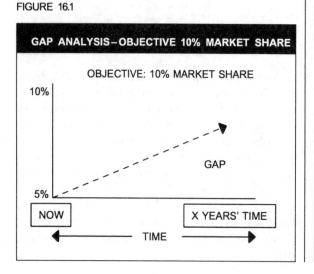

FIGURE 16.2

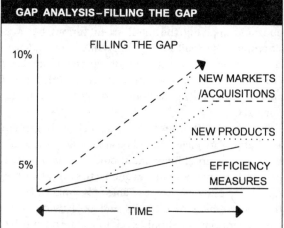

Short-term planning and control

Short-term plans are operational plans, 'short-term' usually referring to a period of one financial accounting year.

When an operational plan is expressed in money terms it is called a *Budget*. Chapter 19, Budgetary Control, covers extensively the techniques and methods used to establish budgets, and discusses the ways in which budgets assist management in running the day-to-day affairs of the business. Actual results can be compared to budget and any over- or under-achievement thus identified. These differences are called *variances*, and they can be analysed to assist management in controlling the actual operations. This facilitates 'management by exception' techniques, whereby management is able to concentrate on those activities that might be out of line with the plan, and to ignore those that are according to plan.

Another form of short-term planning for products is called standard costing. A standard cost is a predetermined estimate of the cost of a product or service. It provides an indication of how much a product or service should cost. Chapter 18 explains how standard costs are set, how they assist in valuing closing stocks, and how they help management in identifying adverse and favourable variances.

The performance or behaviour of costs at different levels of activity also plays a part in short-term planning and decision-making. The analysis of costs between fixed costs and variable costs enables the establishment of the break-even point of the business, and also assists management to make a variety of decisions. For example, whether or not to accept an order from a customer when it might appear, at first glance, that by doing so would cause a loss. *Marginal costing* techniques analyse the behavioural aspects of costs: this is the subject of Chapter 17.

Capital investment appraisal

Money available for investing in fixed assets and other major projects (generally described as *capital expenditure*), is often in short supply. Therefore some form of 'rationing' of the money is usually required. *Investment appraisal* techniques assist management to choose between the choices of investment opportunities by evaluating the forecast returns; for example, ranking the proposals to find those with the 'best' economic return. These techniques are explained and illustrated in Chapter 20.

Profitability analysis methods

In Chapter 21, we shall be looking at various profitability analysis methods, including the use of statistics and trends analysis techniques, which are also designed to assist management in the planning and control of their operations.

Definitions

It should be noted that in this section of the book, as elsewhere, the definitions of terms used are generally in line with CIMA terminology. For convenience, the definitions of some of these planning and control terms (some abridged) which will be referred to in Part III are as follows:

Planning terms

Break even chart
A chart which indicates approximate profit or loss at different levels of sales volume within a limited range.

Break even point
The level of activity at which there is neither profit nor loss.

Cost–volume–profit analysis (CVP)
The study of the effects on future profit of changes in fixed cost, variable cost, sales price, quantity and mix

Forecasting
The identification of factors and quantification of their effect on an entity, as a basis for planning

Limiting factor
Anything which limits the activity of an entity. An entity seeks to optimise the benefit it obtains from the limiting factor.

Projection

An expected future trend pattern obtained by extrapolation. (It is principally concerned with quantitative factors, whereas a forecast includes judgements.)

Sensitivity analysis

A modelling procedure used in planning; changes are made to estimates of the variables to establish whether any will affect the outcome of the plan critically.

Budgeting terms

Budget

A plan expressed in money. It is prepared and approved prior to the budget period and may show income, expenditure and the capital to be employed.

Budgetary control

The establishment of budgets relating the responsibilities of executives to the requirements of a policy, and the continuous comparison of actual with budgeted results, either to secure by individual action the objectives of that policy, or to provide a basis for its revision.

Capital expenditure control

Procedures for authorising and subsequently monitoring capital expenditure.

Cash flow budget

A detailed budget of income and cash expenditure incorporating both revenue and capital items.

Departmental budget

A budget of income and/or expenditure applicable to a particular function (*a function may refer to a department or a process*).

Flexible budget

A budget which, by recognising different cost behaviour patterns, is designed to change as volume of output changes.

Operational budget

Budget of the profit and loss account and its supporting schedules.

Variance

Difference between planned or budgeted cost and actual cost; and similarly revenue.

Standard costing terms

Standard

A predetermined measurable quantity set in defined conditions.

Standard cost

A standard expressed in money. It is built up from an assessment of the value of cost elements. Its main uses are providing bases for performance measurement, control by exception reporting, valuing stock and establishing selling prices.

Standard direct labour cost

The planned average cost of direct labour.

Standard hour or minute

The quantity of work achievable at standard performance in an hour or minute.

Variance

Difference between planned or standard cost and actual cost; and similarly revenue.

Variance analysis

The analysis of performance by means of variances.

17
Marginal Costing and CVP Analysis

In this chapter we shall examine cost behaviour – the way costs behave at different levels of activity – and how the analysis of costs in this manner can help management to make the best choice from a number of alternatives. In addition, we shall be covering the techniques to enable the break-even point to be established and how these calculations can assist in the decision-making process.

The elements of cost – materials, labour and overheads – comprise two different types of cost: *fixed costs* and *variable costs*. As activity rises or falls, some of the costs will increase or decrease in line with the activity.

If a bought-in item which has cost £1 is sold, then, by selling 1000, the costs incurred will be £1000. And if 500 items are sold, the cost will clearly be £500. This type of cost is described as a *variable cost*: it changes in line with output, in this case sales. Other costs, however, remain completely unaffected in the short-term by the changes in the levels of activity, and these are known as *fixed costs*. Costs therefore *behave* differently according to the levels of activity achieved.

There is a further behavioural classification where costs have a combination of both the above characteristics. These are termed *semi-variable* (or alternatively, *semi-fixed*) *costs*.

Over time, it should be noted, all costs change, but in the short term they are generally considered to behave in accordance with the above descriptions.

For accounting purposes, costs are considered to move in an exact linear (straight-line) fashion, fixed costs staying at the same level irrespective of output, variable costs moving directly in line with output, as shown in Figure 17.1.

To illustrate the splitting of costs into these two categories we shall use the typical manufacturing, trading and profit and loss account structure, as shown in Table 17.1. You will note first that no distinction is made in the figures as to the behaviour of costs – whether they are fixed or variable. (You will also note that sales were 1000 units, with 1200 units actually being made in the period. Therefore 200 remained at the end of the accounting period as closing stocks. The valuation of these stocks, using absorption costing methods, will be based on the unit cost of £50 each – £60 000 manufacturing costs divided by the 1200 units made – the value of the closing stocks therefore being £10 000).

Let us work through these accounts, dealing first with the variable costs.

Variable costs

Manufacturing account section

The variable costs will usually comprise raw materials and direct labour – the prime costs of the product.

FIGURE 17.1

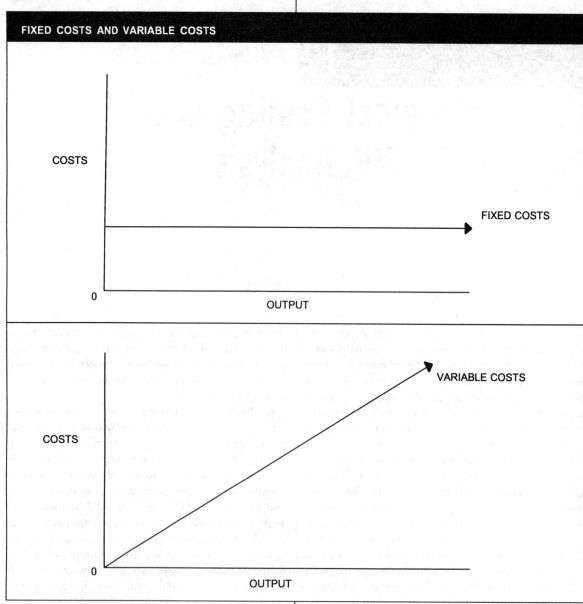

FIXED COSTS AND VARIABLE COSTS

Also, any direct expenses or variable overheads – those costs that can be directly identified within the product and which will therefore vary in line with activity. (An example would be royalties payable.)

Raw materials used in producing a finished product, being a direct cost, are clearly variable – the more products sold the more materials used. But direct labour costs will, in reality, carry some form of fixed or semi-variable cost and should therefore be classified ideally as a semi-variable cost. In many examination questions, however, direct labour is treated as a variable cost, it being considered that the requirement for direct labour will generally move in line with output. (Semi-variable costs are described later and need to be broken down into their two constituent elements – fixed and variable).

TABLE 17.1

TYPICAL MANUFACTURING, TRADING AND PROFIT AND LOSS ACCOUNT STRUCTURE

	£	UNITS
MANUFACTURING ACCOUNT		
MATERIALS	25 000	
DIRECT LABOUR	20 000	
FACTORY OVERHEADS	15 000	
COST OF COMPLETED GOODS	60 000	1 200
TRADING AND PROFIT AND LOSS ACCOUNT		
SALES	**100 000**	1 000
COST OF GOODS SOLD:		
OPENING STOCK	0	0
COMPLETED GOODS	60 000	1 200
CLOSING STOCK	(10 000)	(200)
TOTAL COST OF GOODS SOLD	50 000	1 000
GROSS PROFIT	**50 000**	
SELLING AND ADMINISTRATION COSTS	20 000	
NET PROFIT	**30 000**	

Selling and administration section

Here, some of the costs incurred will relate directly to sales. As sales increase, so too will the related sales cost. An example would be commission payable to commission agents, the cost being directly attributable to the sales achieved in the period.

Fixed costs

By definition, all other costs incurred, not classified as variable, are fixed costs. Examples are: rent and rates; supervision costs; indirect labour; and office and administration expenses. Fixed costs will therefore be included in both the manufacturing section and the sales and administration sections.

For illustration purposes, we shall assume that factory overheads contained £5000 variable costs, and sales and administration costs include £5000 variable

costs. The total costs of £70 000 (£50 000 cost of goods sold plus £20 000 sales and administration costs) can be split between the two types of cost, as shown in Table 17.2.

As previously noted, the production costs relate to 1200 units produced, whereas only 1000 units have been sold. In absorption costing, the costs attaching to the 200 units carried forward include both fixed and variable elements. The variable element is arrived at as follows:

$$\frac{£50\,000}{1200} = £41.66 \text{ per unit}$$

And the fixed element as follows:

$$\frac{£10\,000}{1200} = £8.34 \text{ per unit}$$

But in marginal costing *all fixed costs are treated as period costs and are written off in the accounting period to which they relate*. Therefore *none* of the factory fixed cost overheads will be carried forward in the closing stocks.

Reworking the figures into marginal costing format, the profit statement will appear as shown in Figure 17.2 (with the conventional profit and loss (P&L) account alongside for comparison).

Note the term *contribution*. This is the difference between the sales and the variable costs: it is so called because this is the figure that 'contributes' towards the fixed costs and profit. As already discussed, there is deemed to be a 'straight-line' relationship between the sales and the variable costs directly attributable to those sales. Therefore the contribution will always move precisely in line with the sales figure. In Figure 17.2, if sales had been £200 000 the variable costs would be twice as much (£93 334); and if sales were to drop by half to £50 000, the variable costs would also halve, to £23 333. The relationship between the two is therefore constant and linear, resulting in an undeviating ratio.

The total fixed costs for the period, production, selling and administration, are written off in the period, none of the production costs being carried forward to the next accounting period in the closing stocks. Closing stocks are therefore valued on the basis of variable cost per unit only.

You will have noted that the absorption costing model and the marginal costing model produce different profits. This difference is because of the treatment

TABLE 17.2

TOTAL COSTS SPLIT BETWEEN VARIABLE AND FIXED COSTS				
ANALYSIS OF COSTS	£	VARIABLE	FIXED	UNITS
MATERIALS	25 000	25 000		
DIRECT LABOUR	20 000	20 000		
FACTORY OVERHEADS	15 000	5 000	10 000	
COST OF COMPLETED GOODS	60 000	50 000	10 000	1 200
COST OF GOODS SOLD:				
OPENING STOCK	0			0
COMPLETED GOODS	60 000	50 000	10 000	1 200
CLOSING STOCK	(10 000)	(8 333)	(1 667)	(200)
TOTAL COST OF GOODS SOLD	50 000	41 667	8 333	1 000
SELLING AND ADMINISTRATION COSTS	20 000	5 000	15 000	
TOTAL COSTS	£70 000	£46 667	£23 333	

FIGURE 17.2

PROFIT STATEMENT IN MARGINAL COSTING FORMAT		

MARGINAL COSTING PROFIT STATEMENT		
	£	UNITS
SALES	100 000	1 000
VARIABLE COSTS	46 667	1 000
CONTRIBUTION	53 333	1 000
FIXED COSTS	25 000	
PROFIT	£28 333	

CONVENTIONAL PROFIT AND LOSS PRESENTATION	
	£
SALES	100 000
COST OF GOODS SOLD:	
OPENING STOCK	0
COMPLETED GOODS	60 000
CLOSING STOCK	(10 000)
TOTAL COST OF GOODS SOLD	50 000
GROSS PROFIT	50 000
EXPENSES	20 000
PROFIT	£30 000

of the production fixed costs in the stocks and can be reconciled as follows:

Profit per absorption costing method	£30 000
Less:	
Fixed manufacturing overhead carried forward in closing stocks:	
200 units at £8.33 per unit	
(£1000/1200 units)	£ 1 667
Profit per marginal costing method	£28 333

Worked example

The following examination question provides an illustration of the two methods:

LCCI Management Accounting Third Level (1994)

A department of Thompson Supplies plc manufactures a single product. The following figures apply to a one year period:

Production activity:	100%
Production output:	4 000 units
Production costs:	£32 000 variable
	£ 8 000 fixed
Sales:	£80 000
Selling, distribution and administration costs:	£16 000 variable
	£12 000 fixed
Normal output:	4 000 units per annum

In the first three months of a given year, 1100 units were produced and 800 sold. The variable selling, distribution and administration costs vary with sales.

Required:

(a) Calculate the profit for the first three months using:
   (i) absorption costing; and
   (ii) marginal costing.
(b) Prepare a statement reconciling the profit calculated in a(i) and a(ii).
(c) Calculate the over-/under-absorption of fixed costs for the first three months.

Solution:
(a) (i) and (ii) – see below.

(a)(i)   Profit using absorption costing
                three-month period

	£	Note and calculations
Sales	16 000	£80 000/4 000 × 800 Units
Cost of goods sold		
Opening stocks	0	*Manufacturing account:*
Cost of goods completed	11 000	Variable costs 8 800 £32 000/4 000 × 1100
Closing stocks	(3 000)	Fixed costs 2 200 £ 8 000/4 000 × 1100
	8 000	11 000
		Cost per unit £10.00 £11 000/1 100
Gross profit	8 000	
		Closing stocks 300 units at £10 per unit
Selling, distribution and		
administrative costs:		
Variable costs	3 200	£16 000/4 000 × 800 units
Fixed costs	3 000	£12 000/12 months × 3
	6 200	
Profit – absorption costing	1 800	
Over-absorbed overhead	200 →	Activity expected = 1 000 units; actual production = 1100 units. Therefore 100 units more produced at £2 per unit fixed cost
Profit	2 000	

(a)(ii)   Profit using marginal costing
                three-month period

	£			
Sales	16 000			
Variable costs	9 600	Production	6 400	£32 000/4 000 × 800
		Selling, etc.	3 200	£16 000/4 000 × 800
Contribution	6 400		9 600	
Fixed costs	5 000	Production	2 000	£8 000/4 000 × 1000
		Selling, etc.	3 000	
Profit – marginal costing	1 400		5 000	

(b) Reconciliation of profit:

Profit per absorption costing	£2000
Less: production overhead carried forward in closing stocks:	
300 units at £2 each	£ 600
(£8000/4000 units = £2 each)	
Profit per marginal costing	£1400

(c) Over-absorbed overhead:

1000 units were expected to be produced in the three-month period, but 1100 units were actually produced. The overhead absorption rate per unit for fixed costs was:

$$\frac{8000}{4000 \text{ units}} = £2 \text{ per unit}$$

Therefore 100 more units were produced, resulting in fixed costs being over-absorbed by £200.

Splitting semi-variable costs

As discussed earlier, some costs cannot readily be identified as either fixed or variable and will therefore be classified as semi-variable costs (or alternatively semi-fixed costs). This is because, at different levels of activity, a cost which might normally be considered to be fixed may increase or decrease to a certain extent at the new level of activity. These fixed costs tend to rise or fall in 'steps' – as a higher level of activity is reached, additional costs may be incurred. When normal levels of activity return the additional cost would cease.

The purpose of marginal costing is to split the total costs into the two behavioural elements of fixed and variable costs, to assist in decision-making. Therefore, a method of splitting the semi-variable costs is necessary. There are a number of statistical methods available to enable this to be done and two are described below. The first, an arithmetical system, is known as the *high/low method*.

High/low method

This simple technique uses the difference in units and total costs incurred at one level of activity, compared to the units and total costs incurred at another level, to provide a variable cost per unit. By dividing the *value* difference between the high and low figures by

the *activity* difference this variable cost per unit is thus provided. When this is established, the balance of the costs will represent the fixed cost element.

Example:

Units	Total costs
1000	£ 7000
2000	£11000
3000	£15000
4000	£19000

The first step is to choose both the highest level of activity and the lowest:

	Units	Total costs
High	4000	£19000
Low	1000	£ 7000
Difference	3000	£12000

The next step is to deduct the low figures from the high figures, as in the example. Then simply divide the total costs difference by the units difference. In this example the variable cost per unit will be £4 each (£12000/3000 units).

So, at 4000 units, variable costs will amount to £16000 (4000 × £4). The total cost at this level is £19000. By deducting the variable cost element (£16000) from the total cost £19000, the fixed cost element becomes known: £3000.

A test of the validity of the figures can be gauged from Table 17.3 using the above figures.

Scatter graph method

This other method is to plot both activity and cost data on a graph called a *scatter graph* (or *scatter diagram*). A straight line can then be drawn through the adjudged middle of the points to the vertical axis to

TABLE 17.3

VALIDITY OF DATA IN HIGH/LOW METHOD

UNITS	VARIABLE UNIT COSTS	VARIABLE COSTS	FIXED COSTS	TOTAL COSTS
1000	£4	£ 4000	£3000	£ 7000
2000	£4	£ 8000	£3000	£11000
3000	£4	£12000	£3000	£15000
4000	£4	£16000	£3000	£19000

discover the fixed costs element. The variable cost element can then be calculated. This straight line is termed *the line of best fit* (or *regression line*).

To complete the scatter graph, the horizontal axis (x-axis) is used for the units (or activities) and the vertical axis (y-axis) used for the costs. The x-axis is always used for the independent variable, that is, the units. The y-axis is the dependent variable, because costs are conditional on the various levels of activity achieved.

When the data are plotted, the line of best fit can then be drawn by eye, by judgement. The point where the line connects with the vertical axis represents the fixed costs point. By deducting this amount from the total costs plotted the variable costs become known.

Example:

Prepare a scattergraph from the following data to establish the fixed costs and variable cost elements:

Units	Total costs
1 000	£ 9 000
2 000	£14 000
3 000	£20 000
4 000	£23 000
5 000	£29 000
6 000	£33 000
7 000	£38 000
8 000	£44 000

Solution:
See Figure 17.3.

FIGURE 17.3

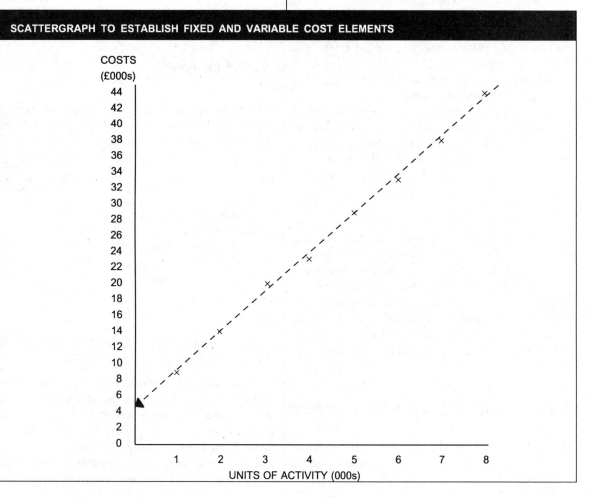

SCATTERGRAPH TO ESTABLISH FIXED AND VARIABLE COST ELEMENTS

The fixed costs element is therefore approximately £4000. By deducting this amount from, say, the 8000-unit cost of £44 000 the variable costs at this level are arrived at: £40 000. Therefore, the variable cost per unit is £5 each (£40 000/8000 units).

Marginal costing as a bookkeeping method

Marginal costing methods can be part of an accounting system. The bookkeeping entries for production activities will record only the variable production costs as product costs, with fixed production costs being written off as period costs to the profit and loss account. The marginal cost valuation of stocks thus excludes the fixed overheads element. Product costs are thus simplified, with no overhead absorption rates to calculate and no over- or under-absorbed fixed overhead computations to be done.

For published accounts purposes, however, marginal costing methods of valuing closing stocks is not acceptable. SSAP 9 (Accounting for stocks and long term contracts) defines the cost of stocks as including the *costs of conversion* of the raw materials, thus embracing production overheads.

The system does not accord either with the accruals (or matching) concept as outlined in SSAP 2 (Disclosure of accounting policies). This states that revenues and costs are matched with one another in the profit and loss account to which they relate. So, for example, the costs of an item (materials, labour, absorbed production overheads) made in Period 1, which is sold in Period 2, will be matched with the income arising in Period 2, the costs having been carried forward as stocks at the end of Period 1. With marginal costing, the fixed costs of conversion are not carried forward in the stock valuation, so therefore costs and revenue cannot be matched in the same accounting period. Thus an adjustment to marginal costing closing stocks will always be needed for financial reporting purposes, to include a proportion of the fixed cost production overheads.

Marginal costing as an aid to decision-making

Marginal costing techniques are especially useful in assisting management in making decisions, some of which are:

Whether to accept one-off special orders from customers.

Whether to continue to make a product, or to buy it in from outside suppliers.

How to select the best course of action from a number of alternatives.

The analysis of costs between fixed and variable elements helps management to decide which way to go: which of the alternatives will be of most benefit. Marginal costing techniques can also help in establishing the maximum profit when certain resources are limited, such as materials or labour. Where, say, two products require the use of one limited resource, the techniques will indicate the best allocation of the scarce resource between the two to achieve the maximum benefit.

Working through these 'decision-making' situations:

Special orders

Worked example

A company manufactures one product, with current production being at 80% of the factory's total capacity. Costs and revenue data are as follows:

	£	Units
Sales	200 000	10 000
Costs		
Variable production costs	150 000	
Fixed production costs	30 000	
Variable selling costs	5 000	
Fixed selling and administration costs	1 000	
Total costs	186 000	
Profit	14 000	

Production cost per unit = £18 using absorption costing
Normal selling price = £20

An overseas customer is interested in placing a one-off bulk order for 2000 units, but the maximum price the customer will pay is £16 per unit. No variable selling costs would be incurred if the order was taken. Should the company accept the order or not?

Initially it appears that the customer wants to pay £2 less than the cost per unit and a loss would therefore ensue if the order were to be taken. But the cost of £18 each is the absorbed cost, and includes £3 of fixed production overheads.

Using marginal costing techniques, the position would appear as follows:

	One-off order	Total	Units
	£	£	£	£
Sales	200 000	32 000	232 000	12 000
Variable costs				
Variable production costs	150 000	30 000	180 000	
Variable selling costs	5 000	0	5 000	
Contribution	45 000	2 000	47 000	
Fixed costs	31 000	0	31 000	
Profit	14 000	2 000	16 000	

So, by taking the job profits overall would increase by over 14% (£16 000/£14 000). In addition, usage of the factory's capacity would rise from 80% to 96% (12 000/12 500 maximum units).

There is always the possibility, however, that existing customers might become aware of the special price offered to the 'one-off customer' and this could affect future trading relationships with those customers. Before accepting orders on a marginal costing basis management need to consider all factors, including this possibility.

'Make or buy' decisions

Often there is an alternative similar product or component that could be purchased from an outside supplier instead of being manufactured by the company itself. A commercial enterprise is in business primarily to maximise profits, so it is therefore necessary for management to investigate all profit opportunities and choose the most beneficial. The following example illustrates the point.

Worked example

ACCA 1982 (abridged)
The budgeted manufacturing cost of a component is as follows:

Variable production costs	£34 per unit
Fixed production costs	£20 per unit
Total production cost using absorption costing	£54

A supplier has offered to supply the item at a guaranteed price of £50. Should the company buy the product or continue making it?

Here, on the face of it, to buy-in the product would appear to represent a cost saving of £4 per unit. But the fixed costs will continue to be incurred and merely 'shifted' from this component to other components or products who will thus have to bear a greater share of the production overheads. The comparison to be made is therefore between the variable production cost – £34 per unit, and the buy-in price of £50. To continue to manufacture is clearly the best option, as each component is £16 cheaper. But other factors may need to be taken into consideration. For example, are the production facilities needed to produce the component capable of being put to more profitable use?

The next part of this question asked: If newly-introduced annual testing costs of £56 000 p.a. are incurred, would this affect the decision to continue to manufacture the component? There is a saving of £16 per unit by continuing to manufacture. This can be considered in marginal costing terms as the 'contribution'. The £56 000 thus becomes the relevant fixed cost of the decision. The number of components manufactured must therefore be sufficient to clear this additional cost if the option to continue to make is to remain cheaper than the buy-in price.

	£
Buy-in cost	50
Production cost	34
'Contribution'	16
Fixed cost	56 000
Number of units to 'break even':	3 500
	(£56 000/£16 per unit)

Check

Units	To buy-in 3 500	To produce 3 500
Variable cost	£175 000	£119 000
Fixed cost	0	£56 000
Total cost	£175 000	£175 000

The point where both costs are equal is a production level of 3500 units as in the computation. So, if the usage of the components is less than 3500 p.a. the bought-in component would be cheaper.

Selecting from a number of alternatives

There are often a number of alternative choices open to management and marginal costing techniques provide assistance by evaluating each proposal to ascertain which is the most financially beneficial for the company.

We shall use the following London Chamber of Commerce question to illustrate how the marginal costing technique of *cost–volume–profit analysis (CVP)* is especially effective in helping management to choose from alternatives. CVP analysis is, using CIMA terminology, *'The study of the effects on future profit of changes in fixed cost, variable cost, sales price, quantity and mix'.*

Worked example

LCCI COSTING – THIRD LEVEL (1994)
Eviver makes only one product which is sold through agents, who receive a commission of 10% on actual selling price. Output has fallen sharply, resulting in the following summarised profit and loss account for the three-month period just ended:

	£
Sales (64 000 units)	5 120
Direct material	1 280
Direct labour	768
Production overhead	1 256
Administration overheads	750
Selling overhead	1 162
Loss	96

The production overhead includes variable costs of £4 per unit, the selling overhead includes the agents' commission. All other overheads are fixed. Capacity exists to increase both production and sales volume by 40 000 units every three-month period.

The following proposals have been put forward at a directors' meeting as alternative strategies to achieve a target profit of £500 000 in the current three-month period:

1. Reduce selling prices by 10%.
2. Spend £250 000 on special advertising.
3. Reduce selling prices by 5% and spend £250 000 on special advertising.
4. Reduce prime costs by £5 per unit, reduce selling prices by 10% and spend £250 000 on special advertising.
5. Increase prime costs by £3 per unit, increase selling prices by 10% and spend £120 000 on special advertising.

Required:
(a) Calculate the number of units (to the nearest unit) required to obtain the target profit in the current three-month period for each of the alternatives.
(b) The break-even point *in sales value* (to the nearest £1000) in each case.

A number of terms and computations will be used in the solution to this question and explanations are given of their meaning and how they are computed as they arise.

The first step is to rearrange the data into marginal costing format.

	£	Units
Sales*	5 120 000	64 000
Variable costs		
Materials	1 280 000	
Labour	768 000	
Production overhead†	256 000	
Agents' commission‡	512 000	
Total variable costs	2 816 000	
Contribution	2 304 000	
Fixed costs§	2 400 000	
Profit (loss)	**(96 000)**	

Notes
*£5 120 000/64 000 units = £80 per unit.
†64 000 units × £4 per unit.
‡10% of £5 120 000.
§£1 000 000 production overhead + admin.
  £750 000 + £650 000.

The question stated that a target profit of £500 000 was required. The contribution figure, as was stated earlier, contributes to fixed costs plus profit. So, to achieve a profit of £500 000 the contribution must be sufficient to pay for the fixed costs of £2 400 000 *plus* the £500 000 target profit. Therefore the contribution to achieve this must be £2 900 000. Thus

> Contribution = fixed costs + profit

As there is deemed to be a constant relationship between sales and variable costs in marginal costing (and thus a linear relationship between sales and contribution), it follows that it is possible to calculate the quantity of sales needed which will be sufficient to achieve the contribution in order to pay for the fixed costs. The formula to do this is as shown below and produces the *break-even point*.

Break-even point

The break-even point is, in CIMA terminology, '*the level of activity at which there is neither a profit nor loss*'.

There are two methods to calculate the break-even point. The first is in *sales value terms* and the formula is as follows:

> $$\frac{\text{Fixed costs}}{\text{Contribution/sales percentage (C/S\%)}}$$

The contribution/sales percentage (or C/S%) represents the ratio of contribution to sales. With variable costs deemed to move precisely in line with sales, this ratio will always be constant. Using this formula, the sales value required to achieve break-even for the existing position of the business will be:

$$\frac{£2\,400\,000}{45\%} \quad (£2\,304\,000/£5\,120\,000)$$

$$= £5\,333\,333 \text{ sales}$$

As the contribution is 45 per cent it follows that the variable costs will be 55 per cent of sales:

Sales	100%
Contribution	45%
therefore, Variable costs =	55%

With sales at £5 333 333 there will be neither profit or loss, as the following demonstrates:

Sales	£5 333 333	100%
Variable costs	£2 933 333	55%
Contribution	£2 400 000	45%
Fixed costs	£2 400 000	
Profit (loss)	0	

The break-even point can also be calculated in *sales unit terms*. That is, the number of units required to be sold to pay for the fixed costs. The formula is:

> $$\frac{\text{Fixed costs}}{\text{Contribution per unit}}$$

The contribution per unit represents the contribution each unit makes to the fixed costs and profit. To arrive at the figure, simply divide the contribution amount by the contribution per unit.

$$\frac{£2\,400\,000}{£36} \quad (£2\,304\,000/64\,000 \text{ units})$$

$$= \mathbf{66\,666} \text{ units}$$

To check this result, multiply the number of units by the sales price per unit of £80: the result will be the same break-even sales value amount as calculated earlier, 66 666 units × £80 per unit = £5 333 280 (to the nearest unit).

Reverting to the worked example above: the first alternative was to reduce the selling prices by 10 per cent. The position would be as shown on page 200.

Option 2, spending £250 000 on special advertising, would require the following calculations:

Contribution
   required: £3 150 000
                  (£2,400,000 + £500 000 + £250 000)
Contribution
   per unit: £36

So the number of units needed to be sold would be:

$$\frac{\text{Fixed costs} + \text{Profit}}{\text{Contribution per unit}} \quad \frac{3\,150\,000}{£36} = 87\,500 \text{ units}$$

Option 3 is to reduce the selling prices by 5 per cent *and* spend the £250 000 on special advertising. The position here is shown on page 200.

Option 4 is to reduce prime costs by £5 per unit, reduce selling prices by 10 per cent *and* spend

Option 1

	£	Units	Present per unit £	Reduction of 10% in selling price
Sales	5 120 000	64 000	80.00	72.00 per unit
Variable costs:				
Materials	1 280 000		20.00	20.00
Labour	768 000		12.00	12.00
Production overhead	256 000		4.00	4.00
Agents' commission	512 000		8.00	7.20
Total variable costs	2 816 000		44.00	43.20 per unit
Contribution	2 304 000		36.00	28.80 per unit

Fixed costs	£2 400 000
Desired profit	£500 000
Contribution required	£2 900 000

Sales in units required $\dfrac{£2\,900\,000}{£28.80}$ = 100 694 units

Option 3

	£	Units	Present per unit £	Reduction of 5% in selling price
Sales	5 120 000	64 000	80.00	76.00 per unit
Variable costs:				
Materials	1 280 000		20.00	20.00
Labour	768 000		12.00	12.00
Production overhead	256 000		4.00	4.00
Agents' commission	512 000		8.00	7.60
Total variable costs	2 816 000		44.00	43.60 per unit
Contribution	2 304 000		36.00	32.40 per unit

Fixed costs	£2 650 000
Desired profit	£500 000
Contribution required	£3 150 000

Sales in units required $\dfrac{£3\,150\,000}{£32.40}$ = 97 222 units

the £250 000. The situation here is shown on page 201:

The fifth and final option is to spend £120 000 on advertising, increase prime costs by £3 and increase selling prices by 10 per cent (see page 201).

Part (b) of the question required the break-even point for each case to be expressed in sales value terms:

Option	Fixed costs (£)	Contribution Sales (%)	Break-even Sales (£)
1	2 400 000	40.0	6 000 000
2	2 650 000	45.0	5 888 889
3	2 650 000	42.6	6 220 657
4	2 650 000	46.9	5 650 320
5	2 520 000	45.7	£5 514 223

Option 4

	£	Units	Present per unit £		Option 5 position £	
Sales	5 120 000	64 000	80.00	− 10%	72.00	per unit
Variable costs:						
Materials	1 280 000		20.00 ⎫	− £5		
Labour	768 000		12.00 ⎭		27.00	
Production overhead	256 000		4.00		4.00	
Agents' commission	512 000		8.00		7.20	
Total variable costs	2 816 000		44.00		38.20	per unit
Contribution	2 304 000		36.00		33.80	per unit
Fixed costs					£2 650 000	
Desired profit					£500 000	
Contribution required					£3 150 000	

Sales in units required $\dfrac{£3\,150\,000}{£33.80} = 93\,195$ units

Option 5

	£	Units	Present per unit £		Option 5 position £	
Sales	5 120 000	64 000	80.00	+ 10%	88.00	per unit
Variable costs:						
Materials	1 280 000		20.00 ⎫	+ £3		
Labour	768 000		12.00 ⎭		35.00	
Production overhead	256 000		4.00		4.00	
Agents' commission	512 000		8.00		8.80	
Total variable costs	2 816 000		44.00		47.80	per unit
Contribution	2 304 000		36.00		40.20	per unit
Fixed costs					£2 520 000	
Desired profit					£500 000	
Contribution required					£3 020 000	

Sales in units required $\dfrac{£3\,020\,000}{£40.20} = 75\,124$ units

Management's decision on which option to choose will depend on their judgement of the achievability of sales for the particular option.

Limiting factors

A limiting factor is, using CIMA terminology '*Anything which limits the activity of an entity*'. If there is a supply shortage of materials, or of labour, or there is a lack of production or storage space, these are limiting factors to a firm's ability to maximise profits. It therefore makes sense for management to ensure that where a limiting factor situation exists, the business is able to maximise profit opportunities by allocating the short-supply resource to products or services in the most effective way.

CVP analysis methods show how this can be achieved.

Example:

A company manufactures four products, each using the same basic raw material. To satisfy the sales demand for all the products, the company will need more raw material than is currently available. But supply is restricted to existing quantities.

Product	A	B	C	D	Total
Selling price – each (£)	100	120	140	160	
Sales demand – units	2 000	3 000	2 500	1 000	
Material usage per unit (kg)	10	12	12	14	
Labour cost per unit (£)	20	26	35	39	
Variable overheads (£)	5	5	6	6	

Material cost per kg = £5.00

Demand for material (kg)	20 000	36 000	30 000	14 000	100 000

Supply of material is restricted to 80 000 kg

So, how best to 'share' the resource of materials, the limiting factor? 100 000 kg could be used but only 80 000 kg is available. The solution is to rank the products by the 'contribution per limiting factor' and then decide on the quantity to produce of each product to ensure the maximum benefit is achieved. This usually results in the top contributor being produced in full while the lowest contributor is restricted to the remaining scarce resource left after production of the other products. First set out the data in the contribution format:

Product	A	B	C	D
	£	£	£	£
Selling price each	100	120	140	160
Variable costs each				
Materials	50	60	60	70
Labour	20	26	35	39
Variable overheads	5	5	6	6
Total variable costs	75	91	101	115
Contribution each	25	29	39	45

Contribution per limiting factor:

	A	B	C	D
per materials (kg)	2.500	2.417	3.250	3.214
	£25/10 kg	£29/12 kg	£39/12 kg	£45/14 kg
per materials (value)	0.500	0.483	0.650	0.643
	£25/£50	£29/£60	£39/£60	£45/£70

Product C, being the most profitable, will be ranked 1, Product D ranked 2, Product A ranked 3 and Product B ranked 4. The scarce resource of materials will thus be allocated to the products in that order, and production will be scheduled as follows:

Ranking	Sales demand	Material required
Product C	2 500 units	30 000 kg (2 500 × 12 kg)
Product D	1 000 units	14 000 kg (1 000 × 14 kg)
Product A	2 000 units	20 000 kg (2 000 × 10 kg)
Product B	1 333 units	16 000 kg (1 333 × 12 kg)
	(max)	80 000 kg

The full demand for materials for products C, D and A can thus be met, but Product B, generating the lowest contribution per the limiting factor, will be restricted. The overall profit position will be as follows:

Product	A	B	C	D	Total
Sales Units	2 000	1 333	2 500	1 000	
	£	£	£	£	£
Sales	200 000	160 000	350 000	160 000	870 000
Variable costs					
Materials	100 000	80 000	150 000	70 000	400 000
Labour	40 000	34 667	87 500	39 000	201 167
Variable overheads	10 000	6 666	15 000	6 000	37 666
Total variable costs	150 000	121 333	252 500	115 000	638 833
Contribution	50 000	38 667	97 500	45 000	231 167

To demonstrate that this was the right financial decision for management to make, imagine instead that the choice had been based on the *contribution* of products. Product A produced the lowest, at £25 per unit, so management might thus decide not to produce that particular product, thereby 'saving' 20 000 kg of the scarce resource. If this had been the choice, the overall position would have been:

Product	A	B	C	D	Total
Sales Units	0	3 000	2 500	1 000	
	£	£	£	£	£
Sales	0	360 000	350 000	160 000	870 000
Variable costs					
Materials		180 000	150 000	70 000	400 000
Labour		78 000	87 500	39 000	204 500
Variable					
overheads		15 000	15 000	6 000	36 000
Total					
variable costs	0	273 000	252 500	115 000	640 500
Contribution	0	87 000	97 500	45 000	229 500

An overall contribution of £229 500 compared to the contribution per limiting factor profit of £231 167. Clearly, the latter method maximises profitability. And it also kept Product A in the market place! (Another name for the limiting factor is the *key factor*.)

Overall C/S percentage with two or more products

When there are two or more products with differing sales and contributions, the break-even point can be calculated by 'weighting' the contributions by the sales mix to produce an overall C/S percentage.

Example:

		Sales mix	
Product A	£10 000	40% contribution
Product B	£20 000	60% contribution
Total fixed costs	£ 8 000	

Required:
Find the overall C/S percentage and the overall sales to break even.

Solution:

		Product A	Product B
	Sales mix (%)	33.33	66.66
		(10/30)	(20/30)
(multiplied by)	Contribution (%)	40	60
=	C/Sm (%)	13.33 +	40
=	**53.33% Contribution sales mix percentage**		

$$\text{Break-even sales} = \frac{£8\,000}{53.33\%} = £15\,000$$

Graphical presentation of cost behaviour

The above examples and exercises demonstrate that CVP is an effective management decision-making tool. To add to its usefulness the analysis of costs into behavioural classifications can readily be depicted graphically. Most people, at all levels in an organisation, are able to absorb financial information more quickly and with greater effect when the information is presented in a chart or in graphical format: the message gets across. One such form of 'visual aid' used to illustrate the way costs behave at various levels of activity is the *break-even chart*.

The break-even chart, according to CIMA terminology 'Indicates the approximate profit or loss at different levels of sales volume within a limited range'.

There are three forms of break-even chart in frequent use:

Conventional break-even chart.
Contribution break-even chart.
Profit–volume chart.

Conventional break-even chart

This chart, also known as the *traditional chart*, appears as shown in Figure 17.4.

Within the 'frame' of the vertical (costs and revenue) line and the horizontal (output) line the break-even chart comprises just three other lines: the fixed costs line, the variable costs line and the sales line.

Setting up the graph

The vertical line is known as the vertical axis (the *y*-axis), and is always used for costs and sales revenue values. The horizontal axis (the *x*-axis) is used to record the levels of sales output; it can be recorded in either output units or sales value, or both. Where the vertical axis meets the horizontal axis a 0 (zero) is placed. This is termed the origin of the graph. Both axes must be scaled evenly and both will begin at 0 at the point of origin.

Taking the vertical y-axis first

The costs and revenue data must be scaled evenly, so that data will not be cramped, difficult to interpret or hard to plot precisely. (It should be remembered that a

FIGURE 17.4

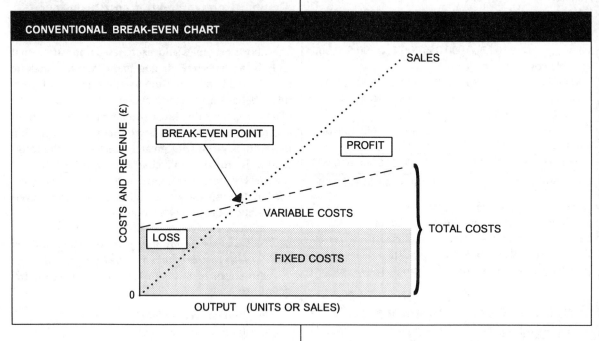

CONVENTIONAL BREAK-EVEN CHART

break-even chart is a visual aid and therefore should be neat and in proportion, easy to read and interpret, and readily understandable.) As an example, if the level of sales is expected to be £10 000 it is better to have the vertical scale plotted at, say, £1000 intervals evenly spread up to a top point of £12 000 or £14 000 than at £500 intervals up to the same top point. This will enhance the visual impact of the graph and achieve the purpose of making the imparted information clearer.

The horizontal *x*-axis must also be scaled precisely, evenly and clearly. It is worth repeating again that it is very important to use sensible, sizeable spacing so that the impact of the graph is immediate and the message it is attempting to convey gets through to the person looking at it. In examinations, a well-presented break-even chart will always score more marks.

The graph should also be correctly titled: (for example, Break-even chart: X Ltd) and the vertical and horizontal axes must be correctly and fully labelled (for example, Sales and Revenue (£) on the vertical axis: Output in Units on the horizontal).

The second step is then to plot the points for the fixed costs, the variable costs and the sales.

Fixed costs

As we have seen, fixed costs tend to remain the same in the short term, irrespective of the level of output. The conventional break-even chart depicts these costs as a *straight line* on the graph. To plot the fixed costs, simply find the cost level applicable to the fixed costs on the vertical axis and draw a straight horizontal line from this point. The line will thus correspond exactly to the horizontal axis. In Figure 17.5, fixed costs have been set at £30 000.

Variable costs

To plot this line, the *total costs* (fixed costs plus variable costs) need to be established at a specific level of output. Say the variable costs incurred at the output level of 1000 units amounted to £70 000 (representing a unit cost of £70 each). The total costs at that precise level of output – 1000 units – would be £100 000: £70 000 variable costs plus fixed costs of £30 000.

On the horizontal scale, find the 1000 units mark and then, on the vertical scale, find the £100 000 position. Where these two intersect represents the total costs at that particular level of output. The variable costs line is then drawn from the fixed costs point on the vertical scale (in the example at the £30 000

FIGURE 17.5

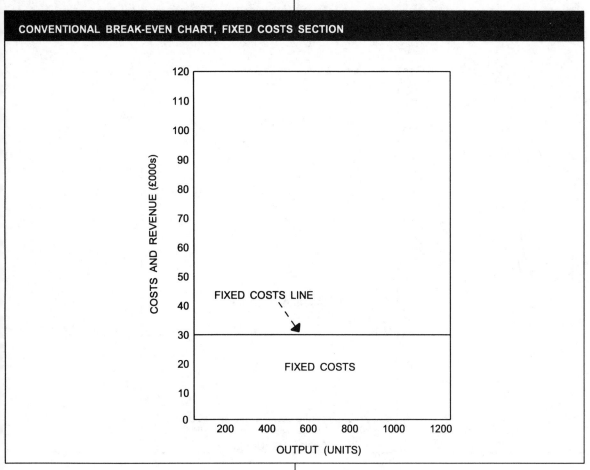

CONVENTIONAL BREAK-EVEN CHART, FIXED COSTS SECTION

FIXED COSTS LINE

FIXED COSTS

OUTPUT (UNITS)

mark) to the £100 000/1000 units intersection point on the graph. You will note in Figure 17.6 that a 'wedge' shape results. As sales increase, so too will the variable costs, in a directly linear manner.

Sales

This line is drawn from the origin of the graph to the level of output/revenue expected. For the example in Figure 17.7, the selling price of each unit is £120. At the 1000-unit level on the horizontal axis the sales value would thus be £120 000. Mark the point where the 1000 units meet the £120 000 on the vertical scale. Then draw the line from zero through to this point.

Combining the three lines produces the completed conventional break-even chart shown in Figure 17.8. Where the sales line intersects with the total costs line is the *break-even point*. If you follow this point down to

the horizontal axis and read off the units this will be the number of units needed to pay for all the fixed costs (600). Now follow the break-even point through to the vertical axis: this gives the sales value needed to pay for the fixed costs (£72 000).

To ensure that the lines have been drawn correctly, the break-even calculation should also be computed:

$$\frac{£30\,000}{41.66\%}\ (£50\,000\ \text{contribution}/£120\,000\ \text{sales})$$

$$= £72\,000$$

You will see that the conventional chart goes further than the calculation, by providing far more information. The profit (or loss) position at various levels of output is depicted: below the break-even point a loss will be sustained; above it a profit is achieved.

FIGURE 17.6

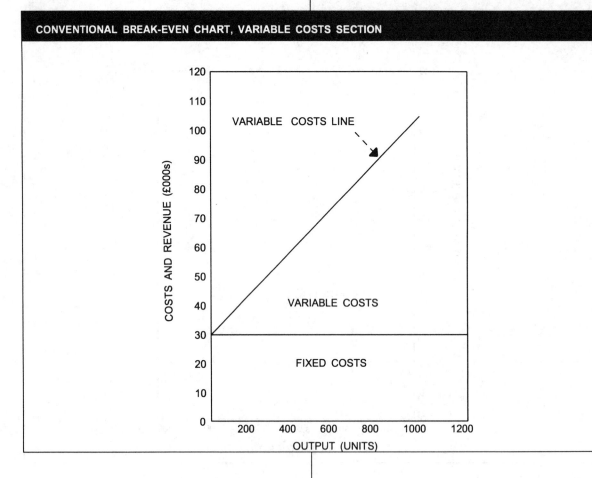

CONVENTIONAL BREAK-EVEN CHART, VARIABLE COSTS SECTION

The actual profit or loss incurred is also calculable visually – it is represented by the 'gap' between the sales line at any level of output and the corresponding total costs line at the same level of sales. By deducting the sales value from the total costs value on the vertical axis the profit or loss becomes known.

Contribution break-even chart

This chart is also composed of the three basic lines – sales, variable costs and fixed costs – within the same y/x frame as described earlier. But in this case the *contribution* made to fixed costs and profit is more clearly revealed.

The scales for both vertical and horizontal axes will be the same as for the conventional break-even chart: that is, plotted at even intervals. Here the *variable*

costs are plotted first. Calculate the variable cost for a particular level of output, 1000 units, say, as before. Find this level on the horizontal output line and also find the calculated cost amount on the vertical line (£70 per unit × 1000 units = £70 000) as in Figure 17.9. Where the two intersect, mark the point. Then draw a straight line from the origin of the graph (zero) through to the marked point and beyond.

Next, on the vertical scale, find the *fixed costs* amount: £30 000 using the same data. Add this to the variable costs amount at the chosen level of output (£70 000, in this case, for 1000 units). This provides the *total costs* value of £100 000. Locate this on the vertical line. Where the 1000 units on the horizontal line intersects with the £100 000 on the vertical line make a point. Then draw a straight line,

FIGURE 17.7

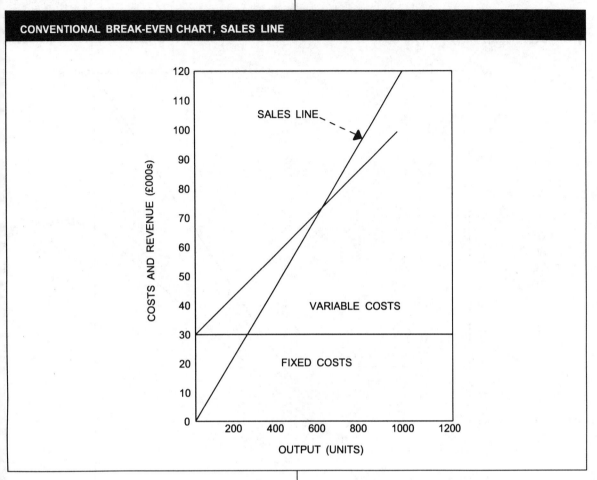

CONVENTIONAL BREAK-EVEN CHART, SALES LINE

joining the £30 000 point on the vertical axis through to the £100 000 mark at the 1000 output level, and extending it as before as in Figure 17.10. The fixed costs and variable costs are thus always equidistant to each other at whatever level of output.

Then draw the sales line from the origin through to the sales revenue value at the 1000 units mark: £120 000 as before (see Figure 17.11).

The contribution area on the chart can readily be gauged, as shown in Figure 17.12.

Profit–volume chart

The purpose of this chart is to indicate the profit or loss arising whenever certain levels of output are achieved. Thus it can act almost as a 'ready reck-

oner' for management, who can use it to gauge the profit or loss for an accounting period whenever the sales for the period becomes known.

It comprises just one line, a contribution line. The vertical line (y-axis) records the profit or loss, and the horizontal line (x-axis) records the sales or output. Taking first its shape, it appears as shown in Figure 17.13.

Where the vertical line intersects with the horizontal line is 0 (zero), the origin of the chart. Above zero on the vertical axis represents profits, below represents losses. The scales used on both axes should be consistent, as before: that is, evenly spaced: 0, 100, 200, 300, etc. Note that on the vertical axis the scales below the output line – the loss area – should mirror exactly the scales in the profit area.

FIGURE 17.8

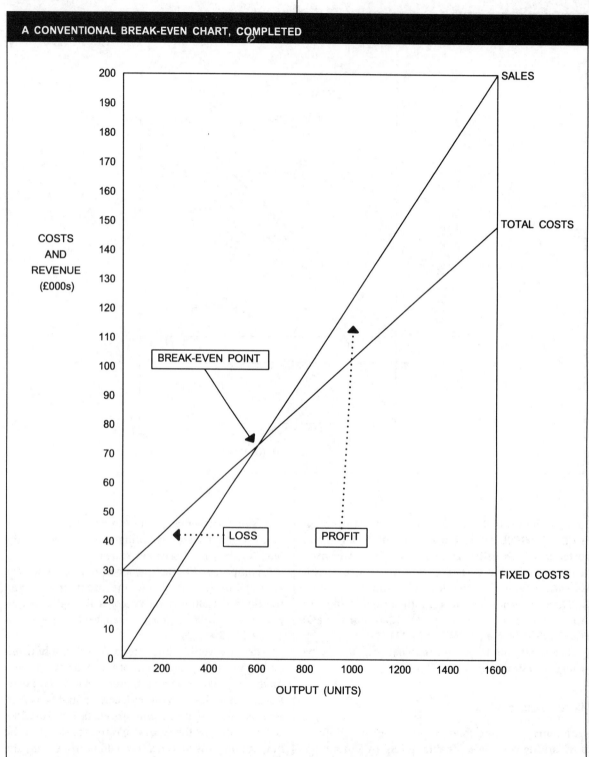

A CONVENTIONAL BREAK-EVEN CHART, COMPLETED

FIGURE 17.9

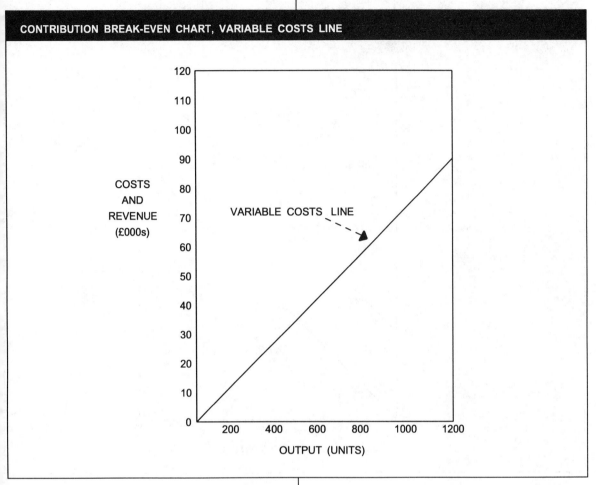

CONTRIBUTION BREAK-EVEN CHART, VARIABLE COSTS LINE

It follows that if sales are 0 on the output line, there will be no variable costs incurred. But *all* the fixed costs will still be incurred. Therefore, at 0 sales there will be a maximum *loss* sustained equal to the fixed costs: no sales = no contribution to the fixed costs.

To complete the profit–volume chart, starting first with the fixed costs: on the vertical line, find the point in the loss area which equals the fixed costs amount – using the figures from the earlier example, £30 000. Next, find the output break-even point on the horizontal output line: (£72 000, or 600 units, as in the example). Note that the break-even point needs to be calculated for the profit–volume chart using the formats previously described.

Draw a straight line from the fixed costs point on the vertical axis through the break-even point. This is the contribution line. From the chart (see Figure 17.14) the profit or loss position at any level of activity can then readily be calculated.

Margin of safety

Another important feature of a break-even chart is that it reveals the *margin of safety*. This is the difference between sales achieved or forecast to be achievable and the break-even point sales. Its purpose is to indicate to management how much sales can fall before break-even point is reached and losses begin. Obviously, the wider the safety margin, the better. It

FIGURE 17.10

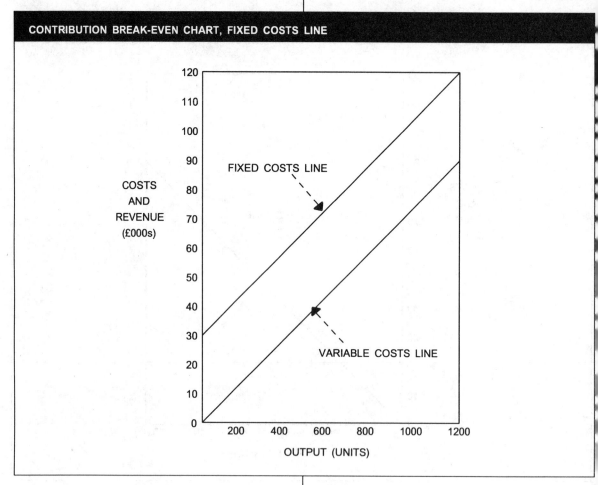

CONTRIBUTION BREAK-EVEN CHART, FIXED COSTS LINE

can be included as a feature on break-even charts as follows, using the conventional model (Figure 17.15).

Example:

Fixed costs	£20 000
Sales	£100 000
Variable costs	£60 000

The margin of safety can also be calculated in percentage terms, as follows:

Expected turnover (or actual turnover achieved)
– breakeven turnover
÷ Expected turnover (or actual turnover achieved)
× 100/1

So for the above example the margin of safety will be:

$$\frac{£100\,000 - £50\,000}{£100\,000} \times \frac{100}{1} = 50\%$$

Sales can therefore fall by 50% before break-even point is reached.

Area of relevance

The three charts described are based on the assumption that all the variables move in strict, straight-line, linear fashion. In fact this is rare. Imagine that sales are falling. Management will instinctively look to see where money can be saved. Therefore fixed costs will

FIGURE 17.11

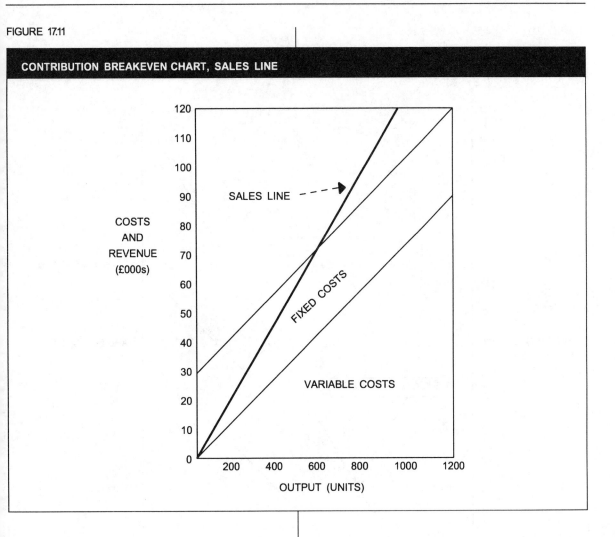

CONTRIBUTION BREAKEVEN CHART, SALES LINE

be pruned to reflect the fall. Similarly, if sales begin to rise, trade discounts allowed to customers who place large orders may perhaps increase disproportionately as customers order more and move into the next trade discount band. And if sales increase, raw materials prices may be reduced to reflect the increased quantity discounts applicable to higher-level purchases the company makes to meet the demand.

So, costs, even in the relatively short term, are inherently semi-variable costs. The lines on the chart should reflect this and be curvilinear rather than straight lines as depicted. When a break-even chart is drawn up to show this curvilinear aspect of costs and revenue it is known as the *economists' model* and would appear approximately as shown in Figure

17.16. Note that in this model there are *two* break-even points.

The straight-line break-even charts described and depicted in this chapter are known as the *accountants' model*. These are not drawn up to reflect precisely the changes in costs and revenue, as is the case with the economists' model, but, instead, they are designed to provide a simplified, and therefore perhaps easier to follow, overview of the likely profit and loss position at various levels of activity. Hence the straight lines. None the less, it is considered that when the accountants' model is superimposed on the economists' version there will be seen to be a relative correlation between the two at certain points. The accountants' single break-even point will

FIGURE 17.12

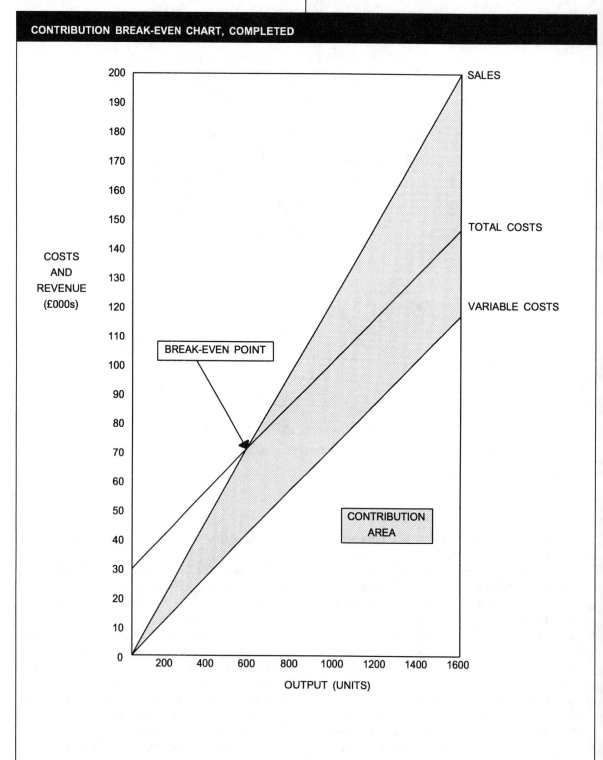

CONTRIBUTION BREAK-EVEN CHART, COMPLETED

FIGURE 17.13

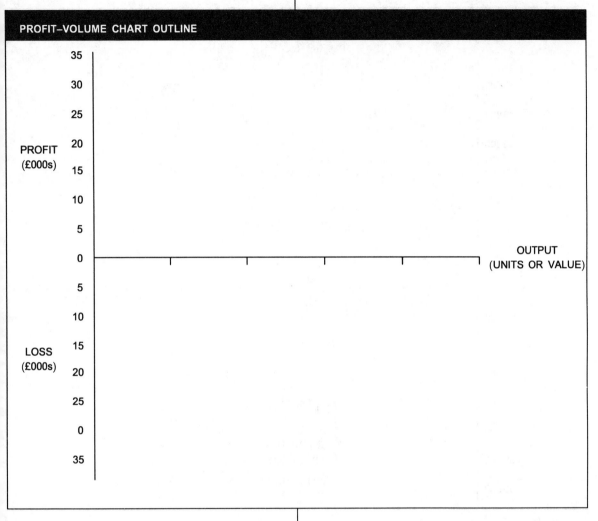

be broadly 'balanced' by the economists' two, with the accountants' break-even point being approximately in the centre of the economists' two break-even points.

This observed parallelism acts as a form of confirmation that the accountants' model is a reliable indicator of the behaviour of costs and revenue within a specified range of activity. This is known as the *area of relevance* or the *relevant range*.

Again, broadly speaking, this area of relevance can be said to be between 70–75 per cent and 120–125 per cent of the break-even point. The area of relevance in Figure 17.16 is therefore as shown in Figure 17.17.

Summary

- Some costs behave differently at varying levels of output. Some move directly in line with outputs and are termed variable costs, others remain more or less the same, irrespective of the change in activity; these are termed fixed costs.
- Other costs increase or decrease in steps as certain levels of activity are reached: these are termed semi-variable costs (or semi-fixed costs).
- Marginal costing techniques use this behavioural

FIGURE 17.14

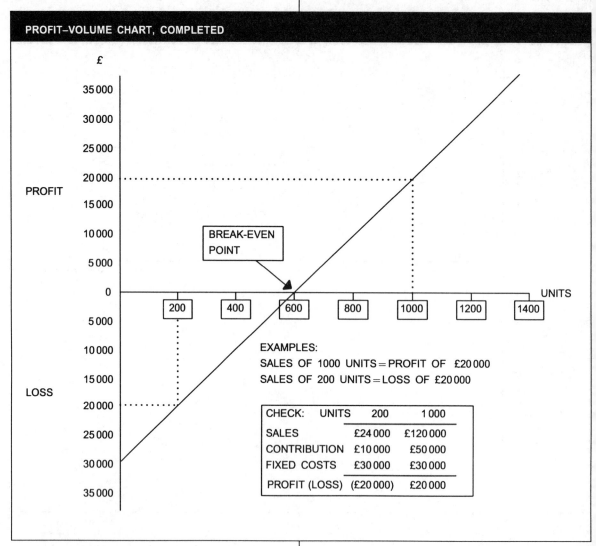

PROFIT–VOLUME CHART, COMPLETED

EXAMPLES:
SALES OF 1000 UNITS = PROFIT OF £20 000
SALES OF 200 UNITS = LOSS OF £20 000

CHECK:	UNITS	200	1 000
SALES		£24 000	£120 000
CONTRIBUTION		£10 000	£50 000
FIXED COSTS		£30 000	£30 000
PROFIT (LOSS)		(£20 000)	£20 000

aspect of costs to provide management with a useful decision-making tool.

- Variable costs generally comprise the direct, prime costs, of production (raw materials, direct labour and direct expenses) plus all other costs that move directly in line with sales, such as agents' commission and royalty payments. Fixed costs are, by definition, all other costs that cannot be classified as variable costs.

- In marginal costing, all the fixed costs (production overheads, sales, administration), are treated as period costs and are written off in the period's profit and loss account, none being carried forward

in closing stocks to future accounting periods. This is a major difference compared to absorption costing, where a proportion of one period's production fixed costs is carried forward to the next accounting period in the closing stock figure. Another difference is the layout of the profit and loss statement. In marginal costing the layout appears as follows:

```
      Sales
      Less Variable costs
  =   Contribution
      Less Fixed costs
  =   Profit (or Loss)
```

FIGURE 17.15

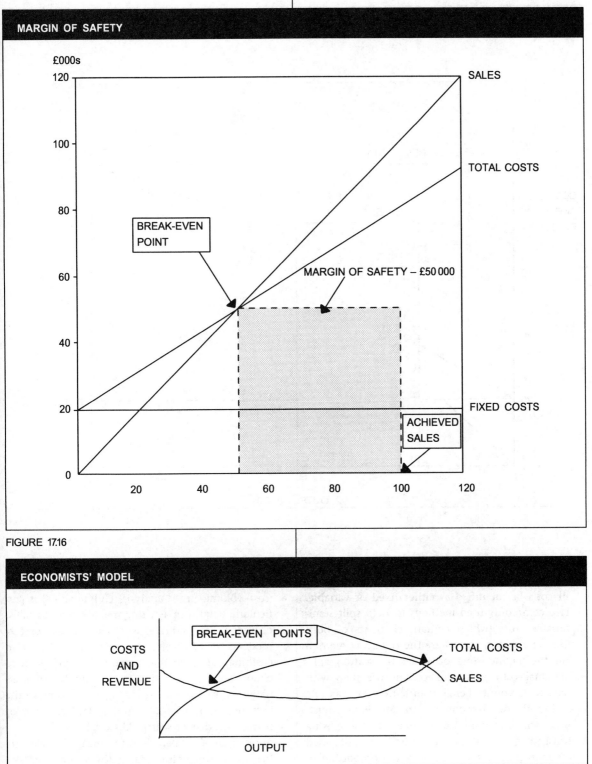

MARGIN OF SAFETY

£000s

- 120 — SALES
- 100
- 80 — TOTAL COSTS
- BREAK-EVEN POINT
- 60 — MARGIN OF SAFETY – £50 000
- 40
- 20 — FIXED COSTS
- ACHIEVED SALES
- 0

20 40 60 80 100 120

FIGURE 17.16

ECONOMISTS' MODEL

BREAK-EVEN POINTS

COSTS AND REVENUE

TOTAL COSTS

SALES

OUTPUT

FIGURE 17.17

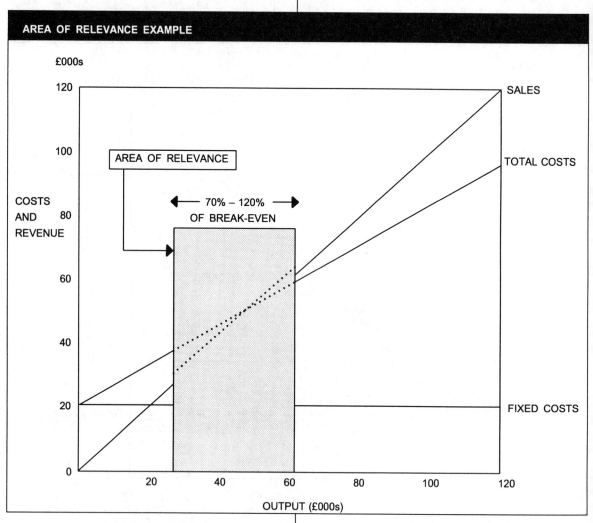

- Marginal costing techniques are used for short-term decision-making purposes, therefore requiring that all costs be identified as either fixed or variable. Two commonly used methods to help split semi-variable costs (which contain elements of both fixed and variable costs) are the high/low method and the graphical method, called the scattergraph.
- Marginal costing is also an accounting system, with separate accounts being maintained for variable and fixed costs. To comply with SSAP 9, an adjustment will be required to be made to the closing finished goods stock valuation for published accounts purposes in order to add a proportion of production overheads to the marginal cost valuations.
- Cost–volume–profit analysis (CVP analysis) is particularly helpful in assisting management to make decisions. For example, whether to make or buy products; or to accept or not one-off orders from customers at lower than usual selling prices; or to choose a course of action from a number of alternatives. It can also assist management to make the best use of restricting limiting factors, such as scarce materials or scarce skilled labour.
- Another key CVP benefit is the means to calculate the break-even point. This is the volume of sales

required to be achieved to pay for the fixed costs. It is calculated using formulae (1) and (2):

$$\frac{\text{Fixed costs}}{\text{C/S\%}} \qquad (1)$$

C/S% is the *contribution* divided by the *sales*, expressed as a percentage. This provides the amount of sales, in value terms, which will pay for all the fixed costs with neither a profit nor a loss ensuing: hence break-even point.

$$\frac{\text{Fixed costs}}{\text{Contribution per unit}} \qquad (2)$$

The contribution per unit is the contribution amount divided by the number of units sold. This indicates the number of units needed to be sold to break even.

- A formula can also be used to arrive at a sales figure needed for a desired profit figure to be achieved:

$$\frac{\text{Fixed costs plus desired profit}}{\text{C/S\%}}$$

- CVP analysis can also be presented graphically through break-even charts. There are three main charts: the conventional break-even chart; the contribution break-even chart, and the profit–volume chart. They show clearly the behaviour of costs at varying levels of activity; the break-even point can readily be identified where the sales line intersects the total costs line.
- The chart can also indicate the margin of safety, which is the difference between the expected (or achieved) sales and the break-even point.
- Break-even charts are constructed with straight lines – linearity – but in reality costs and revenues behave in a curvilinear fashion, as demonstrated in the economists' model of a break-even chart.
- The accountants' model, using straight lines, is thus not completely representative of the likely behaviour of costs at all levels of activity. However, it is generally considered to be a reliable guide, within approximately 25/30 per cent either side of the break-even point. This area is called the area of relevance, or the relevant range.

Examination Questions

1 A LEVEL (ULEAC) 1989

Foxton Industries operates an absorption costing approach to the calculation of profits and applies FIFO (First in, First out) to the valuation of closing stocks. The following are the trading results for the six months ended 31 March 1989:

	£	£
Sales (1500 units)		36 000
Less: direct materials	9 100	
direct labour	6 210	
variable overheads	3 730	
Prime cost (1600 units)	19 040	
Fixed costs	8 960	
	28 000	
Add opening stock (300 units)	5 100	
	33 100	
Less closing stock (400 units)	7 000	
		26 100
Profit		9 900

Required:

Calculate the differences for stock valuation and for profits if a marginal costing approach had been used together with

(i) LIFO (Last in, First out); and

(ii) AVCO (Weighted average cost) methods of valuing stocks.

The prime cost of the units on hand at 1 October 1988 was £11.70 per unit.

2 A LEVEL (ULEAC) 1990

(a) Produce a profit volume graph from the following break-even chart, showing clearly the area of profit, the area of loss, and the break-even point.

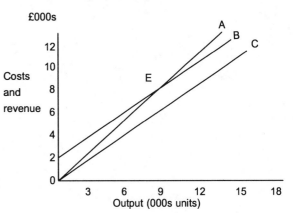

0A = Total revenue
DB = Total cost
0C = Total variable cost
0D = Fixed cost
E = Break-even point

(b) One of the advantages of a break-even chart presented in the above format is that it emphasises the contribution. How does the break-even chart above show the contribution?

3 A LEVEL (ULEAC) 1990

A company's overhead cost items for a year are illustrated by the following graphs. State (a) which graph relates to the following overheads, and (b) give reasons for your answer.

(i)   Factory rent of £50 000 per year.
(ii) Cost of a service: £2 per unit produced up to a maximum of £5000 per year.
(iii) Maintenance in the form of a standing charge of £2500, plus a charge of £5 per unit produced to a maximum of £10 000 per year.

(iv) Depreciation charged on the basis of a cost per unit.
(v) Supervisors' salaries:
     under 500 units produced – one supervisor
     501–1000 units produced – two supervisors
     1001–1500 units produced – three supervisors

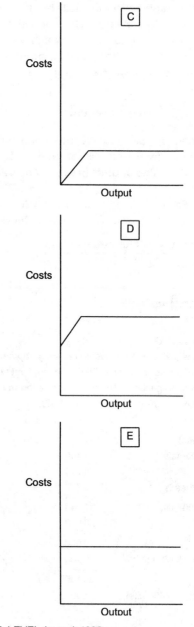

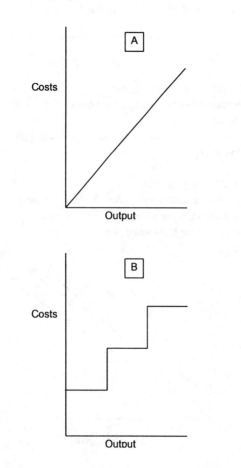

4 A LEVEL (ULEAC) 1992

Barton & Co Ltd make and sell 2000 units per month of a product, 'Barco'. The selling price is £65 per unit, and unit costs are: direct labour £8; direct materials £17; variable overheads £11. Fixed costs per month are £29 400.

The company receives two export orders for completion in September. Order A requests 600 items at a special total price of £20 000; Order B requires 750 items at a total price of £34 000. Order A will require no special treatment, but Order B will demand extra processing at a cost of £6 per item. The company has sufficient capacity to undertake either A or B in addition to its current production, but only by paying its direct labour force an overtime premium of 25%.

Required:

Calculate the company's contribution and the profits for the month if:

(a)   Normal production only takes place.

(b)   Order A is accepted in addition to normal production.

(c)   Order B is accepted in addition to normal production.

5   A LEVEL (ULEAC) 1992

Prepare a break-even chart to accompany the following profit graph if the selling price for the product is £1.50 per unit.

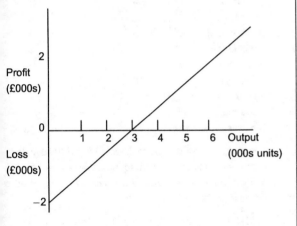

6   A LEVEL (ULEAC) 1993

(a)   The following statement has been drafted on the absorption costing basis. Redraft it showing clearly:
   ● the prime cost;
   ● the marginal cost;
   ● the contribution for the period, and the profit.

	£	£
Sales (1500 units)		72 000
Less: Direct materials	24 100	
Direct labour	11 800	
Variable overheads	8 700	
Fixed costs	19 400	
	64 000	
Less Closing stock (500 units)	16 000	48 000
Profit		24 000

(b)   Prepare a statement to reconcile the profit derived in your answer to (a) above with that shown in the question.

7   A LEVEL (AEB) 1990

Pendulum Ltd manufacture and sell a single product. The following forecast information had been prepared for the financial year ending 30 September, Year 1.

	£000
Sales	5 000
Direct materials	2 000
Direct labour	900
Fixed manufacturing overhead	300
Variable sales and administrative overhead	600
Fixed sales and administrative overhead	200
Variable manufacturing overhead	700

Project unit sales were 50000 units.

The management of Pendulum Ltd called a meeting with the workers' trade union representatives to advise them that in Year 1 the economic environment was about to get much tougher. Material prices are expected to increase and, if the company is to remain profitable, productivity changes and overhead cost reductions must be achieved. The management thought that the company might not reach break-even point. If the company failed to achieve the revised objectives there would have to be labour redundancies.

During the meeting the management presented the following list of adjustments to the Year 1 forecast:

1.   The total direct labour charge would be frozen provided that the workforce produced an extra 10 000 units.

2.   Total material costs would increase by 25% of the original forecast figure. This increase reflects both the price and volume change in the new forecast.

3.   All fixed overheads are to be cut by 10%.

4.   All variable overheads will only be allowed to increase by 5%. This 5% contains any effect of the volume change owing to the increased production.

5.   It should be assumed that all expenses and revenue relationships would be unchanged except where identified.

6.   All goods produced are sold immediately.

The union representatives advised the management that they were unfamiliar with the concept of break-even and asked the management to produce suitable information to help their understanding.

Required:

(a) Prepare a suitable graph to show
   (i)   the break-even points of both the original and the revised forecasts;
   (ii) the area of profit based on the original forecast data; and
   (iii) the margin of safety based on the original forecast data.

(b) Show the formula used to calculate the break-even point in units produced and sold. Calculate the break-even point in units for both the original and the revised forecast data.

(c) Comment on the management's proposals. Indicate whether the proposals can be realistically achieved.

8   A LEVEL (AEB) 1992

Jason Ltd manufactures a product called Dufton. The normal output of this product is 200 000 units.

The following is a cost statement relating to the production of a Dufton:

	£	£
Materials		5.00
Wages		7.00
Factory overheads:		
Fixed	4.50	
Variable	1.00	5.50
Administration overheads:		
Fixed		2.00
Selling overheads		
Fixed	3.50	
Variable	3.00	6.50
		26.00

The selling price of a Dufton is £36.

During the year the company received enquiries about two possible special orders, each involving the production of 2000 units. One enquiry related to the production of a Super Dufton (ref. no. 610) and the other to a Premier Dufton (ref. no. 620). Because of normal production commitments, only one of these possible orders could be handled in the factory.

The conditions of order (ref. no 610) are that the variable costs will increase by 25%, but the selling price cannot exceed £25.00 per unit. The conditions relating to order (ref. no. 620) are that variable costs will decrease by 25%, but the selling price will be £19.00 per unit.

Required:

(a) A computation of the break-even point of normal trading in terms of:

   (i)   sales revenue;
   (ii) units produced; and
   (iii) percentage of normal capacity (assume all units sold).

(b) What profit would be earned in normal trading if:
   (i)   the selling price was increased to £40 per unit and output restricted to 160 000 units; and
   (ii) the selling price was reduced to £28 per unit and output increased to 260 000 units?

(c) Advise the Board as to which of the two special orders should be accepted. Computations must be shown and a reason given for the choice made.

9   A LEVEL (AEB) 1992

Progressive Products Ltd manufacture and sell a single product. The following financial information is available for years ending 31 December:

1.

Costs per unit produced	Budget Year 1	Actual Year 1	Forecast Year 2
	£	£	£
Direct materials	45	48	46
Direct labour	32	30	28
Variable production overhead	10	11	11
Variable sales overhead	5	6	6
Other variable costs	11	12	13

2.   The budgeted fixed costs for Year 1 were £200 000, but after the results were prepared there was a fixed cost adverse variance of £20 000. Fixed costs were expected to increase to £230 000 in Year 2.

3.

Sales	Price per unit	Unit volume
	£	000s
Budget Year 1	120	40
Actual Year 1	125	43
Forecast Year 2	123	47

4.   Assume that all expense and revenue relationships remain unchanged except where identified.

5   The company holds no stocks of finished goods.

Required:

(a) An actual profit statement for the year ended 31 December Year 1.

(b) Calculate the number of sales units necessary to break even for:
   (i)   the budget and actual figures for Year 1; and
   (ii) the forecast figures for Year 2.

(c) Prepare a graph showing a break-even chart for the forecast figures for Year 2

(d) If the fixed costs for Year 2 could be lowered to £200 000, what price would the company be able to charge to maintain the break-even point achieved in Year 1?

10 AAT COST ACCOUNTING AND BUDGETING 1991

The following budgeted information relates to a company that sells one product.

	January	February
Sales	18 000	32 000
Production	25 000	25 000

	£
Selling price per unit	16
Cost per unit:	
Materials	5
Direct labour	3
Variable production cost	2

Fixed production costs: £75 000 per month

There is no opening stock and company policy is to absorb fixed overheads on the basis of direct labour cost.

Required:

(a) Prepared profit and loss statements for the months of January and February on the basis of:
  (i) Marginal costing.
  (ii) Absorption costing.

(b) Calculate the stock valuation at the end of January under each method.

(c) Account for the differences between the two methods.

11 AAT COST ACCOUNTING AND BUDGETING 1992

Your company makes three products: A, B and C. You are given the following information:

	A	B	C
	£	£	£
Selling price	25	30	34
Direct materials	8	11	10
Direct labour	10	12.5	15
Variable overheads	3	3.5	4

Fixed overheads £150 000

You are told:

(i) Maximum sales demand in units:
  A 30 000
  B 20 000
  C 15 000

(ii) The company has a production capacity of 50 000, which can be any mix of A, B and C. Sales of one product does not influence sales of any of the others.

(iii) Direct labour is paid £5 per hour.

Required:

(a) Prepare a statement showing the optimum product mix of A, B and C to maximise profit.

(b) Determine the product mix to maximise profit if you were told that there was a maximum of 105 000 labour hours available.

12 AAT COST ACCOUNTING AND BUDGETING

A building company constructs a standard unit which sells for £30 000. The company's costs can readily be identified between fixed and variable costs.

Budgeted data for the coming six months includes the following:

	Sales in units	Profit £
January	18	70 000
February	20	100 000
March	30	250 000
April	22	130 000
May	24	160 000
June	16	40 000

You are told that the fixed costs for the six months have been spread evenly over the period under review to arrive at the monthly profit projections.

Required:

(a) Prepare a graph for total sales, costs and output for the six months under review that shows:
  (i) the break-even point in units and revenue;
  (ii) total fixed costs;
  (iii) the variable cost line; and
  (iv) the margin of safety for the total budgeted sales.

(b) The company is worried about the low level of sales. The sales director says that if the selling price of the unit was reduced by £5000 the company would be able to sell 10% more units. All other costs would remain the same, you are told. Determine whether the company should reduce the selling price to attract new sales in order to maximise profit. Show clearly any workings.

13 AAT COST ACCOUNTING AND BUDGETING 1993

Your company has the following budgeted costs for the coming year:

Material costs	£1980000	(100% variable)
Labour costs	£1400000	(70% variable)
Production overhead costs	£1300000	(40% variable)
Selling and distribution costs	£ 800000	(15% variable)
Administration costs	£ 820000	
	£6300000	

The planned level of production is 90% of maximum capacity of 50000 units. Each unit sells for £155. Management are worried about the low level of profitability. There has been a request for a special order to produce 4000 units at a price of £95 per unit. The Sales Manager remarks to you that he does not think that we should go ahead with this order as the company does not have the productive capacity and even if it had there would be a loss of £45 per unit.

His proposal to increase profitability would be to drop selling prices for all units by 10%, which would increase demand by 15%. Fixed costs would remain unchanged. Note: costs are either fixed or variable

Required:
(a) Determine whether the company has the productive capacity to make the order.
(b) Show whether the special order should be given the go-ahead, supporting your answers with figures.
(c) Analyse whether the Sales Manager's proposal to increase profitability is preferable to acceptance of the special order, supporting your findings with figures.

14 RSA III ACCOUNTING 1992

Stubby Ltd manufacture two types of widget – the large and the small. Details of the budget for Year 3 are:

	Large	Small
Output in units	10000	15000
Sales price	£12.00	£8.00
Variable manufacturing costs	£ 4.00	£3.00
Variable selling costs	£ 2.00	£1.00
Fixed manufacturing costs	£ 2.00	£1.50
Fixed selling costs	£ 1.00	£0.50

Required:
(a) (i) calculate the contribution made by each product;
    (ii) calculate the total absorption costs of manufacture of each product; and
    (iii) calculate the total fixed costs of the company.

Both products require time on machine Z. Large requires 6 minutes and small 15 minutes. Due to unforeseen circumstances, only 3000 hours will now be available for Year 3.

Required:
(b) (i) calculate the total number of machine Z hours required by the original budget.
    (ii) calculate the quantity of each item that should be made in order to maximise profit under the changed conditions (**NB** Production of either product should not exceed budgeted sales); and
    (iii) calculate the profit which would then be made.

15 RSA III ACCOUNTING 1993

Wonderwand plc produce a hi-fi unit which sells at £80 per unit. Their trading results for the past financial year were as follows:

	£	£
Sales		800000
Cost of raw materials	300000	
Direct labour	200000	500000
		300000
Less:		
Variable selling costs	100000	
Fixed costs	150000	250000
Net profit		50000

For the coming year, the following are relevant:

(i) direct labour costs increase by 10%;
(ii) there is a 10% increase in variable selling costs;
(iii) there will be additional costs of £10000 per annum; and
(iv) materials costs increase by £7.

There are three options shown below:

PLAN A To move to new premises which will involve an additional increase in fixed costs of £15000 per annum.

PLAN B To have any additional units required assembled by an overseas manufacturer. These units would be delivered to your factory at an all inclusive cost of £67 per unit.
        Distribution and selling costs would be the same as for the home produced units.

PLAN C The maximum selling price per unit would be £95. Output would be unchanged from last year.

Required:
(a) Calculate the number of units that need to be sold for each of the above situations in order to:
    (i) Break-even.
    (ii) Earn a net profit of £100000 per annum.
(b) Use your calculations to state which is the best plan.

Note Ignore opening and closing stocks.

16 RSA III ACCOUNTING 1994

(a) Adam and Eve Ltd produce two products – widgets and wotnots. Details of the budget for year 5 are as follows:

	Widgets	Wotnots
Output in units	20 000	25 000
Selling price per unit	£20	£28
Direct labour	£6	£9
(1.5 hours at £4; 2 hours at £4.50)		
Direct materials	£4	£7
Variable selling cost	£1	£1

The annual fixed costs of the company were budgeted at £180 000.

Each widget produced requires 1 hour of machine time, while each wotnot produced requires 1.5 hours of machine time.

Required:

(i) calculate the total contribution made by each product to the overall profit of the company; and

(ii) calculate two overhead absorption rates, one based on direct labour hours and the other based on machine hours.

(b) Both products use an interchangeable raw material which is found to be in short supply and the maximum amount expected to be available for the coming year is expected to have a cost price of £220 000.

Required:

(i) calculate the quantity of each product which should be manufactured under the changed conditions in order to maximise profit (Note Production of either product must not exceed budgeted sales); and

(ii) calculate the profit which will be made.

17 LCCI THIRD LEVEL MANAGEMENT ACCOUNTING 1992

Winters Compressors Ltd manufactures two products and sells them in a very competitive market. Both products are manufactured using the same machinery and skilled labour. The budget for next year shows:

	Product X per unit	Product Y per unit
	£	£
Direct materials	32	32
Direct labour	24	36
(2 hours and 3 hours respectively)		
Variable overhead	8	8
(2 machine hours for each product)		
	—	—
	64	76
Sales – units	30 000	20 000

Fixed cost, which arises largely from the use of the skilled labour, is budgeted at £960 000 for next year. The profit margin is calculated as a 25% addition to full cost.

Required:

(a) Calculate the selling price per unit based upon:

(i) a direct labour hour rate for fixed overheads; and

(ii) a machine hour rate for fixed overheads.

(b) Explain which of the selling prices is most appropriate.

(c) Assuming that skilled labour is restricted to 90 000 hours and that the company chooses to concentrate production on its more profitable product, show

(i) which product this would be, and why; and

(ii) how much profit would be reported if all products were sold.

18 LCCI THIRD LEVEL MANAGEMENT ACCOUNTING 1993

Industrial Tools Ltd manufactures a single product only, which has a variable cost of £16 and is currently sold for £40. The reported profit for the company this year was £800 000 after charging fixed overheads of £400 000. The newly appointed General Manager suggests that, if the selling prices of the product were reduced, sales would increase. He suggests that one of the following policies should be pursued for next year:

Policy	Reduce Selling price by	Volume increase
1	5.0%	10.0%
2	7.5%	20.0%
3	10.0%	30.0%

Required:

(a) Calculate the profits from each of Policies 1, 2 and 3.

(b) State which policy you would recommend, and calculate:

(i) the margin of safety percentage; and

(ii) the contribution to sales ratio.

19 ACCA COST AND MANAGEMENT ACCOUNTING 1 1990

Z Ltd is a retailer with a number of shops selling a variety of merchandise. The company is seeking to determine the optimum allocation of selling space in its shops. Space is devoted to ranges of merchandise in modular units, each module occupying 70 square metres of space. Either one or two modules can be devoted to each range. Each shop has seven modular units.

Z Ltd has tested the sale of different ranges of merchandise and has determined the following sales productivities:

Sales per module per week

	1 Module	2 Modules
	£	£
Range A	6750	6250
Range B	3500	3150
Range C	4800	4600
Range D	6400	5200
Range E	3333	3667

The contribution (selling price – product cost) percentages of sales of the five ranges are as follows:

Range A	20.0%
Range B	40.0%
Range C	25.0%
Range D	25.0%
Range E	30.0%

Operating costs are £5600 per shop per week and are apportioned to ranges based on an average rate per module.

Required:

(a) Determine the allocation of shop space that will optimise profit, clearly showing the ranking order for the allocation of modules.

(b) Calculate the profit of each of the merchandise ranges selected in (a) above and of the total shop.

20 ACCA COST AND MANAGEMENT ACCOUNTING 1990

W Ltd has operated a restaurant for the past two years. Revenue and operating costs over the two years have been as follows:

	Year 1	Year 2
	£000s	£000s
Revenue	1348312	1514224
Operating costs		
Food and beverages	698341	791919
Wages	349170	390477
Other overheads	202549	216930

The number of meals served in Year 2 showed an 8% increase on the Year 1 level of 151156. An increase of 10% over the Year 2 level is budgeted for Year 3.

All staff were given an hourly rate increase of 6% last year (i.e. in Year 2). In Year 3, hourly increases of 7% are to be budgeted.

The inflation on 'other overheads' last year was 5%, with an inflationary increase of 6% expected in the year ahead.

Food and beverage costs are budgeted to average £5.14 per meal in Year 3.

This is expected to represent 53% of sales value.

Required:

(a) From the information given above, and using the high/low method of cost estimation, determine the budgeted expenditure on wages and other overhead for Year 3.

(b)* Calculate the gross profit (i.e. sales less food and beverage costs) percentage of sales, and the net profit percentage of sales, for each of the three years, and comment on the change in these percentages over the period. (Round all figures to the nearest £000 or one decimal place of a per cent).

*Chapter 21 subject material.

21 ACCA COST AND MANAGEMENT ACCOUNTING 1 1991

A company is currently manufacturing at only 60% of full practical capacity, in each of its two production departments, because of a reduction in market share. The company is seeking to launch a new product which it is hoped will recover some lost sales.

The estimated direct costs of the new product, Product X, are to be established from the following information:

Direct materials: every 100 units of the product will require 30 kilos net of Material A. Losses of 10% of materials input are to be expected. Material A costs £5.40 per kilo before discount. A quantity discount of 5% is given on all purchases if the monthly purchase quantity exceeds 25000 kilos. Other materials are expected to cost £1.34 per unit of Product X.

Direct labour (per hundred units):
Department 1: 40 hours at £4 per hour.
Department 2: 15 hours at £4.50 per hour.

Separate overhead absorption rates are established for each production department. Department 1 overheads are absorbed at 130% of direct wages, which is based upon the expected overhead costs and usage of capacity if Product X is launched. The rate in Department 2 is to be established as a rate per direct labour hour also based on expected usage of capacity. The following annual figures for Department 2 are based on full practical capacity:

Overhead: £5424000
Direct labour hours: 2200000

Variable overheads in Department 1 are assessed at 40% of direct wages, and in Department 2 are £1980000 (at full practical capacity).

Non-production overheads are estimated as follows (per unit of Product X)

Variable: £0.70
Fixed: £1.95

The selling price for Product X is expected to be £9.95 per unit, with annual sales of 2 400 000 units.

Required:
(a) Determine the estimated cost per unit of Product X.
(b) Comment on the viability of Product X.
(c) Market research indicates that an alternative selling price for Product X could be £9.45 per unit, at which price annual sales would be expected to be 2 900 000 units. Determine, and comment briefly upon, the optimum selling price.

22 ACCA COST AND MANAGEMENT ACCOUNTING 1 1991

A company markets a range of products, which are sold through agents on a commission basis. Selling costs comprise the commission which is paid at 10% of selling price. The company is considering the introduction of its own sales force to replace the selling of products via agents. Estimates of sales and costs (excluding selling costs) per period have been made at three different levels of activity as follows:

	Low £000s	Medium £000s	High £000s
Sales	600	700	800
Manufacturing costs	350	380	410
Administration costs	160	160	160

Sales and costs (excluding selling costs) are expected to be unaffected by the decision regarding method of selling. If the company's own sales force is introduced, selling costs per period would be expected to total £60 000.

Required:
(a) Calculate the break-even point per period if selling via agents is continued.
(b) Calculate the break-even point per period if the company introduces its own sales force (Note: For (a) and (b) above you do NOT have to provide a break-even chart).
(c) Advise management on the decision regarding the method of selling.

23 ACCA COST AND MANAGEMENT ACCOUNTING 1 1991

B Ltd manufactures a range of products which are sold to a limited number of wholesale outlets. Four of these products are manufactured in a particular department on common equipment. No other facilities are available for the manufacture of these products. Owing to greater than expected increases in demand, normal single shift working is rapidly becoming insufficient to meet sales requirements. Overtime and, in the longer term, expansion of facilities are being considered.

Selling prices and product costs, based on single shift working utilising practical capacity to the full, are as follows:

	Product			
	W	X	Y	Z
(£/unit)				
Selling price	3.6500	3.9000	2.2500	2.9500
Product costs:				
Direct materials	0.8050	0.9960	0.4500	0.6470
Direct labour	0.6040	0.6510	0.4050	0.5090
Variable mfg overhead	0.2400	0.2470	0.2010	0.2170
Fixed mfg overhead	0.8550	0.9500	0.4750	0.7600
Variable selling and admin overhead	0.2160	0.2160	0.2160	0.2160
Fixed selling and admin overhead	0.3650	0.3900	0.2250	0.2950

Fixed manufacturing overheads are absorbed on the basis of machine hours which, at practical capacity, are 2250 per period. Total fixed manufacturing overhead per period is £427 500. Fixed selling and administration overhead, which totals £190 000 per period, is shared among products at a rate of 10% of sales.

The sales forecast for the following period (in thousands of units) is:

W	X	Y	Z
190	125	144	142

Overtime could be worked to make up any production shortfall in normal time. Direct labour would be paid at a premium of 50% above basic rate. Other variable costs would be expected to remain unchanged per unit of output. Fixed costs would increase by £24 570 per period.

Required:
(a) If overtime is not worked in the following period, recommend the quantity of each product that should be manufactured in order to maximise profit.
(b) Calculate the expected profit in the following period if overtime is worked as necessary to meet sales requirements.
(c) Consider the factors which should influence the decision whether or not to work overtime in such a situation.

24 ACCA COST AND MANAGEMENT ACCOUNTING 1 1991

A company manufactures a single product with the following variable costs per unit:

Direct materials	£7.00
Direct labour	£5.50
Manufacturing overhead	£2.00

The selling price of the product is £36.00 per unit. Fixed manufacturing costs are expected to be £1 340 000 for a period. Fixed non-manufacturing costs are expected to be £875 000. Fixed manufacturing costs can be analysed as follows:

Production 1	Production 2	Service Dept	General factory
£380 000	£465 000	£265 000	£230 000

'General factory' costs represent space costs, for example, rates, lighting and heating. Space utilisation is as follows:

Production Department 1	40%
Production Department 2	50%
Service Department	10%

60% of service department costs are labour related and the remaining 40% machine related. Normal production department activity is:

	Direct labour hours	Machine hours	Production units
Dept 1	80 000	2 400	120 000
Dept 2	100 000	2 400	120 000

Fixed manufacturing overheads are absorbed at a predetermined rate per unit of production for each production department, based upon normal activity.

Required:
(a) Prepare a profit statement for a period using the full absorption costing system described above and showing each element of cost separately. Costs for the period were as expected, except for additional expenditure of £20 000 on fixed manufacturing overhead in Production Department 1. Production and sales were 116 000 and 114 000 units respectively for the period.
(b) Prepare a profit statement for the period using marginal costing principles instead.
(c) Contrast the general effect on profit of using absorption and marginal costing systems respectively. (Use the figures calculated in (a) and (b) above to illustrate your answer).

25 ACCA COST AND MANAGEMENT ACCOUNTING 1 1993
A company manufactures and markets a single product. The company's trading results for the year just ending are expected to be:

	£	£
Sales		1 476 461
Direct materials	492 326	
Direct labour	316 764	
Overheads	452 318	1 261 408
Profit		215 053

For the year ahead it is planned to reduce the selling price of the product by 5%. Units sold are estimated to increase by 40%.

Direct materials cost inflation is expected to be 5% in the year ahead and a 5% increase in the hourly wage rate will be payable to the direct labour force for the whole year.

Overhead expenditure in the year prior to the year just ending was £418 232. Overhead cost inflation in the year just ending has been 5%, and production and sales volumes have been 12% higher than in the previous year. The high–low method is to be used to estimate overhead expenditure for the year ahead. Overhead cost inflation is expected to be 6% in the year ahead.

Required:
(a) Prepare a statement showing the estimated trading results for the year ahead.
(b) Calculate (to the nearest £000) the break-even points for each of the two years (i.e. year just ending and the next year)
(c) Comment upon the expected change in break-even point and profit.

26 CIMA COSTING 1990
The owners of a chain of retail petrol filling stations are considering opening an additional station. Initially only one grade of petrol would be sold and the normal selling price would be £0.44 per litre. Variable charges – cost of petrol, delivery and Excise Duty – total £0.40 per litre. The fixed costs for a 4-week period are estimated to be:

	£
Rent	2 000
Rates on business premises	1 000
Wages – 5 people on shifts	3 000
Wage related cost	400
Electricity for continuous opening (24-hour)	300
Other fixed costs	110

After establishing the site for petrol, it is intended at a later stage to develop on the same site a 'motorists' shop' selling the numerous small sundry items often required by motorists. There would be no increase in staff and one cash till only would be operated.

Throughout this question, Value Added Tax is ignored.

Required:
(a) To calculate the break-even point in number of litres and also in £s for a four-week period if
   (i) the above costs applied;
   (ii) the rent was increased by 75%;

(iii) the rent remained at £2000 but commission of £0.002 was given to the employees as a group bonus for every litre sold; and

(iv) the selling price was reduced to £0.43 and no commission was paid (with the rent at £2000).

(b) To state how many litres would need to be sold per 4-week period at £0.44 if costs were as in the original data (that is, with rent at £2,000) to achieve a profit of £700 per week.

(c) To advise the management about the following proposal, assuming sales for a 4-week period at a price of £0.44 per litre are normally:

(i) 275 000 litres; and

(ii) 425 000 litres.

The possibility of operating from 07.00 to 23.00 hours is being considered. The total savings for a 4-week period on the original data would be £120 for electricity and one night-shift person paid £200 per week (wage-related costs £25 per week) would no longer be required. Sales would, however, reduce by 50 000 litres over a 4-week period. Workings should be shown.

27 CIMA COSTING 1990

A manufacturer of glass bottles has been affected by competition from plastic bottles and is currently operating at between 65 and 70 per cent of maximum capacity.

The company at present reports profits on an absorption costing basis but with the high fixed costs associated with the glass container industry and a substantial difference between sales volumes and production in some months, the Accountant has been criticised for reporting widely different profits from month to month. To counteract this criticism, he is proposing in future to report profits based on marginal costing and in his proposal to management lists the following reasons for wishing to change:

1. Marginal costing provides for the complete segregation of fixed costs, thus facilitating closer control of production costs.

2. It eliminates the distortion of interim profit statements which occur when there are seasonal fluctuations in sales volume although production is at a fairly constant level.

3. It results in cost information which is more helpful in determining the sales policy necessary to maximise profits.

From the accounting records the following figures were extracted:

Standard cost per gross (a gross is 144 bottles and is the cost unit used within the business):

	£
Direct materials	8.00
Direct labour	7.20
Variable production overhead	3.36
Total variable production cost	18.56
Fixed production overhead*	7.52
Total production standard cost	26.08

*The fixed production overhead rate was based on the following computations:

Total annual fixed production overhead was budgeted at £7 584 000 or £632 000 per month.

Production volume was set at 1 008 000 gross bottles, or 70 per cent of maximum capacity.

There is a slight difference in budgeted fixed production overhead at different levels of operating:

Activity level % of maximum capacity	Amount per month £000s
50–75	632
76–90	648
91–100	656

You may assume that actual fixed production overhead incurred was as budgeted.

Additional information:

	September	October
Gross sold	87 000	101 000
Gross produced	115 000	78 000
Sales price, per gross	£32	£32
Fixed selling costs	£120 000	£120 000
Fixed administrative costs	£80 000	£80 000

Required:

(a) To prepare monthly profit statements for September and October using

(i) absorption costing; and

(ii) marginal costing.

(b) To comment briefly on the Accountant's three reasons which he listed to support his proposal.

28 CIMA COSTING 1991

Three products – X, Y and Z – are made and sold by a company; information is given below:

	Product X £	Product Y £	Product Z £
Standard costs:			
Direct materials	50	120	90
Variable overhead	12	7	16

	Rate per hour	Hours	Hours	Hours
	£			
Direct labour:				
Dept A	5	14	8	15
Dept B	6	4	3	5
Dept C	4	8	4	15

Total fixed overhead for the year was budgeted at £300 000.

The budget for the current financial year, which was prepared for a recessionary period, was based on the following sales:

Product	Sales in units	Selling price per unit
X	7 500	£210
Y	6 000	£220
Z	6 000	£300

However, the market for each of the products has improved and the Sales director believes that without a change in selling prices, the number of units sold could be increased for each product by the following percentages:

Product	Increase (%)
X	20
Y	25
Z	33.33

When the Sales Director's views were presented to a management meeting, the Production Director declared that although it might be possible to sell more units of product, output could not be expanded because he was unable to recruit more staff for Department B: there being a severe shortage of the skills needed by this department.

Required:
(a) To show in the form of a statement for management, the unit costs of each of the three products and the total profit expected for the current year based on the original sales figures.
(b) To state the profit if the most profitable mixture of the products was made and sold, utilising the higher sales figures and the limitation on Department B.
(c) To identify and to comment on three possible problems which may arise if the mixture in (b) above were to be produced.

29   CIMA COST ACCOUNTING 1992

A company in the civil engineering industry with headquarters located 22 miles from London undertakes contracts anywhere in the United Kingdom.

The company has had its tender for a job in north-east England accepted at £288 000 and work is due to begin in March, Year 3. However, the company has also been asked to undertake a contract on the south coast of England. The price offered for this contract is £352 000. Both of the contracts cannot be taken simultaneously because of constraints on staff site management personnel and on plant available. An escape clause enables the company to withdraw from the contract in the north-east, provided notice is given before the end of November, Year 3 and an agreed penalty of £28 000 is paid.

The following estimates have been submitted by the company's quantity surveyor:

Cost Estimates

	North-east	South coast
	£	£
Materials:		
In stock at original cost, Material X	21 600	
In stock at original cost, Material Y		24 800
Firm orders placed at original cost, Material X	30 400	
Not yet ordered – current cost, Material X	60 000	
Not yet ordered – current cost, Material Z		71 200
Labour – hired locally	86 000	110 000
Site management	34 000	34 000
Staff accommodation and travel for site management	6 800	5 600
Plant on site – depreciation	9 600	12 800
Interest on capital, 8%	5 120	6 400
Total local contract costs	253 520	264 800
Headquarters costs allocated at rate of 5% on total contract costs	12 676	13 240
Contract price	288 000	352 000
Estimated profit	21 804	73 960

Notes:
1. X, Y and Z are three building materials. Material X is not in common use and would not realise much money if resold; however, it could be used on other contracts but only as a substitute for another material currently quoted at 10% less than the original cost of X. The price of Y, a material in common use, has doubled since it was purchased; its net realisable value if resold would be its new price less 15% to cover disposal costs. Alternatively it could be kept for use on other contracts in the following financial year.

2. With the construction industry not yet recovered from the recent recession, the company is confident that manual labour, both skilled and unskilled, could be hired locally on a subcontracting basis to meet the needs of each of the contracts.

3. The plant which would be needed for the south coast contract has been owned for some years and £12 800 is the year's depreciation on a straight-line basis. If the north-east contract is undertaken, less plant will be required but the surplus plant will be hired out for the period of the contract at a rental of £6000.

4. It is the company's policy to charge all contracts with notional interest at 8% on estimated working capital involved in contracts. Progress payments would be receivable from the contractee.

5. Salaries and general costs of operating the small headquarters amount to about £108 000 each year. There are usually ten contracts being supervised at the same time.

6. Each of the two contracts is expected to last from March, Year three to February, Year four which coincidentally, is the company's financial year.

7. Site management is treated as a fixed cost.

Required:

You are required, as the management accountant to the company,

(a) To present comparative statements to show the net benefit to the company of undertaking the more advantageous of the two contracts.

(b) To explain the reasoning behind the inclusion in (or omission from) your comparative financial statements, of each item given in the costs estimates and the notes relating thereto.

30 CIMA COST ACCOUNTING 1993

PM Limited owns the Premier Hotel, which is on a busy main road near an international airport. The hotel has 40 rooms which are let at a rental of £35 per day. Variable costs are £6 per room occupied per day.

Fixed costs per month are:

	£
Depreciation	9 000
Insurance	5 500
Maintenance	4 800
Services	2 700
Management	3 000

Business is not as good in the period October to March as it is in the period April to September. The figures below relate to two six-monthly periods:

	April to September (183 days) £	October to March (182 days) £
Potential room lettings	256 200	254 800
Budgeted room lettings	218 400	165 200

Required:

(a) To calculate the budgeted room occupancy ratio to the nearest percentage figure for each six-month period.

(b) To prepare a statement showing budgeted profit or loss for each of the two six-monthly periods.

(c) To state the number of room days per month which must be let on average each month to break even.

(d) To state, with reason(s), whether or not you believe the hotel should be closed during January and February because in these two particularly poor trading months the fixed costs are not covered by the receipts from letting the rooms.

NON-COMPUTATIONAL, DESCRIPTIVE TYPE QUESTIONS
(NB   Minutes in brackets are a guide to indicate the approximate time your essay should take to complete.)

A   Explain the differences in profit derived from the application of marginal costing and absorption costing. (University Year 1) (15 minutes)

B   Comment briefly on the usefulness of marginal costing for decision making.
CIMA 1994) (10 minutes)

C   You are required, using the accountants' conventional break-even chart as a 'model', to explain how and why a break-even chart drawn by an economist would differ. (CIMA 1993)

D   State and explain three business situations where the use of marginal costing may be beneficial to management in making a decision.
(CIMA 1992) (12 minutes)

E   You are required to compare and contrast the usefulness of a conventional break-even chart with a contribution break-even chart. Your explanation should include illustrative diagrams.
(CIMA 1992) (10 minutes)

F Explain briefly what you understand by the terms 'contribution to sales ratio' and 'margin of safety', illustrating your answer with a diagram or graph.
(CIMA 1990) (12 minutes)

G Discuss the factors which influence cost behaviour in response to changes in activity.
(ACCA 1992) (13 minutes)

H List two advantages and two disadvantages of using marginal costing.
(RSA III 1994) (5 minutes)

I Evaluate whether the assumption that costs are readily identifiable as either fixed or variable throughout a range of production is realistic. Give examples of any alternative classification.
(AAT 1992) (11 minutes)

J List the situations in which marginal costing, as a technique, aids decision-making.
(AAT 1991) (11 minutes)

K Explain what is meant by the accounting term 'contribution'.
(AEB A-level 1991) (10 minutes)

L Compare and contrast the way in which absorption and marginal costing techniques account for fixed costs.
(ULEAC 1993) (10 minutes)

18
Standard Costing and Variance Analysis

A standard cost is a predetermined estimate of the cost of a product. Prior to a product being made, management will have planned its manufacture and determined the quantities of materials and labour needed to make it. They will have considered and evaluated the prime costs involved and decided upon an appropriate method of absorbing the factory overheads into the product. They will thus arrive at the likely manufacturing cost – the expected production cost – of the product.

When the product is made, management, with these predetermined estimates to hand, will be able to compare the two sets of figures. Almost certainly there will be differences between the two: sometimes the estimates will be higher than the actual cost, sometimes lower. These differences are described as *variances*. Management can analyse and investigate these to find the causes that created them and take corrective action if necessary to bring actual costs into line with the predetermined costs. The predetermined estimates, when adopted formally by the firm as a control tool and as part of the cost bookkeeping procedures, are described as *standard costs*.

The establishment of standard costs thus enables management to control actual costs by providing the useful tool of comparison: the actual costs against standard costs.

Additionally, apart from this *management by exception* cost control aspect, standard costs also have other highly practical functions. They can be used to value closing stocks, of which more later, and also to help establish selling prices. Imagine planning to manufacture a new product. How to set its selling price? Management might set it in accordance with current market prices if these exist for similar products, without consideration of the costs involved. But they clearly would not know for certain whether a profit would result. They could, of course, take a chance and price the product to be in line with competitors, but this runs the risk of losses and could be considered to be rash and somewhat reckless.

So the estimated costs of making a new product need to be calculated and taken into consideration when deciding the selling price. Management might still eventually price it exactly in line with the market, but with knowledge of the likely production costs to hand they will know (subject to the reasonableness of those estimates) whether a profit or loss is likely to ensue when the product comes to be sold.

The CIMA definition of a standard cost is:

'a standard expressed in money. It is built up from an assessment of the value of cost elements. Its main uses are providing bases for performance measurement, control by exception reporting, valuing stock and establishing selling prices'.

The definition of a *standard* is *'a predetermined measurable quantity set in defined conditions'*.

The standard cost of a product is therefore a standard *quantity of X* multiplied by the standard *price of X* for each element of cost – materials, labour, and factory variable and fixed overheads.

Take the following position as an example. A furniture manufacturer decides to make a new product, an executive desk for the home market. First, the technical aspects of the product need to be worked out and designed. Starting with *direct materials*, the quantity and quality of the various woods needed to make one of the desks will be determined. Perhaps a prototype desk will be made. The number of handles to be affixed will be decided, along with all other direct material elements such as locks, trays, plastic fitments, etc., needed for its completion. Effectively, a *bill of materials* will be compiled. This is, using CIMA terminology, *'a specification of the materials and parts required to make a product'*.

The next step is then to price those quantities of materials. The buyer or project designer will ascertain the buying prices of the various material elements. When this is done, the total value of the direct materials content of the one desk will become known by the following computation:

> Standard quantity of materials
> × Standard price of materials

The second step is to establish the *direct labour* element. Again, the technical aspects of making the desk will be established by computing the expected hours needed to be spent in each of the production sections to make it. Which machines will be used, what type of direct labour skills are needed and so on. This information may be derived by work study methods, work measurement or other forms of analysis, to ascertain how long it is likely to take for shop floor staff to make the product.

At the end of the assessment management will know how many hours the desk will take to make, split between the various grades of direct labour. The rates of pay of each grade of labour will be established. The direct labour cost to make one desk will then be computed, using the following formula:

> Standard number of direct labour hours
> × Standard rates of pay per hour

If any direct expenses are incurrable, these too will be calculated in similar fashion:

> Standard quantity of direct expenses
> × standard price of the direct expense

The third step (in absorption costing systems) is to make a charge to the product to cover factory *variable and fixed production overheads*. This may be based on one of the traditional methods of absorption – direct labour hours, machine hours and so on, or by using activity based costing (ABC) recovery methods.

Using the direct labour hours method for the example, the number of direct labour hours needed to complete the product, multiplied by the individual variable and fixed overhead absorption rates, will provide the amounts chargeable to the product to cover these overhead costs:

> Standard number of direct labour hours
> × Standard fixed overhead absorption
> hourly recovery rate

The final standard cost of the desk will therefore be:

> Standard cost of direct materials
> + Standard cost of direct labour
> + Standard cost of direct expenses
> + Standard cost of variable overheads
> + Standard costs of fixed overheads absorbed
> = Total standard product cost.

A standard *cost sheet*, or *card* or *computer record*, can then be completed for the product, as seen in Figure 18.1. Obviously, the more accurate the analysis of materials quantities needed and direct labour hours required (and the prices and rates to be paid), the more accurate will be the standard cost. Management will also need to consider the question of wastage of materials and lost time, additional costs which they might decide will have to be borne by the product. If so, allowances will need to be calculated, costed and incorporated into the standard cost.

Types of standards

There are a number of ways for establishing standards, with perhaps the following being the most commonly found:

FIGURE 18.1

STANDARD COST CARD

PRODUCT: EXECUTIVE DESK xx1   DATE PREPARED:
                                                   PREPARED BY:

	QUANTITY	PRICE EACH		TOTAL	
		£	p	£	p
MATERIALS:					
ITEM 1					
ITEM 2					
ITEM 3					
ITEM 4					
ITEM 5					
ITEM 6					
TOTAL DIRECT MATERIALS					

	HOURS	RATE PER HOUR		TOTAL	
		£	p	£	p
LABOUR:					
GRADE 1					
GRADE 2					
GRADE 3					
GRADE 4					
TOTAL DIRECT LABOUR					

	QUANTITY	PRICE EACH		TOTAL	
		£	p	£	p
DIRECT EXPENSES:					
ITEM					
TOTAL DIRECT EXPENSES					

	LABOUR HOURS	ABSORPTION RATE PER HOUR		TOTAL	
		£	p	£	p
VARIABLE OVERHEADS					
FIXED OVERHEADS:					

	£	p
TOTAL STANDARD COST		

Attainable standards;
Ideal standards; and
Basic standards.

Attainable standards

These are standards which are set so that they are achievable or attainable under generally efficient working conditions. As such, they will take into consideration normally expected direct materials losses, spoilages, lost time caused by machine breakdowns (downtime); other possible exigencies and allowances to reflect closely normally achievable production performance.

Attainable standards are thus designed to be *achieved* by production staff and can act as a strong motivational force for staff to 'beat' the standard (and possibly earn a bonus), thus improving the productivity of the firm. They are therefore the most commonly adopted.

CIMA terminology defines an attainable standard as: *'a standard which can be attained if a standard unit of work is carried out efficiently, a machine properly operated or a material properly used. Allowances are made for normal losses, waste and machine downtime'.*

Ideal standards

These standards are based on the assumption that production is carried out under the most favourable conditions: 'the best possible performance in the best of all possible worlds'. In these 'heavenly' conditions there will be no wastage, no spoilages, no idle time – no problems of any kind.

Such standards could, of course, be achieved, but the possibilities of doing so are clearly remote. Because of this element of remoteness about them, they are also known as *potential standards*. Ideal standards are thus considered by many to be too discouraging and demotivating to staff and are therefore not popular.

CIMA define an ideal standard as: *'a standard which can be attained under the most favourable conditions, with no allowance for normal losses, waste and machine downtime'.*

Both attainable standards and ideal standards need to be revised, broadly speaking, every year, usually in time to come into effect in the forthcoming accounting period. This is to reflect changes in production methods, current efficiency levels, rates and prices.

As standard costs are predetermined costs, management may also decide to include any expected price or rate changes in the new standards for the forthcoming period, together with any likely change in production methods and usage patterns.

Occasionally, following the setting of standard costs for the selected period of time, (that is, one year), standards may need to be altered during the period. This may be necessary to reflect temporary, unexpected, forced changes occurring in, say, the supply of materials caused by an event or incident. At the end of the event or incident, supplies or prices would then be expected to return to normal. During this short-term period, alternative sources of supply of the material would be required, maybe at much higher prices.

Rather than produce variances which will simply reflect this temporary situation, management may decide to alter the standard to accommodate the temporary situation. These amendments are often referred to as *current standards* or *temporary standards*. Sometimes, also, it is necessary to change standards during an accounting period because, perhaps, of a change in production methodology. These changes are known as *revised standards*.

Basic standard costs

These are standards set perhaps many years earlier and kept exactly the same, not being altered to allow for price or production method changes in the intervening periods. Used statistically, as base figures, they can indicate the trends in costs and usage, and the monitoring of these movements can be of great assistance to management. Changes from the base year may be presented graphically and compared to other indices, say average wages or the retail price index (RPI), or, if available, the particular industry's own averages, thus providing a comparison benchmark for the trends (see Figure 18.2).

In the example shown in Figure 18.2, there appears to be a correlation between the RPI and the material prices, but the gap is widening. Extrapolations can be made from this information to estimate future periods' prices, using perhaps the government's projected RPI figures as an additional guide.

When basic standard costs are used as a present-day control tool, the variances thrown up when current activity is compared to the basic standards will not

FIGURE 18.2

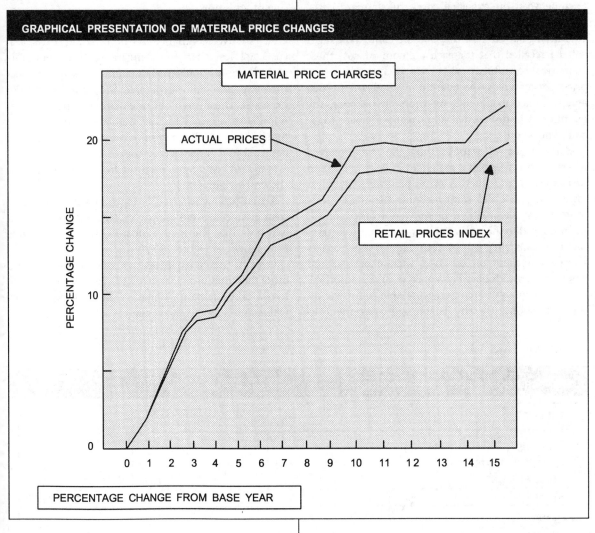

GRAPHICAL PRESENTATION OF MATERIAL PRICE CHANGES

MATERIAL PRICE CHARGES

ACTUAL PRICES

RETAIL PRICES INDEX

PERCENTAGE CHANGE

PERCENTAGE CHANGE FROM BASE YEAR

be very meaningful. As the years pass, the variances become larger and larger, and thus the benefits that standard costs provide to help monitor and control the actual costs will be lost. Adjustments to the basic standards would also be needed for closing stock valuation purposes, as this cost would not necessarily bear 'a reasonable relationship to actual costs obtaining during the period', (SSAP 9). Because of these drawbacks, basic standards are rarely used for everyday control purposes. But as a statistical tool for measuring performance over a period of time and as a basis for projections they are useful.

Variance analysis

A major benefit deriving from standard costs is that by analysing the differences – the variances – between actual costs and standard costs, management is able to identify more quickly problem areas (and areas of success) which need investigating. Variance analysis therefore facilitates *management by exception*, which is, in CIMA Terminology *'the practice of focusing on activities requiring attention and ignoring those that appear to be running smoothly'*.

A variance, as previously stated, is simply the difference between the expected cost – the standard cost – and the actual cost.

Thinking back to how the standard came to be set, it will be recalled that for each element of cost there were two constituent parts: the quantity and the price. For materials, the quantity of materials needed and the price to be paid for them. For labour, the quantity of hours needed and the hourly rate to be paid, and so on.

Management will want to know the costs involved where more (or less) of a material has been used than was expected, and whether prices paid were higher or lower. They will also want to know the costs where more or less direct labour hours were worked, and if the rates paid to the staff were higher or lower. Regarding overheads, they will want to know if more or less money was spent on expenses than expected, and whether overheads have been over- or under-absorbed.

Variance analysis techniques are able to answer all these questions, thereby enabling management to concentrate on those areas that need their most urgent attention.

When actual costs are greater than the standard cost, an adverse variance has occurred; and if actual costs are less than the standard cost, a favourable variance results, 'adverse' therefore means more cost than expected, and 'favourable' means less cost than expected. These are often represented by the symbols A for 'adverse' and F for 'favourable' by the side of the figure. As an illustration, consider the situation depicted in Figures 18.3 to 18.6.

Standard costs have been set for three products as shown in Figure 18.3.

Actual production details together with the actual costs incurred, were shown in Figure 18.4. But you will note that the total standard cost for these units is as shown in Figure 18.5.

Overall, therefore, it has cost the company £1700 more than they anticipated (£330 800 actual compared to £329 100 standard). Management will want to know where and how this has arisen.

FIGURE 18.3

STANDARD COSTS FOR THREE PRODUCTS

PRODUCT	B	C	I
MATERIALS			
QUANTITY – UNITS	50	60	70
PRICE PER UNIT	£2.50	£3.50	£4.00
MATERIAL COST	£125.00	£210.00	£280.00
LABOUR			
HOURS	20	25	18
RATE PER HOUR	£4.00	£5.00	£4.00
LABOUR COST	£80.00	£125.00	£72.00
VARIABLE OVERHEADS			
HOURS	20	25	18
RATE	£10.00	£10.00	£10.00
VARIABLE OVERHEADS COST	£200.00	£250.00	£180.00
FIXED OVERHEADS			
HOURS	20	25	18
RATE	£18.00	£18.00	£18.00
FIXED OVERHEADS COST	£360.00	£450.00	£324.00
TOTAL STANDARD COST	£765.00	£1 035.00	£856.00

FIGURE 18.4

ACTUAL PRODUCTION DETAILS AND COSTS INCURRED				
	B	C	I	TOTAL
UNITS MADE	100	120	150	
COSTS INCURRED:				
MATERIALS	£13 000	£24 800	£44 000	£81 8000
LABOUR	£8 100	£14 500	£11 100	£33 700
VARIABLE OVERHEADS	£20 500	£29 000	£27 200	£76 700
FIXED OVERHEADS – ALLOCATED	£37 000	£55 000	£46 600	£138 600
				£330 800
MATERIAL UNITS USED	5 100	7 300	10 450	
LABOUR HOURS	2 050	2 950	2 800	
BUDGETED UNITS	110	130	140	

By completing a calculation table similar to that shown in Figure 18.6 for each product, an analysis of the variances can be completed. To complete the table, enter the number of units produced in both 'standard' and 'actual' columns. The costs in the 'standard' column will relate to the specific quantity of production, for example, 100 units × material cost per unit of £125 = £12 500 for Product B; 150 unit × labour cost per unit of £72 = £10 800 for Product I, and so on. Then enter the 'actual' costs incurred in the 'actual' column. The differences between the two sets of figures provide the variance amounts.

Note first that the origin of the overall adverse variance of £1700 previously calculated has now been identified:

Product B	£2100 adverse
Product C	£ 900 favourable
Product I	£ 500 adverse
	£1700 adverse

Starting with Product B, you will see that the materials variance is £500 adverse. Actual costs were more than the standard cost. This is the total difference between the two and is described as the *direct material total variance*. A total implies the sum of more than one, and so it is with this variance. You will recall there are two constituents of a cost: quantity and price. So the quantity of materials used may have been more or less than standard and, similarly, the prices paid may have

been higher or lower than the standard prices. The direct material total variance thus comprises these two elements – price and usage – and it can be broken down into two *subvariances*:

direct material price variance
direct material usage variance

You will also see that the direct labour costs were more than standard by £100. This total difference is called the *direct labour total variance*. This too is made up of two subvariances:

direct labour rate variance
direct labour efficiency variance

We shall deal first with how to calculate material and labour subvariances before going on to deal with the overheads variances.

CIMA terminology defines the calculation of each of the above six variances – the total variances and the sub-variances – as follows:

Direct material price variance

(Actual material purchased × Standard price) – (Actual cost of material purchased)

Direct material usage variance

(Standard quantity of material specified for actual production × Standard price) – (Actual material used × Standard price)

FIGURE 18.5

STANDARD COST OF UNITS MADE				
	B	C	I	TOTAL
UNITS MADE	100	120	150	
STANDARD COST – EACH	£765.00	£1 035.00	£856.00	
TOTAL STANDARD COST	£76 500	£124 200	£128 400	£329 100

FIGURE 18.6

CALCULATION TABLE FOR EACH PRODUCT

PRODUCT B

	STANDARD	ACTUAL	VARIANCE	
UNITS PRODUCED	100	100		
	£	£	£	
MATERIALS	12 500	13 000	(500)	ADVERSE
LABOUR	8 000	8 100	(100)	ADVERSE
VARIABLE OVERHEADS	20 000	20 500	(500)	ADVERSE
FIXED OVERHEADS	36 000	37 000	(1 000)	ADVERSE
TOTAL COST	76 500	78 600	(2 100)	ADVERSE

PRODUCT C

	STANDARD	ACTUAL	VARIANCE	
UNITS PRODUCED	120	120		
	£	£	£	
MATERIALS	25 200	24 800	400	FAVOURABLE
LABOUR	15 000	14 500	500	FAVOURABLE
VARIABLE OVERHEADS	30 000	29 000	1 000	FAVOURABLE
FIXED OVERHEADS	54 000	55 000	(1 000)	FAVOURABLE
TOTAL COST	124 200	123 300	900	FAVOURABLE

PRODUCT I

	STANDARD	ACTUAL	VARIANCE	
UNITS PRODUCED	150	150		
	£	£	£	
MATERIALS	42 000	44 000	(2 000)	ADVERSE
LABOUR	10 800	11 100	(300)	ADVERSE
VARIABLE OVERHEADS	27 000	27 200	(200)	ADVERSE
FIXED OVERHEADS	48 600	46 600	2 000	FAVOURABLE
TOTAL COST	128 400	128 900	(500)	ADVERSE
TOTAL COSTS	329 100	330 800	(1 700)	ADVERSE

FIGURE 18.7

PRODUCT B CALCULATION TABLE

PRODUCT B	CALCULATION TABLE		
	STANDARD	ACTUAL	VARIANCE
UNITS	100	100	
MATERIALS	£12 500	£13 000	£500 A

SUB-VARIANCES:

A × A (A)	£13 000		MATERIALS TOTAL VARIANCE
A × S (AS)	£12 750	£250 A	MATERIALS PRICE VARIANCE
S × S (S)	£12 500	£250 A	MATERIALS USAGE VARIANCE
		£500 A	

ONLY THE MIDDLE FIGURE NEEDS TO BE CALCULATED:
ACTUAL QUANTITY – 5100 UNITS MULTIPLIED BY STANDARD PRICE – £2.50 EACH = £12 750

THE DIFFERENCE BETWEEN A AND AS = MATERIALS PRICE VARIANCE; ADVERSE IF A IS GREATER
THAN AS (OR FAVOURABLE IF VICE VERSA)
THE DIFFERENCE BETWEEN AS AND S = MATERIALS USAGE VARIANCE; ADVERSE IF AS IS GREATER
THAN S (OR FAVOURABLE IF VICE VERSA)

Direct material total variance

(Direct material usage variance) + (Direct material price variance)

Direct labour rate variance

(Actual hours worked × Standard direct labour rate) − (Actual hours worked × Hourly rate)

Direct labour efficiency variance

(Standard hours of actual production × Standard direct labour rate) − (Actual direct hours worked × Standard direct labour rate).

Direct labour total variance

(Standard hours of actual production × Standard direct labour rate) − (Actual hours worked × Actual hourly rate)

Calculating materials sub-variances

The formulae for calculating the two subvariances are provided above, but the following 'mnemonic'

method enables the computations to be made with relative ease when a calculation table is used:

$A \times A$
$A \times S$
$S \times S$

First, $A \times A$: this represents the *Actual quantity of materials used* multiplied by the *Actual price paid*. It is thus the actual materials cost in Figure 18.6.

Next, the $A \times S$ figure: this represents the *Actual quantity of materials purchased* multiplied by the *Standard price that should have been paid*.

Finally, the $S \times S$ represents the *Standard quantity of materials that should have been used*, multiplied by the *Standard price*. This amount is also as shown in Figure 18.6.

The difference between the $A \times A$ figure and $A \times S$ represents the *direct materials price variance*. If the actual price paid ($A \times A$) is higher than the standard price ($A \times S$) an adverse price variance has occurred; if vice versa, there will be a favourable variance.

The difference between $A \times S$ (actual quantity) and $S \times S$ (standard quantity) provides the *direct materials usage variance*. Thus, to split the materials variance

FIGURE 18.8

SPLITTING LABOUR SUBVARIANCES				
PRODUCT B		CALCULATION TABLE		
		STANDARD	ACTUAL	VARIANCE
UNITS		100	100	
VARIABLE OVERHEADS		£8 000	£8 100	£100 A

SUB-VARIANCES: DIRECT LABOUR TOTAL VARIANCE

A	£8 100		
AS	£8 200	£100 F	DIRECT LABOUR RATES VARIANCE
S	£8 000	£200 A	DIRECT LABOUR EFFICIENCY VARIANCE
		£100 A	

AGAIN, ONLY THE MIDDLE FIGURE NEEDS TO BE CALCULATED:
ACTUAL HOURS – 2000 UNITS MULTIPLIED BY STANDARD RATE PER HOUR – £4.00 EACH = £2000

THE DIFFERENCE BETWEEN A AND AS = LABOUR RATES VARIANCE; ADVERSE IF A IS GREATER
THAN AS (OR FAVOURABLE IF VICE VERSA)
THE DIFFERENCE BETWEEN AS AND S = LABOUR EFFICIENCY VARIANCE; ADVERSE IF AS IS GREATER
THAN S (OR FAVOURABLE IF VICE VERSA)

into the two subvariances, *only one calculation needs to be made*. This is the middle one: A × S – the actual quantity used multiplied by the standard price of each.

For Product B, the total variance was £500 adverse. This will be split as shown in Figure 18.7.

Direct labour subvariances

The same mnemonic system can be applied for splitting the Labour subvariances, as shown in Figure 18.8.

The reasons why variances occur need to be investigated. An adverse material usage variance may be due to higher than expected wastage of materials; when investigated, this may be found to have been caused by inexperienced direct-labour staff, or perhaps because the wrong specification of materials was used. A favourable material price variance may be as a result of the buyer negotiating a special contract price, or perhaps more favourable trade discounts have been applied than was anticipated when the standard was set. Whatever the reasons, management need to know them, to judge whether any corrective action is called for.

Similarly with direct labour: a favourable rates variance may be because lower-grade staff were used to produce the product; and this could perhaps explain

the increased material wastage, because staff used may not have the same expertise in handling materials. There is often an interplay between the variances. For example, inexperienced staff are paid less, which is a favourable cost outcome, but production may be adversely affected through wastage and other inefficiencies, producing an unfavourable outcome. Management therefore frequently needs to 'balance' one against the other to achieve an overall favourable variance. Variance analysis thus enables management to operate a system of 'responsibility accounting': the Buyer responsible for purchasing materials will be in a position to explain the reasons for any price variances and therefore take the responsibility for them; and on the shop floor, the Production Manager or equivalent will be responsible and therefore in a position to explain the material usage, labour rates and efficiency variances.

Overheads

Dealing now with overheads, variances will arise in both variable production overheads and fixed production overheads.

Variable production overheads variances

Variable overheads are assumed to vary directly in line with production and typically are absorbed into the product, using an absorption method thought by management to be the most appropriate. For an illustration of this, the direct labour hours basis has been used. Both overhead absorption rates (variable and fixed) are usually calculated in advance of an accounting period. For variable overheads the following formula is customary:

$$\frac{\text{Expected (budgeted) variable overheads}}{\text{Expected (budgeted) direct labour hours}}$$
$$= \text{variable overheads absorption rate}$$

It follows that more products produced will generally mean more hours worked, therefore more variable overheads incurred (and vice versa). It further follows that, as the absorption rate is based on an estimate of the expected costs, there could be differences between the actual variable overhead expenses incurred and this predetermined estimate.

Therefore production variable overhead variances can arise because of two factors:

Variable overheads expenditure differences
Direct labour hours differences

Consequently, there are two subvariances for variable production overheads:

Variable overhead *expenditure* variance
Variable overhead *efficiency* variance

The sum of these is called the *variable production overhead total variance*.

CIMA terminology definitions for the calculations to arrive at these variances are:

Variable production overhead expenditure variance

(Actual hours worked × Standard overhead rate)
− (Actual cost)

Variable production overhead efficiency variance

(Standard variable production
overhead cost of actual production)
− (Actual hours worked × Standard overhead rate)

Variable production overhead total variance

(Standard variable production overhead cost of
actual production) − (Actual cost)

The calculation of variable overhead variances can also be fitted into the table format, using the mnemonics A, AS and S as before (see Figure 18.9). Note one change from Figure 18.8 in so far as the hours are required. In the 'actual' column enter the actual hours worked, and in the 'standard' column enter the number of hours that *should have been worked*, to produce the actual output. For Product B the hours worked were 2050 for 100 units. The standard hours expected for 100 units was 2000 hours (20 hours × 100 units.)

Fixed production overheads variances

Fixed production overheads, such as rent, rates, supervisors' salaries and so on, will be absorbed into products, using appropriate overhead absorption rates; for example, the direct labour hours basis, as in this case. The absorption rate will be calculated using budgeted fixed overhead expenditure for an accounting period divided by the number of direct hours expected to be worked in that period:

$$\frac{\text{Budgeted fixed production overheads}}{\text{Budgeted direct labour hours}}$$
$$= \text{Fixed overhead absorption rate}$$

The charge to each product will thus be: *number of direct labour hours worked* multiplied by *the fixed overhead absorption rate*. As with the variable overheads, the actual fixed overheads may be more or less than expected; also, the actual direct labour hours may differ.

These differences give rise to two subvariances:

Fixed production overhead *expenditure* variance
Fixed production overhead *volume* variance

The total of these two subvariances is called the *fixed production overhead total variance*.

CIMA terminology definitions of these variances are as follows:

FIGURE 18.9

CALCULATION OF VARIABLE OVERHEADS VARIANCES

PRODUCT B	CALCULATION TABLE		
	STANDARD	*ACTUAL*	*VARIANCE*
UNITS	100	100	
HOURS EQUIVALENT	2 000	2 050	
VARIABLE OVERHEADS	£20 000	£20 500	£500 A

SUB-VARIANCES:
MNEMONICS   VARIABLE OVERHEADS TOTAL VARIANCE

A	£20 500		
AS	£20 500	£0	VARIABLE OVERHEADS EXPENDITURE VARIANCE
S	£20 000	£500 A	VARIABLE OVERHEADS EFFICIENCY VARIANCE
		£500 A	

AGAIN, ONLY THE MIDDLE FIGURE NEEDS TO BE CALCULATED:
ACTUAL HOURS – 2050 UNITS MULTIPLIED BY STANDARD RATE PER HOUR – £10.00 EACH = £20 500

THE DIFFERENCE BETWEEN A AND AS = VARIABLE OVERHEADS EXPENDITURE VARIANCE; ADVERSE IF
A IS GREATER THAN AS (OR FAVOURABLE IF VICE VERSA)
THE DIFFERENCE BETWEEN AS AND S = VARIABLE OVERHEADS EFFICIENCY VARIANCE; ADVERSE IF
AS IS GREATER THAN S (OR FAVOURABLE IF VICE VERSA)

Fixed production overhead expenditure variance

(Budgeted fixed production overhead)
– (Actual fixed production overhead)

Fixed production overhead volume variance

(Standard absorbed cost)
– (Budgeted fixed production overhead)

Fixed production overhead total variance

(Standard absorbed cost)
– (Actual fixed production overhead)

The volume variance is capable of further subdivision, namely the fixed overhead *capacity* variance and the fixed *overhead* efficiency (or *productivity*) variance.

A calculation table can be used to identify all five variances and appears as shown in Figure 18.10.

Working through Figure 18.10 you will note that it is similar to Figures 18.7–18.9, except that there is an extra column for budgeted fixed overhead expenditure for the period. Here, enter the budgeted units for the period. Then enter the equivalent hours for those units (for Product B, 110 units at 20 hours per unit = 2200 hours). Multiply these hours by the fixed overhead absorption rate (2200 × £18). The figures for the 'standard' column are calculated in similar fashion, with the actual units of output used as the multiplier: (100 units × 20 hours = 2000 hours × £18). Finally, enter the actual output and cost figures in the 'actual' column.

The difference between the standard and actual cost is the fixed overheads *total* variance. The difference between the budget cost and the actual cost is the fixed overheads *expenditure* variance, (in Figure 18.10, A – B). And the difference between the budget cost and the standard cost is the fixed overheads *volume* variance, (in Figure 18.10, B – S).

FIGURE 18.10

CALCULATION TABLE IDENTIFYING FIVE FIXED OVERHEAD VARIANCES

PRODUCT B	CALCULATION TABLE			
	BUDGET	STANDARD	ACTUAL	VARIANCE
UNITS	110	100	100	
HOURS EQUIVALENT	2 200	2 000	2 050	
FIXED OVERHEADS	39 600	£36 000	£37 000	£1 000 A

FIXED OVERHEADS TOTAL VARIANCE

SUB-VARIANCES:

MNEMONICS

A	ACTUAL COSTS	£37 000		
B	BUDGETED COST	£39 600	£2 600 F	FIXED OVERHEADS EXPENDITURE VARIANCE
S	STANDARD COST	£36 000	£3 600 A	FIXED OVERHEADS VOLUME VARIANCE
			£1 000 A	

SUB-DIVISION OF THE VOLUME VARIANCE:

MNEMONICS		STANDARD RATE PER HOUR				
B	BUDGETED HOURS	2200	£18	=	£39 600	
A	ACTUAL HOURS	2050	£18	=	£36 900	£2 700 A CAPACITY VARIANCE
S	STANDARD HOURS	2000	£18	=	£36 000	£ 900 A EFFICIENCY VARIANCE
						£3 600 A

The expenditure variance is simply the difference between management's estimate of the cost that was likely to have been incurred in the accounting period (the budgeted figure) and the actual cost. In this case management forecast expenditure would be £39 600 but it was £37 000 – a favourable variance of £2600.

The volume variance represents the difference between what management expected production would be in the period (110 units) with what was actually achieved (100). So, fewer units were produced and this resulted in an adverse volume variance.

The analysis of the fixed overheads volume variance into the two subdivisions will enable management to discover the reasons why the volume variance occurred. It will be caused by either direct labour *efficiency*, or the usage of the *capacity* of the factory, or a combination of both these factors.

When fixed production overheads are not fully absorbed into products because of direct labour inefficiencies, the cost of this is reflected directly in lower profits. Similarly, if management had decided the factory should be producing products at a certain level, and budgeted accordingly, but the level was not achieved, the under-utilisation of the factory's planned capabil-

ities will also be directly reflected in lower profits. Therefore it is important to management to investigate the causes creating the volume variance.

Fixed overhead capacity and efficiency variances

This split of the volume variance can be achieved using mnemonics as in the bottom section of Figure 18.10. The mnemonics are B (for Budget), A (for Actual) and S (for Standard).

Here, you will note, the hours are analysed. The difference between the budgeted hours and the actual hours (B and A in the Figure) at the standard rate per hour provides the capacity variance. Here, management expected that 2200 hours would be worked, but only 2050 were recorded. The capacity of the factory was not achieved and this has cost £2700.

The difference between the actual hours and the hours considered sufficient to produce the actual quantity of units (the standard hours), represents the efficiency variance. Here, 2050 hours were worked on the 100 units, but it should have taken just 2000 hours. The cost of this was £900 (A – S).

FIGURE 18.11

PRODUCT C: COMPUTATION OF VARIANCES

PRODUCT C	CALCULATION TABLE – VARIABLE COSTS		
	STANDARD	ACTUAL	VARIANCE
UNITS	120	120	
MATERIALS	£25 200	£24 800	£ 400 F
LABOUR	£15 000	£14 500	£ 500 F
VARIABLE OVERHEADS	£30 000	£29 000	£1 000 F
HOURS	3 000	2 950	

MATERIALS VARIANCES:

A	£24 800		
AS*	£25 550	£750 F	MATERIALS PRICE VARIANCE
S	£25 200	£350 A	MATERIALS USAGE VARIANCE
*7300 × £3.50		£400 F	MATERIALS TOTAL VARIANCE

LABOUR VARIANCES:

A	£14 500		
AS*	£14 750	£250 F	LABOUR RATES VARIANCE
S	£15 000	£250 F	LABOUR EFFICIENCY VARIANCE
*2950 × £5.00		£500 F	LABOUR TOTAL VARIANCE

VARIABLE OVERHEADS:

A	£29 000		
AS*	£29 500	£500 F	VARIABLE OVERHEADS EXPENDITURE VARIANCE
S	£30 000	£500 F	VARIABLE OVERHEADS EFFICIENCY VARIANCE
*2950 HOURS AT £10 PER HOUR		£1 000 F	VARIABLE OVERHEADS TOTAL VARIANCE

	CALCULATION TABLE – FIXED COSTS			
	BUDGET	STANDARD	ACTUAL	VARIANCE
UNITS	130	120	120	
HOURS	3250	3 000	2 950	
FIXED OVERHEADS	£58 500	£54 000	£55 000	£1 000 A

SUBVARIANCES:

A	£55 000		
B	£58 500	£3 500 F	FIXED OVERHEAD EXPENDITURE VARIANCE
S	£54 000	£4 500 A	FIXED OVERHEAD VOLUME VARIANCE
		(£1 000) A	FIXED OVERHEAD TOTAL VARIANCE

SUBDIVISION OF VOLUME VARIANCE:

	HOURS	RATE			
B	3 250	£18	£58 500		
A	2 950	£18	£53 100	£5 400 A	CAPACITY VARIANCE
S	3 000	£18	£54 000	£ 900 F	EFFICIENCY VARIANCE
				£4 500 A	VOLUME VARIANCE

The sum of these two variances equals the volume variance.

The computations for the variances for Product C are given in Figure 18.11. As a separate exercise, use the figures given to calculate the variances for Product I.

Materials mix and yield variances

Referring back to the materials usage variance, this can be further subdivided whenever a product comprises a mixture of ingredients in preordained quantities. Occasionally, the mixture may need to be changed on actual production runs, perhaps because of temporary supply difficulties affecting one or more of the ingredients. Imagine a food product with two ingredients, A and B. The standard mix may be A = 25 per cent, and B = 75 per cent. But, in a particular production run, for some reason this may have to be altered to 30 per cent and 70 per cent. Now imagine that A is twice as expensive as B and you will see that additional costs will have been incurred because of this forced change in the mix. This change in mixture may also affect the quantities of finished product yielded: more may have been produced than expected, or less.

Collectively, these changes caused by the variation in the mix are reflected in the materials usage variance. Management may decide that they need to have an indication of the contributing factors to this overall usage variance. These two variances, *mix* and *yield*, provide this further analysis.

CIMA terminology defines the two calculations as follows:

Direct material mix variance

```
(Total material input in a standard mix
              × Standard prices)
 − Actual material input × Standard prices)
```

Direct material yield variance

```
(Standard quantity of materials specified for
       actual production  × Standard prices)
 − (Actual total material input in standard
           proportions × Standard prices)
```

Worked example

As an illustration we shall use the following LCCI (Level 3) 1994 question. Chicko Products uses standard costing in its integrated accounting system. Material price variances are calculated at purchase point and all entries in the materials control account are at standard prices. A product, called PEK, is made by mixing 3 materials to the following standard specification:

Material	Percentage of input	Standard price per kg
P	40%	$13.00
E	25%	$10.00
K	35%	$15.00

A normal loss of 7.5 per cent of total input is allowed for in arriving at the standard cost of the product.

Material stock records for last month show the following:

Material	Opening balance (kg)	Purchases (kg)	Cost	Issues (kg)
P	12 500	11 000	$144 760	11 650
E	7 500	12 000	$117 120	8 200
K	12 000	10 000	$154 800	10 750

During last month 27 950 kg of PEK were produced. There was no opening or closing work in progress.

Required:
Calculate the following material cost variances:
(i) price – for each material and in total;
(ii) Mixture – for each material and in total; and
(iii) yield – in total only.

A table to identify the mix and yield variances might appear as shown on page 246.

The standard cost of the standard mix needs to be established to arrive at the overall standard cost per unit. You will see that the proportion of each ingredient to the whole is multiplied by the appropriate standard cost price of each ingredient. Normal losses need to be provided for, and this is done by grossing up the standard cost by the normal loss percentage. In this question the standard loss is 7.5 per cent so the computation is 7.5%/92.5% = 8.1%; 8.1% of $5.20 gives the normal loss cost of $0.42. (Another method of grossing up is to divide the standard cost by the net of 100 per cent minus the standard loss percentage.

Step 1 Find the overall cost per unit:

		P	E	K	
	Standard mix	40.0%	25.0%	35.0%	100.0%
Multiplied by	Standard cost per kg	$13.00	$10.00	$15.00	
=	Standard cost	$ 5.20	$ 2.50	$ 5.25	$12.95
add normal loss	7.5% of cost	$ 0.42	$ 0.20	$ 0.43	(7.5%/92.5% × STD COST)
	Standard cost per unit	**$ 5.62**	**$ 2.70**	**$ 5.68**	**$14.00**

Step 2 Prepare the calculation table:

		Standard	Actual	Variance	
	Units	27 950	27 950		
27 950 × $5.62 = $157 079	P	$157 079	$151 450	$5 629	11 650 × $13
27 950 × $2.70 = $ 75 465	E	$ 75 465	$ 82 000	($6 535)	8 200 × $10
27 950 × $5.68 = $158 756	K	$158 756	$161 250	($2 494)	10 750 × $15
		$391 300	$394 700	($3 400)	Material usage variance

Step 3 Prepare an additional table to calculate the standard mix of actual input:

	Units	Cost of new mix ($)		Actual input kg	Std mix of Actual input kg	
	P	159 120	12 240 × £13.00	11 650	12 240	40% × 30 600 kg
	E	76 500	7 650 × £10.00	8 200	7 650	25% × 30 600 kg
	K	160 650	10 710 × £15.00	10 750	10 710	35% × 30 600 kg
		396 270		30 600	30 600	

Step 4 Calculation Table:

Standard mix ($)	'New' mix ($)	Actual mix ($)	Mix variance by ingredients
157 079	159 120	151 450	$7 670 F
75 465	76 500	82 000	($5 500) A
158 756	160 650	161 250	($ 600) A
391 300	396 270	394 700	$1 570 F
A	AS	S	

Step 5 Identify material mix and yield variances:

A	£394 700		
AS	£396 270	£1 570 F = mix variance	
S	£391 300	£4 970 A = yield variance	

Material price variance

		Standard ($)	Actual ($)	Variance ($)	
11 000 × £13 = £143 000	P	143 000	144 760	(1 760)	Adverse
12 000 × £10 = £120 000	E	120 000	117 120	2 880	Favourable
10 000 × £15 = £150 000	K	150 000	154 600	(4 800)	Adverse
		413 000	416 680	(3 680)	Adverse

This will give the total standard cost per ingredient inclusive of the normal loss.)

Example:
Standard cost of $2.50, standard loss 7.5% = $2.50 divided by 92.5% = $2.70.

Having completed the standard cost per unit, the calculation table can then be completed. Follow through the calculations given in the example. Note that the question stated that material price variances were calculated at purchase point, so actual issues have been priced at standard cost. The table in Step 2 thus provides just the materials usage variance. A supplementary calculation is also required, namely the standard mix of the actual input. You will see in Step 3 that the input was 30 600 kg. If this quantity had been introduced in accordance with the standard mix (that is, 40%, 25%, 35%) then the quantities of the individual ingredients would have been as shown as in the supplemental table in the example. Using this 'new mix' provides the basis for identifying the mix and yield variances in Steps 4 and 5.

Sales variances

So far, all the variances dealt with have been related to the setting of standard costs for products, resulting in *production cost variances*. But management may in addition set standards for sales and selling prices.

There are two possibilities when management set standards for sales: the actual selling price may be different from the standard selling price, and the actual volume of sales, and therefore gross profit, may be different from that expected, that is, budgeted.

The first possibility, the difference in selling prices, is described as a *selling price variance*; the second is termed a *sales volume profit variance*.

CIMA defines these variances as follows:

Selling price variance

> (Actual sales units × Standard selling price)
> − (Actual sales)

Sales volume profit variance

> (Budgeted sales units × Standard profit per unit)
> − (Actual sales units × Standard profit per unit)

Dealing first with the selling price variance. Management may have set a standard selling price for the product or products. If actual sales are made at differing selling prices then this will create the variance. The calculation to arrive at the variance is straightforward: *actual sales minus (number of units actually sold multiplied by the standard selling price)*. A favourable variance indicates a higher than standard selling price (therefore extra profits); an adverse variance the opposite.

The sales volume profit variance is simply the standard gross profit per unit multiplied by the difference in units. The standard gross profit per unit comprises:

> Standard selling price per unit
> − Standard cost price per unit

Both these variances can be calculated quickly using the following data:

Example:
Budgeted sales: 10 000 units at £70 each
Actual sales: 11 000 units at £75 each
Standard cost per unit: £50
Standard profit: £20

	Budget	Actual	Variance
Units	10 000	11 000	
Sales	£700 000	£825 000	
Standard cost	£500 000	£550 000	
Profit	£200 000	£275 000	£75 000 Favourable

Mnemonics:

A	£275 000	
AB*	£220 000	£55 000 F Selling price variance
B	£200 000	£20 000 F Sales volume profit variance

*11 000 × £20

The sales volume profit variance can be subdivided when there is more than one product sold. There could be, for example, differences in the actual mix of products sold when compared to the budgeted mix of sales. Similarly, if the actual quantity of units sold differs from budget, then this will also create a variance. These subvariances will assist management to discover the reasons for the volume variance. CIMA terminology defines the two as follows:

Sales mix profit variance

(Total actual sales × Budgeted weighted
average standard profit per unit)
− (Actual sales units
× Individual standard profit per unit)

Sales quantity profit variance

(Budgeted sales units
× Standard profit to sales ratio)
− (Total actual sales units × Budgeted
weighted average standard profit)

Again, to separate the two, a table (see Table 18.1) could be used, somewhat similar in style to the previous examples.

As you can see, it is necessary to weight the standard profit per unit to provide the sales mix profit variance. Using the mnemonics, the difference between the actual profit (A) and the budgeted profit (B) is the

sales volume profit variance. The middle calculation, (AB), represents the actual units sold multiplied by the weighted average profit, in this case £2.50 per unit. A minus AB provides the *sales mix profit variance*, and the difference between AB and B is the *sales quantity profit variance*.

To check these figures, a quantity of 2000 more units was sold than expected. At the weighted average standard profit of £2.50 each, an extra profit of £5000 was made – thus a quantity variance. They expected to sell the three products in the ratio of 30% : 40% : 30% and, if this had occurred, the 12 000 units in total would have earned the weighted average standard profit of £30 000 (12 000 × £2.50). However, the actual sales produced a different mix of profits (30% : 30% : 40%), resulting in a profit of £31 500. Therefore an extra £1500 was earned as a result of the change in the mix.

Presentation of variances

The purpose of variances is to assist management by highlighting the differences between planned costs

TABLE 18.1

SEPARATION OF PROFIT VARIANCES

	F	G	H	TOTAL	
WORKINGS					
BUDGETED UNITS	3 000	4 000	3 000	10 000	
STANDARD PROFIT PER UNIT	£2.00	£2.50	£3.00	2.50	WEIGHTED AVERAGE
STANDARD PROFIT	£6 000	£10 000	£9 000	£25 000	
ACTUAL UNITS	3 000	3 000	6 000	12 000	
STANDARD PROFIT PER UNIT	£2.00	£2.50	£3.00		
STANDARD PROFIT	£56 000	£7 500	£18 000	£31 500	

CALCULATION TABLE

	BUDGET	ACTUAL	VARIANCE	
PROFIT	£25 000	£31 500	£6 500	FAVOURABLE
MNEMONICS:				
A	£31 500			
AB*	£30 000	£1 500	F	SALES MIX PROFIT VARIANCE
B	£25 000	£5 000	F	SALES QUANTITY PROFIT VARIANCE
		£6 500	F	SALES VOLUME PROFIT VARIANCE

*12 000 UNITS × £2.50 AVERAGE PROFIT MARGIN

and revenue, and actual costs and revenue, so that they can concentrate their efforts and attention on those areas which are out of line. The conventional trading account does not provide this information, as it deals only with totals.

However, by using standard costs and standard selling prices, this basic information is transformed, enabling management to deal with the setbacks (adverse variances), and to investigate the favourable variances to see if these can be further

FIGURE 18.12

COMPARISON OF TWO FORMS OF DATA PRESENTATION

CONVENTIONAL TRADING ACCOUNT

£

SALES

LESS COST OF GOODS SOLD

GROSS PROFIT

SAME FIGURE

STANDARD COSTING TRADING ACCOUNT

£

BUDGETED TRADING PROFIT

VARIANCES: (A)/F   (ADVERSE) OR
                                                                                                  FAVOURABLE

SALES VARIANCES

SELLING PRICE VARIANCE	
SALES QUANTITY VARIANCE	} SALES VOLUME PROFIT
SALES MIX VARIANCE	VARIANCE

PRODUCTION VARIANCES

DIRECT MATERIALS PRICE VARIANCE	
DIRECT MATERIALS MIX VARIANCE	} DIRECT MATERIALS
DIRECT MATERIALS YIELD VARIANCE	USAGE VARIANCE
DIRECT LABOUR RATES VARIANCE	
DIRECT LABOUR EFFICIENCY VARIANCE	
VARIABLE OVERHEADS EXPENDITURE VARIANCE	
VARIABLE OVERHEADS EFFICIENCY VARIANCE	
FIXED OVERHEADS EXPENDITURE VARIANCE	
FIXED OVERHEADS CAPACITY VARIANCE	} FIXED OVERHEADS
FIXED OVERHEADS EFFICIENCY VARIANCE	VOLUME VARIANCE

ACTUAL TRADING PROFIT

improved. Figure 18.12 compares the two forms of presentation.

To support the standard costing trading account, management will require the data behind the figures in order to carry out meaningful investigations. The various calculation tables used in this chapter to illustrate the computations will provide this detail. These tables, once set up on computer spreadsheet programs, will allow variables to be input readily in each accounting period, with the resulting variances being calculated immediately and supporting schedules available when required.

Standard hour

The *standard hour* represents the amount of work that is able to be done in one hour. Say 1000 units have been made and it has taken 10 hours to make them. This, expressed in standard hours, would be 100 units of output per standard hour. So management should then be able to say that if 15 hours have been worked, the number of units able to be produced in that period of time should be 1500 units.

A standard hour is therefore a measure of work content and is defined in CIMA terminology as '*a quantity of work achievable at standard performance in an hour*'.

Some firms prefer to break down the work into *standard minutes*. So, in the above example, the 1000 units made in 600 minutes gives 1.66 standard minutes per unit. So a job or task can be said to be expected to take so many standard minutes to complete.

The standard hour, once established, can be used to measure the quantity of work produced, to identify overall efficiency. It can also act as a measure of capacity. Assume that the management have set output at 5 units per standard hour, and that 2000 units have been produced. This output would be expected, therefore, to take 400 hours. But the work may have been completed in 380 hours. The work has thus been performed more quickly. This information can be expressed in ratio form to provide management with *performance indicators*.

There are three main standard hour performance indicators, all ratios, as follows:

Volume ratio

$$\frac{\text{Standard hours produced}}{\text{Budgeted capacity}} \times \frac{100}{1}$$

This ratio indicates that, as a percentage of the planned quantity of work for a period, the actual output (volume), expressed also in standard hours, was greater or less than expected.

Example:

Budgeted capacity	3250 standard hours of work
Standard hours of work produced	3000
Actual hours worked	2950

The volume ratio will be: $\dfrac{3000}{3250} \times \dfrac{100}{1} = 92.3\%$

Actual production is therefore performing at only just over 92 per cent of budgeted capabilities.

Efficiency ratio

$$\frac{\text{Standard hours produced}}{\text{Actual direct labour hours}} \times \frac{100}{1}$$

Example:

$$\frac{3000}{2950} \times \frac{100}{1} = 101.6\%$$

The direct labour staff completed the work in less time than anticipated, so achieved an efficiency ratio in excess of 100.

Capacity ratio

$$\frac{\text{Actual direct labour hours}}{\text{Budgeted capacity}} \times \frac{100}{1}$$

Example:

$$\frac{2950}{3250} \times \frac{100}{1} = 90.8\%$$

This ratio explains that the plan was for 3250 hours to be completed but only 2950 was achieved. Thus the planned capacity of the factory was not achieved.

You will note that the above hours are those used when calculating the fixed production overheads variances of capacity, efficiency and volume. So these performance indicators express that information in ratio format. The three ratios are thus inter-linked and by multiplying the capacity ratio by the efficiency ratio, the volume ratio is arrived at.

Capacity Ratio	Efficiency Ratio	Volume Ratio
90.8% ×	101.6% =	92.3%

With these three ratios, management are able to measure quickly the effectiveness of production performance in each accounting period. They are thus key performance indicators.

Standard cost bookkeeping

We have looked extensively at standard costing as a control tool by way of variance analysis, which enables management to operate 'management by exception' techniques. Standard costs can also be used very effectively as part of the double entry book-keeping system, whether this is through integrated accounts or interlocking accounts. When standard costs are used, transfer entries in the following accounts will be made:

Raw materials control account;
Work-in-progress control account;
Production wages control account;
Variable production overheads control account;
Fixed production overheads control account;
Finished goods account;
Cost of goods sold account; and
Variance accounts.

Raw materials control account

The debit entries will be purchases of raw materials at actual cost. The transfer to work in progress will be made at standard cost. Thus, any material price variances arising will be identified at the time purchases are recorded in the account. This variance will be transferred to the raw materials price variance account. Stock gains or losses will be valued at standard cost. The account appears as shown in Table 18.2.

By removing the price variance, the closing stocks of raw materials will thus be valued at standard cost. Alternatively, the transfer of materials to the work-in-progress account can be made at actual cost, in which case the price variance will be identified in that account, and the variance transfer made from there. Using this latter method, the raw materials will be valued at actual cost, not standard.

TABLE 18.2

RAW MATERIALS CONTROL ACCOUNT

DR	£	RAW MATERIALS CONTROL ACCOUNT	CR	£
BALANCE BROUGHT FORWARD AT STANDARD COST	XX			
PURCHASES AT ACTUAL COST	XX	TRANSFER TO WORK-IN-PROGRESS ACCOUNT AT STANDARD COST		XX
TRANSFER TO MATERIALS PRICE VARIANCE ACCOUNT (IF FAVOURABLE)	XX	TRANSFER TO MATERIALS PRICE VARIANCE ACCOUNT (IF ADVERSE)		XX
TRANSFER STOCK DIFFERENCES ACCOUNT (IF GAIN)	XX	TRANSFER STOCK DIFFERENCES ACCOUNT (IF LOSS)		XX
		BALANCE CARRIED FORWARD AT STANDARD COST		XX
	XXX			XXX

TABLE 18.3

WORK-IN-PROGRESS CONTROL ACCOUNT			
DR WORK-IN-PROGRESS CONTROL ACCOUNT			*CR*
	£		£
BALANCE BROUGHT FORWARD – AT STANDARD COST	XX		
TRANSFER RAW MATERIALS FROM RAW MATERIALS ACCOUNT AT STANDARD COST	XX		
TRANSFER DIRECT LABOUR COST FROM PRODUCTION WAGES CONTROL ACCOUNT AT STANDARD COST	XX		
TRANSFER VARIABLE OVERHEADS ABSORBED FROM VARIABLE OVERHEADS CONTROL ACCOUNT AT STANDARD COST	XX	TRANSFER COST OF FINISHED PRODUCT TO FINISHED GOODS ACCOUNT (OR CGSOLD ACCOUNT) AT STANDARD COST	XX
TRANSFER FIXED OVERHEADS ABSORBED FROM FIXED OVERHEADS CONTROL ACCOUNT AT STANDARD COST	XX	TRANSFER TO MATERIALS USAGE VARIANCE ACCOUNT*	XX
		TRANSFER TO LABOUR EFFICIENCY VARIANCE ACCOUNT*	XX
TRANSFER TO MATERIALS USAGE VARIANCE ACCOUNT**	XX	TRANSFER TO VARIABLE COSTS EFFICIENCY VARIANCE ACCOUNT*	XX
TRANSFER TO LABOUR EFFICIENCY VARIANCE ACCOUNT**	XX	TRANSFER TO FIXED COSTS VOLUME VARIANCE ACCOUNT*	XX
TRANSFER TO VARIABLE COSTS EFFICIENCY VARIANCE ACCOUNT**	XX		
TRANSFER TO FIXED COSTS VOLUME VARIANCE ACCOUNT**	XX		
		BALANCE CARRIED FORWARD – AT STANDARD COST	XX
**IF FAVOURABLE	XXX	*IF ADVERSE	XXX

Work-in-progress account

This account, the 'shop floor' account, collects all the elements of cost as follows:

Materials

The cost of raw materials will be debited to the account at standard cost. The actual materials used will be compared with standard usage for the output and any materials *usage* variance identified. This variance will be transferred to the materials usage variance account, or, if further subdivided, to the direct material mix variance account and the direct material yield variance.

Labour

The actual cost of direct labour will have been debited initially to a production wages control account. Any direct labour rates variance will have been identified at that stage and an entry made to transfer it to the direct labour rates variance account (see production wages control account). Thus the charge for direct labour made to the work-in-progress account will be at standard cost, with the credit entry being made to the production wages control account. The direct labour *efficiency* variance will be identified and transferred out of the work-in-progress account to the direct labour efficiency variance account.

Variable production overheads

The actual costs of variable production overheads will be charged to their respective individual variable accounts; the totals of the entries in these accounts will appear in the variable production overheads control account. Any variable overheads expenditure variances will be identified in that account. The charge to the work-in-progress account will thus be made at standard cost, with the credit entry to the variable overheads control account. In the work-in-progress account, variable overheads *efficiency* variances will be identified and transferred to the respective variance account.

Fixed production overheads

Here, actual fixed production overheads will be charged to the fixed production overheads control account. Any expenditure variance will be identified in that account. The amount of fixed overheads

absorbed, based on the standard hours of actual work done, will be transferred from the control account to the work in progress account. Any resultant *volume* variance will be transferred to its variance account. The entries in the work-in-progress account will appear as shown in Table 18.3

The final entry in this account represents the transfer of completed goods in the accounting period (at standard cost) to the finished goods account – or cost of goods sold account if shipped immediately to the customer.

Production wages control account

The wages and salaries paid to all production staff will be debited to this account (with analysis – memorandum – accounts supporting the control account supplying the breakdown details). Payroll on-costs will also be charged here, if management have decided that these costs are to be accounted for as a part of wages and salaries. Note that the debit is for gross wages and salaries, the various payroll creditor accounts having been credited.

The transfer of direct labour costs to the work-in-progress account will be made at standard cost. Any differences between the amounts paid and recovered

TABLE 18.4

PRODUCTION WAGES CONTROL ACCOUNT				
DR	PRODUCTION WAGES CONTROL ACCOUNT			*CR*
	£			£
GROSS PAY FOR PERIOD – DIRECT LABOUR (ACTUAL COST)	XX			
GROSS PAY FOR PERIOD – INDIRECT LABOUR (ACTUAL COST)	XX	TRANSFER DIRECT LABOUR CHARGE TO WORK-IN-PROGRESS ACCOUNT AT STANDARD COST		XX
PAYROLL ON-COSTS (IF MANAGEMENT DECIDE TO CHARGE IT HERE)	XX			
		TRANSFER INDIRECT LABOUR COSTS TO FIXED PRODUCTION OVERHEADS CONTROL ACCOUNT (AT ACTUAL COST)		XX
TRANSFER TO DIRECT LABOUR RATES VARIANCE ACCOUNT (IF FAVOURABLE)	XX	TRANSFER TO DIRECT LABOUR RATES VARIANCE ACCOUNT (IF ADVERSE)		XX
	XXX			XXX

in the charge to production will be identified as a *rates* variance and transferred to the appropriate variance account.

In addition to direct labour staff wages, the control account will also be charged with non-production wages and salary costs. As these are indirect costs, a transfer to the fixed production overheads control account will be made, thus closing the production wages control account each period. The account appears as shown in Table 18.4.

Variable production overheads control account

All variable overheads incurred in the production process will be debited to this account at actual cost, with the transfer to work in progress being made at standard cost. Any *expenditure* variance will be identified at this stage and transferred to the appropriate variance account. The account appears as shown in Table 18.5.

Fixed production overheads control account

Similarly with this account, the actual costs being debited and the transfer to the work-in-progress account are credited at standard cost. The *expenditure* variance will also be identified at this point and transferred to the appropriate account. This account appears as shown in Table 18.6.

Finished goods account

All the entries in this account will be made at standard cost. It appears as shown in Table 18.7.

Cost of goods sold account

This account will be charged with the standard cost of the units sold in the accounting period, as shown in Table 18.8.

TABLE 18.5

VARIABLE PRODUCTION OVERHEADS CONTROL ACCOUNT

DR VARIABLE PRODUCTION OVERHEADS CONTROL ACCOUNT		CR
	£	£
VARIABLE COSTS INCURRED IN THE PERIOD XX	TRANSFER TO WORK-IN-PROGRESS ACCOUNT AT STANDARD COST – (BASED ON APPROPRIATE ABSORPTION RATE)	XX
TRANSFER TO VARIABLE OVERHEADS EXPENDITURE VARIANCE ACCOUNT (IF FAVOURABLE) XX	TRANSFER TO VARIABLE OVERHEADS EXPENDITURE VARIANCE ACCOUNT (IF ADVERSE)	XX
XXX		XXX

TABLE 18.6

FIXED PRODUCTION OVERHEADS CONTROL ACCOUNT

DR FIXED OVERHEADS CONTROL ACCOUNT		CR
	£	£
FIXED COSTS INCURRED FOR PERIOD XX	TRANSFER TO WORK-IN-PROGRESS ACCOUNT AT STANDARD COST – (BASED ON APPROPRIATE ABSORPTION RATE)	XX
TRANSFER TO FIXED OVERHEADS EXPENDITURE VARIANCE ACCOUNT (IF FAVOURABLE) XX	TRANSFER TO FIXED OVERHEADS EXPENDITURE VARIANCE ACCOUNT (IF ADVERSE)	XX
XXX		XXX

TABLE 18.7

FINISHED GOODS CONTROL ACCOUNT

DR	FINISHED GOODS CONTROL ACCOUNT		CR
	£		£
BALANCE BROUGHT FORWARD – AT STANDARD COST	XX		
		TRANSFER TO COST OF GOODS SOLD ACCOUNT – AT STANDARD COST	XX
TRANSFER FINISHED GOODS FROM WORK-IN-PROGRESS ACCOUNT AT STANDARD COST	XX		
		TRANSFER STOCK DIFFERENCES ACCOUNT – AT STANDARD COST (IF LOSS)	XX
TRANSFER STOCK DIFFERENCES ACCOUNT – AT STANDARD COST (IF GAIN)	XX		
		BALANCE CARRIED FORWARD – AT STANDARD COST	XX
	XXX		XXX

Variance accounts

Individual variance accounts may be maintained, or one overall variance account, as shown in Table 18.9.

Note that the variances are written off to the profit and loss account at the end of the accounting period. However, management may decide to carry forward to the next interim period balances on specific variance accounts (such as fixed overheads expenditure variance). The reasoning behind this is that the adverse and favourable variances could 'balance' themselves out over the year.

The flow diagram shown in Figure 18.13 indicates how the cost accounts are linked in a standard costing system.

Summary

- Standard costs are predetermined estimates of how much an individual product or service unit should cost. This information assists management in setting selling prices and in controlling the operations of the business, by analysing differences between actual costs and standard costs (termed variances), and in providing product costs and material prices for stock valuation purposes.
- There are three different types of standard costs: attainable standard costs, ideal standard costs, basic standard costs. Attainable standard costs are

TABLE 18.8

COST OF GOODS SOLD ACCOUNT

DR	COST OF GOODS SOLD ACCOUNT	CR
	£	£
TRANSFER FROM FINISHED GOODS (NUMBER OF UNITS SOLD MULTIPLIED BY STANDARD COST PER UNIT)	XX	TRANSFER TO PROFIT AND LOSS ACCOUNT XX
	XXX	XXX

TABLE 18.9

PRODUCTION VARIANCES ACCOUNT			
DR PRODUCTION VARIANCES ACCOUNT			*CR*
	£		£
TRANSFER RAW MATERIALS PRICE VARIANCE			
TRANSFER RAW MATERIALS USAGE	XX		
TRANSFER DIRECT LABOUR RATES VARIANCE	XX	TRANSFER TO PROFIT AND LOSS ACCOUNT	XX
TRANSFER DIRECT LABOUR EFFICIENCY VARIANCE	XX		
TRANSFER VARIABLE COSTS EXPENDITURE VARIANCE	XX		
TRANSFER VARIABLE COSTS EFFICIENCY VARIANCE	XX		
TRANSFER FIXED COSTS EXPENDITURE VARIANCE	XX	IF THE VARIANCES ARE FAVOURABLE THIS ACCOUNT WILL BE CREDITED AND THE	
TRANSFER FIXED COSTS VOLUME VARIANCE (ALL ABOVE ARE ADVERSE VARIANCES)	XX	TRANSFER TO THE PROFIT AND LOSS ACCOUNT WILL BE DEBITED	
	XXX		XXX

considered to be achievable in a reasonably efficient operation. They can act as a motivating force to spur the workforce to improve their performance. Ideal standards assume no wastage, downtime or any other reduction from 'perfect conditions'. Because of this virtually unachievable quality, ideal standards are also known as potential standard costs. Basic standards remain the same for many years and are generally useful for measuring trends. But because of the remoteness of the figures from current operations, basic standards are not often used as a day-to-day control tool.

- Standards are set for direct materials and direct labour. This is done by assessing the quantities of materials and labour required to make one product and the respective costs of those quantities. The standard cost is therefore built up from the calculation: quantity of items required multiplied by price per item. When all elements of cost have been assessed, a standard total cost for the product will be arrived at.
- The identification of standard cost variances enables management to control their business by using management by exception techniques, enabling them to focus on those activities that need attention. The difference between the total actual production cost of each cost element and

the equivalent standard total cost is termed the total variance, i.e. direct material total variance, direct labour total variance, variable production overheads total variance and fixed production overheads total variance.

- These total variances are broken down into sub-variances:

Materials	Labour	Variable	Fixed
Price	Rate	Expenditure	Expenditure
Usage	Efficiency	Efficiency	Volume

- In addition, there are subdivisions of the materials usage and fixed overhead volume variances. These are:

Materials usage	Fixed overheads volume
Mix	Capacity
Yield	Efficiency

- Mnemonics can be used to help remember the method for splitting the variable cost subvariances, as follows:

Materials

A   Represents the *actual* material total cost

AS The actual *quantity* of materials multiplied by the standard price

S   Represents the *standard* material total cost of the actual quantity made

FIGURE 18.13

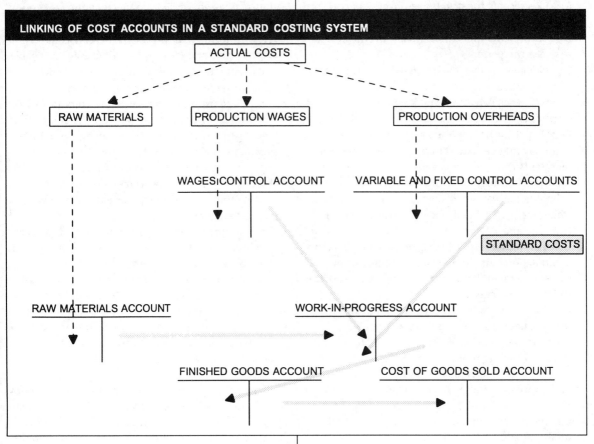

LINKING OF COST ACCOUNTS IN A STANDARD COSTING SYSTEM

- The difference between A and AS represents the material price variance; and the difference between AS and S represents the material usage variance.
- The overall difference between A and S is the materials total variance. When the first figure is greater than the second (i.e. A greater than AS) an adverse variance has occurred; when smaller than the second, there is a favourable variance.

Labour

A Represents the *actual* labour total cost
AS The actual *number of hours* multiplied by the standard rate
S Represents the *standard* labour total cost of the actual quantity made

- The difference between A and AS is the direct labour rates variance; and the difference between AS and S is the direct labour efficiency variance.

The direct labour total variance is the difference between A and S.

Variable overheads

A Represents the *actual* variable overheads total cost
AS Represents the *actual hours worked* multiplied by the standard cost per hour
S Represents the *standard* variable overheads total cost of the actual quantity made

- The difference between A and AS is the variable overheads expenditure variance; and the difference between AS and S the variable overheads efficiency variance. The difference between A and S is the variable overheads total variance.
- The mnemonics for splitting the fixed overheads variances are marginally different from the above pattern.

Fixed overheads

A   Represents the *actual* fixed overhead cost for the period

B   Represents the *budgeted* fixed overhead cost for the period

S   Represents the *standard* fixed overhead cost absorbed

- The difference between A and B represents the fixed overheads expenditure variance; and the difference between B and S represents the fixed overheads volume variance. The difference between A and S represents the fixed overheads total variance.
- Additional mnemonics can be used to split the subdivisional variances related to materials usage (mix and yield) and fixed overhead variances (capacity and efficiency).
- Calculation tables to assist in variance analysis computations also supply supporting information to management if further investigation into the variances is necessary.
- All the above variances arise in production, but management can also set standards for selling prices in order to have a control tool to monitor sales and trading profits.
- There are two sales related standards: the selling price variance and the sales volume profit variance. The standard profit of a product is the net difference between standard selling price and the total standard cost of the item.
- The sales profit volume variance can also be further subdivided into the sales mix profit variance and the sales quantity profit variance.
- Tables and mnemonics can also be used to split these variances.

- The conventional trading account form of presentation does not provide 'management by exception' information as it deals only in totals. But a standard costing format, starting with the expected or budgeted profit and then listing the variances, enables management to identify problem areas quickly and take corrective action where necessary.
- The standard hour represents the amount of work (measured in units of output) that is adjudged by management to be able to be done in one hour at standard performance. This provides management with a further control tool through performance indicators. There are three key indicators, all ratios: the volume ratio; the efficiency ratio; and the capacity ratio.
- The volume ratio shows how much work was actually done (in standard hours format) as a percentage of what the management had budgeted to be completed in the particular period (also in standard hours).
- The efficiency ratio shows the standard hours of actual output as a percentage of the actual hours worked; the capacity ratio shows whether the actual hours were greater or less than the budgeted hours.
- Standard costing can also be part of the cost bookkeeping system, whether integrated with the financial records or kept separately in interlocking accounts. The various stocks accounts – raw materials, work in progress, finished goods, will all generally be valued at standard cost in the system. Separate variance accounts will be maintained to record the analysed differences between actual performance and standard performance.

Examination Questions

1   A LEVEL (ULEAC) 1989

The graph shown opposite depicts labour costs within a standard costing system. All the variances shown are *unfavourable*.

State, with reasons, which areas represent:

(i)   the standard costs;

(ii)   the actual cost;

(iii) the wage rate variance;

(iv)   the labour efficiency variance; and

(v)   the total labour cost variance.

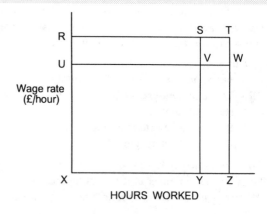

2 A LEVEL (ULEAC) 1990

From the following information calculate:

(i)   the standard machine hour rate;
(ii) the standard hours per unit;
(iii) the variable overhead expenditure variance; and
(iv) the variable overhead efficiency variance.

Budgeted variable overhead	£30 000
Actual variable overhead	£21 000
Budgeted machine hours	500
Actual machine hours	600
Budgeted production	20 units
Actual production	21 units

3 A LEVEL (ULEAC) 1992

Some of the following materials and labour variances have been wrongly calculated, although the figures used are correct. Recalculate the variances, showing clearly the formulae you have used, and state whether the variances are adverse or favourable.

Materials

(i)   Total materials variance

(standard price − actual price) (standard quantity − actual quantity)

= (£8.42 − £8.24) (1940 litres − 2270 litres)

= (£0.18) (330 litres)

= £59.40 adverse

(ii) Materials price variance

(standard price − actual price) standard quantity

= (£8.42 − £8.24) 1940

= £349.20 favourable

(iii) Materials usage variance

(standard quantity − actual quantity) standard price

= (1940 − 2270) £8.42

= £2778.60 adverse

Labour

(i)   Total labour variance

(actual hours − standard hours) (actual rate − standard rate)

= (860 − 800) (£6.14 − £6.53)

= (60 hours) (− £0.39)

= £23.4 adverse

(ii) Wage rate variance

(standard rate − actual price) actual hours

= (£6.53 − £6.14) 860

= £335.4 favourable

(iii) Labour efficiency variance

(actual hours − standard hours) Standard rate

= (860 − 800) £6.53

= £341.80 favourable

4 A LEVEL (AEB) 1990

Pensive Products Ltd manufacture and sell a single product. The company use a standard cost system for the control of direct materials and direct labour. The following information was available for the month of May:

Direct labour:
Budget   11 300 hours at £6 per hour
Actual   11 840 hours at £6.20 per hour
Direct materials usage:
Budget   9400 kg at £2.40 per kg
Actual   9650 kg at £2.10 per kg

Other costs:

	£
Repairs: plant and machinery	1 250
Factory supervisory staff salaries	8 500
Factory heating and lighting	2 400
Factory rent and rates	3 500
Depreciation of plant and machinery	4 800
General factory expenses	8 400

Additional information:
1. The company transfer finished products to the warehouse at a transfer price of 150% of prime costs.
2. Ignore work in progress.
3. During the month of May the target production levels were achieved.

Required:
(a) A manufacturing account for the month of May showing clearly the appropriate classification of costs and the manufacturing profit.
(b) A calculation of the following cost variances for the month of May:

(i)   direct labour: rate and efficiency; and
(ii) direct materials: price and usage.

5 A LEVEL (AEB) 1992

Bragg Ltd manufactures a household product. The standard cost of this article is:

Direct material	3 kg at £1.25 per kg
Direct labour	3 hours at £5.10 per hour

The company manufactures this product in batches of 50 000 units per month and all production is completed by the end of the period.

In June the actual results were:

Direct materials	158 000 kg, costing £189 600
Direct labour	156 000 hours, costing £81 900

Prior to the compilation of the actual results some of the senior management were asked to comment on the possible outcome of the comparison exercise that would take place.

The Purchasing Manager stated that he had obtained very good terms from his suppliers and there should be a favourable price variance. The Personnel Manager reported that no increase in wage rates had been agreed, so there should be no variance emerging in the wage rate calculation. Finally, the Production Manager was of the opinion that the labour force was efficient and the usage of materials would be improved.

Required:

(a) Calculate the following variances:
  (i) total direct cost variance;
  (ii) direct material price and usage variances; and
  (iii) direct labour rate and efficiency variances.

(b) In light of the variances calculated in (a), comment on the managers' views.

6 A LEVEL (AEB) 1993

Nester Ltd manufactures towing equipment and operates a standard costing system. A standard cost sheet for Model A94 is as follows:

Raw materials	3 kg at £2 per kg
Direct labour per model	1 hour at £4 per hour

The actual production of this model for the period 1 January, Year 3 to 31 March, Year 3 resulted in the following details:

Number of items produced	2000
Quantity of material used	6400 kg
Purchase price of material	£2.20 per kg
Labour hours worked	1800 hours
Actual labour rate	£4.10 per hour

There was no defective output and all production was complete.

Required:

(a) Calculate the material and labour variances for the production period 1 January, Year 3 to 31 March, Year 3.

(b) Comment on the labour rate and efficiency variances calculated above.

7 A LEVEL (AEB) 1994

HGW Ltd produces a product called a Lexton. The standard selling price and the manufacturing costs of this product are as follows:

		£
Standard selling price per unit		85

Standard production costs:		
Direct material	1.5 kg at £12 per kg	18
Direct labour	4.4 hours at £7.50 per hour	33
Variable overheads	4.4 hours at £5 per hour	22
		73

The projected production and sales for March were 520 units.

On 1 April the following actual figures were determined:

Sales	550 units at £85 each
Production	550 units
Direct material	785 kg at £12.40 per kg
Direct labour	2400 hours at £7.80 per hour
Overheads	£12 500 (overall variance £400 adverse)

There was no opening stock of the product Lexton.

Required:

(a) Prepare an actual profit and loss statement for HGW Ltd for March

(b) Calculate the following variances and their respective sub-variances:
  (i) sales – price and usage;
  (ii) direct material – price and usage; and
  (iii) direct labour – rate and efficiency.

(c) Prepare a statement reconciling the actual profit calculated in part (a) with the budgeted profit on actual sales (use the variances calculated in part (b) and the given overhead variance).

8 AAT COST ACCOUNTING AND BUDGETING 1991

Your company's Sales division is split on a regional basis, north and south. The sales budget had been set at the following levels for the current year. Your company sells only one product, with the budgeted price set higher in the south than in the north.

	Budgeted units	Price	Budgeted revenue
Northern region	150 000	£10	£1 500 000
Southern region	180 000	£12	£2 160 000
	333 000		£3 660 000

Actual sales for the year turned out to be 350 000 units of which 40% were in the Northern region. The total revenue for the Northern region was £1 470 000, and for the Southern region was £2 310 000. The budgeted and actual cost was £9 per unit.

The Sales Director has asked you to analyse the above figures before he has a meeting with the Sales Managers of the Northern and Southern regions.

Required:

(a) Prepare profit statements to show budgeted profit, actual profit and total sales margin variance for each region and the company as a whole for the year under review.

(b) Prepare sales margin price variances and sales margin quantity variances for each sales region and reconcile to the total sales margin variances calculated in (a) above.

(c) Analyse the above results for the Sales Director, highlighting possible reasons for the variances and the action that should be taken.

9 AAT COST ACCOUNTING AND BUDGETING

A company has two departments, A and B. Its budget and standards for last year included the following data:

	A	B
Units of production	8 000	10 000
Standard labour cost per hour	£4.00	£3.50
Standard labour hours per unit	2.0	1.5
The actual results were:		
Units of production	7 500	9 000
Labour cost	£70 875	£56 700
Labour hours	16 875	15 750

The company is unhappy with these results and wants to relate wage payments to labour effort and hopes to cut its own costs for the coming year.

Using the actual results above as a basis, you are told that the two labour payment schemes under review would have the following features.

Scheme 1

A full-time employee in Department A works 45 hours, while in Department B a full-time employee works 42 hours. They will be paid the actual hourly rate which was paid last year in each department.

Scheme 2

Piecework rates are to be paid on the basis of £8 per unit in Department A and £6 per unit in Department B. You are told that there will be an even flow of work over a 50-week year, and the company has a policy of engaging full- and part-time employees.

Required:

(a) Calculate labour rate, labour efficiency and total labour cost variances for Departments A and B for last year.

(b) Analyse the results achieved in (a), suggesting reasons for any variances.

(c) Calculate the weekly wage that would be paid to a full-time employee in Department A and Department B under Schemes 1 and 2 for the coming year.

(d) Recommend which scheme the company should contemplate using, stating your reasons clearly.

10 RSA III ACCOUNTING 1992

The standard cost of the making of one ladies' skirt in Mr Singh's workshop is:

Materials	3 metres @ £1.50 a metre
Labour	1.5 hours @ £3 an hour.

In Period 25 the actual cost of the 1000 skirts made was calculated at 2700 metres @ £1.60 a metre and 1550 hours @ £2.80 an hour.

Calculate:

(i) material price variance;

(ii) material usage variance;

(iii) labour rate variance; and

(iv) labour efficiency variance.

11 RSA III ACCOUNTING 1993

The standard cost of one widget was made up as follows:

Direct labour	4 hours @ £4.50 per hour
Materials	3 kg @ £2.40 per kg

The factory employs 25 workers who each work a 40-hour week:

20 of the workers are paid £4.60 per hour;
 5 of the workers are paid £4.20 per hour.

During the four-week period ending 1 June, the factory produced 1006 units. There were no breakdowns or absenteeism during the period.

3200 kg of raw materials were used, at a total cost of 7500.

Calculate:

(i)   the total labour variance;

(ii)   the labour efficiency variance;

(iii)   the labour rate variance;

(iv)   the total materials variance;

(v)   the materials usage variance; and

(vi)   the materials price variance.

Note Your variances must refer to the total output of 1006 units.

12 LCCI THIRD LEVEL COST ACCOUNTING 1991

MPV Ltd budgets to make 1000 units per month of a single product, each unit needing 3 kg of one material at a standard price of £5 per kg. At present all the cost accounts are written up at the end of each month. The material stock account is kept on an actual cost basis, using the FIFO pricing routine to calculate the charge to WIP control account. All variances are then calculated and posted at this stage.

During last month, 920 units of product were made, using 2800 kg of material, the stock record of which contained the following input data:

Day	Detail	Quantity (kg)	Actual price per (kg) (£)
1	Opening balance	100	5.20
8	Purchases	1000	5.30
20	Purchases	2500	4.80

It has been suggested that it would be better to calculate the material price variance on receipt of invoice and to make all entries in the material stock account at standard price.

Required:

(a) Using detailed Ledger account format, prepare, for last month, the following accounts as they appear in the present system:

(i)   material stock;

(ii)   WIP control (materials only);

(iii) material price variance; and

(iv)   material usage variance.

(b) Prepare similar accounts as in (a) assuming that the suggested change had been implemented and state by how much monthly profit would increase or decrease as a result.

13 LCCI THIRD LEVEL MANAGEMENT ACCOUNTING 1991

Drymarker plc uses systems of standard costing and budgetary control extensively throughout its organisation. The following are extracts from the records of the Whitemarker cost centre for the months of January and February.

January

Actual production	18 000 units
Actual variable overhead	£2000
Budgeted annual production	240 000 units
Budgeted annual variable overhead	£24 000

February

Actual production	18 000 units
Actual fixed overhead	£5300
Actual hours worked	4800
Budgeted monthly production	20 000 units
Budgeted monthly fixed overhead	£5000
Standard time per unit	15 minutes

Required:

(a) Calculate the following variances:

(i)   variable overhead expenditure for January;

(ii)   fixed overhead expenditure for February; and

(iii) fixed overhead volume for February.

(b) Show how you might subdivide the fixed overhead volume variance.

14 LCCI THIRD LEVEL MANAGEMENT ACCOUNTING 1992

Bellecose Limited has suffered industrial unrest within the last few months which has resulted in trading losses being reported. An extract from the working papers for the most affected department reveals the following:

Standard time per unit	15 minutes
Budgeted output	4 000 000 units
Budgeted fixed overhead	£1 000 000
Actual hours worked	960 000
Actual output	3 600 000 units
Actual fixed overhead	£1 020 000

Required:

(a) Calculate the:

(i)   total fixed overhead variance;

(ii)   fixed overhead expenditure variance; and

(iii) fixed overhead volume variance.

(b) (i)   explain to the management how much of the variance calculated in (a)(iii) is a result of the inefficiency of employees during this period of dispute; and

(ii)   state how many units of output this represents.

15 LCCI THIRD LEVEL COST ACCOUNTING 1992

Favad Ltd makes a single product and operates a system of variance accounting. In Department X, the standard hourly rate for direct workers is set at £4.50 per hour and each unit of product requires 6 standard hours in the department. Fixed overhead in the department is budgeted to cost £165000 per month at a normal monthly level of production of 5000 units of product. There is no opening or closing work in progress.

During last month, 4650 units of product were made, direct workers worked 26800 hours, costing £124350 and fixed overhead incurred in the department was £158650.

Required:
(a) Calculate the total direct labour cost variance and analyse it into appropriate subvariances;
(b) Calculate the total fixed overhead cost variance and analyse it into appropriate subvariances; and
(c) Calculate, to 2 decimal places:
  (i) production volume (or activity) ratio;
  (ii) capacity ratio; and
  (iii) efficiency ratio.

16 LCCI THIRD LEVEL COST ACCOUNTING 1992
Chemico Ltd makes a chemical product called FAB to the following standard specification:

Material	Percentage of input	Standard price per kg (£)
F	35	3.90
A	50	8.07
B	15	4.80

A normal process loss of 15% of total input is allowed for in setting the standard cost of the product. During last month, 30850 kg of good output were produced from the following inputs:

Material	kg	Actual price per kg (£)
F	12500	3.75
A	17650	8.30
B	5350	4.72

Calculate:
(a) the standard material cost of one kilogram of finished FAB;
(b) the following material cost variances:
  (i) price – for each material and in total;
  (ii) mixture – for each material and in total;
  (iii) yield – in total only; and
  (iv) total cost.

17 LCCI THIRD LEVEL COST ACCOUNTING 1992
Jentree Ltd, a manufacturing business, operates an integrated accounting system. Standard costing is used and management

accounts are prepared at monthly intervals. The material price variance is calculated on receipt of purchase invoices.

Required:
Prepare journal entries to record the following events in the accounting system for last month.
(a) The standard price of Fabric Z is £6.20 per metre. 5355 metres of this fabric were received, invoiced at £34272.
(b) 3980 metres of Fabric Z were issued to production;
(c) The fabric is inspected when it is unrolled at the start of the production process; 300 metres, which were found to be faulty, were returned to stores and then sent back to the supplier with a debit note.
(d) The standard direct labour hourly rate is £5. Direct operatives worked 12675 actual hours and were paid £62361. The standard hours of work produced totalled 12435 hours.
(e) Production overhead was absorbed at a standard rate of £6.40 per labour hour.
(f) A debtor, DS Ltd, owed £2500 and was unable to pay; 30 units of stock were accepted back from DS Ltd and taken into Jentree Ltd's stock as a partial settlement. The balance was written off as a bad debt. Jentree's selling price was £60 per unit, which included a mark up for profit of 50% on standard production cost.

Note Narrations are not required.

18 LCCI THIRD LEVEL MANAGEMENT ACCOUNTING 1993
Culling Components Ltd produces a product by mixing two compounds, A and B. The standard materials usage and cost of one load is:

Compound A	10kg @ £4 per kg
Compound B	20kg @ £6 per kg

In February, 160 loads were produced from 2000 kg of A and 2920 kg of B.

Required:
Using individual prices per kg, calculate:
(i) the usage variance;
(ii) the mixture variance; and
(iii) the yield variance.

19 ACCA COST AND MANAGEMENT ACCOUNTING 1 1990
A company manufactures two products which have the following standard costs (per hundred units of output) for direct materials and direct labour:

Product 1:
98 kilos of Material M at £0.78 per kilo
10 hours in Department X at £4.20 per hour.

Product 2:

33 kilos of Material N at £2.931 per kilo

9 hours in Department Y at £4.50 per hour.

The predetermined production overhead rates for the two departments are:

Department X: £3.60 per direct labour hour.

Department Y: £2.90 per direct labour hour.

The following incomplete information is provided of actual production, cost and variances for the period:

Actual production:

Product 1: 42 100 units

Product 2: (vii) units

Actual costs:

Direct materials

41 200 kg of Material M at £0.785 per kg = £32 342

(viii) kg of Material N at (ix) per kg = £23 828

Direct labour:

4190 hours in Department X at £4.20 per hour = £17 598

(x) hours in Department Y at £4.55 per hour = (xi)

Production overhead:

Department X   £14 763

Department Y   (xii)

Variances:

Direct materials:	**Material M**	**Material N**
Price	(i)	£233A
Usage	(ii)	£5F
Total	(iii)	£228A

Direct labour:	**Dept X**	**Dept Y**
Rate	(iv)	(xiii)
Efficiency	(v)	£342F
Total	£84F	(xiv)

Production overhead	(vi)	£142A

Note   A denotes an adverse variance; F denotes a favourable variance.

Required:

(a) Calculate the standard costs of Products 1 and 2 (£ per hundred units to two decimal places).

(b) Calculate the missing cost variances (i) to (vi) relating to Product 1 (to nearest £).

(c) Calculate the missing figures (vii) to (xiv) relating to Product 2. (Calculate variances and total costs to the

nearest £; production, kg and hours to the nearest whole number; and price per kg to two decimal places of a £).

20   ACCA COST AND MANAGEMENT ACCOUNTING 1 1991

B Ltd manufactures a single product in one of its factories. Information relating to the month just ended is as follows:

(i)   Standard cost per hundred units:

	£
Raw materials: 15 kg at £7 per kg	105
Direct labour: 10 hours at £6 per hour	60
Variable production overhead:	
10 hours at £5 per hour	50
	215

(ii)   226 000 units of the product were completed and transferred to finished goods stock.

(iii)   34 900 kg of raw material were purchased in the month at a cost of £245 900.

(iv)   Direct wages were £138 545 representing 22 900 hours work.

(v)   Variable production overheads of £113 800 were incurred.

(vi)   Fixed production overheads of £196 800 were incurred.

(vii)   Stocks at the beginning and end of the month were:

	Opening stock	**Closing stock**
Raw materials	16 200 kg	16 800 kg
Work in progress		4 000 units
		(complete as to raw
		materials but only
		50% as to direct
		labour and overhead)
Finished goods	278 000 units	286 000 units

Raw materials, work in progress, and finished goods stocks are maintained at standard cost. You should assume that no stock discrepancies or losses occurred during the month just ended.

Required:

Prepare the cost ledger accounts relating to the above information in B Ltd's interlocking accounting system. Marginal costing principles are employed in the cost ledger.

21   ACCA COST AND MANAGEMENT ACCOUNTING 1 1992

AB Ltd manufactures a range of products. One of the products, Product M, requires the use of Materials X and Y. Standard material costs for the manufacture of an item of Product M in Period 1 included:

Material X: 9 kg at £1.20 per kg.

Total purchases of Material X in Period 1, for use in all products, were 142 000 kg costing £171 820; 16 270 kg were used in the period in the manufacture of 1790 units of Product M. In Period 2 the standard price of Material X was increased by 6%, whilst the standard usage of the material in Product M was left unchanged; 147 400 kg of Material X were purchased in Period 2 at a favourable price variance of £1031.80. A favourable usage variance of 0.5% of standard occurred on Material X in the manufacture of Product M in the period.

Required:

Calculate:

(i)   the total price variance on purchases of Material X in Period 1;

(ii)   the Material X usage variance arising from the manufacture of Product M in Period 2;

(iii)   the actual cost inflation on Material X from Period 1 to Period 2. Calculate as a percentage increase to one decimal place; and

(iv)   the percentage change in actual usage of Material X per unit of Product M from Period 1 to Period 2. Calculate to one decimal place.

22   ACCA COST AND MANAGEMENT ACCOUNTING 1 1993
One of the cost centres in a factory is involved in the final stage of production. Budgeted fixed overhead costs for the cost centre for a period were:

Apportioned costs	£74 610
Directly incurred costs	£98 328

A predetermined machine hour rate is established for the absorption of fixed production overhead into product cost. Budgeted machine hours for the cost centre in the period were 1900.

Actual overheads (apportioned and directly incurred) in the period were £173 732. The volume variance was £4551 favourable.

Required:

Calculate for the period:

(i)   the predetermined fixed overhead absorption rate;

(ii)   the actual machine hours; and

(iii)   the over-/under-absorption of fixed overhead.

23   CIMA COSTING 1990
A manufacturing company has recently introduced a system of standard costing and you, as the Assistant Management Accountant, wish to demonstrate the value of the system to the management. The following data apply to Period 4, which was a four-week financial period:

Direct materials:

Purchases:	Material A 50 000 kg for £158 750	
	Material B 25 000 kg for £105 000	
Used:	Material A 4 800 kg	
	Material B 1 800 kg	

Direct labour:

	Actual hours worked	Wages paid (£)
Department 1	3 000	11 800
Department 2	2 400	13 250

Budgeted normal capacity expressed in direct labour hours:

Department 1	3200 hours
Department 2	2600 hours

Other information:

Standard cost for 1 unit of finished product:

	Quantity	Price (£)	(£)
Direct material A	10 kg	3.25	32.50
Direct material B	5 kg	4.00	20.00
Direct wages Dept 1	8 hours	4.00	32.00
Direct wages Dept 2	5 hours	5.00	25.00
			109.50

It has been decided to extract material price variance at the time of receipt. 400 finished goods units were produced in the period.

Required:

(a)   To calculate price and usage variances for each of the direct materials A and B.

(b)   To calculate rate and efficiency variances for the direct labour employed by each of Departments 1 and 2.

(c)   To suggest one possible reason for each of the variances shown in your answers to (a) and (b) above, without stating the same reason more than once.

(d)   To calculate for Department 1 and for Department 2
        (i)   the production volume ratio; and
        (ii)   the efficiency ratio.

24   CIMA COST ACCOUNTING 1991
RS Ltd makes and sells a single product J, with the following standard specification for materials:

	Quantity (kg)	Price per (kg)
Direct material R	10	30
Direct material S	6	45

It takes 30 direct labour hours to produce one unit of J with a standard direct labour cost of £5.50 per hour.

The annual sales/production budget is 1200 units evenly spread throughout the year. The budgeted production overhead, all fixed, is £252 000 and expenditure is expected to occur evenly over the year, which the company divides into twelve calendar months. Absorption is based on units produced.

For the month of October the following actual information is provided. The budgeted sales quantity for the month was sold at the standard selling price.

	£	£
Sales:		120 000
Cost of sales:		
Direct material used	58 136	
Direct wages	17 325	
Fixed production overhead	22 000	
		97 161
Gross profit:		22 539
Administration costs:	6 000	
Selling and distribution costs:	11 000	
		17 000
Net profit:		5 539

Costs of opening stocks, for each material, were at the same price per kilogram as the purchases made during the month but there had been changes in the materials stock levels.

	1 October (kg)	30 October (kg)
Material R	300	375
Material S	460	225

Material R purchases were 1100 kg for £35 000.
Material S purchases were 345 kg for £15 180.

The number of direct labour hours worked was 3300 and the total wages incurred £17 325.

Work in progress stocks and finished goods stocks may be assumed to be the same at the beginning and end of October.

Required:

(a) To present a standard product cost for one unit of product J showing the standard selling price and standard gross profit per unit.

(b) To calculate appropriate variances for the materials, labour, and fixed production overheads noting that it is company policy to calculate material price variances *at time of issue to production*.

(c) To present a statement for management reconciling the budgeted gross profit with the actual gross profit;

(d) To suggest a possible cause for each of the labour variances you show under (b) above, stating whether you believe each variance was controllable or uncontrollable

and, if controllable, the job title of the responsible official. Please state the name and amount of each variance about which you write and explain the variance, quantifying it, where possible, in non-financial terms which might be better understood by line management.

25 CIMA COST ACCOUNTING 1992a

RH makes and sells one product, the standard production cost of which is as follows for one unit:

Direct labour	3 hours at £6 per hour	£18
Direct materials	4 kilograms at £7 per kg	£28
Production overheads:	Variable	£ 3
	Fixed	£20
Standard production cost		£69

Normal output is 160 000 units per annum and this figure is used for the fixed production overhead calculation.

Costs relating to selling, distribution and administration are:

Variable	20 per cent of sales value
Fixed	£180 000 per annum

The only variance is a fixed production overhead volume variance. There are no units in finished goods stock at 1 October 1992. The fixed overhead expenditure is spread evenly throughout the year. The selling price per unit is £140.

For the two six-monthly periods detailed below, the numbers of units to be produced and sold are budgeted as:

	Six months ending 31 March Year 3	Six months ending 30 September Year 3
Production	8 500	7 000
Sales	7 000	8 000

Required:

(a) To prepare statements for management showing sales, costs and profits for each of the six-monthly periods, using:
   (i) marginal costing; and
   (ii) absorption costing.

(b) To prepare an explanatory statement reconciling for each six-monthly period the profit using marginal costing with the profit using absorption costing.

26 CIMA COST ACCOUNTING 1992

A labour-intensive production unit operating a standard absorption cost accounting system provides the following information for Period 10:

Normal capacity, in direct

 labour hours   9600

Budgeted variable

 production overhead   £3 per direct labour hour

Budgeted fixed production

 overhead per four-week

 financial period   £120 000

To produce one unit of output takes two hours of working.

Actual figures produced for the four-week period 10 were:

Production, in units	5000
Variable production overhead incurred	£28 900
Fixed production overhead incurred	£118 000
Actual direct labour hours worked	9300

Required:

(a) To calculate, in accordance with the 1991 edition of the Institute's Terminology, the variances for

 (i) variable production overhead expenditure variance;

 (ii) variable production overhead efficiency variance;

 (iii) fixed production overhead expenditure variance; and

 (iv) fixed production overhead volume variance.

(b) To subdivide your volume variance produced for (a)(iv) above into two subvariances and explain the meaning of these in the form of a brief report to management.

27 CIMA COST ACCOUNTING 1993

JB plc operates a standard marginal cost accounting system. Information relating to product J, which is made in one of the company's departments, is given below.

Product J Standard marginal product cost:

		Unit (£)
Direct material	6 kg at £4 per kg	24
Direct labour	1 hour at £7 per hour	7
Variable production overhead*		3
Total variable production cost		34

*Variable production overhead varies with units produced.

Budgeted fixed production overhead,

 per month: £100 000

Budgeted production for Product J: 20 000 units per month.

Actual production and costs for month 6 were as follows:

Units of J produced	18 500

	£
Direct materials purchased and used 113 500 kg	442 850
Direct labour 17 800 hours	129 940
Variable production overhead incurred	58 800
Fixed production overhead incurred	104 000
	735 390

Required:

(a) To prepare a columnar statement showing, by element of cost, the

 (i) original budget;

 (ii) flexed budget;

 (iii) actual costs; and

 (iv) total variances.

(b) To sub-divide the variances for direct material and direct labour shown in your answer to (a)(iv) above to be more informative for managerial purposes.

(Author's note: attempt this question after reading Chapter 19.)

28 CIMA COST ACCOUNTING 1994

NAB Limited has produced the following figures relating to production for the week ended 21 May:

	Production (in units)	
	Budgeted	Actual
Product A	400	400
Product B	400	300
Product C	100	140

Standard production times were: Standard hours per unit

Product A	5.0
Product B	2.5
Product C	1.0

During the week 2800 hours were worked on production.

Required:

(a) Calculate the production volume ratio and the efficiency ratio for the week ended 21 May.

(b) To explain the significance of the two ratios you have calculated and to state which variance may be related to each of the ratios.

29 CIMA COST ACCOUNTING 1994

Show the following information as it would appear in a production overhead control account, complete with all figures and the account balanced off:

	£
Variable overhead incurred	52 000
Variable overhead absorbed	
–5500 hours at £9 per hour	49 500

Variable overhead expenditure variance	?
Fixed overhead incurred	53 750
Fixed overhead absorbed	
– 5500 hours at £9 per hour	49 500
Fixed overhead expenditure variance – adverse	8 750
Fixed overhead volume variance	?

30 CIMA COST ACCOUNTING 1994

The following data have been collected for the month of April by a company which operates a standard absorption costing system:

Actual production of Product EM	600 units

Actual costs incurred:

	£
Direct material E – 660 metres	6 270
Direct material M – 200 metres	650
Direct wages – 3200 hours	23 200
Variable production overhead	
(which varies with hours worked)	6 720
Fixed production overhead	27 000

Variances:

	£
Direct material price:	
Material E	330 Favourable
Material M	50 Adverse
Direct material usage:	
Material E	600 Adverse
Material M	Nil
Direct labour rate	800 Adverse
Direct labour efficiency	1 400 Adverse
Variable production overhead:	
Expenditure	320 Adverse
Efficiency	400 Adverse
Fixed production overhead:	
Expenditure	500 Favourable
Volume	2 500 Favourable

Opening and closing work in progress figures were identical, so can be ignored.

Required:

(a) To prepare for the month of April a statement of total standard costs for Product EM.

(b) To present a standard product cost sheet for one unit of product EM.

(c) To calculate the number of units of product EM which were budgeted for April.

(d) To state how the material and labour cost standards for product EM would originally have been determined.

31 UNIVERSITY OF GREENWICH YEAR 1 BA ACCOUNTANCY AND FINANCE (1992)

In a cost period, Greenwich Ltd sells 70 units of product z for £4480.

Standards for one unit are:

	£	£
Sale price		64.00
Prime cost		
Materials – 13 gallons @ 46p per gallon	5.98	
Wages – 27 hours @ £1.90 per hour	51.30	57.28
Gross profit		6.72

The actual costs for the period were:

Materials:	£563 (1017 gallons)
Wages:	£3572 (1841 hours)
Sales:	£4480

Required:

(a) Calculate the variances for material and labour cost.

(b) Indicate possible reasons for the above variances and describe how the information should be used.

32 UNIVERSITY OF GREENWICH YEAR 1 BA ACCOUNTANCY AND FINANCE (1992)

KA plc produces one brand of shampoo which they market wholesale in cases at £30. Budget production level is 8000 per month, which is the level used to calculate the production overhead absorption rate. There was no opening stock at the beginning of the year. Standard costs per case are as follows:

	Per case (£s)
Direct costs:	
Materials	4.00
Labour	1.50
Production overheads:	
Variable	2.00
Fixed	3.00

Actual results for the first three months of 1992 were:

	Jan	Feb	Mar
Production (cases)	10 000	8 000	6 000
Sales (cases)	8 000	6 000	10 000
Overheads:			
	£	£	£
Production variable	20 000	16 000	12 000
Production fixed	24 000	24 000	24 000
Selling: Variable	24 000	18 000	30 000
Fixed	9 000	9 000	9 000

Direct costs were as standard.

Required:

Prepare, in tabular form, profit statements for each of the three months using:

    (i)   variable costing; and

    (ii) absorption costing.

NON-COMPUTATIONAL, DESCRIPTIVE TYPE QUESTIONS

(**NB**: Minutes in brackets are a guide to indicate the approximate time your essay should take to complete.)

QUESTION

A State how the material and labour cost standards for a product would originally have been determined.

(CIMA 1994) (5 minutes)

B Explain the terms 'attainable standard' and 'ideal standard' and state, with reasons, which ought to be used when setting operational performance standards.

(CIMA 1992) (10 minutes)

C Describe, and contrast, the different types of standards that may be set for raw material usage and labour efficiency.

(ACCA 1992) (18 minutes)

D Describe two advantages a system of standard costing might bring to a company.

(LCCI 1993) (9 minutes)

E Suggest two possible causes for labour variance occurring and two possible causes for material variances occurring.

(RSA III 1993) (8 minutes)

F Define standard costing, and describe how standard costing may be useful to management.

(AEB A Level 1993) (20 minutes)

G How does a system of standard costing enable a business to operate on the principle of management by exception?

(ULEAC 1992) (5 minutes)

19
Budgetary Control

In this chapter we shall examine how short-term plans – budgets – are prepared, and how they enable management to control the affairs of a business.

All commercial and service organisations need to plan for the future in order to be successful. But many firms with sound products and services fail to plan. This weakness does not mean necessarily that their businesses will fail (although this is a likelier possibility), but that they will operate on a day-to-day basis and perhaps miss potential business opportunities that planning for the future opens for them.

Non-planning businesses often stumble financially because they are unprepared for the future. Failure to plan also creates its own costs and lost opportunities. Consider the overdraft position as an example of costs being incurred because of lack of planning: failure to keep within an overdraft limit runs the risk of cheques being unpaid when presented, thus endangering the relationship with suppliers who have extended credit terms to the firm. These suppliers may take court action and insist on future supplies being paid for in cash, or at higher prices because of the poor payments record. It may not be possible to pay by cash, meaning that the company cannot buy stock and so cannot produce or sell on. Trading opportunities are therefore lost. Unauthorised borrowing means that the bank will levy a higher interest rate on the excess overdraft; it will also probably impose financial

penalties each day an excess, unauthorised borrowing situation remains, not to mention the additional cost of bank letters. A further cost is management time which will be fully taken up by resolving such crises, time which could have been spent on more productive matters. It is clear, therefore, that management needs to look forward constantly, to plan the company's operations and objectives carefully – in short, to budget.

There are basically two types of planning, *long-term* and *short-term*. Long-term planning (also called strategic planning or corporate planning), was discussed in general terms in Chapter 16. Its purpose is to set goals for the company (which may take three, five or more years to achieve), and the actions required to attain the ultimate objectives.

Short-term plans slot into the overall strategic plan, usually covering a period of one year (subdivided into months or four/five weekly periods).

Short-term plans are known as *budgets*. CIMA defines a budget as '*A plan expressed in money. It is prepared and approved prior to the budget period*'.

The purpose of the budget is to enable management to *plan* their operations and, during the budget period, to *control* those operations by comparing actual results with budgeted results. Budgets are therefore somewhat similar to standard costs in that they both establish predetermined targets of performance, and they

FIGURE 19.1

ASPECTS OF A BUSINESS QUANTIFIABLE IN TERMS OF MONEY

TRADING INCOME
SALES OF PRODUCTS
SERVICES RENDERED

TRADING EXPENDITURE
MANUFACTURING COSTS
DISTRIBUTION AND SELLING EXPENSES
ADMINISTRATION AND FINANCING COSTS
RESEARCH AND DEVELOPMENT

FIGURE 19.2

FINANCIAL ASPECTS CONTROLLED BY BUDGETS

CAPITAL EXPENDITURE
CASH
LONG-TERM FINANCING

---

both provide a comparison for actual performance (through variances). Budgets, however, are related to the business as a whole, while standard costs are concerned with the production costs of products and manufacturing operations. A budget therefore covers the aspects of a business that can be quantified in money terms (see Figure 19.1).

In addition to these manufacturing and trading operations, a budget will also plan and control the assets and liabilities of the business and its financing (see Figure 19.2). You will recognise these as the structure of the profit and loss account and the balance sheet.

Preparing budgets

The usual steps in preparing a budget are as follows.

The board of directors will appoint a *budget committee* or *budget preparation team*. The board will instruct the committee to prepare a budget for (usually) the upcoming year, in line with financial parameters it lays down.

These parameters may be as agreed at a strategy meeting held to formulate the objectives of the business, therefore being part of the long-term plan. They will probably include target profit returns and general economic guidelines considered appropriate to the business; for example, general inflation rates expected to prevail during the budget period.

The committee may comprise the Sales Director, Production Director and Finance Director, or equivalents, under the general direction of the Managing Director or Chief Executive.

In turn, the committee will appoint a *Budget Officer*, who will be responsible for compiling the budget ready for review and approval by the committee and, finally, by the Board of Directors. The Budget Officer, who will usually be the Financial Controller or Chief Accountant or other accounts-related person, will issue budget instructions (often called the budget manual) to heads of departments and other functionaries.

The Instructions may cover the following areas:

(i)   Objectives of the company for the period. Economic guidelines, such as financial expectations, expected staff pay rates, projected RPI, foreign currency exchange rates, market size, competitors' known plans, limiting factors and so on.

(ii) Definitions of terms used in the budget reports, for example return on capital employed calculation, market share and so on.

(iii) A timetable for when each department's budget is due to be returned to the Budget Officer.

(iv) Budget schedules for completion, to be used to list the income and expenditure expected in the budget period. These will usually be phased to show the income and costs for each accounting period, for example, calendar month or four/five weekly period. In addition, explanations will be given on how to complete the schedules.

(v)   The need for a narrative. This usually consists of a written review by the head of each department and will cover current trading conditions plus results to date for the current year, together with comments and justifications for the budget period figures.

Because most businesses are sales-led it is usual that the sales budget will be completed first, as the requirements of production, distribution and so on will not be able to be computed until the budgeted sales have been established.

FIGURE 19.3

A TYPICAL SALES BUDGET

SALES BUDGET
YEAR 1

SALES BY PRODUCT	JAN	FEB	MAR	APR	MAY	JUN	JUL	AUG	SEP	OCT	NOV	DEC	TOTAL
A													
B													
C													
D													
E													
F													
G													
H													
TOTAL													
LAST YEAR SALES													
% INCREASE (DECREASE)													
SALES BY REPRESENTATIVE													
MR J													
MISS K													
MR L													
MS M													
SALES OFFICE													
TOTAL													
LAST YEAR SALES													
% INCREASE (DECREASE)													
SALES BY CUSTOMER													
AB PLC													
BC PLC													
DE LTD													
FG PLC													
HJ COMPANY													
KL LTD													
OTHER CUSTOMERS													
TOTAL													
LAST YEAR SALES													
% INCREASE (DECREASE)													
HOME/EXPORT SALES													
HOME SALES													
EXPORT SALES													
TOTAL													
LAST YEAR SALES													
% INCREASE (DECREASE)													

On the due date for the return of the budget schedules in accordance with the timetable, the Budget Officer will have the following documents on his/her desk from the various departmental heads and functionaries:

Sales budget
Production budget
Distribution expenses budget
Sales expenses budget
Administration budgets (for each administrative function or department)
Research and development (R&D) budget
Capital expenditure spend requests for the budget year.

These are termed subsidiary budgets and, when collated by the Budget Officer, become the *master budget* subject to approval by the Board. The length of time a budget is in preparation may be several weeks, with many meetings between each section of the business – Sales, Production, Distribution and Administration, to ensure that the budgeted activities are fully co-ordinated. We shall work through each of these budgets in turn.

Sales budget

The sales budget is usually the first to be done. For a manufacturing company selling a number of products through a field sales force, the budget will include the following:

Sales *by product*
Sales *by sales representatives and inside sales staff*
Sales *by major customers/home and export.*

And any other classifications that the company requires.

Each of these classifications will be phased by accounting period and compared to the current year's sales, in both quantity and value. The percentage increase or decrease over the current year will also be provided. Details of the phasing of price increases (or decreases), one-off sales and so on, will be incorporated.

A typical sales budget may appear as shown in Figure 19.3

The Budget Officer will check to see whether the sales are in line with the instructions. For example, the committee may have stipulated that the market

for the firm's products was expected to grow by 5 per cent in the budget period; but the sales budget may show sales increasing by 20 per cent. The reasons why the Sales Department has gone against the guidelines should be set out clearly in the narrative and fully justified before being accepted as part of the budget. Seasonal sales patterns will also be checked against a seasonality model, perhaps based on the past three years' average sales. Here too, any major deviation should be investigated to ensure the budget is meaningful and achievable. Take the seasonality chart shown in Figure 19.4 as an example of a sales budget that appears *not* to have been thought through properly.

You will see that the budget year sales figures have not followed the pattern for the second half of the year. This simple test of the reliability of the phasing of the budget can help to ensure that the budget is sensible and achievable.

There are many matters to be considered in setting the sales budget; the effect of the general economy on the business, likely political factors, the impact of new technology and competition, advertising campaigns, new products or services and so on.

Once the sales budget has been completed and the sales appear to be attainable, a copy will be passed to the Production Department.

Production budget

The production budget will be expected to link into the requirements of the sales budget and also to take account of management's decision on the level of stocks to be carried during the budget year. So, for each product manufactured, the quantity to be made in the budget year will need to be assessed separately, based on the formula shown in Figure 19.5.

The capacity of the factory to produce the quantities required by the sales budget needs to be confirmed. This can be done by converting the quantities of units to be produced into standard hours equivalents. As part of the budgeting process, management will then need to assess the *practical capacity* of the factory. This is the realistic potential output expressed in standard hours that the factory is capable of achieving.

If the sales budget demands are greater than the practical capacity, then this problem needs to be

FIGURE 19.4

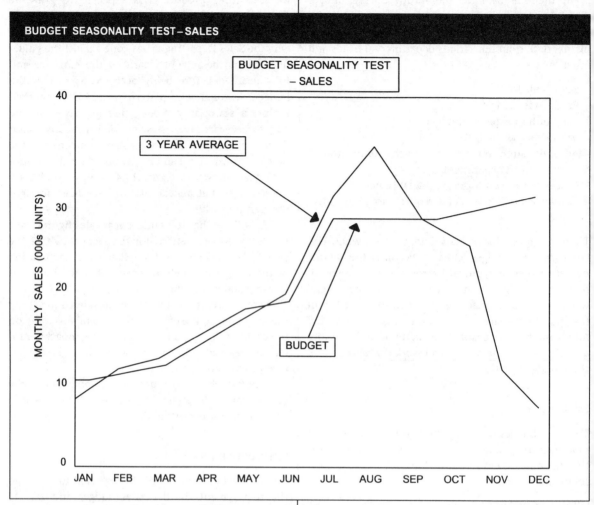

BUDGET SEASONALITY TEST — SALES

BUDGET SEASONALITY TEST
– SALES

3 YEAR AVERAGE

BUDGET

addressed, either by buying in the finished product from third parties, or investing in capital equipment to increase the capacity. If nothing can be done in the short term (that is, over the budget period) to accommodate the sales demands, then the sales budget cannot be achieved and will have to be amended to fall into line with the capabilities of the production function. This is an example of a *principal budget factor*; in CIMA terminology, '*a factor which will limit the activities of an undertaking and which is taken into account in preparing budgets*'. Close co-operation and co-ordination between Sales and Production Departments when compiling the budget is therefore essential. In many cases, the budget instructions themselves will identify the principal budget factor, or *limiting factor* as it is also described.

Once the quantities of production have been reconciled and agreed, the production costs will then be calculated. A typical production cost budget may appear as Figure 19.6. Working through this, assuming standard costs are in operation, the various cost elements involved are as follows.

Raw materials

The calculation is:

> Quantity of items to be produced
> × standard material price per item

The resulting budgeted quantities of materials and the budgeted material costs become a subsidiary budget, which the buyer will use for procurement purposes.

FIGURE 19.5

QUANTITY OF PRODUCT TO BE MADE IN THE BUDGET YEAR									
PRODUCT		A	B	C	D	E	F	G	H
	FINISHED GOODS UNITS:								
	OPENING STOCK – JAN 1								
LESS	BUDGETED CLOSING STOCK – DEC 31								
=	BUDGETED INCREASE (DECREASE) IN STOCK								
	SALES UNITS:								
+	PER SALES BUDGET								
=	PRODUCTION REQUIREMENTS IN BUDGET YEAR								

Direct labour

The calculations will be:

Budgeted direct labour hours required to make
the products × standard direct labour rate
(or rates) applicable in budget period

When converted into staff numbers, this budget may be used by the Personnel Department when planning their own budgets for recruitment and staff benefit expenses. The phasing of likely wage increases will also need to be incorporated into the budget, to ensure that any increase is reflected in the period in which the rise is likely to take effect.

Variable factory overheads

The variable overheads calculation will be:

Number of items to be produced
× budgeted variable overhead cost per item

The budgeted variable overheads absorption rate will be fixed at this stage:

$$\frac{\text{Budgeted variable overheads cost}}{\text{Budgeted direct labour hours}}$$

This rate will be used during the budget period to absorb the variable overheads into actual production.

Fixed factory overheads

Each department involved in production activities (Stores Department, the canteen and so on) will complete a detailed budget which will be used to control expenditure arising during the budget year. When these budgets are completed and collated the budgeted total fixed factory overheads will become known and the absorption rate into products can then be calculated, as follows:

Production Departments' total fixed overheads
for budget period
÷ Budgeted direct labour hours
(or similar denominator)

Budgeted trading account

On completion of the production budget, the budgeted trading account can be prepared and subjected to further checks by the Budget Officer. Budgeted closing stocks for each period will also be available: raw materials, work in progress and finished goods. (With regard to production variances, materials usage, price and so on, the assumption behind the budget is that it is readily achievable through general efficiency – therefore in line with attainable standards. Thus there will not normally be a budget for the production variances.)

FIGURE 19.6

PRODUCTION BUDGET, PRODUCT A

QUANTITY REQUIRED: XX UNITS

COSTS:
. MATERIALS:

	QUANTITY	STD PRICE EACH
ITEM 1		
ITEM 2		
ITEM 3		
		£

SUBSIDIARY BUDGET USED BY BUYING DEPARTMENT

NOTE: ALL FIGURES WILL BE PHASED OVER THE BUDGET PERIOD: E.G. JAN TO DECEMBER

. LABOUR:

	STD HOURS	STD RATE
GRADE 1		
GRADE 2		
GRADE 3		
		£

SUBSIDIARY BUDGET USED BY PERSONNEL DEPARTMENT

VARIABLE OVERHEADS

	STD HOURS*	STD ABSORPTION RATE
CHARGE		£

*OR EQUIVALENT

SUBSIDIARY BUDGET TO CALCULATE THE TOTAL VARIABLE OVERHEAD

FIXED OVERHEADS

	STD HOURS*	STD ABSORPTION RATE
CHARGE		£

*OR EQUIVALENT:

SUBSIDIARY BUDGET TO CALCULATE THE TOTAL FIXED OVERHEADS

BUDGETED PRODUCTION COST FOR XX UNITS   £

At this trading profit stage the budgeted gross profits percentages of each product should be compared to preceding actual gross profits achieved, to ensure that they are reasonably in line. Any marked difference will need to be investigated and justified in the narrative. A budgeted trading statement is shown in Figure 19.7.

Expenses budgets

The expenses budgets comprise distribution and sales, administration, research and development, and financing costs.

Distribution budget

This budget will be based on the projected sales according to the sales budget, with the information perhaps converted into average delivery loads, and will comprise the variable costs of distribution plus the fixed costs of administering this function.

If distribution is through the firm's own fleet of vehicles part of the budget calculations will be to ensure that sufficient delivery capacity is available. This may entail additional capital expenditure or indicate that there are too many vehicles, in which case the excess can be planned to be disposed of.

Sales Department budget

The variable costs aspects of selling, such as commission, will be directly related to the sales budget. Subsidiary budgets will be prepared for advertising and sales promotional costs as well as staff costs and

FIGURE 19.7

BUDGETED TRADING ACCOUNT									
PRODUCT	A	B	C	D	E	F	G	H
SALES								
COST OF GOODS SOLD:								
OPENING STOCKS								
BUDGETED PRODUCTION								
BUDGETED CLOSING STOCKS								
TOTAL COST OF GOODS SOLD								
BUDGETED GROSS PROFIT								
AS PERCENTAGE OF SALES								
PRIOR YEARS' PERCENTAGE OF SALES								

other running costs of the department. Additional subsidiary budgets may also be prepared, linking with the sales budget and the department's budget. One such subsidiary budget might relate to the *budgeted contribution per individual representative*, as shown in Table 19.1.

This budget will enable management to set targets and to investigate why some representatives are below average while others are above. The research into the causes and reasons at the time the budget is being prepared may enable management to alter the methods and structure of the selling activities, perhaps in time for incorporation into the budget period.

Administration budget

Here, there will be a separate budget for each department or function: the Accounts Department, Personnel Department and so on. Each item of administrative expenditure needs to be justified. Although most administration costs are fixed costs and thus will not vary in line with sales in the short term, there should still be a broad correlation between the two when expressed in terms of ratios. This correlation can be checked by expressing the budgeted administration costs as a percentage of the sales, and then comparing this with earlier periods to see if the trend continues or changes. Figure 19.8 illustrates this check.

You will notice that, compared to the two earlier years, the budgeted administration expenses will be taking a bigger 'slice'; this will translate into lower profits. The increase, of course, may be for strategic reasons: perhaps management have decided to engage higher-quality administration staff, or expensive computer equipment has been purchased and is being depreciated over a short period of time. Whatever the reasons, this test will ensure that management are aware of the effect on profits of the relative changes in the costs of the administrative functions.

Budgets will also be prepared for research and development expenditure, bank and loan interest payments and receipts, and other income and expenditure.

The end result will be the *first part* of the master budget: the budgeted profit before tax. A budget for Corporation Tax may also be prepared, to arrive at the profit after tax.

The Budget Officer will have collated these various budgets and produced a pro forma budgeted profit and loss account which will go to the budget committee.

The next stage is to complete the Balance Sheet budget. Most of this work is done by the Budget Officer or his/her delegate.

Balance sheet budget

Fixed assets

Plans for major capital expenditure projects to be undertaken during the budget period will normally have been the subject of investment appraisal techniques (see Chapter 20). These plans will be supplemented by capital expenditure requests that may arise

TABLE 19.1

A TYPICAL SALES BUDGET

	REPRESENTATIVE				
	Mr J £	Miss K £	Mr L £	Ms M £	Sales Office £
BUDGETED SALES					
AVERAGE GROSS PROFIT					
REPRESENTATIVE COSTS:					
SALARY					
PAYROLL ON-COSTS					
COMMISSION					
BONUS					
CAR EXPENSES					
TRAVEL AND SUBSISTENCE					
OTHER COSTS INCURRED					
TOTAL REP COSTS					
REPRESENTATIVE CONTRIBUTION					
AS % OF SALES					

FIGURE 19.8

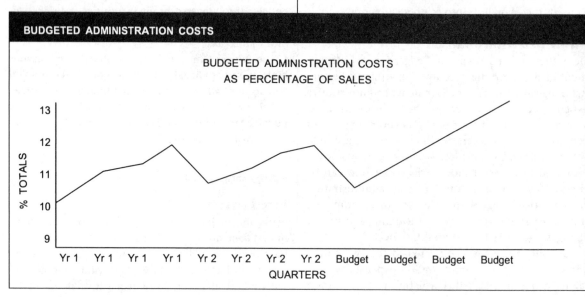

BUDGETED ADMINISTRATION COSTS

BUDGETED ADMINISTRATION COSTS
AS PERCENTAGE OF SALES

when the operating budget is being completed. For example, if it appears from the sales budget that an extra sales representative will be required, then some capital expenditure will arise – a car, portable computer, perhaps a desk and chair and so on.

These requests will be incorporated into an initial pro forma capital expenditure budget by department and, dependent on the overall profitability and liquidity position yet to be decided, the Board may decide that some should be deferred to later periods or not undertaken at all.

The actual capital expenditure in the budget period, once approved by the board, will be phased and incorporated into the balance sheet budget.

A budget for depreciation charges will also be completed once the spend has been approved and incorporated into the various departmental and operational budgets.

The fixed assets budget might appear as shown in Table 19.2.

Working capital budget

The working capital budget will comprise the following subsidiary budgets:

Stocks budget
Trade debtors' budget
Sundry debtors' and prepayments budget
Trade creditors' budget
Sundry creditors and accruals budget
Cash at bank and cash in hand budgets

Stock budget

The value of closing stocks of each category of stock will be as in the production budget discussed earlier in this chapter.

Trade Debtors' Budget

The sales budget will be the base for this budget, with VAT, if applicable, added to the phased sales. The average time taken to collect the debts – the collection period – will then be applied to these grossed sales figures to arrive at trade debtors' amounts collectable for each accounting period. If cash settlement discounts are allowed, these too will be taken into the computation, with the corresponding charge being made in the administration expenses budget (or perhaps as an item in the separate budget for other income and expenses).

TABLE 19.2

FIXED ASSETS BUDGET

PROJECT DETAILS	AUTHORISED AMOUNT £	SPEND IN BUDGET YEAR £	SPEND IN FUTURE YEARS £	PHASING OF BUDGET YEAR SPEND	
				MONTH	AMOUNT £
AUTHORISED ITEMS		–		JAN	10 000
BROUGHT FORWARD				FEB	15 000
FROM PREVIOUS YEAR				MAR	18 000
BALANCE TO SPEND:				APR	8 000
ITEM A	30 000	30 000	–	MAY	19 000
ITEM B	10 000	10 000	–	JUN	30 000
				JUL	5 000
ITEMS AUTHORISED				AUG	9 000
THIS BUDGET YEAR:				SEP	16 000
ITEM C	80 000	60 000	20 000	OCT	10 000
ITEM D	50 000	40 000	10 000	NOV	10 000
ITEM E	20 000	20 000	–	DEC	10 000
	190 000	160 000	30 000		160 000

Acknowledgement of the likelihood of bad debts should also be made and a provision for bad debts allowed for. The balance brought forward from the pre-budget year will also form part of the trade debtors' budget. The trade debtors' budget appears as in Table 19.3.

Sundry debtors' and prepayments budget

Other debtors will also be calculated and phased over the budget period; for example, staff travel loans made, and repayments collected. A prepayments budget will be prepared which will link in with the

TABLE 19.3

TRADE DEBTORS' BUDGET

BASIS	JAN	FEB	MAR	APR	MAY	JUN
	£	£	£	£	£	£
SALES PER SALES BUDGET	10 000	15 000	20 000	25 000	30 000	35 000
ADD VAT	1 750	2 625	3 500	4 375	5 250	6 125
GROSS SALES	11 750	17 625	23 500	29 375	35 250	41 125

PAYMENT TERMS: 60 DAYS
CASH SETTLEMENT: 10% IF 10 DAYS } HALF TAKE ADVANTAGE OF THE DISCOUNT

BAD DEBT PROVISION: 2% OF SALES	235	353	470	588	705	823

TRADE DEBTORS BROUGHT FORWARD:
    NOV   DEC
    £5 000   £7 000

CASH RECEIPT WORKINGS:						
GROSS	11 750	17 625	23 500	29 375	35 250	41 125
LESS PROVISION FOR BAD DEBTS	235	353	470	588	705	823
	11 515	17 273	23 030	28 788	34 545	40 303
HALF = 10% SETTLEMENT	576	864	1 152	1 439	1 727	2 015

COLLECTIONS OF DEBTORS:						
CASH SETTLEMENT DEBTORS	5 758	8 636	11 515	14 394	17 273	20 151
LESS 10% SETTLEMENT DISCOUNT	576	864	1 152	1 439	1 727	2 015
NET COLLECTABLE	5 182	7 773	10 364	12 954	15 545	18 136
60-DAY DEBTORS	5 000	7 000	5 758	8 636	11 515	14 394
TOTAL COLLECTABLE	10 182	14 773	16 121	21 591	27 060	32 530

TRADE DEBTORS' BUDGET	JAN	FEB	MAR	APR	MAY	JUN
DEBTORS BROUGHT FORWARD	12 000	12 993	14 981	21 209	27 554	34 016
SALES FOR PERIOD	11 750	17 625	23 500	29 375	35 250	41 125
CASH COLLECTED IN PERIOD	(10 182)	(14 773)	(16 121)	(21 591)	(27 060)	(32 530)
CASH SETTLEMENT DISCOUNT ALLOWED	(576)	(864)	(1 152)	(1 439)	(1 727)	(2 015)
DEBTORS CARRIED FORWARD	12 993	14 981	21 209	27 554	34 016	40 596

PROVISION FOR BAD DEBTS	235	588	1 058	1 645	2 350	3 173
NET TRADE DEBTORS	12 758	14 394	20 151	25 909	31 666	37 424

operating budgets. For example, rent and rates paid in advance will be charged out each accounting period to the various departments, with the remaining unexpired portion remaining as a prepayment.

Trade creditors' budget

This budget will link into the phased raw materials budget and will also comprise any other expenditure items – revenue or capital – where credit terms are allowed by suppliers/service organisations. Again, adjustments will be needed to the figures to allow for VAT if applicable. The average time the firm takes to pay the creditors will be used to calculate the trade creditors' figure for each of the accounting periods.

If cash discount settlement terms are given by suppliers these too will be included in the computations, with a corresponding credit being made in the other income and expenditure budget, or equivalent.

Sundry creditors' budget

'Sundry creditors' embraces liabilities such as income tax and social security deductions made from staff pay (PAYE and NIC), Corporation Tax payable, and accrued expenses. A subsidiary budget for each of these will be prepared and will link in to the operating budgets.

Cash budget

Working capital also includes cash, and the cash budget is one of the most important of the budgeting functions. It brings together the common denominator of all the other budgets: *cash*. At some stage, sooner or later, every financial transaction the firm undertakes will be reflected in its cash position, either through cash in hand or cash at bank. *Cash in hand* refers to petty cash transactions and sundry small floats the company may operate; *Cash at bank* refers to the firm's bank account.

The cash budget deals with the cash at bank position and reflects the income receivable which will be paid into the bank account, and the payments made from the account via cheques, standing orders, direct debits and so on. This budget interlinks with the capital expenditure budget, with the working capital budgets, and with the profit and loss operating budgets. It will reflect interest payments and interest receipts,

dividends, tax payments and other capital receipts and payments. The cash budget comprises three sections: *receipts*, *payments* and *cash flow*. To demonstrate how it is prepared, the following AAT question from 1991 will be used for illustration:

Worked example

You are presented by your firm with the budgeted data shown in Annex A for the period November to June. It has been extracted from the other functional budgets that have been prepared. You are also told the following:

(i) Sales are 40% cash, 60% credit. Credit sales are paid two months after the month of sale.
(ii) Purchases are paid the month following purchase.
(iii) 75% of wages are paid in the current month and 25% the following month.
(iv) Overheads are paid the month after they are incurred.
(v) Dividends are paid three months after they are declared.
(vi) Capital expenditure is paid two months after it is incurred.
(vii) The opening cash balance is £15 000.

Annex A

	Nov £	Dec £	Jan £	Feb £
Sales	80 000	100 000	110 000	130 000
Purchases	40 000	60 000	80 000	90 000
Wages	10 000	12 000	16 000	20 000
Overheads	10 000	10 000	15 000	15 000
Dividends		20 000		
Capital Expenditure			30 000	

	Mar £	Apr £	Jun £	Jul £
Sales	140 000	150 000	160 000	180 000
Purchases	110 000	130 000	140 000	150 000
Wages	24 000	28 000	32 000	36 000
Overheads	15 000	20 000	20 000	20 000
Dividends				40 000
Capital Expenditure		40 000		

The Managing Director is pleased with these figures, as they show that sales will increase by more than 100% in the period under review. In order to achieve this he has arranged a bank overdraft with a ceiling of £50 000 to accommodate the increased stock levels and wage bill for overtime worked.

Required:
Prepare a cash budget for the 6-month period, January to June.

Solution:

each period, which may be 'positive' or 'negative', plus or minus the opening cash at the beginning of the period, provides the closing cash position. A 'positive' cash flow indicates receipts were greater than payments in the period, a 'negative' cash flow indicates the opposite.

It also follows that the *closing cash* position of one accounting period becomes the opening cash position of the next accounting period. The cash flow budget will thus indicate whether an overdraft is likely to occur in any of the periods or, if there are already

Cash Budget – January to June

	Jan £	Feb £	Mar £	Apr £	May £	Jun £
Receipts						
Trade debtors						
Cash	44 000	52 000	56 000	60 000	64 000	72 000
Credit customers	48 000	60 000	66 000	78 000	84 000	90 000
Total receipts	92 000	112 000	122 000	138 000	148 000	162 000
Payments						
Trade creditors	60 000	80 000	90 000	110 000	130 000	140 000
Wages	15 000	19 000	23 000	27 000	31 000	35 000
Overheads	10 000	15 000	15 000	15 000	20 000	20 000
Dividends				20 000		
Capital expenditure			30 000			40 000
Total payments	85 000	114 000	158 000	172 000	181 000	235 000
Cash Flow						
Opening cash at bank	15 000	22 000	20 000	(16 000)	(50 000)	(83 000)
Cash flow	7 000	(2 000)	(36 000)	(34 000)	(33 000)	(73 000)
Closing cash at bank	22 000	20 000	(16 000)	(50 000)	(83 000)	(156 000)
Workings:						
Trade debtors:						
Sales	110 000	130 000	140 000	150 000	160 000	180 000
Cash sales – 40%	44 000	52 000	56 000	60 000	64 000	72 000
Cash sales – 60%	66 000	78 000	84 000	90 000	96 000	108 000
Wages:						
Current month	12 000	15 000	18 000	21 000	24 000	27 000
Following month	4 000	5 000	6 000	7 000	8 000	9 000

Note first the final section, the *cash flow*. This is simply the difference between the receipts section for each period and the payments section for the same period.

The *opening cash* is the position on day 1 of each accounting period. It follows that the cash flow for

overdraft facilities in existence, whether the limit set is likely to be breached.

This particular question asked for comments in the light of the Managing Director's observations and to offer advice. Clearly, the arranged overdraft will be insufficient to meet the cash flow requirements of the business. He has arranged £50000 but it maximises during the period to £156000. Armed with the cash flow information, the overdraft could perhaps be re-negotiated, or timing changes could be made to the payments – might the capital expenditure and divi-dend payments be delayed?. Or perhaps the ambi-tious build-up of stocks could be reduced, which would in turn reduce the need for overtime and thus conserve cash. Given the cash flow information, man-agement can thus make alternative arrangements to ensure that the company remains within the con-straints of the overdraft.

Budget approval

With the completion of the operating budgets, the balance sheet budget and cash budget, the budget committee will present the result, the master budget, to the Board of Directors for approval. It may show that extra capital long-term funding is required. The Board will then need to decide if this should be in the form of long-term borrowings or an increase in share capital. Once final amendments have been made and approval received from the board, the master budget then becomes fixed as com-pany policy for the forthcoming budget period: *the fixed budget*. An overview of the master budget is given in Figure 19.9.

Budget variances

During the budget year, in each accounting period, actual results will be compared with the budget, and *budget variances* arrived at. This is the difference between the actual results and the equivalent budget figures. Variances enable 'management by exception' techniques to be operated so that management need look only at those areas of performance and activity which are out of line with the budget. They therefore have more time available to deal with the problems and opportunities thrown up by the figures. CIMA defines a budget variance as *'the difference between budget and actual cost for each cost in a budget and for revenue where appropriate'*. Some budget variances that will be computed are as follows:

Administrative cost variance

This is the difference between the actual administra-tion costs incurred and the budgeted cost of adminis-tration. This is a total variance and will be analysed further, by calculating variances for each administra-tive department, and for each expenditure heading within each department.

Marketing cost variance

This is the difference between the actual marketing costs and the budgeted marketing costs. As with the administrative cost variance, this total variance will be further analysed at expenditure heading level (for example, advertising costs) to ascertain the reasons for the variance.

Total profit variance

This is the overall difference between the budgeted profit and the actual profit for the period.

Flexible budget

The master budget, as company policy, is a *fixed budget* and will have been based on forecasts and predictions of sales at a certain level of activity, with the resulting costs incurred applicable to that level of sales. It is a fact of life, however, that budgets are not always achieved: sometimes sales are more than expected, sometimes less.

Comparisons of costs and revenue between the fixed budget, set at one level of output, and the actual results achieved at a different level, will there-fore not be able to be made with ease. This is because of the behavioural nature of costs. Fixed costs, of course, could be compared, for they would not be expected to change in line with the changes in activ-ity. But variable costs will, as they are deemed to have a linear relationship with sales.

To recognise this fact *flexible budgets* are often used. A flexible budget is, to use CIMA terminology *'a budget which, by recognising different cost behaviour patterns, is designed to change as volume of output changes'*. To achieve this, the fixed budget costs need to be ana-lysed between fixed costs and variable costs, using marginal costing techniques. Actual costs incurred will also be analysed by cost behaviour. Then, using

FIGURE 19.9

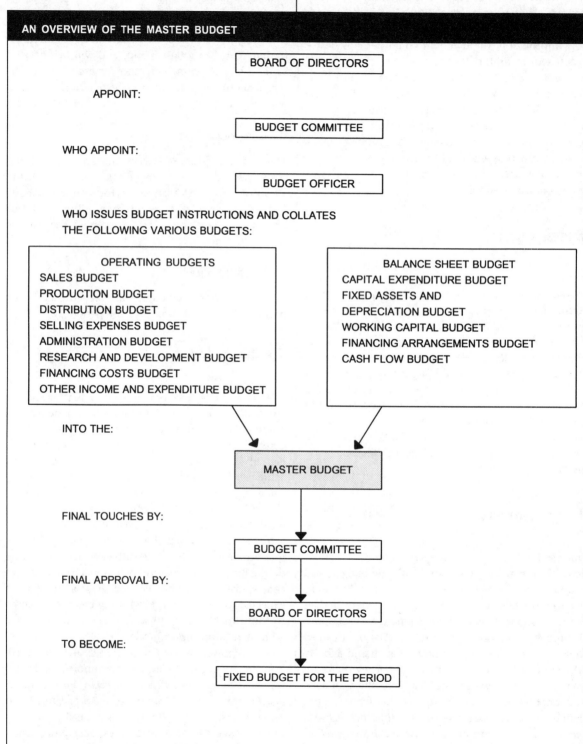

AN OVERVIEW OF THE MASTER BUDGET

BOARD OF DIRECTORS

APPOINT:

BUDGET COMMITTEE

WHO APPOINT:

BUDGET OFFICER

WHO ISSUES BUDGET INSTRUCTIONS AND COLLATES
THE FOLLOWING VARIOUS BUDGETS:

OPERATING BUDGETS
SALES BUDGET
PRODUCTION BUDGET
DISTRIBUTION BUDGET
SELLING EXPENSES BUDGET
ADMINISTRATION BUDGET
RESEARCH AND DEVELOPMENT BUDGET
FINANCING COSTS BUDGET
OTHER INCOME AND EXPENDITURE BUDGET

BALANCE SHEET BUDGET
CAPITAL EXPENDITURE BUDGET
FIXED ASSETS AND
DEPRECIATION BUDGET
WORKING CAPITAL BUDGET
FINANCING ARRANGEMENTS BUDGET
CASH FLOW BUDGET

INTO THE:

MASTER BUDGET

FINAL TOUCHES BY:

BUDGET COMMITTEE

FINAL APPROVAL BY:

BOARD OF DIRECTORS

TO BECOME:

FIXED BUDGET FOR THE PERIOD

the actual sales units as the driver, the fixed budget will be reworked at the actual level of sales achieved. The budgeted variable costs will reflect the actual units sold; the fixed costs will stay the same as the original budget.

Worked example

Breslin Engineering planned to sell 10 000 units of their product and prepared the following budget based on that quantity:

	£	Units
Sales	100 000	10 000 units
Variable costs	50 000	
Fixed costs	20 000	
Budgeted profit	30 000	

However, actual sales for the budgeted period were only 9000, with the following costs and revenue:

	£	Units
Sales	85 500	9 000
Variable costs	47 000	
Fixed costs	22 000	
Actual profit	16 500	

Required:
Prepare a flexible budget for the actual units sold and analyse any variances that may have arisen.

Solution:
Profit and Loss Account – 9 000 units

	Actual	Flexible budget	Variance
Units	9 000	9 000	
	£	£	£
Sales	85 500	90 000	(4 500) Adverse
Variable costs	47 000	45 000	(2 000) Adverse
Fixed costs	22 000	20 000	(2 000) Adverse
Profit	16 500	25 000	(8 500) Adverse

You will see that the flexible budget relates to the actual units sold. Thus, the budgeted variable costs will be amended to this actual level. The budgeted fixed costs will be deemed to remain the same, irrespective of the sales level.

Worked example

LCCI THIRD LEVEL (1994)
Flexit makes a single product which sells at $330 per unit; 12 000 units are budgeted to be produced and sold each month, and unit costs, based on this volume, are:

Direct materials	$104
Direct labour	$ 52
Variable overheads	$ 14
Fixed overheads	$ 90
	$260

During the past month, only 10 400 units were produced and sold. At the start of last month there were unexpected increases of 5% in materials prices and 3% in hourly wage rates. Variable overheads per unit were as budgeted, but total fixed overheads increased by $120 000. Actual material usage per unit and direct labour efficiency were as originally budgeted.

Required:
Prepare a tabular profit and loss statement for the last month showing:

(i)   the original budget;
(ii)   the revised budget adjusted for the fall in volume only; and
(iii) the actual results.

Solution:
See page 286.

Zero-base budgeting

When setting budgets it is often the practice to see what happened in the pre-budget year and, using this as the base, simply add extra costs to those figures, perhaps as a straight percentage increase to that year's actual costs. Some accounting computer packages with integrated nominal ledger/budget programs tend to encourage this approach by providing the facility to increase or decrease budgets of the various expense accounts by a fixed percentage. So, 'Take last year and add, say, 5%', is a common budget approach. This method of budgeting carries with it the likelihood of past excesses and inefficiencies

Solution to Worked Example on page 285:

	Original budget $	Revised budget $	Actual results $
Sales 12 000 × $330	3 960 000		
Sales 10 400 × $330		3 432 000	
Sales 10 400 × $330			3 432 000
Variable costs:			
Materials 12 000 × $104	1 248 000		
Materials 10 400 × $104		1 081 600	
Materials 10 400 × $109.20			1 135 680
Labour 12 000 × $52	624 000		
Labour 10 400 × $52		540 800	
Labour 10 400 × $53.56			557 024
Variable overheads 12 000 × $14	168 000		
Variable overheads 10 400 × $14		145 600	
Variable overheads 10 400 × $14			145 600
Fixed overheads 12 000 × $90	1 080 000		
Fixed overheads 12 000 × $90		1 080 000	
Fixed overheads 12 000 × $90 + $120 000			1 200 000
Profit	840 000	584 000	393 696

being carried forward and added to from one year to the next, thus effectively projecting these negatives into the future as self-perpetuating routines.

The technique of *zero based budgeting* takes the view that every item of expenditure incurred in an activity needs to be re-evaluated and reassessed 'from the beginning' when a budget is being prepared. The previous year's actual results are thereby effectively ignored.

Each expenditure heading starts from '£0': the zero base; each component of cost created by the activity is evaluated and justified, and the budget for the expenditure heading is thus built up. The first question that management ask of the operation is 'Is *any* expenditure necessary in this activity?' Thus, every part of the activity that generates cost will be analysed and alternative methods for completing each will be considered and evaluated.

Take, for example, an expensive report that may be issued daily by a department which, if modified within acceptable limits, could be completed by another section of the business on a less frequent basis at little cost and inconvenience to management. Management may decide to drop the daily report and save its attendant preparation costs.

Zero-base budgeting can therefore take a long time to complete, with each and every activity needing to be broken down and the alternatives considered, costed and justified, with the budget slowly built up using the best considered alternatives.

Summary

- Businesses need to plan for the future through long-term planning to decide on their strategies and objectives for the following three to five years. They also need to plan for the short term: the coming year or another lesser period. These short-term plans are called *budgets*.
- A budget is a plan, expressed in money, that enables the firm to control actual performance during the budget year. It covers all aspects of the business – trading operations as well as the management of current assets, current liabilities and financing requirements.
- Budgets clearly need to be prepared in advance of the budget period; the length of time taken for the completion of a budget may take many weeks.

- At the beginning of the process, the Board of Directors will appoint a budget committee whose job will be to prepare the budget and lay down guidelines to functional management for completion of individual departmental budgets.

- The committee will appoint a Budget Officer, usually an individual with an accounting background. He or she will issue instructions (sometimes called the budget manual) and then collect and collate the various budgets into a master budget. The master budget becomes the profit and loss account budget and balance sheet budget for the coming year.

- The master budget is built up from subsidiary budgets: sales budget, production budget, expenses budgets comprise the budgeted profit and loss account; the fixed assets expenditure budget, current assets budgets, cash flow budgets and financing budgets comprise the budgeted balance sheet.

- The budget committee will ensure that the budgeted production activity matches the sales budget and that all parts of the master budget are co-ordinated and functionaries are thus all 'singing from the same hymn book'.

- Budgets need to be phased to provide budgeted targets for each calendar month or four/five weekly accounting period during the budget period.

- The cash budget is an essential feature of the budgeting process and will interlink with the other budgets. By reflecting the amounts receivable and payable, and the timing of these in the phased periods, the cash budget will enable cash management to be greatly facilitated. When the master budget is approved by the board of directors it becomes policy for the budget period. In each phased period, the actual results will be compared with the budget and variances calculated. This enables management to control the expenditure through the technique of management by exception.

- The approved master budget is a fixed budget and does not take into consideration differing levels of sales units actually achieved.

- Because costs behave differently at varying levels of activity – some costs changing directly in line with activity while others remain relatively fixed irrespective of output levels – it is beneficial to prepare flexible budgets to assist management to identify what the costs should have been at the varying levels of activity actually achieved.

- Another budgeting technique used is zero-based budgeting. This technique looks at each individual activity within a spending department to see if the cost is justified. If there is a benefit arising from the activity the cost will be included in the budget.

- It should be noted that budgets are sometimes imposed by top management, with perhaps unrealistically high expectations, and with lower levels of management not being given the opportunity to be involved in, and generally contribute to, the budgeting process. The 'decreed' budget may have the opposite effect to what was intended, thus becoming demotivational and unachievable.

- However, when there *is* full participation in the budgeting process by all levels of management, and the resulting subsidiary budgets are considered to be attainable by those responsible for their achievement, the budgets can be likened to a 'promissory note' of each manager, thus a very powerful motivating force for their attainment.

Examination Questions

1 A LEVEL (ULEAC) 1990

The information below relates to the business of Madingley Ltd.

Balance Sheet as at 30 May

£(000s)

Fixed Assets	Cost	Aggregate depreciation	Book value
Land and buildings	134.00		134.00
Plant and machinery	9.40	3.76	5.64
Furniture and fittings	2.30	1.05	1.25
	145.70	4.81	140.89

Current Assets		
Stocks: Raw materials		91.70
Finished goods		142.40
Debtors		594.40
Bank		12.40
		840.90
Less: current liabilities		
Creditors: Raw materials		82.20
Overheads		127.40
		209.60

Working capital	631.30
	772.19
Financed by:	
Share capital	500.00
Profit and loss account	272.19
	772.19

The following is a schedule of the budgeted income and expenditure for the six months ended 30 November 1990.

(£000s)

	Sales	Materials	Wages	Overheads
June	193.2	41.20	7.60	123.00
July	201.4	42.40	7.90	119.20
August	216.1	49.60	8.80	131.40
September	200.5	31.40	6.10	91.50
October	190.3	21.20	3.70	59.30
November	183.7	19.80	2.60	42.60

Notes:

(i)   Generally, materials are paid for two months after receipt, and customers pay on average after three months.

(ii)   Payments outstanding for materials at 1 June were: April £38 500; May £43 700.

(iii)   Debtors were: March, £194 300; April £203 600, May, £196 500.

(iv)   Wages are to be paid in the month in which they fall due.

(v)   Overheads are to be paid one month after they are incurred: the figure for May was £127 400.

(vi)   Stocks of raw materials are to be kept at £91 700.

(vii)   The stocks of finished goods at 30 November are to be £136 200.

(viii)   There are no stocks of semi-finished items on 31 May and none are expected in stock on 30 November.

(ix)   Forty per cent of the overheads are to be considered as fixed.

(x)   Depreciation on plant and machinery is to be allowed at 10% per annum on cost; the fixtures and fittings are thought to have a value at 30 November of £980.

(xi)   There are no sales of finished goods or purchases of raw materials for cash planned during the period.

Prepare:

(a)   A forecast operating statement for the period June to November.

(b)   A forecast balance sheet as at 30 November.

2   A LEVEL (ULEAC) 1992

Wimpole Industries cash budget for the period September to December appears below. Since the budget was drafted,

circumstances have changed and the figures now require amending.

Wimpole Industries: Cash Budget September – December

£000s

	S	O	N	D
Receipts				
Sales 2/3	194.0	204.0	208.0	212.0
Sales 1/3	102.0	104.0	106.0	120.0
Sale of equipment				8.8
	296.0	308.0	314.0	340.8
Payments				
Materials	74.0	72.1	79.4	81.2
Wages	15.1	15.7	16.7	17.3
Fixed costs	40.0	40.0	40.0	40.0
Variable costs	125.0	133.4	142.2	66.5
	254.1	261.2	278.3	205.0
Cash Budget				
Opening balance	(108.4)	(66.5)	(19.7)	16.0
Receipts	296.0	308.0	314.0	340.8
Payments	254.1	261.2	278.3	205.0
Closing balance	(66.5)	(19.7)	16.0	151.8

The following changes affect all of the calculations upon which the cash budget is based:

(i)   Sales volume is expected to be 5% less than was originally planned. Material purchases will reflect this reduction.

(ii)   Selling prices are to be increased by 10%.

(iii)   A forecast of worsening trading conditions means that 1% of all sales will result in bad debts.

(iv)   It had been thought that customers would pay one-third of their debts one month after the sale, and the remainder after two months. The introduction of a more aggressive debt management policy is likely to reverse this, with two-thirds of all good debts being collected within the first month after the sale, and only one-third being collected after two months.

(v)   Receipt of monies for the sale of unwanted plant will be received a month earlier than was originally planned.

(vi)   The cost of materials has gone up by 5%, wages by 10% and overheads by 8%.

(vii)   The bank balance at 31 August is now estimated at £100 000 overdrawn.

You are asked to incorporate the above changes into an amended:

(i)   receipts schedule;

(ii)   payments schedule; and

(iii)   cash budget.

3 A LEVEL (AEB) 1990

Pankake Ltd provided the following summarised information for the year ended 30 April, Year 1.

Trading and profit and loss account for the year ended 30 April, Year 1

	£000s	£000s
Sales		2000
Less cost of goods sold		1449
Gross profit		551
Administrative expenses	180	
Selling and distributive expenses	130	
Depreciation of fixed assets	60	370
Net profit		181

Balance sheet as at 30 April, Year 1

	£000s	£000s
50p ordinary shares fully paid		300
Retained earnings		175
		475
Fixed assets: at cost	500	
Less aggregate depreciation	180	320
Current assets		
Stocks	250	
Trade debtors	190	
Cash	20	
	460	
Less current liabilities		
Trade creditors	110	
Accrued expenses	15	
Bank overdraft	180	
	305	155
		475

The Company Accountant provided the following additional information, which will be used as the basis of the company's budget for the year ending 30 April, Year 2.

1. The stock at 1 May, Year 1 was £164 000.
2. Sales values are expected to be 30% higher than the year ended 30 April, Year 1. 40% of all sales will be for cash. The remainder will be on credit and occur at a uniform monthly rate. Credit customers will be allowed 3 months credit. The forecast gross profit margin on sales will be 30%.
3. The average rate of stock turnover will be the same as the year ended 30 April, Year 1.
4. Selling and distributive expenses will be 6% of all sales.
5. Administrative expenses will increase by £20 000.

6. Depreciation will continue to be provided at 10% of cost per annum. On 1 May, Year 2 further expenditure of £150 000 will be incurred on fixed assets. There will be no fixed asset disposals.
7. Other forecast balances as at 30 April, Year 2:

	£000s
Cash	20
Trade creditors	130
Accrued expenses	20
Bank overdraft	101

8. No dividend will be declared for Year 1. However, there will be a bonus issue of one share for every share currently held. The issue will be made on 30 April, Year 1.

Required:
(a) A forecast budget trading and profit and loss account for the year ending 30 April, Year 2.
(b) A forecast budget balance sheet as at 30 April, Year 2.

4 A LEVEL (AEB) 1990

The Managing Director of Pumpkin Ltd was reviewing the results of the company for the financial year ended 31 March. The following summarised information was available:

Balances as at 1 April, Year 1	£
Issued ordinary share capital:	
£1 fully paid shares	150 000
Share premium account	100 000
Balance of retained earnings	40 000
Balances as at 31 March, Year 1	
Net profit for Year 1	70 000
Fixed assets	300 000
Bank overdraft	150 000
Other net current assets	210 000

Note: There were no other accounts with balances. The balances as at 1 April had remained unchanged throughout the year.

The Managing Director was pleased that the company had made a good profit, but he was rather concerned that a healthy bank balance at the beginning of the year had now become a large bank overdraft.

Consequently he asked the Company Accountant to prepare forecast information for Year 2 in order that the cash situation could be improved.

The following information was prepared by the accountant:

1. Company sales – March, Year 1

	£
Cash sales	30 000
Credit sales	65 000

In each month April to September (inclusive) the sales per month would be:

Cash sales	40 000
Credit sales	70 000

All credit sales are settled the month after the sale.

2. All goods purchased are from a single supplier. The goods are purchased on credit and each month's purchases are paid for three months after the month of purchase.

The following purchase schedule had been prepared:

	£	
January	60 000	Actual
February	58 000	Actual
March	61 000	Actual
April	55 000	Forecast
May	55 000	Forecast
June	55 000	Forecast
July	45 000	Forecast
August	45 000	Forecast
September	45 000	Forecast

Note: The company had successfully negotiated lower prices from its supplier, commencing 1 July.

3. Dividends would be paid as follows:
   (i) Final ordinary dividend of 5p per share payable on 31 May, Year 2, in respect of Financial Year 1.
   (ii) Interim ordinary dividend of 2p per share payable on 31 July, Year 2, in respect of financial year 2.

4. Selling and distribution expenses are expected to be 6% of a given month's total/ sales. They are paid one month in arrears.

5. Administration charges would be incurred as follows:
   February, March, Year 1 and April Year 2:
   £10 000 per month
   May to September, Year 2 (inclusive):
   £13 500 per month
   Administration charges are settled two months after the month in which they were incurred.

6. The company decided to make a bonus issue of shares of one share for every three held. The issue would be made on 30 April, Year 2. The bonus shares would not qualify for the final dividend of Year 1 but would qualify for the interim dividend to be paid on 31 July, Year 2.

Required:
(a) Comment on the liquidity of the company as at 31 March, Year 1 and explain to the Managing Director why a company can apparently make a good profit but have no cash in the bank.

(b) Prepare a cash budget for each of the four months ending 31 July, Year 2.

(c) Comment on the forecast bank balance as shown by your cash budget. Identify ways in which the bank overdraft could be reduced over the last five months, August to December, Year 2.

5 A LEVEL (AEB) 1992

Springtime Ltd own a retail store that sells clothes. The company's summarised balance sheet as at 31 March Year 1 was as follows:

	£000s
Called up capital	
200 000 £1 Ordinary shares fully paid	200
General reserve	150
Retained earnings	250
Current liabilities	90
	690
Fixed assets less depreciation	458
Current assets:	
Stocks and debtors	120
Balance at bank	112
	690

The company decided to open a branch store in a neighbouring town. The branch is to be opened on 1 May, Year 2 in newly acquired freehold premises which cost £100 000. Half of this cost will be paid on 1 May, Year 2 and the remainder on 1 July, Year 2. The refurbishment of these premises will cost £20 000, and this amount is due to be paid on 1 July, Year 2. All these amounts are paid by the company's main store.

Additional information:

1.		Main store	Branch
		£	£
	Actual sales		
	February	160 000	–
	March	150 500	–
	April	153 000	–
	Forecast sales		
	May	149 500	8 000
	June	158 000	19 000
	July	161 000	24 000

Main store: Cash from sales is received two months after the month of sale.

Branch: Cash from sales is received one month after the month of sale.

The branch will operate its own bank current account and receipts from debtors will be banked each day. The account was opened on 1 April, Year 2 with an initial balance of £20 000.

2. The following fixed costs are paid:

Main store   £15 000 every month

Branch   £1000 every month, except April.

As a cost transfer the company allocates £2500 of the main store fixed costs every month (except April) to the branch.

3. The company pays variable costs as follows:

	Main store	Branch
	£	£
March	25 000	–
April	30 000	–
May	33 000	2 500
June	31 000	2 700
July	29 000	1 900

All variable costs are paid one month in arrears, except that in May the branch is required to pay them in that month.

4. The main store will be required to pay £5000 legal costs on 1 July, Year 2 in respect of the new freehold premises.

5. Staff salaries paid:

Main store   £12 000 every month

Branch   £1000 every month, except April.

6. Springtime Ltd are due to pay an interim ordinary share dividend of 5% on 1 July, Year 2.

7. All goods for resale are bought by the main store and are charged to the branch store at cost price.

	Goods purchased by main store	Goods received by branch store
	£	£
February	61 000	–
March	58 000	–
April	153 000	8 000
May	48 000	12 000
June	49 500	23 000
July	152 000	24 000

Springtime Ltd receives two months' credit on all its clothing purchases. The branch remits payment for its goods to the main store by credit transfer at the end of the month of receipt.

8. In order to fund further business development, Springtime Ltd plan to issue £100 000 of 11% Debenture at par on 1 July, Year 2. The issue is expected to be fully subscribed and the cash will be received on the same date.

9. The branch store is scheduled to earn a 50% mark-up on cost.

Required:

(a) Separate monthly cash budgets for each store for the four months ending 31 July, Year 2.

(b) For the forecast period ending 31 July Year 2:

  (i) a profit and loss statement for the branch; and

  (ii) a report giving an assessment of the branch's expected profitability during this period.

6   A LEVEL (AEB) 1993

Simon Stylus sells a variety of musical goods. In recent years he has been very successful and has decided to move to new premises. He believes that accounting and budgeting do not really need any great effort and there is not much to learn about them.

Using the balance sheet below he has decided to prepare a budget balance sheet to reflect the financial position he hopes to achieve by 31 March, Year 4.

The balance sheet as at 31 March year 3 was as follows:

	£000s	£000s
Capital		45
Add profit – Year 3		30
		75
Less drawings		15
		60
Loans		10
		70
Represented by:		
Fixed assets:		
Premises	30	
Car	7	37
Current assets:		
Stock in trade	22	
Trade debtors	30	
Balance at bank	8	
	60	
Less trade creditors	27	33
		70

Simon has made the following assumptions in order to draw up his budgeted balance sheet as at 31 March, Year 4:

1. Sales for the year are expected to increase to £270 000. The profit margin is to be one-ninth of sales.

2. Existing premises will be sold for cash at a profit of 20% of balance sheet figure.

3. New premises will cost £16 000 cash and will not be depreciated.

4. Fixtures for the new premises costing £8000 will be purchased. These will be depreciated by 12.5% per annum on cost.

5. The loans will be repaid because of the extra cash received from the sales income forecast.

6. The expansion in sales activity should mean that stock will increase by £8000 and the debtors and creditors by one-third each.
7. Simon will make drawings amounting to four-sevenths of the year's forecast.
8. The balancing figure for the balance sheet will be the bank balance.

Required:

(a) Prepare a budgeted balance sheet for Simon Stylus as at 31 March, Year 4.

(b) Prepare a critical report on Simon's approach to budgeting indicating how effectivè budgeting should be implemented.

7 A LEVEL (AEB) 1993

The following information is a available from the books of Abbington Ltd for the financial year ended 31 October, Year 3:

Trading and Profit and Loss Account for the year ended
31 October, Year 3

	£000s		£000s
Cost of goods sold	910	Sales	1 300
Gross profit	390		
	1 300		1 300
Administration costs	70	Gross profit	390
Selling and			
distribution costs	40		
Financial charges	10		
Depreciation of			
fixed assets	30		
Net profit	240		
	390		390

Balance sheet as at 31 October, Year 3

The newly appointed managing director decided that in order to increase profits it is absolutely necessary to control costs. Thus he decided to introduce budgetary control.

The following forecast information is available for the year ending 31 October, Year 4:

1. The sales are forecast to increase to £1.6m for the year.
2. A more efficient buying programme is expected to increase the gross profit/sales ratio to 32%.
3. In order to finance further expansion as the recession recedes, a rights issue of one new ordinary share for each two shares currently held is to be made on 1 August, Year 4. It is expected that the issue will be fully subscribed and the issue will also be underwritten. The issue price is 65p per share, fully paid.
4. Despite inflationary pressures the managing director is determined to reduce cost. The forecast level of costs is: administration costs will be 5% of forecast sales; and selling and distribution costs will be 3.5% of forecast sales. There will be no change in financial charges as compared to Year 3.
5. Owing to the recession, bad debts are expected to rise substantially and thus the provision for doubtful debts is to be increased to 15% of trade debtors. Forecast trade debts as at 31 October, Year 4 are £150 000.
6. A general reserve will be created on 31 December, Year 4 of £300 000.
7. Land and buildings which cost £350 000 (nil depreciation as at 31 October, Year 3) are to be written down to £200 000 because of falling prices in the property market.
8. Dividends during Year 4 will be restricted to paying:
   (i) the preference dividend for the year; and
   (ii) a final ordinary dividend of 3p per share, but only on the shares issued before 1 August, Year 4.

	£000s	£000s		£000s	£000s
Fixed assets at cost		1 100	Issued capital		
Less aggregate depreciation		230	50p ordinary shares, fully paid		400
		870	11% £1 preference shares, fully paid		50
					450
			Share premium		200
			Retained earnings		700
Current assets			Current liabilities		
Stock	120		Trade creditors	100	
Trade debtors less provision for doubtful debts	90		Accrued expenses	20	120
(100 − 10)					
Balance at bank	390	600			
		1 470			1 470

9. All fixed assets other than land and buildings will be depreciated at 10% per annum, based on the cost of assets held at the end of the financial year. There are to be no additions or disposals of fixed assets during Year 4.

10. Other forecast balances as at 31 October, Year 4:

	£000s
Expense creditors	17.00
Trade creditors	97.00
Stock	290.00
Balance at bank	760.50

Required:

(a) A budgeted trading, profit and loss and appropriation account for the year ending 31 October, Year 4.

(b) A budgeted balance sheet as at 31 October, Year 4.

8 A LEVEL (AEB) 1994

Belinda Raglan owns a clothing factory. Trading over the last two years has been very successful and she feels that having achieved good results it is now time to request an increase in the overdraft facility.

In the past the bank has been willing to offer business overdraft facilities and at present there is an agreed limit of £15 000.

On 1 May, Year 3 the overdraft stands at £5000.

In order to support her request for the increased facility, she has produced a forecast profit statement for the four months ended 31 August, Year 3 as follows:

	May £000	Jun £000	Jul £000	Aug £000
Sales	74	28	116	168
Cost of sales	51	12	78	101
Gross profit	23	16	38	67
Less:				
Rent	4	4	4	4
Other expenses	8	3	10	14
Depreciation	5	5	5	5
	17	12	19	23
Net Profit	6	4	19	44

Although Belinda thought these figures would be sufficient to satisfy the requirements of the bank, the manager has asked for a cash budget for the period concerned to be submitted.

The following additional information concerning the business is available.

1. Rent is paid quarterly in advance on the first day of May, August, November, February.

2. All other expenses are payable in the month in which they are incurred.

3. Purchases for the period are expected to be – May £60 000, June £120 000, July £40 000 and August £43 000. These will be paid for in the month of purchase. Purchases will be unusually high in May and June because they will be subject to a special reduction of 3% of the amounts quoted.

4. 80% of the sales are on a credit basis payable two months later. Sales in March and April were £88 000 and £84 000 respectively.

5. A compensation payment of £10 000 to a former employee for an industrial injury, not covered by insurance, is due to be paid in May.

Required:

Prepare a forecast cash budget on a month-by-month basis for the period May to August, Year 3.

9 AAT COST ACCOUNTING AND BUDGETING

Freewheel is in the process of preparing its master budget for the 6 months ending December, Year 2. The Balance Sheet for the year ended 30 June, Year 1 is estimated to be as follows:

	Cost £	Depreciation provision £	Net book value £
Fixed assets	140 000	14 000	126 000
Current assets			
Stock	25 000		
Trade debtors	24 600		
Bank	3 000	52 600	
Less current liabilities			
Amounts falling due within one year			
Trade creditors	25 000		
Other Creditors	9 000	34 000	
Net current assets			18 600
Total assets less current liabilities			144 600
Capital and reserves:			
Share capital			100 000
Profit and loss account			44 600
			144 600

The Budget Committee have derived the following trading forecasts for the 6 months ended 31 December, Year 2:

	Sales in units	Purchases	Wages and salaries	Overheads excluding depreciation	Purchase of fixed assets	Issue of 20 000 £1 shares	Dividends
May	4 000	12 000	8 000	7 000			
June	4 200	13 000	8 000	7 000			
July	4 500	14 000	8 000	7 000			
August	4 600	18 000	10 000	7 000			
September	4 800	16 000	10 000	7 000		20 000	
October	5 000	14 000	10 000	8 000			10 000
November	3 800	12 000	12 000	8 000	30 000		
December	3 000	12 000	12 000	8 000			

You are given the following information:

1. The selling price in May, Year 1 was £6 per unit and this is to be increased to £8 per unit in October; 50% of sales are for cash and 50% on credit to be paid two months later.
2. Purchases are to be paid for two months after purchase.
3. Wages and salaries are to be paid as follows: 75% in the month incurred and 25% in the following month.
4. Overheads are to be paid in the month after they are incurred.
5. The fixed assets are to be paid for in three equal instalments in the three months following a purchase.
6. Dividends are to be paid three months after they are declared and the receipts from the share issue are budgeted to be received in the month of issue.
7. Fixed assets are depreciated 10% per annum on a straight-line basis on those assets owned at 31 December, Year 2.
8. Closing stock at the beginning of the period under review was equal to the previous two months' purchases. At 31 December, Year 2 it was equal to three months' purchases.

Required:
(a) Prepare the following budgets for the 6 months ended 31 December, Year 2:
  (i) Cash budget;
  (ii) Budgeted profit and loss account; and
  (iii) Budgeted balance sheet.
(b) Comment upon the results, highlighting those areas that you wish to draw to the attention of the Budget Committee.

10 AAT COST ACCOUNTING AND BUDGETING 1992
The board of Mainaction Ltd have had a planning meeting for Year 3. The company produces three products, and a draft budgeted Income Statement is as follows:

	Product X	Product Y	Product Z	Total
	£	£	£	£
Sales				
100 000 units at £15	1 500 000			
80 000 units at £25		2 000 000		
120 000 units at £10			1 200 000	4 700 000
Material	300 000	400 000	480 000	
Labour	700 000	800 000	750 000	
Overheads	225 000	360 000	330 000	
	1 225 000	1 560 000	1 560 000	4 345 000
Profit/(loss)	275 000	440 000	(360 000)	355 000

You are told the following:
(i) All material costs are variable and all production is to be sold.
(ii) The fixed cost element of labour is:

Product X	£100 000
Product Y	£160 000
Product Z	£ 90 000

(iii) Overheads are a mixture of variable and fixed cost. The fixed cost element has been absorbed on the basis of machine hours at the rate of £5 per machine hour. One unit of each product takes the following machine time:

Product X	15 minutes
Product Y	30 minutes
Product Z	15 minutes

(iv) The Board are concerned about the loss on Product Z.
(v) The following separate proposals have been put forward for Year 3:

  1. Allow the budgeted level of activity for all products to stand but cut the labour supervision on Product Z, which will reduce labour fixed costs by £75 000 but increase the variable element of overheads for

Product Z by 10%. In addition, a cheaper material costing 75p per unit less would be introduced for Product Z.

2. Increase the selling price of Product Z by £1 per unit and assume demand will remain constant.

3. Stop making Product Z, which will incur redundancy payments of £50 000 but will also eliminate the fixed labour costs for Product Z.

Required:

(a) Prepare a marginal costing statement to show the budgeted contribution per unit.

(b) Prepare a statement to show the total contribution and profit at the budgeted level of production.

(c) Show what effect each separate proposal made by the Board will have on the budgeted contribution and profitability of the firm.

(d) Outline which strategy proposal you would recommend to the Board, taking both monetary and non-monetary considerations into account. Bear in mind that the current outlook for future sales is likely to be depressed and that the firm has a reputation for the quality of its products.

11 AAT COST ACCOUNTING AND BUDGETING 1992

Secondline Ltd, aware of the uncertain nature of their market for the coming year, have prepared budgeted profit forecasts based on 90%, 100% and 105% activity, as follows:

	£	£	£
Revenue	1 350 000	1 500 000	1 575 000
Less:			
Material costs	337 500	375 000	393 750
Labour costs	440 000	485 000	507 500
Production overhead costs	217 500	235 000	243 750
Administration costs	120 000	130 000	135 000
Selling and distribution costs	70 000	75 000	77 500
	1 185 000	1 300 000	1 375 500
Net profit	165 000	200 000	217 500

In fact, actual activity has turned out far worse than expected, and only 37 500 units have been sold, with the following results:

	£
Revenue	1 075 000
Less:	
Material costs	311 750

	£
Labour costs	351 500
Production overhead costs	171 250
Administration costs	117 500
Selling and distribution costs	66 500
	1 018 500
Net profit	56 500

You are also told that:

(i) The budgeted selling price is £30 per unit.

(ii) All production is sold.

(iii) The fixed element of the budgeted costs will remain unchanged to all levels of production.

Required:

(a) Prepare a statement for the year showing the flexed budget at the actual level of activity, the actual results and the variance for each item of revenue and cost.

(b) Examine the variances of £20 000 or greater, analysing the possible reasons for such variances and the follow up action management can take.

Secondline Ltd had seen that sales were likely to be depressed for the coming year and its sales team had secured a potential order for all the spare capacity from actual activity up to 100% activity. For this order, a special selling price of £25 per unit had been agreed and budgeted variable administration costs would increase by 25%, budgeted variable production overhead costs by 20% and budgeted variable labour costs by £1 per unit. All other costs would remain the same.

Required:

(c) Recommend whether Secondline should have maintained 100% activity for the year by accepting the order detailed above. Clearly state the reasons for your decision and show any workings.

12 AAT COST ACCOUNTING AND BUDGETING 1992

An organisation is constructing its budget for the coming year. It makes three products, Alpha, Beta and Gamma. Sales forecasts for the year are as follows:

	Alpha	Beta	Gamma
Northern region (units)	3 000	5 000	4 000
Southern region (units)	5 000	7 000	6 000
	8 000	12 000	10 000

Selling prices are as budgeted:

Alpha	£ 60.00
Beta	£110.00
Gamma	£ 90.00

You are given the following standard cost data to make one unit:

	Alpha	Beta	Gamma
Material X (kg)	2.00	3.00	2.50
Material Y (kg)	3.00	4.00	1.50
Labour hours – Dept. 1	0.75	1.25	2.00
Labour hours – Dept. 2	1.50	2.00	2.50
Machine hours – Dept. 1	1.00	1.50	2.50
Machine hours – Dept. 2	2.00	2.00	3.00

You are told:

	X	Y
(i) Material cost per kilo	£3	£2

	Dept 1	Dept 2
Labour rates per hour	£4	£3

	Dept. 1	Dept. 2
(ii) Production overheads	£415 000	£567 200

Overheads in Dept. 1 are absorbed on a labour hour basis and in Dept. 2 on a machine hour basis.

(iii) Administration overheads are £350 950 and are to be absorbed on the basis of labour cost.

(iv) Opening and closing stocks are budgeted as follows (in units):

	Alpha	Beta	Gamma	X	Y
Opening stock	1 000	1 200	1 500	5 000	7 500
Closing stock	1 200	1 000	1 800	8 000	10 000

Required:
Prepare the following budgets:
(i)   sales budget in revenue;
(ii) production budget in units for each product;
(iii) material purchase budget;
(iv) departmental labour cost budgets;
(v)   budgeted overhead absorption rates for Departments 1 and 2; and
(vi) standard product cost and standard profit for each product.

13 AAT COST ACCOUNTING AND BUDGETING 1993
Blackarm Ltd makes three products and is reviewing the profitability of its product line. You are given the following budgeted data about the firm for the coming year.

	Product A	Product B	Product C
Sales (units)	100 000	120 000	80 000
	£	£	£
Revenue	1 500 000	1 440 000	880 000
Costs:			
Materials	500 000	480 000	240 000
Labour	400 000	320 000	160 000
Overheads	650 000	600 000	360 000
	1 550 000	1 400 000	760 000
Profit (loss)	(50 000)	40 000	120 000

The company is concerned about the loss on Product A. It is considering ceasing production of it and switching the spare capacity of 100 000 units to Product C.
You are told:
(i)   All production is sold.
(ii) 25% of the labour cost for each product is fixed in nature.
(iii) Fixed administration overheads of £900 000 in total have been apportioned to each product on the basis of units sold and are included in the overhead costs above. All other overhead costs are variable in nature.
(iv) Ceasing production of Product A would eliminate the fixed labour charge associated with it and one-sixth of the fixed administration overhead apportioned to Product A.
(v)   Increasing the production of Product C by 100 000 units would mean that the fixed labour cost associated with Product C would double, the variable labour cost would rise by 20%, and its selling price would have to be decreased by £1.50 in order to achieve the increased sales.

Required:
(a) Prepare a marginal cost statement for a unit of each product on the basis of:
    (i) the original budget; and
    (ii) if product A is deleted.
(b) Prepare a statement showing the total contribution and profit for each product group on the basis of:
    (i) the original budget;
    (ii) if product A is deleted.
(c) Using your results from (a) and (b), advise whether Product A should be deleted from the product range, giving reasons for your decision.

14 AAT COST ACCOUNTING AND BUDGETING 1993
A friend of yours is starting business on her own and has approached you for help. You are given the following budgeted information for the forthcoming six months.

	Sales (units)	Production (units)
July	800	1 000
August	1 000	900
September	1 200	1 200
October	1 400	1 300
November	1 300	1 400
December	1 100	1 000

You establish that:
(i)   Sales policy is to receive 50% of the sale value in the month of sale, 25% the month after sale and the remainder the following month. It is estimated that 20%

of the amount outstanding for the second month after sale will not be collectable.

(ii) Selling price is set at £120 per unit for July, August and September, and £140 for October, November and December.

(iii) Purchases for production are used in the month of purchase and paid for one month after purchase. The cost per unit purchased has been set at £80 for July and August, £85 for September and October, and £90 for November and December.

(iv) Wages and salaries have been set at £16 000 for July and August, £20 000 for September and October and £24 000 for November and December. Policy will be to pay 75% in the month of purchase and 25% in the following month.

(v) Overheads are set at £10 000 for July and are budgeted to rise by £500 per month through to December. The overheads are paid in the month after they are incurred.

(vi) Fixed assets with a total cost of £60 000 will be purchased in July when a 40% deposit will be paid. The balance will be paid in 4 equal instalments commencing 2 months after purchase and every two months thereafter.

(vii) A depreciation policy of 20% straight line per annum is to be adopted and depreciation has been included in the overhead charge on a monthly basis for the period under review.

(viii) An interest-free loan of £50 000 is budgeted to be repaid in December. The loan was raised in July and was used in that month as a goodwill payment to purchase the client base for the business.

Required:

(a) Prepare a cash budget for the business for the period July to December.

(b) Determine the budgeted working capital position at 31st December.

(c) Comment upon the results you have arrived at in (a) and (b), offering sound advice to your friend on matters that you consider appropriate.

15 AAT COST ACCOUNTING AND BUDGETING 1993

Bathgate Ltd had prepared the following budget for year 3:

	£	£
Sales		1 500 000
Less cost of sales:		
Materials	520 000	
Labour	400 000	
Overheads	320 000	1 240 000
Net profit		260 000

Of the above costs, 80% of labour were budgeted as variable and 50% of the overheads were budgeted as fixed. Selling price was set at £75 per unit. During the course of the year it was decided to flex the budget to 22 000 units to reflect increased business confidence.

Actual results for Year 3 were:

	£	£
Sales of 22 000 units		1 680 000
Less cost of sales:		
Materials	680 000	
Labour	420 000	
Overheads	340 000	1 440 000
Net profit		240 000

Required:

(a) Calculate the budgeted break-even in units.

(b) Determine the margin of safety in revenue for the
   (i) original budget; and
   (ii) flexed budget.

(c) Flex the budget to an activity level of 22 000 units and determine variances for sales and each element of cost. (Subvariances are not required.)

(d) Comment upon the results in (c) giving possible reasons to management for the variances and any corrective action that may be taken.

Assume all costs are either fixed or variable.

16 AAT COST ACCOUNTING AND BUDGETING 1993

Your friend is in the process of setting up a service-based business consisting of four departments offering different services to clients.

You ascertain the following information for the coming year.

	Dept. 1	Dept. 2	Dept. 3	Dept. 4
Charge per hour to clients	£20	£25	£30	£40
Budgeted chargeable hours	10 584	6 804	5 292	7 560
Payment per hour to employee	£8	£10	£11	£14

The staff in each department would be expected to work a 35 hour week for 48 weeks per year. 10% of their time is non-chargeable. Other costs include:

	£
Office administration	185 000
Marketing and Selling Expenses	75 000
Rental	160 000

You are told that the flow of work is even throughout the year and that clients pay two months in arrears. The rental cost includes a payment for one quarter in advance charged at the same price as previous quarters. 10% of office expenses are for depreciation and one third of marketing and selling expenses are projected bad debts. All other expenses are paid in the month in which they are incurred. It will be company policy to employ part time as well as full time staff.

Required:

(a) Calculate the following:
  (i) revenue budget by department;
  (ii) number of employees in total and by department;
  (iii) direct wages budget;
  (iv) summary cash budget for the year; and
  (v) summary budgeted profit and loss account for the year.

17 LCCI THIRD LEVEL COST ACCOUNTING 1992
Upsandowns Ltd makes a single product which sells at £120 per unit. Seasonal variations in production and sales volume have become more pronounced because of a recession. At the end of Period 1, 14 000 units were in stock.

Budgets for the next two periods are as follows:

	Period 2	Period 3
Production (units)	14 800	10 400
Sales (units)	11 300	18 500

A system of absorption costing is used and stocks are consistently valued, using the relevant details from the following budgeted unit costs, which is based on a normal level of 12 500 units produced and sold per period:

	£	£
Variable production costs:		
Direct materials	24	
Direct labour	20	
Overheads	10	54
Fixed production overheads		16
Variable selling overheads		4
Fixed selling overheads		12
Fixed administration overheads		14
		100

Fixed selling and administration overheads are treated as period costs when profit and loss accounts are being prepared.

Required:

(a) Prepare budgeted profit and loss accounts in tabular style for Periods 2 and 3.
(b) Provide detailed calculations, which account for the difference in the net profit for Period 3 compared with Period 2.

18 LCCI THIRD LEVEL MANAGEMENT ACCOUNTING 1992
Models Ltd manufactures model tanks which are sold internationally to toy wholesalers at £40 each. Last year's sales were £6 million, when the company was operating at 60% of factory capacity. The desired level of activity this year is 80% of capacity and costs at this volume are likely to be as below:

Model tank

	£	
Prime Cost		
Direct materials	10.00	per tank
Direct labour	5.00	per tank
Production overhead:		
Fixed	1 600 000	per annum
Variable with units	600 000	per annum
Selling and distribution overheads		
Fixed	1 700 000	per annum
Variable with units	400 000	per annum

Required:

(a) Prepare a profit statement for the following situations:
  (i) last year's level of activity; and
  (ii) this year's desired level of activity.
(b) Assuming that an 80% capacity output is achieved, state:
  (i) the price at which the model tank would need to be sold to achieve a profit of £1 500 000; and
  (ii) the point in sales volume at which the company would break even, selling at £40 per tank.

19 ACCA COST AND MANAGEMENT ACCOUNTING 1 1990
Two products are manufactured by a company in one of its factories. The products comprise different mixes of two basic raw materials. One grade of direct labour is employed in the mixing process and another grade in final packaging.

Standard direct material and direct labour costs for the two products in the current period are:

	Product Y (£s per 100 units)	Product Z (£s per 100 units)
Direct materials:		
Raw material A	156.00	78.00
Raw material B	54.00	72.00
Direct labour:		
Mixing	11.25	11.25
Packaging	20.00	20.00

The current standard purchase prices of the raw materials and standard direct labour rates are:

Raw material A	£5.20 per kg
Raw material B	£1.80 per kg
Mixing labour	£4.50 per hour
Packaging labour	£4.00 per hour

A favourable usage variance, currently being achieved on raw material A, is to be incorporated into standard for the following period. Standard material loss on raw material A of 10% of input rather than the existing standard loss of 12%, is to be included. Increases in raw material purchase prices and labour rates, of 5% and 8% respectively, are to be incorporated in the new standards for the following period. The sales budget for the following period for Products Y and Z is as follows:

Product Y	1 700 000 units
Product Z	950 000 units

Stocks of raw materials and finished goods are budgeted as follows for the period ahead:

	Opening Stocks	Closing Stocks
Raw material A (kg)	40 000	25 000
Raw material B (kg)	95 000	90 000
Product Y – units	190 000	200 000
Product Z – units	150 000	125 000

Required:
(a) Calculate, and show in as much detail as possible, the standard direct material and direct labour costs (per hundred units) for the following period.
(b) Establish the budgets for the following period for:
   (i) production of each product – units;
   (ii) purchases of material B (kg); and
   (iii) mixing labour – hours.

20 ACCA COST AND MANAGEMENT ACCOUNTING 1 1990

X Ltd manufactures and sells two varieties of a particular product. Selling prices and variable costs are budgeted for the following period as:

	Variety A £ per unit	Variety B £ per unit
Retail selling price	5.00	6.00
Variable production cost	1.50	1.90
Other variable costs	0.30	0.30

The two varieties are sold by X Ltd direct to retailers at a basic price sufficient to provide the retailers with a gross margin of 30% of sales (before discounts received). Discounts off basic price are given to retailers, depending upon quantities purchased. Discount of 4% is expected on Variety A, and 5% on Variety B, in the following period.

Fixed production costs, jointly incurred by the two varieties of the product, are budgeted to total £225 000. Other fixed costs, also jointly incurred, are budgeted at £73 500.

Budgeted production and sales quantities are:

	Variety 000s units	Variety 000s units
Production	100	150
Sales	105	140

The fixed production costs are absorbed into product costs using a predetermined rate per unit of product, based on budgeted quantities and budgeted costs. The same rate is applied to each variety of the product. Other fixed costs are shared between the two varieties on a similar basis, i.e. a rate per unit of product, based on budgeted quantities and costs.

Required:
(a) Calculate the total revenue, gross profit and net profit that will occur in the following period:
   (i) if actual results in all respects are as per budget; and
   (ii) if actual results are as per budget apart from production of Variety A of 105 000 units.
(b) Using marginal costing principles calculate the expected breakeven sales revenue for the following period.

21 ACCA COST AND MANAGEMENT ACCOUNTING 1 1991

A company is preparing its factory labour budget for the year ahead. In Department X a single product is manufactured. The following information is available about the product:

1. Stocks at the beginning of the budget period are expected to be 48 600 units.
2. Budgeted sales for the year ahead (including 49 000 units in Month 1) are 567 300 units.
3. Stocks at the end of the budget period are required to be sufficient to meet the first month's sales in the following period, when a 10% year-on-year increase is expected.
4. Standard efficiency for direct operatives is 112 units per hour.
5. The standard rate per hour for direct operatives in the budget period is £5.20 per hour.

Required:
Prepare the labour budget for direct operatives (hours and £s) for the year ahead.

In the first month of the budget year, actual results in Department X were as follows:

1. Production of the single product was 50 400 units compared with a budget of 49 700 units.
2. Direct operatives worked 458 hours, including overtime of 6 hours. Overtime is paid at 50% above the basic wage rate. Overtime premium is charged to overhead.
3. Total labour cost of direct operatives was £2 420.25, including employee deductions of £565.35.
4. Indirect labour costs (excluding the overtime premium relating to direct operatives) totalled £1254.85, including employee deductions of £303.90.

Required:
(a) Reconcile the budgeted and actual direct labour costs for Month 1, identifying variances from budget in as much detail as possible.
(b) Prepare Department X's wages control account for Month 1, assuming that efficiency variances are identified in the work-in-progress account.

22 ACCA COST AND MANAGEMENT ACCOUNTING 1 1991

A company is preparing budgets for the year ahead for two of its raw materials that are used in various products which it manufactures. Current year material usage standards are as follows:

In kg per 000 units of product

	Product 1	Product 2	Product 3	Product 4	Product 5
Material A	25	70	15	–	55
Material B	30	5	–	20	–

It has been decided to change standards on Material B for the following year to reflect the favourable usage variances that are occurring for that material on all products. Usage variances on Material B are 10% of standard costs.

Budgeted sales quantities for the following year are:

	Product 1	Product 2	Product 3	Product 4	Product 5
(000s units)	600	350	1850	1200	900

Production quantities are to be budgeted in line with sales, apart from Product 5, where an increase in stock of 30% is required by the end of the budget year. Stocks of the five products at the beginning of the budget year are expected to be:

	Product 1	Product 2	Product 3	Product 4	Product 5
(000s units)	140	80	260	180	100

Stocks of Materials A and B at the end of the budget year are to be 10% of the year's budgeted usage. Stocks at the end of the current year are expected to be:

	kg
Material A	10 030
Material B	4 260

Required:
(a) Prepare material usage and purchases budgets (kg only) for each of Materials A and B for the year ahead.
(b) Prepare summary journal entries for the Material A stock account for the current period.

The following additional information is provided for the current period:

Material A purchases:
116 250 kg at a cost of £280 160 (standard purchase price = £2.40 per kg)
Production:

	Product 1	Product 2	Product 3	Product 4	Product 5
(000s units)	580	330	1900	1200	800

Material A usage has been at standard.

23 ACCA COST AND MANAGEMENT ACCOUNTING 1 1992

Budgeted information for A Ltd for the following period, analysed by product, is shown below:

	Product I	Product II	Product III
Sales units (000s)	225	376	190
Selling price (£s per unit)	11.00	10.50	8.00
Variable costs (£s per unit)	5.80	6.00	5.20
Attributable fixed costs (£000s)	275	337	296

General fixed costs, which are apportioned to products as a percentage of sales, are budgeted at £1 668 000.

Required:
(a) Calculate the budgeted profit of A Ltd, and of each of its products.
(b) Recalculate the budgeted profit of A Ltd on the assumption that Product III is discontinued, with no effect on sales of the other two products. State and justify other assumptions made.
(c) Additional advertising, to that included in the budget for Product I, is being considered. Calculate the minimum extra sales units required of Product I to cover additional

advertising expenditure of £80 000. Assume that all other existing fixed costs would remain unchanged.

(d) Calculate the increase in sales volume of Product II that is necessary in order to compensate the effect on profit of a 10% reduction in the selling price of the product. State clearly any assumptions made.

24 CIMA COST ACCOUNTING 1990
There is a continuing demand for three subassemblies – A, B, and C – made and sold by MW Limited. Sales are in the ratios of A 1, B 2, C 4 and selling prices are A, £215; B, £250; C, £300. Each subassembly consists of a copper frame on to which are fixed the same components, but in differing quantities, as follows:

	Frame	Component D	Component E	Component F
Sub-assembly				
A	1	5	1	4
B	1	1	7	5
C	1	3	5	1
Buying in costs per unit	£20	£8	£5	£3

Operation times by labour for each sub-assembly are:

Sub-assembly	Skilled hours	Unskilled hours
A	2	2
B	1.5	2
C	1.5	3

The skilled labour is paid £6 per hour and the unskilled £4.50 per hour. The skilled labour is located in a Machining Department and the unskilled labour in an Assembly Department. A five-day week of 37.5 hours is worked and each accounting period is for four weeks.

Variable overhead per sub-assembly is A, £5; B, £4; and C, £3.50.

At the end of the current year, stocks are expected to be as shown below but because interest rates have increased and the company utilises a bank overdraft for working capital purposes, it is planned to effect a 10% reduction in all finished sub-assemblies and bought in stocks during Period 1 of the forthcoming year.

Forecast stocks at current year end:

Sub-assembly			
A	300	Copper frames	1 000
B	700	Component D	4 000
C	1 600	Component E	10 000
		Component F	4 000

Work-in-progress stocks are to be ignored.

Overheads for the forthcoming year are budgeted to be Production £728 000, Selling and Distribution £364 000 and Administration £338 000. These costs, all fixed, are expected to be incurred evenly throughout the year and are treated as period costs.

Within Period 1 it is planned to sell one-thirteenth of the annual requirements, which are to be the sales necessary to achieve the company profit target of £6.5 million before tax.

Required:
Prepare budgets in respect of Period 1 of the forthcoming year:
(i) sales, in quantities and value;
(ii) production, in quantities only;
(iii) materials usage, in quantities;
(iv) material purchases, in quantities and value; and
(v) manpower budget, i.e. numbers of people needed in both the Machining Department and the Assembly Department.

25 CIMA COST ACCOUNTING 1992
JM Limited uses absorption costing principles for its variance analysis. The flexible budget for production overheads for the company, which makes one product, shows a budgeted monthly expenditure of £72 000 for an output of 3000 tonnes, and of £108 000 for an output of 7 000 tonnes. The standard overhead absorption rate for absorption purposes is £18 per tonne. During the month of April, the company incurred overhead expenditure of £105 750 (£52 000 variable and £53 750 fixed) for an output of 5500 tonnes.

Required:
Calculate the following:
(i) budgeted variable overhead cost per tonne;
(ii) total budgeted fixed cost per month;
(iii) budgeted output per month on which the standard overhead rate is based;
(iv) budgeted overhead allowance for the actual output in April;
(v) the total overhead absorbed for the month of April;
(vi) variable production overhead expenditure variance for the month of April;
(vii) fixed production overhead expenditure variance for the month of April; and
(viii) fixed production overhead volume variance for the month of April.

26 CIMA COST ACCOUNTING 1992

The following figures have been extracted from a manufacturing company's budget schedules:

	Year 2			Year 3		
	Oct	Nov	Dec	Jan	Feb	Mar
	£000s	£000s	£000s	£000s	£000s	£000s
Sales incl. VAT	1 200	1 100	1 000	1 400	1 200	1 100
Wages and salaries	55	50	65	60	60	60
Purchases of materials	210	280	240	210	240	230
Production overheads	560	500	640	560	500	560
Selling and administration overheads	125	125	125	125	130	130

Other relevant information:

1. All sales are on credit terms of net settlement within 30 days of the date of the sale. However, only 60% of indebtedness is paid by the end of the calendar month in which the sale is made; another 30% is paid in the following calendar month; 5% in the second calendar month after the invoice date; and 5% become bad debts.
2. Assume all months are of equal number of 30 days for the allocation of the receipts and debtors.
3. Wages and salaries are paid within the month they are incurred.
4. Creditors for materials are paid within the month following the purchase.
5. Of the production overheads, 35% of the figure represents variable expenses, which are paid in the month after they were incurred. £164 000 per month is depreciation and is included in the 65% which represents fixed costs. The payment of fixed costs is made in the month in which the cost is incurred.
6. Selling and administration overhead which is payable is paid in the month it is incurred. £15 000 each month is depreciation.
7. Corporation tax of £750 000 is payable in January.
8. A dividend is payable in March: £500 000 net (ignore advance corporation tax).
9. Value added tax (VAT), payable monthly one month later than the sales are made, is to be calculated as follows:
   Output tax
       7/47ths of the sales including VAT figure
       less Input tax of £136 000 for January
                       £125 000 for February
                       £121 000 for March.

10. Capital expenditure commitments are due for payment:
    £1 000 000 in January and £700 000 in March. Both are payments for machinery to be imported from Japan and thus no VAT is involved.
11. Assume that overdraft facilities, if required, are available.
12. The cash at bank balance at 31 December is expected to be £1 450 000.

Required:

(a) To prepare, in columnar form, cash budgets for each of the months of January, February and March (working to nearest £000);
(b) To recommend action which could be suggested to management to effect:
   (i) a permanent improvement in cash flow; and
   (ii) a temporary solution to minimise any overdraft requirements revealed by your answer to (a) above.

27 UNIVERSITY OF GREENWICH YEAR 1
    BA ACCOUNTANCY AND FINANCE (1992)

Collins Manufacturing Ltd are preparing their budgets for Year 3; 90 000 direct labour hours constitutes 100% expected production time.

The following figures for the period emerge from budget meetings:

	£
Estimated fixed costs:	
Depreciation of plant	16 500
Factory salaries	32 250
Other	6 750

Estimated variable costs:	**Per direct labour hour**
Power	30p
Consumables	5p
Direct labour	£1.50

Semi-variable expenses:

During the last two years the following figures were used:

	Direct labour hours	**£**
Year 1	80 000	53 250
Year 2	105 000	63 250

Required:

Prepare Collins' flexible budget at 90%, 100%, and 110% levels of activity.

28 UNIVERSITY OF GREENWICH YEAR 1
    BA ACCOUNTANCY AND FINANCE (1992)

The month-by-month forecast of profitability of a company for the five months May to September is given below:

	May	June	July	Aug	Sept
(In £00s)					
Materials consumed	60	70	80	102	90
Wages	32	32	32	40	32
Depreciation	7	7	7	7	7
Factory expenses	5	5	5	5	5
Rent	3	3	3	3	3
Salaries and office					
expenses	32	32	32	32	32
Advertising and					
publicity	12	14	10	16	20
Sales commission	8	9	10	13	11
	159	172	179	218	200
Sales	160	180	200	260	220
Profit	1	8	21	42	20
Raw materials stock					
(end-month)	70	80	90	70	60

The following information is given:

1. On average payment is made to suppliers one month after delivery.
2. The lag in payment of wages is one-eighth of a month.
3. Factory expenses are paid during the month incurred.
4. Rent is paid quarterly on the last day of March, June, September and December.
5. Salaries and office expenses are paid in the month in which they arise.
6. Advertising and publicity expenditure is paid monthly, but two months' credit is taken.
7. Sales commission is paid one month in arrears.
8. On average, debtors take two months' credit.
9. Cash balance at 1st July is £52 000.
10. In September £30 000 will be paid for machinery. A dividend and tax thereon amounting to £6000 will be paid in August. Investment grants of £20 000 will be received in September.

Required:
Prepare a cash budget for each of the three months to 30th September. (Give figures to the nearest £1000).

NON-COMPUTATIONAL, DESCRIPTIVE TYPE QUESTIONS
(NB Minutes in brackets are a guide to indicate the approximate time your essay should take to complete.)

QUESTIONS
A Describe the major benefits deriving from the preparation of cash budgets.
(Univ. Year 1) (15 minutes)

B 'Budgets and standards are similar but they are not the same.'
   Explain and expand on the above statement, mentioning differences and similarities.
(CIMA 1993) (30 minutes)

C 'Managers may be reluctant to participate in the setting of budgets but when they do, it should lead to better performance.'
   You are required to discuss the above statement, suggesting reasons for the reluctance expressed, how such reservations may be overcome and some of the benefits which may arise from participation in the budgeting process.
(CIMA 1994) (35 minutes)

D Describe the benefits that can be derived from a budgeting system.
(ACCA 1991) (15 minutes)

E Accountants always stress the importance of budgeting for planning and control.
Required: Explain briefly how budgeting aids planning and control within an organisation over a budgetary cycle.
(AAT 1991) (7 minutes)

F A company that manufactures and sells a range of products, with sales potential limited by market share, is considering introducing a system of budgeting.
Required:

(i) list the functional budgets that need to be prepared;
(ii) state which budgets the master budget will comprise; and
(iii) consider how the work outlined in (i) and (ii) can be co-ordinated for the budgeting process to be successful.

(AAT 1991) (13 minutes)

G 'Financial Accounting looks behind, whilst Management Accounting looks ahead.'
   To what extent does this quotation reflect the role of the two branches of accountancy?
(ULEAC 1991) (35 minutes)

H Define budget, budgetary control and flexible budget.
(ULEAC 1993) (11 minutes)

20
Investment Appraisal Techniques

As we have seen from the earlier chapters in this section, well-run businesses plan for the future. They will prepare operational budgets, balance sheet budgets and cash budgets. They will formulate a long-term strategy and endeavour to allow for unforeseen trading conditions in which they will be operating in the future. They will also prepare capital expenditure budgets and forecasts.

Ask any manager in an organisation if he or she requires additional assets, or needs to replace existing assets, and you will be presented with an almost never-ending list. The Production Manager may insist that an old, indispensable machine will not last another six months and really needs replacing immediately; the Sales Manager may say that investment in setting up a new sales line will produce spectacular returns, and the sales force needs much better computer/back-office support; and the Transport Manager may suggest that the distribution budget is not achievable unless he or she is able to get the latest delivery van. The Accountant might insist that the financial accounting system is about to collapse and needs updating with the latest computer equipment; and perhaps the Managing Director may feel that the most recently released telecommunications equipment will help fulfil the Chief Executive's tasks more effectively, and, furthermore, senses that to buy out a small competitor now will strengthen the business dramatically.

However, the funds available to an organisation for investment are generally limited, being restricted to the profits earned (after tax and dividends have been paid), plus any additional capital introduced, plus any receipts from disposals of assets, less any loan repayments to be made, or for working capital needs. The funds for investment are therefore usually narrow and finite and cannot readily accommodate all of these other investment calls, however desirable, as Figure 20.1 indicates. Management will reduce this amount further by making provisions and reserves for future needs.

It is therefore necessary, prudent and 'good business' to restrict or ration capital expenditure and investment ambitions to those projects and schemes which will show the best return on the investment monies available.

Capital expenditure and investment opportunities therefore need to be evaluated and appraised to see if the spend is likely to be financially beneficial to the business and, if so, which schemes or projects should be chosen, and which rejected or shelved. Projects are therefore *ranked* in accordance with these criteria.

It should be noted, however, that some capital expenditure has to be incurred to ensure that legal requirements are met and fulfilled; for example, health and safety regulations demand proper regard to safe working conditions; this may entail essential capital expenditure, which cannot be delayed. The

FIGURE 20.1

INVESTMENT FUNDS AVAILABLE	
	£
BUDGETED PROFIT	
LESS TAXATION	
LESS DIVIDENDS	
= BUDGETED CASH AVAILABLE FROM EARNINGS	
ADD NEW FUNDS FROM SHAREHOLDERS	
ADD NEW LOANS	
ADD SALES OF FIXED ASSETS	
= BUDGETED CASH AVAILABLE	
LESS NEEDED FOR WORKING CAPITAL PURPOSES	
LESS NEEDED TO REPAY LOANS	
= AVAILABLE FOR INVESTING IN ASSETS	£

same goes for urgent replacement of assets caused by wear and tear. But with both of these scenarios there will usually be a choice between competing quotes, and these can be evaluated and appraised.

For other desirable capital expenditure, prudent management tests to see if the proposed expenditure is likely to contribute to the economic success of the business. There are four commonly used management accounting techniques to help them to do this. These are:

Net present value method;
Internal rate of return method;
Payback period method; and
Accounting rate of return method.

Generally, management will evaluate each project using one or more (and in many cases, *all*), of these techniques, and then choose the 'winning projects' which fit well into the overall capital expenditure plans for maximising profitability and efficiency. Inevitably, some will not measure up and are delayed or abandoned.

Time value of money

The first two methods listed above take into consideration the *time value of money*. The decision to invest means that cash available today will be 'locked in' to

the investment and therefore cannot be spent, say, on an advertising campaign to increase sales or pay a dividend. Those alternative opportunities to use the money will have been sacrificed to the investment. The future returns expected from the investment must be greater than the investment if it is to be worthwhile.

Ten pounds to spend today, say, is far more attractive than the same £10 in a year's time: risk and uncertainty eat into its value over that period of time. But if by delaying the spending of the £10 and investing it, with the absolute certainty that in a year's time it would be worth £18, most people would opt for the latter. Thus the reason to invest, the driving force, is the prospect of more cash in the future at an acceptable level to make it worthwhile waiting. Compound interest is the measurement of this 'waiting' time reward.

An illustration of how compound interest works is as follows: If £100 is invested in a building society account at, say, an interest rate of 5% per annum, then after five years the original investment, left untouched, will have grown as shown in Table 20.1. As can be seen from the table, at the end of Year 5, the investment will have grown to £127.63. Conversely, this investment, with its total value in Year 5 of £127.63, has a value as of today of £100. Thus £100 is its *net present value*.

TABLE 20.1

INVESTMENT AT 5% P.A. COMPOUND INTEREST	
	£
ORIGINAL INVESTMENT	100.00
YEAR 1 INTEREST	5.00
	105.00
YEAR 2 INTEREST	5.25
	110.25
YEAR 3 INTEREST	5.51
	115.76
YEAR 4 INTEREST	5.79
	121.55
YEAR 5 INTEREST	6.08
TOTAL VALUE OF INVESTMENT AT END OF YEAR	£127.63

When management is evaluating a project, future cash flows will be prepared to show how much the investment will generate over its economic life. (Cash flows are the difference between the receipts generated by the project and the expenditure incurred by it.) To be able to assess whether the returns from the project will be greater than the original investment it is necessary to discount these cash flows so that both returns and original investment can then be compared meaningfully, using a 'level playing field': that is, the net present value.

Discounted cash flow (DCF)

CIMA defines present value as 'the cash equivalent now of a sum receivable or payable at a future date'.

Forecast future cash flows are *discounted* to arrive at today's net present value. Thus the *discounted cash flow* is the obverse of the compound interest calculation.

The discount factor for Year 5, at 5% pa, is 0.784 on the net present value discount table (see Table 20.2). If £127.63 is multiplied by 0.784 it produces £100: the net present value. Conversely, if £100 is divided by 0.784 it provides the future cash equivalent – £127.63. (Note also that the discount factor can also be arrived at by dividing 100 by the £127.63: 0.784. A method to arrive at the discount factor is shown in the table; but in most examination questions tables are provided so there is no need to calculate the factor.)

The purpose of discounting future cash flows is to arrive at the net present value of those cash flows. This enables management to compare the sum of the flows with the original investment. If the difference between the two is 'positive' (the net present value is greater than the original investment) then the project will provide a return higher than the discount factor anticipated. If 'negative', the opposite is the case.

The discount factor

The discount factor used in net present value calculations is often based on a firm's *weighted average cost of capital*. Each element of capital – equity, long-term loans and debt – is weighted to the total capital employed, as the following example shows.

Example:
A firm pays a dividend of 10% per share; the ordinary share capital is £250 000.

Preference shares receive a dividend each year of 4%; preference share capital is £350 000.

Debenture interest is 16% on debentures of £100 000.

Interest on a long-term bank loan of £300 000 is at the rate of 15%.

Debenture interest and interest on the long-term bank loan are allowable expenses for taxation purposes. For this example, this is 30%.

The weighted average cost of capital for this firm will be as shown in Table 20.3.

The weighted average cost of capital is the most frequently used discount factor, because funds available for investment cannot usually be identified specifically to just one source of capital: the money comes from the total capital available. Therefore it is logical to weight all the elements to arrive at an average figure. If funds to finance a particular project can, however, be identified specifically with the project, then the cost of capital will be the cost of financing those funds. For example, it may be that a machine can be purchased by means of a specific loan. The discount factor will be the rate of interest on the loan.

Another method sometimes used is when the weighted average cost percentage is lower than, say, prevailing market interest rates. In the example above,

TABLE 20.2

NET PRESENT VALUE DISCOUNT TABLE

Year	1%	2%	3%	4%	5%	6%	7%	8%	9%	10%
1	0.990	0.960	0.917	0.962	0.952	0.943	0.935	0.926	0.917	0.909
2	0.980	0.961	0.943	0.925	0.907	0.890	0.873	0.857	0.842	0.826
3	0.971	0.942	0.915	0.889	0.864	0.840	0.816	0.794	0.7672	0.751
4	0.961	0.924	0.888	0.855	0.823	0.792	0.763	0.735	0.708	0.683
5	0.951	0.906	0.863	0.822	0.784	0.747	0.713	0.681	0.650	0.621
6	0.942	0.888	0.837	0.790	0.746	0.705	0.666	0.630	0.596	0.564
7	0.933	0.871	0.813	0.760	0.711	0.665	0.623	0.583	0.547	0.513
8	0.923	0.853	0.789	0.731	0.677	0.627	0.582	0.540	0.502	0.467
9	0.914	0.837	0.766	0.703	0.645	0.592	0.544	0.500	0.460	0.424
10	0.905	0.8290	0.744	0.676	0.614	0.558	0.508	0.463	0.422	0.386
11	0.896	0.804	0.722	0.650	0.585	0.527	0.475	0.429	0.388	0.350
12	0.887	0.788	0.701	0.625	0.557	0.497	0.444	0.397	0.356	0.319
13	0.879	0.773	0.681	0.601	0.530	0.469	0.415	0.368	0.326	0.290
14	0.870	0.758	0.661	0.577	0.505	0.442	0.388	0.340	0.299	0.263
15	0.861	0.743	0.642	0.555	0.481	0.417	0.362	0.315	0.275	0.239

Year	11%	12%	13%	14%	15%	16%	17%	18%	19%	20%
1	0.901	0.893	0.885	0.877	0.870	0.862	0.855	0.847	0.840	0.833
2	0.812	0.797	0.783	0.769	0.756	0.743	0.731	0.718	0.706	0.694
3	0.731	0.712	0.693	0.675	0.658	0.641	0.624	0.609	0.593	0.579
4	0.659	0.636	0.613	0.592	0.572	0.552	0.534	0.516	0.499	0.482
5	0.593	0.567	0.543	0.519	0.497	0.476	0.456	0.437	0.419	0.402
6	0.535	0.507	0.480	0.456	0.432	0.410	0.390	0.370	0.352	0.335
7	0.482	0.452	0.425	0.400	0.376	0.354	0.333	0.314	0.296	0.279
8	0.434	0.404	0.376	0.351	0.327	0.305	0.285	0.266	0.249	0.233
9	0.391	0.361	0.333	0.308	0.284	0.263	0.243	0.225	0.209	0.194
10	0.352	0.322	0.295	0.270	0.247	0.227	0.208	0.191	0.176	0.162
11	0.317	0.287	0.261	0.237	0.215	0.195	0.178	0.162	0.148	0.135
12	0.286	0.257	0.231	0.208	0.187	0.168	0.152	0.137	0.124	0.112
13	0.258	0.229	0.204	0.182	0.163	0.145	0.130	0.116	0.104	0.093
14	0.232	0.205	0.181	0.160	0.141	0.125	0.111	0.099	0.088	0.078
15	0.209	0.183	0.160	0.140	0.123	0.108	0.095	0.084	0.074	0.065

TO CALCULATE THE FACTOR EACH YEAR:

YEAR 1: DIVIDE 1 BY (1 + THE DISCOUNT FACTOR).

EXAMPLE: $14\% = 1/1 + 0.14 =$ 0.877

YEAR 2 ONWARDS: DIVIDE PRIOR YEAR'S FACTOR BY (1 + THE DISCOUNT FACTOR)

EXAMPLE: $14\% = 0.877/1 + 0.14 =$ 0.769

TABLE 20.3

WEIGHTED AVERAGE COST OF CAPITAL			
CAPITAL ELEMENT	VALUE	RATE RETURN	COST OF CAPITAL
	(£)	(%)	(£)
ORDINARY SHARE CAPITAL	250 000	10.0	25 000
PREFERENCE SHARE CAPITAL	350 000	4.0	14 000
DEBENTURES	100 000	11.2	11 200
BANK LOAN	300 000	10.5	31 500
	1 000 000		81 700

WEIGHTED AVERAGE COST
OF CAPITAL = 8.2% (£81 700/£1 000 000)

NOTE: DEBENTURES AND BANK LOAN INTEREST
ARE REDUCED BY TAX RELIEF

the weighted average rate was 8.2%; it may be that market interest rates are 15%. In this case, the company could deposit the amounts available for investment into the market, thus exceeding comfortably its weighted average cost. It is thus logical to use the highest rate of return – *opportunity cost of capital* as the basis for the discount factor.

It should be noted that CIMA, in official terminology, states that '*weighting is usually based on market valuations, current yields and costs after tax*'.

Investment appraisal

Let us look at this in practice. First we need to set the scene in which investment appraisal methods are used. We shall assume the firm in question has adopted a formal capital expenditure authorisation system which includes the following:

Capital expenditure request form
Capital expenditure authorisation form
Periodic reports on actual capital expenditure
Capital expenditure results audit or review

Examples of the layout of forms used for the first two, the capital expenditure request form and authorisation form, are as shown in Figures 20.2 and 20.3.

Obviously, there will be projects that are rejected or shelved and there may be a form issued to this effect.

Once the approval has been granted the company is committing capital for the project and, as with all matters relating to the future, where uncertainty and risk is the norm, the more accurate the financial estimates are, the more likely the success of the project. Thus great care and prudence should be exercised in preparing the figures.

Worked example

Calculating the net present value

For the example, we shall assume that a capital authorisation expenditure request has been submitted for a new production line and associated machinery, with the following financial estimates being carefully calculated, based on market research and supported by a good track record of reliability in forecasting:

The cost to set up and buy the machinery is £500 000. It is expected that the production during its estimated life of six years will be as follows:

Year 1:   50 000 units
Year 2:   80 000 units
Year 3:   90 000 units
Year 4: 100 000 units
Year 5:   70 000 units
Year 6:   30 000 units

Selling prices will be £10 each to start, and expected to rise by 10 per cent each year thereafter. Production will be sold in the year it is produced, thus there will be no opening or closing stocks.

The costs of running the line will be as follows:

Variable costs: £5 per unit, rising by 8 per cent each year.
Fixed costs: £200 000 per annum, rising by £20 000 per annum.

The Manager expects that the line and its equipment can be sold at the end of its economically useful life in Year 6, for £50 000.

The firm's cost of capital is 14 per cent but it is company policy to add a 'risk premium' of 6 per cent to this to cover unforeseen matters. Therefore, on all projects the firm uses a factor of 20 per cent to calculate the net present value.

FIGURE 20.2

CAPITAL EXPENDITURE REQUEST FORM

REQUESTED BY:
DEPARTMENT:

DATE:

I request authorisation for the following capital expenditure:

Signed........................Manager

£

PROJECT DESCRIPTION:

PROJECT NARRATIVE:
[HERE WILL BE GIVEN A DETAILED DESCRIPTION OF THE PROJECT, THE REASONS WHY THE SPEND IS
CONSIDERED NECESSARY, OR IS WORTH INVESTING IN, MARKET STRENGTHS, WEAKNESSES,
OPPORTUNITIES, THREATS, ETC. THE NARRATIVE MAY BE CONSIDERABLE, WITH PERHAPS A SUMMARY
HERE SUPPORTED BY DETAILED CHARTS, TABLES, RESEARCH DOCUMENTATION, ETC.]

REVENUES AND COSTS OVER PROJECT LIFE:

	£	OR		£
REVENUES			PRESENT COSTS	
COSTS			PROPOSED COSTS	
PROFIT			SAVINGS	

INVESTMENT APPRAISAL
NET PRESENT VALUE   (DISCOUNT FACTOR....%)   £XXX
INTERNAL RATE OF RETURN   ....%
PAYBACK PERIOD   ......Years
ACCOUNTING RATE OF RETURN   ....%

SUPPORTING CALCULATIONS WILL BE ANNEXED.

FIGURE 20.3

```
┌─────────────────────────────────────────────┐
│ ███████████████████████████████████████████ │
│  CAPITAL EXPENDITURE AUTHORISATION FORM      │
│                                              │
│  TO: MANAGER              DATE_____       │
│                                              │
│  THE FOLLOWING PROJECT RECEIVED APPROVAL     │
│  AT THE CAPITAL EXPENDITURE AUTHORISATION    │
│  MEETING HELD ON...........................  │
│                                              │
│  ┌─────────────────────────────────────┐    │
│  │ PROJECT:                             │    │
│  │ COST:   £                            │    │
│  │ PROJECT NO:                          │    │
│  └─────────────────────────────────────┘    │
│                                              │
│       SIGNED.................................│
│              AUTHORISERS                     │
│                                              │
│  NOTE: THE PROJECT NUMBER WILL BE QUOTED     │
│  ON ALL PURCHASE ORDERS AND                  │
│  CORRESPONDENCE.                             │
└─────────────────────────────────────────────┘
```

Given this information it is now possible to calculate the cash flows for each of the trading years the production line will be in operation. These figures are marshalled into a table (see Figure 20.4) to produce the *net present value* (NPV) of the project.

Note that the original investment is entered in the '0' column. This is the cost of the project at the time it begins to trade: Day 1 of Year 1. The cash flows, income and expenditure, are entered for each year in accordance with the projections. The proceeds from the sale of the equipment at the end of its life (Year 6) are also entered.

The cash flows deal with cash transactions only: no provisions or reserves are entered: for example, depreciation. The objective is to ascertain the actual monies likely to be generated by the project and to bring these future cash benefits to present values.

Deducting the income from the expenditure produces the net cash flow. The discount factor is then applied, in this case, 20 per cent. Discounting brings the future net cash flows to today's value for each year. These are then totalled to arrive at the total discounted cash flow, which is shown in the '0' column. Deducting this from the original cost produces the NPV. You will see that in this case the figure is £212 389 *positive*. The NPV is greater than the original cost. This means that the project will exceed the firm's

20 per cent cost of capital requirement comfortably and on this one test appears to be a worthwhile project in which to invest.

If the NPV had been lower than the original cost then the project would not have returned the 20 per cent requirement – a *negative* NPV would be the result. Normally a project with a negative NPV would be rejected, or shelved to allow for further thought.

The results from NPV calculations are heavily dependent on reasonably realistic and achievable forecasts. Over-optimism by the proposers in wishing to proceed on a particularly favoured project can result in sales being placed higher than prudence dictates, or costs set lower. One method of overcoming these, and other, natural 'bias' factors is to subject the figures to *sensitivity analysis*. Briefly, this technique looks at all the figures, units to be sold, income and expenditure, and recalculates the table by assuming, say, that units might be 10 per cent less than forecast (or 10 per cent more); costs will be $X\%$ greater, or $X\%$ less; selling prices will be lower or higher than the forecast, and so on.

One or more of these elements may affect the success of the project critically. Sensitivity analysis therefore helps management to judge the risks more effectively by providing answers to questions such as 'If the units in the example were to be 10 per cent less, what would be the effect on the net present value?' When all have been answered, management judgement and entrepreneurial skills will prevail in deciding whether the investment is made or not.

Internal rate of return (IRR)

This technique calculates the *actual* rate of return that the project is forecast to earn. In the above example, a return of 20 per cent as the benchmark had been set so as to cover the cost of capital and the risk premium, and the project exceeded this comfortably. The internal rate of return calculation will provide management with the actual percentage rate of return on the investment.

Establishing this percentage is a relatively easy calculation when using a computer spreadsheet. The IRR is discovered basically through trial and error by changing the discount factor until the NPV sum equals

FIGURE 20.4

NET PRESENT VALUE (NPV) TABLE

DATE:

PREPARED BY :

PROJECT: NEW PRODUCTION LINE AND MACHINERY

	YEAR 0 £	YEAR 1 £	YEAR 2 £	YEAR 3 £	YEAR 4 £	YEAR 5 £	YEAR 6 £
ORIGINAL INVESTMENT	500 000						
CASH FLOWS							
INCOME		500 000	880 000	1 089 000	1 331 000	1 024 800	483 000
DISPOSALS							50 000
EXPENDITURE							
VARIABLE COSTS		(250 000)	(432 000)	(524 880)	(629 856)	(476 171)	(220 399)
FIXED COSTS		(200 000)	(220 000)	(240 000)	(260 000)	(280 000)	(300 000)
NET CASH FLOW		50 000	228 000	324 120	441 144	268 629	12 601
DISCOUNT FACTOR –20%)		0.833	0.694	0.579	0.482	0.402	0.335
DISCOUNTED CASH FLOW	712 389	41 650	158 232	187 665	212 631	107 989	4 221
NET PRESENT VALUE	212 389						

WORKINGS:

	INCOME			VARIABLE EXPENDITURE		
	UNITS	SELLING PRICE	INCOME	UNITS	COST PRICE	COST
1	50 000	£10.00	500 000	50 000	£5.00	250 000
2	80 000	£11.00	880 000	80 000	£5.40	432 000
3	90 000	£12.10	1 089 000	90 000	£5.83	524 880
4	100 000	£13.31	1 331 000	100 000	£6.30	629 856
5	70 000	£14.64	1 024 800	70 000	£6.80	476 171
6	30 000	£16.10	483 000	30 000	£7.35	220 399

zero, or as near to zero as makes no difference to the rounded percentage result. In the example above, the NPV is positive, therefore the IRR will be greater than 20 per cent. If the NPV had been negative the IRR would have been lower than the benchmark.

Using a computer spreadsheet, the easiest method of calculating the IRR is to devote one cell for use as the discount rate. The discount factor cells will then be linked to this cell, so that each time a different discount rate is entered the whole spreadsheet will be recalculated. The formula is shown in Figure

20.5. Note that the IRR for the project in the example is 34 per cent, giving a 'comfort margin' over the cost of capital of 70 per cent (14/20). This comfort margin shows that the financial projections, when subjected to sensitivity analysis, can be adverse by as much as 70 per cent and the project would still be worth investing in. The higher the comfort margin the better, obviously.

Without a computer spreadsheet, the calculations are laborious and time-consuming, but the procedure to find the IRR will be the same: trial and error. As

FIGURE 20.5

FORMULA FOR CALCULATING INTERNAL RATE OF RETURN USING A SPREADSHEET PROGRAM

	A	B	C	D	E	F	G	H	I	J
1										
2										
3										
4										
5				**INTERNAL RATE OF RETURN CALCULATION**				DATE:		
6								PREPARED BY:		
7				PROJECT: *NEW PRODUCTION LINE AND MACHINERY*						
8										
9										
10				*YEAR 0*	*YEAR 1*	*YEAR 2*	*YEAR 3*	*YEAR 4*	*YEAR 5*	*YEAR 6*
11				£	£	£	£	£	£	£
12		ORIGINAL INVESTMENT	500,000							
13										
14		CASH FLOWS								
15		INCOME		500 000	880 000	1 089 000	1 331 000	1 024 800	483 000	
16		DISPOSAL							50 000	
17		EXPENDITURE:								
18		VARIABLE COSTS		(250 000)	(432 000)	(524 880)	(629 856)	(476 171)	(220 399)	
19		FIXED COSTS		(200 000)	(220 000)	(240 000)	(260 000)	(280 000)	(300,000)	
20		NET CASH FLOW		50 000	228 000	324 120	441 144	268 629	12 601	
21										
22		DISCOUNT FACTOR	**34.0%**	0.746	0.557	0.416	0.310	0.231	0.173	
23										
24		DISCOUNTED CASH FLOW	500 175	37 313	126 977	134 707	136 824	62 177	2 177	
25										
26		**NET PRESENT VALUE**	175	– –▶ THE NET PRESENT VALUE SHOULD						
27				APPROXIMATE TO ZERO						
28										
29										
30		LINE 22 ENTRIES	**34.0%**	1/(1 + C22)	+D22/(1 +$C22)	+E22/(1 +$C22)	+F22/(1 +$C22)	+G22/(1 +$C22)	+H22/(1 +$C22)	
31										
32										
33										
34		ENTER THE ADJUDGED DISCOUNT FACTOR								
35										
36		LINK THIS TO EACH CELL ON LINE 22, USING FORMULAE AS ABOVE								
37										
38										
39										
40										

computers are not allowed in the examination room at the present time, questions on the IRR do not usually involve calculations because of the large number of computations required.

The table used to calculate the NPV, where the discount factor is fixed to reflect the cost of capital, can also be used to calculate the IRR as in the table on page 312. Simply change the rate until the NPV approximates to zero, as discussed earlier. The rate resulting in zero (or nearly zero) is the IRR.

These two investment appraisal methods, NPV and IRR, take into consideration the time value of money, bringing the future cash flows through discounting to their present values to see if the project is a worthwhile investment.

To recap, with NPV the discount factor is the firm's cost of capital (usually plus a provision) or the opportunity cost rate – the rate cash could earn if invested elsewhere if this should be higher than the firm's own cost of capital.

A positive NPV means the in-house rate or opportunity cost rate has been exceeded and the project will be acceptable to management on this yardstick; and if negative, vice versa.

With IRR, the discount rate used will produce an NPV of zero, or close to zero. The resulting percentage is the actual return on the investment that can be expected from the project.

The other two appraisal methods, *Payback* and *Accounting Rate of Return* do not take into consideration the time value of money.

Payback

The payback method calculates the period of time a project takes for the future net cash flows to equal the cost of the original investment.

In the worked example above, the original investment was £500 000. This was 'paid back' by the net cash flows *before discounting* as follows:

Year 1:   £50 000 leaving £450 000 to pay back
Year 2:   £228 000 leaving £222 000 to pay back

In Year 3 the net cash flow was £324 120, so the investment was fully recouped during that year. Assuming that the cash flow occurs evenly throughout the year, the month the investment will become

fully paid back will be Month 8. This is calculated as follows:

$$\frac{£222\,000}{£324\,120} \times \frac{12}{1} = 0.68 \text{ or } 8 \text{ months}$$

So the payback for this Project is 2 years 8 months, or 2.68 years.

The payback method therefore indicates how quickly the investment costs will be recovered. A quick payback indicates a reduction in risk, because forecast cash flows become more unreliable over time. Forecasts for, say, the next four years should be more reliable than the four years that follow, and so on. Look back just a few years and note how the economy, and the business climate, has changed. Recessions, booms, inflation, deflation, fashion, new technology, government changes and so on all happen in relatively short time spans. Now imagine preparing revenues and costs for a project with an estimated ten-year life-span. It can readily be seen that an early payback eliminates some of the concerns management might have over the later cash flow projections.

Projects with early paybacks are therefore usually more attractive, and thus more likely to be invested in, than those with protracted paybacks. However, the payback method ignores completely the later cash flows, and it also ignores the NPV of the investment. These are major weaknesses of the method.

Consider the following two projects which are candidates for investment, but the firm can only invest in one of them.

	Project M	Project C
	£	£
Original cost	800 000	800 000
Net cash flows:		
Year 1	400 000	100 000
Year 2	400 000	300 000
Year 3	100 000	400 000
Year 4	50 000	500 000

Project M has a payback period of exactly two years, whereas Project C will take three years. Purely on payback criteria, Project M wins and the company would invest in Project M. But this project earns little in the following years, netting an overall gain of £150 000 in total over its four-year life. Project C, however, nets £500 000. Assuming the later year cash flows to be reasonably reliable, Project C clearly looks to be the better opportunity, bringing in an extra £350 000 over Project M.

This method thus cannot be used in isolation. But it will be one of the four criteria used for selection of investments as indicated on the capital expenditure request form. (See also *ranking of projects* later in this chapter.) It is, however, a useful deciding factor when, say, two projects have virtually the same NPVs but one has a faster payback period. The latter is normally selected.

A refinement sometimes used is the *discounted pay-back method*. This uses the discounted cash flows instead of the net cash flows as the basis for the calculations. In the earlier worked example using the 20 per cent discount factor, the discounted payback period would be:

Year 1:   £41 650 leaving £458 350 to pay back
Year 2:   £158 232 leaving £341 768
Year 3:   £187 665 leaving £112 453

During Year 4, the project investment is paid back – in that year the discounted cash flow amounted to £212 631. So, using the earlier formula, the project will be paid back in 3 years and 6 months, or 3.5 years.

The virtue of this method is that it takes into consideration the time value of money and is therefore more realistic than the basic payback method.

Accounting rate of return method

This method corresponds in certain respects to the financial measurements of return on capital employed (or return on investment) performance measures. Its purpose is to show the profit earned on the investment, expressed as a percentage of the average investment. The formula for its calculation, following CIMA official terminology, is:

$$\frac{\text{Average annual profit}}{\text{Average investment}} \times \frac{100}{1}$$

Note that it is the *average annual profits* used, not the cash flows. Depreciation thus needs to be deducted from the cash flows to arrive at the annual profits. (This is on the assumption that cash flows equate with profit before depreciation with no changes in opening and closing stock figures.)

Using the example above the cost of the asset was £800 000 and this has to be written off over four years. Assuming the company uses straight-line depreciation methods, the average profits for both projects will be as shown in Table 20.4.

The average investment in the projects is calculated as shown in Table 20.5.

As you can see from the tables, both of the above are straightforward averages. From these figures, the accounting rate of return (ARR) can now be computed, as follows:

$$\text{For Project M}: \quad \frac{£37\,500}{£300\,000} \times \frac{100}{1} = 12.5\%$$

$$\text{For Project C}: \quad \frac{£125\,000}{300\,000} \times \frac{100}{1} = 41.7\%$$

The technique may be useful for helping to evaluate the performance of competing projects when other factors are very similar, but it is not recommended as the sole criterion for selection because it ignores the time value of money and also disregards the timing of the profits: the profit average will remain the same whether profits are higher in earlier years, and lower in later years, or vice versa.

TABLE 20.4

AVERAGE PROFITS FOR BOTH PROJECTS

PROJECT M

YEAR	CASH FLOW £	DEPRECIATION £	PROFIT £
1	400 000	200 000	200 000
2	400 000	200 000	200 000
3	100 000	200 000	(100 000)
4	50 000	200 000	(150 000)
	950 000	800 000	150 000

AVERAGE PROFITS = 150 000/4 = 37 500

PROJECT C

YEAR	CASH FLOW £	DEPRECIATION £	PROFIT £
1	100 000	200 000	(100 000)
2	300 000	200 000	100 000
3	400 000	200 000	200 000
4	500 000	200 000	200 000
	1 300 000	800 000	500 000

AVERAGE PROFITS = 500 000/4 = 125 000

TABLE 20.5

AVERAGE INVESTMENT IN PROJECTS

PROJECT M AND C

YEAR	ORIGINAL COST £	ACCUMULATED DEPRECIATION £	NET BOOK VALUE £
1	800 000	200 000	600 000
2		400 000	400 000
3		600 000	200 000
4		800 000	0
			1 200 000

AVERAGE INVESTMENT = 1 200 000/4 = 300 000

Ranking of projects

Finance for investment as discussed is generally limited, with demands for cash usually far exceeding funds available. So investment appraisal methods help management decide which projects to invest in to achieve the best returns for the business. Many firms evaluate each project using all four methods outlined: NPV, IRR, discounted pay back method, and ARR. The weighting of the four in order of impor-

tance is a matter of judgement for management, but those projects with superior NPVs and IRRs will normally be chosen. The other two methods may sway the selection decision when competing projects appear to produce approximately the same time value results.

Periodic reports on capital expenditure

Once the decision has been made to invest in a particular project it will then be necessary to monitor the actual spend to ensure that the costs remain in line with projections. This is best done by including a report within the periodic management accounts and this may take the form shown in Figure 20.6.

Working through this table, the 'authorised amounts' column will provide the authorised value of each project. The 'committed to date' column will show the value of all the orders placed on suppliers up to the date of the report. The 'spend to date' column will record the actual costs incurred on each project to the date of the report (the total of this column should equal the additions figure on the balance sheet plus any balance brought forward from the previous year

FIGURE 20.6

A REPORT ON CAPITAL EXPENDITURE RETURN

CAPITAL EXPENDITURE REPORT

FOR THE MONTH OF _____

PROJECT NUMBER	PROJECT DESCRIPTION	AUTHORISED AMOUNT £	COMMITTED TO DATE £	SPEND TO DATE £	COMMITTED NOT YET SPENT £	PERCENTAGE COMPLETED

described as 'assets under construction'). The 'committed not yet spent' amount is the difference between the committed figure and the spend to date. And finally the 'percentage completed' column will indicate the degree of completion of each project.

In addition to this overall report, further detailed reports will be submitted to management on completion of each project, showing the authorised amount, the actual costs, any under- or over-spend incurred, and the reasons why these occurred, if material. (Materiality in this context may be considered to be any difference decided by the company, for example a 3 per cent variance.)

Capital results audit review (post-audit evaluation)

A review is often made of a project after it has been operating for some time, perhaps after two or three years, to measure the actual results against the original assumptions on which the investment was given the go-ahead. Actual cash flows will be calculated, also the actual NPV and IRR, payback period and ARR. These will be compared with the original request and comparisons made and commented upon.

The original narrative will also be reviewed and compared with actual performance. The object of this *audit review* is to help in identifying the strengths and weaknesses in management projections which may assist in evaluating future projects.

Post-audit evaluations can prove to be salutary, as they can act as a curb to over-enthusiastic, sometimes extremely optimistic assumptions made for favoured projects. But the main purpose of the check is to improve forecasting assumptions and to measure the effectiveness of the investment appraisal techniques.

Summary

- Capital expenditure needs to be planned carefully to ensure that limited funds available are invested in projects that will produce the best results for the business.

- To assist management in this task, investment appraisal techniques are utilised. The four most frequently used methods are: the net present value method (NPV); the internal rate of return method (IRR); the payback period method; and the accounting rate of return (ARR) method.

- The NPV and IRR methods take into consideration the time value of money; these bring future cash flows to present-day value by way of discounted cash flows (DCF). The discount factor used may be the firm's own cost of capital rate plus a provision, or the opportunity rate available if this is higher.

- Net present values can be positive or negative. A positive NPV produces a present-day value of the future cash flows which will be higher than the value of the original investment; and with a negative NPV the opposite occurs. Projects with negative NPVs are usually rejected, shelved or reassessed.

- The IRR method calculates the actual rate of return generated by the investment. It thus uses a discount factor which will produce an NPV of zero. The rate is established by trial and error and can readily be ascertained when a computer spreadsheet is used.

- The payback method calculates the length of time a project is likely to take to pay for itself, and non-discounted net cash flows are used for this. A refinement to payback is the discounted payback method, which uses the discounted cash flows for the calculation.

- The accounting rate of return (ARR) provides the percentage average return the project makes on the average capital employed over its life. This method is not recommended if used as the only basis for appraising projects.

- If there are a number of competing projects for the limited funds available, management may rank them in accordance with the results of the investment appraisal techniques, thus choosing those which are likely to produce the best financial results.

- When funds have been committed to a project it is necessary to control the resulting expenditure. Periodic reports on capital expenditure (usually as part of the management accounts package) will provide management with the details of spend to date compared to authorised amounts. On completion of the project, over- or under-spends, depending on materiality, will be investigated.

- Finally, after perhaps two or three years, the actual performance of the Project will be compared with the original assumptions and projections as part of a formal audit review. This 'hindsight accounting' technique may reveal strengths and weaknesses in management's capital expenditure planning and forecasting abilities.

Examination Questions

1 A LEVEL (ULEAC) 1990

(a)

Capital structure (£000)	Ajax	Borg
Ordinary shares (16%)	700	300
Preference shares (14%)	200	200
Debentures (12%)	100	500

(i) calculate the weighted average cost of capital for each of the companies above, on the assumption that debenture interest is an allowable expense against corporation tax, which stands at 40%; and

(ii) explain fully the reasons for any differences in the weighted average cost of capital for the two companies.

(b) Ajax and Borg both have an opportunity to invest in project Cymberline which requires an initial investment of £300 000, and which is thought will generate the following net cash flows:

	Cymberline £
Year 1	55 000
Year 2	60 000
Year 3	145 000
Year 4	170 000

(i) What is the maximum cost of financing that can be considered when investing in this project?

(ii) From the information given, state with reasons whether you would advise either of the two companies to invest in Cymberline.

Note: Assume that the cash inflow arises at the end of each year.

Present value of £1:

Period	1	2	3	4
12%	0.893	0.797	0.712	0.636
13%	0.885	0.783	0.693	0.613
14%	0.877	0.769	0.675	0.592
15%	0.870	0.756	0.658	0.572
16%	0.862	0.743	0.641	0.552

2 A-LEVEL (AEB) 1990

Ukec plc, a company of diverse interests, was considering the purchase of a factory on the European mainland in order to take advantage of the greater market opportunities that the changes in European Community regulations would bring.

The following information was available on the factories under consideration:

1.

	Factory A £m	Factory B £m	Factory C £m
Purchase cost	50	100	90
Estimated net cash inflows:			
Year 1	3	10	15
Year 2	6	15	19
Year 3	14	30	26
Year 4	16	45	40
Year 5	20	60	45

2. Factory A was still only 70% complete and it was estimated that a further £25m of capital expenditure was necessary in order to complete the factory and be ready for production in Year 1.

3. The company's estimated cost of capital is 10%.

4. The following extract is from the present value table for £1:

	10%
Year 1	0.909
Year 2	0.826
Year 3	0.751
Year 4	0.683
Year 5	0.621

5. Subsequent to the preparation of the forecast information in no. 1 above, the company's economic research department had provided the following additional information:

(i) The EC country in which Factory B was located would have to devalue their currency against the £ by 15% on 1 January, Year 4. It was estimated that the currency/volume effect on the estimated net cash inflows of Factory B would be subsequently to reduce them by 5%.

(ii) Accelerating wage inflation in the EC country where Factory C was located would probably reduce estimated net cash inflows of Factory C by the following amounts:

	£m
Year 2	2
Year 3	3
Year 4	4
Year 5	6

6. It is to be assumed that
   (i) The estimated net cash inflows arise at the end of the relevant year.
   (ii) The factory purchase plus the work necessary to finish Factory A would have been completed by the end of Year 0.

Required:

(a) A detailed table of computations using the net present value method for each of the factories being considered.

(b) A report advising the managing director of Ukec plc as to which factory should be purchased. Your report should pay particular attention to analysing thee factor of risk.

(c) A calculation of the payback period for each of the factories under consideration by Ukec plc.

(d) Compare the results obtained by using the net present value method with the results obtained by using payback.

3   A-LEVEL (AEB) 1992

Eastinteg plc, a major chemical company, had been invited to set up a plant in Eastern Europe in order to provide work in a region of high unemployment. The regional government also hoped that plant modernisation may be possible as well. Eastinteg have the choice of two alternative plants:

(i) **Plant A**   A modern complex from Japan; highly efficient but expensive. Its capital cost is £85m. Its expected annual output is:

Year 1	Year 2	Year 3	Year 4
Tons	Tons	Tons	Tons
30 000	36 000	41 500	80 000

This plant produces a high quality output and fetches the following prices on the open market.

	Year 1	Year 2	Year 3	Year 4
	£	£	£	£
Price per ton	1 000	1 100	950	1 150

(ii) **Plant B**.   This plant is manufacturing locally in Eastern Europe and is relatively unsophisticated and

inefficient. Many experts have reported that it pollutes the environment. The plant will cost £45m, but since many regional government officials were keen to have locally-provided plant, there would be a government grant for the initial capital cost of £20m. In addition, an annual subsidy would also be paid for the first 4 years, of £5m per year. This is to offset some of the plant's running costs. The expected annual output is:

Year 1	Year 2	Year 3	Year 4
Tons	Tons	Tons	Tons
26 000	28 000	27 000	60 000

The output quality of Plant B is relatively inferior to Plant A and is expected to fetch the following lower prices.

	Year	Year 2	Year 3	Year 4
	£	£	£	£
Price per ton	600	650	570	750

Additional information:

1. The forecast operating payments for the plants are as follows:

	Payments per ton of output			
	Year 1	Year 2	Year 3	Year 4
	£	£	£	£
Plant A	400	450	460	500
Plant B	450	500	500	550

2. Both plants have an expected life of 10 years, but it is known that Plant B will become even less operationally efficient after 6 years.

3. While the East European regional government is aware of the pollutive effect of Plant B, it feels that pollution is so common in the region that the additional amount caused by this plant can be ignored.

4. The company's cost of capital is 12% per annum.

5. It should be assumed that all costs are paid and all revenues received at the end of each year.

6. The following is an extract from the present value table for £1:

	11%	12%	13%	14%
Year 1	0.901	0.893	0.885	0.877
Year 2	0.812	0.797	0.783	0.769
Year 3	0.731	0.712	0.693	0.675
Year 4	0.659	0.636	0.613	0.592

Required:

(a) The forecast revenue statements for each of Years 1 to 4, and for each of the plants being considered. Show the expected yearly net cash flows.

(b) Appropriate computations using the net present value method for each of the Plants A and B, for the first four years.

4 A-LEVEL (AEB) 1993

Powerform plc, a company that generates electricity, is considering expanding its power generating capacity in order to meet the rising demand for electricity over the next decade. The following information is available on three new power stations under consideration:

1.

	Power station M £m	Power station P £m	Power station Q £m
Capital cost	45	30	35

In addition, installation costs of 10% of the relevant purchase price will have to be paid. The technical director advised that unforeseen construction difficulties will inevitably lead to higher installation costs, but he could give no firm forecast of the expected rise in these costs.

2. (i) Power station M is gas-fired and very efficient with very low atmospheric pollution, but is relatively expensive.

(ii) Power station P is a conventional coal-fired power station with relatively high atmospheric pollution.

(iii) Power station Q is a new generation coal-fired power station of a Jà sophisticated design which cuts atmospheric pollution significantly.

3. Estimated net cash inflows:

	Power station M £m	Power station P £m	Power station Q £m
Year 1	10	11	9
Year 2	12	12	10
Year 3	15	14	11
Year 4	20	17	13
Year 5	26	20	18

It is to be assumed that the net cash inflows arise at the end of the relevant year.

4. The expected life of each power station is 20 years.

5. Draft regulations from the European Community have indicated that a fuel tax will be imposed on all primary energy resources from Year 3. This would reduce estimated net cash inflows by the following amounts:

	Power station M £m	Power station P £m	Power station Q £m
Year 3	1.0	1.5	1.5
Year 4	1.5	2.5	2.5
Year 5	2.3	3.5	3.5

6. Powerform's estimated cost of capital is 10%.

7. The extract below is from the present value table for £1:

	9%	10%	12%
Year 1	0.917	0.909	0.893
Year 2	0.842	0.826	0.797
Year 3	0.772	0.751	0.712
Year 4	0.708	0.683	0.636
Year 5	0.650	0.621	0.567

8. The company expects that all work will have been completed and that the power station will be operational by the end of Year 0.

Required:

(a) A table of computations using the net present value method for each of the power stations being considered (work to 3 places of decimals).

(b) A report advising the Board of Powerform plc which power station should be purchased. Your report should include a consideration of the short-term and long-term prospects and the social aspects of the project

5 AAT (COST ACCOUNTING AND BUDGETING) 1992

Your company is considering investing in its own transport fleet. The present position is that carriage is contracted to an outside organisation. The life of the transport fleet would be five years, after which time the vehicles would have to be disposed of. The cost to your company of using the outside organisation for its carriage needs is £250 000 for this year. This cost, it is projected, will rise 10% per annum over the life of the project. The initial cost of the transport fleet would be £750 000 and it is estimated that the following costs would be incurred over the following five years:

	Drivers' Costs £	Repairs and Maintenance £	Other costs £
Year 1	33 000	8 000	130 000
Year 2	35 000	13 000	135 000
Year 3	36 000	15 000	140 000
Year 4	38 000	16 000	136 000
Year 5	40 000	18 000	142 000

Other costs include depreciation. It is projected that the fleet would be sold for £150 000 at the end of Year 5. It has been agreed to depreciate the fleet on a straight line basis. To raise funds for the project your company is proposing to raise a long-term loan at 12% interest per annum.

You are told that there is an alternative project that could be invested in, using the funds raised, which has the following projected results:

Payback = 3 years
Accounting rate of return = 30%
Net present value = £140 000

As funds are limited, investment can only be made in one project.

Note: The transport fleet would be purchased at the beginning of the project and all other expenditure would be incurred at the end of each relevant year.

Required:
(a) Prepare a table showing the net cash savings to be made by the firm over the life of the transport fleet project.
(b) Calculate the following for the transport fleet project:
  (i) payback period;
  (ii) accounting rate of return; and
  (iii) net present value.
  The discount factors for 12% are as follows:

Year 1	0.893
Year 2	0.797
Year 3	0.712
Year 4	0.636
Year 5	0.567

(c) Write a short report to the Investment Manager in your company outlining whether investment should be committed to the transport fleet or the alternative project outlined. State clearly the reasons for your decision.

6 AAT COST ACCOUNTING AND BUDGETING 1992

Your company has the option to invest in projects T and R, but finance is only available to invest in one of them.
You are given the following projected data:

	Projects	
	T	**R**
	£	**£**
Initial cost	70 000	60 000
Profits Year 1	15 000	20 000
Year 2	18 000	25 000
Year 3	20 000	50 000
Year 4	32 000	10 000
Year 5	18 000	3 000
Year 6	0	2 000

You are told:
1. All cash flows take place at the end of the year apart from the original investment in the project, which takes place at the beginning of the project.
2. Project T machinery is to be disposed of at the end of Year 5, with a scrap value of £10 000.
3. Project R machinery is to be disposed of at the end of Year 3, with a nil scrap value and replaced with new project machinery that will cost £75 000.
4. The cost of this additional machinery has been deducted in arriving at the profit projections for R for Year 3. It is projected that it will last for three years and have a nil scrap value.
5. The company's policy is to depreciate its assets on a straight-line basis.
6. The discount rate to be used by the company is 14%, and appropriate discount factors are:

Year 1	0.877
Year 2	0.769
Year 3	0.675
Year 4	0.592
Year 5	0.519
Year 6	0.456

Required:
(a) If investment was to be made in Project R, determine whether the machinery should be replaced at the end of Year 3.
(B) Calculate for projects T and R, taking into consideration your decision in (a) above:
  (i) payback period; and
  (ii) net present value;
  and advise which project should be invested in, stating your reasons.

7 AAT COST ACCOUNTING AND BUDGETING 1993

Company TH Ltd is considering investing in one of two mutually exclusive projects. Both projects would require an investment of £150 000 at the commencement of the project and the profile of returns is as follows:

	Project 1 Profit	Project 1 Cash flow	Project 2 Profit	Project 2 Cash flow
	£	**£**	**£**	**£**
Year 1	40 000	60 000	30 000	54 000
Year 2	30 000	50 000	20 000	44 000
Year 3	25 000	45 000	15 000	39 000
Year 4	35 000	55 000	25 000	49 000
Year 5			50 000	74 000

You are told that the machinery associated with Project 1 will be sold for £70 000 at the end of Year 4 and the machinery associated with Project 2 will be sold for £30 000 at the end of Year 5.

The company's cost of capital is 15%, and relevant discount rates are:

Year 1	0.869
Year 2	0.756
Year 3	0.659
Year 4	0.571
Year 5	0.497

Required:

Determine, for both projects:

(i)   payback period;

(ii) accounting rate of return; and

(iii) net present value;

and advise which project should be invested in, giving your reasons.

8   AAT COST ACCOUNTING AND BUDGETING 1993

One of the projects that a company is considering undertaking is the upgrading of a printing machine that will provide considerable cost savings. The two alternatives have the following profiles of returns:

		Ablex machine £	Combat machine £
Year 0	Original investment	90 000	100 000
Year 1	Cash savings	25 000	40 000
Year 2	Cash saving	35 000	60 000
Year 3	Cash savings	30 000	10 000
Year 4	Cash savings	40 000	30 000
	Disposal value of machine at end of Yr 4	10 000	10 000

The company's discount rate is 12% and relevant discount factors are as follows:

Year 1	0.893
Year 2	0.797
Year 3	0.712
Year 4	0.636

Required:

Calculate for both machines:

(i)   payback period;

(ii) accounting rate of return; and

(iii) Net present value.

Recommend which machine to invest in, giving the reasons for your decision clearly.

9   RSA III ACCOUNTING 1993

Your company has to purchase a new machine. The machine will cost £30 000 and is expected to last five years, at the end of which time it will be sold for £2 000. The company has insufficient cash to pay for it, so is investigating two possible methods of financing its purchase:

METHOD A   An immediate payment of £10 000 followed by five further annual payments of £6 400.

METHOD B   Sign a rental contract for five years, paying a rental of £9 000 per annum payable in advance.

Your company's cost of capital is 14% per annum.

Required:

Use the net present value method of investment appraisal to evaluate which method will be the most advantageous way for your company to obtain the machine.

Present value of £1 @ 14%.

Period	
1	0.877
2	0.769
3	0.675
4	0.592
5	0.519

10   RSA III ACCOUNTING 1994

Your company is approached by Lo-tech Ltd with an offer of a new machine to carry out an operation that is at present being carried out by an existing machine. The existing machine is manned by a semi-skilled operative who is paid £12 500 per annum and produces 5000 units a year. The new machine will produce 6000 units a year and will be manned by a skilled operative who will be paid £15 000 per annum.

Each unit produced and sold gives a contribution of £10, and there is a ready market for the extra production.

The new machine will cost £22 000 and will have a working life of 5 years, at the end of which time it will be sold for £300. Lo-tech Ltd are prepared to allow you £2000 on your existing machine if it is traded in against the new machine.

Your company's cost of capital is 12%.

Required:

(a)   Evaluate the proposal to replace the machine using the net present value method of investment appraisal.

Present value of £1 at 12%:

Period	
1	0.893
2	0.797
3	0.712
4	0.636
5	0.567

(b)   Calculate the payback period of the investment.

11   LCCI THIRD LEVEL MANAGEMENT ACCOUNTING 1991
Checkout plc are considering the immediate replacement of
one of their delivery trucks. The choice now lies between two
models, for which data are given below:

Truckall	£
Purchase price	26 000
Trade-in value (Year 6)	4 000
Annual repair costs	3 200
Overhaul cost (year 4)	2 000

Overlander	£
Purchase price	18 000
Trade-in value (Year 3)	8 000
Trade in value (Year 6)	8 000
Annual repair costs	2 800
Overhaul cost (Year 2)	600

If the Truckall model is chosen, it is planned to trade it in at the
end of Year 6. If the Overlander model is chosen, it will be
traded in at the end of Year 3 and replaced immediately with a
new Overlander.

Assume that there is no inflation, and Checkout plc will
borrow money to finance the scheme at 10%. The existing
truck that Checkout plc owns has a written-down value of
£3 500 and a possible trade-in value of £5 000.

Use within your answer the following present values for £1 at
10%:

Period	
1	0.909
2	0.826
3	0.751
4	0.683
5	0.621
6	0.564

Required:
Calculate the present values for both replacement options and
state which is better.

NON-COMPUTATIONAL, DESCRIPTIVE TYPE QUESTIONS
(**NB**:   Minutes in brackets are a guide to indicate the
approximate time your essay should take to complete).

QUESTION
A   Essential to an understanding of the investment appraisal
techniques of payback, accounting rate of return and net
present value is the role of depreciation.

Required:
Explain how you would treat depreciation in a computation
for each of the above appraisal techniques giving reasons
for your decisions.
(AAT 1993) (11 minutes)

B   You have been asked by a manager at TH Ltd why you
might need the expected disposal proceeds of the capital
investment at the end of the project for any investment
appraisal technique, as the capital investment has already
been depreciated.

Required:
Clearly answer the manager's query identifying which
investment appraisal technique, if any, utilises the disposal
proceeds of a capital investment at the end of a project.
(AAT 1993) (7 minutes)

C   Explain why Net Present Value is considered technically
superior to Payback and Accounting Rate of Return as an
investment appraisal technique even though the latter are
said to be easier to understand by management. Highlight
the strengths of the Net Present Value method and the
weaknesses of the other two methods.
(AAT 1992) (15 minutes)

D   What is meant by the terms 'discounting' and 'non-
discounting' methods of investment appraisal? Illustrate
your answer by giving an example of each type of method.
How far do estimated figures reduce the usefulness of
discounting methods of investment appraisal? How do
businesses seek to overcome these problems?
(ULEAC 1993) (35 minutes)

21
Other Control Techniques

In this chapter we shall be examining a number of other cost and management accounting techniques that are of assistance to management in controlling and planning the operations of an enterprise. Some are used to check relative performance, some to control stocks, others to assist management in forecasting, while others are used as an aid in the decision making process.

The techniques covered here are:

Ratios and key performance indicators;
Pareto distribution;
ABC stock classification;
Opportunity costs and sunk costs;
Inter-firm comparisons (uniform costing); and
Trends analysis and forecasting.

Ratios and key performance indicators

By relating one figure to another, one amount as a proportion of another, ratios provide a quick and easy-to-understand key indicator of the performance of both constituents of the ratio. The key indicator, the ratio, can be compared with ratios for earlier periods as well as budgeted ratios, thus providing management with a further control tool.

Ratios can be used to control and measure the trading operations of the business, the working capital and also the performance of assets. There are a number of ratios to do this; the most frequently used are described briefly as follows:

Profitability ratios – profit and loss account

Gross profit (GP) percentage
The calculation formula is:

$$\frac{\text{Gross profit or margin}}{\text{Sales for the period}} \times \frac{100}{1}$$

This ratio has many uses. With this one indicator management are able to ensure that the manufacturing finished product *costs* (or if a retailing or whole-saling business, the buy-in costs of finished products) are in line with *sales*. If so, the ratio will remain relatively constant irrespective of whether the sales are £10000 or £1m. However, if the ratio falls it may indicate that increased costs have not been recovered in selling prices; or there has been shrinkage, stock losses, or discounting of sales prices has taken place. If there is a multiplicity of products sold, the change in the overall gross profit percentage may be caused by a change in the mix of the sales. The GP percentage is a sensitive barometer of the relationship between the two constituent parts. When the ratio changes, the reasons why will need to be investigated. It can be used as a comparison tool for a range of products, ranking the products into low and high earners, with the former being investigated to see whether improvements can be made. It is a useful 'management by exception' tool for a company with, say, a number of outlets selling broadly the same product range. It enables management to identify readily those shops with low GPs and investigate the reasons why.

Another facility it provides is that it can be used to calculate the increase or decrease in the level of sales needed in order to achieve the same gross profit whenever management decide to reduce (or increase) selling prices, thus testing whether the change will be beneficial or otherwise.

The formula for this is:

$$\frac{\text{Old gross profit percentage}}{\text{New gross profit percentage}}$$

Example:
AB Products plan to reduce the selling price of a product by 20% in order to increase its sales and meet the threat of competition. At present they enjoy a gross profit margin of 43 per cent on the item.
Calculate the increase in sales needed so that AB will earn the same gross profit of £50 000. Present selling price per unit is £100.

Solution:

The gross profit statistic is also used by third parties: for example, the Inspector of Taxes will pay due regard to the gross profit percentage when assessing a company's profit and loss account for taxation purposes. He or she can compare an individual firm's GP percentage to the national average for a particular trade, and if there is a marked difference, seek explanations from the trader for the reasons.

Operating expenses to sales percentage
The formula is:

$$\frac{\text{Expenses (distribution, selling, administration)}}{\text{Sales for the period}} \times \frac{100}{1}$$

Each category of expense – distribution, selling, administration – will be expressed as a percentage of sales, and the result compared to the budget and earlier periods to see if there have been any significant changes. Because of the element of fixed costs in the expenses there will not be as strong a correlation to sales as is found in the gross profit percentage. But, even so, as a control measure, the expenses to sales percentage will provide an early indication as to whether various costs within each category are within acceptable parameters. In an organisation with many outlets, an average ratio can be calculated for the whole business and this may be used for comparison purposes. Those outlets that show large differences from the norm will thus be the subject of further analysis.

Net profit percentage

$$\frac{\text{Net profit (gross profit minus expenses)}}{\text{Sales for the period}} \times \frac{100}{1}$$

	Old Gross profit	New Gross profit	Check:	Old Gross profits (%)	New Gross profit (%)	Increase
			Sales units	1 163	2 174	87%
Selling price	100% – 20%	80%	Sales	£116 300 100%	£173 920 100%	
Cost	57%	57%	Costs	£ 66 300 57%	£123 920 71%	
Gross profit	43% – 20%	23%	Gross Profit	£ 50 000 43%	£ 50 000 29%	

Sales units need to increase by: $\dfrac{43}{23}$ = 87%

2174 units × £80 each = £173 920

This is the difference between the gross profit percentage and the operating expenses percentage. It is also known as the *percentage profit on turnover*; the net profit figure used is *before* any charges for interest and taxation payable.

Because of the incidence of fixed costs in the expenses, the correlation of net profit to sales is generally weaker, there being no natural linearity between the two figures. Consider the trading results of a retailing chain over a period of four years, shown in Table 21.1

You will see from the table that there is a reasonably close correlation between the gross profits each year, with all years being close to the average of 38.5 per cent. But the expenses ratio is markedly different. (Over the four-year period sales fell sharply because of a recession. But because of the incidence of high fixed costs associated with retail operations, the expenses, as a percentage of sales rose. Profits consequently fell from 8 per cent to 1.6 per cent, a drop of 80 per cent.

The net profit percentage figure, while being a key ratio, can be subject to major fluctuations and is used primarily as an indicator of general performance, to be compared to other companies in the same field of operations.

Return on capital employed (ROCE)

$$\frac{\text{Profit before interest and tax}}{\text{Average capital employed in the period}} \times \frac{100}{1}$$

This ratio shows the return (the profit) made on the amount invested during the accounting period in which the return was earned. In the above ratio, the *capital employed* (sometimes called *operations management capital employed*) comprises: Fixed assets + *Trading* net current assets (stocks, trade debtors, sundry debtors and prepayments, cash at bank and in hand and trade creditors, sundry creditors and accruals).

It will exclude any amounts payable for tax, interest payable and dividends payable. The average capital employed is usually based on the opening and closing positions, thus:

$$\frac{\text{Opening capital employed plus capital employed}}{2}$$

The return on capital employed can be likened to the interest earned on a deposit account in a building society when expressed as a percentage, for example 5 per cent or 10 per cent gross interest. The interest is the return on the investment. There is, of course, little risk of loss in depositing the money with a building society, so a better return would be expected from the business venture. The ROCE provides a comparative measure of overall management performance and effectiveness in running the business. This ratio is also known as the *primary ratio*.

The term 'operations management capital employed' is so called because it represents the areas under the control and responsibility of the management. Table 21.2 shows the same retail operation over

TABLE 21.1

TRADING RESULTS OVER A FOUR-YEAR PERIOD				
	YEAR 1	YEAR 2	YEAR 3	YEAR 4
	(%)	(%)	(%)	(%)
TURNOVER	100.0	100.0	100.0	100.0
GROSS PROFIT	38.5	38.9	38.7	38.1
EXPENSES:				
DISTRIBUTION	26.6	28.6	30.2	30.4
ADMINISTRATION	3.9	4.3	6.1	6.1
TOTAL EXPENSES	30.6	32.9	36.4	36.5
PROFIT BEFORE INTEREST AND TAX	8.0	6.0	2.4	1.6

TABLE 21.2

OPERATIONS MANAGEMENT CAPITAL				
	YEAR 1 (£000s)	YEAR 2 (£000s)	YEAR 3 (£000s)	YEAR 4 (£000s)
PROFIT BEFORE TAX AND INTEREST	8 500	6 400	3 900	3 200
OPERATIONS MANAGEMENT CAPITAL EMPLOYED	33 400	36 100	37 500	37 200
RETURN ON CAPITAL EMPLOYED	25.4%	17.7%	10.4%	8.6%

the four-year period. You will note the increase in capital employed in Year 2. This was because further shares were issued at a premium which provided management with additional funds. However, due to recession, the profits continued to drop, with a consequent reduction in the return.

It should be noted that there is another method used for calculating the ROCE: profits after interest and tax/divided by total company capital employed (capital and reserves + long-term loans).

Residual income percentage (per division or outlet)

The formula is:

$$\frac{\text{Net profit before tax minus imputed interest charge on invested capital}}{\text{Invested capital}}$$

This ratio may be used by firms with many outlets or divisions (shops, satellite factories and so on) classified as profit centres and thus accountable for their own costs and revenues. By making a charge for notional interest against each division's profits (based on the operations management capital employed in the outlet or division), Head Office management is able to arrive at a ROCE figure (here called *residual income*) for each site, for comparison purposes. This will reveal any laggards and pacemakers but may also reveal a lack of investment in some outlets compared to others. In the short term, returns could be much higher in those outlets where below-average investment has taken place, while those sites with heavier-than-normal investment (therefore considered, perhaps, to have greater potential) may take longer before the returns begin to come through.

As with all ratios and statistics, the underlying causes need to be investigated but, as a guide to problems and opportunities, the residual income percentage comparison acts as a key indicator of performance.

Sales per employee

$$\frac{\text{Sales (turnover) for the year}}{\text{Average number of employees during the year}}$$

This statistic provides management with a useful comparison of the productivity of staff over a period of time. It is expressed in money form (for example, £50 000 per employee). It can also be presented graphically based on moving averages, and also index-based so that the percentage change in the statistic can be seen readily.

The average number of employees may be calculated by taking a head count at the end of each month for the previous twelve-month period and dividing this total by twelve. (For ease of calculation, part-time staff are often counted as 'halves', thus two part-time employees will be counted as one full-time employee.) Similarly, the sales figure will be the rolling total of sales for each previous 12-month period. The graph and statistics in Figure 21.1 provide an illustration.

Profit per employee

$$\frac{\text{Profit for the year before interest and tax}}{\text{Average number of employees in the year}} = \frac{£x \text{ per}}{\text{employee}}$$

This statistic is calculated in similar fashion to the sales per employee statistic and can also be index-based.

Interest cover

$$\frac{\text{Profit before interest and tax}}{\text{All interest payable}} = x \text{ times}$$

This ratio will indicate whether the profits generated have a sufficient margin of safety ('headroom') to pay the interest on borrowings arising from short-term and/or long-term debt. It is therefore a very important indication of vulnerability or sensitivity to increases in interest rates and/or downturns in business, and acts as an early-warning system.

Example:

Profit before interest and tax	= £600 000
Total interest payable	= £ 50 000
Interest cover	= 12 times

Liquidity ratios

The next group of ratios – liquidity ratios – are designed to measure the ability of a company to meet its current liabilities when these fall due.

FIGURE 21.1

SALES PER EMPLOYEE, STATISTICS AND GRAPH

PERIOD	SALES: TOTAL OF LAST 12 PERIODS £	AVERAGE NO. OF STAFF	SALES PER EMPLOYEE £
	TARGET SALES PER EMPLOYEE £50 000		
1	7 200 000	140	51 429
2	7 228 800	140	51 634
3	7 275 715	143	50 753
4	7 286 746	144	50 602
5	7 315 893	145	50 454
6	7 345 157	147	49 967
7	7 374 537	150	49 164
8	7 404 035	152	48 711
9	7 433 652	153	48 586
10	7 463 386	154	48 464
11	7 493 240	153	48 975
12	7 523 213	155	48 537

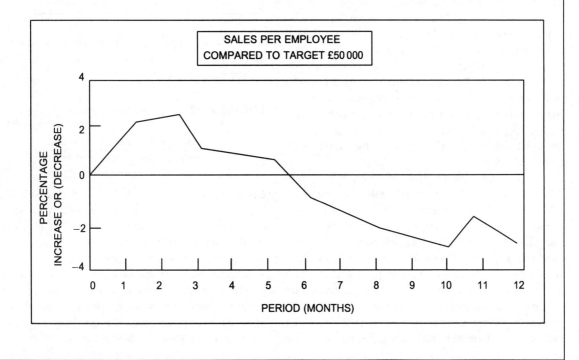

SALES PER EMPLOYEE
COMPARED TO TARGET £50 000

Current ratio

$$\frac{\text{Current assets (ca) at end of period}}{\text{Current liabilities (cl) at end of period}} = \text{ca} : \text{cl}$$

This ratio is expressed as: Current assets : Current liabilities = e.g. 2.00 : 1.00. For every £1.00 of current liabilities the company has £*x.xx* of current assets.

Example:

Current assets £15 000; Current liabilities £7900
Divide the current assets by the current liabilities to provide the current ratio, which is 1.90 : 1; £1.90 of current assets for every £1.00 of current liabilities.

So this company could comfortably meet all its current liabilities by encashing its current assets without recourse to selling fixed assets or raising additional long-term funding. This ratio is often used by banks when assessing overdraft requests; also by providers of long-term funding and by trade and other creditors to ascertain whether a company appears to be able to meet its obligations when they fall due. A low ratio, of, say, 0.50 : 1, usually means that the trader is often not in a position to meet trade creditors' settlement dates and will thus suffer continuing 'cash flow problems' until longer-term money is invested in the business, or assets sold to meet current debts.

Many commentators feel that a ratio of 2 : 1 is ideal, because it indicates that the company is trading well within its capabilities and has adequate working capital to operate the business. However, some industries (for example, food retailing) operating on a cash sales basis, but buying from suppliers on credit and perhaps not having to pay the supplier for six to eight weeks, are usually able to run their business on a ratio much lower than 2.00 : 1.

A ratio of, say, 4.00 : 1 would, however, indicate that the company is carrying surplus cash or excess stock and the cash thus tied up could be better employed elsewhere as it is not required for working capital purposes. As an internal control tool, the current ratio enables management to review and assess their working capital position on a regular basis; it will indicate when additional long-term monies are needed. In the example of another retailing operation shown in Table 21.3 you will see that the working capital, the net current assets, benefited by increasing long-term funding (in this case share capital), disposal

TABLE 21.3

ASSESSING WORKING CAPITAL POSITION		
	YEAR 2	YEAR 1
	£	£
FIXED ASSETS	14 400	16 100
CURRENT ASSETS		
STOCKS	7 700	10 800
DEBTORS	3 600	4 400
CASH AT BANK	3 900	200
	15 200	15 400
CURRENT LIABILITIES		
BANK OVERDRAFT	100	6 500
OTHER CREDITORS	7 800	7 900
	7 900	14 400
NET CURRENT ASSETS	7 300	1 000
CURRENT RATIO	2.08 : 1	1.07 : 1
TOTAL ASSETS	21 700	17 100
CAPITAL, RESERVES AND PROVISIONS:		
SHARE CAPITAL ACCOUNTS	16 300	13 000
RESERVES	4 000	3 100
PROVISIONS	1 400	1 000
	21 700	17 100

of fixed assets, and from the results of a profitable trading year. The company were thus able to double the current ratio cover in the year.

Liquid ratio – 'acid test' ratio

$$\frac{\text{'Quick' assets at end of period}}{\text{Current liabilities at end of period}}$$

Also known as the *quick ratio*, this is expressed 1.00 : 1. For every £1 of current liabilities the company has £1 of 'quick' assets, the 'quick' assets being the current assets which could be realised quickly to pay for the current liabilities in an emergency.

Imagine there is some bad publicity about a company not being able to pay its debts; perhaps *all* the trade creditors and other creditors would demand immediate payment from the company because of these rumours. Faced with these demands, the company would need to realise assets relatively quickly if they could not calm the creditors: the so-called 'quick' assets, being, for example, cash at bank and in hand, trade debtors, short term investments, other cash equivalents and so on. Stocks held are *excluded* from the calculation because they are usually considered to take some time to convert into cash or cash equivalents.

A ratio of 1.00 : 1 is considered by many to be ideal and is used by bankers and creditors to assess the ability of a firm to meet its current liabilities when they fall due. Management need to monitor the ratio each accounting period, and the route it is taking, in order to ensure that the firm can meet its obligations.

Working capital activity ratios

The next ratios examined are those that show the effectiveness of management in controlling working capital. The management of working capital is an area of great importance to any firm, because lack of control of the cash position is one of the most frequently cited reasons why businesses fail.

The following ratios are used to assist management in controlling both current assets and current liabilities and, when budgeted for, will set targets and standards of performance for achievement.

Stock ratios

There are two generally used stock ratios: *number of days stockholding*, and *stock turnover*.

Number of days stockholding ratio

$$\frac{\text{Value of stock held at end of period}}{\text{Average daily cost of sales in the period}}$$

Example:
Stock at close: £185 000
cost of sales for the period: £850 000
Average daily cost of sales: £2329 (£850 000/365)
= 79 days stockholding (£185 000/£2329)

This signifies that if sales continue at the average prevailing rate, with no replenishment of stocks, present stocks would last for 79 days. The usefulness of the statistic is evident when the current stock is compared to the budget or earlier periods, and also to competitors' average stocks. If the budget had indicated a figure, say, of 60 days, then the extra 19 days' stock held represents additional cash tied up of around £45 000 (£185,000 minus £2329 × 60). This unplanned excess will need to be funded; it will also have an adverse affect on costs, with perhaps additional bank interest to pay on an increase in an overdraft, extra insurance costs, perhaps additional storage costs, and so on, including the risks associated with carrying stocks, for example, shrinkage and damage to the stocks.

Stock turnover ratio

This can be calculated as follows:

$$\frac{365}{\text{Number of days stock held}}$$

Or:

$$\frac{\text{Annual cost of sales}}{\text{Value of stock held at end of period}}$$

In the above example, the stock turnover will be 4.6 times (365/79) or £850 000 divided by £185 000. (Conversely, the stock turnover rate can be converted into days simply by dividing 365 by the rate: 365/4.6 = 79 days.)

The number of days' stock ratio also indicates whether stock is increasing or decreasing over time. If the number of days is increasing, it may indicate that dead and slow-moving stocks are being carried, perhaps valued at cost instead of being written down to market value. It may also indicate that the stocks have been 'written up' to ensure profits are reported, although this should not happen with the many safeguards in place to avoid such 'doctoring' of the accounts.

Debtors' average collection period

$$\frac{\text{Trade debtors}}{\text{Average daily sales in the period (inclusive of VAT)}}$$

This ratio gives an indication of how long it takes, on average, for credit customers to pay their accounts.

Example:

Trade debtors: £190 000

Sales for the year inclusive of VAT: £2 114 000

Average daily sales: £5791 (£2 114 000/365)

Average collection period: 33 days (£190,000/£5,791)

This ratio will then be compared to earlier periods and budgeted targets. If the ratio has worsened it may be caused by customers paying more slowly because credit control activity has not been as effective; or the credit terms may have changed. It could also indicate potential bad debt problems. In conjunction with this 'headline'-type figure, an analysis of trade debtors will also usually be prepared, called a *trade debtors' aged analysis report*.

As an example, assume that the normal credit terms granted by a manufacturer to its customers are on a 'net monthly account' basis. Generally speaking, the number of days' credit taken would expect to average around 45 days. For instance, an invoice issued on May 1 would be expected to be paid by the customer no later than June 30. Similarly, invoices dated May 17 and May 31 would also be expected to be paid by June 30, thus averaging out at 45 days' credit.

The aged analysis identifies the slow-paying customers (and also potential bad debts), enabling management to take appropriate action to recover the debts. It also facilitates the 'holding' of any further orders from being despatched to the customer.

A typical trade debtors' aged analysis might appear as shown in Figure 21.2.

Trade creditors' average payment period

$$\frac{\text{Trade creditors}}{\text{Average daily purchases in the period}}$$
(inclusive of VAT)

Example:

Trade creditors: £87 000

Purchases for the year, inclusive of VAT: £512 000

Average daily purchases: £1403 (£512 000/365).

Average payment period: 62 days (£87 000/£1403)

This ratio shows the average time the firm takes to pay its suppliers. Marked differences from budget or past periods will be investigated to find the causes for the

change. Most computer accounting packages produce aged analysis creditor balance reports as well as those for debtors.

Companies often develop their own *key statistics* or *key performance indicators*. These are designed to assist management in assessing activity quickly and effectively. A key performance indicator may be an industry average, which enables the business to compare its own performance against others in the same business. Or it may be an internal benchmark. One such key indicator might be the orders in hand.

Orders in hand

This indicator shows the number of days' work 'in the pipeline' and can be calculated as follows:

$$\frac{\text{Sales value of orders in hand}}{\text{Average sales value of production per day}}$$

Managing the asset of stock

The next two techniques provide management with control tools to manage the asset of stock. The first, the *Pareto distribution method*, is also useful in distinguishing top products and customers.

Pareto (80/20) distribution

This technique is based on the theory that around 20 per cent of the quantity of a group of items, for example, stocks, accounts for 80 per cent of the total value of the item. This tendency, first observed by the economist Vilfredo Pareto, is useful in stock control and for identifying influential factors within the business, for example, customers and product sales. By concentrating resources and effort on the top 20 per cent, the company can make significant savings in time and costs.

To illustrate the Pareto system for the control of stocks, management will firstly identify the top 20 per cent or so of high-value products and set up strict control measures to account fully for the movement of these stocks. For the remaining 80 per cent of low-value stocks (which might account for only 20 per cent of the value of stocks) only general control over the movements will be exercised.

FIGURE 21.2

TRADE DEBTORS' AGED ANALYSIS REPORT

CUSTOMER NAME	CONTACT	TELEPHONE NUMBER	ACCOUNT NUMBER	TOTAL £	CURRENT £	30 DAYS £	60 DAYS £	90 DAYS £	ORDER £	COMMENTS
AB PLC	BRENDA	123456	A1	500	300	200				STATEMENT SENT; PHONED
GMS LTD	MAY	654321	G2	600		600				STATEMENT SENT; PHONED
EB PLC	BRIAN	132465	E7	700		400	200	100		PHONED; CHQ PROMISED FOR £300
DS PLC	RITESH	316524	D2	800	800					STATEMENT SENT
RA LTD	PAM	645312	R1	900	900					STATEMENT SENT
BRB LTD	KATRINA	564123	B3	400				400		INSTRUCTED DEBT COLLECTORS
TE LTD	IAN	432165	T8	300		300				STATEMENT SENT; PHONED
JP PLC	MATTHEW	231465	J2	200				200		INSTRUCTED DEBT COLLECTORS
DC COMPANY	CARL	532146	D3	100	100					STATEMENT SENT
PKS PLC	AVRIL	314256	P1	1 000		1 000				STATEMENT SENT
BB COMPANY	RUPERT	265413	B5	1 200				1 200		INSTRUCTED DEBT COLLECTORS
RE PLC	STEVE	461235	R2	1 300					1 300	COMPANY 'GONE AWAY' – B/DEBT?
TOTALS				8 000	2 100	2 500	200	1 900	1 300	

Thus clerical effort, computer time and costs will be saved. The technique can also be used to classify customers and suppliers. For example, a company with, say, 100 products will find that approximately 20 to 30 will account for around 80 per cent of the turnover. Similarly with customers, the top 20 per cent will again account for the bulk of the business. Thus by paying special attention to the top 20 per cent of a group, management will save time and money and be in a better position to control the whole.

ABC classification of stocks

Allied to the Pareto distribution technique is the stock control system called *ABC classification of stocks*. This method classifies the stocks by value, into high-value items, medium-value items and low-value items. The high-value items, perhaps representing the top 10 per cent in value terms are termed 'A' items and are strictly controlled because of their value; the next 20 per cent of items in value terms (the 'B' items) are also controlled, but not to the same extent as the 'A' items. This leaves the 'C' items, (practically 70 per cent of the whole) which, because of their relatively low value, may not be controlled at all, or in only a superficial manner. Clearly, if there were, say, many thousands of stock items carried, the administrative effort saved by classifying stocks in this way could be significant.

Opportunity costs and sunk costs

These two techniques assist management whenever decisions need to be taken. A decision implies choice: management can choose one option or another. So, when coming to a decision, management should have evaluated the financial opportunities lost to them by making their specific decision, the benefits which would be forgone by making that selection. These forgone benefits are called the *opportunity costs*. They will also need to take into consideration *all* the costs that are relevant to the decision. They need too to be aware of past costs which should be ignored when making the decision – the irrelevant costs. These latter costs are described as *sunk costs* – and, as such are therefore irrelevant to the new decision.

Opportunity costs

Dealing first with opportunity costs, an opportunity cost is, using CIMA terminology, *'the value of a benefit sacrificed in favour of an alternative course of action'*.

All investment decisions should have one thing in common: to make the best possible profit, or save the most cost. When coming to a decision, management need to consider the position that would have prevailed if they had chosen an alternative course, for they will have effectively sacrificed the benefit accruing from that 'second best' alternative by opting for their best choice.

Consider a straightforward position of an investment of £10 000 in a machine. Assume that the machine will make a profit contribution of £2000 per annum. The only other alternative use for the £10 000 would be for management to put the money on deposit with the bank. If the prevailing interest rate is 10 per cent p.a., the interest earned would be £1000 pa. This £1000 is the 'second best', *the opportunity cost* of the investment in the machine. It follows that management should always ensure that, when a decision is taken, the financial result will be a greater profit or a larger cost saving than any of the other alternatives available. Therefore, by considering the opportunity cost in their calculations, management will be able to see whether or not this is the case. The technique is especially useful in 'make or buy' decisions. Many manufacturing firms have the opportunity to buy in products or components instead of making the items themselves.

Example:
A company could buy in a product at a cost of £4.00; the marginal cost of their own manufacture of the item is £2.00. The demand for the item is 10 000 units per annum. On initial perusal, the buy-in price is twice as expensive, so management would, on this basis, continue to manufacture, because the extra costs of buying in would be £20 000. But there could be alternative uses for the machinery tied up in making the item: the machines could perhaps be used to produce a new product. Management therefore needs to take into consideration the profit that would accrue from this new product to be completely sure that *not* buying in the item is the right decision.

Suppose that by utilising the machine to make the new product, a profit of £25 000 would accrue. The opportunity cost of the alternative use is therefore

£25 000. This clearly exceeds the extra buying-in costs. So to manufacture the original item becomes the 'second best' alternative, because an additional profit of £5000 would ensue if they bought in the old item and produced the new item.

Consider now the situation where a firm has a small section of the factory which is empty and has not been required for production. They decide to manufacture a new product and this will entail using that space. In arriving at the costs of the new product they realise there is potential to let the space to a tenant for an annual rental of £10000. The £10000 therefore becomes an opportunity cost of the decision. If the resulting profit from the new product is less than this opportunity cost, then that is not the best alternative, it becomes the second best. Therefore the company should rent out the space.

Example:
Barker Products are holding 1000 units of Product A which has been classified as slow-moving stock. The manufacturing costs amounted to £10 000. An overseas buyer has put in a bid for the whole 1000 units and offered £11 000. Management, when considering this, find that a small modification to the product will make it more saleable generally but will cost £3 per unit. However, there would be some losses in modification, in which 10 per cent of the units would have to be scrapped at the end of the modification process, with no value attached to the scrap. But the Sales Director is confident that the modified Product A would sell quickly for £16 each.

Solution:

	Alternatives	
	Sell	Modify and sell
Sales proceeds	£11 000	£14 400 (900 units x £16)
Costs	0	£ 3 000
Net proceeds	£11 000	£11 400

The best alternative is to modify and sell for £16 per unit. The opportunity cost, the second best alternative, was to sell to the overseas buyer.

Sunk costs

You will note that only the costs and income relevant to the decision were considered in the above example: the existing cost of £10,000 was irrelevant, a sunk cost. A sunk cost is, to use CIMA terminology, '*a past cost not taken into account in decision-making*'.

A decision implies a course of action that affects the future. These actions will attract revenues and costs – future revenues and future costs. So any past costs are ignored, leaving only those future values to be considered. Past costs are described as *sunk costs* and will thus be valued at *nil* in relation to the decision.

Examples:
Spencer, Brandon and Co. have carried out market research into producing a new product. Until it is completed, management will not know whether there is a potential market or not. If not, the market research costs, having been spent, sunk, are written off to profit and loss account at the time the cost is incurred. If the research shows there will be a market, the costs incurred will still be written off to the profit and loss and not included in any subsequent cost calculations for the product. You will note that this cost resulted from an earlier (past) decision and therefore will not be relevant to the cost of the future decision.

Assume now that the same company holds special materials needed to produce a particular product, but this product has now become obsolete and is no longer produced. The materials are related solely to this one product and do not have a scrap value. With prudence in mind, management will have written off the cost of this redundant stock to the profit and loss account, to comply with SSAP 9 requirements that stocks should be valued at the lower of cost or net realisable value. In this case the realisable value was put at *nil*. By chance, a customer is found who requires a special product which can utilise this material.

In the evaluation of the special product, the original cost of the stock will be ignored: it related to the earlier decision and is therefore not a relevant cost related to this decision. If the stockholding is insufficient to complete the order and the firm needs to buy additional quantities, the extra units would be relevant to the decision and thus included in the cost.

Interfirm comparisons (uniform costing methods)

This control technique provides management with a further tool of comparison, an essential feature of cost and management accounting. Being able to compare current results and financial performance against internal benchmarks (such as budgets and standard costs), and against previous results, greatly enhances management's ability to control and plan.

In addition, costs, revenues and operational performance comparisons with other undertakings in the same industry can also be very advantageous. To this end, many trade associations collect cost and revenue data from their members, collate and classify it, and provide performance summaries for the overall industry so that each member company is able to contrast its own results with the industry's averages. As with all comparisons, the basis of the figures being compared must be the same, or similar. For example, if the comparison is 'labour costs per hour' the definition of what constitutes 'labour costs' must be clearly established so that each participant company is reporting comparable information.

If, say, half the members included payroll on-costs in their figures and the other half did not, the resultant industry average labour cost per hour would be misleading, with perhaps half the membership thinking they were overpaying their staff and the other half thinking they were underpaying. The benefits provided by interfirm comparisons have led some industries to embrace uniform accounting systems whereby *all* members of the industry use identical accounting methods and practices. This is called *uniform costing*. The CIMA definition of this is: *'the use by several undertakings of the same costing systems, i.e. the same basic costing methods, principles and techniques'*.

Imagine that a small group of independent companies get together to form a trade association and decide collectively that each member should adopt an identical cost accounting system. Assume that the companies carry out specific orders for customers and therefore use job costing techniques. Each company will use exactly the same methods of accounting for the elements of cost; the same factory overheads absorption rates; the same selling and administration percentage recovery formats; and the same selling price mark-ups or margin computations. The allocation and apportionment of costs will be the same, also the method of dealing with scrap and wastage, the method of evaluating stock, and so on.

Uniform costing methods are also used by enterprises which operate a number of factories or plants producing similar products. For example, a multinational food processor may operate factories throughout the world; each will keep its accounts in accordance with a uniform chart of accounts laid down by the parent company.

Trends analysis

This technique can be used to provide management with a 'visual aid' of actual trading results and also an indication of likely future results if underlying trends within the business continue in the short term. Trend graphs thus form a useful supplement to the periodic management accounts.

Management accounting is concerned with identifying, presenting and interpreting information for management. This applies not only to current trading activities but also to the future position of the business. Thus budgeting and preparation of standard costs are an important part of management accounting.

In addition, projections and forecasts of the likely financial position for the following few weeks or months are also of great importance to management, to give them an indication of where the company is heading. Many companies therefore prepare forecasts as a regular part of their management accounting routines.

Forecasts can be made by management subjectively or with complex mathematical models. They can also be made by careful analysis of trends within the business and the extrapolation of these trends into the near future. Consider the sales position over seven periods and the budgeted sales for the whole year as shown in Table 21.4.

You can see from the table that sales are behind budget cumulatively, but broadly in line with the previous year. With five months to go, are the budgeted sales likely to be achieved for the whole year? From the table, it appears unlikely that the figure of £16 547 000 will be achieved, but it perhaps might be around the previous year's total of £15 759 000. If this were the case, there would be a shortfall in sales of almost £800 000, with correspondingly lower profits. Here, management may consider that, at Period 7, they are just £500 000 off budget, so might consider that, with an extra push, they could get back into line over the remaining five months. But what the figures do not reveal is the underlying trend in the sales. The

TABLE 21.4

PERIOD SALES AND CUMULATIVE SALES

| | PERIOD SALES | | | CUMULATIVE SALES | | |
| | ACTUAL | BUDGET | PREVIOUS YEAR | ACTUAL | BUDGET | PREVIOUS YEAR |
PERIOD	£000s	£000s	£000s	£000s	£000s	£000s
1	1 071	1 113	1 060	1 071	1 113	1 060
2	1 178	1 224	1 166	2 249	2 337	2 226
3	1 285	1 336	1 272	3 534	3 673	3 498
4	1 392	1 447	1 378	4 926	5 120	4 876
5	1 454	1 558	1 484	6 380	6 678	6 360
6	1 558	1 669	1 590	7 938	8 347	7 950
7	**1 544**	**1 654**	**1 575**	**9 482**	**10 001**	**9 525**
8		1 543	1 470		11 544	10 995
9		1 433	1 365		12 977	12 360
10		1 298	1 236		14 275	13 596
11		1 190	1 133		15 465	14 729
12		1 082	1 030		16 547	15 759
	9 482	16 547	15 759			

clues to what is going on remain hidden and unclear, and can easily be overlooked. A study of the underlying trends assists in clarifying the position.

Figures on their own do not always relate the message clearly. Many people are able to relate more effectively to the visual presentation of information provided by graphs and charts. One form of graphical presentation to help see the trends is the use of 'trend graphs'. These show the underlying movements in the figures and can be used, through extrapolation techniques, to forecast the position likely to arise in the short to medium term.

Generally, there is a tendency for trends to continue until something happens to change them. To take an extreme for the example, the current trend in the number of people getting married appears to be on a downward slope. But this might stop (and could reverse sharply), if the government decided to make a large, one-off payment, in cash, to each couple on their wedding day.

A change in course can clearly be seen to occur when new management is appointed with 'new brooms sweeping clean', perhaps altering systems and methods, and thereby altering the existing trends within the business.

Therefore, by measuring trends in the business, management will be provided with an additional control and forecasting tool. Trends are measured as below.

Calculating trends

A trend within a set of figures can be computed by using the technique of *moving annual totals (MATs)*. The MAT (or *rolling average* or *moving average*, as it is also sometimes called) assumes that, at the end of each accounting period, a full year has elapsed; so each period end effectively becomes a 'year end'. The February period end MAT, for example, will represent the 12 periods from March through to the end of February; the June MAT will be the 12 periods from July through to the end of June, and so on. Using the example above, the MATs through to Period 7 will be as shown in Table 21.5.

Through the use of computer spreadsheets the calculations are very much easier to do, as follows. In a separate column adjacent to the data use the @sum command (e.g. @sum(A1..A12)) to add the first 12 figures (here periods 1 to 12). This provides the Period 12 MAT for the previous year (which, of

TABLE 21.5

MOVING ANNUAL TABLES (MATs)					
SALES				**MOVING ANNUAL TOTALS**	
		ACTUAL	*BUDGET*	*ACTUAL*	*BUDGET*
	PERIOD	*£000s*	*£000s*	*£000s*	*£000s*
PREVIOUS YEAR	1	1060			
	2	1166			
	3	1272			
	4	1378			
	5	1484			
	6	1590			
	7	**1575**			
	8	1470			
	9	1365			
	10	1236			
	11	1133			
	12	1030		15759	15759
CURRENT YEAR	1	1071	1113	15770	15812
	2	1178	1224	15782	15870
	3	1285	1336	15795	15934
	4	1392	1447	15809	16003
	5	1454	1558	15779	16077
	6	1558	1669	15747	16156
	7	**1544**	**1654**	15716	16235
	8		1543		16308
	9		1433		16376
	10		1298		16438
	11		1190		16495
	12		1082		16547

course, equates to that year's actual reported results). Copy this format down to the Period 1 cell for the current year and then, by anchoring the format, copy this formula down to all the other period cells for which MATs are required. This provides a *time series* of MATs. These can then be plotted on to a graph to reveal the trends in the figures.

With regard to the budget MATs: here the previous year's actual sales will be used for the budget Period 12 MAT; for each current year period, add the period's budgeted sales and deduct the previous year's period actual sales. So, for Period 1 in the current year, the figure of £15 812 was arrived at as follows:

$$£15\,759 + 1113 - 1060 = £15\,812$$

Plotting the trends

The MAT trends as indicated can be plotted on a graph using the actual MAT sales figures. Or they can be plotted using index numbers, with movements being measured as percentage changes from a base point in time.

We shall first plot the actual MAT figures together with the budgeted MAT amounts, as shown in Figure 21.3. The vertical axis (y-axis) records values, the horizontal axis (x-axis) the accounting periods. Plotting the figures, a discernable trend is apparent; something happened in Period 4 to change the course of the trend. There must have been a cause for this and the reasons should be investigated by management. It may be that a new competitor came on to the scene,

FIGURE 21.3

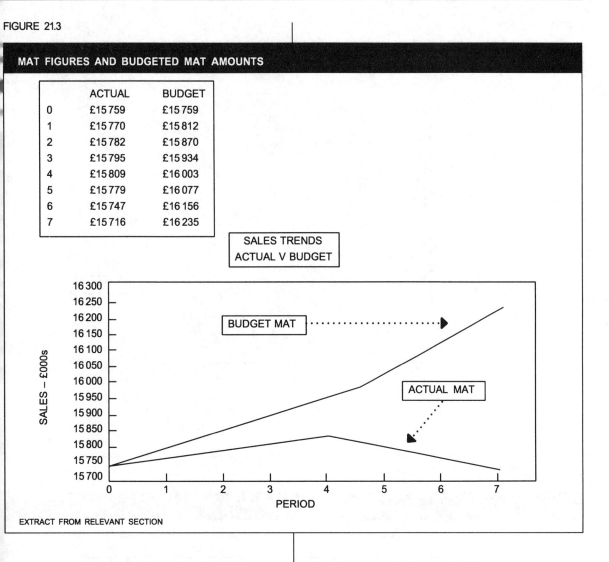

MAT FIGURES AND BUDGETED MAT AMOUNTS

	ACTUAL	BUDGET
0	£15 759	£15 759
1	£15 770	£15 812
2	£15 782	£15 870
3	£15 795	£15 934
4	£15 809	£16 003
5	£15 779	£16 077
6	£15 747	£16 156
7	£15 716	£16 235

SALES TRENDS
ACTUAL V BUDGET

BUDGET MAT

ACTUAL MAT

SALES – £000s

16 300
16 250
16 200
16 150
16 100
16 050
16 000
15 950
15 900
15 850
15 800
15 750
15 700

0 1 2 3 4 5 6 7
PERIOD

EXTRACT FROM RELEVANT SECTION

or perhaps the top sales representative left. Whatever the cause, management should use the knowledge for the purpose of improving future performance.

Plotting the trends using a base year

This type of graph will present the MATs for each period as a percentage increase or decrease over an earlier period's MAT. By taking the previous year's figures as the base the graph for the current year appears as shown in Figure 21.4.

You will notice that the pattern to Period 7 is obviously the same as in the figures graph. But here the percentage movements from the base year can readily be ascertained. The trend in actual sales was slightly up in the first four periods, but from that point they slid back, to below the sales achieved in last year. In contrast, the budgeted sales show a steady expectation of increases. The change to a worsening trend from Period 4 can be seen clearly, but with this graph the reality of falling sales, and the problematical task of recapturing lost ground (to budgeted expectations) comes across more clearly.

As a key task of management accounting is to present information, the chart in Figure 21.4 thus supports the periodic Management Accounts figures, which may be reported as shown in Figure 21.5.

You will notice that the chart in Figure 21.4 provides more information than just the figures on their own, thus assisting management to be more effective.

FIGURE 21.4

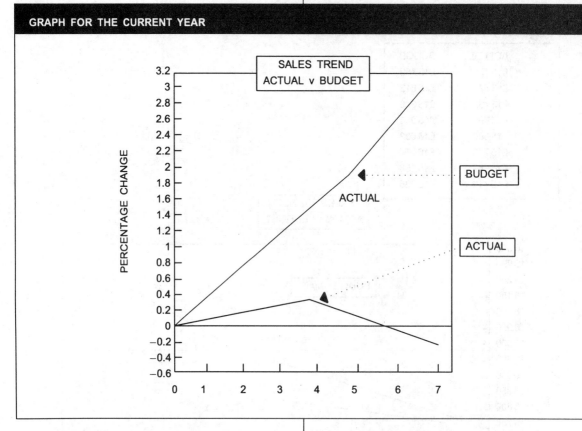

GRAPH FOR THE CURRENT YEAR

FIGURE 21.5

PERIODIC MANAGEMENT ACCOUNT FIGURES

	PERIOD 7			CUMULATIVE TO PERIOD 7		
	ACTUAL *000s*	*BUDGET* *000s*	*LAST YEAR* *000s*	*ACTUAL* *000s*	*BUDGET* *000s*	*LAST YEAR* *000s*
SALES	1 544	1 654	1 575	9 482	10 001	9 525

Extrapolation of the trend line

By straightforward observation of the revealed trends in the graph, a broad estimate could be made of the trading position likely to prevail at the end of the financial year. This is known as extrapolation – a projection or estimation into the future based on known tendencies. In the above example, it looks likely that the trend line will continue to decline, unless something happens to change its direction, with a rough estimate indicating that results for the year will be below those of the previous year, perhaps by around 1 or 2 per cent. Thus, with the previous year's sales being £15 759 000, a reduction of 2 per cent or thereabouts signifies that sales for the current year will be in the order of £15 400 000 - a million off the budgeted target of £16 547 000. The trend graph thus affords management a certain amount of time in which to take some action to try to correct the position, to try to change the course of the trend.

The extrapolation can also be performed using a method called *regression least squares analysis* to find

FIGURE 21.6

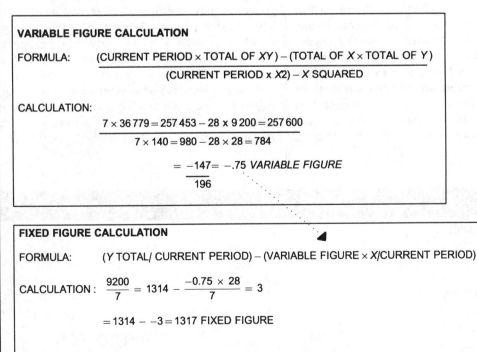

CALCULATION TABLE FOR FIXED AND VARIABLE FIGURES

CALCULATION TABLE

PERIOD	MAT	SALES MAT (DIVIDE BY 12)		
X		Y	XY	X²
1	15 770	1 314.2	1 314.2	1
2	15 782	1 315.2	2 630.3	4
3	15 795	1 316.3	3 948.8	9
4	15 809	1 317.4	5 269.7	16
5	15 779	1 314.9	6 574.6	25
6	15 747	1 312.3	7 873.5	36
7	15 716	1 309.7	9 167.7	49
28		9 200.00	36 779.0	140

VARIABLE FIGURE CALCULATION

FORMULA:
$$\frac{(\text{CURRENT PERIOD} \times \text{TOTAL OF } XY) - (\text{TOTAL OF } X \times \text{TOTAL OF } Y)}{(\text{CURRENT PERIOD} \times X2) - X \text{ SQUARED}}$$

CALCULATION:
$$\frac{7 \times 36\,779 = 257\,453 - 28 \times 9\,200 = 257\,600}{7 \times 140 = 980 - 28 \times 28 = 784}$$

$$= \frac{-147}{196} = -.75 \text{ VARIABLE FIGURE}$$

FIXED FIGURE CALCULATION

FORMULA: (Y TOTAL/ CURRENT PERIOD) – (VARIABLE FIGURE × X/CURRENT PERIOD)

CALCULATION: $\dfrac{9200}{7} = 1314 - \dfrac{-0.75 \times 28}{7} = 3$

$= 1314 - -3 = 1317$ FIXED FIGURE

the 'line of best fit'. This takes the data and finds a 'straight line' through it, this line then being carried through to arrive at the year end figure. The method works by finding a 'fixed' opening figure within the data and also a 'variable' figure. The fixed figure will then be supplemented each period with the variable figure (which can, of course, be a plus or minus amount). For example, the fixed figure may be *1000* and a plus variable figure *15*. So for Period 9, say, the point on the graph will be 1135 (1000 + 9 × 15). The straight line will then be drawn from the opening figure through this point and forecast results can then be read off from the line for any future period (but usually restricted to the current year end position).

Finding the line of best fit

Separate calculations are needed to find the fixed figure and the variable figure, with the calculation table shown in Figure 21.6 being used to find both.

Working briefly through Figure 21.6, in the *X* column list the periods, and add these together to provide a total for the *X* column. Next, in the *Y* column, plot the MATs for each of the figures, dividing by 12 (to make the calculations smaller). This column is also totalled.

The figures in the *XY* column are the product of multiplying columns *X* and *Y*; total this column too. Finally, column X^2 is calculated by squaring the figures in column *X*. Column X^2 should also be totalled.

The variable figure is the first to be calculated. (This is because it forms part of the calculation for the fixed figure computations.) You will note that this is a minus figure because the trend over the whole period is down. If sales had been climbing,

the variable figure would have been positive. To use the information on the chart it will be necessary to multiply by 12 to get back to the MAT. So the fixed figure becomes £15 804 (12 × £1317) and the variable figure is −9 (−0.75 × 12).

The computations can be completed more quickly by using a computer spreadsheet which provides a regression calculation facility. Using Lotus 1-2-3 as an example, with the REGRESSION function, select the *X* range in the table (for the periods to be covered); then select the *Y* range (which will be the *Y* column above, the MAT). Then decide where you want the fixed and variable information to appear on the spreadsheet – the output range. Then simply press GO. The program will produce the information shown in Figure 21.7. You will see that the fixed figure is designated as *constant* and the variable figure is designated *X coefficient*. The small differences compared to the manual model are due to percentage roundings.

The trend graph shown in Figure 21.8, using the line of best fit, indicates the likely year end position for the example. The line of best fit indicates that sales will continue to fall, to about 99.4 per cent of the previous year's actual sales, say £15 600 000. It should be remembered that the line of best fit result is a guideline of what the position *could* be if the present trends continue. But management often have the ability to change trends. This type of graph therefore provides a useful 'early warning', giving them valuable time to plan alternatives to achieve or get close to their original aims.

Trend graphs can also be completed for every major segment of the profit and loss account (sales, cost of sales, expenses, staff position and so on), as well as working capital areas such as debtors.

FIGURE 21.7

REGRESSION OUTPUT OF COMPUTER CALCULATION (LOTUS 1-2-3)		
REGRESSION OUTPUT		
CONSTANT	1317.214	FIXED FIGURE
STD ERR OF Y EST	2.23926	
R SQUARED	0.378272	
NO. OF OBSERVATIONS	7	
DEGREES OF FREEDOM	5	
X COEFFICIENT(S)	−0.738	VARIABLE FIGURE
STD. ERR OF COEFF.	0.4232	

FIGURE 21.8

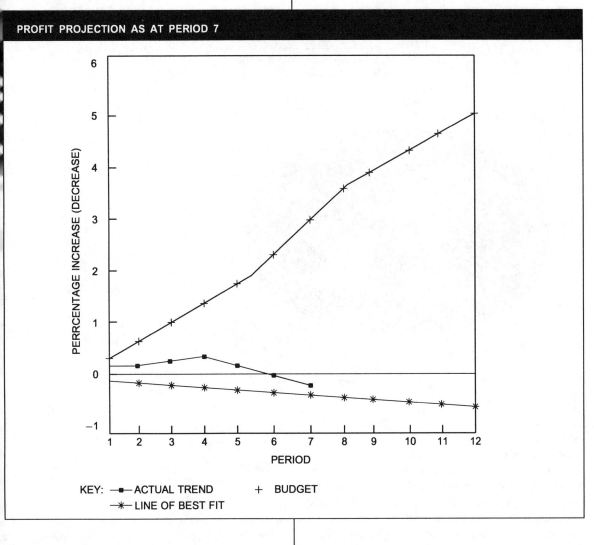

PROFIT PROJECTION AS AT PERIOD 7

KEY: —■— ACTUAL TREND   + BUDGET
     —*— LINE OF BEST FIT

Value added analysis

Another technique which is often used is *value added analysis*. Value added is defined in CIMA terminology as '*sales value less the cost of purchased materials and services. This represents the worth of an alteration in form, location or availability or a product or service*'. (Note also that it is also commonly referred to as *added value*.) Value added thus represents the internally generated costs (broadly, wages and salaries) added to the profit before tax figure.

Example:

Sales	£1 000 000
Purchases and services	£ 250 000
Wages and salaries	£ 500 000
General rates	£ 50 000
Profit before tax	£ 200 000

The value added will be £750 000 (£500 000 wages plus £50 000 general rates plus £200 000 profit).

As a control tool, value added analysis can be used to measure performance by expressing staff costs as a percentage of value added. A value added ratio can be

FIGURE 21.9

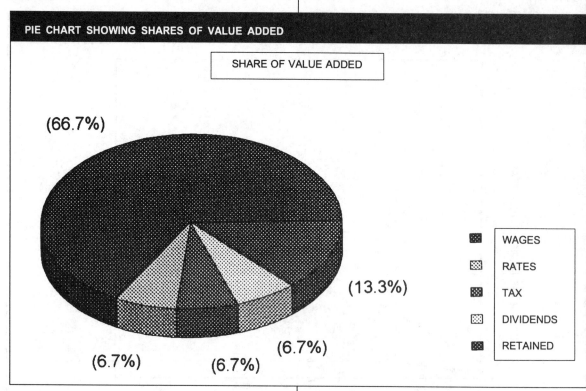

PIE CHART SHOWING SHARES OF VALUE ADDED

SHARE OF VALUE ADDED

(66.7%)

(13.3%)

(6.7%)

(6.7%)   (6.7%)

■ WAGES

▨ RATES

■ TAX

▨ DIVIDENDS

■ RETAINED

produced for each division and department's wages and salaries. In the above example, the overall ratio is 66.6 per cent (500 000/750 000). Over time, this ratio should remain relatively constant. The trend of the ratio can be plotted on a trend graph to reveal any marked changes, thus alerting management to those changes. Target value added ratios can also be set: in the above example, a target of 65 per cent might be set for the wages and salaries.

Value added can also be presented in graphical format, for example by way of a pie chart when reporting financial results. This will show how the value added in an accounting period has been 'spent'. For illustration, we shall assume that taxation on the above example's profits amounted to £50 000 and that the shareholders will receive a dividend of £50 000 (both these payments being appropriations made from the value added amount). The pie chart will appear as shown in Figure 21.9.

Summary

- In addition to the various methods of planning and control discussed in earlier chapters, there are a number of other techniques available to assist management to control the business.
- Some of these have been described and discussed in this chapter: ratios and key performance indicators; Pareto analysis and ABC stock control; opportunity costs and sunk costs analysis for decision-making; uniform cost accounting methods; trends analysis; and value added computations.
- Ratios and statistics provide control by enabling management to relate one figure to another. The major control ratios can be summarised broadly as being concerned with profitability and the management of current assets. Some of the key profitability ratios described were: the gross profit percentage,

the expenses to sales percentage, the net profit percentage and the return on capital employed (ROCE) percentage. Others are the residual income percentage, used to show the relative returns made by various locations or divisions, sales per employee and profit per employee statistics, and interest payable cover.

- The net current assets (working capital) ratios and statistics are : the current ratio (with current assets expressed as a proportion of current liabilities, e.g. £2.00 : £1.00); and the acid test ratio, which concentrates on the current assets that can be expected to be realised in a short period of time to pay for current liabilities.

- Working capital activity ratios are calculated to show the effectiveness of management in controlling the constituent parts of the net current assets. Briefly: stock levels – by the stock turnover ratio and the number of days stock held; the debtors' average collection period (known also as the debtor days ratio), which indicates the average time, in days, that credit customers take to pay their account; and by the number of days it takes to pay creditors.

- Management will also review regularly a trade debtors' aged analysis report as part of the credit control procedures. These are usually prepared monthly and identify slow payers and any doubtful/bad debts customers.

- The trade creditors' average payment period will also indicate how much time the company takes on average to pay its trade creditors, expressed in days. This measurement is also known as the creditor days ratio. Other useful ratios may be the performance of the individual firm compared to an industry average; or the value of orders on hand in a manufacturing or wholesaling operation.

- The Pareto distribution (80/20) observations indicate that broadly 80 per cent of the value of stocks is accounted for by just 20 per cent of the physical quantity of stocks. By controlling the stock with high values strictly, representing approximately 20 per cent of the stockholding, and less control on the remaining 80 per cent low-value items, management can make significant administrative savings in time and cost. Closely allied to this technique is the ABC method of stock classification, in which the top 10 per cent of the stocks in value terms are controlled strictly, the next 20 per cent less

so, and the remaining 70 per cent perhaps not controlled at all.

- When deciding which course of action to take, management needs to consider all the options that are open to them. When these options are evaluated and ranked, the two best alternatives will be revealed. The difference in value between these two best alternatives is the opportunity cost. By choosing the best of the two they will thus have sacrificed the benefit arising from the other alternative. This difference – the opportunity cost – may be added to the relevant costs attached to the favoured decision to ensure that the overall benefit is indeed greater than the rejected alternative. The technique attempts to ensure that management have considered all options and, in making their selection, have, in fact, chosen the alternative that will provide the best benefit or return for the business.

- Sunk costs relate to past decisions taken and therefore are not part of, nor relevant to, the costs and revenues arising from later decisions, therefore being ignored in decision-making.

- When a number of independent companies within the same industry adopt identical accounting methods and procedures so that comparisons of performance can be established, this is called uniform costing or uniform accounting. Large industrial concerns may also use the same chart of accounts and methods for each of their manufacturing plants, perhaps located throughout the world, to assist in comparing performance.

- Management accounting is concerned with identifying and interpreting information for management. This also covers the future short-term position of the business. An important part of management accounting is thus to provide forecasts and projections, and the analysis of trends assists in this task. Trends can be calculated by computing moving annual totals (MATs), or moving averages/rolling averages as they are also sometimes called.

- When MATs are plotted on a graph, management are able to identify the tendency (the trend) of actual figures. Graphical presentation of information can further be enhanced by basing the trend on a base year, thus measuring the percentage change, increase or decrease, from that year. Budgeted MATs can be shown on the same graph.

- By using the technique of regression analysis, a line of best fit trend can be extrapolated to indicate the likely year end position if current trends continue. Extrapolations can be completed for all segments of the profit and loss account and also for working capital control purposes.
- Value added techniques identify the difference between sales and the total of purchases and bought-in items and services. Value added reflects the amount a company 'adds' to this figure to cover wages and salaries, general rates and taxes, and for the profit to arrive at the sale price: The wages and salaries component can be expressed as a percentage of value added for control purposes. The technique is also useful to explain how each £1 of value added is accounted for and this information is often presented in the form of a pie chart.

Examination Questions

1 A-LEVEL (ULEAC) 1991

A company decides to introduce a bonus system whereby the employees receive as a bonus a constant proportion of the added value for the year. It is agreed that the average figure for added value and earnings over Years 1, 2 and 3 is to be used as the basis for the calculation. It is also agreed that the bonus is to be shared out on the basis of 2% of added value, and is to be payable whenever the base ratio (earnings:added value) is reduced – no matter how small the reduction might be.

	Year 1	Year 2	Year 3	Year 4
	£	£	£	£
Direct labour	220 300	233 500	239 200	251 400
Production overheads	54 100	63 300	67 400	61 300
Gross profit	13 600	15 200	17 400	21 700

Calculate:
(i) the amount of added value in each of the three base years;
(ii) the base ratio of earnings to added value;
(iii) the ratio of earnings to added value during Year 4; and
(iv) the amount of bonus payable in Year 4 (if any). If no bonus is payable, state the reasons why.

2 A-LEVEL (ULEAC) 1991

The management of Trends Ltd pays particular attention to the ratios and percentages which they calculate from their annual accounts. For the year ended 31 December they have calculated the following figures, which they are comparing with those of another company, Attractive Figures Ltd, shown alongside.

	Trends Ltd	Attractive Figures Ltd
Gross profit percentage	60%	5%
Net profit percentage	20%	2%
Debtors' collection period	30 days	5 days
Working capital ratio	2 : 1	0.4 : 1
Gearing percentage	20%	70%

One of the two companies is a manufacturing company; the other is a food retailer, with an expanding number of shops.

Required:
(a) Which of the two companies is more likely to be the food retailer? Give two reasons for your choice.
(b) Assuming that the total cost of sales of Trends Ltd was £200 000 for the year, the closing cash and bank balances were £11 005, sales and purchases accrue evenly over the year, and the closing stock for the year was £40 000, calculate:
(i) the total of debtors at 31 December, assuming all sales were on credit terms; and
(ii) the total of current liabilities at 31 December.

3 A LEVEL (AEB) 1991

Bettermake Ltd has been selling household goods as a retailer for several years. On 1 January, Year 1 a decision was taken to open retail shops in Bexville and Amstead, two neighbouring towns. The following summarised information is available for the financial year ended 31 December, Year 1.

	Head office shop £000s	Bexville shop £000s	Amstead shop £000s
Sales	150	30	55
Cost of goods sold	60	15	23
Gross profit	90	15	32
Variable expenses	15	12	16
Fixed expenses	28	13	10
Net profit/loss	47	−10	6

The fixed costs of the two branches consist of the following components:
(i) Head Office has allocated £6000 of its own fixed expenses to each branch.

(ii) The remaining fixed expenses are wholly attributable to the branches.

Required:

(a) Identify the contribution made by each branch to the company for the year 31 December, Year 1.

(b) Prepare a brief report for the Board of Bettermake Ltd, providing a financial analysis of the results of the whole business for the year ended 31 December, Year 1.

4 A-LEVEL (AEB) 1992

The directors of Keats & Co Ltd are faced with strong competition from similar companies and are seeking more information that may help them retain their trading position. It has been suggested that various ratios will give an indication of the performance of the company and help the directors to make vital decisions.

The following are the summarised financial statements of the company:

Trading and profit and loss accounts for the year ended:

	Year 1	Year 2
	£000s	£000s
Turnover	9 000	12 000
Less: Cost of sales	6 300	9 120
Gross profit	2 700	2 880
Less Expenses	1 700	1 820
Net profit	1 000	1 060
Less Corporation tax	560	580
Less Dividends	420	460
	40	20
Retained earnings b/f	240	280
Retained earnings c/f	280	300

Balance sheet as at 31 December

	Year 1		Year 2	
		£000s		£000s
Fixed assets at cost				
Less depreciation		9 300		10 200
Current assets				
Stock	1 560		3 020	
Debtors	1 520		2 940	
Balance at bank	640		0	
	3 720		5 960	

Less Current liabilities

	Year 1		Year 2	
Creditors	1 540		2 780	
Tax and dividends	960		1 040	
Bank overdraft	0		1 800	
	2 500		5 620	
Working capital		1 220		340
		10 520		10 540

Financed by:

	Year 1	Year 2
Share capital (fully issued and paid up)	6 000	6 000
General reserve	1 440	1 440
Profit and loss account	280	300
10% debentures	2 800	2 800
	10 520	10 540

Note: All sales are on a credit basis only.

Required:

(a) Calculate THREE liquidity and THREE profitability ratios for Years 1 and 2.

(b Comment on the company's position as revealed by these ratios.

5 AAT COST ACCOUNTING AND BUDGETING.

The Production Manager of your organisation has approached you for some costing advice on Project X, a one-off order from overseas that he intends to tender for. The costs associated with the project are as follows:

	£
Material A	4 000
Material B	8 000
Direct labour	6 000
Supervision	2 000
Overheads	12 000
	32 000

You ascertain the following:

(i) Material A is in stock and the above was the cost. There is now no other use for Material A, other than the above project, within the factory and it would cost £1750 to dispose of. Material B would have to be ordered at the cost shown above.

(ii) Direct labour costs of £6000 relate to workers that will be transferred to this project from another project. Extra labour will need to be recruited to the other project at a cost of £7000.

(iii) Supervision costs have been charged to the project on the basis of 33.33% of labour costs and will be carried out by existing staff within their normal duties.

(iv) Overheads have been charged to the project at the rate of 200% on direct labour.

(v) The company is currently operating at a point above break-even.

(vi) The project will need machinery that will have no other use to the company after the project has finished. The machinery will have to be purchased at a cost of £10 000 and then disposed of for £5250 at the end of the project.

The Production Manager tells you that the overseas customer is prepared to pay up to a maximum of £30 000 for the project and a competitor is prepared to accept the order at that price. He also informs you the minimum that he can charge is £40 000 as the above costs show £32 000 and this does not take into consideration the cost of the machine and profit to be taken on the project.

Required:

(a) Cost the project for the Production Manager, stating clearly how you have arrived at your figures and giving reasons for the exclusion of other figures.

(b) Write a report to the Production Manager, stating whether the organisation should go ahead with the tender for the project, the reasons why and the price, bearing in mind that the competitor is prepared to undertake the project for £30 000. (Note:The project should only be undertaken if it will show a profit.)

6 RSA III ACCOUNTING 1994

The following are the summarised trading and profit and loss accounts and balance sheets of two retailing concerns Alpha and Beta. Both firms deal in the same kind of goods in the same town.

Trading and profit and loss accounts for the year ended 31 May, Year 4

	Alpha £	Beta £	Alpha £	Beta £
Sales			120 000	120 000
Less cost of sales				
Opening stock	18 000	8 000		
Purchases	92 000	92 000		
	110 000	100 000		
Closing stock	24 000	12 000	86 000	88 000
Gross profit			34 000	32 000
Expenses			11 000	10 500
Net profit			23 000	21 500

Balance sheets

	Alpha £	Beta £
Fixed assets	130 000	110 000
Current assets		
Stocks	24 000	12 000
Debtors	6 200	1 500
Bank	900	6 400
	161 100	129 900
Creditors	7 100	8 900
Proprietor's capital	154 000	121 000
	161 100	129 900

Required:

Calculate the following ratios and use them to compare the performance of the two companies over the past year:

(i) current ratio;
(ii) liquid (acid test) ratio;
(iii) rate of stock turnover;
(iv) collection period for debtors (in days);
(v) net profit as a percentage of sales; and
(vi) gross profit as a percentage of sales.

7 LCCI THIRD LEVEL MANAGEMENT ACCOUNTING 1991

Your company is a member of a scheme using ratio analysis for inter-firm comparison. From last year's accounts, the following ratios were calculated:

1.	Profit/sales	37.2%
2.	Contribution/sales	55%
3.	Profit/capital employed (gross assets)	20%
4.	Margin of safety/sales	63%
5.	Fixed asset turnover ratio	0.61 times
6.	Current ratio	3 to 1
7.	Profit/shareholders funds	21%
8.	Breakeven point/sales	37%

The budgeted accounts in summary form for next year are as follows:

Profit and Loss Account

	£000s	£000s
Sales		320
Variable costs	120	
Fixed costs	80	200
Profit for year		120

Balance Sheet

	£000s	£000s
Fixed assets		810
Current assets	250	
Current liabilities	50	200
Financed by:		
Ordinary shares		760
		(last year £560 000)
Profit and Loss Account		250
		1010

Required:

(a) Calculate the ratios using the budgeted accounts.
(b) Compare the ratios you have calculated with those for last year and explain any changes. (You may make any assumptions necessary but state clearly what they are.)

8 LCCI THIRD LEVEL MANAGEMENT ACCOUNTING 1992
The following information is provided for three separate divisions of a group of companies:

	Division X	Division Y	Division Z
Sales	£180 000	£225 000	£300 000
Profit	(Qa)	£75 000	(Qc)
Investment,	£90 000	(Qb)	£150 000
Return on investment			
(ROI)	15.0%	10.0%	20.0%
Interest rate	10.0%	(Qe)	(Qf)
Residual income (RI)	(Qd)	£15 000	£ 0

Required:
Calculate the six missing figures: Qa, Qb, Qc, Qd, Qe, Qf.

9 ACCA COST AND MANAGEMENT ACCOUNTING 1 1993
Company A expects to have 2000 direct labour hours of manufacturing capacity (in normal times) available over the next two months after completion of current regular orders. It is considering two options in order to utilise the spare capacity. If the available hours are not utilised, direct labour costs would not be incurred.

The first option involves the early manufacture of a firm future order which would as a result reduce the currently anticipated need for overtime working in a few months' time. The premium for overtime working is 30% of the basic rate of £4.00 per hour, and is charged to production as a direct labour cost. Overheads are charged at £6.00 per direct labour hour. 40% of overhead costs are variable with hours worked.

Alternatively, Company A has just been asked to quote for a one-off job to be completed over the next two months and which would require the following resources:

Raw materials:
1. (i) 960 kg of Material X, which has a current weighted average cost in stock of £3.02 per kg and a replacement cost of £3.10 per kg. Material X is used continuously by Company A.
   (ii) 570 kg of Material Y, which is in stock at £5.25 per kg. It has a current replacement cost of £5.85 per kg. If used, Material Y would not be replaced. It has no other anticipated use, other than disposal for £2.30 per kg.
   (iii) Other materials costing £3360.
2. Direct labour: 2200 hours.

Required:
Establish the minimum quote that could be tendered for the one-off job such that it would increase Company A's profit, compared with the alternative use of spare capacity. (Ignore the interest cost/benefit associated with the different timing of cash flows from the different options.)

10 CIMA COSTING 1990
The directors of a family-owned retail department store were shocked to receive the following profit statement for the year ended 31 January:

	£000s	£000s	£000s
Sales		5 000	
Less cost of sales		3 398	1 602
Wages – Departments	357		
– Office	70		
– Restaurant	26	453	
Delivery costs		200	
Departmental expenses		116	
Salaries			
– Directors and management		100	
Directors' fees		20	
Sales promotion and advertising		120	
Store capacity costs,			
i.e. rent, rates, energy		488	
Interest on bank overdraft		20	
Discounts allowed		25	
Bad debts		15	
Miscellaneous expenses	75	1 632	
Net loss		(30)	

Management accounting has not been employed but the following breakdown has been extracted from the financial records:

	Ladies' wear £000s	Men's wear £000s	General £000s	Toys £000s	Restaurants £000s
Sales	800	400	2 200	1 400	200
Purchases	506	220	1 290	1 276	167
Opening stock	90	70	200	100	5
Closing stock	100	50	170	200	6
Wages	96	47	155	59	26
Departmental expenses	38	13	35	20	10
Sales promotion and advertising	10	5	30	75	–
Floor space occupied	20.0%	15.0%	20.0%	35.0%	10.0%

The directors are considering two separate proposals which are independent of each other:

1. Closing the Toy Department.
2. Reducing selling prices on Ladies' Wear and Men's Wear by 5% in the hope of boosting sales.

Required:

(a) To present the information for the year ended 31 January in a more meaningful way to aid decision-making. Include any statistics or indicators of performance that you consider to be useful.
(b) To show and explain the change in profit for a full year if the Toy Department were closed and if all other costs remain the same.
(c) To show for the Ladies' Wear and Men's Wear Departments, if selling prices are reduced by 5% and unit costs remain the same:
  (i) the increase in sales value (to the nearest thousand pounds) that would be required for a full year to maintain the gross profits, in £s, earned by each of these departments; and
  (ii) the increase in (i) above expressed as a percentage of the sales for each department to 31 January.
(d) To state your views on both the proposals being considered by the directors and recommend any alternative action you think appropriate.

11   UNIVERSITY OF GREENWICH YEAR 1 BA
ACCOUNTANCY AND FINANCE (1992)
Robinson Ltd is a small engineering company. It has been asked to tender for a job X123, which is outside normal activities. Since there is surplus capacity, Jim and Paul, the Directors, are keen to quote as low a price as possible. Paul has conducted a survey on this and come up with the following cost:

JOB X123 ESTIMATION

	£
Direct materials	
A: 2000 units at £25 per unit	50 000
B: 200 units at £10 per unit	2 000
C: 50 units at £250 per unit	12 500
Direct labour	
Skilled: 700 hours at £3.50 per hour	2 450
Unskilled: 1500 hours at £2.00 per hour	3 000
Overheads	
Machining department: 400 hours at £20.00 per hour	8 000
Finishing department: 200 hours at £25.00 per hour	5 000
Survey costs	
100 hours at £5.00 per hour	500
Travelling expenses	550
Planning department	
300 hours at £5.00 per hour	1 500
Total	85 500

Jim feels an even lower cost may be obtained. He has asked you as the company's Management Accountant to give an alternative cost. The following information is given:

  Material A: This is regularly required by the business. The original cost was £25 per unit, but the current cost is £20 per unit. There are currently 3000 units in stock.
  Material B: There are 4000 units in stock. The original cost was £10 per unit. B can either be sold for £18 or it can be used as a substitute for Material X, which costs £20 per unit. B's current cost is £24 per unit.
  Material C: This has to be purchased specifically for the project.
  Labour: The workforce is employed on a yearly contract basis. The policy of the company is to make no redundancies. The labour costs included in the cost estimate above are for the mix of labour ideally required for the job. It is likely, however, that skilled staff will perform the full 2200 hours required, since the company has 10 000 hours of skilled labour idle.
  Finishing Department: These facilities are frequently hired out at a charge of £25 per hour.
  Machining Department: This department uses a transfer price of £20 per hour for charging out machine processing time to other departments. This charge is calculated as follows:

	£
Variable cost	8
Fixed cost	9
Department profit	3
Total	20

Survey costs: These costs were incurred in establishing the original cost of the project.

Planning Department: This rate is decided arbitrarily and bears no relation to project X123. It is used to cover other company expenses.

Required:

Restate the cost by using the relevant cost approach. Make any assumptions you deem to be necessary and justify each figure you give and exclude.

NON-COMPUTATIONAL, DESCRIPTIVE TYPE QUESTIONS
(**NB** Minutes in brackets are a guide to indicate the approximate time your essay should take to complete).

A Discuss how opportunity costs assist management in decision making.
   (Univ. Year 1) (10 minutes)

B Explain, and provide illustrations of, the following terms:
   (i)   sunk costs;
   (ii) opportunity cost; and
   (iii) incremental cost.
   (ACCA 1993) (15 minutes)

C Make two brief comments on inter-firm comparison schemes that reflect advantages or disadvantages to participants.
   (LCCI 1991) (4 minutes)

Part IV
Management Accounts

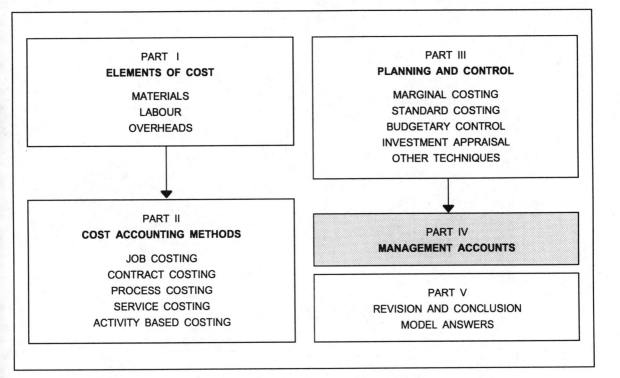

PART I
ELEMENTS OF COST

MATERIALS
LABOUR
OVERHEADS

PART III
PLANNING AND CONTROL

MARGINAL COSTING
STANDARD COSTING
BUDGETARY CONTROL
INVESTMENT APPRAISAL
OTHER TECHNIQUES

PART II
COST ACCOUNTING METHODS

JOB COSTING
CONTRACT COSTING
PROCESS COSTING
SERVICE COSTING
ACTIVITY BASED COSTING

PART IV
MANAGEMENT ACCOUNTS

PART V
REVISION AND CONCLUSION
MODEL ANSWERS

22

Management Accounts for a Manufacturing Company

For limited companies, it is a statutory obligation to prepare *financial statements* each year. The style of the statements (often referred to as *financial reports*), is laid down in accordance with the Companies Act 1985, with the content of the reports rigidly structured. Their main purpose is to inform shareholders and other interested third parties of the trading results for the particular year, together with the values of assets and liabilities as at the date the statements were drawn up. The statements comprise the profit and loss account, the balance sheet and the cash flow statement. Additional information is also contained in the notes to the accounts to support the statements.

However, for management control and planning purposes, their use is limited, as they deal solely with past events, and the detail management need for controlling the day-to-day operations of the business is lacking.

Management accounts, on the other hand, are usually designed to maximise information in order to provide management with the tools to plan and control. The style and content of management accounts (which are usually produced on a calendar month or 4/5-week periodic basis), is dependent on the requirements of management and, to a certain extent, on imagination. Management accounts need to provide information for various levels of manage-

ment and therefore presentation of the data is all important. People are able to measure performance by being able to compare what they thought was going to happen (through budgets and standard costs) with what did in fact, happen; and also with what happened in the past, (for example, last year's comparative results). Management accounts enable them to do this.

A number of examples of regularly prepared reports have been included in various chapters throughout this text. Such reports, for example, staff numbers, will generally be included in the management accounts. The purpose of this chapter is to provide an illustration of a full set of management accounts which a manufacturing company would be expected to prepare on a regular monthly or 4/5-weekly basis. An example of each report is given, along with a brief explanation of the content of each.

As with all sets of documents, it is important that the user of the documentation is able to find his/her way around them so as to locate the information they need relatively quickly and without inconvenience. The first page of a set of management accounts should therefore be the *index* page. The index for this set is as shown in Table 22.1.

Thirty pages of information to help management plan and control. Many firms produce more information than this, many probably much less. But, as

TABLE 22.1

MANAGEMENT ACCOUNTS INDEX (MANUFACTURING COMPANY)

A MANUFACTURING COMPANY
MANAGEMENT ACCOUNTS
PERIOD 7, ENDING 31 JULY
INDEX

PAGE

1	PROFIT AND LOSS ACCOUNT – FIXED BUDGET
2	PROFIT AND LOSS ACCOUNT – FLEXIBLE BUDGET
3	PROFIT AND LOSS VARIANCE REPORT – FLEXIBLE BUDGET
4	BALANCE SHEET
5	CASH FLOW STATEMENT
6	SALES ANALYSIS
7	PRODUCTION COSTS ANALYSIS
8	GROSS PROFIT ANALYSIS
9	DISTRIBUTION – WAREHOUSE COSTS ANALYSIS
10	DISTRIBUTION – PACKING AND DESPATCH COSTS ANALYSIS
11	SELLING – SELLING COSTS ANALYSIS
12	SELLING – MARKETING COSTS ANALYSIS
13	ADMINISTRATION – MANAGING DIRECTOR'S DEPT EXPENSES
14	ADMINISTRATION – ACCOUNTS DEPT EXPENSES
15	ADMINISTRATION – PERSONNEL DEPT EXPENSES
16	ADMINISTRATION – OTHER EXPENSES
17	OCCUPATION COSTS ANALYSIS
18	CAPITAL EXPENDITURE SPEND ANALYSIS
19	FIXED ASSETS ANALYSIS
20	STOCKHOLDING ANALYSIS
21	TRADE DEBTORS' AGED ANALYSIS
22	OTHER DEBTORS' ANALYSIS
23	TRADE CREDITORS' AGED ANALYSIS
24	OTHER CREDITORS' ANALYSIS
25	ANALYSIS OF ACCRUALS AND PREPAYMENTS
26	ANALYSIS OF BORROWINGS
27	KEY RATIOS AND STATISTICS
28	SALES AND PROFITABILITY TRENDS
29	WORKING CAPITAL TRENDS
30	PROFIT PROJECTIONS

'knowledge itself is power', the more details management have of their enterprise the more in control they will be.

Page 1: Profit and loss account – fixed budget

The actual results can be compared with the fixed budget and with the previous year's figures for both the current period and the year to date (cumulative figures) (see Table 22.2). Note that in the percentage columns all the figures will be related to sales. By expressing the figures to sales, management are able to compare results quickly, thus enabling them to concentrate on those areas that might be out of line with expectations. For example, if the selling costs percentage was markedly different from the budgeted percentage and also the previous year's, management would look to the analysis of those costs to find the reasons. The profit and loss account provides totals only and therefore gives an overview of the trading position, the detail being reported on other pages.

Page 2: Profit and loss account – flexible budget

This report (see Table 22.3) reworks the profit and loss figures into their behavioural context, that is variable costs and fixed costs. The fixed budget is also recalculated, using the actual number of units sold as the driver. This enables management to see whether or not the revenue and variable costs are in line with the actual units sold, as well as the extent of any fixed costs variance. Another useful attribute is that it supplies the contribution/sales percentage ratio, useful in decision-making and as the basis for calculating the break-even position and margin of safety information.

Page 3: Profit and loss account – variance report

This report reconciles the budgeted operating profit – in this case the flexible budget – with the actual operating profit, identifying where the variances have occurred. The report enables management to investigate the major variances and to ignore those which are not considered material. See Table 22.4.

Page 4: Balance sheet

The current period's figures can be compared with the budget and with the corresponding period in the previous year. In addition, comparisons can be made with the situation during the previous month. See Table 22.5.

Page 5: Cash flow statement

The cash flow statement, shown in Table 22.6, reports the movement of cash in the business. It shows the source of the receipts and how the money has been spent. The difference between the receipts and payments is the cash flow. If receipts are greater than payments, a positive cash flow for the period results. If payments are greater, a cash outflow occurs. The opening cash at bank is adjusted by the cash flow to provide the closing cash at bank figure.

There are various formats for its presentation, including the financial reporting standards format in accordance with FRS 1 (Financial Reporting Standard 1), and the sources and application of funds format in accordance with the now defunct SSAP 10. In the page 5 version the budgeted cash flows for the later periods are provided so that management are able to see the estimated bank position through to the end of the financial year. An alternative would be to forecast the future periods rather than use the budget.

Page 6: Sales analysis

This schedule (shown in Table 22.7) analyses sales by a number of routes – by product, by customer, by representative and so on. By including a column for the percentage mix, management are able to gauge the importance of the various products, customers and so on, to the whole. The 80/20 rule (Pareto distribution) will often be seen to operate. Any marked increase or decrease in the mix of any of the categories in the current period compared to budget and year-to-date

TABLE 22.2

PROFIT AND LOSS ACCOUNT, FIXED BUDGET

MANAGEMENT ACCOUNTS
PROFIT AND LOSS – FIXED BUDGET

PERIOD 7, ENDING JULY 31

	PERIOD 7						YEAR TO DATE					
	ACTUAL		BUDGET		LAST YEAR		ACTUAL		BUDGET		LAST YEAR	
	£000s	%	£000s	%	£000s	%	£000s	%	£000s	%	£000s	%
SALES		100.0%		100.0%		100.0%		100.0%		100.0%		100.0%
COST OF SALES												
GROSS PROFIT												
OPERATING COST												
DISTRIBUTION												
SELLING												
ADMINISTRATION												
OTHER (INC) EXPENSE												
TOTAL OPERATING COSTS												
OPERATING PROFIT												
INTEREST CHARGES												
PROFIT BEFORE TAX												
TAXATION PROVISION												
PROFIT AFTER TAX												

TABLE 22.3

PROFIT AND LOSS ACCOUNT, FLEXIBLE BUDGET

MANAGEMENT ACCOUNTS
PROFIT AND LOSS – FIXED BUDGET

PERIOD 7, ENDING JULY 31

PERIOD 7

	ACTUAL		FLEXED BUDGET		VARIANCE
	£000s	%	£000s	%	£000s
SALES		100.0%		100.0%	
VARIABLE COSTS					
CONTRIBUTION					
FIXED COSTS					
OPERATING PROFIT					

(ADVERSE) FAVOURABLE

YEAR TO DATE

	ACTUAL		FLEXED BUDGET		VARIANCE
	£000s	%	£000s	%	£000s
		100.0%		100.0%	

TABLE 22.4

PROFIT AND LOSS ACCOUNT, VARIANCE REPORT

MANAGEMENT ACCOUNTS   *PAGE 3*
PROFIT AND LOSS – FLEXIBLE BUDGET VARIANCE REPORT

PERIOD 7, ENDING JULY 31

	PERIOD 7	YEAR TO DATE
FAVOURABLE (ADVERSE)	£000s	£000s
BUDGETED OPERATING PROFIT		
SALES VARIANCES		
SELLING PRICE		
VARIABLE COSTS VARIANCES		
DIRECT MATERIALS PRICE:		
DIRECT MATERIALS USAGE:		
DIRECT LABOUR RATES:		
DIRECT LABOUR EFFICIENCY:		
VARIABLE OVERHEADS EXPENDITURE:		
VARIABLE OVERHEADS EFFICIENCY:		
VARIABLE SELLING COSTS:		
FIXED EXPENSES VARIANCES		
PRODUCTION FIXED OVERHEADS EXPENDITURE:		
DISTRIBUTION COSTS:		
SELLING COSTS:		
ADMINISTRATION COSTS:		
OTHER INCOME (EXPENSE):		
ACTUAL OPERATING PROFIT		

figures may alert management to opportunities and potential problems.

The total sales amount will agree with the profit and loss account sales figure. Returns from customers could also be recorded on the report to indicate the extent of these. For example, if returns for the areas covered by Rep 1 were higher than normal, the reasons for this would need to be investigated.

a whole, which are not shown in Table 22.8) will enable management to see the actual costs compared with the predetermined standard and budgeted output information. A breakdown of the production overheads will also be provided together with details of any under- or over-absorbed overheads. This latter figure will link into the profit and loss variance report.

Page 7:   Production costs analysis

The elements of cost incurred for each product (plus a summary of total production costs for the factory as

Page 8:   Gross profit analysis

The analysis of sales by the various categories will be matched to the cost of sales amounts for each category

TABLE 22.5

BALANCE SHEET AS AT 31 JULY

BALANCE SHEET AS AT 31 JULY   *PAGE 4*

CURRENT MONTH– LAST YEAR £000s		CURRENT MONTH £000s	BUDGET £000s	LAST MONTH £000s
	ASSETS			
	FIXED ASSETS			
	NBV BROUGHT FWD			
	ADDITIONS			
	DISPOSALS			
	DEPRECIATION CHARGE			
	INVESTMENTS			
	CURRENT ASSETS			
	STOCKS			
	TRADE DEBTORS			
	CASH AT BANK			
	CASH IN HAND			
	OTHER DEBTORS			
	PREPAID EXPENSES			
	CURRENT LIABILITIES			
	TRADE CREDITORS			
	BANK OVERDRAFT			
	CORPORATION TAX			
	OTHER PAYABLES			
	ACCRUED EXPENSES			
	NET CURRENT ASSETS (LIABILITIES)			
	TOTAL ASSETS			
	LONG-TERM LIABILITIES			
	NET ASSETS			
	FINANCED BY			
	SHARE CAPITAL			
	SHARE PREMIUM ACCOUNT			
	RETAINED PROFITS B/FWD			
	PROFIT AND LOSS – CURRENT YEAR			
	GENERAL RESERVE			
	REVALUATION RESERVE			
	SHAREHOLDERS' INVESTMENT:			

TABLE 22.6

CASH FLOW STATEMENT

MANAGEMENT ACCOUNTS

CASH FLOW STATEMENT

PERIOD 7, ENDING 31 JULY

	CURRENT PERIOD £000s	BUDGET £000s	YEAR TO DATE £000s	BUDGET PERIOD 8 £000s	BUDGET PERIOD 9 £000s	BUDGET PERIOD 10 £000s	BUDGET PERIOD 11 £000s	BUDGET PERIOD 12 £000s	FORECAST FOR YEAR £000s
RECEIPTS									
PAYMENTS BY CUSTOMERS									
INTEREST RECEIVABLE									
OTHER RECEIPTS									
SALES OF ASSETS									
TOTAL RECEIPTS									
PAYMENTS									
PAYMENTS TO SUPPLIERS									
PAYROLL PAYMENTS									
VAT PAYMENTS									
TAXATION PAYMENTS									
CAPITAL EXPENDITURE									
LOAN REPAYMENTS									
INTEREST CHARGES									
DIVIDENDS									
TOTAL PAYMENTS									
CASH FLOW									
OPENING CASH AT BANK									
CLOSING CASH AT BANK									

TABLE 22.7

SALES ANALYSIS

MANAGEMENT ACCOUNTS

SALES ANALYSIS

PERIOD 7, ENDING 31 JULY

	PERIOD 7						YEAR TO DATE					
	ACTUAL		BUDGET		LAST YEAR		ACTUAL		BUDGET		LAST YEAR	
	£000s	% MIX	£000s	% MIX	£000s	% MIX	£000s	% MIX	£000s	% MIX	£000s	% MIX
SALES BY PRODUCT												
PRODUCT 1												
PRODUCT 2												
PRODUCT 3												
PRODUCT 4												
		100.0		100.0		100.0		100.0		100.0		100.0
SALES BY CUSTOMER												
TOP CUSTOMER												
NEXT TOP CUSTOMER												
THEN NEXT 8 LISTED												
OTHER CUSTOMERS												
		100.0		100.0		100.0		100.0		100.0		100.0
SALES BY REPRESENTATIVE												
REP 1												
REP 2												
REP 3												
REP 4												
SALES OFFICE												
		100.0		100.0		100.0		100.0		100.0		100.0
SALES BY AREA												
HOME SALES												
EXPORT SALES												
		100.0		100.0		100.0		100.0		100.0		100.0

TABLE 22.8

PRODUCTION COSTS ANALYSIS

PRODUCTION COSTS ANALYSIS

PERIOD 7, ENDING 31 JULY

PERIOD 7

PRODUCT 1	ACTUAL COST		STANDARD COST		BUDGETED COST	
	£000s	COST PER UNIT	£000s	COST PER UNIT	£000s	COST PER UNIT
UNITS PRODUCED						
STANDARD HOURS						
COSTS						
RAW MATERIALS						
DIRECT LABOUR						
VARIABLE EXPENSES						
FIXED OVERHEAD ABSORBED						
TOTAL PRODUCTION COST						

PRODUCT 2 ETC.	ACTUAL COST		STANDARD COST		BUDGETED COST	
	£000s	COST PER UNIT	£000s	COST PER UNIT	£000s	COST PER UNIT
UNITS PRODUCED						
STANDARD HOURS						
COSTS						
RAW MATERIALS						
DIRECT LABOUR						
VARIABLE EXPENSES						
FIXED OVERHEAD ABSORBED						
TOTAL PRODUCTION COST						

	PERIOD 7		YEAR TO DATE	
VARIABLE EXPENSES ANALYSIS	ACTUAL	BUDGET	ACTUAL	BUDGET
	£000s	£000s	£000s	£000s
EQUIPMENT HIRE CHARGES				
OTHER DIRECT EXPENSE				

	PERIOD 7		YEAR TO DATE	
FIXED EXPENSES ANALYSIS	ACTUAL	BUDGET	ACTUAL	BUDGET
	£000s	£000s	£000s	£000s
RENT				
RATES				
SUPERVISORY WAGES				
HEAT AND LIGHT				
MACHINE INSURANCE				
DEPRECIATION CHARGES, ETC.				

OVERHEADS INCURRED		
OVERHEADS ABSORBED		
UNDER/OVER-ABSORBED OVERHEAD		

TABLE 22.9

GROSS PROFIT ANALYSIS

MANAGEMENT ACCOUNTS
GROSS PROFIT ANALYSIS
PERIOD 7, ENDING 31 JULY

	PERIOD 7						YEAR TO DATE					
	ACTUAL £000s	% OF SALES	BUDGET £000s	% OF SALES	LAST YEAR £000s	% OF SALES	ACTUAL £000s	% OF SALES	BUDGET £000s	% OF SALES	LAST YEAR £000s	% OF SALES
GROSS PROFIT BY PRODUCT												
PRODUCT 1												
PRODUCT 2												
PRODUCT 3												
PRODUCT 4												
GROSS PROFIT BY CUSTOMER												
TOP CUSTOMER												
NEXT TOP CUSTOMER												
THEN NEXT 8 LISTED												
OTHER CUSTOMERS												
GROSS PROFIT BY REPRESENTATIVE												
REP 1												
REP 2												
REP 3												
REP 4												
SALES OFFICE												
GROSS PROFIT BY AREA												
HOME SALES												
EXPORT SALES												

(see Table 22.9). Note that with regard to the gross profit by representative analysis, a further step can be taken by charging against the gross profits all costs directly attributable to the individual sales representatives. An example is shown in Table 22.28 on page 383 (Page 27 of the accounts – Key ratios and statistics).

Page 9:   Distribution costs – warehouse costs

Warehouse costs cover the storage of finished goods and will include any outside storage facilities used for this purpose. Frequently, the warehouse will also hold raw materials for production. A proportion of the warehouse costs will therefore be chargeable to Production Departments on an equitable basis. A variance column is also added (see Table 22.10) to show the difference between actual and budget figures so that management are able to see quickly the major variations from plan and take appropriate action on those out of line.

Page 10:   Distribution costs – packing and despatch costs

This report, shown in Table 22.11, deals with the costs of order picking in the warehouse, the cost of transporting the finished goods to the customer, the maintenance of the delivery vehicles, and the costs in general of the despatch area. An alternative for order pickers would be to treat them as warehouse staff: their costs would then be included in the warehouse costs analysis report (Page 9 of the accounts). An additional feature might be added to provide management with a key statistic. This could be the cost per picked order, as illustrated, or the cost per tonne-mile, for example.

Page 11:   Selling costs

This report, illustrated in Table 22.12, collects the selling costs and covers the activities of the field force – the 'front line' staff – as well as the supporting sales office function. Sales office staff also sell, through

telesales activities, say, or as 'house sales'. As everything is related to the task of selling, all costs will be related to the sales figure. Additionally, a contribution per sales person can also be reported and an example is given on Page 27 of the accounts (see page 383). Further performance measures can be made by comparing, say, sales office administration costs with the number of orders processed.

Page 12:   Marketing costs

The Department will be responsible for ensuring that market trends affecting the firm's products are closely monitored and also that potential markets and planned launches of new products are assessed and planned. The costs reported in Table 22.13 will be supported by detailed analyses of the various projects and research work the department has carried out.

Page 13:   Managing Director's department costs

As Chief Executive, the Managing Director is responsible for the day-to-day operations of the whole business, and the costs incurred in the performance of this duty may be considerable, because he will be involved in all activities of the firm: for example, seeing potential customers, dealing with major suppliers, deciding on strategy, liaising with other business contacts and so on. In Table 22.14 the costs of the Board of Directors have been shown but these could be reported separately.

Page 14:   Accounts Department costs

The costs of each individual section of the Department could be reported and analysed on separate statements in support of this total report. For example, a report showing the costs of maintaining the sales ledger, including the costs of collecting payments from customers, could be prepared. These costs, on being divided by, say, the number of customers, will thus provide a cost unit control measure (for example, 'sales ledger cost per customer'). See Table 22.15.

TABLE 22.10

DISTRIBUTION COSTS – WAREHOUSE COSTS

MANAGEMENT ACCOUNTS *PAGE 9*

DISTRIBUTION COSTS – WAREHOUSE COSTS

PERIOD 7, ENDING 31 JULY

	ACTUAL £000s	BUDGET £000s	LAST YEAR £000s	ACTUAL £000s	BUDGET £000s	LAST YEAR £000s
STAFF PAYROLL COSTS						
WAREHOUSE MANAGEMENT						
FORK-LIFT DRIVERS						
GENERAL WAREHOUSE						
CLERICAL						
OVERTIME PREMIUM						
DEPRECIATION CHARGES						
FORK-LIFT EXPENSES						
HEAT AND LIGHT						
HIRE OF EQUIPMENT						
INSURANCE						
MAINTENANCE, REPAIRS						
OCCUPATION COSTS						
OUTSIDE STORAGE COSTS						
STATIONERY						
TELEPHONE CHARGES						
WAREHOUSE SUPPLIES						
OTHER WAREHOUSE COSTS						
TOTAL WAREHOUSE COSTS						
LESS CHARGED TO PRODUCTION DEPARTMENT						
NET WAREHOUSE COSTS						
AS PERCENTAGE OF SALES						

TABLE 22.11

DISTRIBUTION COSTS – PACKING AND DESPATCH COSTS

MANAGEMENT ACCOUNTS   *PAGE 10*

DISTRIBUTION COSTS – PACKING AND DESPATCH COSTS

PERIOD 7, ENDING 31 JULY

	ACTUAL £000s	BUDGET £000s	LAST YEAR £000s	ACTUAL £000s	BUDGET £000s	LAST YEAR £000s
STAFF PAYROLL COSTS						
DESPATCH MANAGEMENT						
ORDER PICKERS						
DELIVERY DRIVERS						
VEHICLE MAINTENANCE STAFF						
CLERICAL STAFF						
OVERTIME PREMIUM						
DEPRECIATION CHARGES						
DRIVERS' SUBSISTENCE COSTS						
INSURANCE						
MAINTENANCE, REPAIRS						
MOBILE TELEPHONE COSTS						
OCCUPATION COSTS						
OUTSIDE STORAGE COSTS						
STATIONERY						
SUNDRY DISTRIBUTION COSTS						
TELEPHONE CHARGES						
VEHICLE FIXED COSTS						
VEHICLE RENTAL CHARGES						
VEHICLE RUNNING COSTS						
TOTAL						
AS PERCENTAGE OF SALES						
NUMBER OF ORDERS DESPATCHED						
COST PER ORDER DESPATCHED						

TABLE 22.12

SELLING COSTS

MANAGEMENT ACCOUNTS
SELLING COSTS
PERIOD 7, ENDING 31 JULY

	PERIOD						YEAR TO DATE					
	ACTUAL £000s	% OF SALES	BUDGET £000s	% OF SALES	LAST YEAR £000s	% OF SALES	ACTUAL £000s	% OF SALES	BUDGET £000s	% OF SALES	LAST YEAR £000s	% OF SALES
STAFF PAYROLL COSTS												
MANAGEMENT SALARIES												
SALES OFFICE SALARIES												
SALES REPRESENTATIVES SALARIES												
BONUSES												
ADVERTISING COSTS												
AGENCY COMMISSION												
CAR DEPRECIATION												
CAR EXPENSES												
FURNITURE DEPRECIATION												
MOBILE TELEPHONES												
OCCUPATION COSTS												
PROMOTIONAL MATERIALS												
SALES MEETINGS COSTS												
STAFF RECRUITMENT COSTS												
STATIONERY												
SUNDRY SELLING COSTS												
TELEPHONE AND FAX CHARGES												
TRAVEL AND SUBSISTENCE												
TOTAL												

TABLE 22.13

MARKETING COSTS

MANAGEMENT ACCOUNTS
MARKETING COSTS
PERIOD 7, ENDING 31 JULY

	PERIOD						YEAR TO DATE					
	ACTUAL £000s	% OF SALES	BUDGET £000s	% OF SALES	LAST YEAR £000s	% OF SALES	ACTUAL £000s	% OF SALES	BUDGET £000s	% OF SALES	LAST YEAR 000s	% OF SALES
STAFF PAYROLL COSTS:												
MANAGEMENT SALARIES												
STAFF SALARIES												
CAR DEPRECIATION												
CAR EXPENSES												
FURNITURE DEPRECIATION												
MEETING COSTS												
MOBILE TELEPHONES												
NEW PRODUCT RESEARCH												
OCCUPATION COSTS												
RESEARCH COSTS												
STAFF RECRUITMENT COSTS												
STATIONERY												
SUNDRY COSTS												
TELEPHONE AND FAX CHARGES												
TRAVEL AND SUBSISTENCE												
TOTAL												

TABLE 22.14

MANAGING DIRECTOR'S DEPARTMENT COSTS

MANAGING DIRECTOR'S DEPARTMENT COSTS   *PAGE 13*

DISTRIBUTION COSTS – PACKING AND DESPATCH COSTS

PERIOD 7, ENDING 31 JULY

	ACTUAL £000s	BUDGET £000s	LAST YEAR £000s	ACTUAL £000s	BUDGET £000s	LAST YEAR £000s
				YEAR TO DATE		
STAFF PAYROLL COSTS:						
MANAGING DIRECTOR						
PERSONAL SECRETARY						
PERSONAL ASSISTANT						
NON-EXECUTIVE DIRECTORS' FEES						
CHAIRMAN'S FEES AND EXPENSES						
ANNUAL GENERAL MEETING COSTS						
CAR DEPRECIATION						
CAR EXPENSES						
ENTERTAINING COSTS						
FURNITURE DEPRECIATION						
MEETING COSTS						
MOBILE TELEPHONES						
NON-EXECUTIVE DIRECTORS' COSTS						
OCCUPATION COSTS						
OVERSEAS TRAVEL COSTS						
STAFF RECRUITMENT COSTS						
STATIONERY						
SUNDRY COSTS						
TELEPHONE AND FAX CHARGES						
TRAVEL AND SUBSISTENCE						
TOTAL						

TABLE 22.15

ACCOUNTS DEPARTMENT COSTS

MANAGING DIRECTOR'S DEPARTMENT COSTS   *PAGE 14*

ACCOUNTS DEPARTMENT COSTS
PERIOD 7, ENDING 31 JULY

	PERIOD			YEAR TO DATE		
	ACTUAL £000s	BUDGET £000s	LAST YEAR £000s	ACTUAL £000s	BUDGET £000s	LAST YEAR £000s
STAFF PAYROLL COSTS						
MANAGEMENT SALARIES						
FINANCIAL ACCOUNTS SECTION						
COST ACCOUNTS SECTION						
MANAGEMENT ACCOUNTS SECTION						
OVERTIME PREMIUM						
AUDIT FEES						
BAD DEBTS						
CAR DEPRECIATION						
CAR EXPENSES						
COMPUTER COSTS						
DEBT COLLECTION COSTS						
FURNITURE DEPRECIATION						
MEETING COSTS						
MOBILE TELEPHONES						
OCCUPATION COSTS						
POSTAGE						
PRINTING AND PHOTOCOPYING						
STAFF RECRUITMENT COSTS						
STATIONERY						
SUNDRY COSTS						
TELEPHONE AND FAX CHARGES						
TRAVEL AND SUBSISTENCE						
TOTAL						

Page 15: Personnel Department (human resources) costs

You will note that staff training is included in Table 22.16. This will cover training for all the firm's staff and will be subjected to budgetary control. Recharges to other departments for training costs are then made, so training becomes a cost of the operating department rather than a Personnel Department cost. As the common denominator for this Department is employees, a unit of cost measurement to monitor the costs could be the 'Personnel Department cost per employee': (costs/number of employees).

Page 16: Other income and expenses

This statement (shown in Table 22.17) lists all income and expenses which cannot be identified as being specific to a particular department or function. Management may also decide to charge, or credit, any stock gains or losses and any exceptional trading costs or income that might be considered to be one-off costs.

Page 17: Occupation costs analysis

You will see from Table 22.18 that the building or premises costs are collected as one 'cost centre', then apportioned to the various departments on an equitable basis.

Page 18: Capital expenditure spend analysis

Each project will be listed and the 'spend to date' amount will agree with the 'additions' amount on the balance sheet. Any over- or under-spend arising on completed projects will be subjected to scrutiny if in excess of a specified percentage. See Table 22.19.

Page 19: Fixed assets analysis

This report (see Table 22.20) provides the analysis of the balance sheet fixed assets section. Details of dis-posals may be incorporated, being usually few in number.

Page 20: Stockholding analysis

This provides the analysis of the balance sheet stock figure and, as shown in Table 22.21, will include any provisions for slow or dead stocks. Note that the number of days' stockholding is also shown.

Page 21: Trade debtors' aged analysis

This schedule shown in Table 22.22 summarises the trade debtors' position and will be supported by a detailed aged analysis report similar to the example described in Chapter 21. Note that a provision for bad and doubtful debts is deducted to arrive at the figure reported in the balance sheet.

Page 22: Other debtors' analysis

This report, shown in Table 22.23, will list any amounts receivable other than trade debtors. An example could be staff travel loans.

Page 23: Trade creditors' aged analysis

This schedule (shown in Table 22.24) will enable management to identify any problem areas with suppliers which could affect deliveries or the provision of services. Note that key suppliers are identified on the report: the Pareto distribution observations indicate that these top suppliers will account for a large proportion of the amounts due. This report will be supported by a detailed aged analysis showing the amounts due to all creditors.

Page 24: Other creditors' analysis

This report (see Table 22.25) lists all other creditors (except trade creditors), the bank overdraft position, and corporation tax due. Examples are as indicated.

TABLE 22.16

PERSONNEL DEPARTMENT (HUMAN RESOURCES) COSTS

MANAGEMENT ACCOUNTS

PERSONNEL DEPARTMENT (HUMAN RESOURCES) DEPARTMENT COSTS

PERIOD 7, ENDING 31 JULY

	PERIOD			YEAR TO DATE		
	ACTUAL £000s	BUDGET £000s	LAST YEAR £000s	ACTUAL £000s	BUDGET £000s	LAST YEAR £000s
STAFF PAYROLL COSTS						
MANAGEMENT SALARIES						
STAFF SALARIES						
TRAINEE SALARIES						
OVERTIME PREMIUM						
CAR DEPRECIATION						
CAR EXPENSES						
COMPUTER COSTS						
DEPARTMENTAL MEETING COSTS						
FURNITURE DEPRECIATION						
MOBILE TELEPHONES						
OCCUPATION COSTS						
POSTAGE						
PRINTING AND PHOTOCOPYING						
STAFF RECRUITMENT COSTS						
STATIONERY						
SUNDRY COSTS						
TELEPHONE AND FAX CHARGES						
TRAINING COSTS						
TRAVEL AND SUBSISTENCE						
LESS RECHARGES – TRAINING						
TOTAL						
NUMBER OF EMPLOYEES						
COST PER EMPLOYEE						

TABLE 22.17

OTHER INCOME AND EXPENSES

MANAGEMENT ACCOUNTS *PAGE 16*

OTHER INCOME AND EXPENSES

PERIOD 7, ENDING 31 JULY

	PERIOD			YEAR TO DATE		
	ACTUAL £000s	BUDGET £000s	LAST YEAR £000s	ACTUAL £000s	BUDGET £000s	LAST YEAR £000s
OTHER INCOME						
DISCOUNTS RECEIVED FROM SUPPLIERS						
RENTAL INCOME						
GAINS ON SALE OF FIXED ASSETS						
INTEREST RECEIVABLE						
ROYALTY INCOME						
NON-RECURRING INCOME						
OTHER EXPENSES						
DISCOUNTS ALLOWED TO CUSTOMERS						
LEGAL FEES						
PROFESSIONAL FEES						
LOSS ON SALE OF FIXED ASSETS						
NON-RECURRING LOSSES						

Page 25: Accruals and prepayments

This report (Table 22.26) lists items payable and therefore accrued, at the date of the management accounts. It will also list the prepaid expenses which have been entered in the accounts but relate to later accounting periods.

Page 26: Analysis of borrowings

In addition to the analysis of long-term borrowings and the current short-term borrowing position, this report (see Table 22.27) will show the weighted average cost of servicing debt. This rate may then be used as a constituent of the weighted average cost of capital discount factor calculations for investment appraisal purposes.

Page 27: Key ratios and statistics

The schedule shown in Table 22.28 summarises the activities of the whole firm – production, sales, profitability and so on. Management will use these ratios as the key performance indicators to control the business, seeking explanations for variances in the

TABLE 22.18

OCCUPATION COSTS ANALYSIS

MANAGEMENT ACCOUNTS

OCCUPATION COSTS ANALYSIS

PERIOD 7, ENDING 31 JULY

	PERIOD			YEAR TO DATE		
	ACTUAL £000s	BUDGET £000s	LAST YEAR £000s	ACTUAL £000s	BUDGET £000s	LAST YEAR £000s
WAGES AND SALARIES						
MAINTENANCE STAFF						
SECURITY STAFF						
RENT						
RATES						
ELECTRICITY						
GAS						
WATER						
BUILDINGS INSURANCE						
DEPRECIATION CHARGES						
GROUNDS MAINTENANCE						
TOTAL OCCUPATION COSTS						
ALLOCATED TO FOLLOWING DEPARTMENTS						
PRODUCTION						
WAREHOUSE						
DESPATCH						
SELLING						
MARKETING						
ADMINISTRATION						

TABLE 22.19

CAPITAL EXPENDITURE SPEND ANALYSIS

MANAGEMENT ACCOUNTS

CAPITAL EXPENDITURE SPEND ANALYSIS

PERIOD 7, ENDING 31 JULY

PROJECT NUMBER	DESCRIPTION	AUTHORISED AMOUNT £000s	COMMITTED TO DATE £000s	SPEND TO DATE £000s	NOT YET SPENT £000s	% COMPLETED %	OVER (UNDER) SPENT £000s	% OVER OR (UNDER) SPENT %
PREMISES								
PLANT AND EQUIPMENT								
FIXTURES AND FITTINGS								
MOTOR VEHICLES								
TOTAL								

TABLE 22.20

FIXED ASSETS ANALYSIS

MANAGEMENT ACCOUNTS   *PAGE 19*

FIXED ASSETS ANALYSIS
PERIOD 7, ENDING 31 JULY

	PREMISES £000s	PLANT AND EQUIPMENT £000s	FIXTURES AND FITTINGS £000s	MOTOR VEHICLES £000s	TOTAL ASSETS £000s
ORIGINAL COST/REVALUATION					
BALANCE BROUGHT FORWARD					
ADDITIONS FOR YEAR					
DISPOSALS AT COST					
BALANCE CARRIED FORWARD					
ACCUMULATED DEPRECIATION					
BALANCE BROUGHT FORWARD					
DEPRECIATION ON DISPOSALS					
BALANCE CARRIED FORWARD					
NET BOOK VALUE					

detailed schedules contained in the management accounts.

Page 28: Sales and profitability trends

The three charts in Figure 22.1 show the trends expressed as a percentage change from last year's results. The reasons why the trends are downward will need to be investigated.

Page 29: Working capital trends

The purpose of the graphs seen in Figure 22.2 is to show the trends in stocks, debtors and creditors. In

TABLE 22.21

STOCKHOLDING ANALYSIS

MANAGEMENT ACCOUNTS   *PAGE 20*

STOCKHOLDING ANALYSIS

PERIOD 7, AS AT 31 JULY

	ACTUAL £000S	% MIX	BUDGET £000S	% MIX	LAST YEAR £000S	% MIX
AT STANDARD COST						
RAW MATERIALS						
MATERIAL A						
MATERIAL B						
MATERIAL C, ETC.						
ITEMS LISTED THROUGH TO						
THE TOP 80% IN VALUE						
BALANCE – REMAINING 20%						
LESS: PROVISION FOR						
SLOW AND DEAD STOCK						
TOTAL MATERIALS		100.0%		100.0%		100.0%
WORK IN PROGRESS						
PRODUCTION DEPT 1						
PRODUCTION DEPT 2						
TOTAL WORK IN PROGRESS		100.0%		100.0%		100.0%
FINISHED GOODS						
PRODUCT 1						
PRODUCT 2						
PRODUCT 3						
PRODUCT 4, ETC.						
ITEMS LISTED THROUGH TO						
THE TOP 80% IN VALUE						
BALANCE – REMAINING 20%						
LESS: PROVISION FOR						
SLOW AND DEAD STOCK						
TOTAL FINISHED GOODS		100.0%		100.0%		100.0%
TOTAL STOCKS						
		% MIX		% MIX		% MIX
SUMMARY						
RAW MATERIALS						
WORK IN PROGRESS						
FINISHED GOODS						
		100.0%		100.0%		100.0%

NUMBER OF DAYS' STOCKHOLDING			
RAW MATERIALS	DAYS	DAYS	DAYS
FINISHED GOODS	DAYS	DAYS	DAYS

TABLE 22.22

TRADE DEBTORS' AGED ANALYSIS

MANAGEMENT ACCOUNTS   *PAGE 21*

TRADE DEBTORS' AGED ANALYSIS

PERIOD 7, AS AT 31 JULY

	TOTAL £000s	CURRENT £000s	30 DAYS £000s	60 DAYS £000s	90 DAYS £000s	OLDER £000s
AMOUNTS RECEIVABLE						
HOME CUSTOMERS						
EXPORT CUSTOMERS						
TOTAL TRADE DEBTORS						
LESS PROVISION FOR BAD AND DOUBTFUL DEBTS						
NET TRADE DEBTORS						

NUMBER OF DAYS OUTSTANDING	DAYS	DAYS	DAYS	DAYS	DAYS	DAYS
HOME CUSTOMERS						
EXPORT CUSTOMERS						

AGED ANALYSIS BY TOP CUSTOMERS	TOTAL £000s	CURRENT £000s	30 DAYS £000s	60 DAYS £000s	90 DAYS £000s	OLDER £000s
CUSTOMER AA						
CUSTOMER BB						
CUSTOMER CC						
CUSTOMER DD ETC., LISTED THROUGH TO THE THE 20TH TOP CUSTOMER						
BALANCE OF CUSTOMERS						

TABLE 22.23

OTHER DEBTORS' ANALYSIS

MANAGEMENT ACCOUNTS   *PAGE 22*

OTHER DEBTORS' ANALYSIS

PERIOD 7, AS AT 31 JULY

	ACTUAL £000s	BUDGET £000s	LAST YEAR £000s
INSURANCE CLAIMS			
ROYALTIES RECEIVABLE			
VAT RECOVERABLE			
LOANS TO EMPLOYEES			
BROUGHT FORWARD FROM PERIOD 6			
NEW LOANS			
REPAYMENTS THIS PERIOD			
LOANS CARRIED FORWARD			
SUNDRY DEBTORS			

this example all are increasing. Budgeted trend lines can also be incorporated to indicate whether the increases or decreases in the actual trends were planned or otherwise.

Page 30: Profit projections

This final page of the accounts (see Figure 22.3) provides the latest forecast of results for the remainder of the financial year. The forecasts may be based on subjective estimations or by using short-term forecasting techniques such as extrapolations of current trends.

Summary

- The more information available to management the more in control they will be. Knowledge itself is power; management accounting information, provided each month or 4/5 week periods, has

the power to enable management to alter the course a company is taking and therefore improve profitability.
- This set of accounts can be analysed as follows:

Trading information	Assets/liabilities information
Profit and Loss Account	Balance sheet details
Variances from expectations	Cash flow details
Analyses of sales, production and operating expenses	Capital expenditure details
	Fixed assets details
	Current assets details

In addition, these accounts supply:

Key performance ratios and statistics
Profitability and working capital trends information
Projections of future trading probabilities

They also provide a basis for many management decisions: the starting point for next year's budget perhaps, the formulation of strategy and policy.

TABLE 22.24

TRADE CREDITORS' AGED ANALYSIS

MANAGEMENT ACCOUNTS   PAGE 23

TRADE CREDITORS' AGED ANALYSIS

PERIOD 7, AS AT 31 JULY

	TOTAL £000s	CURRENT £000s	30 DAYS £000s	60 DAYS £000s	90 DAYS £000s	OLDER £000s
AMOUNTS PAYABLE						
HOME SUPPLIERS						
EXPORT SUPPLIERS						
TOTAL TRADE CREDITORS						

	DAYS	DAYS	DAYS	DAYS	DAYS	DAYS
NUMBER OF DAYS OUTSTANDING						
HOME SUPPLIERS						
EXPORT SUPPLIERS						

	TOTAL £000s	CURRENT £000s	30 DAYS £000s	60 DAYS £000s	90 DAYS £000s	OLDER £000s
AGED ANALYSIS BY TOP SUPPLIERS						
SUPPLIER ZZ						
SUPPLIER YY						
SUPPLIER XX						
SUPPLIER WW ETC., LISTED THROUGH TO THE THE 10TH TOP SUPPLIER						
BALANCE OF SUPPLIERS						

- To be an effective management tool, management accounts need to be prepared and issued to management as soon as possible after the end of the period to which they relate. Often, with computer assistance, this is possible within a few days of the period's end. To achieve this speed it is often necessary to use estimates, because information needed to prepare the accounts will not always be available. In this context, it is preferable that management accounts are, say 95 per cent correct within a short time of the period's end than wait for, say, another 20/30 days so that they are 100 per cent correct.

- Graphical presentation of data enhances the impact of the figures, enabling management to see at a glance what is going on.
- The number of reports or schedules included in the management accounts is limited only by imagination. Many firms produce in excess of 50 pages each period, but many have far fewer. It is a certainty, however, that the more aware management are of the movements and activities within the business, the costs and revenues, and the interplay between them, the more in control they will be.

TABLE 22.25

OTHER CREDITORS' ANALYSIS

MANAGEMENT ACCOUNTS   *PAGE 24*

OTHER CREDITORS' ANALYSIS

PERIOD 7, AS AT 31 JULY

	ACTUAL £000s	BUDGET £000s	LAST YEAR £000s
PAYROLL CREDITORS			
VAT PAYABLE			
DIVIDENDS PAYABLE			
COMMISSIONS PAYABLE			
SUNDRY CREDITORS			

TABLE 22.26

ACCRUALS AND PREPAYMENTS

MANAGEMENT ACCOUNTS   *PAGE 25*

ACCRUALS AND PREPAYMENTS

PERIOD 7, AS AT 31 JULY

	ACTUAL £000s	BUDGET £000s	LAST YEAR £000s
ACCRUALS			
RAW MATERIALS PURCHASES			
WAGES PAYABLE			
EXPENSES			
TELEPHONE			
ELECTRICITY			
GAS			
BANK INTEREST			
PROFESSIONAL FEES			
PREPAYMENTS			
RENT TO SEP QUARTER			
RATES TO MARCH 31			
INSURANCE CHARGES			
SUNDRY STATIONERY STOCKS			

TABLE 22.27

ANALYSIS OF BORROWINGS

MANAGEMENT ACCOUNTS   PAGE 26

ANALYSIS OF BORROWINGS

PERIOD 7, AS AT 31 JULY

LONG-TERM DEBT:

	INTEREST RATE	INTEREST CHARGE p.a. £000s	ACTUAL £000s	BUDGET £000s	LAST YEAR £000s
DEBENTURES DETAILS					
LONG-TERM BANK LOAN					
OTHER LOANS					

WEIGHTED AVERAGE COST OF LONG-TERM DEBT (%):

$$\frac{\text{INTEREST CHARGE p.a.}}{\text{TOTAL LONG-TERM DEBT}}$$

	INTEREST RATE % CHARGE p.a.	ACTUAL £000s
CURRENT BORROWINGS		
BANK OVERDRAFT		
OTHER SHORT-TERM LOANS		

TABLE 22.28

KEY RATIOS AND STATISTICS

MANAGEMENT ACCOUNTS
KEY RATIOS AND STATISTICS
PERIOD 7, ENDING 31 JULY

PAGE 27

	PERIOD 7			ACTUAL YEAR TO DATE
	ACTUAL	BUDGET	LAST YEAR	
PRODUCTION SUMMARY				
PRODUCTS MADE (QUANTITY)				
AVERAGE WASTE AS % OF INPUT (%)				
STANDARD HOURS PRODUCED (HOURS)				
EFFICIENCY RATIO (%)				
CAPACITY RATIO (%)				
PROFITABILITY SUMMARY				
GROSS PROFIT (%)				
OPERATING EXPENSES (%)				
NET PROFIT (%)				
RETURN ON CAPITAL EMPLOYED (%)				
INTEREST COVER (TIMES)				
MARGIN OF SAFETY (%)				
SALES SUMMARY				
UNITS OF PRODUCT SOLD (NUMBER)				
ORDERS SHIPPED (NUMBER)				
ORDERS IN HAND (NUMBER)				
EMPLOYEES				
NUMBER OF EMPLOYEES				
PRODUCTION				
DISTRIBUTION				
SELLING				
ADMINISTRATION				
SALES PER EMPLOYEE (£000s)				
PROFIT PER EMPLOYEE (£000s)				

SALES BY REPRESENTATIVE				ACTUAL % TO SALES	BUDGET % TO SALES	LAST YEAR % TO SALES	% TO SALES
REPRESENTATIVE	GROSS PROFIT	REP. COSTS	CONTRIBUTION				
AA	X	Y	X – Y				
BB							
CC							
DD, ETC.							

WORKING CAPITAL				
STOCK – STOCKTURNOVER – TIMES				
T/DEBTORS – NO. OF DAYS OUTSTANDING				
T/CREDITORS – NO. OF DAYS OUTSTANDING				
CURRENT RATIO				

FIGURE 22.1

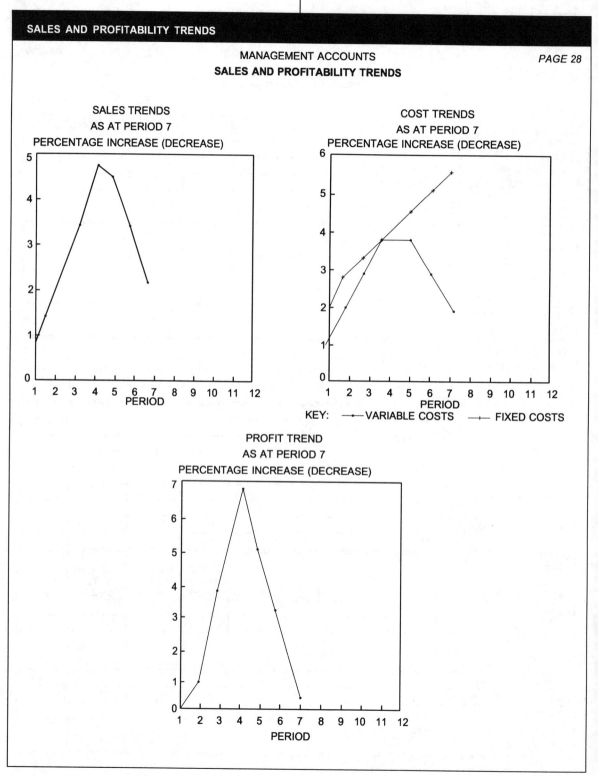

FIGURE 22.2

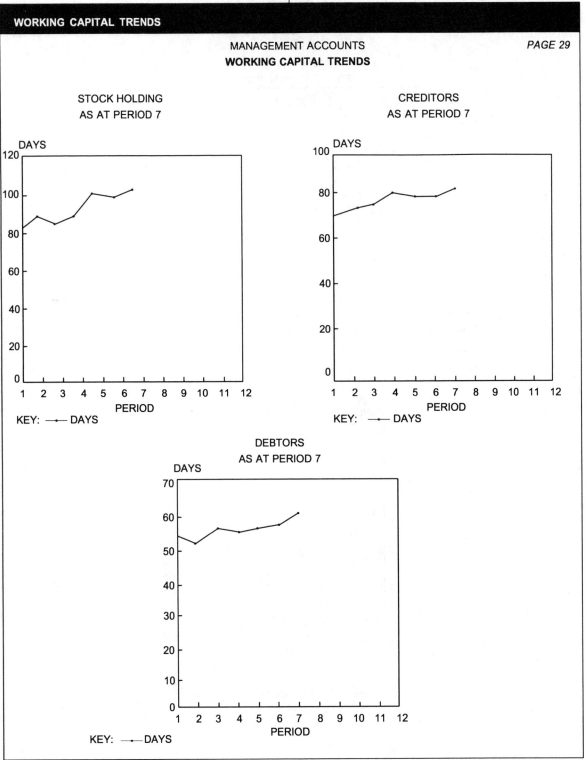

FIGURE 22.3

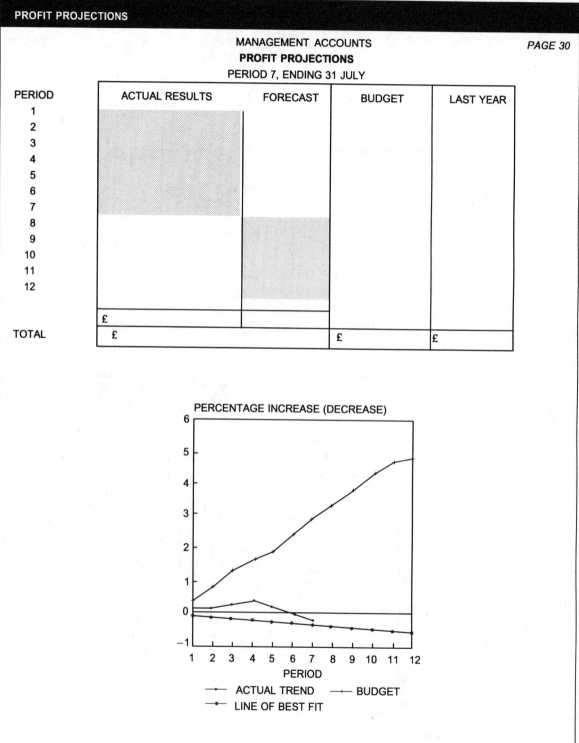

23

Management Accounts of a Retail Company

The aim of this set of management accounts for a retailing operation is the same as the set prepared for the manufacturing firm, described and illustrated in Chapter 22: that is, full and timely information to help management in planning and controlling their business.

You will see from the index shown in Table 23.1 that the contents are very similar to the manufacturing firm's accounts: the profit and loss account analysed in depth; the balance sheet heads subjected to detailed scrutiny; and the key statistics and ratios within the business highlighted and brought prominently to the attention of management. Whenever feasible, graphical interpretation of the information will be included to add dimension and impact, thus enabling management to absorb the details more readily and assisting in the control and decision-making processes. These particular management accounts apply to a retailing organisation which operates a number of branches (outlets), selling a range of merchandise broadly the same throughout.

Other service operators, such as distribution companies, leisure firms, bus companies, computer software houses and so on might produce similar management accounts to those depicted here but, as is to be expected, they will be tailored specifically to meet their own industry and information requirements.

Page 1: Profit and loss account – the company as a whole

The budget and last year figures shown in Table 23.2 provide a comparative yardstick so that the actual results can be put into perspective. In the percentage columns, all figures relate to sales. This facilitates 'management by exception', whereby those ratios which are out of line with the budget and the previous year are identified immediately and can therefore be investigated and checked first.

Page 2: Profit and loss account – by branch

This statement, illustrated in Table 23.3, provides the breakdown by branch of the contribution section of the profit and loss account. Comparisons with budget and the previous year are included. The percentage share of each branch to total sales, gross profit and so on enables management to see immediately the contribution of each branch to the whole, together with the relative changes in these contributions

TABLE 23.1

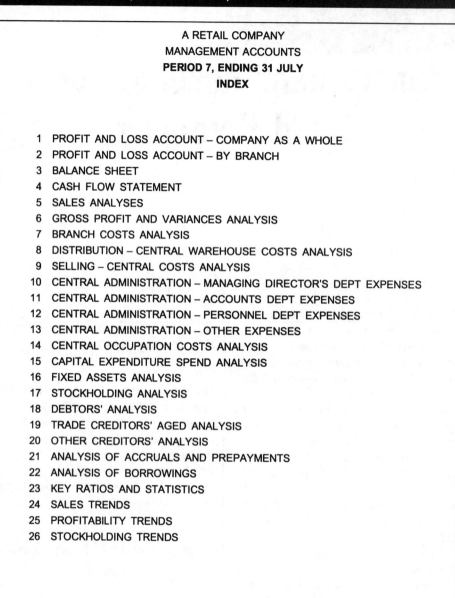

MANAGEMENT ACCOUNTS INDEX (RETAIL COMPANY)

A RETAIL COMPANY
MANAGEMENT ACCOUNTS
PERIOD 7, ENDING 31 JULY
INDEX

1 PROFIT AND LOSS ACCOUNT – COMPANY AS A WHOLE
2 PROFIT AND LOSS ACCOUNT – BY BRANCH
3 BALANCE SHEET
4 CASH FLOW STATEMENT
5 SALES ANALYSES
6 GROSS PROFIT AND VARIANCES ANALYSIS
7 BRANCH COSTS ANALYSIS
8 DISTRIBUTION – CENTRAL WAREHOUSE COSTS ANALYSIS
9 SELLING – CENTRAL COSTS ANALYSIS
10 CENTRAL ADMINISTRATION – MANAGING DIRECTOR'S DEPT EXPENSES
11 CENTRAL ADMINISTRATION – ACCOUNTS DEPT EXPENSES
12 CENTRAL ADMINISTRATION – PERSONNEL DEPT EXPENSES
13 CENTRAL ADMINISTRATION – OTHER EXPENSES
14 CENTRAL OCCUPATION COSTS ANALYSIS
15 CAPITAL EXPENDITURE SPEND ANALYSIS
16 FIXED ASSETS ANALYSIS
17 STOCKHOLDING ANALYSIS
18 DEBTORS' ANALYSIS
19 TRADE CREDITORS' AGED ANALYSIS
20 OTHER CREDITORS' ANALYSIS
21 ANALYSIS OF ACCRUALS AND PREPAYMENTS
22 ANALYSIS OF BORROWINGS
23 KEY RATIOS AND STATISTICS
24 SALES TRENDS
25 PROFITABILITY TRENDS
26 STOCKHOLDING TRENDS

TABLE 23.2

PROFIT AND LOSS ACCOUNT – THE COMPANY AS A WHOLE

MANAGEMENT ACCOUNTS

PROFIT AND LOSS – FIXED BUDGET

PERIOD 7, ENDING JULY 31

PERIOD 7

	ACTUAL		BUDGET		LAST YEAR		YEAR TO DATE					
							ACTUAL		BUDGET		LAST YEAR	
	£000s	%	£000s	%	£000s	%	£000s	%	£000s	%	£000s	%
SALES		100.0%		100.0%		100.0%		100.0%		100.0%		100.0%
COST OF GOODS SOLD												
GROSS PROFIT												
TOTAL BRANCH OPERATING COSTS												
CONTRIBUTION TO CENTRAL COSTS												
CENTRAL COSTS												
CENTRAL DISTRIBUTION COSTS												
CENTRAL SELLING COSTS												
CENTRAL ADMINISTRATION EXPENSES												
OTHER CENTRAL COSTS AND INCOME												
TOTAL CENTRAL COSTS												
OPERATING PROFIT												
INTEREST CHARGES												
PROFIT BEFORE TAX												
TAXATION PROVISION												
PROFIT AFTER TAX												

TABLE 23.3

PROFIT AND LOSS ACCOUNT – BY BRANCH

MANAGEMENT ACCOUNTS

PROFIT AND LOSS – BY BRANCH

PERIOD 7, ENDING 31 JULY

PERIOD 7

BRANCH	SALES £000s	GROSS PROFIT % £000s	PERCENTAGE OF SALES %	BRANCH COSTS £000s	ACTUAL NET PROFIT £000s	BUDGETED NET PROFIT £000s	LAST YEAR NET PROFIT £000s
BRANCH A							
BRANCH B							
BRANCH C							
BRANCH D, ETC.							
TOTAL							

PERCENTAGE SHARE OF TOTAL	SALES %	GROSS PROFIT %	PERCENTAGE OF SALES %	BRANCH COSTS %	ACTUAL NET PROFIT %	BUDGETED NET PROFIT %	LAST YEAR NET PROFIT %
BRANCH A							
BRANCH B							
BRANCH C							
BRANCH D, ETC.							
TOTAL	100.0%	100.0%	100.0%	100.0%	100.0%	100.0%	100.0%

YEAR TO DATE

BRANCH	SALES £000s	GROSS PROFIT % £000s	PERCENTAGE OF SALES %	BRANCH COSTS £000s	ACTUAL NET PROFIT £000s	BUDGETED NET PROFIT £000s	LAST YEAR NET PROFIT £000s
BRANCH A							
BRANCH B							
BRANCH C							
BRANCH D, ETC.							
TOTAL							

PERCENTAGE SHARE OF TOTAL	SALES %	GROSS PROFIT %	PERCENTAGE OF SALES %	BRANCH COSTS %	ACTUAL NET PROFIT %	BUDGETED NET PROFIT %	LAST YEAR NET PROFIT %
BRANCH A							
BRANCH B							
BRANCH C							
BRANCH D, ETC.							
TOTAL	100.0%	100.0%	100.0%	100.0%	100.0%	100.0%	100.0%

when compared to budget and the previous year. This information may also be presented graphically, and, over time, the trends in the contributions of each branch can thus be identified.

Page 3:   Balance sheet as at 31 July

The layout shown in Table 23.4 enables management to compare the current position with three other balance sheets – the budgeted balance sheet; the previous period (previous month); and the equivalent period for the previous year. Additional columns, one showing the figures for the end of the previous financial year, and the other a forecast of the likely position at the end of the current financial year, can also be included.

Page 4:   Cash flow statement

The report in Table 23.5 shows the cash movements within the bank account, the difference between the receipts and payments being the cash flow. Management will find it useful to have details of the 'mix' between cash and credit-card receipts. In addition to the payment items listed, standing orders and direct debits might also be recorded separately. Note that the actual 'year to date' amounts are added to the budgeted amounts for the remainder of the year to provide the forecast for the year.

Page 5:   Sales analysis

The page illustrated in Table 23.6 will show in detail the value of sales of the most popular lines – the top 20 per cent perhaps, as in Pareto distribution observations – and the actual quantity of units sold. The information could also be presented in graphical format and by branch. Selling price variances from budget could also be given on this statement, or on the variances analysis report (see page 395).

Page 6:   Gross profit and variances analysis

This report, shown in Table 23.7, links in with the previous statement. Assuming standard costs have been set for the cost of goods sold, the purchases

variances will also be reported here. These enable management to concentrate on those products which are out of line with expectations. Standard selling prices will also have been set.

Page 7:   Branch costs analysis

In addition to listing the running costs of each branch, an extra table can be incorporated here (see Table 23.8), or as a separate report, to show the residual income percentage return for each branch. A notional interest charge is levied on each branch, based on the capital tied up in the branch. This is also a 'management by exception' measurement technique, providing management with a ROCE (residual income computations) ratio for each branch, thereby enabling suitable action to be taken to improve the performance of branches that fall below expectations.

Page 8:   Central warehouse costs

This report (see Table 23.9) would be used by retailers operating a central warehouse to which suppliers deliver the products, and from where the retailer ships the products to the branches, based on orders received from the shops. Other retailers rely on the supplier to deliver goods directly to the branches, thereby cutting out the need for the central warehouse. The benefits of both systems need periodically to be evaluated carefully, using investment appraisal techniques. Proponents of the central warehouse argue that larger orders can be placed with suppliers and therefore larger trade discounts will apply. In addition, the incidence of an imbalance of stock, overstock and out of stock at the various branches will largely be avoided, as returns can be made to the central warehouse and redistributed to other branches. The advocates of direct delivery by suppliers to branches argue that the costs of running the central warehouse will be saved and reasonable trade discounts could still be negotiated with suppliers.

Page 9:   Central selling costs

This report (see Table 23.10) covers the central selling costs, incurred for the benefit of all the branches and

TABLE 23.4

BALANCE SHEET AS AT 31 JULY

BALANCE SHEET AS AT 31 JULY   PAGE 3

CURRENT MONTH– LAST YEAR £000s		CURRENT MONTH £000s	BUDGET £000s	LAST MONTH £000s
	ASSETS			
	FIXED ASSETS			
	NBV BROUGHT FWD			
	ADDITIONS			
	DISPOSALS			
	DEPRECIATION CHARGE			
	INVESTMENTS			
	CURRENT ASSETS			
	STOCKS			
	TRADE DEBTORS			
	CASH AT BANK CASH IN HAND			
	OTHER DEBTORS			
	PREPAID EXPENSES			
	CURRENT LIABILITIES			
	TRADE CREDITORS			
	BANK OVERDRAFT			
	CORPORATION TAX			
	OTHER PAYABLES			
	ACCRUED EXPENSES			
	NET CURRENT ASSETS (LIABILITIES)			
	TOTAL ASSETS			
	LONG-TERM LIABILITIES			
	NET ASSETS			
	FINANCED BY			
	SHARE CAPITAL			
	SHARE PREMIUM ACCOUNT			
	RETAINED PROFITS B/FWD			
	PROFIT AND LOSS– CURRENT YEAR			
	GENERAL RESERVE			
	REVALUATION RESERVE			
	SHAREHOLDERS' INVESTMENT			

TABLE 23.5

CASH FLOW STATEMENT

MANAGEMENT ACCOUNTS

CASH FLOW STATEMENT

PERIOD 7, ENDING 31 JULY

	CURRENT PERIOD £000s	BUDGET £000s	YEAR TO DATE £000s	BUDGET PERIOD 8 £000s	BUDGET PERIOD 9 £000s	BUDGET PERIOD 10 £000s	BUDGET PERIOD 11 £000s	BUDGET PERIOD 12 £000s	FORECAST FOR YEAR £000s
RECEIPTS									
CASH BANKINGS									
CREDIT-CARD BANKINGS									
INTEREST RECEIVABLE									
OTHER RECEIPTS									
SALES OF ASSETS									
TOTAL RECEIPTS									
PAYMENTS									
PAYMENTS TO SUPPLIERS									
PAYROLL PAYMENTS									
BRANCH CASH PAYMENTS*									
VAT PAYMENTS									
TAXATION PAYMENTS									
CAPITAL EXPENDITURE									
LOAN REPAYMENTS									
INTEREST CHARGES									
DIVIDENDS									
TOTAL PAYMENTS									
CASH FLOW									
OPENING CASH AT BANK									
CLOSING CASH AT BANK									

* ANALYSED SEPARATELY

TABLE 23.6

SALES ANALYSIS

MANAGEMENT ACCOUNTS

SALES ANALYSIS

PERIOD 7, ENDING 31 JULY

SALES BY PRODUCT – £000s

	PERIOD 7						YEAR TO DATE					
	ACTUAL		BUDGET		LAST YEAR		ACTUAL		BUDGET		LAST YEAR	
	£000s	% MIX	£000s	% MIX	£000s	% MIX	£000s	%	£000s	% MIX	£000s	% MIX
PRODUCT 1												
PRODUCT 2												
PRODUCT 3												
PRODUCT 4 ETC., FOR TOP 20% LINES												
BALANCE OF PRODUCTS												
TOTAL SALES		100.0		100.0		100.0		100.0		100.0		100.0

SALES BY PRODUCT – UNITS

	PERIOD 7						YEAR TO DATE					
	ACTUAL		BUDGET		LAST YEAR		ACTUAL		BUDGET		LAST YEAR	
	UNITS	% MIX	UNITS	% MIX	UNITS	% MIX	UNITS	%	UNITS	% MIX	UNITS	% MIX
PRODUCT 1												
PRODUCT 2												
PRODUCT 3												
PRODUCT 4 ETC., FOR TOP 20% LINES												
BALANCE OF PRODUCTS												
TOTAL SALES		100.0		100.0		100.0		100.0		100.0		100.0

TABLE 23.7

GROSS PROFIT AND VARIANCES ANALYSIS

MANAGEMENT ACCOUNTS

GROSS PROFIT AND VARIANCES ANALYSIS

PERIOD 7, ENDING 31 JULY

PERIOD 7

GROSS PROFIT BY PRODUCT (£000s)	ACTUAL £000s	% MIX	BUDGET £000s	% MIX	LAST YEAR £000s	% MIX
PRODUCT 1						
PRODUCT 2						
PRODUCT 3						
PRODUCT 4 ETC., FOR TOP 20% LINES						
BALANCE OF PRODUCTS						
TOTAL SALES		100.0		100.0		100.0

YEAR TO DATE

	ACTUAL £000s	%	BUDGET £000s	% MIX	LAST YEAR £000s	% MIX
PRODUCT 1						
PRODUCT 2						
PRODUCT 3						
PRODUCT 4 ETC., FOR TOP 20% LINES						
BALANCE OF PRODUCTS						
TOTAL SALES		100.0		100.0		100.0

SALES PRICE AND SALES VOLUME CONTRIBUTION VARIANCES

£000s

SELLING PRICES	
PRODUCT 1	
PRODUCT 2	
PRODUCT 3	
PRODUCT 4 ETC., FOR TOP 20% LINES	
BALANCE OF PRODUCTS	

SALES MIX	
SALES QUANTITY	
SALES VOLUME	

TABLE 23.8

BRANCH COSTS ANALYSIS

MANAGEMENT ACCOUNTS
BRANCH COSTS ANALYSIS
PERIOD 7, ENDING 31 JULY

COSTS	BRANCH A ACTUAL £000s	BRANCH A BUDGET £000s	BRANCH B ACTUAL £000s	BRANCH B BUDGET £000s	BRANCH C ACTUAL £000s	BRANCH C BUDGET £000s	BRANCH D ACTUAL £000s	BRANCH D BUDGET £000s	TOTAL ACTUAL £000s	TOTAL BUDGET £000s
STAFF COSTS										
SHOP ASSISTANTS										
MANAGEMENT										
MAINTENANCE										
OTHER STAFF										
CASUAL LABOUR										
CLEANING										
DEPRECIATION										
ELECTRICITY										
GAS										
HEAD OFFICE ALLOCATIONS										
INSURANCE										
LOCAL ADVERTISING										
OTHER SHOP EXPENSES										
RATES										
RENT										
REPAIRS, MAINTENANCE										
SECURITY										
STAFF RECRUITMENT										
STOCK GAINS AND LOSSES										
TELEPHONE AND FAX										
TRANSPORT COSTS										
TOTAL COSTS										

RESIDUAL INCOME (%)	BRANCH A ACTUAL £000s	BRANCH A BUDGET £000s	BRANCH B ACTUAL £000s	BRANCH B BUDGET £000s	BRANCH C ACTUAL £000s	BRANCH C BUDGET £000s	BRANCH D ACTUAL £000s	BRANCH D BUDGET £000s	TOTAL ACTUAL £000s	TOTAL BUDGET £000s
PROFIT										
NOTIONAL INTEREST ON CAPITAL EMPLOYED – x%										
RESIDUAL INCOME										
RESIDUAL INCOME AS PERCENTAGE OF CAPITAL EMPLOYED										

TABLE 23.9

CENTRAL WAREHOUSE COSTS

MANAGEMENT ACCOUNTS   *PAGE 8*

DISTRIBUTION COSTS – CENTRAL WAREHOUSE COSTS

PERIOD 7, ENDING 31 JULY

	ACTUAL £000s	BUDGET £000s	LAST YEAR £000s	ACTUAL £000s	BUDGET £000s	LAST YEAR £000s
STAFF PAYROLL COSTS						
WAREHOUSE MANAGEMENT						
GENERAL WAREHOUSE STAFF						
FORK-LIFT DRIVERS						
ORDER PICKERS						
DELIVERY DRIVERS						
VEHICLE MAINTENANCE STAFF						
WAREHOUSE CLERICAL STAFF						
OVERTIME PREMIUM						
DEPRECIATION CHARGES						
INSURANCE CHARGES						
MAINTENANCE, REPAIRS						
OCCUPATION COSTS						
OUTSIDE CARRIER CHARGES						
STATIONERY						
SUNDRY DISTRIBUTION COSTS						
SUNDRY WAREHOUSE COSTS						
TELEPHONE CHARGES						
VEHICLE FIXED COSTS						
VEHICLE RENTAL CHARGES						
VEHICLE RUNNING COSTS						
TOTAL						
AS PERCENTAGE OF SALES						
NUMBER OF ORDERS DESPATCHED						
COST PER ORDER DESPATCHED						

TABLE 23.10

CENTRAL SELLING COSTS

MANAGEMENT ACCOUNTS
SELLING COSTS—CENTRAL COSTS ANALYSIS
PERIOD 7, ENDING 31 JULY

	PERIOD						YEAR TO DATE					
	ACTUAL £000s	% OF SALES	BUDGET £000s	% OF SALES	LAST YEAR £000s	% OF SALES	ACTUAL £000s	% OF SALES	BUDGET £000s	% OF SALES	LAST YEAR £000s	% OF SALES
STAFF PAYROLL COSTS												
MANAGEMENT SALARIES												
MARKETING STAFF												
CLERICAL STAFF												
ADVERTISING COSTS												
CAR DEPRECIATION												
CAR EXPENSES												
FURNITURE DEPRECIATION												
MOBILE TELEPHONES												
OCCUPATION COSTS												
PROMOTIONAL MATERIALS												
SALES MEETINGS COSTS												
STAFF RECRUITMENT COSTS												
STATIONERY												
SUNDRY SELLING COSTS												
TELEPHONE AND FAX CHARGES												
TRAVEL AND SUBSISTENCE												
TOTAL												
LESS REALLOCATIONS TO BRANCHES												
NET CENTRAL SELLING COSTS												

will include the payroll costs of the area sales management teams, design and promotional work and so on. Some or all of these costs may then be reallocated to the branches on an equitable basis.

Page 10: Managing Director's Department expenses

The Chief Executive has responsibility for the whole business and therefore the costs incurred in the Managing Director's Department may be considerable. Shown in this report (see Table 23.11) are the Board of Directors' costs, such as the Chair costs, non-executive Directors' expenses and so on, although these could be reported separately.

Page 11: Accounts Department expenses

Accounting for cash received and paid out by the branches will be a major part of the Financial Accounts Department's work, with bank reconciliations being completed very frequently. This ensures that monies paid in by the branches agrees with branch returns, and that the cash has been accounted for properly. Additionally, reconciliations of amounts receivable from credit-card companies will also be completed regularly. See Table 23.12.

With no manufacturing costs to account for, the role of the Cost Accountant is somewhat diminished, with his/her functions probably being combined with the Management Accountant's duties.

Page 12: Personnel Department expenses

With the majority of staff employed in the outlets, much of the recruitment work will be carried out at local level, with the central department co-ordinating methods and procedures. The Personnel Department will also be heavily involved in organising training programmes for staff and ensuring that employment policies and procedures are carried out correctly at the outlets. See Table 23.13.

Page 13: Other income and expenses

This report (see Table 23.14) lists all other income and expenses that cannot be identified to specific branches or central departments.

Page 14: Central occupation costs

The costs of the central premises are collected as a cost centre and then apportioned to the various central departments, as shown in Table 23.15.

Page 15: Capital expenditure spend analysis

Each item of capital expenditure will have been authorised prior to the spend in line with investment appraisal and authorisation procedures. The report shown in Table 23.16 provides management with the current spend position. It also reveals any over- or under-spends. If these are higher than the norm set by management, details of the total spend compared to the authorised amounts will be investigated.

Page 16: Fixed assets analysis

This Report (shown in Table 23.17) analyses the balance sheet fixed assets section.

Page 17: Stockholding analysis

The 'mix' of stockholding between branches and the central warehouse will be reported here (see Table 23.18), along with the average number of days' stockholding.

Page 18: Debtors' analysis

You will note that the schedule seen in Table 23.19 includes the amounts receivable from credit-card companies. These balances will be supported by an aged analysis report.

TABLE 23.11

MANAGING DIRECTOR'S DEPARTMENT EXPENSES

MANAGEMENT ACCOUNTS   *PAGE 10*

MANAGING DIRECTOR'S DEPARTMENT COSTS

PERIOD 7, ENDING 31 JULY

	PERIOD			YEAR TO DATE		
	ACTUAL £000s	BUDGET £000s	LAST YEAR £000s	ACTUAL £000s	BUDGET £000s	LAST YEAR £000s
STAFF PAYROLL COSTS:						
MD						
PERSONAL SECRETARY						
PERSONAL ASSISTANT						
NON-EXECUTIVE DIRECTORS' FEES						
CHAIR'S FEES AND EXPENSES						
NON-EXECUTIVE DIRECTORS' COSTS						
ANNUAL GENERAL MEETING COSTS						
CAR DEPRECIATION						
CAR EXPENSES						
ENTERTAINING COSTS						
FURNITURE DEPRECIATION						
MEETING COSTS						
MOBILE TELEPHONES						
OCCUPATION COSTS						
OVERSEAS TRAVEL COSTS						
STAFF RECRUITMENT COSTS						
STATIONERY						
SUNDRY COSTS						
TELEPHONE AND FAX CHARGES						
TRAVEL AND SUBSISTENCE						
TOTAL						

TABLE 23.12

ACCOUNTS DEPARTMENT EXPENSES

MANAGING DIRECTOR'S DEPARTMENT COSTS   *PAGE 11*

ACCOUNTS DEPARTMENT COSTS

PERIOD 7, ENDING 31 JULY

	PERIOD			YEAR TO DATE		
	ACTUAL £000s	BUDGET £000s	LAST YEAR £000s	ACTUAL £000s	BUDGET £000s	LAST YEAR £000s
STAFF PAYROLL COSTS						
MANAGEMENT SALARIES						
FINANCIAL ACCOUNTS SECTION						
MANAGEMENT ACCOUNTS SECTION						
OVERTIME PREMIUM						
AUDIT FEES						
CAR DEPRECIATION						
CAR EXPENSES						
COMPUTER COSTS						
FURNITURE DEPRECIATION						
MEETING COSTS						
MOBILE TELEPHONES						
OCCUPATION COSTS						
POSTAGE						
PRINTING AND PHOTOCOPYING						
STAFF RECRUITMENT COSTS						
STAFF RECRUITMENT COSTS						
STATIONERY						
SUNDRY COSTS						
TELEPHONE AND FAX CHARGES						
TRAVEL AND SUBSISTENCE						
TOTAL						

TABLE 23.13

PERSONNEL DEPARTMENT EXPENSES

MANAGEMENT ACCOUNTS   *PAGE 12*

CENTRAL PERSONNEL DEPARTMENT (HUMAN RESOURCES) COSTS

PERIOD 7, ENDING 31 JULY

	PERIOD			YEAR TO DATE		
	ACTUAL £000s	BUDGET £000s	LAST YEAR £000s	ACTUAL £000s	BUDGET £000s	LAST YEAR £000s
STAFF PAYROLL COSTS						
MANAGEMENT SALARIES						
STAFF SALARIES						
TRAINEE SALARIES						
OVERTIME PREMIUM						
CAR DEPRECIATION						
CAR EXPENSES						
COURSES						
COMPUTER COSTS						
DEPARTMENTAL MEETING COSTS						
FURNITURE DEPRECIATION						
MOBILE TELEPHONES						
OCCUPATION COSTS						
POSTAGE						
PRINTING AND PHOTOCOPYING						
STAFF RECRUITMENT COSTS						
– CENTRAL STAFF						
STATIONERY						
SUNDRY COSTS						
TELEPHONE AND FAX CHARGES						
TRAINING COSTS						
TRAVEL AND SUBSISTENCE						
LESS RECHARGES TO BRANCHES						
TOTAL						

TABLE 23.14

OTHER INCOME AND EXPENSES

MANAGEMENT ACCOUNTS

PAGE 13

OTHER INCOME AND EXPENSES

PERIOD 7, ENDING 31 JULY

	PERIOD			YEAR TO DATE		
	ACTUAL £000s	BUDGET £000s	LAST YEAR £000s	ACTUAL £000s	BUDGET £000s	LAST YEAR £000s
OTHER INCOME						
SETTLEMENT DISCOUNTS FROM SUPPLIERS						
RENTAL INCOME						
GAINS ON SALE OF FIXED ASSETS						
INTEREST RECEIVABLE						
NON-RECURRING INCOME						
OTHER EXPENSES						
LEGAL FEES						
PROFESSIONAL FEES						
LOSS ON SALE OF FIXED ASSETS						
NON-RECURRING LOSSES						

Page 19:   Trade creditors' aged analysis

This statement (see Table 23.20) will report the amounts due to major suppliers. Additional information, such as the total of purchases for the current year, may also be reported, as here or separately.

Page 20:   Other creditors' analysis

The straightforward statement shown in Table 23.21 reports current liabilities except trade creditors and bank overdraft.

Page 21:   Accruals and prepayments

This is another straightforward statement that simply lists the costs and expenses for which no invoice or charge has yet been received (accruals), and those costs and expenses carried forward to the next accounting period (prepayments) (see Table 23.22).

Page 22:   Analysis of borrowings

This analysis (see Table 23.23) also reveals the average cost of long-term capital in percentage terms.

Page 23:   Key ratios and statistics

This report, shown in Table 23.24 provides management with wide-ranging information, enabling comparisons to be made of the actual performance of each of the branches. Note the rankings of each branch. This may be the ROCE (residual income computations), or other yardstick chosen by management. Additionally, the sales per employee for each branch

TABLE 23.15

CENTRAL OCCUPATION COSTS

MANAGEMENT ACCOUNTS   *PAGE 14*

OCCUPATION COSTS ANALYSIS

PERIOD 7, ENDING 31 JULY

	PERIOD			YEAR TO DATE		
	ACTUAL £000s	BUDGET £000s	LAST YEAR £000s	ACTUAL £000s	BUDGET £000s	LAST YEAR £000s
WAGES AND SALARIES						
MAINTENANCE STAFF						
SECURITY STAFF						
RENT						
RATES						
ELECTRICITY						
GAS						
WATER						
BUILDINGS INSURANCE						
DEPRECIATION CHARGES						
GROUNDS MAINTENANCE						
TOTAL OCCUPATION COSTS						
ALLOCATED TO FOLLOWING DEPARTMENTS						
WAREHOUSE						
CENTRAL SALES DEPARTMENT						
ADMINISTRATION DEPARTMENT						

will provide a quick indication that sales and staff are in line with expectations.

Page 24:   Sales trends

The chart shown in Figure 23.1 reports the moving annual total trend for the budget and actual figures. By using regression analysis, the line of best fit can be computed and included on the graph. Here it can be seen that the budget appears unlikely to be achieved when compared to the forecast projection.

Page 25:   Profitability trends

Using MATs and extrapolating the actual results through to the financial year end, management are provided with a forecast of the final year end results if the current trends continue (see Figure 23.2). As each period passes, the prior period's profitability forecasts can be 'superimposed' on to the latest chart. This will strengthen the likelihood of the final results being within the collective area indicated by all the forecasts.

TABLE 23.16

CAPITAL EXPENDITURE SPEND ANALYSIS

MANAGEMENT ACCOUNTS
CAPITAL EXPENDITURE SPEND ANALYSIS
PERIOD 7, ENDING 31 JULY

CLASS OF ASSET (E.G. CARS)	PROJECT NUMBER	DESCRIPTION	AUTHORISED AMOUNT £000s	COMMITTED TO DATE £000s	SPEND TO DATE £000s	NOT YET SPENT £000s	PERCENTAGE COMPLETED	OVER (UNDER) SPENT £000s	PERCENTAGE OVER OR (UNDER) SPENT
BRANCH PROJECTS									
HEAD OFFICE PROJECTS									
TOTAL									

TABLE 23.17

FIXED ASSETS ANALYSIS

MANAGEMENT ACCOUNTS   *PAGE 16*

FIXED ASSETS ANALYSIS

PERIOD 7, ENDING 31 JULY

	BRANCH PREMISES £000s	BRANCH EQUIPMENT £000s	BRANCH VEHICLES £000s	TOTAL ASSETS £000s
ORIGINAL COST/REVALUATION				
BALANCE BROUGHT FORWARD				
ADDITIONS FOR YEAR				
DISPOSALS AT COST				
BALANCE CARRIED FORWARD				

	HEAD OFFICE PREMISES £000s	HEAD OFFICE EQUIPMENT £000s	HEAD OFFICE VEHICLES £000s	TOTAL ASSETS £000s
ORIGINAL COST/REVALUATION				
BALANCE BROUGHT FORWARD				
ADDITIONS FOR YEAR				
DISPOSALS AT COST				
BALANCE CARRIED FORWARD				
TOTAL CARRIED FORWARD				
ACCUMULATED DEPRECIATION				
BALANCE BROUGHT FORWARD				
DEPRECIATION CHARGE CURRENT YEAR				
DEPRECIATION ON DISPOSALS				
BALANCE CARRIED FORWARD				
NET BOOK VALUE				

TABLE 23.18

STOCKHOLDING ANALYSIS

MANAGEMENT ACCOUNTS *PAGE 17*

STOCKHOLDING ANALYSIS

PERIOD 7, AS AT 31 JULY

AT STANDARD COST	ACTUAL £000S	% MIX	BUDGET £000S	% MIX	LAST YEAR £000S	% MIX
FINISHED GOODS AT BRANCHES						
BRANCH A						
BRANCH B						
BRANCH C						
BRANCH D, ETC.						
LESS: PROVISION FOR SLOW AND DEAD STOCK						
TOTAL FINISHED GOODS AT BRANCES		100.0%		100.0%		100.0%
FINISHED GOODS AT WAREHOUSE						
TOTAL FINISHED GOODS		100.0%		100.0%		100.0%
FINISHED GOODS BY PRODUCT						
PRODUCT 1						
PRODUCT 2						
PRODUCT 3						
PRODUCT 4, ETC.						
ITEMS LISTED THROUGH TO THE TOP 80% IN VALUE						
BALANCE – REMAINING 20%						
LESS: PROVISION FOR SLOW AND DEAD STOCK						
TOTAL FINISHED GOODS		100.0%		100.0%		100.0%
OTHER STOCKS						

NUMBER OF DAYS' STOCKHOLDING	ACTUAL	BUDGET	LAST YEAR
BRANCH A	DAYS	DAYS	DAYS
BRANCH B	DAYS	DAYS	DAYS
BRANCH C	DAYS	DAYS	DAYS
BRANCH D	DAYS	DAYS	DAYS
ETC.	DAYS	DAYS	DAYS
WAREHOUSE	DAYS	DAYS	DAYS
COMPANY	DAYS	DAYS	DAYS

TABLE 23.19

DEBTORS' ANALYSIS

MANAGEMENT ACCOUNTS   PAGE 18

DEBTORS' ANALYSIS

PERIOD 7, AS AT 31 JULY

	ACTUAL £000s	BUDGET £000s	LAST YEAR £000s
AMOUNTS DUE FROM CREDIT CARD CO.s			
INSURANCE CLAIMS			
VAT RECOVERABLE			
LOANS TO EMPLOYEES			
BROUGHT FORWARD FROM PERIOD 6			
NEW LOANS			
REPAYMENTS THIS PERIOD			
LOANS CARRIED FORWARD			
SUNDRY DEBTORS			

TABLE 23.20

TRADE CREDITORS' AGED ANALYSIS

MANAGEMENT ACCOUNTS   PAGE 19

TRADE CREDITORS' AGED ANALYSIS

PERIOD 7, AS AT 31 JULY

	PURCHASES THIS YEAR	TOTAL £000s	CURRENT £000s	30 DAYS £000s	60 DAYS £000s	90 DAYS £000s	OLDER £000s
AMOUNTS PAYABLE							
AGED ANALYSIS BY TOP							
SUPPLIERS							
SUPPLIER ZZ							
SUPPLIER YY							
SUPPLIER XX							
SUPPLIER WW ETC.,							
WITH TOP 20% OF							
SUPPLIERS BEING LISTED							
BALANCE OF SUPPLIERS							

TABLE 23.21

OTHER CREDTORS' ANALYSIS

MANAGEMENT ACCOUNTS   *PAGE 20*

OTHER CREDITORS' ANALYSIS

PERIOD 7, AS AT 31 JULY

	ACTUAL £000s	BUDGET £000s	LAST YEAR £000s
PAYROLL CREDITORS			
VAT PAYABLE			
DIVIDENDS PAYABLE			
OTHER SUNDRY CREDITORS			

TABLE 23.22

ACCRUALS AND PREPAYMENTS

MANAGEMENT ACCOUNTS   *PAGE 21*

ACCRUALS AND PREPAYMENTS

PERIOD 7, AS AT 31 JULY

	ACTUAL £000s	BUDGET £000s	LAST YEAR £000s
ACCRUALS			
PURCHASES			
WAGES PAYABLE			
BRANCH EXPENSES ACCRUED			
HEAD OFFICE EXPENSES ACCRUED			
PROFESSIONAL FEES			
PREPAYMENTS			
RENTS			
RATES			
INSURANCES			
STOCKS OF STATIONERY			

TABLE 23.23

ANALYSIS OF BORROWINGS

MANAGEMENT ACCOUNTS   *PAGE 22*

ANALYSIS OF BORROWINGS

PERIOD 7, AS AT 31 JULY

	PERCENTAGE INTEREST		ACTUAL £000s	BUDGET £000s	LAST YEAR £000s
LONG-TERM DEBT:	RATE	CHARGE P.A.			
DEBENTURES DETAILS					
LONG-TERM BANK LOAN					
OTHER LOANS					

WEIGHTED AVERAGE COST OF LONG-TERM DEBT (%)

$$\frac{\text{INTEREST P.A.}}{\text{TOTAL BORROWINGS}} = \quad \%$$

	PERCENTAGE INTEREST		ACTUAL £000s	BUDGET £000s	LAST YEAR £000s
CURRENT DEBT:	RATE	CHARGE P.A.			
BANK OVERDRAFT					
OTHER SHORT-TERM LOANS					

TABLE 23.24

KEY RATIOS AND STATISTICS

MANAGEMENT ACCOUNTS
KEY RATIOS AND STATISTICS
PERIOD 7, ENDING 31 JULY

PAGE 23

	PERIOD 7			ACTUAL YEAR TO DATE
	ACTUAL	BUDGET	LAST YEAR	
PROFITABILITY SUMMARY–COMPANY AS A WHOLE				
GROSS PROFIT (%)				
OPERATING EXPENSES (%)				
NET PROFIT (%)				
RETURN ON CAPITAL EMPLOYED (%)				
INTEREST COVER (TIMES)				
MARGIN OF SAFETY (%)				
PROFITABILITY SUMMARY–BRANCHES BY RANK	RANKING	RANKING	RANKING	RANKING
BRANCH..	1	1	1	1
BRANCH..	2	2	2	2
BRANCH..	3	3	3	3
BRANCH..	4	4	4	4
BRANCH..	5	5	5	5
BRANCH..	6	6	6	6
BRANCH..	7 ETC.	7 ETC.	7 ETC.	7 ETC.
EMPLOYEES				
NUMBER OF EMPLOYEES				
ORDERS SHIPPED (NUMBER)				
ORDERS IN HAND (NUMBER)				
EMPLOYEES	NO.	NO.	NO.	NO.
NUMBER OF EMPLOYEES				
BRANCH..				
BRANCH..				
BRANCH..				
BRANCH..				
BRANCH..				
HEAD OFFICE				
SALES PER EMPLOYEE (£000s)	£000s	£000s	£000s	£000s
BRANCH..				
BRANCH..				
BRANCH..				
BRANCH..				
BRANCH..				
COMPANY AS A WHOLE				
WORKING CAPITAL				
STOCK–STOCK TURNOVER (TIMES)				
T/DEBTORS–NO. OF DAYS OUTSTANDING				
CURRENT RATIO CA:CL				

FIGURE 23.1

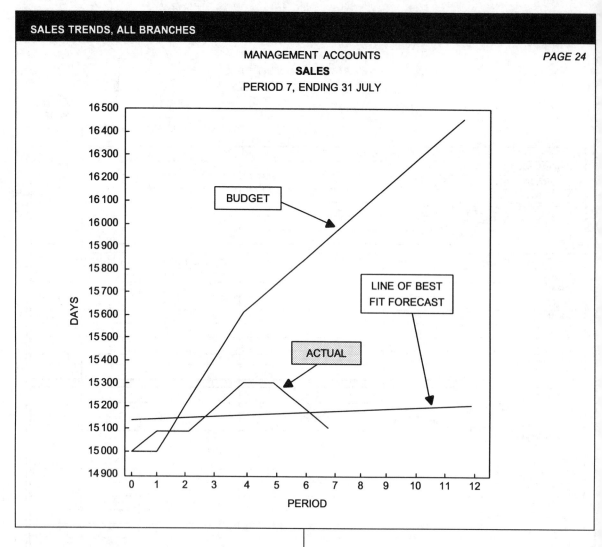

SALES TRENDS, ALL BRANCHES

MANAGEMENT ACCOUNTS
SALES
PERIOD 7, ENDING 31 JULY

PAGE 24

Page 26:   Stockholding trends

This report – showing in Figure 23.3 the position for the whole company – can be broken down to provide the stock position for each of the outlets, as well as for the central warehouse stocks.

Summary

- Management accounts provide management with the ability to control and plan. In this set the emphasis has been on branch profitability analysis and stockholding.
- An additional advantage of accounts that cover a number of branches is that comparisons can be made between them, thereby enabling efficiencies and successes to be identified and adopted throughout.

FIGURE 23.2

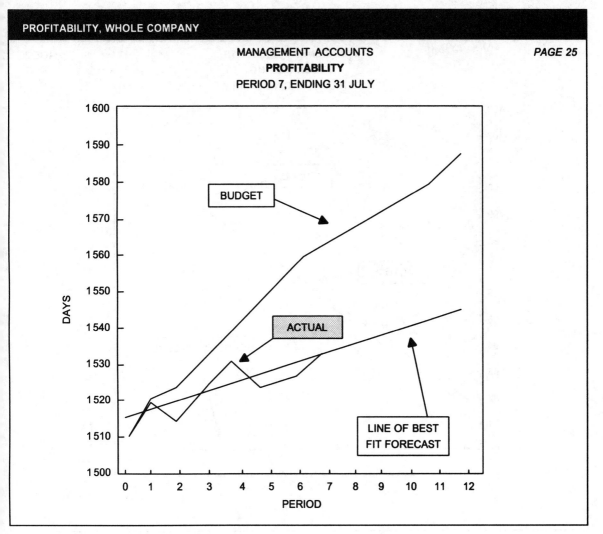

FIGURE 23.3

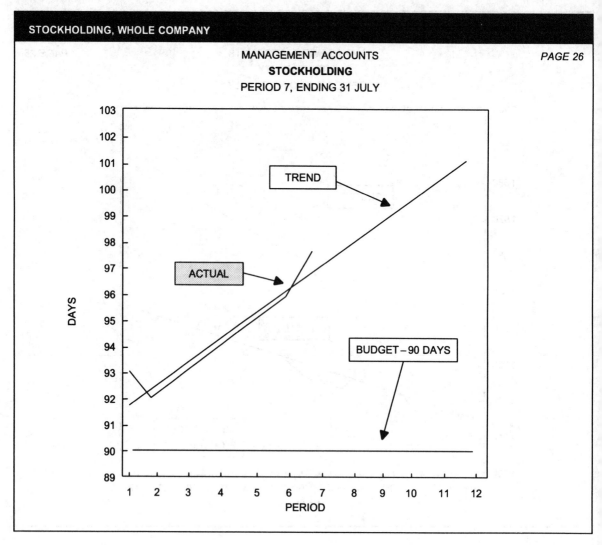

Part V
Revision and Answers

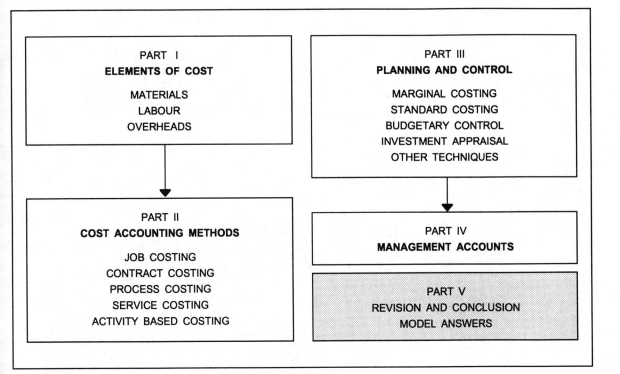

PART I
ELEMENTS OF COST

MATERIALS
LABOUR
OVERHEADS

PART III
PLANNING AND CONTROL

MARGINAL COSTING
STANDARD COSTING
BUDGETARY CONTROL
INVESTMENT APPRAISAL
OTHER TECHNIQUES

PART II
COST ACCOUNTING METHODS

JOB COSTING
CONTRACT COSTING
PROCESS COSTING
SERVICE COSTING
ACTIVITY BASED COSTING

PART IV
MANAGEMENT ACCOUNTS

PART V
REVISION AND CONCLUSION
MODEL ANSWERS

24

Revision and Conclusion

In Parts I and II we saw that a major objective of cost accounting is to calculate the cost of a product, a service or an operation. And in Parts III and IV we examined the various management accounting techniques designed to provide information to management to help them run their business efficiently, effectively and profitably.

In this final chapter we shall be looking back briefly through those earlier chapters as a reminder of the techniques described. We shall also take a brief look at more recent developments in cost and management accounting as a prelude to more advanced studies of the subject.

Elements of cost

In Part I we examined the elements of cost, namely raw materials, direct labour, and overheads.

Raw materials that are identifiable economically as part of the finished product are classified as direct materials; and materials that cannot be so identified are described as indirect materials and classified as production overheads.

Raw materials cost accounting methods enable management to evaluate stocks at the end of each accounting period, for example using FIFO, LIFO, AVCO, actual unit costs or Standard Costing methods. The control of stocks is also facilitated by the setting of various holding levels of stocks: a minimum stockholding level, a maximum level and a reorder level.

Labour cost accounting methods classify this element as being either a constituent part of the finished product, therefore *direct labour costs*, or a supporting service-type cost, that is, *indirect labour costs.*

Labour remuneration methods are also connected with cost accounting, because cost calculations are needed to arrive at gross pay amounts. Labour remuneration systems fall into three main categories: time basis schemes, piecework schemes and premium bonus schemes. An individual on a time basis scheme will receive a rate per hour multiplied by the hours actually worked. The pay of a pieceworker will be how many 'pieces' or units of work have been produced, multiplied by the rate per piece. And the wages of an individual working in a factory where a premium bonus scheme is in operation will comprise the basic (time basis) pay *plus* a bonus based on the amount of time saved to complete a task or job. There are also various 'mixes' of the schemes: for example, with piecework schemes, the pieceworkers might be guaranteed a minimum wage irrespective of the pieces produced.

Overheads are first allocated and apportioned to production and non-production departments or cost centres. Production overheads cover indirect costs incurred on the factory floor (supervisors' wages, cleaning materials, occupation costs and so on), plus the other activities carried out within the production area which 'serve' the manufacturing function, such as the stores department, buying department, canteen and so on.

The production overheads are then absorbed into finished products using a suitable recovery rate, such as machine hours or direct labour hours worked, or activity-based costing techniques.

The final result, the cost of the finished product, will be the costs of the direct materials used plus direct labour costs plus production overhead charged (absorbed) into the product. The resulting *product cost* can then be used to value closing finished goods stocks and also to calculate selling prices.

Overheads, as stated, are allocated and apportioned to non-production departments. 'Non-production' covers all the other functions carried out within the organisation, namely distribution, marketing and selling, and administration. These non-production costs are described as *period costs* – meaning that they will be written off to the profit and loss account in the accounting period in which they were incurred. (Overhead costs included in the product costs, in contrast, are carried forward to the *next* accounting period within the valuation of the closing finished goods stock.)

Distribution costs cover finished goods' warehousing costs and the costs associated with the delivery of the product to customers. Marketing and selling costs cover the costs involved in persuading customers to buy the products and the costs of research into new products. Administration costs are incurred in directing and managing the overall affairs of the business or operation and will embrace the Managing Director's Department, the Accounts Department, Human Resources or Personnel Department and so on.

Cost bookkeeping

There are two major bookkeeping systems used in cost accounting: *integrated accounts* and *interlocking accounts*.

Integrated accounts operate just one general ledger. All postings will therefore be made to this ledger and one trial balance will be extracted, from which financial accounts and costing information will be prepared. Because of the volume of accounts needed to record the information, it is generally necessary to establish *memorandum* or *subsidiary* ledgers to house accounts of the same type. For example, a sales ledger will be maintained to hold all credit customers' accounts; and a raw materials ledger will hold all the individual accounts relating to raw materials. These memorandum ledgers are linked to the general ledger through *control accounts*: a sales ledger control account, a raw materials control account and so on.

The interlocking accounts system splits the financial accounts from the cost accounts, therefore requiring two main ledgers to be kept: the cost ledger and the financial ledger. The cost ledger will maintain the trading accounts, namely stock accounts and manufacturing, trading, and most profit and loss accounts; the financial ledger will hold the assets and liabilities accounts and certain other profit and loss accounts such as financing charges and appropriation accounts. A memorandum cost ledger control account will be maintained in the financial ledger and will be reconciled periodically with the cost ledger's own control account.

Cost accounting methods

Different industries operate different cost accounting methods to account for the elements of cost. These methods can be classified broadly into two main categories: *specific order costing* and *operational costing*.

Specific order costing is used by manufacturers who produce finished goods or projects made or built to a customer's specification. These 'one-off' jobs may be completed relatively quickly, generally meaning within one calendar year, or they may take a number of years to complete. The cost accounting system used for short-term jobs, those finished within the year, is called job costing; the system for longer-term jobs is called contract costing.

Operational costing systems are used by firms which make a product and then sell this from stock, and not to a particular customer's specification. Or, if it is a service organisation, it provides the same ongoing service to a number of customers.

Many products are created through processing basic raw materials into the finished product, the materials passing from one process to the next until the completed article is formed. The operational costing system used for this type of manufacturing is called process costing. In the course of the processing procedures, it often transpires that more than one product emanates from the common processing operations. When this is the case, joint products or by-products are the result. The distinction between these two is made on the basis of value: if two products are produced with broadly the same sales value, the two will be deemed to be joint products; if one product has a much lower value than the other, the lower value product will be considered to be a by-product of the latter. There are different accounting treatments for joint products and by-products.

Operational costing is also used in service industries, such as transport undertakings, hospitals and so on. Here, the operational costing system used is called service costing. A service cost unit is calculated which enables management to control and plan the costs of the service.

With the chosen cost accounting systems in place to account for the elements of cost and revenue, an abundance of information becomes available to management to enable them to plan and control the operations of the business. This information can be presented in a number of ways.

Behavioural aspects of costs

Some costs change depending on different levels of activity achieved; other costs will remain relatively the same irrespective of the output. Thus costs can be split, depending upon the way they behave. Those costs that are seen to move directly in line with output are described as *variable costs*. Those costs that stay the same over the short term are designated *fixed costs*. Some other costs are a mix of the two, changing when different levels of output are achieved, but moving in 'steps' as output increases or decreases. These costs are termed *semi-variable costs* (or *semi-fixed costs*). The analysis of costs by behaviour falls within the planning and control technique called *marginal costing* and *CVP analysis (cost–volume–profit)*. These techniques assist management to make

decisions; for example, whether to make or buy a product, or how to utilise a scarce resource (described as a limiting factor) to maximise profits.

Planning and control

Standard costs

Planning and control go together and there are a number of cost and management accounting techniques designed to assist management to do both.

Management can set a predetermined cost, a *standard cost*, for a product, which will provide a yardstick to compare the actual usage and manufacturing efficiency during the production process. A standard cost comprises two constituents: the quantity needed for a particular item, job or function multiplied by the cost price of the item.

On completion of the work the actual costs will be compared to the standard cost. Any differences are called *variances*. By analysing these variances management will know in respect of raw materials whether (a) too much material has been used (or savings have been made in its use); and (b) whether more or less has been paid for the material than anticipated. Similarly with direct labour. Labour variances will show whether more or less hours have been worked to make the quantity of units produced; and whether the rates of pay to the direct labour staff have been higher or lower than anticipated. Further variances analyse differences between the standard fixed and variable overhead costs with the actual overhead costs incurred.

Variances affect the profit for an accounting period directly. Those that increase the profit are termed *favourable variances*, those that reduce it are termed *adverse variances*.

Budgets

Planning for the whole business falls into two main categories: long-term planning and short-term planning. Long-term planning establishes the objectives and strategy of the firm; short-term planning – often called operational planning – quantifies the long-term plan for the next financial period, usually the next financial year. Short-term plans are generally described as *budgets*.

The sales budget is usually prepared first because most businesses are sales-led, the production budget and other budgets taking their lead from sales. When all budgets are completed and collated, including the balance sheet budget and cash budget, a *master budget* will be the result. This becomes the fixed budget for the budget year. To reflect changes in sales activity, the master budget will be 'flexed' to reflect the behavioural nature of costs, thus producing a flexible budget.

Investment appraisal

Money available for investing in new assets and ventures is usually limited, with demands to spend on capital items often far outstripping the funds available. Management therefore needs to invest carefully, ensuring that the best results for the business are achieved. To assist in this task there are a number of investment appraisal techniques available to management. Those described in the text are the *net present value method*, the *IRR method*, the *payback method*; and the *accounting rate of return method*.

Ratios

Cost and management accounting techniques enable management to control their business by providing the tool of comparison: comparison of actual results with budgets and standard costs; comparison with competitors' results; and comparison through the calculation of key ratios and statistics.

The major control ratios are concerned with profitability and the management of working capital (net current assets). The key ratios for the profit and loss account are the gross profit percentage, the expenses percentage, and the net profit percentage. For the control of working capital, the key statistics are the number of days' stockholding and the number of days' credit taken by customers.

Opportunity costs and sunk costs

By considering the alternatives available when coming to a decision, the management team need to be able to compare their favoured choice with the next best alternative. The difference between the two is called the *opportunity cost*. It follows that the chosen alternative should provide a return greater than the second-best alternative. If not, the other alternative should be chosen. *Sunk costs* are costs that relate to a past decision; they will therefore not be incurred again when a new decision is made that will create future costs and revenue.

Interfirm comparisons

When a number of companies within an industry adopt the same accounting procedures, pooling information, the resulting data can be used by individual members to compare their results with the averages for the whole industry.

Trends analysis

An important part of management accounting is the establishment of the current trading position of the firm in each accounting period (usually calendar monthly or 4/5-weekly periods). Another management accounting purpose is to provide estimates or projections of the likely short-term future trading position. This can be done by the analysis of trends within the business through the calculation of moving annual totals (MATs). These actual trends can then be extrapolated, perhaps to the end of the financial year, to indicate the likely outcome if current trends continue; thus an 'early warning' system is provided.

Management accounts

The purpose of management accounts is to provide management with information to enable them to control and plan the operations of the business. Knowledge itself is power, so the more information presented, the more in control management will be. To be effective, management accounts should be completed within a few days of the end of an accounting period. This enables management to identify strengths and weaknesses as early as possible and therefore to be in a position to take action quickly. Comparison is a key feature of management accounts: for example, actual versus budget; actual versus the previous year. 'Management by exception' techniques are also a feature, bringing to the attention of management those areas that need to be dealt with, while ignoring those areas that are in accordance with plan.

Conclusion

Management decisions are made on the basis of information available. Without relevant information all decisions made become guesses and gambles, based on subjectivity and bias. Like all gambles, some come off (perhaps spectacularly) but most fail. Allied to this, the outcome of poor information reporting and retrieval systems is poor decision-making. The various management accounting techniques described in the text enable management to arrive at considered decisions. 'Quiet, calm deliberation disentangles every knot', is the saying, but this is dependent on the quality of information. So, with the advent of powerful computer programs, the physical problem of retrieving information becomes less onerous; the results should therefore be an improvement in the quality of decisions.

Cost and management accounting is a dynamic subject, with new techniques and methods evolving constantly. For example, one is activity based costing (ABC), which is dependent to a large extent on computer technology to provide the details and analysis of information. An introduction to this technique was given in Chapter 15. The proponents of this method of absorbing production overheads into products, based on the analysis of what drives the overhead costs, argue that it produces more accurate product costs. This, in turn, leads to more accurate selling prices. ABC also ensures that there is a better understanding of the overhead activities that generate costs. The concept of ABC has been advanced to embrace *all* the activities of the business. Here it is called activity based management (ABM). ABM is concerned with the improvement of performance and the value received by the customer by way of analysis of production and non-production activities – the various cost drivers that cause work and therefore overheads. Another development is in budgeting – activity based budgeting (ABB).

Costing, and the presentation of information through management accounting techniques, can be expensive. But the service it performs is highly cost effective and yields benefits that far outweigh the cost.

Costs and revenues are the common factors in all enterprises: the methods and techniques outlined in this text provide management with practical tools to plan and control those costs and revenues, thus ensuring a greater probability that the management goals of efficiency, effectiveness, profitability and overall success are achieved.

25

Model Answers

1   A LEVEL (ULEAC) 1990

(a)   LIFO perpetual system

| December | Receipts | | | Issues | | | Stock | | |
Date	Quantity	£/unit	Total	Quantity	£/unit	Total	Quantity	£/unit	Total
1	Opening balance						8	15.40	123.20
7	11	15.80	173.80				19	15.63	297.00
12				10	15.80	158.00	9	15.44	139.00
14	15	16.00	240.00				24	15.79	379.00
16				13	16.00	208.00	11	15.55	171.00
19	12	16.10	193.20				23	15.83	364.20
21				17	See note*	271.80	6	15.40	92.40
23	14	15.90	222.60				20	15.75	315.00
29				11	15.90	174.90	9	15.57	140.10 *
	52		829.60	51					

*= 3 @ £15.90 + 6 @ £15.40
£47.70 + £92.40

* Note: Dec 21 Issues:

12	16.10	193.20
2	16.00	32.00
1	15.80	15.80
2	15.40	30.80
		£271.80

(b)(i)   AVCO periodic method

	Receipts			Issues			Stock			Average
	Quantity	£/unit	Total	Quantity	£/unit	Total	Quantity	£/unit	Total	cost
December 1	Opening balance						8	15.40	123.20	15.40
Dec purchases	52	15.95	829.60				60	15.88	952.80	15.88
Dec issues				51	15.88	809.88	9	15.88	142.92	15.88

(b)(ii)   LIFO PERIODIC METHOD

	Receipts			Issues			Stock		
	Quantity	£/unit	Total	Quantity	£/unit	Total	Quantity	£/unit	Total
December 1	Opening balance						8	15.40	123.20
Dec purchases	52	15.95	829.60				60	15.88	952.80
Dec issues				51	15.9538	813.65	9	15.46	139.15

2   A LEVEL (ULEAC) 1991

(i)   FIFO

	Receipts units	Receipts price each	Receipts £	Issues units	Issues price each	Issues £	Balance units	Balance £
Opening balance	540	£43.30	23 380				40	1 600
Purchases							580	24 980
Sales				40	£40.00	1 600		
				490	£43.30	21 217	50	2 163
						22 817		

   Profit calculation

Sales	£27 950	
Cost of sales	£22 817	(1 600 + 23 380 − 2 163)
Profit	5 133	

(ii)   LIFO

	Receipts units	Receipts price each	Receipts £	Issues units	Issues price each	Issues £	Balance units	Balance £
Opening balance							40	1 600
Purchases	540	£43.30	23 380				580	24 980
Sales				530	£43.30	22 949		
							50	2 031
						22 949		

   Profit calculation

Sales	£27 950	
Cost of sales	£22 949	(1 600 + 23 380 − 2 031)
Profit	£5 001	

(iii) AVCO

	Receipts units	Receipts price each	Receipts £	Issues units	Issues price each	Issues £	Balance units	Balance £	Average price each
Opening balance							40	1600	£40.00
Purchases	540	£43.30	23380				580	24980	£43.07
Sales				530	£43.07	22827			
							50	2153	£43.07
						22827			

Profit calculation

Sales	£27950
Cost of sales	£22827	$(1600 + 23380 - 2153)$
Profit	£5123

3. A LEVEL (ULEAC) 1990

(i) AVCO perpetual method

Date	Details	Receipts No.	Receipts £	Issues No.	Issues £	Balance No.	Balance £	Average cost
March 1	Opening stock					50	850	£17.000
16	Receipts	100	1750			150	2600	£17.333
24	Issues			90	1560	60	1040	£17.333
April 14		260	4680			320	5720	£17.875
19				150	2681	170	3039	£17.875
22		40	736			210	3775	£17.975
30				160	2876	50	899	£17.975
May 5		190	3648			240	4547	£18.945
20				130	2463	110	2084	£18.945
25		110	2090			220	4174	£18.972
28				120	2277	100	1897	£18.972

(ii) AVCO periodic method

Date	Details	Receipts No.	Receipts £	Issues No.	Issues £	Balance No.	Balance £	Average cost
March 1	Opening stock					50	850	£17.000
March–May	Purchases	700	12904			750	13754	£18.339
March–May	Issues			650	11920	100	1834	£18.339

(iii) LIFO periodic method

Date	Details	Receipts No.	Receipts £	Issues No.	Issues £	Balance No.	Balance £	Average cost
March 1	Opening stock					50	850	£17.000
March–May	Purchases	700	12904			750	13754	£18.434
March–May	Issues			650	11982	100	1772	

4. A LEVEL (ULEAC) 1990

Groceries

	Saleable	Damaged	Total
Sales value	£17 475	£350	£17 825
Cost	£12 200		£12 200
Realisable value		£100	£ 100
Amount to be included in Balance Sheet			£12 300

Frozen foods

Fish	10 000	Realisable value
Vegetables	8 000	Cost
Prepared meals	10 000	Cost
	£18 000	Amount to be included in Balance Sheet

Cigarettes

	Cost	Stolen	Other	Total
	£15 200	£1 800	£1 000	£18 200
Amount to be included in Balance Sheet				£15 200

5. A LEVEL (AEB) 1993

(a) FIFO method

		Receipts units	Receipts £	Sales units	Sales £	Balance units	Balance £
Jan 1	Opening stock					50	8 250
Jan 10	Purchases	200	28 600			250	36 850
Jan 31	Sales			180	26 840	70	10 010
Feb 1	Purchases	120	20 400			190	30 410
Feb 28	Sales			120	18 510	70	11 900
Mar 2	Purchases	220	46 200			290	58 100
Mar 31	Sales			250	49 700	40	8 400
			£95 200		£95 050		

Check: Purchases/opening stock	Jan sales units	Jan sales £	Feb sales units	Feb sales £	Mar sales units	Mar sales £	Total units	Total £
Opening stock	50	8 250					50	8 250
Jan purchases	130	18 590	70	10 010			200	28 600
Feb purchases			50	8 600	70	11 900	120	20 400
March purchases					180	37 800	180	37 800
Closing Stock							40	8 400
	180	26 840	120	18 510	250	49 700	40	8 400
Sales value	£31 500		£25 800		£57 500		£114 800	

Weighted average cost method

		Receipts units	Receipts £	Sales units	Sales £	Balance units	Balance £	Average cost £
Jan 1	Opening stock					50	8 250	165.0
Jan 10	Purchases	200	28 600			250	36 850	147.4
Jan 31	Sales			180	26 532	70	10 318	147.4
Feb 1	Purchases	120	20 400			190	30 718	161.7
Feb 28	Sales			120	19 401	70	11 317	161.7
Mar 2	Purchases	220	46 200			290	57 517	198.3
Mar 31	Sales			250	49 583	40	7 933	198.3
			£95 200		£95 517			

FIFO Stock Value = £8 400; weighted average cost
value = £7 933.

(b) Trading accounts

FIFO			Weighted average cost		
	£			£	
Sales	114 800		Sales	114 800	
Less cost of			Less cost of		
sales			sales		
Opening stock	8 250		Opening stock	8 250	
Purchases	95 200		Purchases	95 200	
Closing stock	(8 400)		Closing stock	(7 933)	
	95 050			95 517	
Profit	19 750		Profit	19 283	

6. AAT COST ACCOUNTING AND BUDGETING 1993
(a)(i) FIFO

		Receipts kg	Receipts £	Issues kg	Issues £	Balance kg	Balance £	
June 1	Balance b/f					1 000	4 000	
June 3	Receipts	2 000	10 000			3 000	14 000	
June 6	Receipts	1 500	8 250			4 500	22 250	
June 9	Issues			2 500	11 500	2 000	10 750	Note: 1000 @ £4; 1500 @ £5.00
June 12	Receipts	3 000	13 500			5 000	24 250	
June 14	Issues			3 500	17 500	1 500	6 750	Note: 500 @ £5; 1500 @ £5.50; 1500 @ £4.50
					29 000			

Cost of issues of Material X using FIFO valuation = £29 000; closing stock valuation = £6 750.

(a)(ii) LIFO

		Receipts kg	Receipts £	Issues kg	Issues £	Balance kg	Balance £	
June 1	Balance b/f					1 000	4 000	
June 3	Receipts	2 000	10 000			3 000	14 000	
June 6	Receipts	1 500	8 250			4 500	22 250	
June 9	Issues			2 500	13 250	2 000	9 000	Note: 1500 @ £5.50; 1000 @ £5.00
June 12	Receipts	3 000	13 500			5 000	22 500	
June 14	Issues			3 500	16 000	1 500	6 500	Note: 3000 @ £4.50; 500 @ £5.00
					29 250			

Cost of issues of Material X using LIFO valuation = £29 250; closing stock valuation = £6 500.

(a)(iii) Weighted average cost

		Receipts		Issues		Balance		Average cost
		kg	£	kg	£	kg	£	£
June 1	Balance b/f					1 000	4 000	4.000
June 3	Receipts	2 000	10 000			3 000	14 000	4.667
June 6	Receipts	1 500	8 250			4 500	22 250	4.944
June 9	Issues			2 500	12 361	2 000	9 889	4.944
June 12	Receipts	3 000	13 500			5 000	23 889	4.678
June 14	Issues			3 500	16 372	1 500	7 017	4.678
					28 733			

Cost of issues of Material X using AVCO valuation = £28 733; closing stock valuation = £7 017.

(b)

$$\sqrt{\frac{2 \times 80\,000 \times £100}{£0.25}} = \frac{£16\,000\,000}{£0.25}$$

$$= £64\,000\,000$$

sq. root thereof: 8 000 units.

(i) Economic order quantity = 8 000 units.
(ii) Average stock = 3 333 units per table below.
(iii) Number of orders per annum = 10 (80 000/8 000).

Month	Receipts	Issues	Balance
1	Opening stock		0
1	8 000	6 666.67	1 333
2	8 000	6 666.67	2 667
3	8 000	6 666.67	4 000
4	8 000	6 666.67	5 333
5	8 000	6 666.67	6 667
6	0	6 666.67	0
7	8 000	6 666.67	1 333
8	8 000	6 666.67	2 667
9	8 000	6 666.67	4 000
10	8 000	6 666.67	5 333
11	8 000	6 666.67	6 667
12	0	6 666.67	0
	40 000	3 333.33 (40 000/12)	

The assumption is that production is evenly spread throughout the year; also, with no lead time nor buffer stock, the company will receive the goods in time for production and therefore an out of stock situation does not arise.

7. LCCI THIRD LEVEL COST ACCOUNTING 1992
Workings and notes:
EOQ formula:

$$\sqrt{\frac{2 \times \text{annual consumption} \times \text{cost per order}}{\text{Holding cost per item p.a.}}}$$

$$\sqrt{\frac{2 \times 100\,000 \times £125}{£1}} = 5\,000 \text{ units}$$

(a) 5000 units

	Receipts	Issues	Balance on order		Total	Allocate free stock	
	kg	**kg**	**kg**	**kg**	**kg**	**kg**	**kg**
Opening position			8 000	10 000	18 000	6 500	11 500
Receipts	5 000		13 000	5 000	18 000	6 500	11 500
Issues		6 400	6 600	5 000	11 600	9 600	2 000
Ordered in period (2)				10 000	21 600	9 600	12 000

(b) Two orders, each of 5 000 kg, will need to be placed to
keep the free stock balance above the 8 000 kg quantity
policy. This is arrived at as follows:

Physical units in stock	6 600
Orders outstanding brought forward	5 000
	11 600
Less allocated to new orders	9 600
	2 000
First new order	5 000
	7 000 – below the 8 000 kg reorder level
Second new order	5 000
Free stock balance at end of period	12 000

(c) (i)   Balance on order from suppliers   15 000 kg
     (ii) Physical stock balance   6 600 kg
     (iii) Balance on allocations   9 600 kg
     (iv) Free stock balance (FSB)   12 000 kg

8. ACCA COST AND MANAGEMENT ACCOUNTING 1 1991

Workings and notes:

Reorder level	5 400 units	1 350 kg × 4 days
Max. level	11 200	5400 + 900 − (800 × 4)
Min. level	1 400	5400 − (1000 × 4)

Stockholding	Order	Receipts	Issues	Balance
0				6 000
1			1 020	4 980
2	9 000		1 020	3 960
3			1 020	2 940
4			1 020	1 920
5			1 020	900
6		9 000	1 200	8 700
7			1 200	7 500
8			1 200	6 300
9			1 200	5 100

10	9 000		900	4 200
11			900	3 300
12			900	2 400
13			900	1 500
14		9 000	900	9 600

(a)   Reorder level   5 400 kg
      Maximum stock level   11 200 kg
      Minimum stock level   1 400 kg

(b)

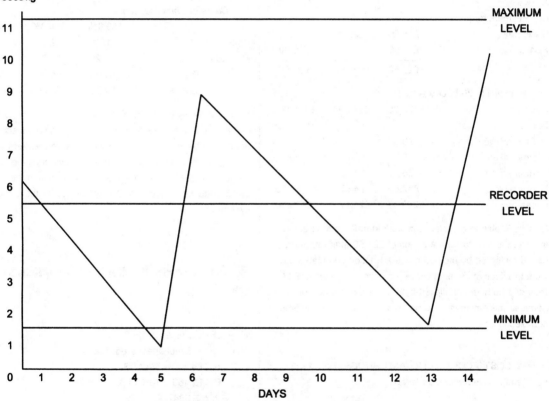

Model answers to examination questions, Chapter 4

1 A LEVEL (ULEAC) 1990

Workings	Daniels	Ericson	Frith
Time allowed – hours	6	6	6
Time taken – hours	3	4	6
Time saved – hours	3	2	0
Bonus – hours	1.5	1	0

Answer

(i) Payment for job:

Basic pay	£15.00	£20.00	£30.00
Bonus	£ 7.50	£ 5.00	£ 0.00
	£22.50	£25.00	£30.00

(ii) Earnings in 35 hour week:

Basic pay	£175.00	£175.00	£175.00
Bonus:			
Time allowed	70	52.5	35
Time taken	35	35	35
Time saved	35	17.5	0
Bonus payment	£87.50	£43.75	£0.00
Gross pay	£262.50	£218.75	£175.00

Daniels is able to complete the work in half the time set so therefore is able to earn a bonus of £87.50 (half the hours saved multiplied by the hourly rate); Ericson completes the work in 2/3rds of the time allowed so earns a bonus of £43.75 (half of 17.5 hours multiplied by £5). Frith earns no bonus because this employee has not been able to save any time in completing jobs.

2 AAT COST ACCOUNTING AND BUDGETING 1993

(i) *Time rate remuneration levels*

	Activity		
	80.0%	**100.0%**	**120.0%**
Hours worked	37.5	37.5	37.5
Rate per hour	£6	£6	£6
Earnings	£225.00	£225.00	£225.00

Piecework remuneration levels

	Activity		
	80.0%	**100.0%**	**120.0%**
Hours worked	37.5	37.5	37.5
Number of pieces made	180	225	270
Rate per piece	£1	£1	£1
Earnings	£180.00	£225.00	£270.00

Bonus scheme remuneration levels

	Activity		
	80.0%	**100.0%**	**120.0%**
Time allowed	30.0	37.5	45.0
Time taken	37.5	37.5	37.5
Time saved	0		7.5
Earnings			
Basic Pay	£225.00	£225.00	£225.00
Bonus			£30.00
			5 hours × £6
	£225.00	£225.00	£255.00

(ii) *Cost per unit produced*

		80.0%	100.0%	120.0%
Units		180	225	270
Method:£	Time	£1.25	£1.00	£0.83
	Piece	£1.00	£1.00	£1.00
	Bonus	£1.25	£1.00	£0.94

As the company wishes to give its employees a minimum wage and an incentive to earn more the premium bonus scheme appears to be the most suitable. This rewards workers for extra achievement and reduces the cost per unit once the targeted production rate has been achieved. In the above the cost per unit is reduced to 94p at 120% against £1 for the piecework system.

Model answers to examination questions, Chapter 5

1 A LEVEL (ULEAC) 1989

Workings – Simultaneous equations

1. A = £4 200 + 5% of B
    B = £2 400 + 10% of A
2. = 20A = £84 000 + 1B
    10B = £24 000 + 1A
3. = 20A – 1B = £84 000
    10B – 1A = £24 000
4. = 200A – 10B = £840 000
    10B – 1A = £24 000
5. = 199A = £864 000 and 10B = £24 000 + £4 342
    A = £4 342
    B = £2 834

Answer:

A's Overheads Apportioned To B = £142 (£4 342 – £4 200)
B's Overheads Apportioned To A = £434 (£2 834 – £2 400)

2 A LEVEL (ULEAC) 1991

Working:

	Technical Services	Administration	Production Departments
	£	£	
Overheads	30 000	20 000	
Administration	2 000	−20 000	18 000
	32 000	0	
Technical services	−32 000	1 600	30 400
	0	1 600	
Administration	160	−1 600	1 440
	160	0	
Technical services	−160	8	152
	0	8	
Administration	1	−8	7
	1	0	
Technical services	−1	0	1
	0	0	50 000

Answer:

(a) Technical services
charge to production = £30 553   30 400 + 152 + 1
Administration charge
to production = £19 447   18 000 + 1 440 + 7
£50 000

(b) Retro Ltd could have used either the elimination method or the algebraic method (simultaneous equations) to apportion the overheads of the two service departments.

3 A LEVEL (ULEAC) 1992

Workings:

	Maintenance	Administration	Production Department
	£	£	
Indirect costs	120 000	86 000	
Maintenance	−120 000	6 000	114 000
	0	92 000	
Administration	9 200	−92 000	82 800
	9 200	0	
Maintenance	−9 200	460	8 740
	0	460	
Administration	46	−460	414
	46	0	
Maintenance	−46	2	44
	0	2	
Administration	0	−2	2
	0	0	206 000

Answer:

Maintenance charge		
to administration	£ 6 462	6 000 + 460 + 2
Administration charge		
maintenance	£ 9 246	9 200 + 46
	£15 708	

Model answers to examinations questions, Chapter 6

1 A LEVEL (ULEAC) 1990

(a)

Department	(I) Overhead absorbed	(ii) Overhead charged	Under or (over) absorbed overhead
	£	£	£
Machine shop	5 720	5 615	(105)
Finishing shop	4 788	4 814	26
Stores	7 512	7 627	115
Assembly bay	24 432	23 180	(1 252)
Stores	42 452		(1 216)

(b)

	Percentage of total materials	Stores overheads apportionment
Machine shop	10.0%	2 443
Finishing shop	60.0%	14 659
Assembly bay	30.0%	7 330
	100.0%	24 432

Basis of apportionment: value of materials charged

2 A LEVEL (ULEAC) 1993

(a) Apportionment of costs:

	Pressing	Fabrication	Painting	Mfg support	Total	Basis
	£	£	£	£	£	
Supervision	6 000	4 500	3 000	1 500	15 000	No. of employees
Rent, power, fire insurance, lighting	7 500	5 500	9 500	2 500	25 000	Area
Plant repairs and depreciation	4 200	3 150	2 100	1 050	10 500	Value of plant
	17 700	13 150	14 600	5 050	50 500	

(b) Apportionment of manufacturing support:

	Pressing	Fabrication	Painting	Mfg support	Total	Basis
	2 244	1 683	1 122	(5 050)	0	No. of employees
	19 944	14 833	15 722	0	50 500	

(c) Absorption rate for the Production Departments:

	Pressing	Fabrication	Painting
Machine hours	13 511		8 290
Labour hours		15 646	
Overhead absorption rate:	£1.48 per machine hour	£0.95 per labour hour	£1.90 per machine hour

3 A LEVEL (ULEAC) 1994

(i) Elimination method

	A	B	C	F	G
	£	£	£	£	£
Overheads	24 000	20 000	14 000	7 000	5 000
Apportionment of overheads: Dept F	1 750	2 800	2 100	(7 000)	350
	25 750	22 800	16 100	0	5 350
Apportionment of overheads: Dept G	2 378	2 081	892	0	(5 350)
	28 128	24 881	16 991	0	0
Hours worked:	3 150	1 890	2 400		
Direct labour hour rate	£8.93		£7.08		
Machine hour rate		£13.16			

(ii) Continuous apportionment method

	A	B	C	F	G	
	£	£	£	£	£	
Overheads	24 000	20 000	14 000	7 000	5 000	
Apportionment of overheads: Dept F	1 750	2 800	2 100	(7 000)	350	
	25 750	22 800	16 100	0	5 350	70 000
Apportionment of overheads: Dept G	2 140	1 872.5	802.5	535	−5 350	
	27 890	24 673	16 903	535	0	70 000
Apportionment of overheads: Dept F	134	214	161	−535	27	0
	28 024	24 887	17 063	0	27	70 000
Apportionment of overheads: Dept G	11	8	4	3	−27	
	28 035	24 895	17 067	3	0	70 000
Apportionment of overheads: DEPT F	1	2	0	−3	0	
	28 036	24 897	17 067	0	0	70 000
Hours worked:	3 150	1 890	2 400			
Direct labour hour rate	£8.90		£7.11			
Machine hour rate		£13.17				

4 A LEVEL (AEB) 1992

(a) Overhead analysis sheet

	Dept X	Dept Y	Dept Z	General Service	Total	Basis of apportionment
	£	£	£	£	£	
Indirect wages	8 000	12 000	18 300	6 700	45 000	Actual
Consumable stores	14 400	9 600	8 000	0	32 000	Stores requisitions
Rent	4 500	6 750	6 000	3 750	21 000	Area M2
Light and heat	3 000	4 500	4 000	2 500	14 000	Area M2
Power	14 000	18 000	900	2 700	36 000	Effective horse power
Depriciation	28 000	36 000	2 000	14 000	80 000	Book value of plant
Insurance – machinery	700	900	50	350	2 000	Book value of plant
	73 000	87 750	39 250	30 000	230 000	
Apportionment of service department	7 500	9 000	13 500	(30 000)		
Apportioned overheads	**£80 500**	**£96 750**	**£52 750**	**£0**	**£230 000**	

(b) Hourly cost rates

Labour hours	100 000		220 000
Machine hours		90 000	
Overhead hourly absorption rate:			
Direct labour hour rate	£0.805		£0.240
Machine hour rate		£1.075	

5 A LEVEL (AEB) 1994

(a) Cost apportionment

	Cutting dept	Machining & finishing	Administration & selling	Total	Basis of apportionment
	£	£	£	£	
Factory power	14 875	44 625		59 500	Kilowatt hours
Sales commission			30 000	30 000	Selling cost
Light and heat	20 533	25 667		46 200	Floor space
Depreciation of equipment	10 000	52 500		62 500	Book value
Repairs to equipment	2 800	14 700		17 500	Book value
Delivery charges			21 700	21 700	Distribution cost
Advertising			15 000	15 000	Selling cost
Supervisory staff	9 100	45 500		54 600	Supervisory staff
Canteen expenses	10 876	28 484		39 360	Factory staff
	£68 184	£211 476	£66 700	£346 360	
Hours worked	36 000	90 000			
Direct labour overhead absorption rate					
	£1.89 per hour	£2.35 per hour			

(b) Unit overhead cost per product

	Cutting dept	Machining & finishing	Total
	£	£	£
Tog A	1.13	8.23	9.36
Tog B	0.95	6.82	7.76
Tog C	0.76	5.64	6.40

6 AAT COST ACCOUNTING AND BUDGETING 1993

(a) Apportionment of production overheads

	Machining	Assembly	Paint shop	Engineering	Stores	Canteen	
Budgeted costs	180 000	160 000	130 000	84 000	52 000	75 000	
Apportionment of canteen	27 000	17 000	13 000	10 000	8 000	(75 000)	basis: no. of staff
	207 000	177 000	143 000	94 000	60 000	0	
Apportionment of stores	24 000	18 000	12 000	6 000	(60 000)		basis: orders
	231 000	195 000	155 000	100 000	0	0	
Apportionment of engineering	45 000	30 000	25 000	(100 000)			basis: service hrs
	276 000	225 000	180 000	0	0	0	

Overhead absorption rates:						
Machining hours	9 200					
Labour hours		11 250				
Labour cost			45 000			
Overhead absorption rates	**£30.00** per machine hour	**£20.00** per labour hour	**£4.00** per £ of labour cost			

(b) Actual results:

	Machining	Assembly	Paint shop
Machine hours	10 000		
Labour hours		7 800	
Labour cost			£35 000
Overhead absorbed	£300 000	£156 000	£140 000
Actual overheads	£290 000	£167 000	£155 000
(Under)/over absorbed overhead	£10 000	(£11 000)	(£15 000)

7 AAT COST ACCOUNTING AND MANAGEMENT ACCOUNTING 1 1992

Workings and notes:

Year 1: machine hours = 132 500 × £18.20 = £2 411 500 budgeted fixed production overheads

Overheads absorbed = £2 442 440 @ £18.20 per hour = 134 200 actual hours

Actual Overheads incurred = £2 317 461

Year 2: Budgeted machine hours = 140 910 (134 200 × 1.05)

Budgeted overhead expenditure = £2 620 926

Budgeted machine hour overhead absorption rate = £18.60 (£2 620 926/140 910)

Actual overheads = £2 695 721;
actual machine hours = 139 260

	Year 1	Year 2
Actual hours worked	134 200	139 260
Overhead absorption machine rate per hour	£18.20	£18.60
Overhead absorbed	£2 442 440	£2 590 236
Overhead incurred	£2 317 461	£2 695 721
Under/(over) absorbed overheads	(£124 979)	£105 485

In Year 1 overhead was overabsorbed by £124 979. More hours were worked than expected − 1 700 − and the overhead additionally absorbed amounted to £30 940 (1 700 × £18.20). In addition, the company budgeted to spend £2 411 500 on fixed overheads but the actual spend was £2 317 461. Thus an additional saving was made here of £94 039. To summarise, more hours worked = £30 940 plus expenditure savings = £94 039 = overabsorption £124 979.

In Year 2 however, there was an underabsorption of £105 485. Less hours were worked than budgeted, 1650 hours, costing £30 690 (1650 × £18.60). In addition, the actual spend was far greater than budgeted, costing an additional £74 795. To summarise: less hours = £30,690 plus greater expenditure = £74 795 = £105 485 underabsorbed. The increase in the machine hour rate between the two years is 40p.

Model answers to examination questions, Chapter 8

1. A LEVEL (ULEAC) 1990
BARRINGTON PRODUCTS LTD
Manufacturing Account as at 31 December

	£
Raw Materials	
Opening stock	8 724
Purchases	146 249
Returns	(1 863)
Closing stock	(9 562)
	143 548
Direct labour	50 503
Prime cost	194 051
Direct expenses	16 679
Factory expenses	
Indirect wages	32 309
General expenses	17 533
Heat and light	5 192
Insurances	6 062
Rates	3 105
Depreciation	4 624
Total factory overheads	64 201
Total production costs	274 931
Add: Opening work in progress	12 842
Less: Closing work in progress	(11 287)
Cost of goods completed	276 486
Manufacturing profit	112 676
Market value	389 162

2. LCCI THIRD LEVEL COST ACCOUNTING 1991
Workings and notes:

	£	Financial ledger £	Cost ledger £
Profit per financial ledger	23 030		
Less sundry income items	(730)		
Less administration diff.	(1 700)	11 800	13 500
Add selling difference	3 750	26 250	22 500
Add factory overheads diff.	3 300	23 500	20 200
	27 650	61 550	56 200
opening stocks	6 770	270 100	263 330
closing stocks	6 330	267 500	273 830
Profit per cost ledger	40 750		

Opening stocks analysis:

	Financial ledger	Cost ledger
	£	£	£
RM	11770	107250	95480
WIP	(14750)	79600	94350
FG	9750	83250	73500
	6770	270100	263330

Closing stocks analysis:

	Financial ledger	Cost ledger
	£	£	£
RM	21650	98800	120450
WIP	(5650)	80300	74650
FG	(9670)	88400	78730
	6330	267500	273830

Answer A   Stock values in cost ledger:

	(i) Opening	(ii) Closing
	£	£
RM	95480	120450
WIP	94350	74650
FG	73500	78730

Answer B   Balance on the Cost Ledger Control Account at the start of quarter 1 will be:

£270100 credit

(To balance the debit entries on the stock accounts brought forward.)

Answer C

Factory:

Factory costs	£20200
Direct labour cost	£25250
Overhead absorption rate	80.0% on direct labour cost

Administration:

Administration costs	£13500
Sales value	£450000
Overhead absorption rate	3.0% on sales value

Selling:

Selling costs	£22500
Sales value	£450000
Overhead absorption rate	5.0% on sales value

3. ACCA COST AND MANAGEMENT ACCOUNTING 1 1990

Workings and notes:

Raw materials		Receipts kg	Receipts £	Issues kg	Issues £	Balance kg	Balance £	Ave. cost £
	o/balance					21 600	28 944	1.3400
1st	Issues			7 270	9 742	14 330	19 202	1.3400
7th	Purchases	17 400	23 490			31 730	42 692	1.3455
8th	Issues			8 120	10 925	23 610	31 767	1.3455
15th	Issues			8 080	10 872	15 530	20 895	1.3455
20th	Purchases	19 800	26 730			35 330	47 625	1.3480
22nd	Issues			9 115	12 287	26 215	35 338	1.3480
			50 220		43 826			

DR	Raw materials stock control account				CR	
		Kilos	£		Kilos	£
Balance b/fwd		21 600	28 944			
Purchases		37 200	50 220	Issues	32 585	43 826
				Balance c/fwd	26 215	35 338
		58 800	79 164		58 800	79 164

DR	Work in progress account				CR	
		Units	£		Units	£
Materials			43 826			
Labour and overheads			35 407	Cost of goods made trfrd to f/goods	17 150	79 233
			79 233			79 233

DR	Finished goods stock control account				CR				
		Units	£		Units	£		FIFO	
Balance b/fwd		16 960	77 168	Transfer to cost of sales account	17 030	77 491	→	16 960	£77 168
Transfer from work in progress account		17 150	79 233					70	£ 323
				Balance c/fwd	17 080	78 910		17 030	£77 491
		34 110	156 401		34 110	156 401			

4. CIMA COST ACCOUNTING 1992

(i) Journal for the payroll entries:

Payroll journal	DR £	CR £
Wages control account	199 230	
National insurance payable account		32 890
PAYE payable account		27 800
Pension fund account		7 200
Court order retentions payable account		1 840
Trade union subscriptions payable account		1 200
Private health care contributions payable account		6 000
Net pay control account		122 300
	199 230	199 230

(ii) Wages control account:

Wages control account analysis journal		DR £	CR £
Work in progress control account		94 260	
Production overhead control account:		102 670	
Indirect labour account	48 600		
Overtime premium account	9 000		
Shift premiums account	13 000		
Idle time account	4 300		
Sick pay account	9 000		
Company national ins'ce a/c	18 770		
Fixed assets under construction account		2 300	
Wages control account			199 230
		199 230	199 230

5. CIMA COST ACCOUNTING 1993

Production overhead included in work in process for Process 1 = £125 000.

Direct wages for Process 1 included in work in process = £50 000

Overhead absorption rate per £1 of direct wages cost = £2.50.

Production overhead included in work in process for Process 2 = £105 000.

Direct wages for Process 1 included in work in process = £70 000.

Overhead absorption rate per £1 of direct wages cost = £1.50.

DR	Raw materials control account		CR
	£000		£000
Balance b/fwd	400		
Purchases	210	Returns to suppliers	10
		Issues to Process 1	136
		Issues to Process 2	44
		Balance c/down	420
	610		610

DR	Work in Process 1 account		CR
	£000		£000
Balance b/fwd	246		
Materials	136	Transfer to Process 2	483
Direct wages	84	Abnormal loss	20
Production overhead	210		
		Balance c/down	173
	676		676

DR	Work in Process 2 account		CR
	£000		£000
Balance b/fwd	302		
Transfer from			
Process 1	483		
Materials	44	Transfer to f/goods	908
Direct wages	130	Abnormal loss	33
Production overhead	195		
		Balance c/down	213
	1 154		1 154

DR	Finished goods account		CR
	£000		£000
Balance b/fwd	60		
Transfer from		Transfer to cost of	
Process 2	908	goods sold account	844
		Balance c/down	124
	968		844

DR	Wages control account		DR
	£000		£000
Direct wages paid	200	Transfer to Process 1	84
Production salaries paid	170	Transfer to Process 2	130
		Transfer to production	
		overhead	170
Balance c/down	14		
	384		384

DR	Production overhead control account		CR
	£000		£000
Production expenses			
paid	250		
Transfer from wages		Transfer to Process 1	210
control account	170	Transfer to Process 2	195
Depreciation charge	8		
		Transfer to under-	
		absorbed account	23
	428		428

DR	Debtors control account		CR
	£000		£000
Balance b/fwd	1 120		
Sales	1 100	Cash received	1 140
		Transfer to Process 2	
		Balance c/fwd	1 080
	2 220		2 220

DR	Creditors control account		CR
	£000		£000
		Balance b/fwd	300
Cash payments	330	Purchases	210
Purchase returns	10		
Balance c/fwd	170		
	510		510

DR	Administration overheads account		CR
	£000		£000
Balance b/down	120		
Payments	108		
		Balance c/down	228
	228		228

DR	Selling and distribution overheads account		CR
	£000		£000
Balance b/down	80		
Payments	84		
		Balance c/down	164
	164		164

DR	Cost of goods sold account		CR
	£000		£000
Balance b/down	888		
Transfer from finished			
goods account	844	Balance c/down	1 732
	1 732		1 732

DR	Freehold buildings account		CR
	£000		£000
Balance b/fwd	800		
		Balance c/down	800
	800		800

DR	Plant and equipment account		CR
	£000		£000
Balance b/fwd	480		
		Balance c/down	480
	480		480

DR	Provision for depreciation – P & E account		CR
	£000		£000
		Balance b/fwd	100
		Charge – October	96
Balance c/down	196		
	196		196

DR	Capital account		CR
	£000		**£000**
		Balance b/fwd	2 200
Balance c/down	2 200		
	2 200		2 200

DR	Profit retained account		CR
	£000		**£000**
		Balance b/fwd	220
Balance c/down	220		
	220		220

DR	Bank account		CR
	£000		**£000**
		Balance b/down	464
Debtors	1 140	Wages control	200
		Wages control	170
		Production overhead control	250
		Creditors	330
		Admin control	108
		Selling & distn control	84
Balance c/down	466		
	1 606		1 606

DR	Sales account		CR
	£000		**£000**
		Balance b/down	1 200
		October sales	1 100
Balance c/down	2 300		
	2 300		2 300

DR	Abnormal loss account		CR
	£000		**£000**
Balance b/down	9		
Process 1 loss	20		
Process 2 loss	33	Balance c/down	62
	62		62

DR	Over/under absorbed overhead		CR
	£000		**£000**
		Balance b/down	21
Transfer from overhead control	23	Balance c/down	2
	23		23

Model answers to examination questions, Chapter 10

1 A LEVEL (ULEAC) 1991

(a) Cost of Batch No. 23 if all units pass inspection:

	Total	Per unit	
	£	£	
Materials	480.00	1.60	
Labour	84.00	0.28	$300/15 \times £4.20$
Overheads	72.00	0.24	$300/15 \times £3.60$
Set up of machine	21.00	0.07	
Total	**£657.00**	**£2.19**	$£657/300 = £2.19$

(b) Actual cost of Batch No. 23:

	Total	
	£	
Materials	480.00	$300 \times £1.60$
Labour	84.00	$300/15 \times £4.20$
Overheads	72.00	$300/15 \times £3.60$
Set up of machine	21.00	
Rectification work:		
Set up of machine	18.00	
Labour – 9 hours	37.80	$9 \times £4.20$
Overheads – 9 hours	32.40	$9 \times £3.60$
Scrap value – 20 units (17.20)		$20 \times £0.86$
Total cost	**£728.00**	
Cost per unit	**£2.60**	£728/280

(c) Loss incurred because of defective work:

280 units should have cost	£613.20	$280 \times £2.19$
Actual cost	£728.00	
Loss incurred:	**£114.80**	

2 A LEVEL (AEB) 1993

Workings and notes:

Depreciation = £3000 p.a.   (£24 000/8 years)

Heat and light:

XR8 proportion: $250/8750 \times £7000$

$$= £200$$

Supervision:

XR8 proportion: $1/20 \times £6000$

$$= £300$$

XR Repair equipment = £110

Power cost = $2500 \times 5p = £125$

Labour Costs:

Set up = 200 Hours × £4.80 = 960 (assumed treated as a machine dept overhead because no details of set-up hours have been provided for Z22)

Insurance:

XR8 proportion:

24 000/768 000 × £8 000 = £250

(a) Statement

Machine hour rate for XR8

	Cost per annum £
Depreciation charge	3 000
Heat and light proportion	200
Supervision proportion	300
Repair equipment	110
Insurance	250
Set up costs	960
	4 820
Machine hours	2 300
Machine hour rate	**£2.10**

(b) Cost of Job Z22

	£	
Materials	37.50	15 kg × £2.50 per kg
Labour – Machinist	19.20	12 hours × £4.80/3
Labour – Assembly	10.80	3 hours × £3.60
Overheads	25.20	12 hours × £2.10
	£92.70	

Cost of job Z22 = £92.70

3 AAT COST ACCOUNTING AND BUDGETING 1991

(a)

	Direct labour cost	Direct labour hours	Machine hours
Production overhead	£600 000	£600 000	£600 000
Direct labour cost	£200 000		
Direct labour hours		£40 000	
Machine hours			£50 000
Overhead absorption rate	**£3.00** per labour cost	**£15.00** per direct labour hour	**£12.00** per machine hour

(b) As the company has invested heavily in machinery and reduced its workforce, the more appropriate overhead absorption rate the company should use is the machine hour rate of £12 per machine hour.

(c) Cost of Job AX

	£	
Materials	3 788	
Direct labour	1 100	
Direct expenses	422	
Production overhead	1 440	120 Hours × £12 Per hour
	6 750	
Administration overhead	1 350	20% of £6 750
	8 100	
Profit	900	Difference
Selling price	**£9 000**	£8 100/.90

4 AAT COST ACCOUNTING AND BUDGETING 1993

Workings and notes:

Budget		£	
Materials		763 000	
Labour	Dept A	152 000	
Labour	Dept B	125 000	
Overhead	Dept A	760 000	£20.00 Per labour hour
Overhead	Dept B	750 000	600.0% of labour cost
Production cost		2 550 000	
Administration overhead		510 000	

Administration as percentage of production cost = 20%

Cost of zeron

		£	
Material	RAYEX	44 000	
	NAYON	20 000	
Labour	Dept A	10 000	
	Dept B	8 000	
Overheads	Dept A	50 000	
	Dept B	48 000	
		180 000	
Administration Cost		36 000	
		216 000	60%
Profit		144 000	40%
BID Price		360 000	100%

5 ACCA COST AND MANAGEMENT ACCOUNTING 1 1991

Workings and notes:

Material P – priced on weighted average basis:

	Receipts (units)	Receipts (£)	Issues (units)	Issues (£)	Balance (units)	Balance (£)	Average (£)
Opening Stock					3 100	5 594	1.8045
Purchases	3 500	6 335			6 600	11 929	1.8074
Purchases	3 800	6 916			10 400	18 845	1.8120
Issues			7 060	12 793	3 340	6 052	1.8120

Material wastage not charged to individual jobs, therefore cost becomes an overhead: 60 kg wasted @ £1.812 per kg = £108.72.

Rectification work not charged to individual jobs, therefore cost becomes an overhead: 340kg @ £1.812 per kg = £616.08.

Other materials: Wastage and rectification also not charged to jobs so become an overhead: wastage = £236; rectification work = £197.

Labour

Normal hours	3640 @ £6 p/hr	£21 840.00	
Overtime hours	290 @ £6 p/hr	£1 740.00	
Premium – 30%		£522.00	Becomes an overhead

Idle time treated as an overhead:
  82 hours @ £6 = 492.00

Rectification work treated as an overhead:
  37 hours @ £6 = £222.00

Productive hours: 3640 + 290 – 82 – 37 = 3 811 hours

Overheads

Supervisory labour	3 760.00	
Depreciation	585.00	
Cleaning materials	63.00	
Stationery/telephone	275.00	
Rent and rates	940.00	
Vehicle running costs	327.00	
Other administration	688.00	
Material P wastage	108.72	as above
Material P rectification	616.08	as above
Other materials waste	236.00	as above
Other materials rect'n	197.00	as above
Labour o/time premium	522.00	as above
Labour idle time	492.00	as above
Labour rectification	222.00	as above
Total overhead	9 031.80	

Recovered on a direct labour hour basis: 3 811 hours

Answer:

Absorption rate per hour   £2.3699

(a) Statement of Costs – Job 126

	£	
Material P	1 739.52	960 kg @ £1.812
Other Material	2 030.00	
Less wastage Material	(42.00)	
Less rectification material	(33.00)	
Labour	2 976.00	496 hours @ £6
Less idle time	60.00	10 hours @ £6
Less rectification work	72.00	12 hours @ £6
Direct costs	6 538.52	
Overheads	1 123.33	474 @ £2.3699
Total cost – job 126	£7 661.85	

(b) Wastage = 42 kg = 1.11% of material input. Target is 1%.
Rectification cost = £105 = 1.61% of direct cost. Target is 1.5%.
Actual idle time = 10 hours = 2.11% of labour hours charged. Target is 2%.

None of the targets set have been achieved on Job 126. The under-performance may be more widespread, and similar comparisons of actual results with the targets should be calculated for the factory as a whole. Job 126 can then be compared with these results. The actual additional costs borne because the targets were not achieved on Job 126 are as follows:

Wastage	7.54	42 – (42/1.11 × 1)
Rectification	7.17	105 – (105/1.61 × 1.5)
Idle time	3.13	60 – (60/2.11 × 2)
	17.84	

Model answers to examination questions, Chapter 11

1 A LEVEL (ULEAC) 1991

Contract no. 1234

DR	Contract account		CR
	£		£
Materials	120 480	Materials returns	1 460
		Materials carried down	
		to next accounting	
Direct wages	134 200	period	15 340
Wages accrued	5 220		
Plant at cost	82 600	Plant carried down at	
		valuation to next	
		period	63 200
Sub-contractors'			
charges	27 560		
Head office expenses	71 430		
Direct expenses	42 570		
Direct expenses		Balance carried	
accrued	2 840	down	406 900
	486 900		486 900
Balance brought			
down	406 900	Work certified	500 000
Attributable profit	68 255	Work not yet certified	27 350
Profit provision	52 195		
	527 350		527 350

Workings:

Notional profit = £120 450   (527 350 − 406 900)

$$\frac{2 \times £425\,000 \times £120\,450}{3 \times £500\,000 \times 1} = £68\,255 \text{ attributable profit}$$

Prudency test:

Work completed to date	£500 000
Contract price	£850 000

= 59% completed, it is assumed that management are reasonably certain that an overall profit will be earned from the contract.

2 A LEVEL (ULEAC) 1994

Contract 93/5

DR	Contract account		CR
	£		£
Materials	110 000	Materials returns	1 000
		Materials carried down	
		to next accounting	
Direct wages	96 000	period	11 000
Wages accrued	4 000		
Plant at cost	60 000	Plant carried down at	
		valuation to next	
		period	40 000
Establishment			
expenses	50 000		
Direct expenses	30 000		
Direct expenses		Balance carried	
accrued	2 000	down	300 00
	352 000		352 000
Balance brought			
down	300 000	Work certified	320 000
Attributable profit	27 778	Work not yet certified	20 000
Profit provision	12 222		
	340 000		340 000

Workings:

Notional profit = £40 000

$$\frac{2 \times £300\,000 \times £40\,000}{3 \times £320\,000 \times 1} = £25\,000 \text{ attributable profit}$$

Prudency test:

Work completed to date	£320 000
Contract price	£600 000

= 53.3% completed, it is assumed that management are reasonably certain that an overall profit will be earned from the contract.

Contract 93/9

DR	Contract account £	CR £
Materials	80 000	Materials returns	2 000
		Materials carried down to next accounting	
Direct wages	64 000	period	8 000
Wages accrued	5 000		
Plant at cost	90 000	Plant carried down at valuation to next period	80 000
Establishment expenses	30 000		
Direct expenses	20 000		
Direct expenses accrued	1 000	Balance carried down	200 000
	290 000		290 000
Balance brought down	200 000	Work certified	160 000
		Work not yet certified	30 000
		Loss transferred to P & L	10 000
	200 000		200 000

Prudency test:
Work completed to date   £160 000
Contract price   £800 000
= 20% completed.
A loss has arisen and the contract is only 20% complete. If management consider that further losses will be sustained, these should be recognised in the above account period and written off to profit and loss account.

Model answers to examination questions, Chapter 12

1   A LEVEL (ULEAC) 1989
(i)

DR	Primary process account		CR	
	kg	£	kg	£
Materials	65 000	39 000	Normal loss	6 500	0
Labour		5 730	Transfer to		
Overheads		3 240	secondary process	55 000	45 100
			Abnormal loss	3 500	2 870
	65 000	47 970		65 000	47 970

Cost per unit = £47 970/58 500 = £0.82 each

DR	Secondary process account		CR	
	kg	£	kg	£
Transfer from primary process			Normal loss	2 750	0
			Transfer to finishing		
account	55 000	45 100	process	53 000	67 840
Materials		6 300			
Labour		7 200			
Overheads		8 280			
Abnormal gain	750	960			
	55 750	67 840		55 750	67 840

Cost per unit = £66 880/52 250 = £1.28 each

DR	Finishing process account		CR	
	kg	£	kg	£
Transfer from secondary			Normal loss	2 650	3 313
			Transfer to		
process	53 000	67 840	finished goods		
Labour		8 280	account	48 000	74 328
Overheads		5 160	Abnormal loss	2 850	3 639
	65 000	81 280		53 000	81 280

Cost per unit = £77 967.50/50 350 = £1.5485 each

(ii)

DR	Abnormal gains account £	CR £
Transfer to profit and loss account	960	Transfer from secondary account	960
	960		960

DR	Abnormal losses account £	CR £
Transfer from primary account	2 870	Sale receipts re: losses from finishing account	2 938
Transfer from finishing account	3 639	Transfer to profit and loss account	3 571

2 A LEVEL (ULEAC) 1990

(a) Apportionment of overheads

	A	B	C	X	Y
	£	£	£	£	
Indirect costs	15 000	12 000	10 000	6 000	4 000
Dept Y	1 600	1 200	800	400	(4 000)
	16 600	13 200	10 800	6 400	0
Dept X	2 880	1 600	1 920	(6 400)	
	19 480	14 800	12 720	0	0

Overhead absorption rate:

Hours worked	2 000	2 200	2 500
Rate per hour	**£9.740**	**£6.727**	**£5.088**

(b) Process accounts

DR		Process A account			CR
	kg	£		kg	£
Materials	5 000	50 000	Normal loss	250	0
Labour		2 331	Transfer to		
Overheads:			Process B	4 600	51 811
120 hours					
@ £9.740		1 169	Abnormal loss	150	1 689
	5 000	53 500		5 000	53 500

Cost per unit = £53 500/4 750 kg = £11.2632

DR		Process B account			CR
	kg	£		kg	£
Transfer			Normal loss	115	0
from A	4 600	51 811	Transfer to		
Material		4 000	finished		
Labour		1 651	goods	4 500	58 194
Overheads:					
80 hours					
@ £6.727		538			
Abnormal gain	15	194			
	4 615	58 194		4 615	58 194

Cost per unit = £58 000/4 485 kg = £12.9320

Cost of the order processed during April: £58 194

3 A LEVEL (ULEAC) 1990

Equivalent units table

Units	Material	Labour	Overheads
Completed units made	6 000	6 000	6 000
Work in progress	600	520	440
(a) Total equivalent units	6 600	6 520	6 440
Costs	£12 540	£8 476	£7 084
Costs per element	£1.90	£1.30	£1.10

(b) Cost per complete unit £4.30

(c) Value of work in progress

Materials	£1 140	600 × £1.90
Labour	£676	520 × £1.30
Overheads	£484	440 × £1.10

Total value of work in progress £2 300

4 A LEVEL (ULEAC) 1992

(a) Calculation of work in progress.

Units	Materials	Labour	Overheads
Completed product	8 000	8 000	8 000
Work in progress	270	210	180
	8 270	8 210	8 180
Notes	(0.9 × 300)	(0.7 × 300)	(0.6 × 300)

Cost			
Materials	72 776		as below
Labour		59 112	as below
Overheads			109 908 as below
Cost per element	£8.80	£7.20	£13.44

Valuation of work in progress:

	Units	Cost Per element	Value
Materials	270	£8.80	2 376
Labour	210	£7.20	1 512
Overheads	180	£13.44	2 418
			6 306

Cost per unit £29.436

(b) Manufacturing account.

Toft Processing

Manufacturing Account for the three months ended 31 May

		£
Materials		
Opening stock	5 576	
Purchases	76 110	
Returns	(2 510)	
Closing stock	(6 400)	
		72 776
Labour		
Direct factory wages	58 042	
Less accrual b/fwd	(3 450)	
Add accrued wages	4 520	
		59 112

Prime Cost			**131 888**

Factory Overheads			
Indirect factory wages		40 573	
Accrued wages		5 490	46 063
Heating and lighting		11 803	
Less accrual b/fwd		−1 860	
Add accrued heating		1 320	11 263
General factory expenses		10 839	
Less prepaid expenses		−810	
Add accrued expenses		760	10 789
Insurance of plant		6 664	
Less prepaid insurance		−1 490	5 174
Rates of factory premises		15 151	
Less prepaid rates		−4 012	11 139
Depreciation			25 480
			109 908

Manufacturing costs	241 796
Add opening work in progress	0
Less closing work in progress	(6 306)
Total cost of product manufactured	**235 490**
	(= 8 000 × £29.436)
Manufacturing profit	**35 510**
Manufacturing output at market price	£271 000

5 A LEVEL (ULEAC) 1994

(i) Raw materials valuation

Material X	£2 400	
Material Y	£ 480	(being the lower of cost or net realisable value)
Material Z	£1 060	
	£3 940	

(ii) Work-in-progress valuation

Units	Material	Labour	Overheads
Completed	4 000	4 000	4 000
Work in progress	200	200	200
	4 200	4 200	4 200
Costs	£3 300	£4 320	£780
Cost per element	£0.79	£1.03	£0.19
Cost per unit	£2.00		

Work in progress valuation:

Materials	£157	200 × £0.79
Labour	£206	200 × £1.03
Overheads	£37	200 × £0.19
	£400	

(iii) Finished goods valuation

4 000 units at £2.00 each = £8 000

6 AAT COST ACCOUNTING AND BUDGETING

(a) Process account

DR		Process account–product XY			CR
	kg	£		kg	£
Materials	25 000	62 000	Normal loss	1 000	2 000
Labour		44 000	Transfer to		
Overheads		63 000	finished stock	15 000	112 500
			Work in progress	6 000	32 000
			Abnormal loss	3 000	22 500
	25 000	169 000		25 000	169 000

Equivalent units table

Units	Material	Labour	Overheads	Total
Completed	15 000	15 000	15 000	
Abnormal loss	3 000	3 000	3 000	
Work in progress	6 000	4 000	3 000	
	24 000	22 000	21 000	
Costs	£60 000	£44 000	£63 000	
Costs per element	£2.50	£2.00	£3.00	
Cost per unit				**£7.50**
Work-in-progress valuation	£15 000	£8 000	£9 000	£32 000

(b) Abnormal loss account

DR	Abnormal loss account		CR
	£		£
Transfer from process account	22 500		
		To profit and loss account	22 500
	22 500		22 500

Note: Only normal losses had any scrap value, with no value being attached to abnormal losses. Therefore no receipts for sale have been credited to the abnormal loss account.

7 AAT COST ACCOUNTING AND BUDGETING

Weighted average method used = AVCO method

(a) Process 1 account

DR		Process 1 account – November		CR
	Units	£	Units	£
Materials	15 000	26 740	Normal loss 750	0
Labour		36 150	Transfer to	
Overheads		40 635	Process 2 10 000	85 000
Abnormal gain	150	1 275	Closing WIP 4 400	19 800
	15 150	104 800	15 150	104 800

Equivalent units table

Units	Materials	Labour	Overheads
Completed units	10 000	10 000	10 000
Less abnormal gain	−150	−150	−150
Closing WIP	3 520	2 200	1 760
Equivalent units	13 370	12 050	11 610
Costs	£26 740	£36 150	£40 635
Costs per element	£2.00	£3.00	£3.50

Cost per unit £8.50

Valuations

WIP	£7 040	£6 600	£6 160	£19 800
Transfer to Process 2				**£85 000**

(10 000 × £8.50)

Abnormal gain **£1 275**

(150 × £8.50)

(b) Process 2 account

DR		Process 2 account – November		CR
	Units	£	Units	£
Opening stock	2 000	26 200		
Transfer from			Normal loss 600	5 100
Process 1	10 000	85 000	Transfer to	
Labour		40 000	finished goods 9 500	175 750
Overheads		59 700	Abnormal loss 100	1 850
			Closing WIP 1 800	28 200
	12 000	210 900	12 000	210 900

Equivalent units table, AVCO method

	Materials	Labour	Overheads
Completed units	9 500	9 500	9 500
Abnormal gains	100	100	100
Closing WIP	1 800	1 200	1 350
Equivalent units	11 400	10 800	10 950

Costs:

Brought forward	£17 000	£3 200	£6 000
Current period	£79 900	£40 000	£59 700
	£96 900	£43 200	£65 700 £205 800
Costs per element	£ 8.50	£4.00	£6.00

Cost per unit £ 18.50

Valuations:

Closing WIP	£15 300	£4 800	£8 100 £28 200
Transfer to f/goods			£175 750

(9 600 × £18.50)

Abnormal loss £1 850

(100 × £18.50)

(c) Normal loss account

In process costing the normal loss income is usually credited directly to the process account as shown above, so a separate account is not generally required.

(d) Abnormal loss/gain account

DR		Abnormal loss/gain account		CR
		£		£
Abnormal loss			Abnormal gain	
transferred from			transferred from	
Process 2 account		1 850	Process 1 account	1 275
			Loss for November	
			transferred to P & L a/c	575
		1 850		1 850

8 LCCI THIRD LEVEL COST ACCOUNTING 1992

DR		Product WYE – Process 2 account		CR
	Units	£	Units	£
Opening			Normal loss 1 750	4 375
balance	5 000	77 300		
Transfer from				
Process 1	30 000	361 300	Transfer to	
Materials added		44 000	finished stock 29 800	545 370
Conversion costs		118 700	Abnormal loss 450	8 235
			Closing work in	
			progress c/d 3 000	43 320
	35 000	601 300	35 000	601 300
Balance b/d	3 000	43 320		

Equivalent units table

Units	Materials	Conversion cost
Completed units	28 500	29 800
Abnormal losses	450	450
Work in progress e/units	2 400	2 250
	32 650	32 500

Costs		
WIP brought forward	£65 400	£11 900
Cost during period	£361 300	
	£44 000	£118 700
	(£4 375)	
	466 325	130 600 Total
Cost per unit	£14.28	£4.02 £18.30

Valuation of completed units: 29 800 × £18.301 = £545 370
Valuation of abnormal losses = 450 units × £18.301 = £8 235
Valuation of work in progress:
  Materials – 2400 × £14.283 = £34 279
  Conversion costs: 2 250 units × £4.018 = £9 041
  Total = £34 279 + £9 041 = £43 320

(a) Cost per unit = £18.301
  Total value of finished stock transfer = £545 370
(b) Value of closing work in progress = £43 320 total
  Value of closing materials work in progress = £34 279
  Value of closing conversion costs work in progress
  = £9 041
(c) Charge to profit and loss for abnormal loss:

Per process account	£8 235
Less recovered through	
sale of 450 units @ £2.50 each	£1 125
Net cost	£7 110

9 LCCI THIRD LEVEL COST ACCOUNTING 1992
(a)

DR		Process A account		CR
	Units	£	Units	£
Balance b/fwd	2 000	67 000		
Materials	6 000	143 000	Transfer to	
Conversation			finished stock	6 500 318 500
costs		166 700	Closing WIP	1 500 58 200
	8 000	376 700		8 000 376 700

Equivalent units table

Units	Material Units	Conversion cost £
Completed	6 500	6 500
Closing WIP	1 500	900
	8 000	7 400

Costs	£188 000	£188 700
Cost per element	£23.50	£25.50
Cost per unit	£49.00	

Valuation of completed units:
  6 500 units × £49.00 = £318 500
Valuation of closing material work in progress =
  1500 units × £23.50 = £35 250
Valuation of closing conv/costs work in progress =
  900 × £25.50 = £22 950

(b)

DR		Process A account			CR
	Units	£		Units	£
Opening WIP	2 000	64 800			
Materials	6 000	143 000	Transfer to		
Conversion			finished stock	6 500	312 000
costs*		166 700			
Transfer to			Transfer to		
conversion costs			materials total		
variance a/c		4 900	variances a/c		11 000
			Closing WIP	1 500	56 400
	8 000	379 400		8 000	379 400

*Equivalent to 6 600 units: b/fwd 800; completed 6 500, c/fwd
900; therefore 6 600.

Variances	Standard	Actual
Materials 6000 × £22	£132 000	£143 000
		£11 000 Adverse price variance
Conversion costs	£171 600	£166 700
		£4 900 Favourable variance

10 ACCA COST AND MANAGEMENT ACCOUNTING 1 1990
Workings and notes:
Standard purchase price: £3.50 per kg, usage = 5kg : standard
cost = £17.50 per unit

Materials	Receipts kg	Receipts £	Issues kg	Issues £	Balance kg	Balance £
Opening Stock					5 240	18 340
Purchases	7 600	26 600			12 840	44 940
Issues			7 460	26 110	5 380	18 830
Discrepancy			70	245	5 310	18 585

Raw material price variance	304 Adverse	Accounted for separately
Indirect materials:		
Opening stock	1 484	Assumed to be accounted for
Purchases	2 107	separately from the raw
Issues	(1 963)	materials stock
Closing Stock	1 628	

(a)

DR	Raw materials stock control account £		CR £
Balance brought forward	18 340	Issues to work in progress	
Purchases	26 600	progress control account	26 110
		Stock discrepancy w/off	245
		Balance carried forward	18 585
	44 940		44 940

(b)

DR	Production wages control account £		CR £
Net pay	7 524		
Employees deductions	3 381	Transfer to work in progress control account	7 950
		Transfer to production overhead control account	2 955
	10 905		10 905

(c)

DR	Production overhead control account £		CR £
		Balance b/fwd (accruals)	3 840
Indirect materials used	1 963		
Transfer from production wages control account	2 955	Transfer to work in progress account	15 900
Expenditure	9 252		
Accruals	4 170		
Transfer over-absorbed overheads	1 400		
	19 740		19 740

(d)

DR	Work in progress control account				CR
	Units	£		Units	£
Balance b/fwd:					
Materials	260	4 550	Transfer to		
Lab/ohead		1 950	F/goods a/c	1 450	48 354
Transfer			Work in	310	8 373
materials			progress		
control a/c	1 492	26 110			
Transfer Wages					
control a/c		7 950			
Transfer Production					
o/head a/c		15 900			
Abnormal gain	8	267			
	1 760	56 727		1 760	56 727

Equivalent units table

Units	Materials Units	C/cost £	
Completed	1 450	1 450	
Abnormal gain	(8)	(8)	
Closing WIP	310	186	
	1 752	1 628	
Costs	£30 660	£25 800	
Cost per element	£17.50	£15.85	£33.35
WIP valuation	£5 425	£2 948	£8 373

(e)

DR	Finished goods control account				CR
	Units	£		Units	£
Balance b/fwd	1 470	47 775			
Transfer from			Transfer to cost		
Work in Progress			of sales	1 520	49 442
account	1 450	48 354			
			Balance c/fwd	1 400	46 687
	2 920	96 129		2 920	96 129

11 ACCA COST AND MANAGEMENT ACCOUNTING 1 1990

Workings and notes:

FIFO table units	Materials	Conversion	
Completed Goods	181 940	181 940	
Abnormal loss	60	60	
Less WIP b/fwd	(14 000)	(8 000)	
Add closing WIP	16 200	12 600	
Equivalent units	184 200	186 600	
Current costs	£504 720	£76 506	
Cost per element	£2.74007	£0.41000	£3.150065

Valuation of completed units

Units completed			
this period:	167 940	173 940	
Cost per element	£2.740070	£0.410000	
Valuation	£460 167	£71 315	£531 482
Add costs brought forward			£55 160
			£586 642
WIP valuation	£44 389	£5 166	£49 555

Valuation of abnormal loss: 60 units at £3.150065 each £189

(a)

DR		Process 3 account			CR
	Units	£		Units	£
Balance					
b/forward	20 000	55 160			
Transfer			Transfer to		
from 2	180 000	394 200	Finished		
Materials		110 520	Goods	181 940	586 642
Conversion costs		76 506	Work in		
			progress		
			carried		
			forward	18 000	49 555
			Abnormal loss	60	189
	200 000	636 386		200 000	636 386

(b) If a normal loss of 60 units had been expected the proceeds from the sale of the rejects would be credited to the process account, thus reducing the costs of processing. However, as no losses were expected, an abnormal loss has arisen and management need to know the extent of this (in this case it has cost the firm £189). Any proceeds from the sale are credited to the abnormal loss account.

12 ACCA COST AND MANAGEMENT ACCOUNTING 1 1992

Workings and notes:

Process Account – Units

21 700	Losses		6 700	@ 45p
105 600			92 400	per kg
			28 200	
127 300			127 300	
			5 280	normal losses
			1 420	abnormal losses

(a)(i)

Equivalent units table, AVCO method

	Materials	Conversion costs	
Units			
Completed units	92 400	92 400	
Closing WIP	28 200	14 100	
	120 600	106 500	
Costs			
Opening Balance	£56 420	£30 597	
Period costs	£276 672	£226 195	
Sale of scrap	(£3 015)	£0	
	£330 077	£256 792	Total
Cost per element	£2.7370	£2.4112	£5.1481

(a)(ii)

Equivalent units table, FIFO method

	Materials	Conversion costs	
Units			
Completed units	92 400	92 400	
Abnormal losses	1 420	0	
Closing WIP	28 200	14 100	
	122 020	106 500	
Less: opening WIP	−21 700	−13 020	
	100 320	93 480	
Costs			
Period costs	£276 672	£226 195	
Sale of scrap	(£2 376)	£0	
	£274 296	£226 195	
Total cost per element	£2.7342	£2.4197	£5.1539

(b)

DR			Process account		CR
		£			£
Balance			Normal losses	5 280	2 376
b/fwd	21 700	87 017			
Materials	105 600	276 672	Transfer to finished		
Conversion			goods stock	92 400	472 403
costs		226 195			
			Abnormal losses	1 420	3 883*
			Balance		
			c/down	28 200	111 223
	127 300	589 884		127 300	589 884
Balance					
b/down	28 200	111 223			

*Note: Incurred at beginning of process, therefore priced at materials value

Valuation of completed units

	Completed	Opening WIP	This period units	Valuation	
Materials	92 400	−21 700	70 700	£193 309	(@ £2.7342)
Conversion	92 400	−13 020	79 380	£192 077	(@ £2.4197)
				£87 017	B/fwd costs
				£472 403	

Closing WIP valuation:

Units	£
£28 200	£77 105
£14 100	£34 118
	£111 223

13 ACCA COST AND MANAGEMENT ACCOUNTING 1 1993

(a)

DR			Process 2 account		CR
	Units	£		Units	£
WIP b/forward	1 200	3 009	Normal loss	5 600	0
Transfer from			Transfer to finished		
Process 1	112 000	187 704	goods	105 400	296 273
Materials		47 972			
Conversion			Abnormal losses	600	1 329
costs		63 176	(@ £2.215 each)		
			WIP carried		
			down	1 600	4 259
	113 200	301 861		113 200	301 861
WIP brought					
down	1 600	4 259			

Equivalent units table, FIFO

Units	Materials	Conversion costs	
		£	
Completed units	105 400	105 400	
Abnormal losses	600	0	
Closing WIP	1 600	1 200	
Less opening WIP	−1 200	−600	
	106 400	106 000	
Current costs	£235 676	£63 176	
Cost per element	**£2.2150**	**£0.5960**	**£2.8110**

Valuation of completed units:

	Completed	Opening WIP	This period units	Valuation	
Materials	105 400	−1 200	104 200	£230 803	(@ £2.215)
Conversion	105 400	−600	104 800	£62 461	(@ £0.596)
				£3 009	B/fwd costs
				£296 273	

Closing WIP valuation:

	Units	£	
Materials	1 600	£3 544	(@ £2.215)
Conversion costs	1 200	£715	(@ £0.596)
		£4 259	

(b)   If wastage had occurred at the end of the period the abnormal losses would have incurred some conversion costs. These costs would therefore need to be included in the valuation of the abnormal losses. The equivalent units table would have included the 600 units in the conversion costs column, (as well as in the materials column), and a unit cost arrived at: here £2.8076 each. The abnormal losses valuation would therefore be priced at this unit cost = £1 685, instead of £1 329. This would also have affected the valuation of the completed units and the closing WIP. It would also be probable that the percentage expected loss, in this case, 5%, would alter as the losses would be based on the expected output of the process rather than the input, as here.

14   CIMA COST ACCOUNTING 1990

(i)

DR		Process account – period 10		CR	
	Units	£		Units	£
Materials	5 000	14 700	Normal loss	150	150
Additional					
materials		13 830			
Direct wages		6 555	Transfer to finished		
			goods	3 930	36 549
Overhead		7 470			
			Closing WIP		
			carried down	800	5 160
			Abnormal loss	120	696
	5 000	42 555		5 000	42 555
Balance					
b/down	800	5 160			

Workings and notes:

Equivalent units table

Units	Materials	Added materials	Wages	Overheads
Completed units	3 930	3 930	3 930	3 930
Abnormal losses	120	80	40	20
Closing WIP	800	600	400	200
	4 850	4 610	4 370	4 150
Costs	14 700	£13 830	£6 555	£7 470
Normal loss credit	(150)			
	14 550			
Total cost				
per element	**£3.00**	**£3.00**	**£1.50**	**£1.80** **£9.30**

Valuation of Completed Units: 3930 × £9.30

Valuation of abnormal loss units:

Materials	Added materials	Wages	Overheads
£360	£240	£60	£36 **£696**
120 × 3	80 × 3	40 × 1.50	20 × 1.80

Valuation of WIP units:

£2 400	£1 800	£600	£360 **£5 160**

(ii)

DR	Abnormal loss account		CR
	£		£
Transfer from		Sale of scrap	120
process account	696		
		Transfer to P & L account	576
	696		696

15 CIMA COST ACCOUNTING 1990

(i)

DR		Process A account			CR
	kg	£		kg	£
Materials	2 000	10 000	Transfer normal loss	400	200
Labour		7 200	Transfer Process B	1 400	26 005
Plant time		8 400	Transfer abnormal loss	200	3 715
Overhead		4 320			
	2 000	29 920		2 000	29 920

Cost per unit: £29 720/1 600 units = £18.575

(ii)

DR		Process B account			CR
	kg	£		kg	£
Transfer from A	1 400	26 005			
Materials	1 400	16 800	Transfer normal loss	280	511
Labour		4 200	Transfer finished goods	2 620	56 989
Plant time		5 800			
Overhead		2 520			
Abnormal gain	100	2 175			
	2 900	57 500		2 900	57 500

Cost per unit: £54 814/2520 units = £21.7516

(iii)

DR		Normal loss/gain account			CR
	kg	£		kg	£
Transfer from A	400	200	Sales proceeds		
Transfer from B	280	511	A	400	200
			B	280	511
	680	711		680	711

(iv)

DR		Abnormal loss/gain account			CR
	kg	£		kg	£
Transfer from A	200	3 715	Transfer from B	100	2 175
Proceeds adj. B	100	183	Proceeds: A	200	100
			Transfer to P&L		1 623
	300	3 898		300	3 898

(v)

DR		Finished goods account			CR
	kg	£		kg	£
Transfer from B	2 620	56 989			
			Balance c/down	2 620	56 989
	2 620	56 989		2 620	56 989

(vi)

Profit and loss account extract

	£
Sales	
Cost of sales	
Opening stock	0
Good manufactured	56 989
Closing stock	(56 989)
	0
Abnormal loss	1 623

16 CIMA COST ACCOUNTING 1994

(a)

	Cum. % completed	
Direct Labour:		
Stamping and forming	25.0%	25.0%
First assembly	25.0%	50.0%
Machining and cleaning	12.5%	62.5%
Second assembly	25.0%	87.5%
Spray painting	12.5%	100.0%

Metal Issues: 50 000 kg − 2 900 kg = 47 100 kg @ £1.00 per kg = £47 100

Material A Issues: 40 000 units − 2 500 units = 37 500 units @ £0.80 per unit = £30 000

Material B Issues: 75 000 units − 3 000 units = 72 000 units @ £0.40 per unit = £28 800

DR		Process account			CR
	Units	£		Units	£
Metal	37 500	47 100	Completed units	33 500	133 464
Material A		30 000			
Material B		28 800	Work in process	4 000	13 549
Paint		2 144			
Wages		22 268			
Overhead		16 701			
	37 500	147 013		37 500	147 013

Equivalent units tables

Units	Metal	Material A	Material B	Paint	Labour	Overhead	
Completed	33 500	33 500	33 500	33 500	33 500	33 500	*Notes:*
WIP – ready for second assembly	1 500	1 500	0		938*	938*	*62.5% Completed
Assembled not painted	2 500	2 500	2 500		2 188**	2 188**	**87.5% Completed
Equivalent units	37 500	37 500	36 000	33 500	36 625	36 625	
Costs	£47 100	£30 000	£28 800	£2 144	£22 268	£16701	
Cost per element	£1.256	£0.800	£0.800	£0.064	£0.608	£0.456	£3.984
Valuation of WIP	£5 024	£3 200	£2 000	£0	£1 900	£1 425	£13 549

Valuation of completed goods: 33 500 × £3.984 = £133 464

(b) Cost of production statement – period 1

		(ii)	(iii)
		Equivalent production	
	£	units	£
Metal	47 100	37 500	£1.256
Material A	30 000	37 500	£0.800
Material B	28 800	36 000	£0.800
Painting	2 144	33 500	£0.064
Wages	22 268	36 625	£0.608
Overhead	16 701	36 625	£0.456
(i) Total production cost	147 013		
(iii) Cost of one component			£3.984
(iv) Cost of completed unit	133 464		
(v) Value of work in process at end of Period 1:			£13 549

Model answers to examination questions, Chapter 13

1. A LEVEL (ULEAC) 1993

(i) Process accounts

DR		Primary process account			CR
	Litres	£		Litres	£
Materials	60 000	24 000	Normal losses	6 000	1 500
Labour and overheads		29 340			
Abnormal gain	1 200	1 152	Transfer to secondary process	55 200	52 992
	61 200	54 492		61 200	54 492

Cost per litre: (£24 000 + £29 340 − £1500)/54 000 litres
= £0.96 per litre).

DR		Secondary process account account			CR
	Litres	£		Litres	£
Transfer from primary process	55 200	52 992	Cost of output	54 000	135 000
Direct labour and overheads		83 568			
Refining of by-product		240	Sale of by-product	1 200	1 800
	55 200	136 800		55 200	136 800

Summary

Cost of output from the primary to the secondary process: £52 992

Net saving arising from abnormal gain in the primary process: £1 152

(Note: 4 800 litres would have been sold for 25p per litre, resulting in sales receipts of £1 200; as £1 500 has been credited to the primary process account, a debit of £300 will be made in the abnormal gain account, reducing the abnormal gain to £852.)

Cost of output from the secondary process: £135 000

(ii) Valuation of closing stocks

	Adamite	Bondite	
Litres	18 000	36 000	
Sales value	£113 400	£111 600	£225 000
Apportionment of output cost:			
Volume of output method	£45 000	£90 000	£135 000
Cost per unit	£2.50	£2.50	
Market value method	£68 040	£66 960	£135 000
Cost per unit	£3.78	£1.86	
Closing stocks valuation			
Closing stocks – units	8 100	7 200	
Volume of output method	£20 250	£18 000	£38 250
Market value method	£30 618	£13 392	£44 010

2 ACCA COST AND MANAGEMENT ACCOUNTING 1 1990

Workings and notes:

DR			Process account			CR
	Units	£		Units	£	Cost per unit
Common costs	744 000	509 640	W	276 000	189 060	£0.685
			X	334 000	228 790	£0.685
			Y	134 000	91 790	£0.685
	744 000	509 640		744 000	509 640	

W, X – no further processing
Y – further processing

	W	W	X	X
	Units	£	Units	£
Sales	255 000	240 975	312 000	277 680

Closing stocks:

	W	X	Y
Made	276 000	334 000	134 000
Sold/transferred	255 000	312 000	128 000
C/balance	21 000	22 000	6 000
C/bal value	14 385	15 070	4 110 @ £0.685 33 565

DR		Product Z Process A/C			CR
	Units	£		Units	£
Materials	128 000	87 680	Transfer		
			f/goods	96 000 104 640	£1.09
Labour		10 850	By product	8 000	960
Overhead		7 070			
		105 600			105 600

DR		Product Z finished goods account			CR
	Units	£		Units	£
Opening Stock	8 000	8 640	Transfer cost		
Transfer			of sales	94 000	102 380
f/goods	96 000	104 640	Closing		
			stock	10 000	10 900
	104 000	113 280		104 000	113 280

(a) Profit and loss account

Profit and loss account for the period

	W	X	Y	Z	Total
	£	£	£	£	£
Sales	240 975	277 680	0	100 110	618 765
Cost of sales					
Opening stock	0	0	0	8 640	8 640
MFG costs	189 060	228 790	91 790	16 960	526 600
Transfer			(87 680)	87 680	0
Closing stock	(14 385)	(15 070)	(4 110)	(10 900)	(44 465)
	174 675	213 720	0	102 380	490 775

Gross profit	66 300	63 960	0	(2 270)	127 990	
Selling and administration	24 098	27 768	0	10 011	61 877	
Net profit (loss)	**£42 203**	**£36 192**	**£0**	**(£12 281)**	**£66 114**	

(b) Alternative offer for Product Y

The profit and loss position if the offer of 62p per kg was accepted for Product Y, would be as follows (134 000 kg × 62p = £83 080):

	W	X	Y	Z	Total
Sales	240 975	277 680	83 080	0	618 765
Common costs					509 640
Less closing stocks					(29 455)
				(43 000 kg × £0.685 (W + X))	
Cost of goods sold					480 185
Gross profit					138 580
Selling and administration costs					61 877
Profit					76 703

Therefore, the acceptance of the alternative is the better choice.

3 CIMA COSTING 1990

Workings and notes:

Net sales value is taken to mean sales less the additional processing costs.

Apportionment of costs:

	Sales	Additional cost	Net sales value	Percentage share %	Share of cost (£000s)
Q	768	160	608	62.30	456
R	232	128	104	10.66	78
S	32	0	32	3.28	24
T	240	8	232	23.77	174
	1272	296	976	100.00	732

DR	Common process account		CR
	£000		
		Transfer to Q processing a/c	456
Materials	268	Transfer to R processing a/c	78
Conversion	464	Transfer to S finished goods a/c	24
		Transfer to T processing a/c	174
	732		732

(a) Budgeted profit statement

	Q £000s	R £000s	S £000s	T £000s	Total £000s
Sales	768	232	32	240	1272
Costs					
Common costs	456	78	24	174	732
Additional costs	160	128	0	8	296
	616	206	24	182	1028
Profit	152	26	8	58	244

(b) Alternative strategy

Sales	Output	Value
Q	400000	512000
R	90000	144000
S	5000	32000
T	9000	180000
		868000

	Q £000s	R £000s	S £000s	T £000s	Total £000s
Sales	512	144	32	180	868
Costs					
Common costs	456	78	24	174	732
Profit	56	66	8	6	136

(c) The apportionment of common costs is unhelpful to management when comparing alternatives. Instead, only the costs and revenues arising from a decision should be considered. The common costs are attributable to the whole, cannot be identified precisely with the individual products and should therefore be ignored. The following table indicates which is the most profitable decision for management to make.

	Q £000s	R £000s	S £000s	T £000s	Total £000s
Sales	768	232	32	240	1272
Costs					
Additional cost	160	128	0	8	296
Net	608	104	32	232	976
Compared to–					
Sell off at split	512	144	32	180	868
Difference	96	−40	0	52	

As can be seen, if Product R were to be sold at the split-off point, the company would earn an extra £40000. The optimum profit position, and therefore the recommendation, would be:

	Q £000s	R £000s	S £000s	T £000s	Total £000s
Sales	768	144	32	240	1184
Costs					
Additional costs	160	0	0	8	168
Contribution	608	144	32	232	1016
Common costs					732
Profit					284

Recommendation: Process further (Q), Sell at split-off point (R), Same (S), Process further (T)

4 CIMA COST ACCOUNTING 1992

Joint costs apportioned on litres produced:

DR		Common process account		CR
	Litres	£	Litres	£
Joint costs	8000	40000	Transfer to B 3500	17500
			Transfer to K 2500	12500
			Transfer to C 2000	10000
	8000	40000	8000	40000

(a) Profit and loss for June

	Product B £	Product K £	Product C £	Total £
Sales	35000	50000	60000	145000
Production costs				
Common costs	17500	12500	10000	40000
Post-separation costs	20000	10000	22500	52500
	37500	22500	32500	92500
Profit (loss)	(2500)	27500	27500	52500

(b) Comparison

	B £	K £	C £	Total £
Sales after split-off	35000	50000	60000	145000
Costs				
Additional costs	20000	10000	22500	52500
Net	15000	40000	37500	92500
Compared to–				
Sell off at split	21000	20000	18000	59000
Difference	(6000)	20000	19500	33500

If the company sold B at split-off point, profits would be maximised as follows:

Profit and loss for June

	Product B	Product K	Product C	Total
	£	£	£	£
Sales	21 000	50 000	60 000	131 000
Production costs				
Post-separation				
costs	0	10 000	22 500	32 500
	21 000	40 000	37 500	98 500
Less common				
costs	17 500	12 500	10 000	40 000
Profit	3 500	27 500	27 500	58 500

Model answers to examination questions, Chapter 14

1 AAT COST ACCOUNTING AND BUDGETING 1992

(a) Cost statement

	Accom-modation	Catering	Leisure	Outings	Total
	£	£	£	£	
Labour	110 000	100 500	35 000	38 500	284 000
Materials	19 000	36 000	16 000	13 000	84 000
Power	20 000	10 000	50 000	4 000	84 000
(kwh hours)					
Rent and rates	36 000	12 000	18 000	6 000	72 000
(area)					
Depreciation	5 000	10 000	30 000	15 000	60 000
(machinery)					
Advertising	30 000	24 000	16 000	6 000	76 000
	220 000	192 500	165 000	82 500	660 000
Office expenses	80 000	70 000	60 000	30 000	240 000
	300 000	262 500	225 000	112 500	900 000
Customer days	15 000	12 000	8 000	3 000	
Cost per					
customer day	£20.00	£21.88	£28.13	£37.50	

(b) Calculation of charge to married couple:

Facility	Usage	Cost per day	Charge
Accommodation	7 days	£20.00	£140.00
Catering	7 days	£21.88	£153.13
Leisure	3 days	£28.13	£ 84.38
Outings	3 days	£37.50	£112.50
			£490.00 per person

Charge:

Two customers at £490.05 each plus 30% profit:

	£490.00
	£490.00
	£980.00
Profit	£420.00 30% on price
	£1 400.00

(c) Under/over-absorption of costs per cost centre

	Accom-modation	Catering	Leisure	Outings	Total
	£	£	£	£	
Absorbed costs	305 000	284 375	191 250	120 000	900 625
Actual Costs	320 000	275 000	200 000	125 000	920 000
Under/(over)-absorbed costs	15 000	(9 375)	8 750	5 000	19 375

2 AAT COST ACCOUNTING AND BUDGETING 1993

(a)

Days	Black	White
Number of working days	260	260
Holiday entitlement + public holidays	40	35
Actual number of working days	220	225
Less 10% non-chargeable	22	22.5
Number of working days chargeable	198	202.5
Number of working hours (x8) associated with project:	1584	1620

Costs		
Gross annual salary	£42 500.00	£35 000.00
Add pension contribution	£3 400.00	£2 100.00
Add cost of car per annum	£3 732.00	£3 220.00
Overheads associated with project	£26 400.00	£18 000.00
	£76 032.00	£58 320.00
Cost per hour	**£48.000**	**£36.000**

£44 400 pro rata (overheads)

(b)

	Black	White	Total
49.5 days work (198/4) at 8 hours per day × £48 per hour	19 008.00		£19 008.00
49.5 days work (202.5/4) at 8 hours per day × £36 per hour		£14 580.00	£14 580.00
			£33 588.00 80%
Add profit of 20%			£ 8 397.00 20%
			£41 985.00 100%

Chargeable to government
department each quarter
* 1584 × £15 = £23 760 = 59.5%
  1620 × £10 = £16 200 = 40.5%
Total   £39 960
Apportionment of £44 400 based on above mix.

3 ACCA COST AND MANAGEMENT ACCOUNTING 1 1992
Workings and notes:
(Part (b) of this question should be attempted after study of marginal costing techniques – Chapter 17)

Purchased vehicles
Fleet of 40 vehicles. New vehicle cost = £35 000 each
  = £1 400 000
35 drivers at £13 000 p.a. = £455 000 + employer costs 15%
  = £68 250
Other fixed costs = £1 240 per vehicle p.a. = £49 600
  (40 × £1 240)
Disposal after three years = 40 × £11 000 = £440 000
Disposal after five years = 40 × £5000 = £200 000
Depreciation = 3 years = £960 000 /3 = £320 000
  (£1 400 000 – £440 000)
Depreciation = 5 years = £1 200 000/5 = £240 000
  (£1 400 000 – £200 000)
Number of journeys per annum = 40 × 52 × 5 = 10 400
  journeys.
But idle time = 20% so actual journeys = 8 320 (10 400 – 2 080)
Variable costs per journey = £37.80;
  Cost = 8 320 × £37.80 = £314 496 p.a.

Contract vehicles
£100 per day

Variable costs £0.20 per km
52 weeks × 5 days per week = 260 days
But required for above less 20% = 208 days
Hire charges = 208 × £100 = £20 800 × 40 = £832 000
Kilometres per annum cost = 1 747 200 × £0.20 = £349 440

Costs per annum

Own fleet	Own fleet – 3 years	Own fleet – 5 years
	£	£
Depreciation	320 000	240 000
Drivers costs	455 000	455 000
Employer costs	68 250	68 250
Other costs	49 600	49 600
Variable costs	314 496	314 496
Cost per annum	£1 207 346	£1 127 346
Journeys	8 320	8 320
Cost per journey	£145.11	£135.50
Contract cost p.a.	£1 181 440	£1 181 440
Journeys	8 320	8 320
Cost per journey	£142.00	£142.00

(a)(i) For the three-year contract, the minimum annual price CD Ltd could quote would be £1 181 440 to cover the total costs of the cheaper of the two options open to them.

(ii) With the five-year contract, the lowest price CD Ltd could quote would be on the basis of the cheaper (purchase) option above. Here the minimum price should be £1 127 346 to cover their total costs.

(b) Calculations:

8320 units =		Per journey
Fixed costs	£ 892 850	£107.31
Variable costs	£ 314 496	£ 37.80
	£1 207 346	£145.11

Excess variable costs of contract hire =		
Contract hire variable	£142.00	
Less: own fleet variable	£ 37.80	
'Saving' per unit	£104.20	
Fixed Costs per unit	£107.31	
'Saving' per unit	£104.20	= 1.0298 × 8 320 units

To break even	8 568 journeys			
Maximum journeys =	10 400 journeys			
Percentage utilisation of fleet to equate the two costs	82.38%			

Check:

Fixed costs	£892 850	
Variable costs	£323 870	8568 journeys @ £37.80
Total cost	£1 216 720	
Journeys	8568	
Cost per journey	£142.01	

Model answers to examination questions, Chapter 15

1. CIMA COST ACCOUNTING 1991

Workings and notes:

	A	B	C	D	Total
Machine hours	480	300	160	360	1300

Production runs:
  21 (420/20)

Number of sales:
  42 (420/10)

Total production overhead:	£26 000
Machine hour absorption rate	£ 20.00 per machine hour

(a) Total costs using machine hour rate

	A	B	C	D	Total
	£	£	£	£	£
Direct materials	4 800	5 000	2 400	7 200	19 400
Direct labour	3 360	2 100	1 120	2 520	9 100
Production overheads	9 600	6 000	3 200	7 200	26 000
Total costs	17 760	13 100	6 720	16 920	54 500

(b) Total costs using ABC:

	A	B	C	D	Total
Set up costs:					
Production run	6	5	4	6	21
Set up costs apportionment	£1 500	£1 250	£1 000	£1 500	£5 250
Stores receiving requisitions					
Number	20	20	20	20	80
Cost apportionment	£900	£900	£900	£900	£3 600
Inspection/quality control					
Production runs	6	5	4	6	21
Cost	£600	£500	£400	£600	£2 100
Materials handling and dispatch					
Orders executed	12	10	8	12	42
Cost apportionment	£1 320	£1 100	£880	£1 320	£4 620
Machine department					
Machine hours	480	300	160	360	1300
Cost	£3 851	£2 407	£1 284	£2 888	£10 430
Production overhead costs	£8 171	£6 157	£4 464	£7 208	£26 000
Add material and labour	£8 160	£7 100	£3 520	£9 720	£28 500
Total costs using ABC	£16 331	£13 257	£7 984	£16 928	£54 500

(c) Comparison of unit product costs

Product	Total cost machine hour basis	Per unit	Total cost ABC basis	Per unit	Difference per unit
	£		£		
A	17 760	£148.00	16 331	£136.09	£11.91 more than ABC
B	13 100	£131.00	13 257	£132.57	(£ 1.57) less than ABC
C	6 720	£ 84.00	7 984	£ 99.80	(£15.80) less than ABC
D	16 920	£141.00	16 928	£141.07	(£ 0.07) less than ABC
	54 500		54 500		

The total cost of Product A using the machine hour absorption system is much higher than ABC, which endeavours to identify more precisely how the production costs have arisen. The selling price of this product, if based on costs using the former method, will therefore be higher. The pricing implication is that by 'over-pricing' sales will be lost, perhaps encouraging competitors to undercut the price and win greater market share. Conversely, with Product C, this product may be underpriced, again if the selling price is based on cost. The profit implications of both over- and underpricing may be lower income for the company.

Model answers to examination questions, Chapter 17

1   A LEVEL (ULEAC) 1989

(i)   LIFO marginal costing valuation
Workings:

	Manufactured		Sold		Balance	
	Units	Cost £	Units	Cost £	Units	Cost £
October 1						
Opening stock					300	3 510
					(at £11)	
Units made	1 600	19 040			1 900	22 550
Units sold			1 500	17 850	400	4 700
		(at Last in price of £11.90 (£19 040/1 600))				

Trading results for the six months ended 31 March:
(marginal costing LIFO stock valuation)

Sales	36 000
Less: variable cost of sales	
Opening stock	3 510
Variable costs	19 040
Closing stock	−4 700
	17 850
Contribution	18 150
Fixed Costs	8 960
Profit	**9 190**

(ii)   AVCO marginal costing valuation
Workings:

	Manufactured		Sold		Balance	
	Units	Cost £	Units	Cost £	Units	Cost £
October 1						
Opening stock					300	3 510
					(at £11.70 each)	
Units made	1 600	19 040			1 900	22 550
		(giving an average prices of £11.8684 each)				
Units sold			1 500	17 803	400	4 747
		(at average price of £11.8684 each)				

Trading results for the six months ended 31 March:
(marginal costing AVCO stock valuation)

Sales	36 000
Less: variable cost of sales	
Opening stock	3 510
Variable costs	19 040
Closing stock	−4 747
	17 803
Contribution	18 197
Fixed Costs	8 960
Profit	**9 237**

2 A LEVEL (ULEAC) 1990

Profit Volume graph

(a) Workings:

From observation of the contribution graph, fixed costs are £2 000 000 and break even in units is 9 000 units.

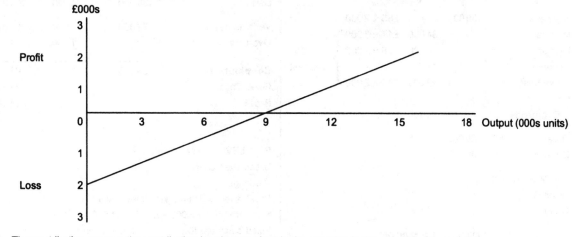

(b) The contribution area on the contribution break-even chart in the question is the area 0A–C0, as follows:

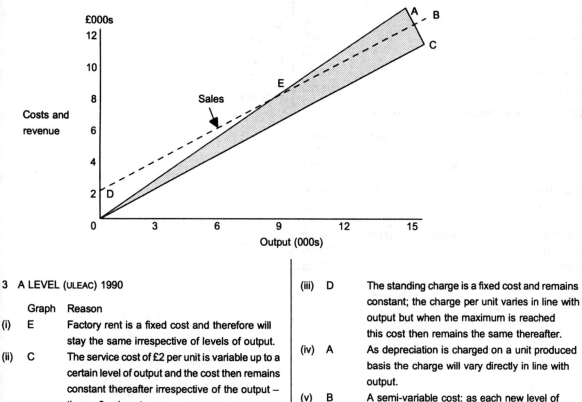

3 A LEVEL (ULEAC) 1990

Graph	Reason
(i) E	Factory rent is a fixed cost and therefore will stay the same irrespective of levels of output.
(ii) C	The service cost of £2 per unit is variable up to a certain level of output and the cost then remains constant thereafter irrespective of the output – thus a fixed cost.

(iii) D — The standing charge is a fixed cost and remains constant; the charge per unit varies in line with output but when the maximum is reached this cost then remains the same thereafter.

(iv) A — As depreciation is charged on a unit produced basis the charge will vary directly in line with output.

(v) B — A semi-variable cost: as each new level of output is reached the number of supervisors required will increase.

4 A LEVEL (ULEAC) 1992
Workings and notes:

	Sales	Costs		
	£	£		
Normal sales	130 000		£65 × 2 000	
Materials		34 000	£17 × 2 000	
Labour		16 000	£8 × 2 000	= £36
Variable				per unit
overheads		22 000	£11 × 2 000	
Fixed				
Overheads		29 400		

Order A	600	20 000	21 600
Order B	750	34 000	31 500

Overtime premium:

Order A	1 200
Order B	1 500

(a) Contribution and profit for September
Normal production

		£
Sales	2 000 units	130 000
Variable costs		72 000
Contribution		58 000
Fixed Costs		29 400
Profit		28 600

(b) Order A accepted with normal production

	Normal	Order A	Total
	£	£	£
Sales	130 000	20 000	150 000
Variable costs	72 000	21 600	93 600
Variable costs		1 200	1 200
Contribution	58 000	(2 800)	55 200
Fixed Costs			29 400
Profit			25 800

(c) Order B accepted with normal production

	Normal	Order B	Total
	£	£	£
Sales	130 000	34 000	164 000
Variable costs	72 000	27 000	99 000
Overtime premium	–	1 500	1 500
Contribution	58 000	5 500	63 500
Fixed Costs			29 400
Profit			34 100

5 A LEVEL (ULEAC) 1992
Break-even chart
Workings:
Break-even is 3 000 units; sales value
therefore will be 3 000 × £1.50 = £4 500
Fixed costs are £2 000, so to break even
the contribution must also be £2 000:

	£
Sales	4 500
Variable costs	2 500
Contribution	2 000
Fixed costs	2 000
Profit/loss	0

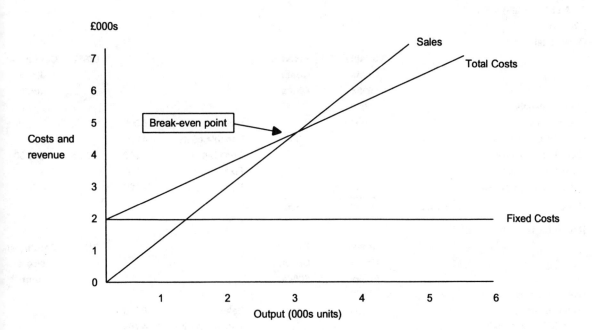

£000s

6 A LEVEL (ULEAC) 1993
(a) Redrafted statement showing the prime cost, marginal
     cost, contribution and profit.

	£
Sales	72 000
Variable Costs:	
Materials	18 075
Labour	8 850
Prime cost	26 925
Variable overheads	6 525
Marginal cost	**33 450**
Contribution	38 550
Fixed costs	19 400
Profit	**19 150**

(b) Reconciliation statement.

	£
Profit per absorption costing	24 000
Less fixed costs carried forward in closing stocks:	
$\dfrac{500}{2000} \times £19\,400$	4 850
Profit per marginal costing statement	19 150

7   A LEVEL (AEB) 1990

Workings:

Original data:

	Variable Costs £000s	Fixed Costs £000s			C/S%	Cont'n per direct unit
Direct materials	2 000					
Direct labour	900		Sales	5 000		
Fixed MFG overhead		300	Variable costs	4 200		
Variable sales/admin	600		Contribution	800	16.0%	£16.00
Fixed Sales/admin		200	Fixed costs	500		
Variable MFG overhead	700		Profit	300		
Units: 50 000	4 200	500				

Revised data:

	Variable Costs £000s	Fixed Costs £000s			C/S%	Cont'n per direct unit
Direct materials	2 500					
Direct labour	900		Sales	6 000		
Fixed MFG overhead		270	Variable costs	4 765		
Variable sales/admin	630		Contribution	1 235	20.6%	£20.58
Fixed Sales/admin		180	Fixed costs	450		
Variable MFG overhead	735		Profit	785		
Units: 60 000	4 765	450				

(a)   Break-even chart – original data

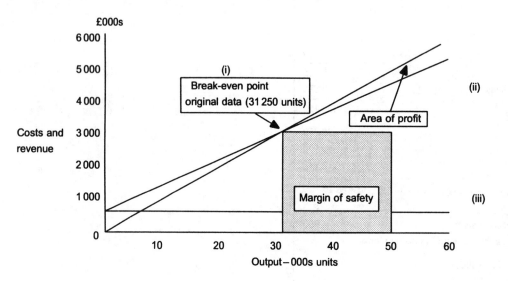

Break-even chart – revised data

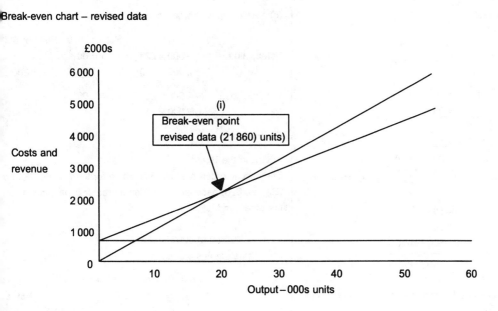

(b) Break-even formula.
Formula:

	FC	FC
	CS %	Contribution Per Unit

FC = Fixed Costs

	Value	Units
Original data	500	500
	16.0%	£16
Break-even	£3 125 000	31 250 units
Revised data	450	450
	20.6%	£20.58
Break-even	£2 186 000	21 860 units

(c) Comment

The revised data increases the number of units to be produced by 10 000, representing an increase of 20% over the previous forecast. With the economic environment about to get much tougher, according to management, it is questionable whether the company will be able to increase their sales to such an extent.

Direct labour staff will also need to increase their productivity by 20%, with no improvement in rates of pay. Whether this would be acceptable to the workers and their representatives is also open to question.

Fixed costs too may be difficult to cut by 10%; for example, rent and rates cannot usually be reduced, which means that other fixed overheads will need to be cut further to achieve the overall blanket reduction.

Similarly with variable overheads. With a 20% increase in volume it is to be expected that variable overheads would be in line with this. However, an increase of only 5% has been allowed in the revisions, indicating that the price paid per unit of variable overhead consumed will be reduced dramatically. This would appear to be unachievable.

8 A LEVEL (AEB) 1992

(a) Workings:

	£	£
Sales price (each)		36.00
Variable costs (each)		
Materials	5.00	
Wages	7.00	
Overheads		
Factory	1.00	
Sales	3.00	16.00
Contribution per unit		20.00 55.5556% = C/S%
Fixed costs:		
Factory	4.50	
Administration	2.00	
Sales	3.50	10.00
Profit per unit		10.00

(i) Break-even point in sales revenue terms (normal trading of 200,000 units)

$$\frac{\text{Fixed costs}}{\text{C/S\%}} \quad \frac{£2\,000\,000}{55.6\%} \quad £10 \times 200\,000$$

$$= \quad £3\,600\,000 \text{ sales to break-even.}$$

(ii) Break-even point in units produced (normal trading of 200\,000 units)

$$\frac{\text{Fixed costs}}{\text{cont'n per unit}} \quad \frac{£2\,000\,000}{£20.00}$$

$$= \quad 100\,000 \text{ units to break even.}$$

(iii) Break-even as a percentage of normal capacity:

$$\frac{£100\,000}{£2\,000\,000} \quad \frac{\text{break even}}{\text{normal capacity}}$$

$$= \quad 50.0\%.$$

(b)

(i) Profit if selling price is £40 and output is 160\,000 units:

Sales	£6\,400\,000	£40 × 160\,000
Variable costs	£2\,560\,000	£16 × 160\,000
Contribution	£3\,840\,000	
Fixed costs	£2\,000\,000	
Profit	**£1\,840\,000**	

(ii) Profit if selling price is £28 and output is 260\,000 units:

Sales	£7\,280\,000	£28 × 260\,000
Variable costs	£4\,160\,000	£16 × 260\,000
Contribution	£3\,120\,000	
Fixed costs	£2\,000\,000	
Profit	**£1\,120\,000**	

(c) Which special order to accept:

		Ref no. 610	Ref no. 620
Sales value	2\,000 × £25	50\,000	
	2\,000 × £19		38\,000
Variable costs	2\,000 × £20	40\,000	
	2\,000 × £12		24\,000
Contribution		10\,000	14\,000

Advice to the Board:

The special order to accept should be for the Premier Dufton (Ref no. 620) because it provides a greater contribution than the other product.

9 A LEVEL (AEB) 1992

(a) Actual profit statement

Profit Statement for year 1

	Actual £	Notes:
Sales	5\,375\,000	43\,000 × £125
Less variable costs	4\,601\,000	43\,000 × £107
Contribution	774\,000	
Fixed Costs	220\,000	200\,000 + 20\,000
Profit	**554\,000**	

(b) Break-even in units

(i) Budget year 1

Notes

$$\frac{\text{Fixed costs}}{\text{Cont'n per unit}} \quad \frac{£200\,000}{£17}$$

$$120 - 103$$

$$= \quad 11\,765 \text{ units}$$

(i) Actual year 1

$$\frac{£220\,000}{£18}$$

$$125 - 107$$

$$= \quad 12\,222 \text{ units}$$

(ii) Forecast year 2

$$\frac{£230\,000}{£19}$$

$$123 - 104$$

$$= \quad 12\,105 \text{ units}$$

(c) Graph

Break-even chart – year 2 forecast = 12 105 units

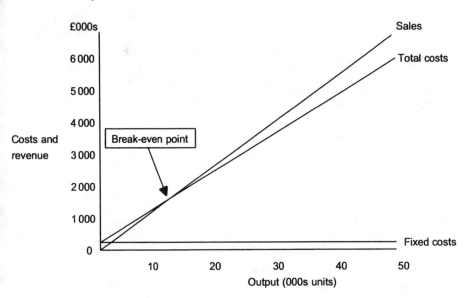

Sales = 47 000 units × £123 = £5 781 000

Variable costs = 47 000 × £104 = £4 888 000 +

   Fixed costs £230 000 = Total costs of £5 118 000

Contribution = £893 000; Contribution per unit
   = £893 000/47 000 = £19

Break-even = £230 000/£19 = 12 105 units

(d) If fixed costs were £200 000 in year 2
£200 000/12 222 units = £16.36 contribution per unit
Therefore:

Variable costs	**=£104**
Contribution	=£16.36
Selling price	=£120.36

The selling price could be reduced to £120.36

10 AAT COST ACCOUNTING AND BUDGETING

(a) Profit and loss statement – marginal costing

	January	February
	£	£
Units	18 000	32 000
Sales – £16 each	288 000	512 000
Variable costs – £10 each	180 000	320 000
Contribution	108 000	192 000
Fixed costs	75 000	75 000
Profit	33 000	117 000

Profit and loss statement – absorption costing

	January	February
	£	£
Sales	288 000	512 000
Cost of goods sold:		
Opening stock	0	91 000
Goods produced*	325 000	325 000
Closing stock – 7000 Units	(91 000)	0
	234 000	416 000
Profit	54 000	96 000

*Production	January	February
Units	25 000	25 000
	£	£
Materials	125 000	125 000
Labour	75 000	75 000
Variable costs	50 000	50 000
Fixed costs	75 000	75 000
Cost per unit: £13	325 000	325 000

(b) Stock valuation at end of January:
Marginal costing: 7000 units at £10 each = £70 000
Absorption costing: 7000 units at £13 each = £91 000

(c) Reconciliation of differences in profit:

	January	February
Profit per marginal costing	£33 000	£117 000
Add/deduct fixed costs written off as period costs:		
January		£21 000 (7 000 × £3 Per Unit)
February		(£21 000)
Profit per absorption costing	£54 000	£96 000

11 AAT COST ACCOUNTING AND BUDGETING 1992
(a) Optimum product mix

	A	B	C	Total
Selling price each	£25.00	£30.00	£34.00	
Variable costs each:				
Materials	£ 8.00	£11.00	£10.00	
Labour	£10.00	£12.50	£15.00	
Overheads	£ 3.00	£ 3.50	£ 4.00	
	£21.00	£27.00	£29.00	
Contribution each	£ 4.00	£ 3.00	£ 5.00	
Optimum product mix (units)	30 000	5 000	15 000	50 000
Contribution	£120 000	£15 000	£75 000	£210 000
Less fixed costs				£150 000
Net profit				£ 60 000

(b) Limiting factor of labour hours

	A	B	C	Total
Hours required per unit	2.00	2.50	3.00	
Contribution per unit	£4.00	£3.00	£5.00	
Contribution per limiting factor:	£2.00 per hour	£1.20 per hour	1.67 per hour	
Allocation of hours:	60 000	0	45 000	105 000
Product mix (units)	30 000	0	15 000	

Profit Statement	A	B	C	Total
Sales	750 000	0	510 000	
Variable costs each	630 000	0	435 000	
Contribution	120 000	0	75 000	195 000
Less fixed costs				£150 000
Net profit				£45 000

12 AAT COST ACCOUNTING AND BUDGETING (1992)
Workings and notes:

	Sales (£)	Profit	Diff = Total Costs (£)
Jan	540 000	70 000	470 000
Feb	600 000	100 000	500 000
Mar	900 000	250 000	650 000
Apr	660 000	130 000	530 000
May	720 000	160 000	560 000
Jun	480 000	40 000	440 000

High/low method to split costs into fixed and variable:

	Units	Cost
High	30	650 000
Low	16	440 000
	14	210 000

Variable cost per unit = £210 000/14 = £15000

Check:	Variable	Fixed	Total
High	£450 000	£200 000	£650 000
Low	£240 000	£200 000	£440 000

Break even point: units = £200 000/£15 000 = 13.33 units
Break even point: value = £200 000/50% = £400 000

Six months Budget:
Sales	£3 900 000	
Variable cost	£1 950 000	
Contribution	£1 950 000	£15 000 P/unit or 50% C/S%
Fixed costs	£1 200 000	
Profit	£ 750 000	

(a) BREAK-EVEN CHART

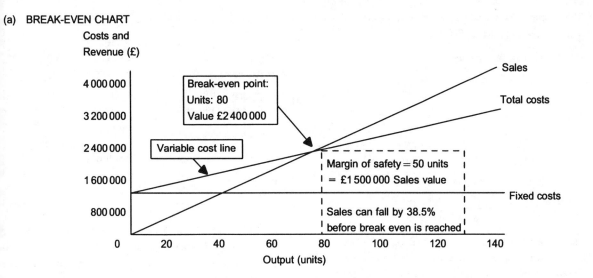

(b) Workings:

	Present position per unit	Proposed position per unit	
Selling price	100.0%	83.3%	
Costs	50.0%	50.0%	
Contribution	50.0%	33.3%	1.50 in units
C/S%	50.0%	40.0%	

Formula: $\dfrac{50\%}{40\%} = 25\%$ increase in sales required

Therefore the reduction would not be beneficial to the company as a 25% increase in sales value would be required to achieve the same profit:

	Present position	Proposed position	Required position
Units	130	143	195
Sales	£3 900 000	£3 575 000	£4 875 000
			(25% increase)
Variable costs	£1 950 000	£2 145 000	£2 925 000
Contribution	£1 950 000	£1 430 000	£1 950 000
Fixed costs	£1 200 000	£1 200 000	£1 200 000
Profit	£ 750 000	£ 230 000	£ 750 000

13   AAT COST ACCOUNTING AND BUDGETING 1993

Workings and notes:

Analysis of cost:	Variable £	Fixed £
Materials	1 980 000	0
Labour	980 000	420 000
Prod'n overhead	520 000	780 000
Selling overhead	120 000	680 000
Administration	0	820 000
Total	3 600 000	2 700 000

Above = 90% of production = 45 000 units (50 000 × 90%)
Variable cost per unit = £80 each (£3 600 000/45 000)
Selling value of production = £6 975 000 (45 000 × £155)

(a) Productive capacity

	Units
Maximum capacity	50 000
Budgeted capacity	45 000
Special order	4 000
Total	49 000

The company has the productive capacity to make the order of 4 000 units.

(b) Acceptance of special order.

	£	
Selling value	380 000	4 000 units at £95 each
Variable costs	320 000	4 000 units at £80 each
Contribution	60 000	

The special order should be given the go-ahead as it will increase overall profits by £60 000.

(c) Sales Manager's proposal.

	Budget plus special order	Proposal	
	£	£	
Sales	7 355 000	6 975 000	See note below
Variable costs	3 920 000	4 000 000	
Contribution	3 435 000	2 975 000	
Fixed costs	2 700 000	2 700 000	
Profit	735 000	275 000	

Note: The selling price would drop to £139.50, but sales could not increase by 15% because this would take the units above the maximum capacity (45 000 × 1.15 = 51 750). The above sales figure takes the maximum position of 50 000 units. As can be seen, the Sales Manager's proposals would result in a substantially lower profit and the special order should be made.

14   RSA III ACCOUNTING 1992

(a)

	Large	Small	Total
Units	**10 000**	**15 000**	
	£	£	
Sales	120 000	120 000	240 000
Variable costs	60 000	60 000	120 000
Contribution	60 000	60 000	120 000
Fixed costs absorbed by each product	30 000	30 000	60 000
Profit	30 000	30 000	60 000

(i)   Contribution of £30 000 from each product.
(ii)   Total costs absorbed by each product = £90 000.
(iii)   Total fixed costs of the company = £60 000.

(b)   Workings:

	Large	Small	
Number of minutes per unit	6	15	
Number of units per hour	10	4	
Number of units required	10 000	15 000	
Therefore, number of hours required for budget	1 000	3 750	4 750

Contribution per limiting factor:

	£	£
Selling price	12.00	8.00
Variable costs	6.00	4.00
Contribution	6.00	4.00
Contribution per hour	60.00	16.00

Production schedule:

	Hours	Contribution	No. of
		£	Units
Large	1 000	60 000	10 000
Small	2 000	32 000	8 000

(i)   Total number of machine Z hours required by original budget = 4 750 hours.
(ii)   Quantity of each items to maximise profit = 10 000 Large; 8 000 Small.
(iii)   Profit to be made with production limited:

	Large	Small	Total
Sales	120 000	64 000	184 000
Variable costs	60 000	32 000	92 000
Contribution	60 000	32 000	92 000
Fixed costs			60 000
Profit			32 000

15   RSA III ACCOUNTING 1993

Workings and notes:

Number of units sold last year:	10 000	(£800 000/£80)

Variable costs per unit in last year:

Materials	£ 30.00	(£300 000/10 000)
Labour	£ 20.00	(£200 000/10 000)
Selling costs	£ 10.00	(£100 000/10 000)
Contribution per unit	£ 20.00	(£80 − £60)
Fixed costs	£150 000	

Variable costs in the coming year:

Materials	£ 37.00	plus £7
Labour	£ 22.00	plus 10%
Selling costs	£ 11.00	plus 10%
Contribution per unit	£ 10.00	(£80 − £70)
Fixed costs in coming year	£160 000	

(a)(i) Break even

	Plan A	Plan B	Plan C
Fixed costs			
As table above	£160 000	£160 000	£160 000
Additional costs	£ 15 000	–	–
Adjusted fixed costs	£175 000	£160 000	£160 000
Contribution per unit			
Sales price	£ 80.00	£80.00	£95.00
Variable costs	£ 70.00	£67.00	£70.00
Variable selling cost	–	£11.00	–
Contribution	£10.00	£ 2.00	£25.00
Break-even in units	**17 500**	**80 000**	**6 400**

(ii) Earn a net profit of £100 000

	Plan A	Plan B	Plan C
Fixed costs as above	£175 000	£160 000	£160 000
Add desired profit	£100 000	£100 000	£100 000
	£275 000	£260 000	£260 000
Contribution per unit	£10.00	£2.00	£25.00
Number of units required	**27 500**	**130 000**	**10 400**

(b) Plan C appears to be the best plan, assuming that the price can be increased by nearly 19%, as this provides a contribution of £25 per unit.

16 RSA III ACCOUNTING 1994

(a)(i) Contribution made by each product.

	Widget	Wotnots	Total
Units	20 000	25 000	
	£	£	£
Sales	400 000	700 000	1 100 000
Variable costs	220 000	425 000	645 000
Contribution	180 000	275 000	455 000
Fixed Costs			180 000
Profit			275 000

(a)(ii) Calculation of overhead absorption rates

	Widgets	Wotnots	Total
Labour hours			
1.5 Hours per unit	30 000		30 000
2 Hours per unit		50 000	50 000
			80 000
			hours

Machine hours			
1 hour per unit	20 000		20 000
1.5 Hours Per Unit		37 500	37 500
			57 500
			hours

Overhead absorption rates:
Labour hour overhead absorption rate: £2.25 per labour hour
Machine hour overhead absorption rate: £3.13 per machine hour

(b)(i) Raw materials limiting factor.

	Widgets £	Wotnots £
Selling price	20	28
Materials	4	7
Labour	6	9
Selling cost	1	1
	11	17
Contribution	9	11
Contribution per limiting factor	2.25	1.57

Apportionment of limiting resource spend:

Widgets	£ 80 000 = 20 000 units (£4 per unit)
Wotnots	£140 000 = 20 000 units (£7 per unit)
	£220 000

(b)(ii) Profit

	Widgets	Wotnots	Total
Units	20 000	20 000	
	£	£	£
Sales	400 000	560 000	960 000
Variable costs	220 000	340 000	560 000
Contribution	180 000	220 000	400 000
Fixed Costs			180 000
Profit			**220 000**

17 LCCI THIRD LEVEL MANAGEMENT ACCOUNTING 1992

Workings and notes:

Labour hour rate

	X	Y
Sales (units)	30 000	20 000
	£	£
Costs		
Materials	960 000	640 000
Labour	720 000	720 000
Variable overheads	240 000	160 000
Fixed overheads	480 000	480 000
	2 400 000	2 000 000
Profit margin	600 000	500 000
Sales value	3 000 000	2 500 000
Selling price each	£100.00	£125.00

Machine hour rate

	X	Y
Sales (units)	30 000	20 000
	£	£
Costs		
Materials	960 000	640 000
Labour	720 000	720 000
Variable overheads	240 000	160 000
Fixed overheads	576 000	384 000
	2 496 000	1 904 000
Profit margin	624 000	476 000
Sales value	3 120 000	2 380 000
Selling price each	104.00	119.00

Labour Hours	60 000	60 000	120 000
Fixed overheads			£960 000
Direct labour hours absorption rate:			£8.00 per hour
Machine hours	60 000	40 000	100 000
Fixed overheads			£960 000
Machine hours absorption rate:			£9.60 per hour

(a) Selling price per unit:

X   Y
(i) £100.00 £125.00 Based on direct labour hour rate
(ii) £104.00 £119.00 Based on machine hour rate

(b) The most appropriate to use would be the direct labour hour rate, because the question pointed out that the fixed costs arise largely from the use of the skilled labour.

(c) Workings and notes:

Contribution per limiting factor:

	X	Y
	£	£
Selling price	100	125
Variable costs:		
Materials	32	32
Labour	24	36
Overheads	8	8
	64	76
Contribution	£36	£49

Contribution limiting factor:

	X	Y
Labour Hours	2	3
Contribution per labour hour	£18	£16.33

(i) The most profitable product is Product X, because it contributes £18 for each direct labour hour – the limiting factor.

(ii) Profit and loss account with all units sold when labour restricted:

	X	Y	Total	D/lab Hours
Sales (units)	30 000			60 000
Sales (units)		10 000		30 000
	£	£	£	
Sales value	3 000 000	1 250 000	4 250 000	
Variable costs	1 920 000	760 000	2 680 000	
Contribution	1 080 000	490 000	1 570 000	
Fixed Costs			960 000	
Profit			610 000	

18 LCCI THIRD LEVEL MANAGEMENT ACCOUNTING 1993

Workings and notes:

Selling price = £40; Variable costs = £16; therefore contribution = £24 per unit.

	£	
Profit	800 000	
Fixed Costs	400 000	
= Contribution	1 200 000	(£1 200 000/£24 = no. of units = 50 000)
Variable costs	800 000	50 000 × £16
Sales	2 000 000	50 000 × £40

(a)

	Present position	Policy 1	Policy 2	Policy 3
Sales Price	£40.00	£38.00	£37.00	£36.00
No. of Units	50 000	55 000	60 000	65 000
	£	£	£	£
Sales	2 000 000	2 090 000	2 220 000	234 000
Variable cost	800 000	880 000	960 000	1 040 000
Contribution	1 200 000	1 210 000	1 260 000	1 300 000
				(55.556%)
Fixed Costs	400 000	400 000	400 000	400 000
Profit	**800 000**	**810 000**	**860 000**	**900 000**

(b) The most favourable option is Policy 3, which increases the profits by £100 000 over the present position.

Margin of safety calculation:

Break even position – sales of 65 000 units:

			units	sales value
Fixed costs	400 000	=	20 000	720 000
Cont'n per unit	£20			
Forecast sales			65 000	2 340 000
Margin of safety			45 000	1 620 000
As percentage of forecast			69.2%	69.2%

Contribution/sales ratio calculation:

Sales	£2 340 000
Contribution	£1 300 000
Ratio	**55.6%**

19 ACCA COST AND MANAGEMENT ACCOUNTING 1 1990

Workings and notes:
1 module = 70 sq metres
Seven per shop = 490 sq. metres

1 module contribution per week:

	A	B	C	D	E
Sales	£6 750	£3 500	£4 800	£6 400	£3 333
Contribution	£1 350	£1 400	£1 200	£1 600	£1 000
Contribution per limiting factor	£19.29	£20.00	£17.14	£22.86	£14.28
Ranking	3RD	2ND	4TH	1ST	

2 modules contribution per week:

	A	**B**	**C**	**D**	**E**
Sales	£12 500	£6 300	£9 200	£10 400	£7 334
Contribution	£ 2 500	£2 520	£2 300	£ 2 600	£2 200
Therefore second					
module contribution =	£ 1 150	£1 120	£1 100	£ 1 000	£1 200
Ranking	2ND	3RD	4TH	5TH	1ST

(a) Allocation of floor space on basis of contribution per limiting factor.

	A	**B**	**C**	**D**	**E**
1 Module	70	70	70	70	0
2 Module	70	70	70	0	0
Total	140	140	140	70	0

(b) Profit statement.

		A £	**B** £	**C** £	**D** £	**Total** £
Contribution	D				1 600	1 600
	A	2 500				2 500
	B		2 520			2 520
	C			2 300		2 300
		2 500	2 520	2 300	1 600	8 920
Operating costs		1 600	1 600	1 600	800	5 600
Profit		900	920	700	800	3 320

20 ACCA COST AND MANAGEMENT ACCOUNTING 1 1990
Workings and notes:

	Year 1	**Year 2**	**Year 3**
Meals served	151 156	163 248	179 573

Wages high/low analysis:

	£	**Units**
High	368 375	163 248
Low	349 170	151 156
	19 205	12 092

£1.59   Variable wage cost per unit

	Check	Variable cost £	Fixed cost £	Total £
Year	1151 156	240 066	109 104	349 170
Year 2	163 248	259 271	109 104	368 375
plus 6%		15 556	6 546	22 102
Total		274 827	115 650	390 477
Year 3	179 573	302 310	115 650	417 960
plus7%		2 162	8 096	29 258
		323 472	123 746	447 218

Overheads high low analysis:

	£	Units
High	206 600	163 248
Low	202 549	151 156
	4 051	12 092

£0.34 Variable overheads cost per unit

	Check	Variable cost £	Fixed cost £	Total £
Year 1	151 156	50 640	151 909	202 549
Year 2	163 248	54 691	151 909	206 600
plus 5%		2 735	7 595	10 330
Total		57 425	159 505	216 930
Year 3	179 573	63 177	159 505	222 682
plus 6%		3 791	9 570	13 361
		66 967	169 075	236 042

(a) Budgeted expenditure on Wages in Year 3: £447 218

Budgeted expenditure on Overheads in Year 3: £236 042

(b)

	Year 1	Year 2	Year 3
Meals served	151 156	163 248	179 573
	£000s	£000s	£000s
Sales	1 348	1 514	1 742
			(£923 007/
			53%)

Cost of sales:

Food and beverage costs	698	792	923
			(£5.14 ×
			179 573)
Gross profit	650	722	819
Expenses:			
Wages	349	390	447
Overheads	203	217	236
	552	607	683
Net profit	98	115	135
Gross profit percentage	48.2%	47.7%	47.0%
Net profit percentage	7.3%	7.6%	7.8%

Comment:

The gross profit percentage shows a steady fall from Year 1. The following analysis per meal served indicates the reasons for this:

Selling price	£8.92	£9.28	£9.70
Percentage increase		4.0%	4.6%
Food, etc. costs	£4.62	£4.85	£5.14
Percentage increase		5.0%	6.0%

It can be seen that the selling prices have not kept pace with the increase in the food and beverage costs, with the 'gap' widening again in Year 3. Management will need to address this, either by increasing the selling price or by endeavouring to find cheaper sources of supplies, or a mixture of both, if this erosion in gross profit was not of itself part of a planned strategy.

The net profit percentage however shows an increase each year. The reason for this is because the fixed costs are 'falling' as a percentage of sales because to sales have grown at a faster rate than the fixed costs:

Sales increase	8%	10%
Increase in fixed wages costs	6%	5%
Increase in fixed overheads costs	5%	6%

The profit statement becomes clearer when the behavioural nature of the costs are shown as either fixed or variable costs:

	Year 1	Year 2	Year 3
Sales	1 348 312	1 514 224	1 741 522
Variable costs	989 047	1 124 171	1 313 446
Contribution	359 265	390 053	428 077
Fixed costs	261 013	275 155	292 820
Profit	98 252	114 898	135 256
C/S%	26.6%	25.8%	24.6%

	£	£
Increase in contribution	30 788	38 024
Increase in fixed costs	14 142	17 665
Overall increase	16 646	20 359

It may be that the comparative reduction in the contribution/sales ratio is the result of management policy, as indicated earlier, and the 'lower' selling prices have attracted more customers, allowing the fixed costs to be absorbed more quickly.

21   ᴀᴄᴄᴀ COST AND MANAGEMENT ACCOUNTING 1 1991
Workings and notes:

Per 100 units

Direct materials	
Requirement – net	30 kg
Losses – 10%	3.33 kg
Requirement – gross	33.33 kg
	£
Cost	5.4 per kg
Discount	0.27 per kg→0.33 kg × 200 000 units per

month = 66 666 kg net

Net	5.13 per kg	so exceeds the 25 000 kg threshold
Cost per 100 units	171.00	
Other materials	134.00	
	305.00	

Direct labour:		*Notes:*
Department 1	160.00	
Department 2	67.50	15 hours × £4.50
	227.50	

Overheads absorbed:			
Department 1:	Fixed and variable	208.00	130% of £160
Department 2:			

	Annual cost	Hours		
Variable	£1 980 000	2 200 000	13.50	15 hours @ 90p per hour (£1 980 000/

2 200 000)

Fixed	£3 444 000	1 320 000		2 200 000 × 0.60
Total overhead:	£5 424 000			
Plus hours required for Product X		360 000		
(2 400 000 × 0.15 hours each)		360 000		
Fixed overhead rate per hour	£2.05		30.75	15 hours @ £2.05 per hour
Estimated production cost			784.75	per 100 units
Non-production overheads: variable			70.00	£0.70 × 100
fixed			195.00	£1.95 × 100
Total estimated cost of X			1 049.75	per 100 units
(a) Estimated cost per unit			10.50	

(b) Comment.

The selling price of £9.95 is lower than the above estimated cost per unit. Thus it would appear not to be viable. However, the cost of £10.50 includes elements of fixed costs, and these costs will still remain to be paid if Product X is produced or not. The charge to Product X for fixed costs amounts to:

Department 1	90% of £160	£144.00 per 100 units
Department 2		£ 30.75 per 100 units
Non-production		£195.00 per 100 units
		£369.75

The fixed costs per unit is therefore £3.70, so the marginal cost of Product X is £6.80. The product will therefore contribute to overall fixed costs and profits as follows:

Sales price	£9.95
Variable costs	£6.80
Contribution	£3.15

And the extra profit earned will be: £7 560 000

$$(2\,400\,000 \times £3.15)$$

Therefore Product X is viable based on the information supplied.

(c) If the selling price is reduced and the volume increased, the extra profit generated by Product X will be as follows:

Sales price	£9.45
Variable costs	£6.80
Contribution	£2.65

2 900 000 × £2.65 = £7 685 000 profit.

the assumption is that the extra units sold will not affect the fixed costs position and can be sold. The additional 500 000 units is within the capacity of the factory, raising the manufacturing level to 80% (1 755 000/2 200 000 hours).

22 ACCA COST AND MANAGEMENT ACCOUNTING 1 1991

Workings and notes:

Manufacturing costs	Sales	Costs
High	800	410
Low	600	350
	200	60

Variable cost per £ sales = £60/200 = £0.30

Situation with selling agents:

	Variable costs	Fixed costs	Total costs
Sales at £800 k	£	£	£
Manufacturing	240	170	410
Administration	0	160	160
Selling agents	80	0	80
	320	330	650

Situation with own selling force:

	Variable costs	Fixed costs	Total costs
Sales at £800k	£	£	£
Manufacturing	240	170	410
Administration	0	160	160
Selling agents	0	60	60
	240	390	630

(a) Break even point using selling agents:

	£000s	
Sales	800	
Variable costs	320	
Contribution	480	60.0%
Fixed costs	330	
Profit	150	

Fixed costs	£330 000
C/S%	60%
Break even =	£550 000 sales

(b) Break even point using own sales force:

	£000s	
Sales	800	
Variable costs	240	
Contribution	560	70.0%
Fixed costs	390	
Profit	170	

Fixed costs	£390 000
C/S%	70%
Break even =	£557 143 sales

(c) The break even point is higher with the firm's own sales force but the difference between the two is not great – just £7 143 – approximately 1% separates them. All the estimates are in excess of the break even point. The option of the firm's own sales force, which has a much higher contribution/sales percentage than the selling agent alternative, should prove to be the more profitable selection, if sales achieve the medium and high levels expected. At the £600 000 sales level both schemes achieve the same net profit:

	Selling agents	Own sales force
	£	£
Sales	600 000	600 000
Contribution	360 000	420 000
Fixed costs	330 000	390 000
Profit	30 000	30 000

23 ACCA COST AND MANAGEMENT ACCOUNTING 1 1991

Workings and notes:

Absorption of fixed manufacturing overheads:

Cost per period	£427 500
Machine hours per period	2 250
Machine hour rate =	£190.00 per hour

Forecast Requirements:

Forecast sales (units)	Fixed overhead absorbed	Divide by £190 for m/c hours	Units per hour
W 190 000 @ £0.855	£162 450	855	222.22
X 125 000 @ £0.95	£118 750	625	200.00
Y 144 000 @ £0.475	£ 68 400	360	400.00
Z 142 000 @ £0.76	£107 920	568	250.00
	£457 520	2 408	

Contribution per limiting factor calculations:

	W	X	Y	Z
	£	£	£	£
Selling price	3.6500	3.9000	2.2500	2.9500
Variable costs				
Materials	0.8050	0.9960	0.4500	0.6470
Labour	0.6040	0.6510	0.4050	0.5090
Production overheads	0.2400	0.2470	0.2010	0.2170
Selling overheads	0.2160	0.2160	0.2160	0.2160
	1.8650	2.1100	1.2720	1.5890
Contribution	1.7850	1.7900	0.9780	1.3610
Machine hours	222.2	200	400	250
Contribution per machine per hour:	£396.63	£358.00	£391.20	£340.25
Ranking	1	3	2	4

(a)

Production:	Quantity	Hours	Cum./ hours
W	190 000	855	
Y	144 000	360	1 215
X	125 000	625	1 840
Z	102 500	410	2 250

Balance of hours available

Workings and notes:

Product Z

Requirement	142 000 units	
Normal time production	102 500 units	
Shortfall	39 500 units	= @ £0.2545 extra per unit
		= £10 053

(b) Profit Statement:

	W	X	Y	Z	Total
Units	190 000	125 000	144 000	142 000	
	£	£	£	£	
Sales	693 500	487 500	324 000	418 900	
Variable costs	354 350	263 750	183 168	225 638	
Add additional					
labour charge	354 350	263 750	183 168	225 638	
Contribution	339 150	223 750	140 832	193 262	896 994

Fixed production costs	427 500
Additional fixed costs	24 570
Selling costs	190 000
Forecast profit	254 924

(c) By working overtime the company will increase profits as follows:

Additional contribution from	
Product Z – 39 500 × £1.361 each	£53 760
Less additional costs: overtime premium	£10 053
fixed costs	£24 570
Extra profit	£19 137

This represents an increase of 8% and is normally sufficient incentive for management to decide in favour of working overtime to fulfil the orders. Against the decision, however, may be that the opportunity to earn more through overtime may be denied to some workers, and this may cause some problems with the workforce, with perhaps a reduction in labour efficiency. In addition, although the fixed costs are shown to increase, there may be further 'hidden' costs which would reduce the extra profit.

24 ACCA COST AND MANAGEMENT ACCOUNTING 1 1991
Workings and notes:
Materials costs:
  Production : 116 000 units at £7 each = £812 000
Labour costs:
  Production: 116 000 units at £5.50 each = £638 000

Production overheads:
Apportionment of overheads:

	Dept 1	Dept 2	Service	General Factory	Total
	£	£	£	£	£
	380 000	465 000	265 000	230 000	1 340 000
General factory	92 000	115 000	23 000	(230 000)	
			288 000		
Service:					
Labour related	76 800	96 000	(172 800)		
Machine related	57 600	57 600	(115 200)		
	606 400	733 600	0	0	1 340 000
Production					
units	120 000	120 000			
Absorption					
rate	£5.0533	£6.1133		per production unit	
Total per unit	£11.1667				

Cost per production unit:

Materials	£ 7.0000
Labour	£ 5.5000
Variable	
overheads	£ 2.0000
Fixed	
overheads	£11.1667
	£25.6667

(a) Profit statement – absorption costing

	£	
Sales	4 104 000	114 000 × £36
Cost of sales		
Opening stock	0	
Goods manufactured	2 977 337	116 000 × £25.6667
Closing stock	51 333	2 000 × £25.6667
	2 926 004	
Gross profit	1 177 996	
Fixed expenditure		
under-absorbed	64 666	£1 360 000 –
		(116 000 × £11.1667)
Other non-manufacturing		
costs	875 000	
	939 666	
Profit for the period	238 330	

(b) Profit statement – marginal costing

	£	
Sales	4 104 000	
Variable costs	1 653 000	114 000 × £14.50
Contribution	2 451 000	
Fixed Costs	2 235 000	£1 360 000 + £875 000
Profit for the period	216 000	

(c) In the absorption profit statement, fixed production costs have been carried forward in the closing stocks, amounting here to £22 330 (2000 units × £11.1667). But in marginal costing all fixed costs incurred in the accounting period are written off in the period and so the marginal costing profit statement shows a lower profit. In the following period, however, assuming no closing stocks are carried forward at the end of it, those fixed costs brought forward from this period will be written off, resulting in the marginal costing profit statement producing a higher profit than the absorption system.

25 ACCA COST AND MANAGEMENT ACCOUNTING 1 1993

Workings and notes:

Overheads:	Value	Units	
High	£452 318	112	
Low + 5%	£439 144	100	(£418 232 × 1.05)
	13 174	12	

Variable cost per unit		£1 098	
Check:	Variable	Fixed	Total
High – 112 units	£122 961	£329 357	£452 318
Low – 100 units	£109 787	£329 357	£439 144

(a)	Year just ended	Year ahead	
	£	£	
Sales	1 476 461	1 963 693	£1 476 461 × 1.40 × 95%
Materials	492 326	723 719	(£492 326 × 1.40 × 1.05)
Labour	316 764	465 643	(£316 764 × 1.40 × 1.05)
Overheads:			
Fixed	329 357	349 119	increase of 6%
Variable	122 961	182 474	(£122 961 × 1.40 × 1.06)
	1 261 408	1 720 955	
Profit	215 053	£242 738	

(b) Break even.

	Year just ended		Year ahead	
	£		£	
Sales	1 476 461		1 963 693	
Variable cost	932 051		1 371 837	
Contribution	544 410	36.87%	591 857	30.14%
Fixed costs	329 357		349 119	
Profit	215 053		242 738	
Break even	£893 000		£1 158 000	
	(£329 357/36.87%)		(£349 119/30.14%)	

(c) Comment.

As can be seen, the break-even point in the year ahead has risen sharply. The reason is twofold: first, the contribution/sales percentage has fallen substantially, and secondly the fixed costs have risen. The company's policy of reducing the selling price to stimulate sales, however, would appear to be successful if they achieve the 40% increase in sales, for the overall profits will increase by over £27 000.

26 CIMA COSTING 1990

Workings and notes:

	(i)	(ii)	(iii)	(iv)
Fixed costs	£6 810	£8 310	£6 810	£6 810
Contribution per litre	£ 0.04	£ 0.04	£0.038	£ 0.03
Break-even in units	170 250	207 750	179 211	227 000
Increase in rent		£1 500		

(a) Break-even.

	Option I	Option II	Option III	Option IV
In litres	170 250	207 750	179 211	227 000
In value	74 910	91 410	78 853	97 610

(b) For profit of £700 per week.

	Option I
Fixed costs + profit	9 610
Contribution	£0.04
Litres required	240 250

(c) Four-week normal trading.

	(i)	(ii)
Litres sold	275 000	425 000
	£	£
Sales	121 000	187 000
Cost of sales	110 000	170 000
Gross profit	11 000	17 000
Fixed costs	6 810	6 810
Profit	4 190	10 190

Four-week trading – reduced hours

	(i)	(ii)
Litres sold	225 000	375 000
	£	£
Sales	99 000	165 000
Cost of sales	90 000	150 000
Gross profit	9 000	15 000
Fixed costs	5 790	5 790
Profit	3 210	9 210

Change in hours = reduction in profits of £980

Fixed Costs:		6 810
Less: electricity		120
Less: staff wages	200	
Less: wage related costs	25	
	225	
	× 4	900
		5 790

27 CIMA COST ACCOUNTING 1990

Workings and notes:

	September	October
Production overhead absorbed:		
Production	115 000	78 000
Capacity	120 000	120 000
As % of capacity	95.8%	65.0%
Therefore overhead spend =	£656 000	£ 632 000
Production Account		
Gross made	£ 115 000	£ 78 000
Materials	£ 920 000	£ 624 000
Direct Labour	£ 828 000	£ 561 600
Variable costs	£ 386 400	£ 262 080
Fixed overhead		
Absorbed	£ 864 800	£ 586 560
	£2 999 200	£2 034 240
Cost per unit	26.08	26.08

Closing stock valuation: 28 000 units at £26.08 = £730 240   5 000 units at £26.08 = £130 400

(a)(i) Absorption costing monthly profit statements

	September	October
	£	£
Sales	2 784 000	3 232 000
Cost of sales:		
Opening stock	0	730 240
Goods manufactured in period	2 999 200	2 034 240
Closing Stock	(730 240)	(130 400)
	2 268 960	2 634 080
Gross profit	515 040	597 920
Under (over)absorbed overhead	(208 800)	45 440
Fixed selling costs	120 000	120 000
Fixed administrative costs	80 000	80 000
	(8 800)	245 440
Profit for the month	£523 840	£352 480

(a)(ii) Marginal costing monthly profit statements

	September	October
	£	£
Sales	2 784 000	3 232 000
Variable costs	1 614 720	1 874 560
Contribution	1 169 280	1 357 440
Fixed costs	856 000	832 000
Profit	313 280	525 440

(b) Comment.

1. The Accountant is right to point out that marginal costing segregates fixed costs, treating them as period costs chargeable to the period profit and loss account to which they relate. With regard to the control of production costs, the company appears to operate a standard costing system and therefore control of costs will be exercised through variance analysis, covering both variable costs and fixed production expenditure costs.

2. As can be seen from the two profit statements, the treatment of the fixed production costs creates a large difference; the closing stock of September includes £210 560 of September fixed overheads and this has been carried forward to October to be written off in that month thus 'increasing' September profits at the 'expense' of October's. With marginal costing, the revenues and variable costs are matched precisely, with the fixed costs written off in the period incurred. Profits reported on the marginal costing system, however, will depend completely on the volume of sales in the month, so if sales are very low in one month, profits will also be low (or losses arise). Therefore marginal costing will not eliminate the distortions in the net profit caused by seasonal fluctuations.

3. By splitting costs into the way they behave according to output, variable and fixed costs, management have a useful decision-making tool with which to make short term decisions to maximise profits, as the Accountant has pointed out.

28 CIMA COST ACCOUNTING 1991

(a) Unit costs of each product

Unit Costs	X	Y	Z
	£	£	£
Materials	50.00	120.00	90.00
Labour:			
Dept A	70.00	40.00	75.00
Dept B	24.00	18.00	30.00
Dept C	32.00	16.00	60.00
Variable overhead	12.00	7.00	16.00
Total unit cost	188.00	201.00	271.00

(a) Answer
Profit expected for the current year

	X	Y	Z	Total
	£	£	£	£
Sales	1 575 000	1 320 000	1 800 000	4 695 000
Variable costs	1 410 000	1 206 000	1 626 000	4 242 000
Contribution	165 000	114 000	174 000	453 000
Fixed costs				300 000
Profit based on the original sales figures				153 000

(b) Hours required

	X	Y	Z	Total
	£	£	£	£
Dept B	30 000	18 000	30 000	78 000
	(4 × 7 500)	(3 × 6 000)	(5 × 6 000)	

Contribution based on new selling prices:

	£	£	£
Selling price	210.00	220.00	300.00
Variable cost	188.00	201.00	271.00
Contribution	22.00	19.00	29.00

Contribution per limiting factor:

Dept B Hours	4	3	5
Contribution	£22.00	£19.00	£29.00
	£5.50	£6.33	£5.80
Ranking	3rd	1st	2nd

(c) Answer
Profit using most profitable mixture of Product

	X	Y	Z	Total
Units	3 875	7 500	8 000	
Dept B hours 1	15 500	22 500	40 000	78 000
	£	£	£	£
Sales	813 750	1 650 000	2 400 000	4 863 750
Variable costs	728 500	1 507 500	2 168 000	4 404 000
Contribution	85 250	142 500	232 000	459 750
Fixed Costs				300 000
Profit				£159 750

29 CIMA COST ACCOUNTING 1992
Workings and notes
Material X:

In stock	£21 600
On order	£30 400
	£52 000
10% thereof:	£5200 Additional cost of South Coast contract (opportunity cost)

Material Y:

In stock	£24 800
Present cost	£49 600

(a)

North-east contract	£	South-coast contract	£
Contract price	288 000	Contract price	352 000
Material X:		Material Y:	
In stock	21 600	Replacement cost	49 600
On order	30 400	Material X:	
Not yet ordered	60 000	Additional cost if north-east Contract cancelled –	
		as above	5 200
		Material Z:	71 200
Labour	86 000	Labour	110 000
Staff accommodation	6 800	Staff accommodation	5 600
Income from rental of equipment	(6 000)	Cancellation charge	28 000
Relevant cost	198 800	Relevant cost	269 600
Net benefit	89 200	Net benefit	82 400

The most beneficial contract is therefore the north-east contract as it produces an extra £6 800 profit.

(b) The reasoning is as follows:

North-east contract

Material X – a direct variable cost, therefore relevant to the decision and included in the statement.

Labour – a variable cost also so included for the same reason.

Site management – a fixed cost: if the contract does not go ahead this cost will remain – therefore not relevant to the decision.

Staff accommodation – a variable cost therefore relevant and so included.

Depreciation – the plant is already owned and therefore not specifically purchased for the contract; therefore not included as not relevant.

Interest on capital – a notional charge allocated to the contract so therefore not relevant to the decision.

Headquarters costs are fixed and allocated to the contract, therefore not relevant; these costs will remain irrespective of the decision. The receipts from the hiring out of the surplus plant arise from taking the North-east contract; therefore this is relevant to the contract and credited to it.

South-coast contract

Material Y – a variable cost therefore relevant to the decision; as the material is in common use, the new price is used.

Material X – If the South-coast contract is taken Material X cannot be used except as a substitute material; the additional costs incurrable, i.e., £5 200, of using X for other materials will arise by taking the South-coast contract. Therefore this is a relevant cost to be included in the South-coast contract.

Material Z: a direct cost of the contract.

Staff accommodation – a variable cost therefore relevant and so included.

Cancellation charge: arises only if the South-coast contract taken – therefore a relevant cost of this contract.

30 CIMA COST ACCOUNTING 1993

Workings and notes:

Number of potential room lettings:

£256 200/£35 = 7 320 rooms – April to September

Number of potential room lettings:

£254 800/£35 = 7 280 rooms – October to March

Budgeted room lettings:

£218 400/£35 = 6 240 rooms – April to September

Budgeted room lettings:

£165 200/£35 = 4 720 rooms – October to March

(a)

	April–September	October–March
Potential room lettings	7 320	7 280
Budgeted room lettings	6 240	4 720
Room occupancy ratio	85%	65%

(b)

Budgeted profit and loss account

	April–September	October–March
Rooms let	6 240	4 720
	£	£
Sales	218 400	165 200
Costs		
Variable costs	37 440	28 320
Fixed costs:		
Depreciation	54 000	54 000
Insurance	33 000	33 000
Maintenance	28 800	28 800
Services	16 200	16 200
Management	18 000	18 000
Total costs	187 440	178 320
Profit	30 960	(13 120)

(c) Workings:

Contribution per room = £29 (£35 – £6)

Fixed costs per month = £25 000

Number of room days per month to break even

= 862 (£25 000/£29)

(d) If the hotel were to be closed for January and February, there would clearly be no income receivable and therefore no contribution towards the fixed costs. Each room contributes £29, so by closing down for the two months the loss would be higher, as no fixed costs would be recovered from trading.

Model answers to examination questions, Chapter 18

1 A LEVEL (ULEAC) 1989

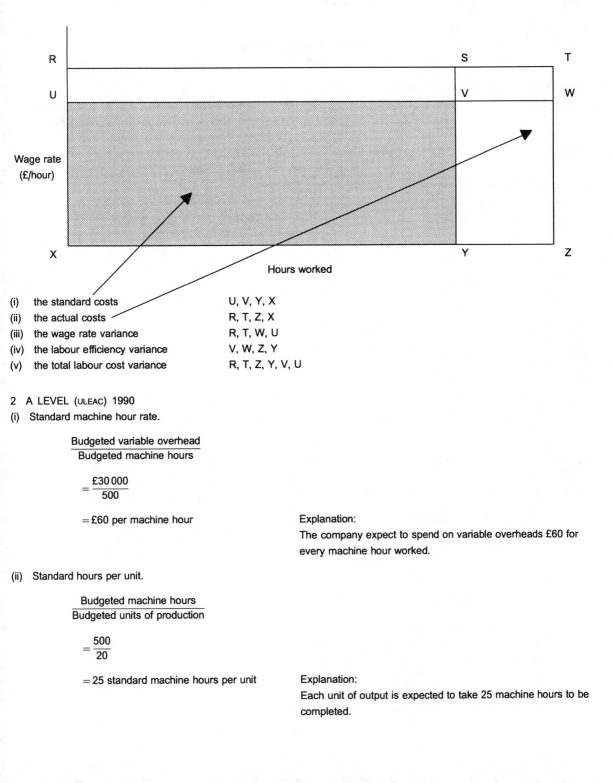

(i)	the standard costs	U, V, Y, X
(ii)	the actual costs	R, T, Z, X
(iii)	the wage rate variance	R, T, W, U
(iv)	the labour efficiency variance	V, W, Z, Y
(v)	the total labour cost variance	R, T, Z, Y, V, U

2 A LEVEL (ULEAC) 1990

(i) Standard machine hour rate.

$$\frac{\text{Budgeted variable overhead}}{\text{Budgeted machine hours}}$$

$$= \frac{£30\,000}{500}$$

$$= £60 \text{ per machine hour}$$

Explanation:
The company expect to spend on variable overheads £60 for every machine hour worked.

(ii) Standard hours per unit.

$$\frac{\text{Budgeted machine hours}}{\text{Budgeted units of production}}$$

$$= \frac{500}{20}$$

$$= 25 \text{ standard machine hours per unit}$$

Explanation:
Each unit of output is expected to take 25 machine hours to be completed.

(iii) and (iv)   Variance analysis – variable overheads.

	Standard	**Actual**	**Variance**		
Units	21	21			
Costs	£31 500	£21 000	£10 500	Favourable	21 units × 25 hours × £60 per hour
A		£21 000			
AS	600 × £60	£36 000	£15 000	Favourable expenditure variance	
SS	525 × £60	£31 500	£ 4 500	Adverse efficiency variance	

(iii)   Variable overhead expenditure variance
= £15 000 Favourable

Explanation:
The company expected to spend £60 for each machine hour worked and 600 hours were actually worked; thus £36 000 would be expected to have been spent on variable overheads. But only £21 000 was spent. Thus £15 000 was saved – a favourable variable overheads expenditure variance.

(iv)   Variable overhead efficiency variance = £4500 Adverse

Explanation:
25 standard machine hours were expected for each unit and for 21 units the hours should have been 525. But they produced the 21 in 600 hours so were therefore less efficient.

3   A LEVEL (ULEAC) 1992

Note: The question states that the figures are correct but the variances have been calculated wrongly.

Materials		**Standard**	**Actual**	**Variance**	
Litres		1 940	2 270		
Costs		£16 334.80	£18 704.80	£2 370.00	Adverse materials total variance
A	2 270 × £8.24	£18 704.80			
AS	2 270 × £8.42	£19 113.40	£ 408.60		Favourable materials price variance
S	1 940 × £8.42	£16 334.80	£2 778.60		Adverse materials usage variance
			£2 370.00		Adverse materials total variance

Labour		**Standard**	**Actual**	**Variance**	
Hours		800	860		
Costs		£5 224.00	£5 280.40	£56.40	Adverse labour total variance
A	860 × £6.14	£5 280.40			
AS	860 × £6.53	£5 615.80	£335.40		Favourable labour rates variance
S	800 × £6.53	£5 224.00	£391.80		Adverse labour efficiency usage variance
			£ 56.40		Adverse labour total variance

Summary:

Materials (i)   £2 370.00 Adverse materials total variance
(ii)   £408.60 Favourable materials price variance
(iii) £2 778.60 Adverse materials usage variance

Labour   (i)   £56.40 Adverse labour total variance
(ii)   £335.40 Favourable labour rates variance
(iii) £391.80 Adverse labour efficiency usage variance

4   A LEVEL (AEB) 1990

(a) Manufacturing account.

Manufacturing Account for the month of May

	£
Materials:	
Usage: 9650 kg at £2.40	23160
Labour:	
11840 hours at £6 per hour	71040
Prime cost	94200
Factory overheads:	
Repairs: plant and machinery	1250
Factory supervisory staff salaries	8500
Factory heating and lighting	2400
Factory rent and rates	3500
Depreciation of plant and machinery	4800
General factory expenses	8400
	28850
Total manufacturing costs	123050
Factory profit	18250
Transfer price to warehouse	141300 (150% of prime cost)

(b) Variance analysis.

Materials		Standard £	Actual £	Variance £	
		22560	20265	2295	Favourable materials total variance

Analysis:

Materials:

A			20265		
AS	9650 × £2.40		23160	2895	Favourable materials price variance
S			22560	600	Adverse materials usage variance

Labour		Standard £	Actual £	Variance £	
		67800	73408	5608	Adverse labour total variance

Analysis:

Materials:

A			73408		
AS	11840 × £6		71040	2368	Adverse labour rates variance
S			67800	3240	Adverse labour efficiency variance

Summary:

(i)   Direct labour rate variance   = £2368 Adverse

      Direct labour efficiency variance = £3240 Adverse

(ii) Direct materials price variance   = £2895 Favourable

      Direct materials usage variance = £ 600 Adverse

5 A LEVEL (AEB) 1992

(a) Variances.

	Standard £	Actual £	Variance £	
Units	50 000	50 000		
Materials	187 500	189 600	2 100	Adverse materials total variance
Labour	765 000	819 000	54 000	Adverse labour total variance
Total	952 500	1 008 600	56 100	Adverse total direct cost variance

Analysis of variances:

Materials:		£	
A		189 600	
AS	158 000 × £1.25	197 500	£ 7 900 Favourable materials price variance
S		187 500	£10 000 Adverse materials usage variance
Labour:			
A		819 000	
AS	156 000 × £5.10	795 600	23 400 Adverse labour rates variance
S		765 000	30 600 Adverse labour efficiency variance

Summary:

(i)	Total direct cost variance	£56 100 Adverse
(ii)	Direct materials price variance	£ 7 900 Favourable
	Direct materials usage variance	£10 000 Adverse
(iii)	Direct labour rate variance	£23 400 Adverse
	Direct labour efficiency variance	£30 600 Adverse

(b) Comment.

Purchasing Manager

The good terms negotiated by the Purchasing Manager have resulted in a favourable variance, as anticipated by him.

Personnel Manager

As no increase in wage rates had been agreed the large, adverse labour rates variance must be caused by more expensive staff being used to produce the product. The actual cost per hour is £5.25 compared to the standard cost of £5.10.

Production Manager

Contrary to this manager's opinion, the materials usage was higher than the standard set, which has cost the company £10 000; 158 000 kilogrammes being used instead of 150 000 kilogrammes.

In addition, the efficiency of the (more expensive) labour force was lower than expected and this has cost £30 600. The work force should have taken 150 000 to produce the 50 000 units, but instead it took them 156 000 hours.

6 A LEVEL (AEB) 1993

(a) Actual materials cost = 6 400 kg × £2.20 per kg = £14 080

Actual labour cost = 1 800 hours × £4.10 per hour

	Standard cost £	Actual cost £	Variance £	
Units	2 000	2 000		
Materials	12 000	14 080	2 080	Adverse direct materials total variance

Labour		8 000	7 380	620	Favourable direct labour total variance

Variance analysis

Materials:

A			14 080		
AS	6400 × £2		12 800	1 280	Adverse materials price variance
S			12 000	800	Adverse materials usage variance
				2 080	Adverse materials total variance

Labour:

A			7 380		
AS	1800 × £4		7 200	180	Adverse labour rates variance
S			8 000	800	Favourable labour efficiency variance
				620	Favourable direct labour total variance

Summary:

Materials price variance	£1 280 Adverse
Materials usage variance	£ 800 Adverse
Materials total variance	£2 080 Adverse
Labour rates variance	£ 180 Adverse
Labour efficiency variance	£ 800 Favourable
Labour total variance	£ 620 Adverse

(b) Comment

The adverse materials price variance of £1280 has arisen because the company has paid an extra 20p for each kilo purchased (6400 × 20p). The reason may be caused by a price increase by the supplier, or emergency purchases were necessary because of an out-of-stock situation, or because the standard cost price was incorrectly set.

The adverse materials usage variance of £800 has arisen because the company should have used 6000 kg to manufacture 2000 items but instead used 6400 kg. The reason could be due to inefficient or inexperienced labour. As there was no defective output, excess wastage does not appear to have been the cause. Another possibility is that materials have been lost due to pilferage.

The adverse labour rates variance of £180 has arisen because the company paid an extra 10p for each hour worked (1800 × 10p). This may be because of a recent wage increase, or higher-grade staff were used. If the latter had been the case it would normally be expected that the materials usage would have been lower to compensate, but this has not occurred in this instance.

The favourable efficiency variance of £800 has arisen because the workforce should have completed the 2000 units in two hours but they only took 1800 hours (200 × £4). This adds weight to the possibility that higher-grade staff were used, who, being generally more skilled,would be expected to take less time to complete the work. Another reason for both these variances could be that the standards have been incorrectly set.

7   A LEVEL (AEB) 1994

(a)   Actual profit and loss statement.

HGW Ltd

Profit and loss statement for March

	£
Sales	46 750
Cost of sales:	
Materials	9 734
Labour	18 720
Variable overheads	12 500
	40 954
Profit	5 796

(b)   Variances

(i)   Sales variances

	Budget	**Actual**	**Variance**
Units	520	550	
	£	**£**	**£**
Sales	44 720	46 750	
Standard cost	37 960	40 150	
Profit	6 760	6 600	− 160 Adverse

Variance analysis:

A	6 600		
AB	550 × £13	7 150	550	Adverse selling price variance
B		6 760	390	Favourable sales volume profit variance

(ii)   Production variances

	Budget	**Actual**	**Variance**
Units	550	550	
	£	**£**	**£**
Costs:			
Materials	9 900	9 734	166	Favourable materials total variance
Labour	18 150	18 720	570	Adverse labour total variance
V/overheads	12 100	12 500	400	Adverse var/overheads total variance

Variance analysis:

Materials

A		9 734	
AS	785 kg × £12	9 420	314	Adverse materials price variance
S		9 900	480	Favourable materials usage variance

Labour

A		18 720	
AS	2 400 × £7.50	18 000	720	Adverse labour rates variance
S		18 150	150	Favourable labour efficiency variance

(b) Summary:

(i)	Selling price variance	(£550) Adverse
(i)	Sales volume profit variance	£390 Favourable
(i)	Sales variance	(£160) Adverse
(ii)	Materials price variance	(£314) Adverse
(ii)	Materials usage variance	£480 Favourable
(ii)	Materials total variance	£166 Favourable
(iii)	Labour rates variance	(£720) Adverse
(iii)	Labour efficiency variance	£150 Favourable
(iii)	Labour total variance	(£570) Adverse

(c) Reconciliation statement – month of March

	£
Budgeted trading profit	6 760
Sales variances:	
Selling price	(550)
Sales volume profit	390
Production variances:	
Materials price	(314)
Materials usage	480
Labour rates	(720)
Labour efficiency	150
Variable overheads total	(400)
Actual trading profit	5 796

8 AAT COST ACCOUNTING AND BUDGETING 1991

Workings and notes:

	North	South	
Actual sales	140 000	210 000	350 000 units
Actual sales value	£1 470 000	£2 310 000	
Cost per unit = £9	£1 260 000	£1 890 000	

(a) Profit statements.

North region

	Budget	Actual	
Units	150 000	140 000	
Sales	£1 500 000	£1 470 000	
Standard cost	£1 350 000	£1 260 000	
Profit	£ 150 000	£ 210 000	£60 000 Favourable total sales variance

South region

	Budget	Actual	
Units	180 000	210 000	
Sales	£2 160 000	£2 310 000	
Standard cost	£1 620 000	£1 890 000	
Profit	£ 540 000	£ 420 000	(£120 000) Adverse total sales variance

Summary:

	North	South	Company
Budgeted profit	£150 000	£540 000	£690 000
Actual profit	£210 000	£420 000	£630 000
Total sales variance	£ 60 000	£120 000	£ 60 000
	Favourable	Adverse	Adverse

(b) Variance Analysis.

North region

A		£210 000		
AB	140 000 × £1	£140 000	£70 000	Favourable selling price variance
B		£150 000	£10 000	Adverse sales volume profit variance
			£60 000	

South region

A		£420 000		
AB	210 000 × £3	£630 000	£210 000	Adverse selling price variance
B		£540 000	£ 90 000	Favourable sales volume profit variance
			£120 000	

Summary:

	North		South	
Selling price variance	£70 000	Favourable	£210 000	Adverse
Sales volume profit variance	£10 000	Adverse	£ 90 000	Favourable
Total sales variance	£60 000	Favourable	£120 000	Adverse

(c) Report to Sales Director.

To: Sales Director

Subject: Sales and profit performance – North and South Regions   Date:

From: Accountant

As requested, I have completed an analysis of the performance of both regions and enclose two reports (A and B) to assist at your forthcoming meeting. Table A shows the actual profit compared to budget for each division. You will note that the North did better than budget and a favourable variance of £60 000 was earned. However, South fell short of budget and there was an adverse profit variance of £120 000.

Table B analyses both these variances to find the underlying causes and I summarise these as follows:

North: The £60 000 favourable variance has arisen through an increase in the selling price of 50p per unit, resulting in extra income of £70 000. However, the number of units actually sold was lower than budget by 10 000. As we had budgeted for a profit per unit of £1 (£10 − £9) this reduction in the units has cost the company £10 000. It may be that the increase in the price affected the number of units sold, with some customers perhaps resisting the higher price.

Unit sales were down in percentage terms by nearly 6.7% but could have fallen by 33.3% to earn the same budgeted profit (£1/ £1.50): 100 000 units at £1.50 = £150 000. Therefore the selling price increase has succeeded and the new price should be continued.

South: The £120 000 adverse variance is mainly because of the reduction in the selling price, from £12 per unit to £11. This cost the company £210 000. However the price reduction seems to have attracted more customers and sales increased by 30 000 units, bringing in an extra profit of £90 000. The increase in the units sold represents an increase over budget of 16.7%. But to achieve the budgeted profit at the lower selling price an increase of 50% in the number of units to be sold was required (£3/£2): 270 000 units at £2 profit = £540 000.

Therefore the reduction has not succeeded and consideration should be given to increasing the price.

(Signed)

9 AAT COST ACCOUNTING AND BUDGETING
(a) Variances

Department A

	Standard	Actual	Variance	
Units	7 500	7 500		
	£	£	£	
Costs	60 000	70 875	10 875	Adverse

Analysis of variance:

A		70 875		
AS	16 875 × £4	67 500	3 375	Adverse labour rates variance
S		60 000	7 500	Adverse labour efficiency variance
			10 875	Adverse labour total variance

Department B

	Standard	Actual	Variance	
Units	9 000	9 000		
	£	£	£	
Costs	47 250	56 700	9 450	Adverse

Analysis of variance:

A		56 700		
AS	15 750 × £3.50	55 125	1 575	Adverse labour rates variance
S		47 250	7 875	Adverse labour efficiency variance
			9 450	Adverse labour total variance

(b) Both departments have recorded adverse variances in both rates and efficiency. The reasons could be as follows:

Labour rates variance:

The company could have increased the rates of pay for its staff but not changed the standard rate. Higher paid staff could have been used.

Labour efficiency variance:

The staff took longer than expected to complete the work. This may have been caused by waiting for materials, inexperienced or untrained staff used, machine breakdowns, poor supervision or the standards may have been incorrectly set.

(c) Weekly wage rates;

Department A hourly rate = £70 875/16 875 =   £4.20   per hour
Department B hourly rate = £56 700/15 750 =   £3.60   per hour

Scheme 1

	Department A	**Department B**
Weekly wages:		
Hours	45	42
Wages per week	£189.00	£151.20

Scheme 2

	Department A	**Department B**	
Actual hours per unit	2.25	1.75	
Number of units made	7 500	9 000	
Number of hours worked	16 875	15 750	per annum
Hours per week	337.5	315	above divided by 50
Hours per person per week	45	42	
Therefore number of staff	7.5	7.5	people
Cost:			
A	£1 200		7 500 units × £8/50
B		£1 080	9 000 units × £6/50
Wages per person per week	**£160.00**	**£144.00**	

(d) For Department A piecework (Scheme 2) would seem to be more appropriate, as the cost per unit will be lower: 150 units produced per week at a cost of £180 compared to £189 under Scheme 1.
Similarly for Department 2: Scheme 2 would cost £144 for 180 units per week compared to £151.20 under Scheme 1.
The recommendation therefore should be for the company to adopt the piecework scheme.

10   RSA III ACCOUNTING 1992
Workings

	Standard	Actual	Variance	
Units	1 000	1 000		
	£	£	£	
Materials	4 500	4 320	180	Favourable
Labour	4 500	4 340	160	Favourable
	9 000	8 660		
Materials				
A		4 320		
AS	2 700 × £1.50	4 050	270	Adverse price variance
S		4 500	450	Favourable usage variance
Labour				
A		4 340		
AS	1 550 × £3	4 650	310	Favourable rates variance
S		4 500	150	Adverse efficiency variance

(i)   Material price variance   = £270 adverse
ii)   Material usage variance   = £450 favourable
(iii) Labour rates variance   = £310 favourable
(iv) Labour efficiency variance = £150 adverse

11   RSA III ACCOUNTING 1993

Workings and notes:

Actual labour cost: £14 720.00   20 × (40 hours @ £4.60) × 4
                     £ 3 360.00   5 × (40 hours @ £4.20) × 4
                     ──────────
                     £18 080.00

	Standard	Actual	Variance	
Units	1 006	1 006		
	£	£	£	
Materials	7 243.20	7 500.00	256.80	Adverse
Labour	18 108.00	18 080.00	28.00	Favourable
	25 351.20	25 580.00	284.80	

Materials

A		7 500.00		
AS	3200 × £2.40	7 680.00	180.00	Favourable price variance
S		7 243.20	436.80	Adverse usage variance

Labour

A		18 080.00		
AS	4000 × £4.50	18 000.00	80.00	Adverse rates variance
S		18 108.00	108.00	Favourable efficiency variance

Summary:
(i)   Total labour variance   = £28.00 favourable
(ii)   Labour efficiency variance = £108.00 favourable
(iii) Labour rate variance   = £80 adverse
(iv)   Total materials variance   = £256.80 adverse
(v)   Materials usage variance   = £436.80 adverse
(vi)   Materials price variance   = £180.00 favourable

12   LCCI THIRD LEVEL COST ACCOUNTING 1991

Workings and notes:
Valuation of issues:

Day	Detail	Receipts Units	Receipts £	Issues Units	Issues £	Balance Units	Balance £
1	Opening balance					100	520
8	Purchases	1 000	5 300			1 100	5 820
20	Purchases	2 500	12 000			3 600	17 820
				2 800	13 980	800	3 840

(100 @ £5.20; 1 000 @ £5.30; 1 700 @ £4.80)

	Standard	Actual	Variance	
Units	920	920		
Materials	£13 800	£13 980	£180	Adverse
A		£13 980		
AS	2 800 × £5	£14 000	£20	Favourable price
S		£13 800	£200	Adverse usage

(a) Ledger accounts: present system

(i) **DR** — **Material stock account** — **CR**

	£		£
Opening balance	520		
Purchases	17 300	Issues – transfer to WIP account	13 980
		Closing balance	3 840
	17 820		17 820

(ii) **DR** — **WIP control account (materials only)** — **CR**

	£		£
Material issues transfer	13 980	Transfer material usage variance	200
Transfer material price variance	20	Transfer to finished goods store	13 800
	14 000		14 000

(iii) **DR** — **Material price variance account** — **CR**

	£		£
Transfer to profit & loss account	20	Transfer from WIP control account	20
	20		20

(iv) **DR** — **Material usage variance account** — **CR**

	£		£
Transfer from WIP control account	200	Transfer to profit & loss account	200
	200		200

(b) Entries using standard costs

(i) **DR** — **Material stock account** — **CR**

		£		£
Opening balance	100 × £5	500		
Purchases	3 500 × £5	17 500	Issues – transfer to WIP Account	
			2 800 × £5	14 000
			Closing balance	4 000
		18 000		18 000

(ii) **DR** — **WIP control account (materials only)** — **CR**

	£		£
Material issues stock transfer	14 000	Transfer material usage variance	200
		Transfer to finished goods store	13 800
	14 000		14 000

(iii)

DR	Material price variance account		CR
	£		£
Adjustment to opening stock value	20		
Transfer to profit & loss account	180	Purchase price variances	200
	200		200

(iv)

DR	Material usage variance account		CR
	£		£
Transfer from WIP control account	200	Transfer to profit & loss account	200
	200		200

Profit and loss position

	Present system	Proposed system
Price variance	£20	£180
Usage variance	(£200)	(£200)
	(£180)	(£20) = increase in profit

13 LCCI THIRD LEVEL MANAGEMENT ACCOUNTING 1991

(a)(i) Variable overhead expenditure variance for January.

	Standard	Actual	Variance	
Units made	18 000	18 000		
Costs	£1 800	£2 000	£200	Adverse

Variance analysis:

A		2 000		
AS 18 000 × £0.10		1 800	200	Adverse expenditure variance
S		1 800	0	Efficiency variance

Variable overhead expenditure variance = £200 Adverse

(ii) and (iii) Fixed production overheads variances for February.

	Budget	Standard	Actual	Variance	
Units made	20 000	18 000	18 000		
Hours equivalent	5 000	4 500	4 800		
Costs	£5 000	£4 500	£5 300	£800	Adverse

Mnemonics:

A	£5 300			
B	£5 000		£300	Adverse expenditure
S	£4500		£500	Adverse volume

(ii)   Fixed overhead expenditure variance for February = £300 adverse

(iii) Fixed overhead volume variance for February = £500 adverse

(b) The fixed overhead volume variance can be further sub-divided as follows:

Mnemonics: (Hours × standard rate per hour)

B		£5000		
A	4800 × £1	£4800	£200	Adverse capacity variance
S		£4500	£300	Adverse efficiency variance

14 LCCI THIRD LEVEL MANAGEMENT ACCOUNTING 1992
Workings and notes:

	Budget	Standard	Actual	Variance	
Units made	4 000 000	3 600 000	3 600 000		
Hours equivalent	1 000 000	900 000	960 000		
Costs	£1 000 000	£900 000	£1 020 000	£120 000	Adverse total fixed overhead variance

Variance analysis:

A		£1 020 000		
B		£1 000 000	£ 20 000	Adverse expenditure
S		£ 900 000	£100 000	Adverse volume

(a)(i)   Total fixed overhead variance   =£120 000 adverse

  (ii)   Fixed overhead expenditure variance = £20 000 adverse

  (iii) Fixed overhead volume variance   =£100 000 adverse

Sub-variances calculation: (Hours × Standard rate per hour)

B		£1 000 000		
A	960 000 × £1	£ 960 000	£40 000	Adverse capacity variance
S		£ 900 000	£60 000	Adverse efficiency variance

(b)(i) and ii)   The fixed overhead volume variance can be broken down into two sub-variances, namely fixed overhead capacity variance and the fixed overhead efficiency variance. As can be seen from the above analysis, the factory should have worked 1 million hours but instead only worked for 960 000 hours. Thus the factory's capacity to produced was reduced by 40 000 hours, which cost £40 000.

With regard to the efficiency of the employees during the dispute period, the other variance, the fixed overhead efficiency variance, shows that relative inefficiencies cost the firm £60 000, which represents 240 000 units: in the hours worked, production should have been 3 840 000 units (960 000 × 4) but only 3 600 000 were produced.

Adverse efficiency variance therefore = £60 000

Number of units this represents   = 240 000

15 LCCI THIRD LEVEL COST ACCOUNTING 1992
Workings and notes:

Standard hourly rate: £4.50 per hour

Standard hours per unit: 6

Fixed overhead budget: £165 000 p/month

Level of production: 5000 units p/month

Actual units in month: 4650

Number of labour hours: 26 800; cost £124 350

Actual fixed overhead: £158 650

	Standard	Actual	Variance	
Units made	4 650	4 650		

	£	£	£	
Costs	125 550	124 350	1 200	Favourable
A		124 350		
AS 26 800 × £4.50		120 600	3 750	Adverse rates
S		125 550	4 950	Favourable efficiency

(a) Direct labour cost variance   £1 200   Favourable
      Direct labour rates variance   £3 750   Adverse
      Direct labour efficiency variance   £4 950   Favourable

(b) Workings:

	Budget	Standard	Actual	Variance	
Units made	5 000	4 650	4 650		
Hours equivalent	30 000	27 900	26 800		

	£	£	£	£	
Costs	165 000	153 450	158 650	5 200	Adverse
A		158 650			
B		165 000		6 350	Favourable expenditure
S		153 450		11 550	Adverse volume
				5 200	Adverse total f/overhead

Total fixed overhead cost variance   £ 5 200   Adverse
Fixed overhead expenditure variance   £ 6 350   Favourable
Fixed overhead volume variance   £11 550   Adverse

(c) Budgeted capacity   30 000 Hours
      Standard hours of work produced   27 900 Hours
      Actual hours worked   26 800 Hours

      Volume ratio   = S/B × 100/1   93.00%
      Capacity ratio = A/B × 100/1   89.33%
      Efficiency ratio = S/A × 100/1   104.10%

16 LCCI THIRD LEVEL COST ACCOUNTING 1992

	F	A	B	Total
Standard mix	35.0%	50.0%	15.0%	
Standard cost per kg	£3.90	£8.07	£4.80	
Standard cost	£1.37	£4.04	£0.72	£6.12
Normal loss (15%)	£0.24	£0.71	£0.13	
Standard cost per unit	£1.61	£4.75	£0.85	£7.20

(a) Standard material cost of 1 kg of FAB = £7.20

Calculation of variances:

Materials usage

	Standard	Actual	Variance	
Units made	30 850	30 850		
	£	£	£	
F	49 541.47	48 750.00	791.47	Favourable
A	146 446.76	142 435.50	4 011.26	Favourable
B	26 131.76	25 680.00	451.76	Favourable
	222 120.00	216 865.50	5 254.50	Favourable

Cost of changed mix

	Actual input kg	Std mix of input	New cost	
F	12 500	12 425	£ 48 457.50	(12 425 × £3.90)
A	17 650	17 750	£143 242.50	(17 750 × £8.07)
B	5 350	5 325	£ 25 560.00	(5 325 × £4.80)
	35 500	35 500	£217 260.00	

Mix/yield table

	Std mix	New mix	Actual mix	Mix variance	
Units made	30 850	30 850	30 850		
	£	£	£	£	
F	49 541	48 458	48 750	292.50	Adverse
A	146 447	143 243	142 436	807.00	Favourable
B	26 132	25 560	25 680	120.00	Adverse
	222 120.00	217 260.00	216 865.50	394.50	Favourable

Analysis Of Variances:

	£	£	
A	216 865.50		
AS	217 260.00	394.50	Favourable mix variance
S	222 120.00	4 860.00	Favourable yield variance
		5 254.50	Favourable usage variance

Material price variance

	Standard	Actual	Variance	
	£	£	£	
F	48 750.00	46 875.00	1 875.00	Adverse
A	142 435.50	146 495.00	4 059.50	Adverse
B	25 680.00	25 252.00	428.00	Favourable
	216 865.50	218 622.00	5 506.50	Adverse

) Summary of variances

	(i)	Price	F	1 875.00	Adverse
			A	4 059.50	Adverse
			B	428.00	Favourable
			Total	5 506.50	Adverse
	(ii)	Mixture	F	292.50	Adverse
			A	807.00	Favourable
			B	120.00	Adverse
			Total	394.50	Favourable
	(iii)	Yield	Total	4 860.00	Favourable
	(iv)	Total cost		218 622.00	Actual

7 LCCI THIRD LEVEL COST ACCOUNTING 1992

Workings and notes:

Material price variance $= 5\,355\,m \times £6.20 - £34\,272 = £33\,201 - £34\,272 = £1\,071$ adverse

Issues to production $= 3\,980\,m \times £6.20 = £24\,676$

Returns to stores $= 300\,m \times £6.20 = £1860$

Returns to supplier $= 300\,m \times £6.40 = £1920$ ($£34\,272/5355\,m = £6.40$ per metre)

Labour:

Std hours	Actual hours	Variance		
12 435	12 675			
£62 175	£62 361	£186		Adverse
A		62 361		
AS	12 675 × £5	63 375	1 014	Favourable rate
S		62 175	1 200	Adverse efficiency
			186	

Overhead absorbed:

	Standard	Actual		
	12 435	12 675		
	79 584	81 120	1 536	Adverse efficiency

) S Ltd debt: 30 units @ £60 = £1800; bad debt = £700

Sales returns = £1800

Standard production cost = £40 per unit (£40 + 50% markup, £20 = selling price of £60)

Taken into finished stock = 30 units @ £40 each = £1200

Journal entries

J/E No:	Account name	DR	CR	
		£	£	
a	Material price variance account	1 071		
	Material stock control account	33 201		
	Purchases ledger control account		34 272	and credited to suppliers' accounts
b	Work in progress control account	24 676		
	Material stock control account		24 676	

c	Material stock control account	1 860		
	Work in progress control account		1 860	
	Purchases ledger control account	1 920		and debited to suppliers' accounts
	Material stock control account		1 860	
	Material price variance account		60	
d	Work in progress control account	62 361		
	Wages control account		62 361	
	Work in progress control account	1 014		
	Direct labour rates variance account		1 014	
	Direct labour efficiency variance account	1 200		
	Work in progress control account		1 200	
e	Sales returns account	1 800		
	Bad debts account	700		
	Sales ledger control account		2 500	and credited to D S Ltd's account
	Finished stock control account	1 200		
	Cost of goods sold account		1 200	

18 LCCI THIRD LEVEL MANAGEMENT ACCOUNTING 1993
Workings and notes:

	A	B	Total
Standard mix – kg	10	20	30
Standard cost per kg	£4.00	£6.00	
Standard cost	£40.00	£120.00	£160.00

Calculation table

	Standard	Actual	Variance	
Loads	160	160		
	£	£	£	
Costs				
A	6 400	8 000	1 600	Adverse
B	19 200	17 520	1 680	Favourable
	25 600	25 520	80	Favourable

Cost of changed mix

	Actual input (kg)	STD mix of input (kg)	New cost
	2 000	1 640	£ 6 560.00
	2 920	3 280	£19 680.00
	4 920	4 920	£26 240.00

Mix/yield table

	Std mix	New std mix	Actual mix	Mix variance	
Loads made	160	160	160		
	£	£	£	£	
Costs					
A	6 400	6 560	8 000	1 440	Adverse
B	19 200	19 680	17 520	2 160	Favourable
	25 600	26 240	25 520	720	Favourable

Variance Analysis

	£	£	
A	25 520		
AS	26 240	720	Favourable mix variance
S	25 600	640	Adverse yield variance

(i)   Usage variance = £80 favourable
(ii) Mixture variance = £720 favourable
(iii) Yield variance = £640 adverse

19 ACCA COST AND MANAGEMENT ACCOUNTING 1 1990

Materials calculation table: Product 1 – Material M

	Standard	Actual	Variance	
Units made	42 100	42 100		
Costs				
M	32 181	32 342	161	A

Variance analysis:
Material M:

A		32 342			
AS	41 200 × £0.78	32 136	206	A	Price
S		32 181	45	F	Usage
			161	A	Total

Materials calculation table: Product 2 – Material N

	Standard	Actual	Variance	
Units made	24 400	24 400		
Costs				
N	23 600	23 828	228	A

Variance analysis:
Material N:

A		23 828			
AS	8 050 × £2.931	23 595	233	A	Price
S		23 600	5	F	Usage
			228	A	Total

Labour calculation table: Product 1 – Dept X

	Standard	Actual	Variance	
Units made	42 100	42 100		
Costs				
Dept X	17 682	17 598	84	F
	£0.420			

Variance analysis:

Labour

A		17 598			
AS	4 190 × £4.20	17 598	0		Rate
S		17 682	84	F	Efficiency
			(84)	F	Total

Labour calculation table: Product 2 – Dept Y

	Standard	Actual	Variance	
Units made	24 400	24 400		
Costs				
Dept Y	9 882	9 646	236	F

Variance analysis:

Labour

A	2 120 × £4.55		9 646		
AS	2 120 × £4.50	9 540	106	A	Rate
S		9 882	342	F	Efficiency
			236	F	Total

Production overhead absorbed:

		Absorbed	Actual	Variance	
Dept X	4 190 hours × £3.60 per hour	15 084	14 763	321	F
Dept Y	2 120 hours × £2.90 per hour	6 148	6 290	142	A
		21 232	21 053	179	

(a)   Standard costs of product 1 and 2.

	1	2	
Materials	£0.76	£0.97	
Labour	£0.42	£0.41	
Overheads	£0.36	£0.26	
	£1.54	£1.63	each
Multiplied by 100	£154.44	£163.32	

(b) and (c)   Summary.

(i)   Material M price variance: £206 adverse.

(ii)   Material M usage variance: £45 favourable.

(iii)   Material total variance = £161 adverse.

(iv)   Direct labour rate variance – Dept X = £0.

(v)   Direct labour efficiency variance – Dept X = £84F.

(vi) Production overhead variance – Dept X = £321 favourable.

(vii) Product 2 units: 24 400 units.

(viii) Material N kilos: 8050 kg.

(ix) Material N price per kg: £2.96.

(x) Dept Y hours: 2120 hours.

(xi) Dept Y labour cost: £9646.

(xii) Production overhead – Dept Y: £6290.

(xiii) Direct labour rate variance – Dept Y = £106 adverse.

(xiv) Direct labour total variance – Dept Y = £236 favourable.

20 ACCA COST AND MANAGEMENT ACCOUNTING 1 1991

Workings and notes:

Standard cost per unit = £2.15 each.

Material price variance: 34 900 @ £7 = £244 300; actual £245 900; variance = £1 600 Adverse

Equivalent units table:

Units

	Material	**Conversion costs**
Completed	226 000	226 000
WIP	4 000	2 000
Equivalent units	230 000	228 000

Materials

	Standard	**Actual**	**Variance**	
Units	230 000	230 000		
Costs	£241 500	£240 100	£1 400	Favourable usage

Labour

	Standard	**Actual**	**Variance**		
Units	228 000	228 000			
Costs	£136 800	£138 545	(£1 745)		Adverse
A		138 545			
AS	22 900 × £6	137 400	£1 145	Adverse rates	
S		136 800	£600	Adverse efficiency	

Variable overheads

	Standard	**Actual**	**Variance**	
Units	228 000	228 000		
Costs	£114 000	£113 800	200	Favourable
A		£113 800		
AS		£114 500	£700	Favourable expenditure
S		£114 000	£500	Adverse efficiency

DR   **Raw materials control account**   **CR**

	Kg	£		Kg	£
Balance brought forward	16 200	113 400			
Cost ledger control a/c:			Transfer: Work in progress account	34 300	240 100
Purchases	34 900	244 300			
			Balance carried down	16 800	117 600
	51 100	357 700		51 100	357 700
Balance brought down		117 600			

DR   **Work in progress control account**   **CR**

	Units	£		Units	£
Balance b/fwd		0			
Materials, transferred from raw					
materials control account	230 000	240 100	Transfer to finished goods control	226 000	485 900
Material usage variance		1 400			
Direct wages, transferred from wages					
control account		137 400	Transfer wages efficiency variance		600
Variable overhead, transferred from					
variable overheads control account		114 500	Transfer variable overheads efficiency		
			variance		500
			Work in progress carried down	4 000	6 400
	230 000	493 400		230 000	493 400
Balance brought down	4 000	6 400			

DR   **Finished goods control account**   **CR**

	£		£
Balance brought forward	597 700		
Transfer from work in progress account	485 900	Transfer to cost of sales account (P&L)	468 700
		Balance carried forward	614 900
	1 083 600		1 083 600
Balance brought down	614 900		

DR   **Wages control account**   **CR**

	£		£
Balance brought forward	0		
Cost ledger control a/c:		Transfer to direct labour rates variance a/c	1 145
Wages paid	138 545	Transfer to work in progress account	137 400
		Balance carried forward	0
	138 545		138 545
Balance brought down	0		

DR   **Variable overhead control account**   **CR**

	£		£
Balance brought forward	0		
Cost ledger control a/c:			
expenses paid	113 800	Transfer to work in progress account	114 500
Transfer to variable overhead expenditure			
variance a/c	700	Balance carried forward	0
	114 500		114 500

Balance brought down   0

DR	Fixed overheads control account		CR
	£		£
Balance brought forward	0		
Cost ledger control a/c:			
expenses paid	196 800	Transfer to profit and loss account	196 800
		Balance carried forward	0
	196 800		196 800

Balance brought down   0

DR	Cost ledger control account		CR
	£		£
		Balance brought forward	711 100
Transfer costing profit and loss account	667 245	Transfer from financial ledger:	
		Material purchases	245 900
		Wages paid	138 545
		Variable overheads	113 800
Balance carried down	738 900	Fixed overheads	196 800
	1 406 145		1 406 145
		Balance brought down	738 900

DR	Production variances account		CR
	£		£
Materials price variance	1 600	Materials usage variance	1 400
Labour efficiency variance	600		
Labour rates variance	1 145	Overheads expenditure	700
Variable overheads efficiency	500	Transfer to costing P&L a/c	1 745
	3 845		3 845

DR	Costing profit and loss account		CR
	£		£
Transfer finished goods	468 700		
Transfer fixed overheads	196 800	Transfer to financial ledger (cost ledger	
Transfer variances	1 745	control a/c)	667 245
	667 245		667 245

Trial balance

	DR	CR
Raw materials account	£117 600	
Work in progress account	£ 6 400	
Finished goods account	£614 900	
Cost ledger control a/c		£738 900
	£738 900	£738 900

21 ᴀᴄᴄᴀ COST AND MANAGEMENT ACCOUNTING 1 1992
Workings and notes:

Period 1

Standard material cost of Material X per unit of Product M = £10.80
142 000 kg purchased = £171 820 = £1.21 per kg
Standard cost of 142 000 kg = £170 400
Material price variance = £1 420 adverse

Usage Period 1

	Standard	Actual	Variance	
Units made	1 790	1 790		
Costs	£19 332.00	£19 524.00	£192.00	Adverse
A		£19 524.00		
AS	16 270 × £1.20	£19 524.00		
S		£19 332.00	£192.00	Adverse usage

(i)   Material X price variance in Period 1 = £1 420 Adverse
(ii) Material X usage variance in Perlod 1 = £192.00 Adverse

Period 2

Standard price = £1.20 (£10.80 × 1.06) = £1.272 per kg
147 400 × £1.272 = £187 492.80
£187 492.80 − £1 031.80 = £186 461.00 actual spend
Cost per kg in Period 2 = £186 461/147 400 = £1.265 per kilo

(iii) Cost inflation on Material X in Perlod 2.

Perlod 1 cost per kg	£1.2100
Perlod 2 cost per kg	£1.2650
Inflation	£0.0550
As percentage over Period 1	4.5% Additional cost

Standard usage = 9 kg; saving of 0.5% in Period 2. Therefore actual usage per unit = 8.955 kg per unit.

(iv) Period 1 usage = 16 270 kg/1790 units = 9.0894 kg per unit

Perlod 1 usage	9.0894
Perlod 2 usage	8.9550
Difference per kg	0.1344
As a percentage over period 1	1.5% Reduction in usage

22 ᴀᴄᴄᴀ COST AND MANAGEMENT ACCOUNTING 1 1993
Workings and notes:

Total budgeted costs = £172 938
Budgeted machine hours = 1900

(i) Predetermined fixed overhead absorption rate

$$\frac{£172\,938}{1\,900} = £91.02$$

(ii) Actual machine hours

	Budget	Standard	Actual		
	£	£	£	£	
	172 938	177 489	173 732	3 757	Favourable total
A		173 732			
B		172 938		794	Adverse expenditure
S*		177 489		4 551	Favourable volume
				3 757	Favourable total

*Arrived at by adding favourable volume variance to the budgeted figure.

Actual machine hours = £177 489 divided by £91.02 = 1950

(iii) Overabsorption of overhead = £3757

23 CIMA COSTING 1990
Workings and notes:
Material price variance identified on receipt

	Standard	Actual	Variance	
Purchases A	50 000 kg	50 000 kg		
Cost	£162 500	£158 750	£3 750	Favourable
Purchases B	25 000 kg	25 000 kg		
Cost	£100 000	£105 000	£5 000	Adverse

Material usage:

	Standard	Actual	Variance	
Units made	400	400		
Material A	£13 000	£15 600	£2 600	Adverse
Material B	£ 8 000	£ 7 200	£ 800	Favourable

(a)

	Material A	Material B
Price variance	£3 750 Favourable	£5 000 Adverse
Usage variance	£2 600 Adverse	£ 800 Favourable

Labour:

	Standard	Actual	Variance	
Units made	400	400		
Dept 1	£12 800	£11 800	£1 000	Favourable
Dept 2	£10 000	£13 250	£3 250	Adverse

Variance analysis:

Dept 1

A		£11 800		
AS	3 000 × £4.00	£12 000	£200	Favourable rate
S		£12 800	£800	Favourable efficiency

Dept 2

A		£13 250		
AS	2 400 × £5.00	£12 000	£1 250	Adverse rates
S		£10 000	£2 000	Adverse efficiency

(b)

	Dept 1	**Dept 2**
Direct labour rate variance	£200 Favourable	£1 250 Adverse
Direct labour efficiency variance	£800 Favourable	£2 000 Adverse

(c) The favourable material price variance for Material A may be caused by a reduction in the price per kg negotiated with the supplier.

The adverse material price variance for Material B may be caused by a change in supplier who charges more per kg for perhaps a better quality product.

The adverse usage variance for Material A may be because of greater wastage because of inefficient handling of the material.

The favourable usage variance for Material B may be because of better-quality material purchased.

The favourable direct labour rate variance for Department 1 may be because of using lower-grade staff to complete the work.

The adverse direct labour rate variance for Department 2 may be caused by an increase in the rate per hour negotiated for Department 2 staff.

The favourable labour efficiency variance in Department 1 may be because of extra effort of staff with perhaps greater supervision, and the adverse labour efficiency variance in Department 2 may be because of a hold up in the flow of work, necessitating a diversion of direct labour to other work, or idle time classifications.

(d) Dept 1

	Budget	**Standard**	**Actual**
Hours	3 400	3 200	3 000
Volume ratio	94.12% (3 200/3 400)		
Efficiency ratio	106.67% (3 200/3 000)		

Dept 2

	Budget	**Standard**	**Actual**
Hours	2 600	2 000	2 400
Volume ratio	76.92% (2 000/2 600)		
Efficiency ratio	83.33% (2 000/2 400)		

24 CIMA COST ACCOUNTING 1991

(a) Standard cost of unit J:

	£
Materials	
Material R 10 kilograms @ £30 per kg	300
Material S 6 kilograms @ £45 per kg	270
Labour	
30 hours @ £5.50 per hour	165
Fixed production overheads absorption:	210
	945

$$\text{Absorption rate} = \frac{£252\,000}{1\,200}$$

$$= £210.00 \text{ per unit}$$

Product J

	£
Standard selling price	1 200
Standard cost price (as above)	945
Standard gross profit	255

(b) Workings and notes for part (b)

Stock account R

	Receipts £	Issues £	Balance £	
Opening stock			9 545	
Receipts	35 000		44 545	£31.8182
Issues		32 616	11 930	

Stock Account S

	Receipts £	Issues £	Balance £	
Opening stock			20 240	
Receipts	15 180		35 420	£44 0000
Issues		25 520	9 900	

Variance table

	Standard	Actual	Variance	
Units made	100	100		
	£	£	£	
Materials				
R	30 000	32 616	2 616	Adverse total
S	27 000	25 520	1 480	Favourable total
Labour	16 500	17 325	825	Adverse total
Fixed overhead	21 000	22 000	1 000	Adverse total
	94 500	97 461	2 961	Adverse

Fixed overheads

	Budget	Standard	Actual		
Units	100	100	100		
	£	£	£	£	
Cost	21 000	21 000	22 000	1 000	Adverse

Analyses:

A		22 000			
B		21 000	1 000		Adverse expenditure
S		21 000	0		Volume variance
B	3 000 hrs × £7	21 000			
A	3 300 hrs × £7	23 100	2 100		Capacity (F)
S	3 000 hrs × £7	21 000	2 100		Efficiency (A)

Variance analysis

Material R

		£	£	
A		32 616		
AB	1 025 × £30	30 750	1 866	Adverse price variance
S		30 000	750	Adverse usage variance

Material S

		£	£	
A		25 520		
AB	580 × £45	26 100	580	Favourable price variance
S		27 000	900	Favourable usage variance

Labour

		£	£	
A		17 325		
AB	3 300 × £5.50	18 150	825	Favourable rates variance
S		16 500	1 650	Adverse efficiency variance

Summary Of Variances:

	£	
Material R price variance	1 866	Adverse
Material R usage variance	750	Adverse
Material S price variance	580	Favourable
Material S usage variance	900	Favourable
Labour rates variance	825	Favourable
Labour efficiency variance	1 650	Adverse
Overhead expenditure variance	1 000	Adverse
Overhead capacity variance	2 100	Favourable
Overhead efficiency variance	2 100	Adverse

(c) Reconciliation statement

	£
Budgeted gross profit:	
100 units at £255 per unit	25 500
Add favourable production variances:	
Material S price	580
Material S usage	900
Labour rates	825
Overhead capacity	2 100
	29 905
Less adverse production variances	
Material R price	1 866
Material R usage	750
Labour efficiency	1 650
Overhead expenditure	1 000
Overhead efficiency	2 100
	7 366
Actual gross profit	22 539

(d)

	Amount controllable	(Y/N)	Responsible official	Possible cause
Favourable variances:				
Labour rates	£ 825	Y	Personnel manager/ Production Manager	Lower grade staff used or actual rates of pay less than that anticipated when standards set because of negotiations by Personnel Office.
Adverse variance				
Labour efficiency	£1 650	Y	Production Manager	Here, the workforce took 300 hours longer to produce the 100 units. This may have been caused by the relative inefficiencies of lower grade staff or because of machine breakdowns or other delays.

25 CIMA COST ACCOUNTING 1992

Workings and notes:

	6 months to March	6 months to September
Sales	£980 000	£1 120 000

Fixed production overheads:

16 000 × £20 = £320 000 per annum

Production costs:

Units produced	8 500	7 000
	£	£
Variable costs	416 500	343 000
Fixed costs	170 000	140 000
	586 500	

Fixed production overhead volume variance:

Absorbed	170 000	140 000
Cost	160 000	160 000
	10 000	(20 000)

(a)(i) Statement using marginal costing.

	Six months ending 31 March	Six months ending 30 September
Sales units	7 000	8 000
	£	£
Sales	980 000	1 120 000
Variable costs	539 000	616 000
Contribution	441 000	504 000
Fixed costs	250 000	250 000
Profit for the period	191 000	254 000

(a)(ii) Statement using absorption costing.

	Six months ending 31 March	Six months ending 30 September
Sales units	7 000	8 000
	£	£
Sales	980 000	1 120 000
Cost of sales		
Opening stock	0	103 500
Goods manufactured	586 500	483 000
Closing stock	(103 500)	(34 500)
	483 000	552 000
Gross profit	497 000	568 000
Fixed production overhead		
volume variance	(10 000)	20 000
Selling, distribution, admininistration		
Variable	196 000	224 000
Fixed	90 000	90 000
	276 000	334 000
Profit for the period	221 000	234 000

(b) Reconciliation statement.

	Six months ending 31 March	Six months ending 30 September
Profit per absorption costing	221 000	234 000
Less fixed production overhead		
carried forward	(30 000)	(10 000)
Add fixed production overhead		
brought forward		30 000
Profit per marginal costing	191 000	254 000

In absorption costing the fixed production overhead on units unsold at the end of the period is carried forward to the next accounting period. In marginal costing, all fixed costs are treated as period costs and therefore written off in the period the cost has arisen.

26 CIMA COST ACCOUNTING 1992

Workings and notes:

Variable production overhead variances:

	Standard	Actual	Variance	
Units	5 000	5 000		
Costs	£30 000	£28 900	£1 100	Favourable

Analysis

A		28 900			
AS	9 300 × £3	27 900	1 000	Adverse expenditure	
S		30 000	2 100	Favourable efficiency	

Fixed production overhead variances:

	Budget	Standard	Actual variance		
Units	4 800	5 000	5 000		
Hours	9 600	10 000	9 300		
Cost	£120 000	£125 000	£118 000	£7 000	Favourable

Analysis

A	£118 000		
B	£120 000	£2 000	Favourable expenditure
S	£125 000	£5 000	Favourable volume

Analysis of sub-variances

		Hours			
B		9 600	£120 000		
A	9 300 hours × £12.50		£116 250	£3 750	Adverse capacity
S		10 000	£125 000	£8 750	Favourable efficiency

(a)(i)   Variable production overhead expenditure variance = £1000 Adverse

  (ii)   Variable production overhead efficiency variance = £2100 Favourable

 (iii)   Fixed production overhead expenditure variance = £2000 Favourable

 (iv)   Fixed production overhead volume variance = £5000 Favourable

(b)   Fixed production overhead capacity variance = £3750 Adverse
Fixed production overhead efficiency variance - £8750 Favourable

Report to management

Subject: Fixed production overhead sub-variances   Date:

From: Cost accountant

The volume variance of £5000 favourable has arisen because the actual quantity of work produced was greater than anticipated in the budget: 200 more units were produced. The volume variance can be further divided into sub-variances to ascertain its causes. The sub-variances are called the capacity variance and the efficiency variance. An adverse capacity variance has arisen because the level of work expected and budgeted for was set at the equivalent of 9600 hours. But only 9300 hours actual were worked. Therefore the capacity of the factory was not utilised to the extent expected, resulting in an adverse capacity variance of £3750 (300 hours × £12.50). However, the amount of work carried out during the 9300 hours was equivalent to 10 000 hours. Therefore the workforce have been more efficient, producing a favourable efficiency variance of £8750 (700 hours × £12.50).

(Signed)

27   CIMA ACCOUNTING 1993

(a)   Cost statement – month 6

	(i) Fixed budget	(ii) Flexed budget	(iii) Actual	(iv) Total variances	
Production (units)	20 000	18 500	18 500		
	£	£	£	£	
Direct materials	480 000	444 000	442 650	1 350	Favourable
Direct labour	140 000	129 500	129 940	440	Adverse
Variable overhead	60 000	55 500	58 800	3 300	Adverse
Fixed overhead	100 000	100 000	104 000	4 000	Adverse
Total production costs	780 000	729 000	735 390	6 390	Adverse

(b)   Analysis of direct material and direct labour variances:

Material

A		£442 650		
AS	113 500 kg × £4	£454 000	£11 350	Favourable price
S		£444 000	£10 000	Adverse usage

Labour

A		129 940		
AS	17 800 hrs × £7	124 600	5 340	Adverse rate
S		129 500	4 900	Favourable efficiency

Summary:
Material price variance = £11 350 Favourable
Material usage variance = £10 000 Adverse
Labour rates variance = £5340 Adverse
Labour efficiency variance = £4900 Favourable

28 CIMA COST ACCOUNTING 1994

Workings:

	A	B	C
Budgeted hours	400 × 5.0	400 × 2.5	100 × 1.0
Standard hours	400 × 5.0	300 × 2.5	140 × 1.0

	Total	A	B	C
Budgeted hours	3 100	2 000	1 000	100
Actual hours	2 800			
Standard hours	2 890	2 000	750	140

a) Volume Ratio

$$\frac{\text{Standard hours}}{\text{Budgeted hours}} = \frac{2\,890}{3\,100}$$

$$= 93.2\%$$

Efficiency Ratio

$$\frac{\text{Standard Hours}}{\text{Actual Hours}} = \frac{2\,890}{2\,800}$$

$$= 103.2\%$$

b) Significance of the ratios.

Volume ratio

This ratio relates actual production, expressed in standard hours, with that planned in the budget. If the ratio is below 100%, as in this case, the factory has not produced the quantity of goods that the management expected. It therefore acts as a performance indicator. The volume ratio, when expressed in money terms is called the fixed overhead volume variance.

Efficiency ratio

This ratio measures the actual time it took to complete the work compared to the time it should have taken in accordance with the pre-determined standards. Here, 2890 hours of work were produced in 2800 hours. Therefore greater efficiency than expected was achieved. The efficiency ratio, expressed in money terms, is called the fixed overhead efficiency variance.

29 CIMA COST ACCOUNTING 1994

Workings:

Variable overheads

	Standard	Actual	Variance	
Hours	5 500	5 500		
	£	£	£	
Cost	49 500	52 000	2 500	Adverse
A		52 000		
AS	5 500 × £9	49 500	2500	Expenditure – adverse
S		49 500	0	Efficiency

Fixed overheads

	Budget	Standard	Actual	
Hours	5 500	5 500		
	£	£	£	£
Cost		49 500	53 750	4 250	Adverse
A		53 750		
B	5 000 × £9	45 000*	8 750		Adverse expenditure
S		49 500	4 500		Favourable volume

*As actual expenditure was £53 750 and an adverse expenditure variance of £8750 has arisen, the budgeted expenditure must be the net of the two: £45 000

DR	Production overhead control account		CR
	£		£
Cash – variable costs	52 000	Transfer to work in progress:	
Cash – Fixed costs	53 750	Variable overhead absorbed	49 500
Transfer to fixed overhead volume		Transfer to work in progress:	
variance account	4 500	Fixed overhead absorbed	49 500
		Transfer to variable overhead:	
		Expenditure variance account	2 500
		Transfer to fixed overhead:	
		Expenditure variance account	8 750
	_____		_____
	110 250		110 250

30 CIMA COST ACCOUNTING 1994

Workings and notes:

Variable costs:

	Standard	Actual	Variance	
Units	600	600		
	£	£	£	
Costs:				
Material E	6 000	6 270	270	Adverse (330F − 600A)
Material M	600	650	50	Adverse (50A − 0)
Labour	21 000	23 200	2 200	Adverse (800A + 1400A)
Overheads	6 000	6 720	720	Adverse (320A + 400A)
	33 600	36 840	3 240	Adverse

Material E

A		£6 270		
AS	660 × £10*	£6 600	£330	Fav. price
S	600 × £10	£6 000	£600	Adv. usage

*(£6 600/660 = £10)

Material M

A		£ 650		
AS	200 × £3*	£ 600	£50	Adv. price
S	200 × £3	£ 600	£ 0	

*(£600/200 = £3)

Labour

A	3 200 × £7.25	£23 200		
AS	3 200 × £7*	£22 400	£ 800	Adv. rate
S	3 000 × £7	£21 000	£1 400	Adv. efficiency

* (£22 400/3200 = £7)

Variable overheads

A		£6 720		
AS	3 200 × £2*	£6 400	£320	Adv. spend
S	3 000 × £2	£6 000	£400	Adv. efficiency

* (£6400/3200 hours = £2)

Fixed Costs:

		Budget	**Standard**	**Actual**		
				variance		
Units		550	600	600		
Hours		2 750	3 000	3 200		
Cost		£27 500	£30 000	£27 000	£3 000	Favourable (500F + 2500F)
A			£27 000			
B	2 750 × £10		£27 500	£ 500 F		
S	3 000 × £10		£30 000	£2 500 F		

(a)   Total Standard costs statement – product EM

	£
Direct material E	6 000
Direct material M	600
Direct Wages	21 000
Variable overheads	6 000
Fixed overheads	30 000
	63 600

(b)   Standard Product Cost sheet - Product EM

		£
Material E	1 metre at £10 per metre	10.00
Material M	1/3 metre at £3 per metre	1.00
Labour	5 hours at £7 per hour	35.00
Overheads:		
Variable	5 hours at £2 per labour hour	10.00
Fixed	£50 per unit	50.00
		106.00

Check: 600 units @ £106 each = £63 600

Variable	£33 600
Fixed	£30 000
	£63 600

(c)   Number of units budgeted for April = 550 Units

(d) The standards would have been set by reference to technical specifications and, assuming attainable standards have been used, modified by allowance for any wastage and expected inefficiencies. The attainable standards thus arrived at will then enable management to control the actual costs and usage through variance analysis: price and usage for materials; rate and efficiency for labour.

31 UNIVERSITY OF GREENWICH YEAR 1 BA ACCOUNTANCY AND FINANCE (1992)

	Standard	Actual	Variance	
Units	70	70		
Costs				
Material	£ 418.60	£ 563.00	£144.40	Adverse
Labour	£3 591.00	£3 572.00	£ 19.00	Favourable
	£4 009.60	£4 135.00	£125.40	

Variance analysis:

Materials:

A		£563.00		
AS	1 017 × 46p	£467.82	£95.18	Adverse price
S		£418.60	£49.22	Adverse usage

Labour:

A		£3 572.00		
AS	1 841 × £1.90	£3 497.90	£74.10	Adverse rate
S		£3 591.00	£93.10	Favourable efficiency

(a) Summary:

Material price variance = £95.18 Adverse
Material usage variance = £49.22 Adverse
Labour rate variance = £74.10 Adverse
Labour efficiency variance = £93.10 Favourable

(b) Possible reasons:

The material price variance of £95.18 adverse may have arisen because of an increase in price by the supplier not being taken into consideration when the standard cost was set.

The adverse material usage variance may be because of greater wastage arising from inefficient handling of the material.

The adverse labour rate variance may be caused by higher-grade staff being used instead of the grade expected by the standard.

The favourable labour efficiency variance may be because of greater efficiency of the higher-grade staff.

32 UNIVERSITY OF GREENWICH YEAR 1 BA ACCOUNTANCY AND FINANCE (1992)

Workings and notes:

	Jan	Feb	Mar
Sales units	8 000	6 000	10 000
Sales value	£240 000	£180 000	£300 000
Standard cost per case £10.50 (absorption costing)			
Production units	10 000	8 000	6 000
Production costs (absorption costing)	£105 000	£84 000	£63 000

(i) Profit statement – three months ending March 31

Variable costing method

	Jan	Feb	Mar	Total
	£	£	£	
Sales	240 000	180 000	300 000	
Variable costs				
Production	60 000	45 000	75 000	
Selling	24 000	18 000	30 000	
	84 000	63 000	105 000	
Contribution	156 000	117 000	195 000	
Fixed costs	33 000	33 000	33 000	
Profit	123 000	84 000	162 000	£369 000

(ii) Profit statement – three months ending March 31

Absorption costing method

	Jan	Feb	Mar	Total
	£	£	£	
Sales	240 000	180 000	300 000	
Cost of sales				
Opening stock	0	21 000	42 000	
Goods made	105 000	84 000	63 000	
Closing stock	21 000	42 000	0	
	84 000	63 000	105 000	
Gross profit	156 000	117 000	195 000	

Model Answers to examination questions, Chapter 19

1 A LEVEL (ULEAC) 1990

(a) Operating statement workings:

		£	
Sales		1 185 200	$193.2 + 201.4 + 216.1 + 200.5 + 190.3 + 183.7$
Material Purchases		205 600	$41.2 + 42.4 + 49.6 + 31.4 + 21.2 + 19.8$
Wages		37 000	$7.6 + 7.9 + 8.8 + 6.1 + 3.7 + 2.6$
Overheads		5 67 000	$123 + 119.2 + 131.4 + 91.5 + 59.3 + 42.6$
	Fixed	226 800	
	Variable	340 200	
Stocks:			
R/Material	Opening	91 700	
	Closing	91 700	
F/Goods	Opening	142 400	
	Closing	136 200	
Depreciation:			
	P & M	940	
	F & F	270	$1 250 - 980$

Note: It has been assumed that the closing stocks of finished goods have been valued using marginal costing techniques; therefore the fixed overheads and depreciation charges have been included as period costs

Madingley Ltd
Forecast operating statement – for the six months
June to November

	£	£000s
Sales	1 185 200	1 185.20
Manufacturing costs		
Materials		
Opening stock	91 700	
Materials	205 600	
Closing stock	(91 700)	
	205 600	
Wages	37 000	
Overheads Variable	340 200	
Cost of goods completed	582 800	
Opening finished goods	142 400	
Cost of goods completed	582 800	
Closing finished goods	(136 200)	
Cost of goods sold	589 000	589.00
Gross profit	596 200	596.20
Fixed overheads	226 800	596.20
Depreciation P&M	940	
Depreciation F&F	270	
Profit for the period	**368 190**	**368.19**

(b)   Balance sheet working:

		£	
Fixed assets costs		No change	
Fixed assets depreciation (P&M)		4 700	3 760 + 904
Fixed assets depreciation (F&F)		1 320	1 050 + 270
Current assets:			
Raw material stocks		91 700	
Finished goods stocks		136 200	
Debtors		574 500	200.5 + 190.3 +
Bank	See below	281 900	183.7
C/liabilities	Creditors R/matls	41 000	21.2 + 19.8
	Creditors Overheads	42 600	November
Share capital		No change	
P&L account		640 380	272.19 + 368.19

Bank Account

Balance b/fwd	12 400	R/m payments	
Receipts			
M,A,M,J,J,A	1 205 100	A,M,J,J,A,S	246 800
		O/hds payments	
		M,J,J,A,S,O	651 800
		Wages	37 000
		Balance c/fwd	281 900
	1 217 500		1 217 500

Madingley Ltd
Forecast balance sheet as at 30 November

Fixed Assets	Cost £000s	Aggregate depreciation £000s	Book value £000s
Land and buildings	134.00		134.00
Plant and machinery	9.40	4.70	4.70
Furniture and fittings	2.30	1.32	0.98
	145.70	6.02	139.68

Current assets		
Stocks:		
Raw materials		91.70
Finished goods		136.20
Debtors		574.50
Bank		281.90
		1 084.30
Less: current liablities		
Creditors:		
Raw materials		41.00
Overheads		42.60
		83.60
Working capital		1 000.70
		1 140.38
Financed by:		
Share capital		500.00
Profit and loss account		640.38
		1 140.38

2   A LEVEL (ULEAC) 1990

Working:

Sales	Original Budget	Explanation:
July	291	2/3rds paid in September
August	306	1/3rd paid in September, 2/3rds in October
September	312	1/3rd paid in October, 2/3rds in November
October	318	1/3rd paid in November, 2/3rds in December
Novermber	360	1/3rd paid in December

Re note (iv)

Adjustments to sales budget:

	July	August	September	October	November	
Original	291 000	306 000	312 000	318 000	360 000	
Less 5%	(14 550)	(15 300)	(15 600)	(15 900)	(18 000)	Re note (i)
	276 450	290 700	296 400	302 100	342 000	
Add 10%	27 645	29 070	29 640	30 210	34 200	Re note (ii)
	304 095	319 770	326 040	332 310	376 200	
Less 1%	(3 041)	(3 198)	(3 260)	(3 323)	(3 762)	Re note (iii)
	301 054	316 572	322 780	328 987	372 438	

Cash received		S	O	N	D	Total	
July		100 351				100 351	
August		211 048	105 524			316 572	
September			215 187	107 593		322 780	Re note (iv)
October				219 325	109 662	328 987	
November					248 292	248 292	
		311 399	320 711	326 918	357 954		

Materials	S	O	N	D
Original budget	74 000	72 100	74 900	81 200
Less 5%	−3 700	−3 695	−3 970	−4 060
	70 300	68 495	75 430	77 140
Add 5%	3 515	3 424.75	3 771.50	3 857
	73 815	71 920	79 202	80 997

Wages	S	O	N	D
Original Budget	15 100	15 700	16 700	17 300
Add 10%	1 510	1 570	1 670	1 730
	16 610	17 270	18 370	19 030

Variable costs	S	O	N	D
Original budget	125 000	133 400	142 200	66 500
Less 5% volume drop	−6 250	−6 670	−7 110	−3 325
	118 750	126 730	135 090	63 175

Overheads	S	O	N	D
(Assumed refers to fixed costs)				
Original budget	40 000	40 000	40 000	40 000
Add 8%	3 200	3 200	3 200	3 200
	43 200	43 200	43 200	43 200

Wimpole Industries:
Cash Budget September–December

	£000s			
	S	O	N	D
(i) Receipts				
Sales 2/3	211.0	215.2	219.3	248.3
Sales 1/3	100.4	105.5	107.6	109.7
Sale of equipment			8.8	
	311.4	320.7	335.7	358.0
(ii) Payments				
Materials	73.8	71.9	79.2	81.0
Wages	16.6	17.3	18.4	19.0
Variable costs	118.8	126.7	135.1	63.2
Fixed costs	43.2	43.2	43.2	43.2
	252.4	259.1	275.9	206.4
(iii) Cash Budget				
Opening balance	(100.0)	(41.0)	20.6	80.4
Receipts	311.4	320.7	335.7	358.0
Payments	252.4	259.1	275.9	206.4
Closing balance	(41.0)	20.6	80.4	232.0

3   A LEVEL (AEB) 1990

Working:

Sales budget

Sales year 1	2 000 000 plus 30% = £2 600 000	
Gross profit budget		
30% of £2 600 000		£ 780 000
Therefore cost of goods sold budget =		£1 820 000
Administrative expenses		
budget	£180 000 plus £20 000	£ 200 000
Selling and distributive		
budget	6% of Sales	£ 156 000
Depreciation 10% existing equipment		£ 50 000
Plus new		
equipment	10% of £150 000	£ 15 000

Stock budget	
Stock turnover	
Opening stock	164 000
Closing stock	250 000
Average stock	£ 207 000
Cost of goods sold	£1 449 000

Stock turnover =   7 times

£1 449 000/£207 000

Therefore stock turnover for Year 2 will be:

£1 820 000/7 =	£260 000
Opening stock	£250 000
Closing stock	£270 000
Average stock	£260 000

Share capital

budget	= 1 200 000 shares	£300 000

Fixed assets

budget	£500 000 plus £150 000	£650 000

Aggregate depreciation

budget	£180 000 plus £65 000	£245 000

Trade debtors budget

Sales	£2 600 000
Less 40% cash sales	£1 040 000
= Credit sales	£1 560 000
Monthly sales	£ 130 000
Debtors at 31 May year 2	£2 390 000

Cash budget	£ 20 000
Trade creditors budget	£130 000
Accrued expenses budget	£ 20 000
Bank overdraft budget	£101 000

(a)   Forecast budget trading and profit and loss account

Pankake Limited

Forecast budget trading and profit and loss account
for the year ending 30 April, Year 2

	£	£
Sales		2 600 000
Less cost of goods sold		1 820 000
Gross profit		780 000
Administrative expenses	200 000	
Selling and distributive expenses	156 000	
Depreciation of fixed assets	65 000	421 000
Net profit		359 000

Pankake Limited

Forecast balance sheet as at 30 April, Year 2

	£	£
50p ordinary shares fully paid		
(1 200 000 shares)		300 000
Retained earnings:		
Brought forward		175 000
Budget year		359 000
		£834 000

Fixed assets: at cost	650 000	
Less aggregate depreciation	245 000	405 000
Current assets		
Stocks	270 000	
Trade debtors	390 000	
Cash	20 000	
	680 000	
Less current liabilities		
Trade creditors	130 000	
Accrued expenses	20 000	
Bank overdraft	101 000	
	251 000	429 000
		834 000

Note: The format for the P&L account and balance sheet used by the Examiner ideally should be reproduced in the answer.

4   A LEVEL (AEB) 1990

(a)   Report to Managing Director
Subject: Liquidity of the company
From: Company Accountant   Date:

The cash position on 1 April, Year 1 was £290 000 with the balance sheet appearing as follows:

Cash	£290 000	Share capital	£150 000
		Share premium account	£100 000
		Retained earnings	£ 40 000
	£290 000		£290 000

The balance sheet one year later, at 31 March, Year 1 is as follows:

Fixed Assets	£300 000	Share capital	£150 000
		Share premium account	£100 000
Other net current assets	£210 000	Retained earnings	£110 000
		Bank overdraft	£150 000
	£510 000		£510 000

You will see that the company has invested £300 000 in fixed assets, and other net current assets have increased from nil at the beginning of the year to £210 000 at the end. These assets, totalling £510 000, have been paid for as follows:

By utilising the cash at bank available	£290 000
From profits earned during the year	£ 70 000
From the bank by way of an overdraft	£150 000
	£510 000

Although the profit for the year was good it was insufficient to pay for the increase in these assets, thus an overdraft was necessary.

(Signed)

(b) Cash Budget
Workings

	March £	April £	May £	June £	July £		
Sales	95 000	110 000	110 000	110 000	110 000		
Cash	30 000	40 000	40 000	40 000	40 000		
Credit	65 000	70 000	70 000	70 000	70 000		
Receipts							
Cash		40 000	40 000	40 000	40 000		
Credit		65 000	70 000	70 000	70 000		
		105 000	110 000	110 000	110 000		

	January	February	March	April	May	June	July
Purchases	60 000	58 000	61 000	55 000	55 000	55 000	
Paid				**60 000**	**58 000**	**61 000**	**55 000**

Dividends
15 000 × 5p per share   7 500 Final dividend
200 000 × 2p per share   4 000 Interim dividend

Selling and distribution expenses

	March	April	May	June	July		
Sales	95 000	110 000	110 000	110 000	1 10 000		
6% thereof	5 700	6 600	6 600	6 600	6 600		
Paid		5 700	6 600	6 600	6 600		

	February	March	April	May	June	July
Administration charges						
Cost	10 000	10 000	10 000	13 500	13 500	13 500
Paid			**10 000**	**10 000**	**10 000**	**13 500**

Pumpkin limited
Cash budget for the period April to July, Year 2   Cash Budget for
                                                                                     August and September

Receipts	April £	May £	June £	July £	August £	September £
Cash sales	40 000	40 000	40 000	40 000	40 000	40 000
Credit sales	65 000	70 000	70 000	70 000	70 000	70 000
	105 000	110 000	110 000	110 000	110 000	110 000
Payments						
Purchases	60 000	58 000	61 000	55 000	55 000	55 000
Dividends		7 500		4 000		
Selling costs	5 700	6 600	6 600	6 600	6 600	6 600
Administration	10 000	10 000	10 000	13 500	13 500	13 500
	75 700	82 100	77 600	79 100	75 100	75 100
Cash flow	29 300	27 900	32 400	30 900	34 900	34 900
Opening cash	(150 000)	(120 700)	(92 800)	(60 400)	(29 500)	5 400
Closing cash	(120 700)	(92 800)	(60 400)	(29 500)	5 400	40 300

(c) Comment

A cash budget prepared for the two months August and September, based on the information supplied, indicates that the company will move back into the 'black' in August.

With no expenditure on fixed assets or other non current assets outflows, the cash position will continue to improve as the following profit summary indicates:

Sales	£660 000
Purchases	£300 000
	(Assuming stock levels, if any, remain the same)
Selling	£ 39 600
Administration	£ 77 500
Profit	£242 900

If the overdraft had continued for the final five months of the calendar year, the company could have reduced it by any number of ways. For example, by delaying further the payments to suppliers, cancelling credit facilities offered to customers, increasing the profit margins, reducing selling and administration costs, and delaying or cancelling the payment of the dividends.

5   A LEVEL (AEB) 1992

(a) Workings and notes:

Opening bank balance at 1 April, year 2: £112 000

New branch cost £100 000: payable May (£50 000) and July (£50 000)

Refurbishment cost £20 000: payable July

Opening cash £20 000 on April 1 (transfer from main account)

Receipts: main store receive two months after sale:

	April	May	June	July
Feb	160 000			
Mar		150 500		
April			153 000	
May				149 500

Receipts: Branch receive one month after sale:

	April	May	June	July
May			8 000	
June				19 000

Expenses:	April	May	June	July
Fixed costs:				
Main	15 000	15 000	15 000	15 000
Branch		1 000	1 000	1 000
Variable costs:				
Main	**April**	**May**	**June**	**July**
March	25 000			
April		30 000		
May			33 000	
June				31 000

Branch:	April	May	June	July
May		2 500		
June				2 700

Legal costs of £5 000 payable by main store in July

Salaries	April	May	June	July
Main:	12 000	12 000	12 000	12 000
Branch:		1 000	1 000	1 000

Interim dividend payable in July (main account) : £10 000

Purchases:				
Main	April	May	June	July
Feb	61 000			
March		58 000		
April			153 000	
May				48 000

Purchases transfer: branch pay main – receipt for main; payment for branch

	April	May	June	July
April	8 000			
May		12 000		
June			23 000	
July				24 000

Issue of Debentures in July: £100 000

Main store cash budget

Four months to 31 July Year 2

Receipts	April	May	June	July
	£	£	£	£
Debtors	160 000	150 500	153 000	149 500
Branch transfer	8 000	12 000	23 000	24 000
Debenture issue				100 000
	168 000	162 500	176 000	273 500
Payments				
New branch cash	20 000			
New branch purchase		50 000		50 000
Refurbishment of branch				20 000
Fixed costs	15 000	15 000	15 000	15 000
Variable costs	25 000	30 000	33 000	31 000
Legal costs				5 000
Salaries	12 000	12 000	12 000	12 000
Interim dividend				10 000
Purchases	61 000	58 000	153 000	48 000
	133 000	165 000	213 000	191 000
Cash flow	35 000	(2 500)	(37 000)	82 500
Opening cash Balance	112 000	147 000	144 500	107 500
Closing cash Balance	147 000	144 500	107 500	190 000

Branch cash budget

Four months to 31 July Year 2

Receipts	April £	May £	June £	July £
Transfer from main store	20 000			
Debtors			8 000	19 000
	20 000	0	8 000	19 000
Payments				
Fixed costs		1 000	1 000	1 000
Variable costs		2 500		2 700
Salaries		1 000	1 000	1 000
Transfer to main (purchases)	8 000	12 000	23 000	24 000
	8 000	16 500	25 000	28 700
Cash flow	12 000	(16 500)	(17 000)	(9 700)
Opening cash balance	0	12 000	(4 500)	(21 500)
Closing cash balance	12 000	(4 500)	(21 500)	(31 200)

(b) Profit and loss statement for the branch

(i) Forecast profit and loss acount

Branch

Four months ending 31 July Year 2

	£
Sales	51 000
Cost of sales:	
Opening stock	0
Purchases	67 000
Closing stock	(33 000)
	34 000
Gross profit	**17 000**
Expenses	
Variable costs	7 100
Fixed costs	3 000
Salaries	3 000
Main stores charge	7 500
	20 600
Forecast net loss for the period	**3 600**

(ii) Report

Report on the Profitability of the new Branch for the period four months to July 31, Year 2

To:

From: Accountant

The forecast net loss for this period is after charging £7500 from the main store. If this is added back, the Branch is planned to make a contribution of £4000 in the period.

(Signed)

6   A LEVEL (AEB) 1993

(a)   Workings and notes:

Budget for Year 4:

Sales = £270 000; Gross profit = £30 000 (one-ninth)

Premises sold for £30 000 + 20% = £36 000

New premises = £16 000; no depreciation

New fixtures = £8000; depreciation = £1 000 (12.5%)

Loans repaid = £10 000

Stock to increase to £30 000 (+£8 000)

Debtors to increase to £40 000 (£30 000 + one-third)

Creditors to increase to £36 000 (£27 000 + one-third)

Profit = £30 000 − depreciation − £1000 = £29 000

Gain on sale of premises = £6000. Therefore profit for Year 4 = £35 000

Drawings = four-sevenths of profit = £20 000.

Simon Stylus

Budgeted balance sheet as at 31 March, Year 4

	Original Cost	Accumulated Depreciation	£
Fixed assets			
Premises	160 00	16 000	
Fixtures	8 000	1 000	7 000
Car	7 000	0	7 000
	31 000	1 000	30 000
Current assets			
Stock in trade		30 000	
Trade debtors		40 000	
Balance at bank		11 000	
		81 000	
Less trade creditors		36 000	45 000
Total assets			75 000
Represented by			
Capital brought forward			60 000
Profit – Year 4			35 000
Less drawings			(20 000)
			75 000

(b) Report

To:

Subject: Budgeting

From: Accountant   Date:

The preparation of a budget is an important part of management control as it provides a measure against which actual results can be assessed. The budget is a plan quantified in money terms and to be effective needs to be properly thought through. This entails detailed preparations of expected revenues and costs in the budget period.

Simon appears to prepare only the balance sheet, but budgets should also be prepared for the profit and loss account, the cash position, and other operating activities.

Simon, for example, has assessed sales at £270 000, but this may be over-optimistic or otherwise. To support this figure, a sales budget should be prepared analysing the sales by customer, product, period and so on. An arbitrary calculation of the profit margin is also not the correct way to budget. For example, sales are expected to increase, but some of the costs related to those sales may stay at the old level (fixed costs) and some move in line with the increase (variable costs). Simon needs to analyse the present costs and revenue position in order to assess this costs behavioural effect.

In addition, by working systematically through the expected costs and revenues, oversights and omissions are avoided. For example, Simon has not allowed for depreciation on the car but has allowed for it on the new equipment. Capital expenditure also needs to be planned carefully to ensure that the investment is worthwhile.

Another area lacking in Simon's approach is in the management of working capital. Simon has stated that stocks, debtors and creditors will increase but there is no indication of how the working capital is to be controlled, that is, by setting budgets for the number of days' stockholding, debtors' and creditors' outstandings. Finally, the budgeted balance sheet should be part of the master budget which collates all the activities of the business, so balancing figures, such as Simon has used for the balance at bank just to make the balance sheet agree, will not arise.

(Signed)

A LEVEL (AEB) 1993

Workings and notes:

Year 4 Sales = £1 600 000

Gross profit = 32% of £1 600 000 = £512 000

Issue of shares: 400 000 shares at 65p each = £260 000 (share premium = £60 000) (800 000 shares × 1/2)

Administration costs = 5% × £1 600 000 = £80 000

Selling Costs = 3.5% × £1 600 000 = £56 000

Financial charges = £10 000

Doubtful debts new provision = 15% of £150 000 = £22 500

Doubtful debts charge to P&L = £22 500 − £10 000 = £12 500

General reserve = £300 000

Land and buildings written down by £150 000

Preference dividend = 11% × £50 000 = £5 500

Ordinary dividend = 3p × 800 000 shares = £24 000

Depreciation = 10% × £750 000 (£1 100 000 − 350 000) = £75 000

Other balances per question

(a) Profit and loss account

Budgeted trading and profit and loss account

	£
Sales	1 600 000
Less cost of goods sold	1 088 000
Gross profit	512 000
Expenses	
Administration	80 000
Selling and distribution	56 000
Financial charges	10 000
Doubtful debts provision	
Increase	12 500
Depreciation	75 000
	233 500
Budgeted net profit	**278 500**

Budgeted profit and loss appropriation account

	£
Budgeted net profit	278 500
Add: retained earnings b/fwd	700 000
	978 500
Exceptional charge:	
Write down of land and buildings	150 000
Dividends	
Preference dividend	5 500
Interim dividend − ordinary shares	24 000
Transfer to general reserve	300 000
Retained earnings carried forward	**499 000**

(b) Balance sheet

Budgeted balance sheet budgeted balance sheet as at 31 October Year 4

	Cost or valuation	Aggregate depreciation	£
Fixed assets			
Land and buildings	200 000	0	200 000
Other fixed assets	750 000	305 000	445 000
	950 000	305 000	645 000
Current assets			
Stock		290 000	
Trade debtors less	150 000		
Provision for			
doubtful debts	22 500	127 500	
Balance at bank		760 500	
		1 178 000	
Less current liabilities			
Trade creditors		97 000	
Expenses creditors		17 000	
		114 000	1 064 000
Total assets			1 709 000

Financed by:

Issued capital:		
50p Ordinary shares fully paid		600 000
11% Preferences shares, fully paid		50 000
Share premium account		260 000
Retained earnings		499 000
General reserve		300 000
		1 709 000

---

8 A LEVEL (AEB) 1994

Workings and notes:

Agreed overdraft = £15 000; opening overdraft = £5 000

Rent payments: (£4 000 × 12) = 48 000/4 = £12 000 per quarter –

May payment = £12 000; August = £12 000

Other expenses: in month incurred

	Purchases		Other expenses
May	60 000	Less 3%	8 000
June	120 000	Less 3%	3 000
July	40 000		10 000
Aug	43 000		14 000

Sales:	80%	Paid in:	80%		2%
March		May	70 400		
April		June	67 200		
May		July	59 200		14 800
June		Aug	22 400		5 600
July		Sep			23 200
Aug		Oct			33 600

Compensation payment = £10 000 in May

Belinda Raglan

Cash budget for the four months ending 31 August, Year 3

Receipts	May £	June £	July £	August £
Cash Sales	14 800	5 600	23 200	33 600
Credit sales	70 400	67 200	59 200	22 400
	85 200	72 800	82 400	56 000
Payments				
Rent	12 000			12 000
Other expenses	8 000	3 000	10 000	14 000
Purchases	58 200	116 400	40 000	43 000
Compensation	10 000			
	88 200	119 400	50 000	69 000
Cash flow	(3 000)	(46 600)	32 400	(13 000)
Opening cash	(5 000)	(8 000)	(54 600)	(22 200)
Closing cash	(8 000)	(54 600)	(22 200)	(35 200)

9 AAT COST ACCOUNTING AND BUDGETING

Working and notes:

Cash received

Sales:	Units	Value	Cash	Credit	Total cash
May	4 000	£24 000			
June	4 200	£25 200			
July	4 500	£27 000	£13 500	£12 000	£25 500
Aug	4 600	£27 600	£13 800	£12 600	£26 400
Sep	4 800	£28 800	£14 400	£13 500	£27 900
Oct	5 000	£40 000	£20 000	£13 800	£33 800
Nov	3 800	£30 400	£15 200	£14 400	£29 600
Dec	3 000	£24 000	£12 000	£20 000	£32 000

Purchases two months credit

Wages and salaries:		75%	25%	Total
June	£ 8 000			
July	£ 8 000	£6 000	£2 000	£ 8 000
Aug	£10 000	£7 500	£2 000	£ 9 500
Sep	£10 000	£7 500	£2 500	£10 000
Oct	£10 000	£7 500	£2 500	£10 000
Nov	£12 000	£9 000	£2 500	£11 500
Dec	£12 000	£9 000	£3 000	£12 000

Overheads in following month

Fixed assets: Dividends

Dec   £10 000   Dec   £10 000

Shares issue   Fixed assets depn = £170 000 × 10% = £17 000/2 = £8 500

Sept   £20 000

Closing Stocks = £14 000 + £12 000 + £12 000 = £38 000

(a)(i)   Cash budget

Freewheel
Cash budget for the six months ending 31 December

	July £	August £	September £	October £	November £	December £
Receipts						
Cash sales	13 500	13 800	14 400	20 000	15 200	12 000
Credit sales	12 000	12 600	13 500	13 800	14 400	20 000
Share issue			20 000			
	25 500	26 400	47 900	33 800	29 600	32 000
Payments						
Purchases	12 000	13 000	14 000	18 000	16 000	14 000
Wages & Salaries	8 000	9 500	10 000	10 000	11 500	12 000
Overheads	7 000	7 000	7 000	7 000	8 000	8 000
Fixed assets						10 000
Dividends						
	27000	29 500	31 000	35 000	35 500	44 000
Cash flow	(1 500)	(3 100)	16 900	(1 200)	(5 900)	(12 000)
Opening Cash	3 000	1 500	(1 600)	15 300	14 100	8 200
Closing Cash	1 500	(1 600)	15 300	14 100	8 200	(3 800)

(ii) Budgeted profit and loss account

Freewheel

Budgeted profit and loss account for the six months ending 31 December, Year 2

	£
Sales	177 800
Cost of sales:	
Opening stock	25 000
Purchases	86 000
Closing stock	(38 000)
	73 000
Gross profit	104 800
Expenses	
Wages and salaries	62 000
Overheads	45 000
Depreciation	8 500
	115 500
Budgeted net loss	(10 700)
Profit and loss account b/f	44 600
Dividend	10 000
Profit and loss account c/f	23 900

(iii) Budgeted balance sheet

Freewheel

Budgeted balance sheet as at 31 December Year 2

	Cost	Acc. depn	
Fixed assets	170 000	22 500	147 500
Current assets			
Stock		38 000	
Debtors		27 200	
		65 000	
Less current liabilities			
Trade creditors		24 000	
Wages due		3 000	
Fixed assets due		20 000	
Dividends due		10 000	
Overheads due		8 000	
Bank overdraft		3 800	
		68 800	
Net current liabilities			(3 600)
Total assets less current liabilities			143 900
Financed by:			
Share capital			120 000
Profit and loss account			23 900
			143 900

(b) Comment

The cash budget reveals that an overdraft situation will arise in August and December. The company will need to arrange overdraft facilities with the bank for these two periods. If this cannot be arranged, the company has perhaps the options of either bringing forward from September to August the issue of the additional shares, which will eliminate the overdraft for August, or looking again at the capital expenditure spend of £30 000 and the way this will be paid for. Perhaps the payment terms can be extended further. Another possibility is to look again at the stock policy of increasing this to three months purchases.

This latter decision represents £12 000 and if reversed would eliminate the overdraft in December completely.

The profit and loss account budget shows the serious situation of a loss being incurred in this period. Unless this is reflective of a normal trend for the first six months of the year the company clearly needs to look again at the following: level of sales; gross profit percentage achieved; the level of the expenses.

With regard to the balance sheet, the working capital position is very serious. With no funds being generated from trading and the additional share capital issue being used to pay for the additional fixed assets and dividend, the company will be in a difficult position come December. There will be insufficient working capital and this is reflected in the working capital ratio, which has dropped from a reasonable 1.55 : 1 to a dire 0.95 : 1. Clearly the company will not be able to pay its way and urgent steps need to be taken to avoid the problems the budget has indicated.

10 AAT Cost ACCOUNTING AND BUDGETING 1992

Workings and notes:

Materials all variable

Labour	X	Y	Z
Fixed	£100 000	£160 000	£ 90 000
Variable	£600 000	£640 000	£660 000
			(by deduction)
Total	£700 000	£800 000	£750 000

Overheads

Machine times:	X	Y	Z
Units per hr	4	2	4
= No. of units	100 000	80 000	120 000
= M/c hours	25 000	40 000	30 000
=			
Fixed costs	£125 000	£200 000	£150 000
Var. o/heads	£100 000	£160 000	£180 000
Total	£225 000	£360 000	£330 000

a) Marginal costing statement

	Product X	Product Y	Product Z
Sales price per unit	£15.00	£25.00	£10.00
Variable costs per unit			
Materials	£ 3.00	£ 5.00	£ 4.00
Labour	£ 6.00	£ 8.00	£ 5.50
Overheads	£ 1.00	£ 2.00	£ 1.50
	£10.00	£15.00	£11.00
Contribution per unit	£ 5.00	£10.00	(£ 1.00)

(b) Statement of total contibution and profit at budgeted level

	Product X	Product Y	Product Z	Total
Units	100 000	80 000	120 000	
	£	£	£	£
Sales	1 500 000	2 000 000	1 200 000	4 700 000
Variable costs	1 000 000	1 200 000	1 320 000	3 520 000
Contribution	500 000	800 000	(120 000)	1 180 000
Fixed Costs:				
Labour	100 000	160 000	90 000	
Overheads	125 000	200 000	150 000	
	225 000	360 000	240 000	825 000
Profit	275 000	440 000	(360 000)	355 000

Total contribution = £1 180,000; total profit = £355 000

(c) **Proposal 1**

Effect on

	Contribution	Profitability	
Budgeted figures	£1 180 000	£355 000	
Reduce Z supervision		£ 75 000	
Increase variable			
overheads – Z	(£ 18 000)	(£ 18 000)	120 000 × £0.15
Reduce material			
prices – Z	£ 90 000	£ 90 000	120 000 × £0.75
	£1 252 000	£502 000	

Proposal 2

Effect on

	Contribution	Profitability	
Budgeted figures	£1 180 000	£355 000	
Increase Z selling			
price by £1	£ 120 000	£120 000	120 000 × £1
	£1 300 000	£475 000	

Proposal 3

Effect on

	Contribution	Profitability	
Budgeted figures	£1 180 000	£355 000	
			Negative
Stop making Z	£ 120 000	£120 000	Contribution
Incur redundancy			
costs		(£ 50 000)	
Save fixed labour			
costs		£ 90 000	
	£1 300 000	£515 000	

(d) The most profitable alternative is Proposal 3, but this removes Product Z completely from the company. The Board have to consider whether this short-term solution is also better for the long-term interests of the business.

Proposal 1 is the next best alternative. Here, though, the company's reputation for quality may be damaged if inferior product is despatched to customers. Again, the longer-term effect of adopting this strategy should be considered and assessed.

Proposal 2 would appear to be difficult to introduce because of the continuing outlook for sales to be depressed. However, if the price can be raised without affecting the demand this might prove to be the most appropriate strategy in the short term, otherwise Proposal 3 should be chosen.

11 AAT COST ACCOUNTING AND BUDGETING

Workings and notes:

	90%	100%	105%
Units	45 000	50 000	52 500
Material cost per unit	£7.50	£7.50	£7.50
Labour cost per unit	£9.78	£9.70	£9.67

(Therefore includes an element of fixed cost)

High/low method:	Units	Cost
High	52 500	£507 500
Low	45 000	£440 000
	7 500	£ 67 500

= variable cost per unit of £9.00

Labour fixed	£ 35 000	£ 35 000	£ 35 000
Labour variable	£405 000	£450 000	£472 500

Overheads cost per unit:

Production	£4.83	£4.70	£4.64

(Therefore includes fixed costs)

High/low method:

	Units	Cost
High	52 500	£243 750
Low	45 000	£217 500
	7 500	£ 26 250

= variable cost per unit of £3.50

Fixed	£ 60 000	£ 60 000	£ 60 000
Variable	£157 500	£175 000	£183 750

Administration costs:

Cost per unit	£2.67	£2.60	£2.57

Also contains some variable costs

High/low method:

	Units	Cost
High	52 500	£135 000
Low	45 000	£120 000
	7 500	£ 15 000

= variable cost per unit of £2.00

Fixed	£30 000	£ 30 000	£ 30 000
Variable	£90 000	£100 000	£105 000

Selling etc overheads:

Cost per unit	£1.56	£1.50	£1.48

Also contains some variable costs

High/low method:

	Units	Cost
High	52 500	£77 500
Low	45 000	£70 000
	7 500	£ 7 500

= variable cost per unit of £1.00

Fixed	25 000	25 000	25 000
Variable	45 000	50 000	52 500

(a)

	Flexed Budget	Actual	Variance	
Sales – Units	37 500	37 500		
	£	£	£	
Sales	1 125 000	1 075 000	50 000	Adverse
Less: Variable costs				
Materials	281 250	311 750	30 500	Adverse
Labour	337 500	316 500	21 000	Favourable
Production overheads	131 250	111 250	20 000	Favourable
Administration costs	75 000	87 500	12 500	Adverse
Selling and distribution costs	37 500	41 500	4 000	Adverse
	862 500	868 500	6 000	Adverse
Contribution	262 500	206 500	56 000	Adverse

Fixed Costs:

Labour	35 000	35 000		
Production overheads	60 000	60 000		
Administration costs	30 000	30 000		
Selling and distribution costs	25 000	25 000		
	150 000	150 000	0	
Net profit	**112 500**	**56 500**	**56 000**	**Adverse**

(b) Analysis of Variances:

Sales variance £50 000

This variance has arisen because the price per unit has dropped from £30 budgeted to an actual £28 666. This may have been as a result of giving trade discounts to customers over and above that expected by the budget forced on the company by the uncertainties of their market. It could also perhaps indicate that not all the units have been invoiced in the period due to administration oversights. Management need to investigate the reasons, perhaps looking through the invoices raised during the period to see which did not reach the £30 per unit and reappraising the budget price of £30 per unit to see if this is sustainable.

Materials Variance £30 500

This adverse variance has arisen because the company paid an average £8.313 per unit instead of the budgeted £7.50 per unit. This may have been because of a large price increase by the supplier, or 'panic' buying due to an out of stock situation. It could also be due to less efficient use of the materials with larger wastage than expected. Management need to establish the quantity of materials used in order to establish the exact reasons.

Labour Variance £21 000

The favourable variance has arisen because the average cost per unit was lower than budgeted – £8.44 compared to £9. This may be because the workforce were more efficient and completed the work more quickly than budgeted, or it could be that lower cost staff were used. Again, management need to investigate how many labour hours have actually been used to complete the units and compare this with the budgeted hours to find out the underlying reasons.

Production Overheads Variance £20 000

A favourable variance which could have arisen because the actual overhead expenditure was lower than expected; or because the efficiency of production was greater than budgeted. Here again, management need to analyse the overhead recovery figures (quantity of hours) and compare actual with budget to ascertain the reasons for this total variance.

(c)   Potential order position

	Actual activity	Potential order	Total	
Sales – Units 3	7 500	12 500	50 000	
	£	£	£	
Sales	1 075 000	312 500	1 387 500	
Variable costs:				
Materials	311 750	93 750		£7.50 × 12 500
Labour	316 500	125 000		£10 × 12 500
Production overheads	111 250	52 500		£4.20 × 12 500
Administration costs	87 500	31 250		£2.50 × 12 500
Selling and distribution costs	41 500	12 500		
	868 500	315 000	1 183 500	
Contribution	206 500	(2 500)	204 000	
Fixed costs			150 000	
Net profit			54 000	

A loss of £2500 would arise if the potential order were to be taken and therefore the company should not accept it. Perhaps management could revisit those variable costs which will increase to see if these could be contained and therefore make the order feasible.

12   AAT COST ACCOUNTING AND BUDGETING 1992

(i)   Sales budget in revenue

	Alpha	Beta	Gamma	Total
Units	8 000	12 000	10 000	
Selling price per unit	£60	£110	£90	
Sales value	£480 000	£1 320 000	£900 000	£2 700 000

(ii)   Production budget in units

	Alpha	Beta	Gamma
Opening stock	1 000	1 200	1 500
Units to be produced	8 200	11 800	10 300
Sales	−8 000	−12 000	−10 000
Closing stock	−1 200	−1 000	−1 800
Production budget =	8 200	11 800	10 300 units

(iii)   Material purchase budget

		X	Y
Units			
Opening stock		5 000	7 500
Issues:			
Alpha	8 200 × 2;		
	8 200 × 3	16 400	24 600
Issues:			
Beta	11 800 × 3;		
	11 800 × 4	35 400	47 200

Issues:

Gamma	10 300 × 2.5;		
	10 300 × 1.5	25 750	15 450
Total issues		77 550	87 250
Closing stock		8 000	10 000
Purchases		80 550	89 750
		issues + c/stock − o/stock	
Purchases in units		80 550	89 750
Cost (×£3; ×£2)		£241 650	£179 500

(iv)   Departmental labour cost budgets

	Alpha	Beta	Gamma	
Units	8 200	11 800	10 300	
Hours:				
Dept 1	6 150	14 750	20 600	
			41 500 hours	
Dept 2	12 300	23 600	25 750	
Costs:				
Dept 1:				
at £4 per hour	£24 600	£ 59 000	£ 82 400	£166 000
Dept 2:				
at £3 per hour	£36 900	£ 70 800	£ 77 250	£184 950
	£61 500	£129 800	£159 650	£350 950

(v)   Budgeted overhead absorption rates

	Dept 1	Dept 2
Overheads	£415 000	£567 200
Labour hours	41 500	
Machine hours:		
Alpha	2 × 8 200	16 400
Beta	2 × 11 800	23 600
Gamma	3 × 10 300	30 900
		70 900

Overhead absorption rate: labour hour £10.00 per hour
Overhead absorption rate: machine hour £8.00 per hour

(vi)   Standard product cost and standard profit for each product

	Alpha	Beta	Gamma	
Budgeted selling price	£60.00	£110.00	£90.00	
Standard product costs:				
Material X	£ 6.00	£ 9.00	£ 7.50	
Material Y	£ 6.00	£ 8.00	£ 3.00	
Labour: Dept 1	£ 3.00	£ 5.00	£ 8.00	
Labour: Dept 2	£ 4.50	£ 6.00	£ 7.50	
Overheads: Dept 1	£ 7.50	£ 12.50	£20.00	
Overheads: Dept 2	£16.00	£ 16.00	£24.00	
Total standard cost	£43.00	£ 56.50	£70.00	
Administration costs	£ 7.50	£ 11.00	£15.50	100% of
Standard Profit	£ 9.50	£ 42.50	£ 4.50	labour

13 AAT COST ACCOUNTING AND BUDGETING 1993

Workings and notes:

	A	B	C	Total
Labour costs:				
Fixed	£100 000	£ 80 000	£ 40 000	£220 000
Variable	£300 000	£240 000	£120 000	
Overhead costs:				
Fixed	£300 000	£360 000	£240 000	£900 000
Variable	£350 000	£240 000	£120 000	£1 120 000

Product A ceasing affect:

Fixed labour eliminated	£100 000	
Fixed o/hd eliminated	£50 000	

Product C affect increase:

Fixed labour cost	(£40 000)	
Saving if A stopped	110 000	Fixed Costs

Variable labour cost +20%
Reduction in selling price
to £9.50 each
(£11 − £1.50)

(a)(i) Marginal cost

Statement per unit	A	B	C
Original budget			
Selling price	£15.00	£12.00	£11.00
Variable costs			
Material	£ 5.00	£ 4.00	£ 3.00
Labour	£ 3.00	£ 2.00	£ 1.50
Overhead	£ 3.50	£ 2.00	£ 1.50
	£11.50	£ 8.00	£ 6.00
Contribution per unit	£ 3.50	£ 4.00	£ 5.00

(a)(ii) With Product A deleted

	B	C
Selling Price	£12.00	£9.50
Variable costs:		
Material	£ 4.00	£3.00
Labour	£ 2.00	£1.80
Overhead	£ 2.00	£1.50
	£ 8.00	£6.30
Contribution per unit	£ 4.00	£3.20

(b)(i) Original Budget

	A £	B £	C £	Total £
Units	100 000	120 000	80 000	
Sales	1 500 000	1 440 000	880 000	3 820 000
Variable costs	1 150 000	960 000	480 000	2 590 000
Contribution	350 000	480 000	400 000	1 230 000
Fixed costs				1 120 000
Profit				110 000

(b)(ii) With Product A deleted

	B £	C £	Total £
Units	120 000	180 000	
Sales	1 440 000	1 710 000	3 150 000
Variable costs	960 000	1 134 000	2 094 000
Contribution	480 000	576 000	1 056 000
Fixed costs			1 010 000
Profit			46 000

(c) Product A should be retained as it is contributing towards overall profits. By keeping it the profit will be £64 000 higher than with it deleted.

Table (b)(i) shows that A is contributing £350 000 towards the fixed costs. If the savings in fixed costs which would arise from its deletion are deducted from this contribution, it can be seen that the company would lose £200 000 if production of A ceased. This loss would be offset somewhat by the increase in sales of Product C which, as can be seen from table (b)(ii) would contribute an extra £176 000. However the extra £40 000 fixed labour costs reduces this to £136 000.

The difference in favour of retaining A is therefore £200 000 less £136 000 additional profit from C = £64 000.

14   AAT COST ACCOUNTING AND BUDGETING 1993

Workings and notes

Sales	Jul	Aug	Sep	Oct	Nov	Dec	
Units	800	1 000	1 200	1 400	1300	1100	
Price each	£ 120	£ 120	£ 120	£ 140	£ 140	£ 140	
Sales value	£96 000	£120 000	£144 000	£196 000	£182 000	£154 000	£892 000
Receipts:							
Cash sales	£48 000	£ 60 000	£ 72 000	£ 98 000	£91 000	£ 77 000	
Credit sales:							
July		£24 000	£ 19 200				
Aug			£ 30 000	£ 24 000			
Sep				£36 000	£ 28 800		
Oct					£ 49 000	£ 39 200	
Nov						£ 45 500	
Dec							
	£48 000	£ 84 000	£121 200	£158 000	£168 800	£161 700	
Purchases							
Units	1 000	900	1 200	1 300	1 400	1 000	
Price each	£ 80	£ 80	£ 85	£85	£90	£ 90	
Purchases value	£80 000	£ 72 000	£102 000	£110 500	£126 000	£ 90 000	£580 500
Payments:		£80 000	£ 72 000	£102 000	£110 500	£126 000	
Wages and salaries	£16 000	£ 16 000	£ 20 000	£ 20 000	£ 24 000	£ 24 000	£120 000
Payment	£12 000	£ 12 000	£ 15 000	£ 15 000	£ 18 000	£ 18 000	
		£ 4 000	£ 4 000	£ 5 000	£ 5 000	£ 6 000	
	£12 000	£ 16 000	£ 19 000	£ 20 000	£ 23 000	£ 24 000	
Overheads	£10 000	£ 10 500	£ 11 000	£ 11 500	£ 12 000	£ 12 500	£ 67 500
Less depreciation	£ 1 000	£ 1 000	£ 1 000	£ 1 000	£ 1 000	£ 1 000	
	£ 9 000	£ 9 500	£ 10 000	£ 10 500	£ 11 000	£ 11 500	£ 61 500
Payment		£ 9 000	£ 9 500	£ 10 000	£ 10 500	£ 11 000	
Fixed assets	£60 000						
Payment	£24 000		£ 9 000		£ 9 000		
Loan							
Received	£50 000						
Used for goodwill	(£50 000)						
Repaid						£50 000	

(a) Cash budget – Six months ending December 31

	Jul £	Aug £	Sep £	Oct £	Nov £	Dec £
Receipts						
Cash sales	48 000	60 000	72 000	98 000	91 000	77 000
Credit sales	0	24 000	49 200	60 000	77 800	84 700
Loan	50 000					
	£ 98 000	£ 84 000	£121 200	£158 000	£168 800	£161 700
Payments						
Purchases	0	80 000	72 000	102 000	110 500	126 000
Wages and salaries	12 000	16 000	19 000	20 000	23 000	24 000
Overheads	0	9 000	9 500	10 000	10 500	11 000
Fixed assets	24 000	0	9 000	0	9 000	0
Goodwill purchase	50 000					
Repayment of loan	0	0	0	0	0	50 000
	£ 86 000	£105 000	£109 500	£132 000	£153 000	£211 000
Cash flow	12 000	(21 000)	11 700	26 000	15 800	(49 300)
Opening Cash	0	12 000	(9 000)	2 700	28 700	44 500
Closing Cash	12 000	(9 000)	2 700	28 700	44 500	(4 800)

(b) Budgeted working capital

at December 31

Stock	£ 0	
Debtors	(£105 700)	(Nov: £36 400 + Dec: £69 300)
T/creditors	(£ 90 000)	December due
Wages	(£ 6 000)	25% of December due
Overheads	(£ 11 500)	December due
Bank overdraft	(£ 4 800)	Per cash flow
Fixed assets	(£ 18 000)	2 instalments due
	(£130 300)	
Working capital	(£ 24 600)	Negative

(c) Comment

As can be seen from the cash budget, there will be an overdraft in two of the six months and steps will need to be taken to arrange facilities with the bank to cover this position. If an overdraft facility cannot be arranged it will be necessary for the friend to reorganise her receipts and payments to avoid the situation. It may be that the loan repayment can be made over a period of time instead of one payment after just six months' trading. Or she may try to stop the number of bad debts, which is costing her 5% of her turnover, a substantial amount in cash terms.

With regard to the working capital position, a major problem is revealed by the budget in so far as there will be insufficient assets to pay creditors when they fall due. The working capital ratio is just 0.81 : 1.00 and this will cause her to 'ration' payments, which might create serious trading problems for her. The following profit and loss account provides a clue to the potential difficulties indicated by the budget:

Sales	£892 000
Cost of sales	£580 500
Gross profit	£311 500
Expenses	
Wages	£120 000
Overheads	£ 61 500
Depreciation	£ 6 000
Bad debts	£ 89 200
	£276 700
Profit	£ 34 800

With capital expenditure of £60 000 and the purchase of goodwill costing £50 000, she has non-working expenditure of £110 000 but only £40 800 of operational earnings (including depreciation) to pay for them. This gap needs to be made good by either capital being invested by her, or long-term loans being raised.

15 AAT COST ACCOUNTING AND BUDGETING 1993

Workings and notes

Budget:	Materials	Labour	Overheads	Total
Variable cost	520 000	320 000	160 000	£1 000 000
Fixed costs	0	80 000	160 000	£240 000

Number of units: £1 500 000/£75 = 20 000
Variable cost

per unit	£26	£16	£8	£50

(a) Budget break even in units

	£	Units
Sales	1 500 000	20 000
Variable Costs	1 000 000	
Contribution	500 000	£25.00 per unit
Fixed Costs	240 000	
Profit	260 000	

Break even in units:

$$\frac{\text{Fixed costs}}{\text{Contn per unit}}$$

$$= £240 000/£25 \qquad 9 600 \text{ units}$$

(b) Margin of safety in revenue

(i) Original budget

$$\frac{\text{Budgeted sales}}{£1 500 000} - \frac{\text{Break even sales}}{£720 000}$$

$$= £780 000 \qquad \text{Margin of safety}$$

(ii) Flexed budget

$$\frac{\text{Budgeted sales}}{£1 650 000} - \frac{\text{Break even sales}}{£720 000}$$

$$= £930 000 \qquad \text{Margin of safety}$$

(c) Flexed budget

	Flexed Budget	Actual	Variance	
Units	22 000	22 000		
	£	£	£	
Sales	1 650 000	1 680 000	30 000	Favourable
Less cost of sales:				
Materials	572 000	680 000	108 000	Adverse
Labour	432 000	420 000	12 000	Favourable
Overheads	336 000	340 000	4 000	Adverse
	1 340 000	1 440 000	100 000	Adverse
Net profit	310 000	240 000	70 000	Adverse

(d) Comment

An adverse variance has occurred of £70 000. The reasons for this may be as follows: Sales variance £30 000 favourable: the company appears to have increased the price from £75 to £76.36 or, alternatively, varying trade discounts may not have been taken up by the customers. Materials variance of £108 000 adverse. The price per unit was budgeted at £26 but the actual cost per unit was £30.91. Suppliers may have increased the price, or alternatively usage of materials may have been much higher than anticipated and wastage greater. Labour variance £12 000 favourable: rates of pay may have been lower than anticipated or labour efficiency may have been better than budgeted. Overheads variance of £4 000 adverse. This may be due to either higher than anticipated expenditure or lower-than-expected levels of production achieved in a specified period of time.
The most serious variance is for materials, and management need to investigate the reasons for this. If it is due primarily to price increases from suppliers thought will need to be given to a possible increase in the selling price to recoup the cost. Alternatively, management may look for other materials which may be at lower prices. If the reason is because of to an excess use of materials management will need to find the causes and take corrective action to avoid a reccurrence.

16 ᴀᴀᴛ COST ACCOUNTING AND BUDGETING 1993
Workings and notes

Revenue

budget	Dept 1	Dept 2	Dept 3	Dept 4	Total
Chargeable					
hours	10584	6804	5292	7560	
Rate per					
hour	£20	£25	£30	£40	
Revenue	£211680	£170100	£158760	£302400	£842940

Staff numbers

	Dept 1	Dept 2	Dept 3	Dept 4	Total
Chargeable					
hours	10584	6804	5292	7560	
Non chargeable					
hours	1176	756	588	840	
Total					
hours pa.	11760	7560	5880	8400	
Hours per					
person	1680	1680	1680	1680	
Number of					
employees	7.0	4.5	3.5	5.0	20.0

Direct wages budget

Hours	Dept 1	Dept 2	Dept 3	Dept 4	Total
worked	11760	7560	5880	8400	
Rate per					
hour	£8	£10	£11	£14	
Cost	£94080	£75600	£64680	£117600	£351960

Summary cash budget

Receipts:	£842940/12 × 10 months	£702450

Payments	
Wages	£351960
Office admin£185000 − £18500	
depreciation	£166500
Marketing and selling	
£75000 − £25000 bad debts	£50000
Rental £32000 × 5	£160000
	£728460

(i) Revenue budget by department:

	£
Dept 1	211680
Dept 2	170100
Dept 3	158760
Dept 4	302400
	£842940

(ii) Number of employees

Dept 1	7.0
Dept 2	4.5
Dept 3	3.5
Dept 4	5.0
	20.0

(iii) Direct wages budget £351960

(iv) Summary cash budget:

Receipts	£
Customer payments	702450
Payments	
Wages	351960
Office administration	166500
Marketing and selling	50000
Rental	160000
	728460

Cash flow	(26010)
Opening cash	0
Closing cash	(£26010) overdrawn

(v) Summary budgeted profit and loss account:

	£
Sales	842940
Expenses	
Wages	351960
Administration costs	185000
Marketing and selling	75000
Rental charges	128000
	739960
Budgeted profit for the year	£102980

17 ʟᴄᴄɪ THIRD LEVEL COST ACCOUNTING 1992
Workings and notes:

Stocks		Manufactured	Sold	Balance
Period 2	Opening stock			14000
	Manufactured	14800		28800
	Sold		11300	17500
Period 3	Manufactured	10400		27900
	Sold		18500	9400

Product costs

12 500 units level:

	Unit price	Value
Materials	24	£300 000
Labour	20	£250 000
Overhead – variable	10	£125 000
Overhead – fixed		£200 000
		£875 000

Budgeted cost per unit at 12 500 level   £   70

Absorption of fixed overheads

		Period 1	Period 2	
224 000	Absorbed cost	£236 800	166 400	403 200
150 400	Budgeted cost	£200 000	200 000	400 000
73 600	Under/over absorbed	£36 800	−33 600	3 200
−70 400				

(a)   Ups and Downs Ltd budgeted profit and loss account

	Period 2	Period 3	Notes:
Unit sales	11 300	18 500	
	£	£	
Sales	1 356 000	2 220 000	At £120 each
Cost of sales:			
Opening stock	980 000	1 225 000	
Goods manufactured	1 036 000	728 000	
Closing Stock	(1 225 000)	(658 000)	
	791 000	1 295 000	At £70 each
Gross profit	565 000	925 000	£50 per unit
Expenses			
(Over)/under-absorbed overhead	(36 800)	33 600	Per table above
Variable selling overheads	45 200	74 000	At £4 per unit
Fixed selling overheads	150 000	150 000	Fixed costs set at 12 500 level (×£12 p/unit)
Fixed administration overheads	175 000	175 000	Fixed costs set at 12 500 level (×£14 p/unit)
	333 400	432 600	
Profit for period	£231 600	£492 400	

(b)   The profit in Period 3 is greater than
        Period 2 by £260 800. This can be accounted
        for as follows:

Higher sales are forecast to be achieved in
Period 3 compared to Period 2 and this will
increase Period 3's gross profit by: 7200
units at £50 per unit gross profit   £360 000

But the additional sales will attract higher
variable selling costs (7200 × £4 per unit)   (28 800)

In Period 2 an over-absorption of fixed production over-heads has resulted because an extra 2300 units over the normal level of production has been achieved: 2300 × £16 per unit.   £36 800

Conversely, in Period 3, production fell below the norm and fixed production overheads were not fully absorbed: 2100 × £16.   (£33 600)

Finally, the opening stock for Period 2 included £224 000 of fixed overheads from earlier periods; at the end of Period 2 fixed production overheads carried forward to Period 3 amounted to £280 000 (17 500 × £16). So the difference, namely £56 000, represents Period 2's fixed production costs carried forward to Period 3.   £56 000

However, in Period 3 the closing stocks include only 9400 × £16 - £150 400 – so Period 3 effectively bears the cost represented by the difference between the opening stock fixed cost element (£280 000) and the amount carried forward to Period 4 (£150 400).   (£129 600)

	£260 800

---

18 LCCI THIRD LEVEL MANAGEMENT ACCOUNTING 1992
Workings and notes:

Selling price = £40; sales = £6 000 000; therefore units sold = 150 000
100% capacity = 150 000/0.6 = 250 000; therefore 80% = 250 000 × 0.8 = 200 000 units

(a)(i) Last year's level of activity

Number of model tanks	150 000	
	£	**Per unit**
Sales	6 000 000	£40.00
Less variable costs:		
Materials	1 500 000	£10.00
Labour	750 000	£ 5.00
Production overheads	450 000	£ 3.00
Selling overheads	300 000	£ 2.00
	3 000 000	£20.00
Contribution	3 000 000	£20.00
Fixed costs	3 300 000	
Loss for period	(£300 000)	

(ii) This year's desired level of activity:

Number of model tanks	200 000	
	£	**Per unit**
Sales	8 000 000	£40.00
Less variable costs:		
Materials	2 000 000	£10.00
Labour	1 000 000	£ 5.00
Production overheads	600 000	£ 3.00
Selling overheads	400 000	£ 2.00
	4 000 000	£20.00
Contribution	4 000 000	£20.00
		(50.0%)
Fixed Costs	3 300 000	
Profit for period	£700 000	

(b)(i) Formula: Fixed costs + desired profit/number of units = contribution

$$\frac{4\,800\,000}{200\,000} = £24.00 \text{ contribution per unit}$$

Add variable costs	
per unit	£20.00
Selling Price	£44.00 Each

(ii) Formula: Fixed costs/C/S%

$$\frac{£3\,000\,000}{0.5} \quad C/S = 50\%$$

Break-even point   £6 600 000 Sales

19 ACCA COST AND MANAGEMENT ACCOUNTING 1 1990

Workings and notes:

Current costs and usage Materials:

		Product Y			**Product Z**	
A		**A**			**A**	
Current	Usage – kg	30.00	£156/5.20		15.00	£78/£5.20
	Cost	£156.00	per 100 units		£78.00	per 100 units
New	Usage – kg	29.46	30/1.12 × 1.10		14.73	15/1.12 × 1.10
	Price	£5.46	£5.20 × 1.05		£5.46	£5.20 × 1.05
	Cost	£160.87	per 100 units		£80.44	per 100 units

		Product Y			**Product Z**	
		B			**B**	
Current	Usage – kg	30.00	kg per 100 units		40.00	kg per 100 units
	Cost	£54.00	per 100 units		£72.00	per 100 units
New	Usage – kilos	30.00	kg per 100 units		40.00	kg per 100 units
	Price	£1.89	£1.80 × 1.05		1.89	£1.80 × 1.05
	Cost	£56.70	per 100 units		£75.60	per 100 units

Current costs and usage: Labour – Product Y

		Mixing Dept			**Mixing Dept**	
Current	Hours	2.50	£11.25/£4.50	Hours	5.00	£11.25/£4.50
	Cost	£11.25		Cost	£20.00	
New	Hours	2.50			5.00	
	Cost	£12.15	2.5 hours × £4.50 + 8%		£21.60	5 × £4.32

Current costs and usage: Labour – Product Z

		Packaging Dept			**Packaging Dept**	
Current	Hours	2.50	£11.25/£4.50	Hours	5.00	£11.25/£4.50
	Cost	£11.25		Cost	£20.00	
New	Hours	2.50			5.00	
	Cost	£12.15	2.5 hours × £4.50 + 8%		£21.60	5 × £4.32

(a) Summary

	Product Y	**Product Z**
	£	**£**
Raw material A	160.87	80.44
Raw material B	56.70	75.60
Mixing labour	12.15	12.15
Packaging	21.60	21.60
Cost per 100 units	251.33	189.79

(b)(i)   Production budget

	Product Y	Product Z
Sales	1 700 000	9 500 000
Closing Stock	200 000	1 250 000
	1 900 000	1 750 000
Less Opening Units	190 000	1 500 000
Production Budget	1 710 000	9 250 000 units

(ii)   Purchases of Material B

	Product Y	Product Z	
Production	513 000	370 000	883 000
Closing Stock			90 000
			973 000
Opening stock			(95 000)
Purchases of B			878 000 kg

(iii)   Mixing labour – hours

	Product Y	Product Z	Total
Units to produce	17 100	9 250	
Hours per 100 units	2.5	2.5	
Number of hours	42 750	23 125	65 875 hours

20   ACCA COST AND MANAGEMENT ACCOUNTING 1 1990
Workings and notes

	A	B
	£	£
Retail selling price	5.00	6.00
Less 30% retailer margin	1.50	1.80
	3.50	4.20
Less quantity discounts	0.14	0.21
X Ltd selling price	3.36	3.99 each

	A	B	
Production costs:			
Units to produce	100 000	150 000	250 000
Costs			
Variable	£150 000	£285 000	
Fixed costs	£ 90 000	£135 000	225 000 = 90p per unit
	240 000	420 000	
Cost per unit	£ 2.40	£ 2.80	

(a)(i)   Profit and loss account – budget achieved

	Product A	Product B	Total	Notes
	105 000	140 000		
	£	£		
Sales	352 800	558 600	911 400	
Cost of Sales:				
Opening stock	12 000	0		1
Goods manufactured	240 000	420 000		
Closing stock	0	(28 000)		2
	252 000	392 000		
Gross profit	100 800	166 600	267 400	
Variable costs	31 500	42 000	73 500	3
Fixed costs	31 500	42 000	73 500	4
Net profit	37 800	82 600	120 400	

Notes:

1.   As only 100 000 units were budgeted to be produced but 105 000 were sold it follows that there must have been 5000 units (at least) as opening stocks. The same cost per unit has been used for the valuation of these stocks.

2.   Similarly with Product B closing stocks. As 150 000 were produced and 140 000 sold the closing stocks must be 10 000 units.

3.   The period variable costs will vary in line with the sales achieved, e.g. 30p per unit.

4.   The period fixed costs are apportioned between A and B on the basis of number of units sold.

(ii)   With production of Variety A increased to 105 000 the position will be:

	£	Units	
Opening stock	12 000	5 000	brought forward
Goods manufactured	252 000	105 000	
Closing stock	(12 000)	(5 000)	carried forward

As 5000 more units were produced than budgeted an over-absorption of production overheads has occurred: £90 000 (100 000 × 90p) should have been absorbed, but £94 500 has been charged to production (105 000 × £90p): £4500 overabsorbed. As only £90 000 was actually spent, the overabsorption will be credited to profit and loss account, increasing the profit for Variety A to £42 300 and total profits to £124 900.

(b) Break even for the following period.

Contribution per unit:

	A	B
Sales	£ 3.36	£ 3.99
Variable costs	£ 1.80	£ 2.20
Contribution	£ 1.56	£ 1.79
Number of units	105 000	140 000
Revenue	£352 800	£558 600	£911 400
Contribution	£163 800	£250 600	£414 400
C/S%			45.47%
Fixed costs	£298 500		
Break even =	£298 500/45.47%	656 477	

21 ACCA COST AND MANAGEMENT ACCOUNTING 1 1991

(a) Workings and notes:

	Units	
Opening stocks	− 48 600	
Budgeted sales	567 300	
Closing stocks	53 900	49 000 + 10%
Production required	572 600	

Standard efficiency 112 per hour
= 5112.5 hours required

At £5.20 per hour £26 585.00

(a) Labour budget – direct operatives budget year

Production required	572 600 Units
Standard Efficiency	112 Units per hour
Number of hours requirement	5 112.5 hours
Direct operatives labour budget	£26 585

(b) Workings and notes:

	Actual	Budget
Direct labour		
Production	50 400	49 700
Hours worked	458	
Overtime premium	3 hours	
	461	

		Hours paid	Rate per hour	O/T premium
Cost – net	£2 420.25	461	5.25	15.75
Deductions	£ 565.35			
Total cost	£2 985.60			

Indirect labour	
Cost	1 254.85
Deductions	303.90
Total cost	£1 558.75

	Standard	Actual	Variance	
Units made	50 400	50 400		
Cost	£2 340.00	£2 404.50	£64.50	Adverse
A		£2 404.50		
AS	458 × £5.20	£2 381.60	£22.90	Adverse
S		£2 340.00	£41.60	Adverse

(a)

Budgeted labour cost		£2 340.00	
Add direct labour rate variance		£ 22.90	Adverse
Add direct labour efficiency variance		£ 41.60	Adverse
Actual labour cost		£2 404.50	

(b)

DR	Wages control account			CR
	£			£
Direct operatives:				
Cash	1 854.90	Transfer to work in		
Deductions	565.35	progress account	2 381.60	
Indirect labour:		Transfer to direct labour		
Cash	950.95	rates variance		
Deductions	303.90	account	22.90	
		Transfer to production		
		overheads accounts	1 254.85	
		Transfer to overtime		
		premium account		
		(OVERHEADS)	15.75	
	3 675.10		3 675.10	

22 ACCA COST AND MANAGEMENT ACCOUNTING 1 1991

Workings and notes:

Material A

Product	Sales budget	Closing stock	Opening stock	Production	Kg per unit	Kg required for production
1	600	140	140	600	25	15 000
2	350	80	80	350	70	24 500
3	1 850	260	260	1 850	15	27 750
4	1 200	180	180	1 200	0	0
5	900	130	100	930	55	51 150
						118 400

Material B

Product	Sales budget	Closing stock	Opening stock	Production	Kg per unit*	Kg required for production
1	600	140	140	600	27	16 200
2	350	80	80	350	4.5	1 575
3	1 850	260	260	1 850	0	0
4	1 200	180	180	1 200	18	21 600
5	900	130	100	930	0	0
						39 375

* Adjusted by 10%.

(a) Material usage budget

	Material A kg	Material B kg
	118 400	39 375

Purchases

	Production	Closing stock	Opening stock	Purchases
Material A	118 400	11 840	10 030	120 210.0
Material B	39 375	3 938	4 260	39 052.5

Material purchases budget

	Material A kg	Material B kg
	120 210	39 052.5

	Production	kg each	Usage at std
1	580	25	14 500
2	330	70	23 100
3	1 900	15	28 500
4	1 200	0	0
5	800	55	44 000
		110 100	£264 240

£279 000 116 250 kg at £2.40
£280 160 Actual cost
£   1 160 Adverse price variance

(b) Journal entries

	DR	CR
Work in progress control account	£264 240	
Material A stock control account		£264 240
Material A stock control account	£280 160	
Suppliers accounts (CRs control a/c)		£280 160
Material price variance account	£ 1 160	
Material A stock control account		£ 1 160

23 ACCA COST AND MANAGEMENT ACCOUNTING 1 1992

(a)

	Product I £	Product II £	Product III £	Total £
Sales	2 475 000	3 948 000	1 520 000	7 943 000
Variable costs	1 305 000	2 256 000	988 000	4 549 000
Contribution	1 170 000	1 692 000	532 000	3 394 000
Attributable	275 000	337 000	296 000	908 000
Apportioned	519 741	829 065	319 194	1 668 000
Profit for the period	375 259	525 935	(83 194)	818 000

(b)

	Product I £	Product II £	Total £
Sales	2 475 000	3 948 000	6 423 000
Variable costs	1 305 000	2 256 000	3 561 000
Contribution	1 170 000	1 692 000	2 862 000
Attributable	275 000	337 000	612 000
Apportioned	642 737	1 025 263	1 668 000
Profit for the period	252 263	329 737	582 000

Assumptions are that (a) the fixed costs of £1 668 000 would not be reduced by the discontinuance of Product III; and (b) that the apportionment of this sum will continue to be made on sales.

(c) Additional cost = £80 000.
Contribution per unit = £1 170 000/225 000 = £5.20
Additional sales units required to pay for the advertising:

$$\frac{£80\,000}{£5.20} = 15\,385 \text{ units}$$

(d)

	Present	Proposed
Selling price	£10.50	£ 9.45
Variable costs	£ 6.00	£ 6.00
Contribution	£ 4.50	£ 3.45
C/S%	42.86%	36.51%
Increase in sales volume required		17.3913% (42.86%/36.51%)

Check

			Per unit
Sales	£3 948 000	£4 634 609	£9.45
Variable costs	£2 256 000	£2 942 609	£6.00
Contribution	£1 692 000	£1 692 000	£3.45
Units	376 000	490 435	

Calculations: £3 948 000 × 1.173913 = £4 634 609
in units: £4 634 609/£9.45 = 490 435 units

It is assumed that the increase in volume will not affect the fixed costs position of Product II.

24 CIMA COST ACCOUNTING 1990

Workings and notes:

Per unit costs

	A	B	C
Materials costs			
Frame	£20	£20	£20
Component D	£40	£ 8	£24
Component E	£ 5	£35	£25
Component F	£12	£15	£ 3
	£77	£78	£72

	A	B	C
Labour			
Skilled hours	2	1.5	1.5
Cost	£12.00	£ 9.00	£ 9.00
Unskilled hours	2	2	3
Cost	£ 9.00	£ 9.00	£13.50
	£21.00	£18.00	£22.50
Variable overheads	£ 5.00	£ 4.00	£ 3.50
Variable cost per unit	£103.00	£100.00	£ 98.00
Selling price per unit	£215.00	£250.00	£300.00
Contribution per unit	£112.00	£150.00	£202.00

				Total
Ratio of sales	1	2	4	
Sales mix	£215	£500	£1 200	£1 915
Contribution mix	£112	£300	£ 808	£1 220
C/S (%)	52.093%	60.000%	67.333%	63.7076%
Sales mix (%)	11.23%	26.11%	62.66%	100.00%

(i) Sales in quantities and value.

Budgeted profit for the year	£ 6 500 000
Fixed costs for the year	£ 1 430 000
Contribution required for the year	£ 7 930 413

Therefore sales for the year =	£12 448 149	(£7 930 413/0.637 076)
Sales period 1 =	£ 957 550	(1/13 of £12 448 149)
Sales mix A = 11.23%	£ 107 533	
B = 26.11%	£ 250 016	
C = 62.66%	£ 600 001	
	£ 957 550	

Sales units	A	500
	B	1 000
	C	2 000
		3 500

(ii) Production in quantities.

	A	B	C
Opening stock	300	700	1 600
Sales	500	1 000	2 000
Closing stock	270	630	1 440
Production	470	930	1 840

(iii) Materials usage, in quantities.

	Frames	D	E	F
Production – A	470	2 350	470	1 880
Production – B	930	930	6 510	4 650
Production – C	1 840	5 520	9 200	1 840
Usage	3 240	8 800	16 180	8 370

(iv) Material purchases in quantities and value.

	Frames	D	E	F
Opening stock	1 000	4 000	10 000	4 000
Materials usage	3 240	8 800	16 180	8 370
Closing stock	900	3 600	9 000	3 600
Purchases	3 140	8 400	15 180	7 970
Cost of purchases	£62 800	£67 200	£75 900	£23 910

(v) Manpower budget.

	A	B	C	
Units	470	930	1 840	
Hours:				
Skilled	940	1 395	2 760	
Unskilled	940	1 860	5 520	
Hours per period per person	150	150	150	
Number of people				
Machining	6	9	18	34.0
Assembly	6	12	37	55.5

25 CIMA COST ACCOUNTING 1992

Workings and notes:

Budgeted monthly overhead expenditure:
£72 000 – output 3000 tonnes

Budgeted monthly overhead expenditure:
£108 000 – output 7000 tonnes

Standard overhead absorption rate:
£18 per tonne

High/low split:

	Output	Cost
High	7 000	£108 000
Low	3 000	£ 72 000
	4 000	36 000 = variable cost per tonne of £9

Actual overheads:

Variable	£ 52 000
Fixed	£ 53 750
	£105 750
Output	5 500 tonnes

(i) Variable cost per tonne: £36 000/4000 = £9 per tonne

	High	Low
Variable	£ 63 000	£ 27 000
Fixed	£ 45 000	£ 45 000
	£108 000	£720 000

(ii) Fixed cost per month = £45 000

(iii) Variable cost per tonne	£ 9.00
Fixed cost per tonne	£ 9.00
Standard overhead absorption rate	£18.00

Fixed cost divided by absorption rate per tonne = budgeted output:

$$\frac{£45\,000}{£9} = 5000 \text{ units}$$

Budgeted output per month = 5000 units

Check	5 000 units
Variable cost	£45 000
Fixed cost	£45 000
	£90 000
Rate per tonne	£18

(iv) Budgeted overhead allowance for the actual output in April:
5500 tonnes × £9 plus £45 000 = £94 500

(v) Total overhead absorbed for the month of April:
5500 units at £18 per tonne = £99 000

(vi) Variable production overhead expenditure variance for the month of April

	Standard	Actual	Variance
Output	5 500	5 500	
Variable costs	£49 500	£52 000	£2 500 Adverse

Adverse expenditure variance of £2500.

(vii)/(viii)   Fixed production overhead variances:

	Budget	Standard	Actual	Variance	
Output	5 000	5 500	5 500		
Fixed costs	£45 000	£49 500	£53 750	£4 250	Adverse
A			£53 750		
B		£45 000		£8 750	Adverse expenditure
S		£49 500		£4 500	Favourable volume

(vii)   Fixed production overhead expenditure variance for April: £8750 adverse.

(viii)   Fixed production overhead volume variance for April: £4500 favourable.

26   CIMA COST ACCOUNTING 1992

Workings and notes:

	Nov	Dec	Jan	Feb	Mar
Receipts from debtors (£000)					
November	660	330	55		
December	–	600	300	50	
January	–	–	840	420	70
February	–	–	–	720	360
March	–	–	–	–	660
			1 195	1 190	1 090
Wages and salaries			60	60	60
Creditors			240	210	240
Production overhead analysis					
Variable	224	196	175	196	
Fixed	416	364	325	364	
Depreciation	164	164	164	164	
Fixed – net of depreciation	252	200	161	200	
Payments:					
Variable			224	196	175
Fixed			200	161	200
Selling and admin overhead			125	130	130
Depreciation			15	15	15
Net of depreciation			110	115	115
Corporation tax			750		
Dividend					500

VAT computations

Sales	1 000	1 400	1 200	1 100
7/47ths thereof = Output tax	149	209	179	164
Payable		149	209	179
Input tax		136	125	121
VAT payable		13	84	58

Capital expenditure	1 000		700

(a) Cash budget – January, February and March

	January	February	March
Receipts			
Debtors	1 195	1 190	1 090
	1 195	1 190	1 090
Payments			
Wages and salaries	60	60	60
Creditors	240	210	240
Production overhead:			
Variable	224	196	175
Fixed	200	161	200
Selling and administration	110	115	115
Corporation tax	750		
Dividend			500
VAT	13	84	58
Capital expenditure	1 000		700
	2 597	826	2 048
Cash flow	(1 402)	364	(958)
Opening cash	1 450	48	412
Closing cash	48	412	(546)

(b)(i) A permanent improvement in cash flow can be effected by raising additional share capital to pay for the capital expenditure. The cash budget shows that £1 700 000 will be paid out during the three months, creating an overdraft position at the end of March. If these capital expenditures were to be financed by long-term funds, such as additional share capital, or long-term loans, the company would avoid the strain of financing fixed assets from its working capital. In addition, the company could endeavour to improve its debtors' collection by reducing the incidence of bad debts. Perhaps more rigorous credit vetting of customers and stronger credit control. Ongoing cost control could also be carried out.

(ii) A temporary solution to minimise the March overdraft would be: to pay the dividend at a later date; to delay the capital expenditure payment by negotiatng with the supplier; and to arrange to pay creditors later than at present.

27 UNIVERSITY OF GREENWICH YEAR 1
BA ACCOUNTANCY AND FINANCE (1992)

Workings and notes:

Split of semi-variable costs:

	Hours	Cost (£)
High	105 000	63 250
Low	80 000	53 250
	25 000	10 000

Variable cost per hour	£0.40		

	Variable	Fixed	Total
High	42 000	21 250	63 250
Low	32 000	21 250	53 250

Collins budget for Year 3

Level of activity:	90.0%	100.0%	110.0%
Hours	81 000	90 000	99 000
Costs	£	£	£
Variable costs:			
Power	24 300	27 000	29 700
Consumables	4 050	4 500	4 950
Direct labour	121 500	135 000	148 500
Semi-variable costs:			
Variable element	32 400	36 000	39 600
Fixed costs:			
Semi-variable:	21 250	21 250	21 250
Fixed:			
Depreciation	16 500	16 500	16 500
Factory salaries	32 250	32 250	32 250
Other	6 750	6 750	6 750
Total budget	259 000	279 250	299 500

28 UNIVERSITY OF GREENWICH YEAR 1
   BA ACCOUNTANCY AND FINANCE (1992)

Workings and notes:

	May	Jun	Jul	Aug	Sep
Materials (£000s)					
Opening stock		70	80	90	70
Purchases		£80	£90	£82	£80
Consumed	60	70	80	102	90
Closing stock	70	80	90	70	60
Payment			80	90	82
Wages accrued	32	32	32	32	32
Paid – 7/8	28	28	28	28	28
Paid – 1/8		4	4	4	4
			32	32	32
Factory expenses			5	5	5
Rent					9 (36/4)
Salaries and expenses			32	32	32
Advertising and publicity			12	14	10
Sales commission			9	10	13
Debtors' receipts			160	180	200
Machinery payments					30
Dividend				6	
investment grants received					20

Cash budget for the three months ending September

	July £000s	August £000s	September £000s
Receipts			
Debtors' receipts	160	180	200
Investment grants		6	
	160	186	200
Payments			
Materials	80	90	82
Wages	32	32	32
Factory expense	5	5	5
Rent			9
Salaries/expense	32	32	32
Advertising	12	14	10
Commission	9	10	13
Machinery			30
Dividend		6	
	170	189	213
Cash flow	(10)	(3)	(13)
Opening cash	52	42	39
Closing Cash	42	39	26

Model answers to examination questions, Chapter 20

1 A LEVEL (ULEAC) 1990

(a)(i) Weighted average cost of capital:

Ajax

	Capital £000s	Rate %	Cost £000s
Ordinary shares	700	16	112.0
Preference shares	200	14	28.0
Debentures	100	12	7.2 (less tax at 40%)
	1 000		147.2
Weighted average cost of capital:		**14.72%**	(147.2/1 000)

Borg

	Capital £000s	Rate %	Cost £000s
Ordinary shares	300	16	48.0
Preference shares	200	14	28.0
Debentures	500	12	36.0 (less tax at 40%)
	1 000		112
Weighted average cost of capital:		**11.20%**	(112/1 000)

(ii) The difference between the weighted average cost of capital of the two companies is because a larger proportion of Ajax's capital comprises ordinary shares (70% against Borg's 30%), which attract a larger return. This difference increases Ajax's cost of capital by £64 000; but this is partially offset by the extra costs of financing the debentures in Borg, costing that company £28 800 more.

(b)(i) The maximum cost of financing for the project is 16%.

(ii) investment appraisal – Ajax

	0	1	2	3	4
Investment	£300 000				
Net cash flows		55 000	60 000	145 000	170 000
Discount factor					
– 15%		0.870	0.756	0.658	0.572
Discounted cash flow	£285 860	47 850	45 360	95 410	97 240
Net present value	**(£14 140)**				

Investment appraisal – Borg

	0	1	2	3	4
Investment	£300 000				
Net cash flows		55 000	60 000	145 000	170 000
Discount factor					
– 12%		0.893	0.797	0.712	0.636
Discounted					
cash flow	£308 295	49 115	47 820	103 240	108 120
Net present					
value	**£ 8 295**				

For Ajax, the project results in a negative net present value, indicating that the return will be lower than the 15% discount factor. Therefore the advice would be for Ajax not to invest. But for Borg, the NPV shows a surplus of £8295 and therefore the project would be worthwhile.

2   A LEVEL (AEB) 1990
(a)   NPV calculations

Factory A

			£m			
	Year 0	1	2	3	4	5
Investment	75.00					
Net cash						
inflows		3.000	6.000	14.000	16.000	20.000
Discount factor						
– 10%		0.909	0.826	0.751	0.683	0.621
Discounted						
Cash flow	41.55	2.73	4.96	10.51	10.93	12.42
NET present						
value	(33.46) Negative					

Factory B

			£m			
	Year 0	1	2	3	4	5
Investment	100.00					
Net cash						
inflows		10.000	15.000	30.000	42.75	57.00
Discount factor						
– 10%		0.909	0.826	0.751	0.683	0.621
Discounted						
Cash flow	108.61	9.09	12.39	22.53	29.20	35.40
NET present						
value	8.61 Positive					

Factory C

	Year 0	1	2	3	4	5
				£m		
Investment	90.00					
Net cash inflows		15.000	17.000	23.000	36.00	39.00
Discount factor – 10%		0.909	0.826	0.751	0.683	0.621
Discounted Cash flow	93.76	13.64	14.04	17.27	24.59	24.22
NET present value	3.76 Positive					

(b) Report.

Report to Managing Director

Subject: Investment in European factory

From: Accountant   Date

We have completed the Investment Appraisal review of the three European factories with the following results:

	Capital Cost	Discounted Cash Flow	Net Present Value
	£m	£m	£m
Factory A	75.00	41.55	−33.46
Factory B	100.00	108.61	8.61
Factory C	90.00	93.76	3.76

You will see that the cash flow from Factory A is insufficient to repay the original investment at the cost of capital of 10%. Factory B appears to be a better investment than Factory C as the NPV is greater for that factory. However, because the above results are necessarily based on estimations it would be advisable to subject the figures to sensitivity analysis techniques. In addition it may be of benefit to investigate the possibilities of European Union (EU) grants for new factories in particular development areas.

(Signed)

(c) Payback.

	Factory A Cash flow	Factory A Balance	Factory B Cash flow	Factory B Balance	Factory C Cash flow	Factory C Balance
Year 0		−75		−100		−90
Year 1	3	−72	10	−90	15	−75
Year 2	6	−66	15	−75	17	−58
Year 3	14	−52	30	−45	23	−35
Year 4	16	−36	42.75	−2.25	36	1
Year 5	20	−16	57	54.75	39	40

Project has no payback period

Payback is in Year 5:
5.039 Years
2.25/57 = 0.039

Payback is in Year 4:
4.972 Years
35/36 = .972

appropriate investment.

(d)   Factory C has the faster payback, but only marginally over Factory B, whereas Factory B provides the superior net present value. With regard to Factory A, both investment appraisal techniques indicate that this would not be an

3   A LEVEL (AEB) 1992
(a)   Forecast revenue statements

Workings and notes:

Plant A

	1	2	3	4
Capital cost: £85 000 000				
Revenues	£30 000 000	£39 600 000	£39 425 000	£92 000 000
Payments	£12 000 000	£16 200 000	£19 090 000	£40 000 000
Depreciation	£ 8 500 000	£ 8 500 000	£ 8 500 000	£ 8 500 000

Plant B

	1	2	3	4
Capital cost: £45 000 000 less govt grant of of £20 m = £25 m				
Revenues	£15 600 000	£18 200 000	£15 390 000	£45 000 000
Payments	£11 700 000	£14 000 000	£13 500 000	£33 000 000
Depreciation	£ 2 500 000	£ 2 500 000	£ 2 500 000	£ 2 500 000
Govt subsidy	£ 5 000 000	£ 5 000 000	£ 5 000 000	£ 5 000 000

Forecast revenue statement – Plant A

Year	1	2	3	4	Total
Revenues	£30 000 000	£39 600 000	£39 425 000	£92 000 000	
Costs	£12 000 000	£16 200 000	£19 090 000	£40 000 000	
Net cash flow	**£18 000 000**	**£23 400 000**	**£20 335 000**	**£52 000 000**	
Depreciation	£ 8 500 000	£ 8 500 000	£ 8 500 000	£ 8 500 000	
Forecast net revenue	**£ 9 500 000**	**£14 900 000**	**£11 835 000**	**£43 500 000**	**£79 735 000**

Forecast revenue statement – Plant B

Year	1	2	3	4	Total
Revenues	£15 600 000	£18 200 000	£15 390 000	£45 000 000	
Costs	£11 700 000	£14 000 000	£13 500 000	£33 000 000	
Less subsidy	£ 5 000 000	£ 5 000 000	£ 5 000 000	£ 5 000 000	
Net cash flow	**£ 8 900 000**	**£ 9 200 000**	**£ 6 890 000**	**£17 000 000**	
Depreciation	£ 2 500 000	£ 2 500 000	£ 2 500 000	£ 2 500 000	
Forecast net revenue	**£ 6 400 000**	**£ 6 700 000**	**£ 4 390 000**	**£14 500 000**	**£31 990 000**

(b) Net present value of projects

Plant A

Year	0	1	2	3	4
Original investment	£85 000 000				
Net cash flows		£18 000 000	£23 400 000	£20 335 000	£52 000 000
Discount factor – 12%		0.893	0.797	0.712	0.636
Discounted cash flow	£82 274 320	£16 074 000	£18 649 800	£14 478 520	£33 072 000
Net present value	£2 725 680 Negative				

Plant B

Year	0	1	2	3	4
Original investment	£25 000 000				
Net cash flows		£8 900 000	£9 200 000	£6 890 000	£17 000 000
Discount factor – 12%		0.893	0.797	0.712	0.636
Discounted cash flow	£30 997 780	£7 947 700	£7 332 400	£4 905 680	£10 812 000
Net present value	5 997 780 Positive				

Note: on this four year evaluation basis, Plant B should be the project to invest in. But both projects have a life of 10 years and the later years net cash flows need to be evaluated, especially as Plant B becomes less effective after six years. In addition, the social aspect of the additional pollution caused by Plant B needs to be considered for unexpected, government imposed, costs may be incurred in later years to protect the environment. Because of these negatives with respect to Plant B, the recommendation would be to extend the appraisal period for the full 10 years, including an additional provision for possible costs incurrable to reduce the pollution aspects of Plant B.

4   A LEVEL (AEB) 1993

Notes and workings:

	M	P	Q
Capital cost – £m	45.0	30.0	35.0
Installation – £m	4.5	3.0	3.5
Net cash flows after deduction of fuel tax			
	£m	£m	£m
1	10.0	11.0	9.0
2	12.0	12.0	10.0
3	14.0	12.5	9.5
4	18.5	14.5	10.5
5	23.7	16.5	14.5

(a) Net present value table: power station M

£m

	0	1	2	3	4	5
Original cost	49.500					
Net cash flows		10.000	12.000	14.000	18.500	23.700
Discount factor		0.909	0.826	0.751	0.683	0.621
Discounted cash flow	56.869	9.090	9.912	10.514	12.636	14.718
Net present value	7.369 Positive					

Net present value table: power station P

£m

	0	1	2	3	4	5
Original Cost	33.000					
Net cash flows		11.000	12.000	12.500	14.500	16.500
Discount factor		0.909	0.826	0.751	0.683	0.621
Discounted cash flow	49.449	9.999	9.912	9.388	9.904	10.247
Net present value	16.449 Positive					

Net present value table: power station Q

£m

	0	1	2	3	4	5
Original Cost	38.500					
Net cash flows		9.000	10.000	9.500	10.500	14.500
Discount factor		0.909	0.826	0.751	0.683	0.621
Discounted cash flow	39.752	8.181	8.260	7.135	7.172	9.005
Net present value	1.252 Positive					

(b) Report.

To: Board of Powerform plc

Subject: Purchase of Power Station

From: Accountant   Date:

The net present values of each of the three Power Stations under consideration have been calculated and the results are enclosed. The following summarises the position:

	Capital cost	Net present value
	£m	£m
M	49.5	7.4
P	33.0	16.4
Q	38.5	1.3

The net present value has been calculated using the company's estimated cost of capital of 10%.

Power station P – the conventional coal-fired power station – is clearly the better investment in the short term on net present value criteria, and the advice would be that this alternative should be purchased. However, the Technical Director has advised that the installation costs of all three projects may be higher than has been allowed for in the attached tables. In light of this it may be prudent to ascertain more accurate estimations of the installation costs before a final decision is made. Furthermore, if possible, realistic estimations for later years should also be calculated to see if, over the longer term, Station P should prove to be the better investment. In addition, other costs which cannot be quantified easily need to be considered. Pollution, for example, and employment prospects. The figures include an estimation of the likely European fuel tax from Year 3. However, other measures over the life-span of the projects may be introduced to curb pollution and this would have a major affect on Station P. It could be that heavy capital expenditure in the later years may be incurred to bring the coal-fired station emissions down to acceptable levels. Employment prospects in the raw materials supply industries might also be considered by the board, because the coal-fired stations will employ more people than the gas-fired industry. Another method of project appraisal the Board may wish to consider in conjunction with the NPV is the payback; that is, how long each project will take to pay for itself from net cash flows (undiscounted) as follows:

M	P	Q
3.73 years	2.8 years	3.95 years

Station P, again, appears the better investment using this criterion. Therefore, in the short term, the overall advice would be to invest in Station P .

5   AAT COST ACCOUNTING AND BUDGETING 1992
Workings and notes:

Life of fleet = 5 years
Cost of outside organisation:

Year	1	2	3	4	5
	£	£	£	£	£
	250 000	275 000	302 500	332 750	366 025
Cost of fleet:					
Drivers	33 000	35 000	36 000	38 000	40 000
Repairs	8 000	13 000	15 000	16 000	18 000
Other	130 000	135 000	140 000	136 000	142 000
Less depreciation	(120 000)	(120 000)	(120 000)	(120 000)	(120 000)
	51 000	63 000	71 000	70 000	80 000

(a) Net cash savings table/net present value – transport fleet

	Year 0	Year 1	Year 2	Year 3	Year 4	Year 5
	£	£	£	£	£	£
Investment	750 000					
Cash flows:						
Outside organisation costs		250 000	275 000	302 500	332 750	366 025
Own fleet costs		(51 000)	(63 000)	(71 000)	(70 000)	(80 000)
Disposal of fleet						150 000
Net cash savings		199 000	212 000	231 500	262 750	436 025
Discount factor		0.893	0.797	0.712	0.636	0.567
Discounted cash flow	925 855	177 679	169 005	164 777	166 982	247 412
Net present value	175 855 Positive					

Net cash savings therefore =						
Running costs	1 191 275	199 000	212 000	231 500	262 750	286 025
Investment	600 000					
Net cash savings	591 275					

(b)   Calculations:
(i) Payback period: 3.41 years

(ii) Accounting rate of return:

	Average Annual Saving	Average Investment
1	79 000	630 000
2	92 000	510 000
3	111 500	390 000
4	142 750	270 000
5	166 025	0
	591 275	1 800 000
= (Divide by 5)	£118 255	£360 000

Accounting rate of return = £118 255/£360 000 = 32.3%

(iii) Net present value = £175 855

(c)   Report.

To: Investment Manager

Subject: Investment in Transport Fleet

From: Accountant   Date:

The following table provides a comparison of the proposed
cost savings of investing in the transport fleet with the
alternative project:

	Fleet	Alternative
Payback period	3.41 years	3 years
Accounting rate of return	32.3%	30%
Net present value	£175 855	£140 000

As you will see, an investment in the transport fleet will provide
a substantially better net present value. The other appraisal
methods are broadly similar. In view of the superior NPV of the
transport fleet I would recommend this investment.

(Signed)

6   AAT COST ACCOUNTING AND BUDGETING
Workings and notes:

T disposed of in year 5 = £10 000; cost = £70 000; = £60 000
over 5 years = depreciation of £12 000 pa
R disposed of in year 3 = nil value; cost = £60 000 over
3 years = depreciation of £20 000
New R cost £75 000 over 3 years = £25 000 depreciation; no
scrap value

T

	Profit	Depreciation	Cash flow
Year 1	15 000	12 000	27 000
Year 2	18 000	12 000	30 000
Year 3	20 000	12 000	32 000
Year 4	32 000	12 000	44 000
Year 5	18 000	12 000	30 000 + Disposal of £10 000
Year 6	0		0

R

	Profit	Depreciation	Cash flow
Year 1	20 000	20 000	40 000
Year 2	25 000	20 000	45 000
Year 3	25 000	20 000	45 000
Year 4	10 000	25 000	35 000
Year 5	3 000	25 000	28 000
Year 6	2 000	25 000	27 000

(a) Investment in project R

Year	0	1	2	3	4	5	6
First investment	£ 60 000						
Cash flows		£40 000	£45 000	£45 000			
Discount factor – 14%		0.877	0.769	0.675			
Discounted cash flow	£100 060	£35 080	£34 605	£30 375			
Net present value	**£ 40 060 Positive**						
Second investment				£75 000			
Cash flows					£35 000	£28 000	£27 000
Discount factor – 14%				0.675	0.592	0.519	0.456
Discounted cash flow	(£3 061)			(£50 625)	£20 720	£14 532	£12 312
Net present value	**£3 061 Negative**						
Overall NPV	£36 999 Positive						

The first machine should not be replaced because the second machine has a negative NPV.

(b) Investment in project T

Year	0	1	2	3	4	5
Investment	£70 000					
Cash flows		£27 000	£30 000	£32 000	£44 000	£40 000
Discount factor – 14%		0.877	0.769	0.675	0.592	0.519
Discounted cash flow	£115 157	£23 679	£23 070	£21 600	£26 048	£20 760
Net present value	**£ 45 157 Positive**					

	T	R (3 year inv)
(i) Payback period	2.41 years	1.44 years
(ii) Net present value	£45 157	£40 060

Project T has the superior NPV and should be the one selected. R's payback period is the better of the two, but as the difference is only one year, is insufficient to outweigh the NPV difference

7 ᴀᴀᴛ COST ACCOUNTING AND BUDGETING 1993

Project 1: net present value table

	Year 0	Year 1	Year 2	Year 3	Year 4
	£	£	£	£	£
Original investment	150 000				
Cash flows		60 000	50 000	45 000	125 000
Discount factor – 15%		0.869	0.756	0.659	0.571
Discounted cash flow	190 970	52 140	37 800	29 655	71 375
Net present value	40 970 Positive				

Project 2: net present value table:

	Year 0	Year 1	Year 2	Year 3	Year 4	Year 5
	£	£	£	£	£	£
Original investment	150 000					
Cash Flows		54 000	44 000	39 000	49 000	104 000
Discount factor – 15%		0.869	0.756	0.659	0.571	0.497
Discounted cash flow	185 558	46 926	33 264	25 701	27 979	51 688
Net present value	35 558 Positive					

(i) Payback period

		Project 1	Project 2
Balance end of year	1	90 000	96 000
	2	40 000	52 000
	3	40 000/45 000	13 000
	4		13 000/49 000
Payback periods		**2.89 Years**	**3.27 Years**

(ii) Accounting rate of return.

		Project 1			**Project 2**	
Year	Profit	Investment	Year		Profit	Investment
1	40 000	130 000	1		30 000	126 000
2	30 000	110 000	2		44 000	102 000
3	25 000	90 000	3		39 000	78 000
4	35 000	0	4		49 000	54 000
	£130 000	£330 000	5		74 000	0
Divide by 4	£ 32 500	£ 82 500			£236 000	£360 000
			Divide by 5		£ 47 200	£ 72 000

Accounting rate of return 39.4%   **65.6%**

(iii) Net present value.

As table above

	Project 1	**Project 2**
	£40 970	£35 558

Summary

	Project 1	**Project 2**
Payback period	2.89 Years	3.27 Years
Accounting rate	39%	66%
Net present value	£40 970	£35 558

Based on the above appraisals, Project 1 should be invested in because of its superior net present value and payback period.

8 AAT COST ACCOUNTING AND BUDGETING 1993
Net present value table – Ablex machine

	Year 0 £	Year 1 £	Year 2 £	Year 3 £	Year 4 £
Original investment	90 000				
Cash Flows		25 000	35 000	30 000	50 000
Discount factor – 12%		0.893	0.797	0.712	0.636
Discounted cash flow	103 380	22 325	27 895	21 360	31 800
Net present value	13 380 Positive				

Net present value table – Combat machine

	Year 0 £	Year 1 £	Year 2 £	Year 3 £	Year 4 £
Original investment	100 000				
Cash Flows		40 000	60 000	10 000	40 000
Discount factor – 12%		0.893	0.797	0.712	0.636
Discounted cash flow	116 100	35 720	47 820	7 120	25 440
Net present value	16 100 Positive				

(i) Payback period

		Ablex	Combat
Balance at end of	year 1	65 000	60 000
	year 2	30 000	0
	year 3	0	
Payback period		**3 years**	**2 years**

(ii) Accounting rate of return

Note assets	Ablex profits	Ablex investment	Combat profits	Combat investment
Depreciation on s/l method				
1	5 000	70 000	17 500	77 500
2	15 000	50 000	37 500	55 000
3	10 000	30 000	−12 500	32 500
4	20 000	0	7 500	0
	50 000	150 000	50 000	165 000
Average: divide by 4	12 500	37 500	12 500	41 250
Accounting rate of return		**33.3%**		**30.3%**

(iii) Net present value

	Ablex	Combat
As table above	£13 380	£16 100

Summary:

	Ablex	Combat
Payback period	3 Years	2 Years
Accounting rate of return	33%	30.3%
Net present value	£13 380	£16 100

The machine to invest in should be Combat because it has a superior net present value, and the payback period is shorter. The accounting rate of return is not generally recommended as a method of choosing between alternatives.

9 RSA III ACCOUNTING 1993

Method A Evaluation: Purchase

	0	1	2	3	4	5
	£	£	£	£	£	£
Original deposit	10 000					
Cash payments		6 400	6 400	6 400	6 400	4 400
Discount factor		0.877	0.769	0.675	0.592	0.519
Discounted cash payments	20 927	5 613	4 922	4 320	3 789	2 284

Payments net
present value £30 927

Method B Evaluation: Rental

	0	1	2	3	4
	£	£	£	£	£
Original rental payment	9 000				
Cash payments		9 000	9 000	9 000	9 000
Discount factor		0.877	0.769	0.675	0.592
Discounted cash payments	26 217	7 893	6 921	6 075	5 328

Payments net
present value £35 217

The most advantageous way of obtaining the machine would
be to purchase it over the five years.

10 RSA III ACCOUNTING 1994
Workings and notes:

Existing machine fixed costs $= £12 500$ pa.
Contribution $= £10 \times 5000 = £50 000$ pa.
Profits $= £37 500$ pa.

New machine fixed costs $= £15 000$ pa.
Contribution $= £10 \times 6 000 = £60 000$ pa.
Profits $= £45 000$ pa.

Therefore additional cash flows with new machine $= £7 500$ pa.

Net present value table

	Year					
	0	**1**	**2**	**3**	**4**	**5**
	£					
Investment	20 000					
Additional						
cash flows		7 500	7 500	7 500	7 500	7 800
Discount						
factor – 12%		0.893	0.797	0.712	0.636	0.567
Discounted						
cash flow	27 208	6 698	5 978	5 340	4 770	4 423
Net present						
value	**£7 208 Positive**					

(a) The investment in the new machine will produce a
positive net present value using a 12% discount factor of
£7208 and therefore should be invested in.

(b) Payback period.

Balance at end of period	1	12 500	
	2	5 000	
	3	5 000/7 500	0.67
	4	0	

Payback period = 2.67 years

11 LCCI THIRD LEVEL MANAGEMENT ACCOUNTING 1991
Truckall present value table

	Year						
	0	**1**	**2**	**3**	**4**	**5**	**6**
Purchase							
price	£21 000						
Cash flows							
– costs		3 200	3 200	3 200	5 200	3 200	– 800
Discount							
factor		0.909	0.826	0.751	0.683	0.621	0.564
discounted							
cash flow	£13 043	2 909	2 643	2 403	3 552	1 987	(451)
Net present							
value	£34 043						

Overlander present value table

	0	1	2	3	4	5	6
				Year			
Purchase price	£13 000						
Cash flows – costs		2 800	3 400	12 800	2 800	3 400	– 5 200
Discount factor		0.909	0.826	0.751	0.683	0.621	0.564
Discounted cash flow	£16 057	2 545	2 808	9 613	1 912	2 111	(2 933)
Net present value	£29 057						

It is assumed that the company would trade-in the existing truck and receive £5 000 – the trade-in value – and this has been deducted from the purchase price.

Based on the above information, with interest charges to cover the monies borrowed being ignored, the Overlander truck should prove to be the better investment option because of the lower total costs incurred.

Model answers to examination questions, Chapter 21

1   A LEVEL (ULEAC) 1991

Workings:

Added value:

	Year 1	Year 2	Year 3	Total	Year 4
Wages	220 300	233 500	239 200	693 000	251 400
Profit	13 600	15 200	17 400	46 200	21 700
Added value	233 900	248 700	256 600	739 200	273 100

Base ratio:

	Year 1	Year 2	Year 3	Total	Year 4
Earnings	220 300	233 500	239 200	693 000	251 400
Added value	233 900	248 700	256 600	739 200	273 100
Base ratio				0.9375	0.9205

(i)   Added value for the three base years:

	Year 1	£233 900
	Year 2	£248 700
	Year 3	£256 600

(ii)   Base ratio of earnings to added value: 93.75%

(iii)   Ratio of earnings to added value in Year 4:   92.05%

(iv)   Amount of bonus payable in Year 4:   £5 462   £273 100 × 2%

2 A LEVEL (ULEAC) 1991

(a) Which company is the retailer?

Food retailers usually operate on low margins on high-volume turnover products. Other retailers, with low turnover products, will normally have a higher margin to compensate for lower volume sales.

As an illustration, the profit margin for the retailer selling, say, cigarettes will receive a lower profit margin on each packet of cigarettes, but will probably sell a great many packets. Another retailer, selling, say, furniture, will not sell so many units as the cigarette vendor and therefore the volume of sales will be lower; but this will be compensated by a greater profit margin.

This is one reason why 'Attractive Figures' would seem to be the retailer and 'Trends' the manufacturing company.

Another reason is cash. Retailers' sales are usually cash sales, the customer paying at the time of the purchase. Manufacturers, on the other hand, normally extend credit terms to their trade customers.

This is the second reason why 'Attractive Figures' is more likely to be the retailer and 'Trends' the manufacturer.

(b) Debtors and current liabilities at 31 December for Trends Ltd

	£	
Sales	500 000	(£200 000/0.40)
Cost of sales	200 000	
Gross profit	300 000	60.0%

Total debtors at 31 December:

Sales	£500 000	
Average daily sales	£ 1 370	(£500 000/365)
No. of days collection period	30	

(i) Debtors at 31 December   £ 41 096   £1 370 × 30

(ii) Current Assets:

Stock	£40 000	
Debtors	£41 096	
Cash account	£11 005	
	£92 101	= 2
Current liabilities	£46 050	= 1
Net current assets	£46 051	Ratio 2 : 1

Current liabilities are therefore £46 050

3 A LEVEL (AEB) 1991

(a) Contribution.

	Head office shop	Bexville shop	Amstead shop	Company as a whole
	£	£	£	£
Sales	150 000	30 000	55 000	235 000
Variable costs	75 000	27 000	39 000	141 000
Contribution	75 000	3 000	16 000	94 000
Fixed costs –				
Branch	40 000	7 000	4 000	51 000
Profit/loss	35 000	(4 000)	12 000	43 000

The contribution made by each branch to the company is as follows:

Head Office branch	£35 000
Bexville branch	(£ 4 000)
Amstead branch	£12 000
	£43 000

It is assumed that all the fixed costs incurred by Head Office are allocatable (as running costs) of the Head Office shop and are therefore not related to the administrative costs of the business as a whole. However, if all these costs were for the general administration of the company as a whole, the position would be as follows:

	Head office shop	Bexville shop	Amstead shop	Company as a whole
	£	£	£	£
Sales	150 000	30 000	55 000	235 000
Variable costs	75 000	27 000	39 000	141 000
Contribution	75 000	3 000	16 000	94 000
Fixed costs –				
Branch		7 000	4 000	11 000
	75 000	(4 000)	12 000	
Fixed costs – Administration costs				40 000
Profit/loss				43 000

The contribution made by each branch to the company is as follows:

Head Office branch	£75 000
Bexville branch	(£ 4 000)
Amstead branch	£12 000
	£83 000

(b) Report.

To: Board of Bettermake Ltd

Subject: Financial Analysis of the Company

From: Accountant   Date:

I have prepared an analysis of the branches using marginal costing methods and enclose a copy of the results [(a) above]. The company made a profit of £43 000 in the year but you will see that the Bexville shop was not able to clear its fixed costs from trading and therefore failed to make a contribution to the company as a whole.

Analysing the figures further, the gross profit margins earned by each shop are as follows:

Head Office	60.0%	(90/150)
Bexville	50.0%	(15/30)
Amstead	58.2%	(32/55)

The reason why Bexville is 'out of step' with the other two branches needs to be investigated. If that branch had achieved the same ratio as Head Office (i.e. 60%) the loss would have been reduced by £3000.

A comparison of the variable expenses as a percentage of sales is as follows:

Head Office	10.1%	(15/150)
Bexville	40.0%	(12/30)
Amstead	29.1%	(16/55)

Again, Bexville is significantly out of line with the others and the reasons why need to be investigated. If these could be reduced, Bexville branch would make a contribution. Similarly, the reasons why Amstead's variable costs are nearly three times higher than those of Head Office should also be investigated.

Fixed costs too at Bexville are nearly twice as high as the Amstead shop and a comparison of each cost heading needs to be completed to find which of the fixed costs is causing the difference.

(Signed)

4 A LEVEL (AEB) 1992

(a) Ratios.

	Year 1	Year 2	Notes: Year 1	Year 2
Profitability ratios				
			£000s	£000s
Gross profit %	30.0%	24.0%	2 700/9 000	2 880/12 000
Net profit %	11.1%	8.8%	1 000/9 000	1 060/12 000
Return on capital employed	8.7%	9.2%	1 000/11 480	1 060/11 580

	Capital employed:	£000s	£000s
	Fixed assets	9 300	10 200
	Current assets	3 720	5 960
	Current liabilities	− 1 540	− 4 580
		11 480	11 580

Liquidity/activity ratios

	Year 1	Year 2	£000s	£000s
Current ratio	1.49 : 1	1.06 : 1	3 720/2 500	5 960/5 620
Acid test ratio	0.86 : 1	0.52 : 1	2 160/2 500	2 940/5 620
No. of days receivables	62	89	1 520/(9 000/365)	2 940/(12 000/365)

Note: The number of days receivables is a working capital activity ratio.

(b) Comment.

Although the turnover increased by one-third in Year 2, up from £9m to £12m, profitability has not kept pace. The gross profit ratio has fallen from 30% to 24% – a fall of over 20% – so the £3m improvement in sales has resulted in an increase in the gross profit of only £180 000. Expenses have increased by £120 000, or 7% and the net profit increased by £60 000 – just 6% higher than Year 1. The return on capital employed has improved slightly.

With only £60 000 being generated from trading, and fixed assets increasing by £900 000, the company's liquidity has suffered, as revealed in the current ratio. For every £1 of liabilities in Year 1 the company had £1.49 of current assets. This has fallen to £1.06 of current assets for each £1 current liability. The acid test ratio indicates that the company will have difficulties in meeting current liabilities when they fall due. It will be necessary for the Directors to consider raising additional long-term financing to regularise the working capital position.

With regard to the management of working capital, it is clear that the number of days' credit given to customers has contributed to the overdraft position. If the number of days outstanding could be reduced to Year 1's 62 days, the overdraft would be lower by £886 000 (£12m/365 × 27 days).

5 AAT COST ACCOUNTING AND BUDGETING 1991

Workings and notes:

Material A cost is a sunk cost and is ignored in the decision.

Disposal cost = £1750; will be incurred if Project X not proceeded with.

Direct labour cost attributable to this job: £7000 = relevant cost.

Cost of special machine: £10 000 − £5250 = £4750 = relevant cost.

(a) Relevant costs of Project X.

		Reasons
Material A	− 1 750	1
Material B	8 000	2
Direct labour	7 000	3
Machine	4 750	4
	18 000	

Reasons:

1. As material A was a sunk cost the disposal costs 'saved' by not having to dispose of it becomes a benefit to Project X.
2. Material B will need to be purchased for the Project, therefore this is a relevant cost.
3. The extra labour costs arise specifically because of Project X, therefore are relevant to this project.
4. The cost of the machine is also relevant just to this project.

The overhead costs and supervision, having been apportioned to the project, are unaffected whether or not the project goes ahead. These costs are therefore irrelevant to the decision whether to accept or reject the job.

(b) Report.

To: Production Manager

Subject: Project X Opportunity

From: Accountant   Date:

I have costed the project as requested, with the following results:

	Cost £
Materials:	
A	0
B	8 000
Saving on not having to dispose of Material A	− 1 750
Labour	7 000
Depreciation of machinery	4 750
	18 000
Selling price	30 000
Profit	12 000

Working through this table compared to the costs previously drawn up:

Materials

Material A, although costing £4000, was considered not to have any further use and would therefore have been written down to nil for stocktaking purposes. This is therefore a sunk cost and so is not relevant to the decision to make this project. If the enquiry had not been received, a further cost of £1750 would have been incurred in disposing of Material A. Therefore it is correct to say that Project X will save this extra cost. Project X has thus been credited with this saving. Material B will need to be purchased at the cost of £8000 and is therefore relevant to the decision to manufacture X.

Labour

The relevant cost associated with Project X is £7000 because this will be the cost incurrable if the project goes ahead, having arisen because of the decision to make X.

Machine

The machinery will need to be purchased specifically for the project and is therefore relevant to the decision whether or not to go ahead.

Overheads

You will note that there are no overhead costs related to Project X. This is because these costs will be incurred irrespective of whether or not the project goes ahead; they are therefore not relevant costs but sunk costs, not related to this particular decision.

Overall, therefore, the total costs attributable to Project X amount to £18 000. The competitor has met the customers maximum price of £30 000. You will see that if the same price is quoted, a profit of £12 000 will be earned. But if our price were, say, £29 000 a reasonable profit would still be made.

(Signed)

6 RSA III ACCOUNTING 1994

		Alpha	Beta
(i)	Current ratio	4.38:1	2.24:1
(ii)	Acid test ratio (liquid ratio)	1.00:1	0.88:1
(iii)	Stock turnover	102 days	50 days
(iv)	Debtors' collection period	19 days	5 days
(v)	Net profit (%)	19.2%	17.9%
(vi)	Gross profit (%)	28.3%	26.7%

Comparison:

As both firms deal in the same kinds of goods and both are located in the same town, it would be expected that the ratios and statistics would be broadly similar, but this is not the case.

Alpha's current ratio is exceptionally high, indicating that money could be used for other purposes, e.g. short-term interest bearing investments, instead of being tied up in the current assets (stocks in this case). Beta's ratio is in line with the generally accepted 'ideal ratio' of 2:1, although, being in retailing, it would normally be expected to be lower than this.

The acid test for Alpha is exactly in line with the ideal of 1:1; Beta, on the other hand, would find some difficulty in paying all the creditors if they should be asked for immediate payment.

The number of days stock for Alpha is twice that of Beta: 102 days to 50 days. This could indicate that Alpha are carrying old stock, which might be considered 'dead' or 'slow-moving'. It could also indicate poor buying performance, with drastic overstocking. Clearly the extra stocks have not increased sales for Alpha, indicating that it is not being displayed to customers but is held in their warehouse.

Alpha is again out of step on the number of days debtors are outstanding. Retailing is generally a cash trade and outstandings are usually minimal compared to other industries. The reasons why Alpha allow extended credit need to be investigated.

Both the net profit and gross profit percentages are broadly in line with each other, with Alpha being marginally better than Beta. However, this could also indicate that Alpha have not allowed for stock write-offs in the period.

To summarise, both companies have similar trading results, but Alpha's management of working capital is poor compared to Beta.

7 LCCI THIRD LEVEL MANAGEMENT ACCOUNTING 1991

(a) Budgeted accounts ratios.

			Budget	Last year
1.	Profit/sales	120/320	37.5%	37.2%
2.	Contribution/sales	200/320	62.5%	55.0%
3.	Profit/capital employed (gr/assets)	120/1060	11.3%	20.0%
4.	Margin of safety/sales	192/320	60.0%	63.0%
5.	Fixed asset turnover ratio	810/320	0.39 times	0.61 times
6.	Current ratio	250/50	5:1	3:1
7.	Profit/shareholders funds	320/1010	31.7%	37.0%
8.	Breakeven point/sales	128/320	40.0%	37.0%

(b) Comparison.

Ratio 1, Profit to Sales is broadly similar to the previous year, but it will be seen that the Contribution/Sales ratio (2) has increased markedly, from 55% to 62.5% – a 13% increase. This may be because of an increase in the selling prices or a reduction in the marginal costs, or a combination of these two. As this ratio has increased but the Profit/Sales ratio has remained the same, it reveals that the fixed costs have increased substantially. They are now 25% of sales as compared with 17.8% the previous year. The reasons for this need to be investigated. It may be caused by a reduction in the volume of sales or a management decision to increase administration costs, or rent and rates or other fixed costs may have increased substantially.

The Margin of Safety (4) and Breakeven Ratios (8) provide further evidence that fixed costs have risen, thereby increasing the break even point and reducing the Margin of Safety.

There has been a fall in Ratio 3 and this has happened because of the increase in fixed and current assets. This latter conclusion is confirmed by the drop in both the Fixed Asset Turnover Ratio (5) – down from 0.61 times to 0.39 times and by the increase in the Current Ratio (6). More assets are being employed because the company have had an increase in share capital – an extra £200 000 has been raised – and the profit generated appears to have been fully reinvested in the business. But the extra funds have not, in the budget year at least, resulted in additional profits being earned. Further evidence for this is provided in Ratio 7, Profit to Shareholders Funds, which show a lower return caused by the increased investment. The excess current assets ratio of 5 : 1 indicates the company need to consider how best to use this surplus liquidity to improve the profit performance of the business.

8 LCCI THIRD LEVEL MANAGEMENT ACCOUNTING 1992

	Division X	Division Y	Division Z
Sales	£180 000	£225 000	£300 000
Profit	**£13 500**	£75 000	**£30 000**
Interest charge	£9 000	**£60 000**	£30 000
Residual income	**£4 500**	£15 000	£0
Investment	£90 000	**£750 000**	£150 000
Interest rate	10.0%	**8.0%**	**20.0%**

Qa	£13 500	15% × £90 000 = £13 500
Qb	£750 000	£75 000/10% = £750 000
Qc	£30 000	£150 000 × 20% = £30 000
Qd	£4 500	£13 500 − £9 000 = £4 500
Qe	8%	£60 000/£750 000 = 8%
Qf	20%	£30 000/£150 000

9 ACCA COST AND MANAGEMENT ACCOUNTING 1 1993

Workings and notes:

2000 hours spare capacity

Option 1 statistics

Hourly rate = £4; Overtime premium = £1.20 per hour = direct labour cost

Overheads £6 per direct labour hour

Variable overheads = £2.40; fixed overheads £3.60 per direct labour hour

Option 2 statistics

Raw materials X: Current cost £3.02 with 960 kg available; replacement cost = £3.10. Used continuously.

Raw materials Y: Current cost £5.25 with 570 kg; replacement cost £5.85. Available 570 kg.

Material Y can only be used for this option. But it can be disposed of for £1311 (570 kg × £2.30).

Plus other materials £3360.

Option 1 Bring forward manufacture of future order.

Hours available	2 000
Rate per hour	£4.00
Direct labour cost	£8 000.00

Notes:

Overtime premium saved:	£2 400	£8 000 × 30%

Option 2 One-off job alternative

	£	
Materials		
Cost of Material X	2 976	960 kg @ £3.10 – the replacement cost as this material is used continuously and the extra quantity would also be required.
Cost of Material Y	1 311	Material Y cannot be used for any other purpose so is a sunk cost. However, by not disposing of it Company A will forgo the sale proceeds (the opportunity cost) and this therefore becomes a cost of the one-off job.
Other materials	3 360	
Direct labour:		
2 200 hours at £4	8 800	
Overtime working:		
200 hours at £1.20	240	
Variable overheads:		
2 200 hours at £2.40 per hour	5 280	
	21 967	

The minimum quote for the one-off job should therefore be sufficient to cover the relevant costs of this job, plus the opportunity cost of the next best alternative, i.e. £2400.

Therefore the quote should be £24 367 plus an amount to increase the profit over the next best alternative, i.e. £1 to make the price £24 368.

10 CIMA COSTING 1990

(a) Profit and loss account – Year ended 31 January

	Ladies' wear	Men's wear	General	Toys	Restaurant	Total	
Sales	800	400	2 200	1 400	200	5 000	
Less: cost of sales	496	240	1 320	1 176	166	3 398	
Gross profit	304	160	880	224	34	1 602	
As % of sales	38.0%	40.0%	40.0%	16.0%	17.0%	32.0%	
Direct expenses:							
Wages	96	47	155	59	26	383	
Expenses	38	13	35	20	10	116	
Sales promotion	10	5	30	75	0	120	
	144	65	220	154	36	619	
Contribution	160	95	660	70	−2	983	
As % of sales	20.0%	23.8%	30.0%	5.0%	−1.0%	19.7%	

							As % of sales
Allocated costs:							
Occupancy costs*	97.6	73.2	97.6	170.8	48.8	488	9.8%
Discount allowed	4.0	2.0	11.0	7.0	1.0	25	0.5%
Bad debts**	2.4	1.2	6.6	4.2	0.6	15	0.3%
	104.0	76.4	115.2	182.0	50.4	528.0	10.6%
Net contribution	56.0	18.6	544.8	(112.0)	(52.4)	455.0	9.1%

		As % of sales
Less central costs		
Delivery costs	200	4.0%
Salaries – Office	70	1.4%
Salaries – Directors and management	100	2.0%
Directors fees	20	0.4%
Interest on bank overdraft	20	0.4%
Miscellaneous expenses	75	1.5%
	485	9.7%
Net loss for period	(30)	−0.6%

*Based on floor area occupied
**Based on sales – attempts should be made to identify precisely the departments to which these costs relate.

	Ladies' wear	Men's wear	General	Toys	Restaurant
Cont'n per floor space occupied per 100 area	£8	£6.33	£33	£2	−£0.20

Sales per floor space occupied } Other performance indicators
Sales per employee

(b) If the toy department were to be closed, the company would lose the contribution it provides of £70 000. Therefore the loss for the year would rise to £100 000.

(c)

	Ladies' wear	Men's wear
Present selling price equivalent	£1.00	£1.00
Present cost of sales equivalent	£0.62	£0.60
Gross profit	£0.38	£0.40
Profit (%)	38.00%	40.00%

Reduction of 5%

	Ladies' wear	Men's wear
Sales	0.95	0.95
Cost of sales	0.62	0.60
Profit	£0.33	£0.35
Profit (%)	34.74%	36.84%

Increase in sales required to earn the same gross profit in £s   9.5101% (38/34.7)   8.6957 (40/36.8)

Check:

	Ladies' wear	Men's wear
Sales	£876	£435
Gross profit	£304	£160
Gross profit (%)	34.74%	36.84%

(i) Ladies' wear increase = £76 000
Men's wear increase = £35 000

(ii) Ladies' wear percentage increase = 9.51%
Men's wear increase   = 8.70%

(d) Comment.

The first alternative, closing the Toy Department, should be avoided because it would worsen the position, the loss would increase by £100 000. However, the Department clearly does not warrant the use of the largest area in the store – 35%, contributing just £2 per floor area occupied compared with up to £33 in the General Department. With regard to the reduction of selling prices in the Ladies' and Men's Wear Departments, management need to judge whether the reduction in the selling prices will boost sales by a percentage amount greater than the above figures.

The General Department produces the greatest profit per area occupied and management should consider allocating more space to it, reducing the Toy Department accordingly. Management need also to deal with the negative contribution performance of the Restaurant, which lost £2000 in the period, before any allocation of costs. Unless the Restaurant is considered to be a 'service', attracting customers into the store with low-priced meals, with the purpose of encouraging them to spend in the main departments, management may need either to increase the selling prices or to reduce the running costs, or a combination of both.

11 UNIVERSITY OF GREENWICH YEAR 1
    BA ACCOUNTANCY AND FINANCE (1992)

	Job X123 £	Notes
Direct materials		
Material A: 2000 units at £20	40 000	1
Material B: 200 units at £20	4 000	2
Material C: 50 units at £250	12 500	3
Direct labour	0	4
Machining department overheads		
400 hours at £8 per hour	3 200	5
Finishing department		
200 hours at £25 per hour	5 000	6
Survey costs	0	7
Planning department	0	8
Total	64 700	

Notes:
1. Material A is used regularly by the business, so the relevant cost will be the current cost for this job.
2. The opportunity cost for this material is £20 per unit and is included in the cost.
3. This is required specifically for this job so is a relevant cost.
4. As the labour force will continue to be employed whether this job is taken or not, this cost is irrelevant to the decision.
5. The variable element of the Machining Department will be relevant to the job and therefore included in the costs.
6. The opportunity cost of hiring out the Finishing Department is relevant to this job and will thus be included.
7. Survey costs are sunk costs and therefore irrelevant.
8. Planning Department costs relate to fixed costs and therefore will be irrelevant to this job.

Index

REVISION DISKS

These two unique spreadsheet disks provide examples of all the cost and management accounting formats and formulae described in this text book. Designed as useful additional revision aids, each disk explains and illustrates the concepts of all of the major topics described in detail in the chapters in the book.

Disk A1 covers the elements of cost (materials, labour, overheads) and absorption costing, and also cost accounting methods (job and contract costing, service costing, process costing, and ABC). Disk A2 covers planning and control - marginal costing and CVP analysis, standard costing and variance analysis, budgetary control, investment appraisal and other control techniques.

The disks are interactive, allowing students to complete exercises and to instantly check and correct their answers, which are provided. The programs are an easy way to learn and enable students to see how the formats and formulae are set up on spreadsheets. The disks are suitable for students studying up to intermediate level for all the professional bodies examinations and also A-level, LCCI, BTEC etc

Written on Lotus 123, release 4 each disk is windows compatible. Other spreadsheet versions are also available.

ORDER FORM

To: Accountancy Aid
Unit 41, Hobbs Industrial Estate
Newchapel, Lingfield, Surrey, RH7 6HN
Or fax: 0181 462 0401

Name _____

Address_____

_____

_____

_____

Postcode_____

Tel. No_____
Please supply me with
_____copies of   Disk A1.......Cost Accounting and Cost Accounting Methods
                          at £9.95 each inclusive of post and packing
_____copies of   Disk A2......Planning and Control Methods
                          at £9.95 each inclusive of post and packing.
                          State version required if not Lotus 123, release 4
I enclose a cheque for: **£**_____
(UK only. Please enquire for overseas prices)
I wish to pay by Visa/Mastercard:

My number is:| | | | |

Expiry date_____

Signed_____

Allow 21 days for delivery.
Lotus and 123 are registered trade marks of Lotus Development Corporation

Management Accounting: Official Terminology

Divided into key subject areas for easy reference, this terminology defines the terms covering the vital elements of management accounting. Prepared by CIMA on the basis of standard usage and practice, it covers the vital topics of cost accounting, planning, budgeting, financial accounting, financial management, and performance measurement to provide a comprehensive lexicon management accounting terms.

Ref 32   pp157   £8.95   ISBN 0 901308 67 6

Computing Terminology (3rd edition)

As information technology continues to transform all areas of the business scene, managers and accountants need to keep abreast of basic computing terms and concepts. Whatever your role is in business you will benefit from reading this 'easy to use' guide to computing language.

Ref 155   pp87   £8.95   ISBN 1 874784 15 9

Terminology of Business and Company Law (2nd edition)

This dictionary of legal terms is an excellent reference source for business professionals and students. Covering topics included in most Business and Company Law courses, the book provides concise and jargon-free explanations to promote a clear understanding of the issues.

Ref 99   pp143   £8.95   ISBN 1 874784 13 2

Order Form

Please indicate publication(s) required and quantity below. Please enclose payment with order and allow for Postage and Packing: UK & rest of Europe £1.00 for up to the first £10.00 worth of books ordered plus £1.00 per £10.00 unit thereafter. Overseas £2.00 per £10.00 unit etc.

**To: Publishing Sales Department,
CIMA, 63 Portland Place, London W1N 4AB
Tel: 0171 637 2311, Fax: 0171 631 5309**

I wish to order:

Ref No: Quantity: Price:

Name _____

Address _____

Postage: _____

I enclose a cheque for: _____

I wish to pay by Visa/Mastercard my number is:

_____

Postcode _____

Expiry date _____

I am a: CIMA member ☐   CIMA student ☐   Non-member ☐
(Please tick appropriate box)

O

A free set of OHP Masters is available for all adopters of this text. For your set contact:

Jane Powell
Commissioning Editor
Macmillan Press
Houndmills
Basingstoke
Hants
RG21 6XS